# LIVING AND WORKING

# IN

# AUSTRALIA

## A SURVIVAL HANDBOOK

by

### David Hampshire

**SURVIVAL BOOKS • LONDON • ENGLAND**

First published in 1998
Reprinted 1999, 2000 (with changes)
Second edition 2001
Reprinted 2002
Reprinted 2003

Survival Books Limited, 1st Floor, 60 St James's Street
London SW1A 1ZN, United Kingdom
☎ +44 (0)207-493 4244, 📱 +44 (0)207-491 0605
✉ info@survivalbooks.net
💻 www.survivalbooks.net

British Library Cataloguing in Publication Data.
A CIP record for this book is available from the British Library.
ISBN 1 901130 51 7

Printed and bound in Finland by WS Bookwell Ltd

# ACKNOWLEDGEMENTS

My sincere thanks to all those who contributed to the successful publication of this book, in particular the many people who took the time and trouble to read and comment on the draft versions, including Graeme Dargi, Yolande Pierece-Holmes, Alan Allebone, Ron and Pat Scarborough, John Holmes, James Burton, Dianne Rodgers, Eugene Benham, Louise Stapleton, Pam Miller, Charles King, Adèle Jekgan, Nassem Mohammed, Vera Poole and everyone else who contributed in any way and whom I have omitted to mention. **Many thanks also to Joanna Styles, who updated this second edition, and to Joe and Kerry Laredo, who were responsible for proof-reading, editing and formatting the book.** Last, but certainly not least, a special thank-you to Jim Watson for the superb cover, cartoons, illustrations and maps.

**By The Same Publisher**

The Alien's Guide to Britain
The Alien's Guide to France
The Best Places to Live in France
The Best Places to Live in Spain
Buying a Home Abroad
Buying a Home in Britain
Buying a Home in Florida
Buying a Home in France
Buying a Home in Greece & Cyprus
Buying a Home in Ireland
Buying a Home in Italy
Buying a Home in Portugal
Buying a Home in Spain
How to Avoid Holiday & Travel Disasters
Living and Working Abroad
Living and Working in America
Living and Working in Britain
Living and Working in Canada
Living and Working in France
Living and Working in Germany
Living and Working in Holland,
Belgium & Luxembourg
Living and Working in Ireland
Living and Working in Italy
Living and Working in London
Living and Working in New Zealand
Living and Working in Spain
Living and Working in Switzerland
Retiring Abroad
Rioja and its Wines
The Wines of Spain

# What Readers and Reviewers

When you buy a model plane for your child, a video recorder, or some new computer gizmo, you get with it a leaflet or booklet pleading 'Read Me First', or bearing large friendly letters or bold type saying 'IMPORTANT – follow the instructions carefully'. This book should be similarly supplied to all those entering France with anything more durable than a 5-day return ticket. It is worth reading even if you are just visiting briefly, or if you have lived here for years and feel totally knowledgeable and secure. But if you need to find out how France works then it is indispensable. Native French people probably have a less thorough understanding of how their country functions. – Where it is most essential, the book is most up to the minute.

**Living France**

We would like to congratulate you on this work: it is really super! We hand it out to our expatriates and they read it with great interest and pleasure.

**ICI (Switzerland) AG**

Rarely has a 'survival guide' contained such useful advice  This book dispels doubts for first-time travellers, yet is also useful for seasoned globetrotters – In a word, if you're planning to move to the USA or go there for a long-term stay, then buy this book both for general reading and as a ready-reference.

**American Citizens Abroad**

It is everything you always wanted to ask but didn't for fear of the contemptuous put down – The best English-language guide – Its pages are stuffed with practical information on everyday subjects and are designed to complement the traditional guidebook.

**Swiss News**

A complete revelation to me – I found it both enlightening and interesting, not to mention amusing.

**Carole Clark**

Let's say it at once. David Hampshire's *Living and Working in France* is the best handbook ever produced for visitors and foreign residents in this country; indeed, my discussion with locals showed that it has much to teach even those born and bred in *l'Hexagone*. – It is Hampshire's meticulous detail which lifts his work way beyond the range of other books with similar titles. Often you think of a supplementary question and search for the answer in vain. With Hampshire this is rarely the case. – He writes with great clarity (and gives French equivalents of all key terms), a touch of humour and a ready eye for the odd (and often illuminating) fact. – This book is absolutely indispensable.

**The Riviera Reporter**

The ultimate reference book – Every conceivable subject imaginable is exhaustively explained in simple terms – An excellent introduction to fully enjoy all that this fine country has to offer and save time and money in the process.

**American Club of Zurich**

# Have Said About Survival Books

What a great work, wealth of useful information, well-balanced wording and accuracy in details. My compliments!

**Thomas Müller**

This handbook has all the practical information one needs to set up home in the UK – The sheer volume of information is almost daunting – Highly recommended for anyone moving to the UK.

**American Citizens Abroad**

A very good book which has answered so many questions and even some I hadn't thought of – I would certainly recommend it.

**Brian Fairman**

A mine of information – I may have avoided some embarrassments and frights if I had read it prior to my first Swiss encounters – Deserves an honoured place on any newcomer's bookshelf.

**English Teachers Association, Switzerland**

Covers just about all the things you want to know on the subject – In answer to the desert island question about the one how-to book on France, this book would be it – Almost 500 pages of solid accurate reading – This book is about enjoyment as much as survival.

**The Recorder**

It's so funny – I love it and definitely need a copy of my own – Thanks very much for having written such a humorous and helpful book.

**Heidi Guiliani**

A must for all foreigners coming to Switzerland.

**Antoinette O'Donoghue**

A comprehensive guide to all things French, written in a highly readable and amusing style, for anyone planning to live, work or retire in France.

**The Times**

A concise, thorough account of the DOs and DON'Ts for a foreigner in Switzerland – Crammed with useful information and lightened with humorous quips which make the facts more readable.

**American Citizens Abroad**

Covers every conceivable question that may be asked concerning everyday life – I know of no other book that could take the place of this one.

**France in Print**

Hats off to Living and Working in Switzerland!

**Ronnie Almeida**

# CONTENTS

# 4. ARRIVAL 109

# 5. ACCOMMODATION 119

# 6. POST OFFICE SERVICES 151

# 7. TELEPHONE 163

## 12. HEALTH — **279**

## 13. INSURANCE — **301**

# 14. FINANCE 325

# 15. LEISURE 365

# 16. SPORTS 397

# 19. THE AUSTRALIANS 471

# 20. MOVING HOUSE OR LEAVING AUSTRALIA 479

# APPENDICES 485

# INDEX 499

# ORDER FORMS 510

# IMPORTANT NOTE

**A**ustralia is a diverse country with many faces, a plethora of ethnic groups, languages, religions and customs, and continuously changing rules, regulations (particularly regarding social security, health care, education and taxes) and prices. Note that a change of government in Australia, which can occur every three years, can have far-reaching repercussions for many important aspects of daily life in Australia. **I cannot recommend too strongly that you always check with an official and reliable source (not always the same) before making any major decisions, or taking an irreversible course of action. However, don't believe everything you're told or read – even, dare I say it, herein!**

Useful addresses and references to other sources of information are included in all chapters and in **Appendices A** and **B**, to help you obtain further information and verify details with official sources. Important points have been emphasised in **bold** print, some of which it would be expensive, or even dangerous, to disregard. **Ignore them at your peril or cost.** Unless specifically stated, the reference to any company, organisation or product in this book doesn't constitute an endorsement or recommendation. Any reference to any place or person (living or dead) is purely coincidental. There's no such place as Wogga Wogga.

# AUTHOR'S NOTES

- The federal or Commonwealth government refers to the Australian national government which has its seat in Canberra (Australian Capital Territory). State government refers to the government of a particular state (such as New South Wales) or territory (such as the Northern Territory). Unless otherwise specified, the term 'state' also applies to territories. Note that the term 'state capital' refers to the capital of an Australian state, e.g. the capital of New South Wales is Sydney, while the capital of the Commonwealth of Australia is Canberra.

- The following (official) abbreviations for the Australian states and territories are used in this book: Australian Capital Territory (ACT), New South Wales (NSW), Northern Territory (NT), Queensland (QLD), South Australia (SA), Tasmania (TAS), Victoria (VIC) and Western Australia (WA).

- All times are shown using am (ante meridiem) for before noon and pm (post meridiem) for afternoon. Most Australians don't use the 24-hour clock. All times are local, so check the time difference when making inter-state or international telephone calls (see **Time Difference** on page 468).

- All prices shown are in Australian dollars (A$) unless otherwise noted. **Prices should be taken only as estimates, although they were mostly correct at the time of publication.**

- His/he/him also means her/she/her (please forgive me ladies). This is done to make life easier for both the reader and (in particular) the author, and *isn't* intended to be sexist.

- Most spelling is (or should be) British English.

- Warnings and important points are shown in **bold** type.

- The following symbols are used in this book: ☎ (telephone), 📠 (fax), ✉ (e-mail), 🖥 (Internet).

- Lists of **Useful Addresses** and **Further Reading** are contained in **Appendices A** and **B** respectively.

- For those unfamiliar with the metric system of weights and measures, imperial conversion tables are included in **Appendix C**.

- A map of Australia is contained in **Appendix D**.

# INTRODUCTION

Whether you're already living or working in Australia or just thinking about it, this is **THE BOOK** for you. Forget about all those glossy guide books, excellent though they are for tourists – this amazing book was written especially with you in mind and is worth its weight in amber nectar (beer). *Living and Working in Australia* is designed to meet the needs of anyone wishing to know the essentials of Australian life, including immigrants, temporary workers, business people, students, retirees, long-stay tourists and even extra-terrestrials. However long your intended stay in Australia, you'll find the information contained in this book invaluable.

General information isn't difficult to find in Australia, where a multitude of books are published on every conceivable subject. However, reliable and up-to-date information specifically intended for foreigners living and working in Australia isn't so easy to find, least of all in one volume. My aim in writing this book was to help fill this void and provide the comprehensive *practical* information necessary for a relatively trouble-free life down under.

You may have visited Australia as a tourist, but living and working there is a different matter altogether. Adjusting to a different environment and culture and making a home in any foreign country can be a traumatic and stressful experience, and Australia is no exception. You need to adapt to new customs and traditions and discover the Australian way of doing things, for example finding a home, paying bills and obtaining insurance. For most foreigners in Australia, finding out how to overcome the everyday obstacles of life has previously been a case of pot luck. **But no more!** With a copy of *Living and Working in Australia* to hand, you'll have a wealth of information at your fingertips – information derived from a variety of sources, both official and unofficial, not least the hard won personal experiences of the author, his family, friends, colleagues and acquaintances.

*Living and Working in Australia* is a comprehensive handbook on a wide range of everyday subjects and represents the most up-to-date source of general information available to foreigners in Australia. It isn't, however, simply a monologue of dry facts and figures, but a practical and entertaining look at life in Australia.

Adapting to life in a new country is a continuous process and, although this book will help reduce your 'beginner's' phase and minimise the frustrations, it doesn't contain all the answers (most of us don't even know the right questions). What it *will* do is help you make informed decisions and calculated judgements, instead of uneducated guesses and costly mistakes. **Most important of all, it will help you save time, trouble and money, and repay your investment many times over!**

Although you may find some of the information a bit daunting, don't be discouraged. Most problems occur only once and fade into insignificance after a short time (as you face the next half a dozen!). The majority of foreigners in Australia would agree that, all things considered, they love living there. A period spent in Australia is a wonderful way to enrich your life, broaden your horizons, and maybe even please your bank manager. I trust this book will help you avoid the pitfalls of life in Australia and smooth your way to a happy and rewarding future in your new home.

**Good luck!**

**David Hampshire**
**August 2001**

# 1.

# FINDING A JOB

Finding a job in Australia may be easier than you expect, especially with its relatively low unemployment rate, as there are vacancies for skilled tradesmen and professionals throughout the country. However, if you don't automatically qualify to live or work in Australia (e.g. as a citizen of New Zealand), obtaining a visa is likely to be more difficult than finding a job. Australia is no longer the fabled 'land of opportunity' or 'the lucky country', at least not for the hundreds of thousands of migrants it previously welcomed. It now hopes to become 'the clever country' through the importation of highly educated and skilled workers. Not surprisingly, it's a popular destination among prospective migrants, and few countries offer such an attractive lifestyle and high standard of living, and such good business and employment prospects.

**Immigrants:** Australia is a country of immigrants and is the second most polyglot, multicultural nation in the world after Israel, with huge ethnic communities and migrants from over 125 nations. Before the Second World War, Australian migrants were predominantly from Britain and Ireland; even 40 years ago, Britain dominated Australia's migrant intake, when Australia would take virtually anyone and even offered a £10 assisted passage scheme. Britain has provided over 2 million migrants since 1945 and over 7 million in total. Today, however, only some 10 per cent of new migrants are British, although Britain still remains the largest source of skilled migrants (and second overall to New Zealand).

Since the war, there has also been an influx of migrants from continental Europe, including large numbers of Greeks and Italians, plus Lebanese, Turks, Yugoslavs and various others. All major cities contain suburbs with predominantly 'foreign' communities and atmospheres, including Chinese, Greek, Italian, Lebanese and Yugoslav. Sydney is home to more New Zealanders than most cities in New Zealand and Melbourne's Greek population is the third-largest in the world (after Athens and Thessalonica). Since the end of the official 'white Australia' policy in 1975, Australia has admitted large numbers of Asian immigrants, including many refugees from Indochina. There are also many immigrants from the Pacific, Middle East, southern Europe, Central and South America, and South Africa. In 2000, over 90 per cent of the population was of European descent, 5 per cent Asian and 1.5 per cent Aboriginal. Over 60 per cent of the 4 million immigrants who were born overseas have come from a non-English speaking country, and immigrants account for a sizeable portion of the country's population growth, as well as around a quarter of the labour force.

Today, Australia has a multicultural migration policy and settlers are encouraged to retain their ethnic languages, lifestyles and artistic traditions. Many immigrants now originate from Asia, which is the fastest growing ethnic group and expected to outnumber immigrants from Britain in the next decade. However, some Australians are alarmed about what they call the 'Asianisation' of Australia's immigration policy – within the next 50 years around 25 per cent of Australia's population is likely to be of Asian origin. Nevertheless, it isn't all one-way traffic and around 30,000 people leave Australia each year, and many immigrants return home after a relatively short period (around 20 per cent of new arrivals in the last decade have left again). Around 5 to 10 per cent of Australians have also emigrated to other countries.

Migrant numbers have fallen dramatically in recent years, from around 140,000 per year in the '80s to a quota of just 85,000 in 2001–02 (up by almost 20,000 from late '90s levels). Australian embassies and consulates receive enquiries from around a million people a year, of whom some 400,000 make applications. Of those accepted, almost half have relatives in Australia, around 45 per cent are professionals or skilled workers, and some 15 per cent are refugees. In recent years, debate has centred on how migration affects employment, with those claiming it increases unemployment in the ascendancy. Many analysts believe it's a knee-jerk reaction to make migrants the scapegoats for Australia's economic woes and that no link has been established between migration and high unemployment. Indeed, in the USA it has been calculated that immigration boosts the economy by $billions a year.

**Employment Prospects:** Australia has a small labour force of around 9.1 million people, some three-quarters of whom are employed full-time, and an unemployment rate of 6.7 per cent in mid-2001. You shouldn't plan on obtaining immediate employment in Australia unless you have a firm job offer or special qualifications and experience for which there's a strong local demand, for example in information or communication technology. If you want a good job, you must usually be well qualified and speak fluent English (if you're an independent migrant, you won't be accepted without these qualifications). Unemployment is high among non-English speaking adult migrants, particularly those from North Africa, the Middle East and the Indian subcontinent. This mostly applies to those who came to Australia under the Family Reunion Program (although two-thirds have professional qualifications), many of whom believe that they were better off at home.

It's important to obtain the latest information concerning jobs (official information sometimes lags behind the real situation); if possible, try to secure a position before your arrival. Most states publish data on current job prospects, indicating occupations with shortages or surpluses of experienced workers. It's advantageous to make a fact-finding visit to Australia to check your job prospects first hand, although this may not be feasible (a research trip will also help you to judge more accurately whether you're likely to enjoy the Australian way of life). This may also help you to find a prospective employer willing to sponsor you, which will make the task of obtaining a visa much easier. If you plan to arrive in Australia without a job, you should have a detailed plan for finding employment on arrival and try to make some contacts before you arrive.

The Australian job market changed dramatically in the '90s, during which most new jobs shifted from manufacturing, construction and finance to the property, communications and service industries (e.g. retailing and computing). There has been huge job growth in the white-collar services sector in recent years (the growth industry of the '90s), particularly in property and business support services, which now employ some 80 per cent of the workforce and are responsible for 20 per cent of export earnings. Agriculture (including horticulture, fishing, forestry, horses and the service industries to agriculture and agribusiness) has also created over 20,000 jobs in the last decade. Retailing is the largest source of jobs in Australia with some 1.36 million workers, and a further 1.1 million are employed in manufacturing, although its share of national employment has halved to below 15 per cent since the mid-'60s. In recent years, most new jobs have been created in Queensland and Western Australia.

Australian manufacturers and the Australian labour market have been relatively slow to embrace new technology and to adjust to the rapidly changing world economy, although there's now an intensive government drive to rectify this. Many companies depend on (declining) assistance (worth $4 billion a year) through tariffs on imports, production bounties and export incentives, rather than improving productivity, reducing costs and eradicating restrictive working practices. Australian productivity is just half that of the USA and some 60 per cent of that of many developed countries. Like most western countries, Australia has found it increasingly difficult to compete with cheap imports from countries (e.g. in Asia) where labour costs are very low.

The information technology age has spawned a new class of low skilled, low paid, part-time and casual workers, and one of the trade unions' main fears is that new technology will create an 'underclass' and dump thousands of people on the job scrap heap. Although there was major job-shedding by banks and utility companies in the mid-'90s, in recent years economic growth and the 2000 Olympics have led to greater employment. Indeed, although new technology may be putting people out of work in some industries, it's credited with creating jobs overall. Australia's job market, like that of most western countries, was transformed in the '90s and it's vital for workers to keep their skills up to date in order to stay ahead of the pack. There's currently a chronic shortage of IT specialists in Australia (some 100,000 vacancies in 2001) and the government has introduced a special visa class to try to combat this problem.

Although it isn't as easy to find work as in the '80s, there's a steady demand for skilled workers in most regions and a shortage in some areas, which has been exacerbated by a sharp reduction in apprenticeships and training in recent years. If you have a choice, compare the job or business opportunities in all states and territories before deciding where to live, as job prospects vary considerably from city to city and state to state (as does the lifestyle, culture and to a lesser extent, the weather). Some states (such as South Australia) have a shortage of skilled workers and offer incentives to migrants such as job matching schemes, subsidised accommodation and low-interest loans. It's also easier to qualify for immigration if you're willing to settle outside the major cites in a 'designated' low-growth area (in recent years, job prospects have grown faster in regional centres than in state capitals).

**Changing Workforce:** The jobs lost in the last decade or so have generally been well paid skilled and semi-skilled manufacturing jobs, which have often been replaced by low paid, part-time or temporary jobs with few benefits (comprising some 40 per cent of all jobs in Australia). Labour experts believe that the era of secure, full-time employment with comprehensive employee benefits and lifetime guarantees has gone for ever (not just in Australia, but world wide). Today, there's a new psychological contract between employers and employees, where job security isn't part of the deal. In the last few decades, the country has gone from boom to bust, with the prosperous '80s followed by the worst recession (which hit Australia earlier than most other western countries) since the great depression of the 1930s. However, the years 1998–2000 have seen strong annual economic growth (around 4 per cent), which is expected to continue at least until the end of 2002, and, for the first time since the Asian crisis in 1997–98, net exports increased significantly in the period 2000–01.

Australia has undergone an economic revolution in recent years, during which many sacred cows have gone (or are going) to the wall, including protectionism, state ownership, the welfare state and the power of the unions. Today, employees must be flexible with diverse and up-to-date skills, constantly renewed through further education and training. Australia has a highly mobile labour force (around a quarter of the workforce changes jobs each year), particularly among the young, and even managers and executives often need to change careers or move to another city to find a job. Nowadays, an increasing number of people are 'tele-working' (working from home via telephone, fax and computer), either from choice or because their employers have closed offices to reduce costs. There are over a third of a million home-based workers in Australia – a number which is growing at three times the rate of overall employment – and it's estimated that homeworkers will comprise some 25 per cent of the workforce in the next decade.

**Industrial Relations:** Industrial relations have historically been poor in Australia, although there has been a huge reduction in strikes during the last two decades due among other things to the 'accord' between unions and employers instigated by the Labor Party when it came to power in the early '80s. This altered the constant cycle of confrontation between workers, management and the government and heralded an era of relative industrial peace. In place of demands for higher wages, workers were given better working conditions and benefits, which helped put a brake on runaway inflation and strengthened the economy. Between 1981 and 1990, the number of days lost to strikes fell from some 800 per thousand employees to just over 200. However, the reduction in strikes was also influenced by the recession and the consequent sharp rise in unemployment.

For many years, Australian workers were blessed with falling working hours, high wages (which kept pace with or exceeded inflation) and extensive employee protection. However, this was won at the cost of higher unemployment, low productivity and reduced competitiveness in international markets. In 2000, the number of working days lost to industrial action was 413,800, a decrease of almost 11 per cent on the 1999 figure. Over the same period, the number of employees involved in industrial disputes (either directly or indirectly) decreased by 47 per cent. Industrial action occurred in a number of key industries both in the private sector, with disputes in the metal producing and manufacturing industries, and in the public sector, where education and the health and community service industry bore the brunt of strikes. In 2000, all states except Tasmania and the Northern Territory recorded a decrease in the number of working days lost. A survey in 2000 found that Australia's industrial relations system is widely seen as unfair, open to political manipulation and susceptible to conflict.

**Unemployment:** In the new millennium, reducing unemployment is the biggest challenge facing the nation. During the early '90s, Australian workers were hit by a combination of recession and 'restructuring', with many companies slashing their staff in order to become 'lean and mean' and compete more effectively. Companies quickly realised that they could operate with smaller workforces, and today Australia's largest employers are continually reducing their staff and have become ruthless in making employees redundant. Downsizing by government (the number of federal employees has halved in the last ten years) and businesses has made over 3 million full-time workers redundant in the last decade. Increasing competition (at home and overseas), new technology and greater automation have all exacerbated the problem and led to relatively high levels of unemployment, particularly for a country that has traditionally enjoyed low unemployment compared with the rest of the world.

However, after peaking at 11.3 per cent in 1992, the number of jobless has fallen slowly and in mid-2001 stood at around 6.7 per cent (over 650,000 people, 200,000 of whom are long-term unemployed, i.e. out of work for a year or longer) and forecasts are that it will fall below 6 per cent by mid-2002. Unemployment is highest in Tasmania and Queensland, lowest in New South Wales and Victoria. It's also much higher in rural areas, which is why most migrants head for the cities. Unskilled and semi-skilled workers have been hardest hit by the downturn, as have the younger and older age groups (most long-term unemployed are under 25 or over 45). Age discrimination is widespread in Australia, although it's illegal to specify age in job advertisements in some states, and the older you are, the more difficult it is to find a job.

Unemployment is, not surprisingly, much higher than average among migrants who don't speak fluent English. In recent years, many migrants who have been unable to find a job have experienced great hardship as they can no longer claim social security during their first two years in the country (although some migrants have successfully challenged the new law). Working holidaymakers no longer find it easy to find work, as unemployed young Australians are snapping up the temporary and casual low-paid jobs which were once the preserve of the itinerant 'backpacker'. In the last few years, the government has introduced a number of job creation schemes, such as Jobsearch and Newstart (see page 307), in an effort to boost employment, particularly among the young and long-term unemployed.

**Work Ethic:** Australians aren't renowned for their work ethic ('sickies' – days off work for no reason – are widespread) and Australian industry is noted for its low productivity. However, Australians believe in working (and playing) hard, and they generally work as hard and efficiently as workers in other western countries. Don't be misled by the informality and casual atmosphere and dress in many companies, as Australian employers can be ruthless when it comes to the bottom line. Although the usual working week is just 35 to 40 hours for most wage earners (the average in 1999 was 39.5 hours), overtime is normally available. Twelve-hour days aren't uncommon among managerial and professional staff. In fact, the higher you climb the ladder of success, the harder you're expected to work (burn-out is common among managers and executives). Redundancies and cost-cutting in recent years have increased the pressure on all employees, particularly white-collar workers, many of whom now do the work of a number of people. Job dissatisfaction is rife in Australia, one survey showing that (incredibly) over 60 per cent of employees would like a new job.

**Further Information:** There are numerous books written for those seeking a job in Australia, including *Getting a Job in Australia* by Nick Vandome (How To Books), the *Australia & New Zealand Contact Directory* (Expat Network, UK ☎ 020-8760 5100, 💻 www.expatnetwork.com) and *Graduate Opportunities* published by the Graduate Careers Council of Australia, PO Box 28, Parkville, VIC 3052 (☎ 3-9348 4300, 💻 www.gradlink.edu.au). A range of reports and information is available at Australian missions abroad, and the Department of Employment, Education, Training and Youth Affairs (DETYA), which projects employment trends for the next ten years in a wide range of industries, trades and professions, publishes a number of booklets. The Australian Bureau of Statistics (ABS) also publishes job figures and employment forecasts (💻 www.abs.gov.au). Finally, a wealth of job information can be found via the Internet (e.g. 💻 www.jobsearch.com.au) – see page 34.

## QUALIFICATIONS

The most important qualification for working in Australia is the ability to speak English fluently. If you have a degree or a certificate from a recognised educational establishment in an English-speaking country, language usually presents no problems. However, applicants from non-English speaking countries or backgrounds must usually pass an English test and possibly also an occupational English examination, where the pass mark depends on your profession or trade. The failure rate is high.

Once you have overcome this hurdle, you should establish whether your trade or professional qualifications and experience are recognised in Australia. While you may be well qualified in your own country, you may need to pass professional examinations or trade tests to satisfy Australian standards (overseas trained doctors recently went on hunger-strike claiming that they were denied the right to practise by discriminatory qualification tests). If you aren't experienced, Australian employers will expect your studies to be in a relevant discipline and to have included work experience.

The points system (see page 88) on which most immigration is based, depends to a large extent on the skills and qualifications of applicants. Points are awarded for skill levels based on your current or previous employment and whether your qualifications are adequate, including occupational training. Theoretically, qualifications recognised by professional and trade bodies overseas should be recognised in Australia. However, recognition varies depending on the country and in some cases foreign qualifications aren't recognised by Australian employers or professional and trade associations. All academic qualifications should also be recognised, although they may be given less prominence than equivalent Australian qualifications, depending on the country and the educational institution in which they were obtained.

To practise a profession or trade in Australia, you require evidence of an appropriate level of education and practical experience; the usual minimum number of years' experience is three but it can be much higher for some jobs. To work in Australia as a licensed tradesman your qualifications must be assessed by a Vocational Training Board or similar state organisation; you may also need a special licence to work in some states, trades or professions (or pass an examination). Trades Recognition Australia (TRA) provides a trades assessment service and assesses migrants' qualifications, skills and experience against comparable standards in Australia. For example, the metal and electrical trades have a system whereby overseas-trained tradesmen can be awarded an Australian Recognised Tradesman's Certificate.

The recognition of professional qualifications is usually the responsibility of the relevant professional body, which migrants are normally required to join to practise in Australia. Note, however, that a favourable assessment isn't a guarantee that you will be professionally recognised or be able to gain employment in your field of expertise, as some professional bodies require overseas practitioners to pass examinations conducted or supervised by themselves. In some cases, it's necessary for foreign professionals to work under the supervision of a registered professional Australian for a period, e.g. a year, or to undertake further training. Medical practitioners must have studied medicine in Australia or New Zealand to work in some states, e.g. NSW, and foreign doctors cannot work for Medicare (the state health scheme).

The Australian government no longer lists the skills and qualifications necessary for occupations. However, you can check the qualifications required for a particular job in the ***Australian Standard Classification of Occupations (ASCO)*** dictionary, available for reference at Australian High Commission offices and other Australian government offices overseas and at offices of the Department of Immigration and Ethnic Affairs in Australia or on the website ⌨ www.abs.gov.au. Additional information can be obtained from the National Office of Overseas Skills Recognition (NOOSR), PO Box 1407, Canberra City, ACT 2601 (☎ freecall 1800-020 086, ⊠ noosr@detya.gov.au).

Whatever kind of job you're looking for in Australia, whether temporary or permanent, part or full-time, always take proof of your qualifications, training and experience with you, plus copies of references and an up-to-date *curriculum vitae* (see page 36.

## GOVERNMENT EMPLOYMENT SERVICES

In Australia, there are two government authorities in charge of employment at federal level: Centrelink (🖳 www.centrelink.gov.au) and Employment National (🖳 www. employmentnational.com.au).

**Centrelink:** Centrelink offices provide a range of customer services covering: employment, education, training and youth affairs; social security; health and family services; and primary industries and energy. Centrelink offices also provide many services including: registration and acceptance of new applicants for income support and employment assistance; self-help job facilities, including computer access to a national job vacancies database; advice and information regarding the government Jobs, Education and Training (JET) program; and specialist labour market assistance services for disadvantaged groups, including Aboriginals and Torres Strait Islanders, single parents, people with disabilities, migrants and young people. Centrelink has a comprehensive website and an online magazine, *Update Employment*, which provides latest information on Centrelink services. The Centrelink employment service can be reached on ☎ 13-2850 (local call cost from anywhere in Australia).

**Employment National:** Employment National is a government-owned company run on market lines advertising itself as Australia's largest recruitment solutions provider. The company, with some 120 offices throughout Australia, aims to provide information on services, job vacancies, apprenticeships and harvest work. A monthly online magazine called *Employ*, which aims to provide latest information on job and apprenticeship opportunities as well as help and advice was launched in mid-2001. It competes head on with a host of community-based 'job brokers', including community job centres (such as Work Ventures and Work Solutions in Sydney), employer organisations, local councils and private job search companies, which have contracts with the government and are paid by results, i.e. getting people jobs. The Employment National scheme is perceived by most Australians to be inefficient and poorly run and to have done little to solve the problem of long-term unemployment. Concern about the scheme is frequently raised by the media and the general public, mainly in the belief that the government manipulates the statistics to boost claims of success.

## PRIVATE EMPLOYMENT AGENCIES

Private employment agencies abound in all major cities and towns in Australia and are big business. Private employment agencies employ some 85,000 people annually, of whom nearly two-thirds are engaged in casual work. Many large companies are happy to engage agents and consultants to recruit employees, particularly executives, managers, professionals and temporary staff. There are four main types of employment agencies in Australia: personnel consultants, employment agencies, labour hire contractors and student employment services. Personnel consultants (head-hunters) handle mostly executive, managerial and professional positions (lawyers are in demand, so if you're feeling unloved in your home country, you can go to Australia and be unloved there also), although there's some overlap with 'general' employment agencies. Labour hire contractors handle jobs for skilled, semi-skilled and unskilled manual workers and tend to be located in industrial areas rather than the main streets of major cities.

The largest number of agencies simply come under the generic term 'employment agencies'. Some specialise in particular fields or industries: accounting; agriculture; au pairs and nannies; banking; carers; computing; engineering and technical; hospitality; industrial and manual work; legal; medical and nursing; mining; outback jobs; sales; secretarial; resort work; and tourism. Others deal with a range of industries and professions. Some agencies deal exclusively with temporary workers in a variety of occupations, including office staff, baby-sitting, housekeeping, cooks, gardeners, chauffeurs, hairdressing, security, cleaners, labourers and industrial workers. Nursing, nanny and care agencies are common and usually cover the whole range of nursing services. Many agencies handle both permanent and temporary positions.

There's a plethora of employment agencies in Australia, many operating nationally with offices in all major cities, while others operate in one or two cities only. Among the largest agencies operating nationwide or in most major cities are Accountancy Placements, ADIA, Alfred Marks, BDS Challenge International, Brook Street, Catalyst Recruitment Systems, Centacom, Centastaff, Computer People, Dial-an-Angel, Drake Personnel, Ecco Personnel, Forstaff, IPA Personnel, Job Network, Julia Ross Personnel, Kelly Services, Key People, Manpower, Metier Personnel, Morgan & Banks, Select Appointments, Skilled Work Force, Temporary Solutions, Templine and Western Staff Services. Check the yellow pages for local offices of these and other agencies. If you're travelling around Australia and plan to work in a number of major cities, you may find it advantageous to work for a national agency with offices nationwide.

Agencies are usually prohibited from charging a fee to job applicants, as they receive their fees from clients, although in some states they may charge a registration fee (check first). For permanent staff, the fee paid by the employer is a percentage of the annual salary (e.g. 10 per cent) and for temporary, hourly-paid staff they take a percentage of the hourly rate paid by employers. If you take a temporary job through an agency, you'll be paid by the agency, usually weekly or fortnightly, which may include paid public and annual holidays after a qualifying period. Always obtain a contract and ensure that you know exactly how much you'll be paid and when, and the conditions regarding the termination of a job.

Agencies must deduct income tax from gross pay and you're required to give an agency your tax file number (see page 327) within a few weeks of starting work; otherwise they must deduct tax at the highest marginal tax rate. Salaries vary considerably according to the type of job, but most secretarial jobs pay between $12 and $18 per hour or $325 to $475 per week net (after tax). You usually receive extra pay (loading) for weekend and night work, and there are allowances (called tropical loading or remote area allowances) for jobs in remote areas of the Northern Territory and Western Australia (above the Tropic of Capricorn).

When visiting employment agencies, you should dress appropriately for the type of job you're seeking, and take with you your passport (with a visa if applicable), tax file number (TFN), *curriculum vitae* (CV), references and your bank details (if you want to get paid!). Office staff may be given a typing or literacy test (if applicable) and some agencies have in-house training programmes for secretarial staff. You should register with a number of agencies to maximise your chances of finding work. Keep in close contact and try to provide a telephone number where you can be contacted; otherwise you should ring in every day.

Employment agencies earn a great deal of money from finding people jobs so, provided you have something to offer their clients, they'll be keen to help you (if you're an experienced accountant, nurse or secretary you may get trampled in the rush). If they cannot help you, they'll usually tell you immediately and won't waste your time. To find local agencies, look in the yellow pages under 'Employment Agencies' and in local newspapers. Employment agencies are increasingly using the Internet to advertise job vacancies, which speeds up the response and processing of job applications. Many Australian agencies employing temporary staff advertise overseas in publications (see **Appendix A**) targeted at those with working holidaymaker visas. A list of agencies specialising in particular jobs or fields is contained in *Live, Work & Play in Australia* by Sharyn McCullum (Kangaroo Press).

## CONTRACT JOBS

Contract or freelance jobs are available through specialist employment agencies in Australia. Contracts are usually full-time and for a fixed period, although they may be open-ended. There's a thin dividing line between contract and temporary jobs (see page 29) which are often one and the same. In recent years, many companies have been shifting from full-time employees to contract workers and contracting out jobs such as cleaning, building maintenance, catering, construction work, computer installation and even parts of the manufacturing process.

Many contract positions are for specialists, in fields such as accountancy, computing, engineering, electronics and mining, although there's also a strong market in providing cleaning, catering and maintenance services. Rates vary considerably, e.g. from around $12 per hour for a clerk up to $100 or more an hour for a computer specialist. Contractors may work at home or on a client's or contract company's premises. There used to be a lucrative market in contract jobs in Australia, particularly for information technology specialists, although the recession in the '90s put paid to many jobs. Consultant companies (also called bodyshops) specialise in supplying contract staff to major companies. Note that the usual visa regulations apply to contract workers, unless they're employed to work outside Australia.

## PART-TIME JOBS

Part-time jobs are available in most industries and professions in Australia and are most common in offices, pubs, shops, factories, cafes and restaurants. In the last few years the number of part-time workers in Australia has risen considerably, particularly among women, and now totals around 3 million – some 25 per cent of the workforce. Over 75 per cent of part-time jobs in larger workplaces (with a minimum of 20 staff) are in the retail, accommodation, cafe and restaurant, education, health and community service sectors. Part-time jobs apply to all levels (from executives to clerks) and all businesses, many turning to part-time work for lifestyle, health or family reasons. Job satisfaction is generally higher among part-time workers than those in full-time employment (wouldn't you be happier working fewer hours?).

A part-time job is generally defined as less than 20 hours per week. Part-time workers are usually paid on an hourly basis and don't have the same rights as full-time workers, but pay awards normally contain provisions to protect part-time workers' rights. They don't, however, usually receive annual leave, sick pay, maternity leave or the other entitlements that full-time workers get, although the balance is being redressed in various industries. Part-time workers are also generally poorly paid compared to full-time employees. Part-time jobs may be advertised in Employment National offices (see page 26).

## TEMPORARY & CASUAL JOBS

Temporary and casual jobs differ from part-time jobs in that they're usually for a limited (fixed) period, e.g. from a few hours to a few months, or even intermittent. Most Australian companies employ temporary or casual staff at some time (around 50 per cent on a regular basis), particularly in clerical positions when staff are sick or on holiday, for special projects and to supplement permanent employees. The casual job market has grown considerably in recent years, particularly in the food, beverage and manufacturing sectors and some 18 per cent of employees identify themselves as casual workers. The temporary job market was hit hard during the recession in the early '90s, although there has been a huge increase in demand in the last few years, particularly in the major cities. Downsizing and the cost of making full-time employees redundant (and unfair dismissal claims) have led many companies to employ an army of temporary employees, which is often more time-efficient and cost-effective.

Many people choose to make careers in temporary and contract work, which provides them with maximum flexibility when it comes to travel, working hours, time off and holidays. Although there's less security than with a full-time job and you don't usually receive any benefits, you're generally compensated by a higher hourly rate of pay. Temporary work also provides an opportunity to try your hand at a range of jobs which you would otherwise probably never do. The easiest way to find temporary work in the major cities is through an employment agency (see page 26), when, providing you have a marketable skill (e.g. accountancy, computing or nursing), it's relatively easy to find well paid temporary work. Hourly rates range from around $12 per hour for clerical staff to over $100 for IT professionals.

**Working Holidaymakers:** Temporary work particularly applies to foreigners with working holidaymaker visas, which permit you to work for any employer for up to three months. Note that it isn't easy to find temporary or casual work in many areas and you often need to hustle to get a job and may require experience or qualifications. It's important to ensure that you have sufficient funds to tide you over until you can find work. The easiest work to find is on farms, usually picking fruit or vegetables (see below). Note that you should be prepared to splash out on some smart clothes if a job requires them (or arrange to have them sent to you from overseas).

During university holiday periods, you'll have stiff competition from students so, if you're planning to work in a major city, try to get there before the local students break for their holidays. Most holiday jobs are available in retailing, fast food, harvesting and hospitality. Recruiting is often done a few months prior to holiday periods, e.g. companies hire in August to October for the summer period of December to February. Well known department and chain stores are generally the best employers. Avoid jobs offering unpaid 'trial' periods, which is illegal and is usually simply a con trick to get you to work for nothing. You should also avoid door-to-door selling requiring advance payment (e.g. $200) for sample kits (selling them is how some companies make their money) and jobs which pay only commission.

You'll usually have better job prospects if you plan to stay put for a number of months rather than just a few weeks. Note that you may be entitled to a tax rebate when you leave Australia, although claiming it may be more trouble than it's worth. Good sources of information for working holidaymakers are *Live, Work & Play in Australia* by Sharyn McCullum (Kangaroo Press), *Workabout Australia* by Barry Brebner, and the TNT *Australia & New Zealand Travel Planner* (see address in **Appendix B**), which contains advice on finding casual and temporary work. The British Universities North America Club (BUNAC, 16 Bowling Green Lane, London EC1R 0BD, UK ☎ 020-7251 3472, 🖳 www.bunac.org) has a 'Work Australia' programme which helps graduates with working holidaymaker visas to find temporary work.

**Farm Work:** One of the most common forms of temporary work in Australia is fruit and vegetable picking, which can be done somewhere in Australia throughout the year (many people manage to stay in work all year round). Pay varies considerably (from excellent to poor) and is either an hourly rate or, more often, piece work, where the more you pick the more you earn. Doing piece work you can earn around $100 per day, although you'll need to work between 50 and 80 hours per week, possibly seven days a week. You should expect to earn from around $300 per week after tax from most harvesting jobs. Always establish your hours, conditions and pay in advance, as there are unscrupulous employers around who will happily take advantage of you given half a chance.

Farming is a rough and ready experience and involves hard, often dirty work – definitely not for softies. You must usually have a tent or vehicle to sleep in; some employers provide basic accommodation and food (there may be a charge), but it's usually terrible and it's better to provide your own. It pays to have your own transport as farms are generally situated in remote areas (there aren't too many in downtown Sydney). Note that large farms are sometimes targeted by immigration officials, resulting in deportation for illegal workers. The government publication, *Harvest Table*, carries job advertisements from local fruit-growers' associations and there are harvest labour offices in many country areas. There's also a Harvest Hotline with latest information (☎ 1300-720 126 local call rate). An up-to-date state by state harvest guide is included on the *Harvest Trail* link on the Jobsearch website (🖳 www.jobsearch.gov.au).

Visitors to Australia with Working Holiday Visas (see **Chapter 3**) may be interested in the Visitoz Scheme, which is a work placement scheme designed particularly with working holiday visa holders in mind. Those who are accepted by the selection process for the scheme are guaranteed jobs and on-the-spot training during their stay in Australia. Jobs offered are mainly outdoors in the agricultural or rural hospitality industries, although there are jobs available in education, health care and maintenance. For more information on the scheme contact the Visitoz Scheme: in Australia, Springbrook, MS 188, Goomeri, 4601 Queensland (☎ 07-4168 6106,

⌨ www.visitoz.org) and in Britain, 4c Queens Gate Place, London SW7 5NT (☎ 020-7581 8627, ✉ wdtb@aol.com).

**Salary & Tax:** Employers or agencies require your tax file number (see page 327) and when you leave an employer you should receive a group certificate (for tax purposes). If you don't provide a tax file number, your employer must deduct tax at the highest marginal tax rate (47 per cent). If you earn over $450 per week, your employer must pay 3 per cent of your salary into a superannuation fund. This is intended to be rolled over from employer to employer until you reach retirement age but, if it amounts to less than $500, it's usually paid to you in cash. Many employers illegally pay temporary staff in cash without making any deductions for tax (see **Working Illegally** on page 43). Rates of pay for temporary jobs are often higher than for permanent jobs, as there's no entitlement to holiday or sick pay or other benefits, and no notice period may be required by either party.

**Casual Work:** Casual workers are usually employed on a daily, first-come-first-served basis. The work often entails hard labouring and is therefore better suited to men, although if you're a female weightlifter there's no bar against the fairer sex. Pay for casual work is usually low (from $5 per hour) and is usually paid cash in hand.

Temporary jobs may be advertised in Employment National offices (see page 26). See also **Employment Agencies** on page 26.

## VOLUNTARY WORK

The minimum age for voluntary work in Australia is usually 18, and most organisations require good or fluent English to be spoken. No special qualifications are required, and the minimum length of service varies from one month to one year (often there's no maximum length of service). Handicapped volunteers are also welcomed by many organisations. Voluntary work (not surprisingly) is unpaid, although meals and accommodation are usually provided and some organisations also pay pocket money. However, this is usually insufficient for your living expenses (entertainment, drinks, etc.), so make sure that you bring sufficient money with you. People over 50 years of age who are receiving unemployment benefit can do voluntary work with an approved organisation, subject to a minimum of 32 hours every two weeks.

It's essential, before coming to Australia to do voluntary work, that you check whether you're eligible and will be permitted to enter Australia under the immigration and employment regulations. The usual visitor's visa regulations apply to voluntary workers, but you don't require a special visa for unpaid work. Volunteers are usually required to pay a registration fee, pay for their own travel to and from a workcamp, and they may also be expected to contribute towards the cost of their board and lodging.

The main Australian voluntary organisations include:

● Volunteer Search, run by the government and offering more than 11,000 vacancies in volunteer work throughout Australia (⌨ www.volunteersearch.gov.au);

● The Involvement Volunteers (PO Box 218, Port Melbourne, Victoria 3207, ☎ 03-9646 5504; ⌨ www.volunteering.org.au), who maintain a register of voluntary positions and offer some paid work, e.g. on farms;

- The Australian Trust for Conservation Volunteers (ATCV, PO Box 423, Ballarat, Victoria 3353, ☎ freecall 1800-032501 or 03-5333 1483, 🖥 www.atcv.com.au), which has projects such as tree planting, track conservation, and flora and fauna surveys. Most projects are for a weekend or a week only and all accommodation, food and transport is provided in return for a small contribution (e.g. $20 a day) to help defray costs;

- The Australia & New Zealand Scientific Exploration Society (PO Box 174, Albert Park, Victoria 3206, ☎ 03-9866 8699, 🖥 http://home.vicnet.net.au), a non-profit organisation that undertakes scientific expeditions into wilderness areas of Australia. Volunteers are sent into the field under the guidance of an experienced leader;

- The international organisation, Willing Workers on Organic Farms (WWOOF), Mt Murrindal Co-Op, Gelantipy Road, Buchan, 3885 Victoria (☎ 03-5155 0235/ 0218, 🖥 www.wwoof.com.au), which has around 500 participating farms in Australia (a booklet is available listing all members). You receive food, accommodation and experience, but no pay. Membership costs $45 for a single person and $50 for any two people travelling together;

- The Wilderness Society (130 Davey St., Hobart, TAS 7000, ☎ 03-6234 9799, 🖥 www.wilderness.org.au), which requires a constant supply of volunteers.

Many other organisations require voluntary workers, including the Red Cross Society, the Salvation Army and the St. John's Ambulance Association.

## WORKING WOMEN

Some 55 per cent of Australian women work and comprise around 45 per cent of the total Australian workforce, including 35 per cent of full-time employees and 75 per cent of part-time workers (half of all women in paid employment work part-time). A woman doing the same or broadly similar work to a man and employed by the same employer is legally entitled to the same pay and terms of employment as a man ('equal pay for work of equal value'). However, as in most western countries, although there's no *official* discrimination, in practice this often isn't the case. Despite equal pay legislation (enshrined in the Sex Discrimination Act of 1984), women have found it impossible to close the pay gap between themselves and men, and in the mid-'90s men's wages were increasing at around twice the rate of women's. Women are disadvantaged in terms of pay scales at all levels of employment in all industries and professions, and most employers pay only lip service to equal pay. Women receive an average of around 70 per cent of men's wages (higher in professional jobs) and, although this is influenced by the fact that more women do menial jobs than men, the percentage of female executives and managers is low and women are consistently paid less for doing the same work. Women's only advantage is probably that unemployment amongst women is lower than amongst men.

Careers in which women predominate, such as nursery and primary school teaching, speech and occupational therapy, nursing, and librarianship, are comparatively poorly paid compared with those where men dominate. The concentration of women in part-time work and the failure of award wages to keep pace with enterprise agreements is also widening the gap between male and female earnings. Women working full-time are likely to be paid less than men and are less likely to have had a recent pay rise or to receive bonuses.

In recent years, women have been moving into male-dominated professions in increasing numbers, including accountancy, auditing and mathematics. However, although more women are breaking into the professions, they don't usually reach the top, where the 'old-boy' network thrives. The main discrimination among women professionals isn't in salary or title but in promotion opportunities, as many companies and organisations are loath to elevate women to important positions (ostensibly because of fears that they may leave and start a family or at least take long breaks from work – in 2000, only around 21 per cent of men took leave from work for family reasons compared with some 40 per cent of women). This invisible barrier is known as the 'glass ceiling'. The saying 'the best man for the job is often a woman' is seldom acknowledged by Australian employers, most of whom prefer male candidates. Male chauvinism is alive and positively thriving in Australia, where women employees also face the additional hazard of sexual harassment.

Although the glass ceiling is less of an obstacle to success than previously (cracks have been appearing in recent years), men are four times more likely than women to be managers and administrators. Women are almost non-existent among the directors of major companies and, although 25 per cent of the representatives on government authorities and boards are officially supposed to be women (a figure which should rise to 50 per cent in the long term), in reality it's much lower. Just 6 per cent of company directors and 10 per cent of top management positions are held by women. Most successful businesswomen are forced to put their career before their family (most don't have children) and personal life, most female executives working over 50 hours a week. Employers are (not surprisingly) wary of female employees becoming pregnant, as after one year's employment they're entitled to 12 months' unpaid maternity leave, after which they have the right to return to the same job with the same pay.

Self-employment is the best bet for women who want to get to the top and, not surprisingly, it has increased steadily during the last decade, despite the fact that banks and other financial institutions are usually loath to lend women money. See also **Discrimination** on page 51.

## JOB HUNTING

When looking for a job in Australia (or anywhere for that matter), you shouldn't put all your eggs in one basket, as the more job applications you make the better your chances of success. Contact as many prospective employers and employment agencies as possible, either by writing, telephoning or calling on them in person. Whatever job you're looking for, it's important to market yourself correctly and appropriately, which depends on the type of job you're seeking. For example, the recruitment of executives and senior managers in Australia is usually handled by consultants, who advertise in the Australian national press (and also overseas) and interview all applicants prior to presenting clients with a shortlist. At the other end of the scale, manual jobs requiring no previous experience may be advertised at Employment National offices, in local newspapers or even in shop windows, where the first suitable able-bodied applicant may be offered the job on the spot.

When writing for a job, address your letter to the personnel director or manager (try to obtain his name) and include your *curriculum vitae* (CV). Note, however, that writing for jobs from overseas is usually a hit and miss affair and it's probably the least successful method of securing employment (although it can be successful for those seeking 'temporary' jobs for up to four years). If you're applying from overseas and are planning to visit Australia, you should tell prospective employers when you will be available for interview and should arrange as many interviews as you can fit into your timetable (companies may wish to see a copy of your visa before interviewing you). Note that visiting Australia for an interview usually impresses prospective employers of your commitment. Your method of job hunting obviously depends on your circumstances, qualifications and experience, and the sort of job you're seeking, and may include the following:

- Visit local Employment National offices in Australia (see page 26). This is mainly for non-professional skilled and unskilled jobs.

- Check the TV teletext job service and other bulletin boards.

- Check employment sites on the Internet (which is increasingly being used by Australian agencies and headhunters). There are numerous sites and the Department of Employment (DEWRSB) maintains a regularly updated site with a list of most employment websites (⌨ www.dewrsb.gov.au). Some useful employment websites are: ⌨ www.jobsearch.gov.au (this government-run website is the largest – some 38,000 job vacancies in 2001 – and most comprehensive with daily additions), www.mycareer.com.au (thousands of jobs from recruitment agencies and employers), www.seek.com.au, www.jobnet. com.au (recruitment site for IT jobs), www.dma.com.au (specialist IT recruitment), www.employment.com.au, www.bluecollar.com.au (bluecollar jobs only), www.ambitionconnect.com.au (accounting and finance jobs), www.health work.com.au (jobs for health personnel), www.tempsonline.com.au (thousands of temporary job vacancies).

- Contact private recruitment consultants and employment agencies (see page 26).

- Obtain copies of Australian daily newspapers (see page 436), all of which contain 'positions vacant' sections (the Saturday editions are the best), including job advertisements dedicated to particular industries or professions on certain days. Most local and national newspapers are available in the reading rooms of local libraries in Australia, so you don't usually need to buy them. Jobs are also advertised in industry and trade newspapers and magazines. Australian newspapers are available in some countries from international news agencies, Australian embassies and consulates, Australian trade and commercial centres, and Australian social clubs (although they don't always contain the 'situations vacant' sections).

In Britain, single copies of the major Australian newspapers can be purchased from Smyth, International Media Representatives, 1 Torrington Park, London N12 9GG, UK (☎ 020-8446 6400). Subscriptions to Australian newspapers are available from TNT Express World, Unit 6, Spitfire Way, Spitfire Estate, Hounslow, Middx. TW5 9NW (☎ freephone 0800-777 999), but are expensive. The 'jobs vacant' sections of major Australian newspapers can also be perused via the Internet (a useful resource for anyone who isn't in Australia).

- Networking (basically getting together with like-minded people to discuss business) is a popular way of making business and professional contacts in Australia. It can be particularly successful for executives, managers and professionals when job hunting.

- If you have a professional qualification that's recognised in Australia, you can write to an Australian professional organisation for information and advice (addresses are obtainable from Australian chambers of commerce overseas); membership of the organisation may be obligatory to work in Australia. All associations publish journals containing 'positions vacant' advertisements, where members can also offer their services to prospective employers.

  Information about specific professions, trades and industries, particularly job opportunities in individual states, cities or areas, can be obtained from local chambers of commerce in Australia.

- Apply to international and national recruiting agencies acting for Australian companies. Agencies mainly recruit executives and key managerial and technical staff, and some have offices overseas, e.g. in Britain.

- Apply to foreign multi-national companies with offices or subsidiaries in Australia and make written applications directly to Australian companies. You can obtain a list of companies working in a particular field from trade directories, copies of which are available at reference libraries in Australia (they can also be consulted at Australian missions and chambers of commerce overseas).

- Place an advertisement in the 'Situations Wanted' section of a national newspaper in Australia or a local newspaper in the area where you wish to work. If you're a member of a recognised profession or trade, you could place an advertisement in a newspaper or magazine dedicated to your profession or a particular industry.

- Ask relatives, friends or acquaintances working in Australia whether they know of an employer looking for someone with your experience and qualifications.

- If you're already in Australia, contact or join expatriate social clubs, churches, societies and professional organisations, particularly your country's chamber of commerce.

- Students can use the Internet to contact prospective employers via Gradlink, established by the Graduate Careers Council of Australia.

- Apply in person to Australian companies (see **Personal Applications** below).

*Always* obtain a job offer in writing and a contract; steer clear of an employer who won't provide them. An official job entitles you to accident insurance, unemployment benefit, state pension and superannuation, redundancy payments and official protection from exploitation, among other benefits (see also **Working Illegally** on page 43).

## Personal Applications

Your best chance of obtaining some jobs (particularly temporary jobs) in Australia is to apply in person, when success is often simply a matter of being in the right place at the right time. When looking for a job for which no special qualifications or experience are required, it isn't necessarily *what* you know, but *who* you know. Many companies don't advertise but rely on attracting workers by word of mouth and their own vacancy boards. Always leave your name and address with a prospective employer and (if possible) a telephone number where you can be contacted, particularly if a job may become vacant at short notice. Advertise the fact that you're looking for a job with friends, relatives and acquaintances, and anyone you come into contact with who may be able to help. You can give lady luck a helping hand by your persistence and enterprise in:

- cold calling on prospective employers;
- checking wanted boards;
- looking in local newspapers;
- checking notice and bulletin boards in large companies, shopping centres, embassies, clubs, sports centres, stores, universities, churches and hostels;
- asking friends, acquaintances (etc.) and other temporary workers.

When leaving a job in Australia, you should ask for a written reference (one isn't usually provided automatically), particularly if you intend to look for further work in Australia or you think your work experience will help you to obtain employment overseas.

## CURRICULA VITAE & INTERVIEWS

*Curricula vitae* (CVs) are important in Australia when looking for a job, particularly when jobs are thin on the ground. Don't forget that the purpose of your CV is to obtain an interview, not a job, and it must be written with this in mind. This means that it must be tailored to every job application. If you aren't up to writing a good CV, you can employ a professional writer who should be able to turn your boring working life into something of which Indiana Jones would be proud. A good CV should be: brief (four pages or less); typed/printed on white A4 sheets (one side only); without strange fonts or bizarre layouts; word perfect and user-friendly; without ego, verbosity, salary demands or unexplained gaps in employment. Include a paragraph on your achievements. Your covering letter also needs to be word perfect and to grab the reader's attention. The government organisations Centrelink and Employment National offer free advice on the writing of CVs and job applications (see page 36). **The standard of most CVs in Australia is abysmal, so if yours is exceptional you're way ahead of the pack already.**

Job interviews shouldn't be taken lightly, as making a good impression can be the difference between getting a foot on the ladder of success and standing in the dole queue. Although dress rules in Australia aren't as strict as in some other countries, you should always dress smartly and appropriately when applying for a job (shorts and thongs are out). The secret of success is in your preparation, so do your homework on prospective employers and try to anticipate every question (and then some more) that you may be asked, and rehearse your answers. Be prepared to answer questions about why you came to Australia and what you think of the country and its people. Questions may be blunt and to the point and answers should be positive – you should avoid criticising your home country or former employers (or, needless to say, Australia!).

In recent years, Australian employers and recruitment agencies have been increasingly using psychology and personality tests to select staff. Some employers also require prospective employees to complete aptitude and other written tests. Employers may also require the names of a number of personal or professional referees, whom they may contact. You should take evidence of your educational, trade and professional qualifications and references from former employers. You may also be required to produce your passport and visa entitling you to live and work in Australia (if already issued), plus your driving licence.

## SALARY

It can be difficult to determine the salary you should command in Australia, as salaries aren't always listed in job advertisements, except for public sector employees (who are paid according to fixed grades). Salaries may vary considerably for the same job in different parts of Australia. In general, wages are highest in New South Wales (particularly Sydney, which has the highest cost of living) and Canberra, and lowest in Queensland and South Australia. However, salary variations aren't uniform across Australia and people living in areas with a low cost of living can sometimes earn as much as those in cities with a much higher cost of living. Australia generally has a lower cost of living (see page 360) than most European countries (similar to the USA). However, although Australians have traditionally been highly paid, some analysts believe that Australia's future may be low-tech, low-pay (compared with other OECD countries, Australia is going backwards).

There isn't a national statutory minimum wage in Australia, where minimum or 'award' wage are set for different industries, trades and professions through a unique system, decided at federal or state level by pay agreements between unions and employers. There are some 5,000 federal and state awards, each with six to eight wage classifications, making a total of around 35,000 different award wages. These cover over 80 per cent of Australian workers, although many employers pay above the award rate. Small businesses are more likely to pay above award wages than big companies (over two-thirds of small companies pay above award wages compared with around 50 per cent of large companies). Overtime rates are usually one and a half times the normal hourly award rate, but can be twice the normal rate for weekend work.

Employees not on awards often receive the federal minimum wage, which in 2001 was $400.40 per week (equal to a minimum hourly rate of $10.54 for a 38-hour week). Many analysts think that the high minimum wage is partly responsible for high unemployment, although it's effectively cut by employers hiring part-time and casual workers (many employers, particularly restaurant owners, pay below the legal rate of pay). Many people believe that there should be a lower minimum wage for unskilled workers, who are currently priced out of jobs.

Government surveys of average weekly earnings are published regularly for a wide range of trades and professions, both nationally and for individual states and cities. The govnerment-run organisiation Wagenet has a website where you can consult wages and conditions of employment information (🖳 www.wagenet.gov.au). There are also a number of books which detail wages in different occupations, including *What Jobs Pay* by Rod Tilson (Hobsons Press).

In 2000, the average weekly wage for adult males in full-time employment was around $833 ($885 with overtime) and $698 ($714.50 with overtime) for women. A third of employees earn less than $400 a week (many migrants from non-English speaking countries earn below $300 a week), while around 10 per cent earn over $1,000 a week. Average weekly wages have been increasing more slowly in recent years than in the '80s, although they're usually ahead of inflation. However, real wages for many workers fell over the last decade and many families receive social security payments (e.g. a 'family payment') to top up their incomes. Government employees earn more on average than employees in the private sector and receive higher wage increases. The highest paid jobs are usually in mining, finance and insurance, while the lowest paid are in retailing, catering and tourism. Under a scheme called 'leave loading', full-time employees are paid an extra 17.5 per cent of their normal wage when they're on holiday (usually paid in December).

Graduates can expect to start on annual salaries of around $34,000 for men and $32,000 for women (the gap is narrowing). At the other end of the scale, managing directors earn between $300,000 and $500,000 a year in Sydney (it isn't unusual for companies to pay executives 10 to 25 per cent more when they move to Sydney) compared with $175,000 to $350,000 in Melbourne and $125,000 to $200,000 in Perth. Executive salaries in Australia are fast catching up with the rest of the world, and expatriate American bosses of top Australian companies earn $millions a year (including $tens of millions in bonuses in the form of share incentives/options and performance-related bonuses).

Usually, salaries are negotiable, and it's up to you to ensure that you receive a level of salary and benefits commensurate with your qualifications and experience (or as much as you can get!). If you have friends or acquaintances working in Australia or who have worked there, ask them what an average or good salary is for your trade or profession. Salaries paid by some foreign companies (e.g. American or Japanese companies) may be higher on average than those paid by Australian companies, particularly for executives and managers imported from overseas. Your working hours (see page 59) in Australia may differ from those in other countries and will vary according to your profession and where you work. The standard working week is between 37 and 40 hours, although many employees work up to ten hours a week overtime. Hourly paid workers are paid overtime for extra hours and higher 'penalty' rates for night, shift and weekend work. In contrast, executives, professionals and managers often work over 50 hours per week without extra pay. There are allowances (called 'tropical loading' or 'remote area allowances') for work in remote areas of the Northern Territory and Western Australia (above the Tropic of Capricorn).

Women have fallen behind in the pay stakes in recent years, particularly those employed in part-time and temporary jobs, where wage growth has been minimal. Pay increases are often linked to improved productivity and performance, and pay generally rises in line with inflation. The 'accord' between workers, management and the former Labor government (from 1983 to 1996) generally heralded the end of massive pay rises for workers in return for better working conditions and fringe benefits. In 2000, average pay rose 3.75 per cent; in 2001, it's expected that average official pay rises will be around 3 per cent (in line with the rate of inflation) – considerably below those demanded by the unions, although at the bottom of the scale those without industrial clout and working outside the formal award system will receive little or nothing at all.

For many employees, particularly executives and senior managers, their 'salary' is much more than what they receive in their weekly or monthly pay packets. Many companies offer a number of fringe benefits (or perks) for executives and managers, which may even continue into retirement. These include company cars used for private purposes, private health insurance, children's private education and expense accounts (see also **Managerial & Executive Positions** on page 55). However, such benefits have declined considerably in recent years with the introduction of a fringe benefits tax (FBT), which is levied at 47 per cent on the taxable value of employee fringe benefits. There has also been a tax crackdown on executive pay packages, particularly 'salary sacrifice' schemes, where executives sacrifice part of their pay in return for higher superannuation payments and other benefits.

The most common forms of fringe benefits are subsidised company restaurants or canteens, allowances for living away from home, and superannuation (which is compulsory), all of which are covered by union awards and aren't liable to FBT. Under the mandatory Superannuation Guarantee (introduced in 1992), employers must pay a percentage of your salary into a superannuation fund (see page 310). Most employees consider fringe benefits to be important, particularly superannuation, income protection insurance, flexi-days, life insurance, company cars, staff discounts and child care on business premises. The opportunity to work overtime is also seen as an important 'fringe benefit' by most hourly paid workers, many of whom earn around a quarter of their wages from overtime. Always check whether a quoted salary is salary only or a total salary package, including for example superannuation and a company car.

# SELF-EMPLOYMENT & STARTING A BUSINESS

Anyone who's an Australian citizen or a permanent resident can work in a self-employed capacity in Australia, which includes sole proprietors, partnerships, co-operatives, franchises and private limited companies. There are numerous opportunities for entrepreneurs in Australia, where everyone (or at least most people) has equal opportunity and is judged on his merits. However, if you're planning to enter Australia as a business migrant, you need to have considerable financial resources and pass a points test (see page 88). Business migrants in the past three years brought in over $500,000 each and created around 4,000 jobs (on average each migrant created seven jobs).

Although new businesses have a high failure rate within the first few years, working for yourself is still the best way to become (and remain) rich in Australia (and most other countries). There's considerable red tape for those wishing to start a business in Australia, although it isn't as restrictive as in many other countries, where the average small businessman spends as much as four hours per week on government paperwork. Much of the fall in unemployment in recent years has been a result of self-employment or jobs created by small companies. Some 20 per cent of working Australians run their own business. Redundancy (and the difficulty in finding full-time employment) is often the spur for those aged over 45 to start their own business and around 20 per cent of retrenched (redundant) employees turn to self-employment. **However, it isn't a panacea for unemployment.**

**Research:** For many people, starting a business is one of the quickest routes to bankruptcy. In fact, many people who start businesses would be better off investing in lottery tickets – at least they would then have a chance of getting a return on their investment! **If you're going to work for yourself you must be prepared to fail (despite your best efforts), as almost two out of three new businesses fail within three to five years.** The key to starting or buying a successful business is research, research and yet more research (plus innovation, value for money and service). Bear in mind that choosing the location for a business is vital. Always thoroughly investigate an existing or proposed business (including the location, catchment area, competition and history) before investing a cent. Generally speaking, it isn't wise to run a business in a field in which you have no experience, although obviously this isn't always possible (and some businesses require little experience, specialist knowledge or training). When experience or training is necessary, it's often better to work for someone else in the same line of business to gain experience, rather than jump in at the deep end. Assistance (including hands-on training) from the seller could be made part of a purchase contract. **Like most countries, Australia isn't a place for amateur entrepreneurs, particularly those who don't do their homework and are unfamiliar with Australians and the Australian way of doing business.**

**Business Structure:** There are three main types of business structure you can choose if you're self-employed: a sole proprietorship, a partnership or a limited company, which can be public or proprietary (which means private). Because of the ever-changing and complex Australian tax laws, you should consult a tax expert before deciding on the best one for you. You must also decide whether to buy an established business or a franchise or start a new business from scratch. Note that, although franchises have a higher success rate than other start-up businesses, it may take years to make a profit (often the only people to get rich are the franchise companies). A *Franchisees Guide* can be obtained from The Franchise Council of Australia Ltd., Box 1498 GPO Melbourne, VIC 3001 (☎ 03-9650 1667, ✉ jim. mccrackend@franchise.org.au).

**Buying A Business:** Businesses for sale are advertised in specialist magazines and some daily newspapers. There are also business migration agents in Australia and overseas who can help you buy or establish a company in Australia, although their fees can be high. Note that the purchase of a business *must* always be conditional on obtaining visas, licenses, permits, loans and other necessary funding, and anything else that's vital to its successful establishment. While it's easier to buy an existing business (which gives you an immediate cash flow) than start a new one, you must thoroughly investigate the financial status, turnover and value of a business (*always* obtain an independent valuation). It's important to engage an accountant and lawyer at the earliest opportunity. Note that a lawyer should be acting solely for you, not for any other parties in a transaction, and shouldn't be receiving commission from anyone involved. **Take care, as there are crooks around who prey on innocent foreigners!**

**Finance & Cash Flow:** Most people are far too optimistic about the prospects for a new business and over-estimate income levels (it often takes years to make a profit). Be realistic or even pessimistic when estimating your income; overestimate the costs and underestimate the revenue (then reduce it by up to 50 per cent!). While hoping for the best, you should plan for the worst and have sufficient funds to last until you're established and profitable. New projects are rarely, if ever, completed within budget. Make sure you have sufficient working capital and that you can survive until a business takes off. Australian banks are wary of lending to new businesses, especially those run by new immigrants. If you wish to borrow money for a business venture in Australia, you should carefully consider where and how you plan to raise it. Under-capitalisation is the main reason for small business failures and isn't helped by cash-flow problems caused by late payers.

**Grants & Incentives:** The Australian government welcomes successful business people and investors to apply for residence in Australia, although applicants are generally required to invest at least $500,000 in a business (see page 89). The Australian Business Migration scheme provides prospective migrants with a link to professional and commercial advisors who provide specialist advice and other services. Compare your business prospects in all states and territories, all of which compete to attract foreign investors and business people with incentives such as tax rebates, free counselling, cash grants and loan guarantees. Some state governments publish lists of business opportunities for migrants. For information about government backed finance, contact the Australian Trade Commission (AUSTRADE), AIDC Tower, Maritime Centre, 201 Kent Street, Sydney, NSW 2000 (☎ 02-9390 2000, 💻 www.austrade.gov.au).

**Information & Professional Advice:** A wealth of free advice and information for budding entrepreneurs is available from Australian embassies and high commissions, federal government and state agencies, chambers of commerce, professional associations, trade unions, and local councils. The Australian Securities and Investments Commission has a wealth of free information available both from their regional offices and on their website. The ASIC can be contacted at GPO Box 5179AA, Melbourne, VIC 3001 (☎ 03-9280 3300, 💻 www.asic.gov.au). The Office of Small Business is a government agency with offices in all major cities, offering free advice and assistance to those planning to start their own business. It publishes an abundance of information and publications, particularly concerning raising finance for a new business. Employment National and Centrelink (see page 26) publish various booklets about starting a new business and running the finances. There are Business Enterprise Centres (BECs) in some states and territories (e.g. NSW and the ACT), where you can obtain free advice and support on a wide range of business-related subjects.

Most international firms of accountants have offices in major cities in Australia (and in many other countries) and are an invaluable source of information (in English and other languages) on a wide range of subjects, including forming a company, company law, taxation and social security. Many publish free books about doing business in Australia, including *Doing Business in Australia* (Ernst & Young and Price Waterhouse) and *Establishing a Business in Australia* (Minter Ellison). Information about starting a small business in Australian can also be obtained from the Department of Fair Trading, Office of Small Business, 3rd Floor, Enterprise House, 1 Fitzwilliam Street, Parramatta, NSW 2150 (☎ 02-9895 0555), the Australian Small Business Association, GPO Box 2315, Adelaide SA 5001 (☎ freecall 1800-808 463, 💻 www.cpsu.asn.au) and Australian Small Business & Investing, 180 Bourke Street, Alexandria, NSW 2015 (☎ 02-9353 6666). Australia's major banks have small business centres providing free banking, financial and other advice to new businesses. The Australian Tax Office publishes a numerous helpful booklets including *How to Keep Your Business Records*. There are a number of journals published for prospective business buyers, including *Business and Properties FOR SALE* (Pacific O'Brien Publications, PO Box 2170, Southport, QLD 4215, ☎ 07-5571 1103, 💻 www.aresj.com.au).

**Local Information:** There are many state and local government agencies and departments providing information and advice about starting and running a business. All states operate business advisory, development, investment, industry and technology corporations or departments. One of the best places to start is your local chamber of commerce, which is a mine of information about every aspect of business and relocation to particular towns or areas (many produce relocation and business information packages). Public libraries are also an excellent source of information about starting a business.

## AU PAIRS

Single females aged between 17 and 27 (usually referred to as 'girls') are eligible for a job as an au pair in Australia. The au pair system provides you with an excellent opportunity to travel, improve your English and generally broaden your education by living and working in Australia. Au pairs are usually contracted to work for a minimum of three to six months and a maximum of two years, although shorter assignments may be available. You may work as an au pair on a number of separate occasions, providing the total period doesn't exceed two years. You require a visa to enter Australia to work as an au pair.

A good basic knowledge of English is expected of all au pairs, although English classes (see page 214) are available at language schools and colleges in most towns. When applying, you should state whether you wish to attend English classes so that you can be placed with a family living within a reasonable distance of a language school. As an au pair, you receive free meals and accommodation and have your own room. You're usually required to pay your own fare to and from Australia, although some families may pay towards the fare home for au pairs staying six months or longer. Au pairs may be required to holiday with the family or be free to take holidays at home or with friends. Check in advance.

Most families prefer non-smokers (smokers aren't accepted by some families) and girls with a driving licence (so you can take little Bruce or Sheila to school, sports events, etc.). Working hours are officially limited to 30 per week, five hours per day (morning or afternoon), six days per week, plus a maximum of three evenings' baby-sitting. You should have at least one full day and three evenings free of household responsibilities each week and should be free to attend religious services if you wish. Au pairs are paid the 'princessly' sum of between $125 and $200 per week pocket money (rates are highest in the major cities), which means you stand little chance of getting rich unless you marry a wealthy Australian.

Au pairs are usually placed in families with children. Duties consist of light housework, including simple cooking for children, clothes washing (with a machine) and ironing (for children only), washing up and drying dishes, making beds, dusting, vacuum cleaning, and other light jobs around the home. In order to endure (or possibly even enjoy) the work, you should be used to helping around the house and working with children. You aren't a general servant or cook (although extra services are often taken for granted) and shouldn't be expected to look after physically or mentally handicapped children. Unfortunately, abuses of the au pair system are common (in all countries) and you may be expected to work long hours and spend many evenings baby-sitting while the family are out enjoying themselves.

Some families may also expect you to act as a language teacher for members of the family, which you should refuse (unless they offer you lots of money!). On the other hand, you shouldn't expect the family to teach you English, although most are only too willing to help. If you have any questions or complaints about your duties, you should refer them to the agency which found you your position (if applicable). Make sure you have a return ticket (or the money to buy one), so that if you're faced with an intolerable situation you can at least go home (some agencies will find you another family). You're usually required to give notice if you wish to go home before the end of your agreement, although this won't apply if the family has abused the arrangement.

Au pair positions must be arranged privately, either directly with a family or through a private agency (there's no official government agency). There are dozens of agencies who specialise in finding au pair positions (both in Australia and overseas) and au pair positions can also be found through magazines and newspapers in Australia, but you're usually better off using an agency. The best agencies vet families in advance, make periodic checks on your welfare and help you overcome any problems you may have (either personal or with your family). If you're ill or have an accident during your stay in Australia, you can obtain treatment under the Medicare national health scheme (see page 283).

Some agencies offer a two-week trial period, after which either the au pair or the family can terminate the arrangement without notice. If the arrangement is terminated after the trial period, an agency will usually try to find you another family. Write to a number of agencies and compare the conditions and pocket money offered. Agencies must provide a letter of invitation clearly stating your duties, hours, free time and pocket money (which must be shown to the immigration officer on arrival in Australia). Most agencies provide you with a list of other au pairs in your area and may also put you in touch with local youth and social centres. **Au pair agencies aren't permitted to charge au pairs a fee, which is paid by the family.**

Agencies will send you an application form (questionnaire) and usually ask you to provide character references, a medical certificate, a number of photographs, a letter addressed to a prospective family and possibly a number of international reply coupons. You can choose a particular city or area, although most agencies prefer applicants who are willing to be located anywhere (take care, though, or they may send you to Kalgoorlie or Wagga Wagga). When completing the form, be careful with your answers and get help if there's anything you don't understand, e.g. when asked if you have any allergies, it wouldn't be wise to write 'children'. A useful book for prospective au pairs planning to work in Australia is the *Au Pair and Nanny's Guide to Working Abroad* by Susan Griffith & Sharon Legg (Vacation Work).

## WORKING ILLEGALLY

An estimated 50,000 people live illegally in Australia, some 60 per cent of whom also work illegally. The illegal labour market (usually called the black economy) thrives in Australia and is estimated to cost the government up to $15 billion in lost tax revenue annually. Most illegal workers are young people who overstay their working holiday visas or who arrive as tourists and stay on. The vast majority are employed on farms (e.g. fruit picking) and in factories and restaurants. Many unscrupulous employers use illegal labour in order to pay low wages for long hours and poor working conditions, particularly in the farming industry. However, there has been a crackdown in recent years and immigration officials link tax file numbers with immigration details and make routine swoops on fruit farmers and other suspect employers. **It's strictly illegal to work in Australia without a valid visa.** If you're tempted to work illegally, you should be aware of the consequences, as the black economy is a risky business for both employers and employees. When people are discovered working illegally, they're usually given the choice of voluntary (rapid) departure from the country or deportation (around 7,500 people are deported annually). A foreigner caught working illegally is usually fined and deported and may be barred from re-entering Australia for one to three years. Fines of up to $4,000 and suspended prison sentences of up to six months can also be imposed. People deported for criminal or security reasons are permanently excluded.

Employees without a valid visa permitting them to work in Australia have no entitlement to state or company pensions, unemployment benefits, accident insurance at work and have no legal job protection.

# LANGUAGE

English is the most important and most widely spoken language in the world and is spoken by some 1.4 billion people as their first or second language. It's the world's *lingua franca* and is the language of the United Nations antechamber, international peacekeeping, world banking and commerce, air traffic control, academic research, computers, the Internet, space travel, scientific discovery, news gathering and world entertainment. If you're planning to live or work in Australia, you'll need to speak, read and write English well enough to find your way around the country, deal with government officials, shop, and understand and hold conversations with the people you meet. Independent migrants from non-English speaking backgrounds will need to take an English test. Your chances of obtaining a good job (or any job) in Australia are greatly diminished if you don't speak English fluently, and many immigrants from non-English speaking backgrounds are unemployed because their lack of English would endanger other employees and reduce workplace efficiency. English proficiency is also important if you have a job requiring a lot of contact with others or which involves speaking on the telephone or dealing with other foreigners, many of whom speak their own 'dialect' of English.

Surprisingly, an estimated million migrants cannot speak English, a huge number in a country of fewer than 18 million people, and some 2.5 million residents (around 15 per cent of the population) speak a language other than English at home. Sydney is Australia's most multicultural city (closely followed by Melbourne), where four out of six people in some suburbs speak a language other than English at home (overall some 30 per cent of the population of Sydney doesn't speak English at home). Sydney and Melbourne are home to around 65 per cent of all non English-speaking migrants, who together speak a total of some 240 foreign languages. Many migrants predominantly use their mother tongue (e.g. Arabic, Cantonese, German, Greek, Hindi, Italian, Korean, Lebanese, Serbo-Croat, Spanish, Turkish or Vietnamese) on a day-to-day basis and have only a smattering of English. Australia's failure to train migrants in English is handicapping them in respect of social, economic and political life, and ghettos are emerging where Australian-born children don't speak fluent

English. There's a thriving ethnic radio and TV broadcasting network, the Special Broadcasting Service (SBS), which was established in 1978 and broadcasts in the main cities.

It's particularly important for students (unless they are studying English) to have a high standard of English, as they must be able to follow lectures and take part in discussions in the course of their studies. This may also require a much wider and more technical or specialised vocabulary. For this reason, most universities and colleges won't accept students who aren't fluent in English and many require a formal qualification or require students to take a written test. Whether you speak British English, American English or some other variety is irrelevant, although some foreigners have a problem understanding the natives (even Americans and Britons occasionally have problems understanding Australians).

Australian English is similar to British English but has its own colourful vernacular, called 'strine' (from the way 'Australian' is pronounced with a heavy Australian accent), thrown in for good measure. Strine (also called Ozspeak) is Australia's greatest creative form and is full of abbreviations, word-tweaking, profanities, hyperbole and vulgar expressions (or flash, filth and fun). Strine is the language of a rebellious subculture and has its origins in the Cockney (London) and Irish slang of the early convicts. The use of strine and slang words varies with the state or region. The Australian language also includes many words adopted from Aboriginal languages (see below).

There are slight regional variations in the Australian accent, although foreigners usually find it difficult to detect them. Accents are broader in isolated country areas than among the middle class city dwellers, many of whom are of British ancestry. Newcomers have difficulty distinguishing between Australians and New Zealanders (who, like Americans and Canadians, don't take kindly to being confused). Australians tend to speak through their noses (not moving your lips when talking keeps the flies out) with a broad nasal drawl. The use of expletives is widespread; many of them are used as a sign of familiarity and even affection (bloody is in everyday use and no longer considered a swear word in Australia). Aussies believe in calling a spade a spade and to hell with the consequences! Absurd comparisons are frequently used for emphasis such as 'as busy as a bricklayer in Beirut' (idle), 'as useful as a wether at a ram sale' (useless) and 'as straight as a dog's hind leg' (bent).

Australians often cannot decide whether to use American or British spelling (e.g. program/programme, labor/labour, etc.) and consequently misspellings abound. In everyday use, many words have a completely different meaning in Australia than they do in other English-speaking countries such as crook (ill), game (brave), globe (light bulb), knock (criticise), ringer (a top performer), shout (a round of drinks) and tube (a can of beer). Everything and anything is abbreviated in Australia, often by shortening any word with more than two syllables and adding the vowel e or o on the end of it as in derro (derelict), garbo (dustman), reffo (refugee) and rego (car registration), or adding a suffix such as ie, y or i. Common Ozspeak includes, chrissy (Christmas), barbie (barbecue), brickie (bricklayer), postie (postperson), mozzie (mosquito), cossie (swimming costume), truckie (truck driver), blowie (blowfly), tinny (can of beer), Aussie (Australian) and footy (football).

Many books have been written about Australian vernacular speech, including the *Aussie Talk-Macquarie Dictionary* by Arthur Delbridge (Macquarie Library), *The Dinkum Dictionary* by Leni Johannsen (Viking O'Neil), *The Dinkum Aussie Dictionary* by Richard Beckett (Child and Henry) and the *Australian Phrasebook*

(Lonely Planet). The standard Australian English dictionary is the *Macquarie Dictionary* (compiled by the Macquarie University, Sydney), the bible of Aussie English (2,500 pages!).

**Aboriginal Languages:** Australian Aboriginal (literally meaning 'indigenous') society has the longest unbroken cultural history in the world, dating back 70,000 years to the ice age. When the First Fleet arrived in Australia in 1788, there were estimated to be around 250 Australian languages (all believed to have evolved from a single language family) comprising some 700 dialects (although the British didn't do any surveys before massacring the natives). Of the original 250 or so languages, only around 20 survive today and are spoken regularly and taught in schools. Kriol, spoken mostly in northern Australia, is the most widely used Aboriginal language and the native language of many young Aboriginals. It contains many English words but the meanings are often different and the spelling is phonetic.

If you wish to improve your English before starting work or a course of study in Australia, there are English-language schools throughout the country where you can enrol in a part or full-time course lasting from a few weeks to a year or longer (see **Language Schools** on page 214).

# 2.

# WORKING CONDITIONS

Working conditions in Australia are among the best in the western world and are regulated in most fields of employment at federal or state level, where legislation covers such matters as annual and public holidays, long service leave, workers' compensation, occupational health and safety, discrimination, and redundancy procedures and payment. Working conditions and wages in Australia aren't usually determined by the free market but are decided in negotiations between the unions and employers and are subject to approval by the Australian Industrial Relations Commission. The result of this process is termed the 'award' for a particular job or industry. It sets minimum wages and 'penalty' rates of pay for overtime and unsociable hours and includes such matters as working hours, holiday entitlement, sick leave, redundancy and termination of employment. Many employers' pay and conditions are more generous than the statutory minimum decided under industry awards. Employees in Australia are also protected by a comprehensive federal social security (welfare) system which includes pensions, unemployment benefits, sickness and disability allowances, and family payments (see page 306).

There are three types of awards: federal or state awards, Australian Workplace Agreements (AWAs), and certified agreements. Federal awards, which are made by the Australian Industrial Relations Commission (AIRC), were simplified under the Workplace Relations Act, 1996 and may include regulations relating only to twenty 'allowable' matters, such as rates of pay and allowances, overtime, shift penalty and other penalty rates, hours of work, and leave provisions. Matters that are better dealt with at the workplace are not included in an award. State awards are the responsibility of State industrial tribunals and are similar in content to federal awards.

AWAs also set out minimum working conditions but under these agreements workers usually give up certain rights (such as agreeing to a longer standard working week or giving up high penalty rates for overtime) and renounce restrictive practices in return for increased wages or bonuses. AWAs must be approved by the Australian Industrial Relations Commission, which has approved more than 1,000 since they were introduced in April 1998.

Certified agreements are collective agreements made directly between an employer and a group of employees, or between an employer and a union. All certified agreements must meet approval by the AIRC and satisfy certain conditions, e.g. the agreement must be approved by the majority of employees; a dispute settlement procedure must be included; and the agreement must include a nominal expiry date, which cannot be more than three years after approval.

Industrial disputes in Australia are usually resolved by arbitration, all parties agreeing to abide by the final decision of the Conciliation and Arbitration Commission, the highest legal authority in the Australian industrial system. In recent years, many trades and industries have been encouraged to enter into enterprise working agreements and decentralised bargaining with individual employees and groups of employees, which are eating into the unions' traditional authority in the workplace.

Workers are generally well paid in Australia and enjoy extensive fringe benefits, especially in professional and executive positions, where 'perks' constitute a sizeable slice of pay packets. However, despite relatively high salaries and generally good working conditions, employees in Australia are becoming increasingly dissatisfied with their lot, including pay and conditions, work-related stress, long hours and high workload, poor treatment by management, job insecurity, and the balance between work and family life. Many people work too hard and too many hours, and it has been estimated that as many as one in four employees has taken time off work in connection with work-related stress.

Information about employment conditions and workers' rights can be obtained from the Australian Industrial Relations Commission, Level 35, Nauru House, 80 Collins St., Melbourne VIC 3000 (postal address: GPO Box 19945, Melbourne VIC 3001 ☎ 03-8661 7777, 🖳 www.airc.gov.au) and the Department of Industrial Relations, 1 Oxford Street, Darlinghurst, NSW 2010 (☎ 02-9243 8888, 🖳 www.dir. nsw.gov.au).

# DISCRIMINATION

It's illegal under the Racial Discrimination Act, 1975 and Sex Discrimination Act, 1984 to discriminate against an employee because of sex (unless a person's sex is an essential qualification for a job), because he's married or because of his race, nationality, colour, sexual orientation, or ethnic or national origin. It's also illegal to discriminate against an employee because he does or doesn't wish to join a trade union. A woman doing the same or broadly similar work to a man or work of equal value is legally entitled to the same salary and other terms of employment as a man (see **Working Women** on page 32). Discrimination applies to selection, appointment, training, promotion and dismissal. Note that discrimination is particularly rife where young employees are concerned, most of whom are unaware of their rights. Some companies have a policy of employing disabled or handicapped applicants whenever possible (or at least not discriminating against them), taking into account their ability, safety and comfort.

Note, however, that employers may discriminate against smokers, and over three-quarters of Australia's top companies restrict smoking (and the consumption of alcohol) in the workplace. Around half of all companies have a total ban on smoking at work and a third have restricted areas where employees are permitted to smoke. It's legal for employers to specify in job advertisements whether they'll hire smokers (employers are fearful of law suits from non-smokers regarding 'passive' smoking). Smoking breaks (called 'smokos') in Australia are estimated to cost business $billions a year!

It's difficult to prove discrimination on the grounds of sex and almost impossible on the grounds of race, although it's acknowledged that discrimination is widespread. If you're subjected to sexual harassment (which can happen to both women *and* men) you should report it to your supervisor or manager, as many companies have internal procedures to deal with such matters. However, if you don't receive satisfaction, you can report it to your union or the police and take legal advice. The Human Rights and Equal Opportunities Commission (HREOC) handles sexual harassment and discrimination cases in the utmost confidence and can advise you whether you have legal grounds for a complaint (which must be submitted in writing). The HREOC's national office is in Sydney (GPO Box 5218, Level 24, American Express Building, 388 George Street, Sydney, NSW 1042, ☎ local rate 1300-656 419; 🖳 www.hreoc. gov.au) and it has regional offices in Brisbane, Darwin and Hobart. Complaints in NSW are handled by the NSW Anti-Discrimination Board and in other states by Equal Opportunity Commissioners.

Note, however, that victims of discrimination who win compensation payments are often left frustrated and empty-handed. Rulings by the HREOC aren't legally enforceable and compensation ordered by it is rarely paid without victims being forced to take further legal action (many just give up). To combat this sense of frustration, since April 2000 the Federal Court has ruled in around 15 per cent of cases that HREOC had not been able to enforce. Rulings made by the Federal Court on discrimination are legally enforcible and, as a result, employers are now increasingly aware of their liability. The government has also introduced educational campaigns and workplace training in an attempt to combat discrimination in the workplace and the general opinion that Australia's discrimination laws are a sham.

# TERMS OF EMPLOYMENT

Negotiating an appropriate salary is just one aspect of your remuneration, which, for many employees, consists of much more than what they receive in their pay packets. When negotiating your terms of employment for a job in Australia, the checklists on the following pages should prove helpful. The points listed under **General Positions** below apply to most jobs, while those listed under **Managerial & Executive Positions** (on page 55) usually apply only to executive and top managerial appointments. Many companies offer a number of benefits (often referred to as perks) for executives, managers and key personnel, and it isn't unusual for the perks of board members to comprise as much as half their total remuneration. Note, however, that since the introduction of fringe benefits tax (FBT), employees must pay tax on fringe benefits and you should therefore check their real cash value (see page 356). Employees being relocated to Australia by their overseas employers are exempt from paying tax on some fringe benefits.

## General Positions

- **Salary:**
  - Is the total salary adequate, taking into account the cost of living in Australia (see page 360)? Is it index-linked?
  - Does it include an allowance for working (and living) in an expensive city (e.g. Sydney) or remote area?
  - How often is the salary reviewed?
  - Does the salary include commission and bonuses (see page 59)?
  - Does the employer offer profit-sharing, share options or share-save schemes?
  - Is overtime paid or time off given in lieu of extra hours worked?
  - Is a 'golden hello' (i.e. a 'signing on' fee) paid?
  - Is the total salary (including expenses) paid in Australian dollars or is it paid in another country (in a different currency) with expenses for living in Australia?

- **Relocation Expenses:**
  - Are relocation expenses or a relocation allowance paid?
  - Do the relocation expenses include travelling expenses for all family members?
  - Is there an upper limit and, if so, is it adequate?

- Are you required to repay your relocation expenses (or a percentage) if you resign before a certain period has elapsed?
- Are you required to pay for your relocation expenses in advance (which could run into many thousands of dollars)?
- If employment is for a fixed period, are your relocation expenses paid when you leave Australia?
- If you aren't shipping household goods and furniture to Australia, is there an allowance for buying furniture locally?
- Do relocation expenses include the legal and estate agent's fees incurred when moving home?
- Does the employer use the services of a relocation consultant (see page 121)?

- **Accommodation:**
  - Will the employer pay for a hotel (or pay a lodging allowance) until you find permanent accommodation?
  - Is subsidised or free, temporary or permanent accommodation provided? If so, is it furnished or unfurnished?
  - Must you pay for utilities such as electricity, gas and water?
  - If accommodation isn't provided by the employer, is assistance in finding suitable accommodation given? What does it consist of?
  - What will accommodation cost?
  - While living in temporary accommodation, will you be paid travelling expenses to your permanent home? How far is it from your place of employment?
  - Are your expenses paid while looking for accommodation?

- **Working Hours:**
  - What are the weekly or monthly working hours?
  - Does the employer operate a flexi-time system (see page 60)? If so, what are the fixed (core time) working hours? How early must you start? Can you carry forward extra hours worked and take time off at a later date (or carry forward a deficit and make it up later)?
  - Are you required to clock in and out of work?
  - Can you choose to take time off in lieu of overtime worked or to be paid for it?

- **Part-time or Periodic Working:**
  - Is part-time or school term-time working permitted?
  - Are working hours flexible or is part-time working from home permitted?
  - Does the employer have a job-sharing scheme?
  - Are extended career breaks permitted with no loss of seniority, grade or salary?

- **Leave Entitlement:**

- What is the annual leave entitlement? Does it increase with age?
- What are the paid public holidays?
- Is free air travel to your home country or elsewhere provided for you and your family and, if so, how often? Are other holiday travel discounts provided?
- Is maternity/paternity leave provided?

- **Insurance:**
  - Is health insurance or regular health screening provided for you *and* your family? If so, what does it include (see page 312)?
  - Is free life assurance provided?
  - Is accident or any special insurance provided by the employer?
  - For how long is your salary paid if you're ill or have an accident?

- **Company Pension (Superannuation):**
  - Is there a company superannuation (super) fund (see page 310)?
  - Can you pay a lump sum into the fund in order to receive a full or higher pension?
  - What are the rules regarding early retirement?
  - Is the pension index-linked and based on your final salary?
  - Do the pension rules apply equally to full *and* part-time employees?

- **Employer:**
  - What are the employer's prospects?
  - Is his profitability and growth rate favourable?
  - Does he have a good reputation?
  - Does he have a high staff turnover and, if so, why?

- **Women:**
  - What is the employer's policy regarding equal opportunities for women?
  - How many women hold positions in middle and senior management or at board level (if the percentage is low in relation to the number of women employees, perhaps you should be wary if you're a career woman)?
  - Is paid maternity leave provided and, if so, for how many weeks?

- **Training:**
  - What initial or career training does the employer provide?
  - Is training provided in-house or externally and will the employer pay for training or education overseas, if necessary?
  - Does the employer have an on-going training programme for employees in your trade or profession (e.g. technical, management or language)? Is the employer's training recognised for its excellence (or otherwise)?
  - Will the employer pay for a part of or the total cost of non-essential education, e.g. a computer or language course?
  - Will the employer allow paid day release for you to attend a degree course or other studies?

- What are the promotion prospects?

- Does the employer provide a free nursery or crèche for children below school age or a day care centre for the elderly?

- Are free or subsidised English language lessons provided for you and your spouse (if necessary)?

- Is a free or subsidised employee restaurant provided? If not, is a lunch allowance paid? Is any provision made for shift workers, i.e. breakfast or evening meals?

- Is a travelling allowance paid from your Australian home to your place of work?

- If the job involves a lot of air travel, are you entitled to claim frequent-flyer points?

- Is free or subsidised parking provided at your place of work?

- Are free work clothes, overalls or a uniform provided? Does the employer pay for the cleaning of work clothes?

- Does the employer offer inexpensive or interest-free home loans or mortgage assistance? Note that an inexpensive home loan can be worth $thousands a year.

- Is a company car provided? What sort of car? Can it be used privately, and if so, does the employer pay for petrol?

- Does the employer provide fringe benefits such as subsidised in-house banking services, a car discount scheme, cheap petrol, travel discounts, employees' discount shop, product discounts, free sports and social facilities, and subsidised tickets for social and sports events?

- Do you have a written list of your job responsibilities?

- Have the employment conditions been confirmed in writing?

- If a dispute arises over your salary or working conditions, under the law of which country will your contract be interpreted?

## Managerial & Executive Positions

- Is private schooling paid for or subsidised by the employer? If necessary or desired, will the employer pay for a boarding school in Australia or another country?

- Is the salary index-linked or protected against devaluation and cost of living increases? This is particularly important if you're paid in a foreign currency that fluctuates wildly or could be devalued. Are you paid an overseas allowance for working in Australia?

- Is there an executive superannuation scheme? Note that the Australian Taxation Office has clamped down on salary sacrifice packages, whereby executives and other highly-paid employees sacrifice a large part of their salaries in return for higher superannuation payments (see page 310).

- Is a housing allowance paid or a rent-free house or apartment provided?

- Are paid holidays (perhaps in a company owned house or apartment) or 'business' conferences in exotic places provided?

- Are the costs incurred by a move to Australia reimbursed? For example, the cost of selling your home, employing an agent to let it for you or storing household effects.

- Will the employer pay for domestic help or contribute to the cost of a servant or cook?

- Is a car provided (possibly with a chauffeur)?

- Are you entitled to any miscellaneous benefits such as private club membership, free credit cards, or tickets for sports events and shows?

- Is there an entertainment allowance?

- Is extra compensation paid if you're made redundant or fired? Redundancy or severance payments (see page 71) are compulsory for all employees in Australia (subject to length of service), but executives often receive a generous 'golden handshake' if they're made redundant, e.g. after a take-over.

## CONTRACT OF EMPLOYMENT

Under Australian law, a contract of employment exists as soon as an employee proves his acceptance of an employer's terms and conditions of employment, e.g. by starting work, after which both employer and employee are bound by the terms offered and agreed. A contract isn't always in writing (it can be verbal and sealed by a handshake), although a company must usually provide employees who are normally employed in Australia with a written statement containing certain important terms of employment and additional notes, e.g. regarding discipline and grievance procedures. A written contract of employment usually contains all the terms and conditions agreed between the employer and employee. Note that employees have the right to review a contract for 14 days before signing it.

Under the Workplace Relations Act,1996, employers have increasingly been offering employees individual contracts, i.e. non-union certified agreements and Australian Workplace Agreements (AWAs). AWAs are valid for a maximum of three years and are effectively fixed-term contracts for three years. A non-union certified agreement must be approved by the Industrial Relations Commission, which will happen provided a majority of workers vote in favour; individual workers aren't required (or even entitled) to sign or veto an agreement. Contracts are subject to a no-disadvantage test and must meet seven minimum conditions, including no reduction in pay when compared with awards. However, in some cases employers have been permitted to offer non-union employment agreements that reduce living standards, if they can show that the deals increase job security.

Under AWAs, many companies reserve the right to use contractors, part-time, casual and temporary workers as required, recruit, transfer or retrench on the basis of merit rather than prior agreement from industry or seniority, and use staff, production or engineering employees to perform any task within their competence, thus breaking down existing demarcations. Employees may also be required to work shifts of up to 12.5 hours. In return, workers usually receive guaranteed annual pay rises, performance bonuses and a guarantee that AWA pay rates will equal or outstrip wages under any certified agreement negotiated with unions. In many cases, employees with individual contracts are worse off, as contracts seek to cash out sick leave and other leave entitlements and allowances for employees in skilled trades, cut penalty rates, leave-loading and overtime, and tailor working hours to meet peaks and troughs in demand, as well as undermining restrictive work practices in heavily unionised industries. Around 10 per cent of employees have individual contracts, which have become a potent weapon against the union movement and have reduced the cost of labour. However, many workers have rejected the agreements and stayed with collective agreements negotiated through their union.

Contracts may consist of a simple sheet of paper or be comprehensive multi-page documents, e.g. from a multi-national company. You should usually receive some form of contract, even for part-time and temporary jobs, although you won't usually receive a contract for casual work such as fruit picking (but you should get written confirmation of your wages and hours). A contract for a temporary position must state the period of the contract and should guarantee you compensation in the event that employment is terminated without notice. Note that either party can sue for breach of contract.

You usually receive two copies of your contract of employment (which may be called a 'statement of terms and conditions' or an 'offer letter'), both of which you should sign and date. One copy must be returned to your prospective employer, assuming you agree with the terms and want the job, and the other is for your own records. There are usually no hidden surprises or traps for the unwary in an Australian contract of employment, although as with any contract you should know exactly what it contains before signing it. If your knowledge of English is poor, you should ask someone to explain anything you don't understand in simple English (Australian companies rarely provide foreigners with contracts in a language other than English). Your contract of employment usually contains the following details:

- name of the employer and employee;
- date employment begins and whether employment with a previous employer counts as part of the employee's continuous period of employment;
- job title;
- salary details, including overtime pay and piece-rates, commission, bonuses and agreed salary increases or review dates;
- when the salary is to be paid, e.g. weekly, fortnightly or monthly;
- hours of work;
- annual and public holiday entitlements and pay;
- sickness and accident benefits;
- pension (superannuation) scheme details;
- probationary and notice periods (or the expiry date, if employment is for a limited period);
- disciplinary and grievance procedures (which may be contained in a separate document).

If there are no agreed terms under one or more of the above headings, this may be stated in the contract. Any special arrangements or conditions you have agreed with an employer should also be contained in the contract. If all or any of the above particulars are contained in a collective agreement, an employer may refer employees to a copy of this, including other documents such as work rules or handbooks, wage regulation orders, sick pay and superannuation scheme conditions, and the rules relating to flexible working hours and company holidays. Before signing your contract of employment, you should obtain a copy of any general employment conditions (see below) or documents referred to in the contract and ensure that you understand them.

Your employment is usually subject to satisfactory references being received from your previous employer(s) and/or character references. In the case of a school-leaver or student, a reference may be required from the principal of your last school, college or university. For certain jobs, a pre-employment medical examination is required and periodic examinations may be a condition of employment, e.g. where good health is vital to the safe performance of your duties. If you require a visa to work in Australia, your contract may contain a clause stating that the contract is subject to a visa being granted by the authorities. Employees must usually be notified in writing of any changes in their terms and conditions of employment, e.g. within one month of their introduction.

## EMPLOYMENT CONDITIONS

The term employment conditions (as used here) refers to an employer's general employment terms and conditions (including benefits, rules and regulations) that apply to all employees, unless otherwise stated in individual contracts of employment. General employment conditions are usually referred to in employment contracts and employees normally receive a copy on starting employment (or in some cases beforehand). Employment conditions are explained in this chapter or a reference is made to the chapter where the subject is covered in more detail.

## Validity & Applicability

Employment conditions usually contain a paragraph stating the date from which they are valid and to whom they apply.

## Place of Work

Unless there's a clause in your contract stating otherwise, your employer cannot change your place of work without your agreement. Note that the place of work usually refers to a town or area of a large city, rather than a specific office or building. If applicable, a contract may state that you may occasionally be required to work at other company locations.

## Salary & Benefits

Your salary is stated in your contract of employment and salary reviews, overtime rates, piece and bonus rates, planned increases and cost of living rises may also be included. Only general points, such as the payment of your salary into a bank or other account, and the date of salary payments, are usually included in employment conditions. You should usually receive an itemised pay statement (or wage slip), either with your salary (if it's paid weekly or fortnightly in cash) or separately (when your salary is paid monthly into a bank account). **Always ensure that you receive a pay slip containing the legally-required information, as it's almost impossible to dispute pay claims without one.**

Salaries in Australia are generally reviewed annually, although the salaries of professional employees and all employees in some businesses may be reviewed every six months. The salaries of new employees may also be reviewed after six months. A percentage of your annual salary increase is usually to compensate for a rise in the cost of living, although some employees receive pay rises below the annual rate of inflation. Annual increases may be negotiated separately by employees on individual contracts, by an independent pay review board or by a union (or unions), when an industry is covered by an award (see **Salary** on page 58). Employees not on awards often receive the federal minimum wage, which in 2001 was $400.40 per week (equal to a minimum hourly rate of $10.54 for a 38-hour week).

# Commission & Bonuses

Your salary may include commission or bonus payments, calculated on your individual performance (e.g. based on sales) or the company's performance as a whole, which may be paid regularly (e.g. monthly or annually) or irregularly. Some employers pay employees a special annual bonus (not to be confused with a general award holiday pay bonus) at the end of the year, although this isn't normal practice in Australia. When a bonus is paid, it may be stated in your contract of employment, in which case it's obligatory. If applicable, an annual bonus is usually paid pro rata if you don't work a full calendar year, e.g. in your first and last years of employment with a company. CEOs in Australia typically receive a bonus averaging 25 to 30 per cent of their gross salary.

Some employers operate an annual voluntary bonus scheme, based on each employee's individual performance or the company's profits (a profit-sharing scheme), although this may apply only to senior managers and executives. Profit-sharing schemes aren't common in Australia, although performance-related bonuses or commissions are common in the finance industry. In some companies, employees are offered company shares at a favourable price, usually well below the market price. If you're employed on a contract basis for a fixed period, you may also be paid an end-of-contract bonus. When discussing your salary with a prospective employer, always take into account the total salary package, including commission, bonuses and fringe benefits such as a company car or a low-interest home loan. In industry, particularly in small firms, blue-collar workers are often paid bonus or 'piece-work' rates based on their individual productivity.

# Working Hours

Working hours in Australia vary according to your employer, your position and the type of industry in which you're employed. A national 38-hour working week was introduced in 1981, since reduced to 37 hours. However, many people work longer hours, particularly employees in factories, who often work ten or more hours overtime per week. A survey for 1999–2000 showed that the average working week is 39.5 hours, men working an average of 43 hours and women an average of 38 hours. A standard working day (without overtime) for a blue-collar worker is from 7 or 8am to 3.30 or 4.30pm, while working hours in most offices and shops are from 8.30 or 9.30am until 4.30 or 5.30pm, with an hour's break for lunch.

Most employees work a five-day week, although over 25 per cent of men work weekends and some 20 per cent work shifts. In the last few years, many companies have switched from eight-hour to 12-hour shifts, which means working only 11 or 12 days per month or ten days in a three-week roster. Twelve-hour shifts are common in enterprise deals where the advantage for employers is that they entail no overtime payments. Employees also gain, as they earn around the same as previously (when they worked overtime) and have much more leisure time. Most workers prefer 12-hour shifts after having tried them, although there's a safety risk, particularly in factories, where it's estimated that there's double the risk of accidents due to fatigue. The Australian government is encouraging employers to adopt 'family-friendly practices' whereby employees enjoy more flexible working hours and leave arrangements.

Hourly paid workers are usually paid overtime (see below) for extra hours and higher penalty rates for night, shift and weekend work. On the other hand, executives, professionals, managers (and an increasing number of non-union workers) often work overtime without extra pay. Many people work much longer hours now than they did in the '70s and '80s, and stress and illness from overwork is a constant threat for managers and executives. Tea or coffee breaks may be scheduled at set times during mid-morning and mid-afternoon, particularly in factories (employers usually provide free tea and coffee and many also provide biscuits). Tea and coffee breaks are estimated to cost the country around $12 billion a year. Long business lunches (two hours or more) are becoming less common, although it's still customary to find employees finishing their lunch late in the afternoon on Thursdays and Fridays.

Your working hours may not be increased above the hours stated in your employment conditions without compensation or overtime being paid. Similarly, if you have a guaranteed working week, your hours cannot be reduced (i.e. short-time working) or changed without your agreement, unless there's a clause (sometimes referred to as a 'mobility clause') in your contract. In reality, an employer is unlikely to change or reduce your hours without agreement if he wants to retain your goodwill and services. If you refuse short-time working and are subsequently dismissed, you can usually regard yourself as being retrenched (see page 70), in which case you should receive compensation. Some employers operate a system of flexible working hours and may also permit employees to take part in job-sharing, voluntary reduced hours and working part of the time at home. Around a third of Australian workers (usually blue-collar) are required to sign on or clock in and out of work (employees caught cheating may be summarily dismissed).

## Flexi-Time & Days Off

Many Australian companies operate flexi-time working hours or a system of rostered days off (RDO). The conditions and rules relating to flexi-time and RDO schemes vary according to your employer (they're most common in public service) and are more likely to apply to those in managerial, administrative and professional occupations. At their peak, RDOs applied to almost a third of wage and salary earners, although they're now being lost through enterprise bargaining. RDOs are usually taken on a Monday so that they provide a long weekend, but this has proved disruptive to companies' operations. In recent years, employers have been cutting back on RDOs, e.g. from 12 to six per year, converting them to annual or special accrued leave, swapping them for superannuation payments or replacing them with time off in lieu spread over different days.

Many employees can work flexible hours if they need to and working parents are usually permitted to leave work for up to an hour at any time for personal reasons. A flexi-time system usually requires all employees to be present between certain hours, known as the core or block time. For example, from 9 to 11.30am and from 1.30 to 4pm. Employees may make up their required working hours by starting earlier than the required core time, reducing their lunch break or working later. Many business premises are open from around 7am until 6pm or later, and smaller companies may allow employees to work as late as they wish, provided they don't exceed the maximum permitted daily working hours.

## Overtime

The opportunity to work overtime is seen as a lucrative fringe benefit by most blue-collar workers, many of whom earn around a quarter of their wages from overtime. In some industries there's an ingrained 'overtime culture', although for many workers overtime is a matter of economic necessity; without it, many families would find it difficult to pay their bills. Of the six million or so people in full-time employment, almost half regularly work overtime and some 25 per cent of men work over 50 hours a week. Overtime is generally paid at time-and-a-half for the first three hours and double-time thereafter (plus Sundays and public holidays), or as detailed in the award for the trade or industry (workers in some industries receive 2.5 times the day shift rate for Sundays). Penalty rates of pay are paid for regular night, shift and weekend work, and there are allowances (called 'tropical loading' or a 'remote area allowances') for work in remote areas of the Northern Territory and Western Australia (above the Tropic of Capricorn).

In order to reduce overtime costs, many companies have been extending the normal working week and changing to 12-hour shifts. In non-union agreements, workers are three times more likely to have a standard working week longer than 38 hours, and overtime may be paid at the standard rate (more likely in non-union workplaces). As much as half of all overtime worked is unpaid and fewer than 40 per cent of workers work standard hours. Many enterprise agreements stipulate that employees work longer hours at ordinary time (e.g. up to 50 a week) in return for higher wages and bonuses. Some companies pay overtime only when work is urgent and officially approved, and many prefer salaried (i.e. monthly paid) employees to take time off in lieu of overtime worked or expect them to work unpaid overtime. Working hours for employees who work a flexi-time system (see above) are usually calculated on a monthly basis, with employees being permitted to carry forward extra hours worked and take time off at a later date, or carry forward a deficit and make it up later.

## Travel & Relocation Expenses

Your travel and relocation expenses to Australia (or to a new job in another region of Australia) depend on your agreement with your employer and are usually detailed in your contract of employment or conditions. If you're hired from outside Australia, your air ticket (or other travel costs) to Australia is usually booked and paid for by your employer. You can usually also claim any additional travel costs, for example the cost of transport to and from airports.

Australian employers may also pay your relocation expenses to Australia up to a specified amount. This may be paid as a percentage of your salary, a block allowance or only specific expenses, such as removal, legal and estate agent's fees. The allowance should be sufficient to move the contents of an average house (castles aren't usually catered for) and you must normally pay any excess costs yourself. Companies may ask you to obtain two or three removal estimates when they're liable for the total cost of removal. If you don't want to bring your furniture to Australia or have only a few belongings to ship, you may be given an allowance to purchase furniture locally (check with your employer). Generally, you're required to organise and pay for the removal yourself. Your employer usually reimburses the equivalent amount in Australian dollars *after* you've paid the bill, although it may be possible to get him to pay the bill directly or make an advance payment. If you change jobs within Australia, your new employer may pay your relocation expenses when it's necessary for you to move home. Don't forget to ask, as he may not offer to pay (it may depend on how keen he is to employ you). See also **Relocation Consultants** on page 121.

## Social Security

The Australian social security system is non-contributory and funded out of general taxation, with the exception of a Medicare levy of 1.5 per cent of gross taxable income (above $13,807 a year). For information see page 62.

## Medical Examination

Many Australian companies require prospective employees to have a pre-employment medical examination, which is performed by a company doctor (or a doctor nominated by the employer). An offer of employment is usually subject to you being given a clean bill of health. This may be required for employees over a certain age (e.g. 40 years) or just for those in particular jobs, e.g. where good health is of paramount importance for reasons of safety. Thereafter, a medical examination may be required periodically (e.g. every year or two) or when requested by your employer. Medical examinations may be required as a condition of membership of a company health, pension or life insurance scheme. Some companies insist on key employees having regular health screening, particularly senior managers and executives.

## Company Cars

Many Australian employers provide senior employees such as directors, senior managers and professionals with a company car as a fringe benefit, in addition to employees who need a car to do their job (e.g. sales reps). Most companies provide executives with a luxury car (worth over $55,134) under a lease arrangement, which allows the employer to claim fringe benefits tax on cars provided as part of employee packages. Note that, although the company provides the car, if you leave for any reason you're responsible for the balance of the finance. If you're provided with a company car, you usually receive details regarding its use and your obligations on starting employment. If you lose your licence (e.g. through drunken driving) and are unable to fulfil the requirements of your job, your employment may be terminated (i.e. you'll be fired), and you may not be entitled to any compensation. If a company car is provided, check what sort of car it is and whether you'll be permitted to use it privately. Note that employees are required to pay fringe benefit tax (FBT) on the value of a company car that's used privately (see page 356). Many companies allow employees to buy secondhand company cars at favourable prices.

# Superannuation

A compulsory superannuation (or company pension) was introduced in 1992 to help persuade trade unions to accept moderate pay rises (the rules have since been extended to include part-time workers and those who leave the workforce for up to two years). In 2001, employers must contribute up to 8 per cent (2001) of an employee's monthly salary, depending on the size of their payroll (a few companies with few staff contribute less than the maximum); this is usually paid into an approved superannuation fund. From 2002 most employers will have to contribute 9 per cent. In 2000, almost 90 per cent of employees received this benefit. For further information see page 310.

# Accident Insurance

All employers in Australia are required to have occupational accident insurance (called workers' compensation insurance or WorkCover) for employees working on their premises, whether in a factory, office, shop, warehouse or residential accommodation. Schemes, many of which operate at a loss, are financed by a levy on salaries, e.g. 2.18 per cent in Victoria. Some states have overhauled their workers' compensation schemes in recent years, e.g. Victoria, where proposed changes in 2001 were met with massive opposition culminating in widespread strikes. The new scheme in Victoria aims amongst other things to change benefits and to ensure that the system is fully self-funding, as in schemes operated by South Australia, the Northern Territory and the Commonwealth government.

In order to reduce accidents, employees must obey all safety regulations such as those relating to smoking , the use of safety equipment and clothes such as hard hats, steel-capped boots and goggles, the securing of long hair or ties, and the wearing of jewellery. However, unless an employee is grossly negligent and recklessly ignores safety rules and regulations, he's invariably deemed to be entitled to compensation. A worker is paid compensation (commonly called 'compo') if he's injured or sick as the result of an accident in the workplace or when travelling to or from work or on company business. Compensation covers medical and other expenses and loss of earnings, and a worker's dependants are entitled to compensation if he's killed on the job. Note that Australians tend to claim compo for the slightest injury at work. However, although bogus claims are rife, particularly concerning the health effects of work-related stress, making a claim for compo often carries a stigma and many workers try to avoid it (particularly those on contracts).

Occupational health and safety is dealt with by both federal and state governments and at the federal level is determined by the National Occupational Health and Safety Commission. The conditions of payment and the amount of compensation payable are laid down in various state acts, although in some states Workers' Compensation Boards decide on individual claims. If a claim is rejected, a worker can take his case to his union and it will be decided by a workers' compensation commission.

## Sick Pay

Most employees are entitled to take up to two weeks paid sick leave each year, depending on the award for the trade or industry. Because there's an allowance for sick days (called 'sickies'), many employees feel that they should take them whether they're sick or not (poor health is usually the last reason employees take sickies), particularly those in the public sector. It's estimated that around 15 per cent of companies with five or more employees have between 10 and 25 per cent of their workers absent 'sick' each day. Some 40 million working days (or an average of 5 per cent of the total) are lost to sickies each year, costing employers $billions.

Usually, you must have been employed for a minimum period before you're entitled to sick pay, e.g. three or six months, which may coincide with your probationary period. If you're sick during this period, your pay will be docked but, when you've completed three or six month's service, you may be reimbursed. A doctor's certificate isn't required for sick days taken within your annual allowance, although a certificate is required for additional sick days (for which you may not be paid). These are apparently easy to obtain even if you aren't sick! An employee cannot usually be dismissed when he's sick, although this depends on the period and the frequency of sick days and should be stipulated in your employment contract. In some states (e.g. NSW), up to five days of an employee's sick leave can be used to care for a partner (even same sex partners) or family member.

Some employers have an occupational sick pay (OSP) scheme, under which you receive your full salary for a number of months (depending on your length of service) in the event of sickness or after an accident. OSP may be provided by your employer as part of a company pension scheme.

## Miscellaneous Insurance

Other insurance provided by your employer is usually detailed in your employment conditions. This may include free life and health insurance, which also covers travel overseas on company business. Some companies provide free membership of a private health insurance scheme, although this may apply only to executives, managers and key personnel. Where applicable, check whether health insurance includes your family. Companies may also operate a contributory group health insurance scheme, offering reduced subscriptions for individual members.

## Notification of Sickness or Accident

You're usually required to notify your employer as soon as possible of sickness or an accident that prevents you from working, i.e. within a few hours of your normal starting time. Failure to do so may result in your not being paid for that day. You're required to keep your boss or manager informed about your illness and when you expect to return to work. For sick days that fall within your annual entitlement (see **Sick Pay** above), you aren't required to provide a doctor's certificate, although one is required for additional sick days.

## Annual Holidays

All permanent employees in Australia are entitled to at least four weeks' annual holiday and many receive up to six weeks, depending on the award for their trade or industry. Many employers offer four weeks in the first year of employment and six weeks thereafter; employees in some industries and professions receive as many as eight or nine weeks paid annual holiday. Under a scheme called holiday or leave 'loading', full-time employees are paid an extra 17.5 per cent of their normal wage (a sort of booze allowance) when they take their annual holidays, although this is increasingly being eliminated by AWAs. Some companies pay leave loading only to employees below a certain salary level, e.g. $50,000. In some industries and professions (e.g. teaching), employees are required to take paid holidays at certain times (what a hardship!).

Holiday entitlement is calculated on a pro rata basis (per completed calendar month of service) if you don't work a full calendar year. Part-time staff may also be entitled to paid holidays on a pro rata basis. Holidays must usually be taken within the year in which they're earned, although many companies allow employees to carry any outstanding annual holiday entitlement over to the next year. Employers may also allow employees to take their total annual holiday entitlement in one block, rather than split it into periods throughout the year.

Before starting a new job, check that any planned holidays will be approved by your new employer. This is particularly important if they fall within your probationary period (usually the first three months or 13 weeks), when holidays may not be permitted. Holidays may usually be taken only with the prior permission of your manager and in many companies must be booked up to one year in advance. If you resign your position or are given notice, most employers will pay you in lieu of any outstanding holidays, although this isn't an entitlement and you may be obliged to take the holiday at your employer's convenience.

## Public Holidays

The number of statutory public holidays in Australia varies from state to state between 10 and 12. There are eight national public holidays plus two to four state public holidays, the dates of which vary according to the state or territory (some companies and industries also have special holidays such as a company outing or a union picnic day). All states also celebrate Labour Day (in addition to the holidays shown below), although the date varies from state to state. Schools, banks, businesses and most shops are closed on public holidays.

The following days are public holidays throughout Australia:

| Date | Holiday |
| --- | --- |
| 1st January | New Year's Day |
| 26th January | Australia Day (the actual date varies from state to state and is usually on the Monday following the 26th unless the 26th is a Monday) |
| March/April | Good Friday (the date changes each year) |
| March/April | Easter Monday (the Monday after Good Friday) |
| 25th April | Anzac Day (in memory of those who died in the two world wars) |
| 2nd Monday in June | Queen's birthday (except Western Australia, which celebrates the Queen's birthday in September) |
| 25th December | Christmas Day |
| 26th December | Boxing Day (called Proclamation Day in South Australia) |

If a public holiday falls at a weekend, there's usually a substitute holiday on the following Monday (but not always). Some companies close during Christmas and New Year, e.g. 25th December until 1st January inclusive. To compensate for this shutdown and perhaps other extra holidays during the year, employees may be required to work extra hours throughout the year, or may be required to take part of their annual holiday entitlement. Part-time staff may be paid for a public holiday only when it falls on a day when they would normally be working.

You aren't required to work on public holidays unless otherwise stated in your contract of employment. When it's necessary to work on public holidays, you normally receive the same or a higher rate of pay than is paid for working on a Sunday (e.g. double the normal rate) and/or time off in lieu. When a job involves working at weekends and on public holidays (e.g. shift working), you usually receive a penalty rate or are paid a shift allowance.

# Compassionate & Special Leave

Whether or not you're paid for time off work or time lost through unavoidable circumstances (e.g. public transport strikes or car breakdowns) depends on your employer, on whether you're paid weekly or monthly (e.g. with an hourly rate of pay), and not least, whether you're required to punch a clock. The attitude to paid time off may also depend on your status and position. Executives and managers (who often work much longer hours than officially required) have much more leeway regarding time off than factory workers. Certain employees are allowed, by law, to take time off work under certain circumstances, as follows:

- An expectant mother is entitled to 'reasonable' paid time off for ante-natal care.

- A trade union official is entitled to paid time off for trade union duties and training for such duties; employees may also be paid to attend union meetings during working hours. Similarly, a safety representative is allowed paid time off in connection with his safety duties.

- All employees are allowed time off for public duties such as service as a juror or court witness, councillor or school governor, or as a member of a statutory tribunal or authority, although your employer isn't usually required to pay you.
- If you're made redundant, you're entitled to take one day off each week to look for a new job or to arrange training in connection with a new job.

Many Australian companies also provide paid compassionate or special leave on certain occasions, which may include your own or a family marriage, the birth of a child and the death of a family member or close relative. Many employers allow special leave, including long service leave, family leave, carers' leave and unpaid leave. However, only some 25 per cent of employees have the right to specific family or carers' leave and only around 20 per cent of enterprise agreements contain specific provisions addressing work and family issues, e.g. through special leave provisions. Women are far more likely to take leave for family reasons than men and in 2000 some 40 per cent of women took leave compared to just 21 per cent of men.

After 10 or 15 years' continuous service with an employer, you may be entitled to up to six months' leave on full or half pay. Some employers also permit unpaid career breaks (sabbaticals) of up to three years. The terms and conditions for special leave vary considerably according to the employer and, where applicable, should be detailed in your employment conditions.

# Expenses

Expenses paid by your employer are usually listed in your employment conditions. These may include travel costs from your home to your place of work, which (if applicable) may consist of a bus or rail season ticket or the equivalent in cash (paid monthly with your salary). Companies without a company restaurant or canteen may pay employees a lunch allowance or provide luncheon vouchers. Expenses paid for travel on company business or for training courses may be detailed in your employment conditions or listed in a separate document. Most companies pay a 'km' allowance to staff authorised to use their private motor vehicles on company business (but you must ensure that business use is covered by your car insurance).

# Probationary & Notice Periods

For most jobs there's a probationary period, which may vary from two weeks for weekly paid employees to three months (13 weeks) for permanent employees. Your notice period normally depends on your method of salary payment, your employer, your profession and your length of service, and is detailed in your contract of employment and employment conditions. Note that probationary and notice periods apply equally to employers and employees. The notice period for weekly paid workers is usually as follows:

| Length of Service | Notice Period |
| --- | --- |
| less than 1 year | 1 week |
| 1–3 years | 2 weeks |
| 3–5 years | 3 weeks |
| over 5 years | 4 weeks |

Employees aged over 45 years with more than two years' service are entitled to an extra week's notice or pay in lieu of notice. Most monthly paid employees have a one-month (or four-week) notice period, which takes effect after any probationary period. The notice period may be longer for executive or key employees, e.g. three or six months, or may be extended after a number of years' service (in which case it will be noted in your employment conditions).

If an employer doesn't give you the required notice in writing, he's liable to pay you in full for the period of official notice (see **Discipline & Dismissal** on page 70). If you resign, you must usually do so in writing. If you resign or are given notice, your company may not require you to work your notice period, particularly if you're joining a competitor or your boss feels that you may be a disruptive influence on your colleagues. However, if he doesn't want you to work your notice, he must pay you in full for the notice period, plus any outstanding overtime or holiday entitlement.

If an employer goes bankrupt and cannot pay you, you may terminate your employment without notice, but your employer cannot legally do this. Other valid reasons for an employee *not* to give notice are assault or abuse on him or a colleague by the employer, and failure to pay or persistent delay in paying his wages. Nevertheless, employees can usually leave a job without giving notice and the chances of an employer having any legal rights worth enforcing are negligible. However, you may lose any bonuses or other monies owed to you, plus any possibility of receiving a reference.

# Education & Training

Education and training provided by your employer may be stated in your employment conditions. It's in your own interest to investigate courses of study, seminars and lectures which you feel will be of direct benefit to you and your employer. Most employers will give reasonable consideration to a request to attend a course during working time, provided you don't make it a full-time occupation. In addition to relevant education and training, employers must also provide the essential tools and equipment for a job (although this is open to interpretation). It's compulsory for companies to provide appropriate and adequate safety and health training for all employees. However, Australian employers are notoriously lax in providing adequate training, and only around half the workforce receives education or training during a year (which may be on-the-job or in formal courses). To encourage employers to improve the quantity and quality of their training programmes, an Industry Training Levy was introduced in 1990 requiring employers to pay a penalty when specified minimum training levels weren't met.

If you need to improve your English, language classes may be paid by your employer. If it's necessary to learn a foreign language (other than English) in order to perform your job, the cost of language study should be paid by your employer. An allowance may be paid for personal education or hobbies (e.g. flower arranging, kite flying or break-dancing) which aren't work related or of direct benefit to your employer (unless he's in the flower, kite or dancewear business).

# Pregnancy & Confinement

Time off work for sickness in connection with a pregnancy is usually given without question, but it may not be paid unless authorised by a doctor if it exceeds your annual sick leave allocation. Depending on the industry or sector in which they're employed, most female employees are entitled to 12 months' unpaid maternity leave and those in the public sector are entitled to 12 weeks' paid maternity leave. Around 35 per cent of employees in the private sector receive paid maternity leave (Australia is one of the few countries in the world that has no laws requiring paid benefits in the private sector), although companies are increasingly scrapping it and it's also under threat from the outplacement of jobs. A few employers give employees with 12 months' continuous service six weeks' paid maternity leave. Part-time employees may be entitled to pro rata maternity leave and pay. A woman usually has the right to return to her job with the same pay within 12 months of giving birth. Around 20 per cent of employers provide paid paternity leave for fathers and most employers allow fathers to take unpaid leave when their partner gives birth.

## Part-Time Job Restrictions

Restrictions on part-time employment for an employer other than your regular employer may be detailed in your employment conditions. Many Australian companies don't allow full-time employees to work part-time (i.e. moonlight) for another employer, particularly one in the same line of business. You may, however, be permitted to take a part-time teaching job or similar part-time employment (or you can write a book).

## Confidentiality & Changing Jobs

If you disclose any confidential company information, either in Australia or overseas (particularly to competitors), you may be liable to instant dismissal and may also have legal action taken against you. You may not steal any secrets or confidential information (e.g. customer mailing lists) from a previous employer, but you may use any skills, know-how, knowledge and contacts acquired during his employ. If you make any inventions while an employee, they remain your property unless you sell or license them to your employer, the invention was made as part of your 'normal duties', or you were specifically employed to invent, e.g. in research and development.

You may not compete against a former employer if there's a valid, binding restraint clause in your contract of employment. Your contract may also contain a clause defining the sort of information that the employer considers to be confidential, such as customer and supplier relationships and details of business plans. If there's a confidentiality or restraint clause in your contract that's unfair (e.g. inhibits you from changing jobs), it will probably be invalid in law and therefore unenforceable. If you're in doubt, consult a solicitor who's an expert in company law about your rights. If you're a key employee, you may have a legal binding contract preventing you from joining a competitor or starting a company in the same line of business as your employer for a period, and in particular, enticing your former colleagues to join your company. However, such a clause is usually valid for a limited period, e.g. one year.

## Acceptance of Gifts

With the exception of those employed in the public sector, employees are normally permitted to accept gifts of a limited value from customers or suppliers, e.g. bottles of wine or spirits or other small gifts at Christmas. Generally, any gifts given and received openly and above board aren't considered a bribe or unlawful. Nevertheless, you should declare any gifts received to your immediate superior, who will decide what is to be done with them. Most bosses pool gifts and divide them among all employees. (If you accept a real bribe, make sure it's a big one and that you have a secret Swiss bank account!)

## Long Service Awards

Most large companies present their employees with long service awards after a number of years, e.g. 15, 20 or 25. These are usually in the form of a gift such as a watch or clock (so you can count the hours to your retirement). Periods of absence on maternity leave may count as continuous employment when calculating your length of service.

## Retirement

Your employment contract may be valid only until the official state retirement age, currently 61 for women (although it's gradually being increased to 65) and 65 for men. In many large companies, early retirement is possible from the age of 55. If you wish to continue working after you've reached retirement age, you may need to negotiate a new contract of employment (you should also seek psychiatric help). If your employer has a compulsory retirement age, usually 65, he isn't required to give you notice. Many companies present employees with a gift on reaching retirement age (e.g. the key to your ball and chain), the value of which usually depends on your number of years' service. See page 69 for more information.

## Discipline & Dismissal

Most large and medium size companies have comprehensive grievance and disciplinary procedures, which must usually be followed before an employee can be suspended or dismissed. Some employers have disciplinary procedures whereby employees may be suspended with or without pay, e.g. for breaches of contract. Employees may also be suspended (usually with pay) pending investigation into an alleged offence or impropriety. Disciplinary procedures usually include both verbal and official written warnings, e.g. first verbal warning, second verbal warning, first written warning, second written warning, interview with board, etc., and official records must be kept by your employer. These procedures are both to protect employees from unfair dismissal and to ensure that dismissed employees cannot (successfully) sue their employer. If you have a grievance or complaint against a colleague or your boss, there may be an official procedure to be followed in order to obtain redress. If an official grievance procedure exists, it will usually be detailed in your employment conditions.

It's illegal to dismiss employees on grounds other than those detailed in government and union agreements. In instances where employment was terminated on unjustified grounds, there may be a review by an industrial court, and wrongful dismissal can result in a claim for damages. There has been a massive increase in unfair dismissal claims in recent years running into several thousands annually as a result of the government's tightening of federal industrial relations laws. However, employees dismissed for 'serious misconduct' such as disobedience of management decisions, fraud or any other illegal activity aren't entitled to notice or benefits. If you believe that you've been unfairly dismissed, you can take your case to the Conciliation and Arbitration Commission. There's a filing fee for a claim for unfair dismissal and provisions allowing costs to be awarded against employees who make frivolous claims. Those earning over $71,200 a year are excluded from claiming for unfair dismissal, along with casuals on short-term arrangements, those on probation for three months or less, and apprentices.

# Redundancy

Redundancy (called retrenchment in Australia) has become a common occurrence in recent years, particularly during the recession in the early '90s. Retrenchment is defined as 'where an employer has made a definite decision that he no longer wishes the job that an employee has been doing to be done by anyone, and this is not due to the ordinary and customary turnover of labour'. Retrenched workers are entitled to severance pay in accordance with the Termination Change and Redundancy (TCR) case in 1984. The amount of severance pay (in terms of normal weeks' pay) for those employed under federal awards depends on the length of service of an employee, as shown below:

| Length of Service | Severance Pay |
| --- | --- |
| less than 1 year | 0 weeks |
| 1–2 years | 4 weeks |
| 2–3 years | 6 weeks |
| 3–4 years | 7 weeks |
| over 4 years | 8 weeks |

Employees aged over 45 years with more than two years' service are entitled to an extra week's notice or pay in lieu of notice. Severance pay is higher in some states, e.g. 16 weeks in NSW plus an extra 25 per cent for those over 45. Many enterprise agreements allow for three or four weeks' pay for each year of service when an employee takes forced redundancy. Severance pay may not exceed the amount an employee would have earned had he remained in employment until his normal retirement date and is paid at ordinary time rates for the standard working week. If an employee receives a superannuation payment (see page 310), the amount is generally deducted from his entitlement to severance pay.

The average severance pay for executives is usually around six months' salary, although some executives, managers and key personnel have a clause in their contract whereby they receive a generous 'golden handshake' if they're retrenched, e.g. after a take-over. Employers have no unfettered right to dismiss executives and must safeguard themselves against compensation claims by executives they sack. This applies even if they obtain an indemnifying deed of release, which is supposed to protect employers from further suits, claims or demands when an employee accepts a retrenchment package.

When an employee has been notified of his retrenchment, he's permitted to take a day off each week with pay to look for another job. Employers must contact a Centrelink office and inform them of the number of proposed retrenchments, the category of employees affected, and the period over which the retrenchments will be made. Some companies provide 'outplacement' consultancy or agency services for employees who are retrenched. This includes advice and counselling on future job prospects, job hunting, state benefits, retirement, retraining, setting up in business, and financial advice for employees who receive large redundancy payments.

Australia has no unemployment benefit scheme, but unemployed people receive social security payments under either the Jobsearch or Newstart schemes (see page 307). Retrenched employees are entitled to a 'statement of employment' (reference). It's also possible for employees to take voluntary redundancy or early retirement and receive an early pension, e.g. in the event of ill health.

# References

Employers in Australia aren't legally obliged to provide employees with a written reference or 'statement of employment', except in the case of retrenchment. However, if you leave an employer on good terms, he'll usually provide a written reference on request. If your employer refuses to give you a written reference or gives you an unwarranted 'bad' reference, you should ask your immediate boss or a colleague for a personal reference. In Australia, prospective employers may contact your previous employer (or employers) directly for a reference, either orally or written. This can be bad news for employees, as you have no idea what has been said about you and whether it's true or false. However, an employer cannot (legally) maliciously defame you, although should he do so verbally, it's almost impossible to successfully sue him.

# Trade Union Membership

Trade unions have been active in Australia since the mid-19th century, when many professional agitators were deported from Britain and Ireland. Australia has a long tradition of supporting workers' rights, better working conditions and improved pay, all of which unions have fought hard for over the years. However, unions earned themselves a terrible reputation during the '60s and '70s, when the country and the economy was frequently crippled by strikes. This was brought to an end in the mid-'80s with the accord between employers, unions and government, brokered by the Labor government elected in 1983 (the unions have traditionally had strong links with the Australian Labor Party). In recent years, there has been a series of confrontations between the Liberal/National coalition government and the unions, after the government brought in tougher 'anti-union' laws, which included anti-strike provisions and tough sanctions against some primary and secondary boycotts. This has led to some bitter disputes between employers wishing to end outdated restrictive work practices (and the resulting low productivity), which are rampant in industries with strong unions such as mining and the docks.

Today, there are over 300 trade unions in Australia, around half of which are affiliated to the Australian Council of Trade Unions (393 Swanston St., Melbourne, VIC 3000, ☎ 03-9663 5266, 🖳 www.actu.asn.au). Union membership in Australia is among the highest in the world at around 31 per cent of the workforce (some 2.8

million people), although in the last few decades they've been losing ground in their areas of traditional strength and have largely failed to recruit young workers, women, workers in small businesses and those in growth industries. There was a net loss of 25 per cent of union membership between 1992 and 1999, and some 60 per cent of workers believe unions are no longer relevant to them (a survey in 1997 found that non-union members are more likely to be satisfied at work, have more positive attitudes to management and feel more secure than those in unions).

Nevertheless, despite their reduced membership, unions have a great deal of influence, particularly in companies and industries which previously had 'closed shop' agreements, where all employees had to join a union (the Workplace Relations Act, 1996 abolished compulsory union membership). However, although union membership isn't compulsory, some union representatives or trades put a lot of pressure on employees to join. The public sector is the most heavily unionised with around 55 per cent of employees being members; membership in the private sector is below 25 per cent. Large companies with over 100 employees have the highest rates of unionisation and small businesses with fewer than ten employees the lowest (unions are now active in less than 20 per cent of workplaces).

Whether you're better off as a member of a trade union will depend on the industry in which you're employed. There are benefits to be gained from union membership and, in addition to negotiating better pay and conditions for members, unions also offer members legal and medical assistance in work-related disputes. In most industries which recognise trade unions, members' pay and conditions are decided by collective bargaining between employers and trade unions. Employers aren't allowed to discriminate against an employee in selection, promotion, transfer, training or dismissal because he belongs (or wishes to belong) to a trade union.

# 3.

# PERMITS & VISAS

**B**efore making any plans to live or work in (or even travel to) Australia, you *must* ensure that you have the appropriate visa, without which you will be refused permission to enter the country. With the exception of New Zealanders, anyone wishing to enter Australia as a visitor or for any other purpose requires a visa. Australia is a nation of migrants and only the 1.5 per cent Aboriginals represent the indigenous population; everyone else is an immigrant or descended from an immigrant. After the second world war Australia instituted a mass immigration policy ('populate or perish') and accepted virtually anybody who applied, even providing assisted passages where migrants paid only a small sum (e.g. £10 in Britain) towards their fare to Australia. However, immigration policy has altered dramatically since then and Australia's entry qualifications for independent migrants (those without family in Australia) are now among the most stringent in the world. In the '60s, Australia accepted around 140,000 migrants a year, peaking at 172,000 in 1988, although in the '90s the quota allocation was reduced considerably, although a review of immigration policy found that the quotas were too low, particularly regarding skilled migrants, and could stifle economic growth. In the period 2001–02 there was an allocation of 85,000 visas, of which over half were for skilled migrants.

Immigration is a sensitive subject in Australia, where the majority of people are against large-scale immigration (although many also believe that it provides real benefits for the country and stimulates economic growth). Migrants bring $billions into Australia each year and migration is the country's third-largest, foreign-currency earner after tourism and agriculture, to say nothing of the wealth created by migrants. However, not everybody welcomes immigrants and issues such as over-crowding and over-population, and protecting Australia's environment, culture and economy, are arguments frequently cited by those opposed to large-scale immigration. Despite its vast size, Australia has a relatively small population (around 19 million) and is actually considered by many Australians to be over-populated owing to its lack of productive land, shortage of water and generally over-crowded cities.

Many Australians feel that migrants are a strain on the economy and take jobs away from 'real' Australians, a view which has become more prominent in recent years. The ethnic background of migrants is also a thorny issue and although race and ethnic origin aren't officially an immigration issue, almost half of all Australians believe that the country accepts too many Asians and some would also like fewer migrants from the Middle East (settlers from Asia, Africa and the Middle East have borne the brunt of the government's cuts in immigration in recent years).

Note that there's a huge unsatisfied demand for emigration to Australia, which is much more difficult than emigrating to the USA, Canada, New Zealand or South Africa (the regulations are designed to keep people out rather than let them in). It's becoming increasingly difficult to obtain a visa as an independent migrant and it's also more difficult (or impossible) for immigrants who don't speak fluent English. Australian missions receive over a million enquiries a year and 400,000 applications, of which around 85,000 are accepted for emigration. Over a third of those accepted already have family in Australia, around 50 per cent are professionals or skilled workers and as many as 15 to 20 per cent are refugees.

Applying for a visa as a migrant (permanent residence) is time consuming, confusing, difficult and expensive, and has spawned a wealth of migration consultants and keeps thousands of civil servants in 'employment'. The Australian government is constantly changing the rules and sometimes introduces retrospective changes that apply to applications already lodged (but not processed). Before making an application, check the latest regulations and criteria for visa applications. Note that even when new requirements have been announced, they may not be introduced for many months or even years, and could even be rejected by the upper house (Senate) of the Australian parliament after being passed by the lower house. Application fees for migrant visas are high and aren't refundable, so you should ensure that you have a *very* good chance of being accepted before making an application (otherwise you would be better off spending your money on lottery tickets!). **Note that a two-year waiting period has been introduced in recent years before most migrants can claim social security, which has caused many unemployed migrants to become destitute and homeless (particularly those from third world countries with little money).**

Permanent foreign residents of Australia don't receive the same rights as Australian citizens with regard to their freedom to leave and enter Australia. If you migrated to Australia in 1987 or later, your initial visa gives you permission to return to Australia for three, four or five years after first entry. After this time, if you choose not to apply for Australian citizenship, you must obtain a 'resident return visa' (RRV) before leaving the country, which allows a permanent resident to return to Australia within a period of either three months or five years. Whether the visa is granted depends on how long you have spent in Australia during the previous five years. If you migrated prior to 1987 you will have been issued with either an Authority to Return (ATR) or a Return Endorsement (RE), which are valid providing you have not been out of Australia for more than three years and you have not become a citizen.

An RRV cannot be extended and you should not wait until the visa expires before applying for a new one. You should check well in advance if you are eligible for a new visa. If it expires, you must apply for a new one and the amount of time you have spent outside Australia in the five years immediately prior to your application will determine whether you're eligible for a new visa, and if so, what type. For example, if you have lived in Australia for at least two years within the last five, you will probably be eligible for an RRV which gives you the right to remain outside Australia for up to five years. If you aren't eligible for a five-year RRV you may be eligible for a three-month RRV. If you choose to return to Australia just before your visa expires, you will be obliged to remain there for at least 12 months before you're eligible for another RRV. If you need to leave because of an emergency during this period, you will allowed to do so only once.

**The information in this chapter is intended as a guide only and the rules and regulations concerning visas change frequently. It's important to check the latest regulations with an Australian mission or immigration consultant (such as The Emigration Group – see inside covers) before making a visa application.**

# VISAS

With the exception of New Zealanders, anyone wishing to enter Australia requires a visa, which must be obtained before arrival in the country. New Zealanders receive a special category visa on arrival and nothing is stamped in their passports. There are no formalities and they can live and work in Australia for as long as they wish. **If you need a visa and arrive without one, you'll be sent back to your home country at your own expense.** The type of visa issued depends on the reason for your planned trip to Australia, which may be anything from a few weeks holiday or a short business trip to permanent residence.

There are three main categories of visas: migration, temporary residence and visitors. Multiple-entry visas are issued to those who need to visit Australia frequently over a long period, such as businessmen, the parents of children living there, entertainers and sportsmen. Note that there are fees for anything other than a three-month visitor's visa, which have increased considerably in recent years (see page 96). The processing of visa applications in some categories can take a considerable time in some countries owing to the large number of applications to be processed, and approval can take anything from a few weeks to a number of years.

Information about visas, charges and forms can be obtained from offices of the Department of Immigration and Multicultural Affairs (DIMA) in Australia (🖥 www. immi.gov.au) and Australian missions overseas. General information about visa applications is contained in *making and processing Visa applications* (form 1025i). It's important to obtain and complete the correct form, pay the correct fee and satisfy other requirements such as being inside or outside Australia, as required. You must be careful to indicate the visa class under which you wish to be considered, as your application cannot be considered under any class other than the one noted on your application form. An *Application for Migration to Australia* form (47) must be completed by all applicants wishing to travel to Australia to live permanently and applications must be sent or delivered to a DIMA office or an Australian mission overseas with all relevant documentation and the fee.

Family members who apply at the same time can usually apply on the same form and pay just one fee (a child born after an application is made, but before it's decided, is included in the parents' application). In certain circumstances, a spouse or dependent child can be added to an application. Applications for some visas, such as visitors' visas, may be decided while you wait. In this case, if you're granted a visa you're usually given a visa label in your passport. If your application for a visitors' visa is refused, you will be given a notice of refusal. For all other visas, you're notified of the decision by letter. If you're refused a visa, you will be notified why and, if applicable, where you can apply for a review of the decision and the time limit for doing so.

If you plan to travel to or from Australia while your visa application is being considered (assuming this is possible), you should inform the DIMA, as a visa will be refused if you're in the 'wrong place' when a decision is made. For most visas where an application is made overseas, you must be outside Australia when a decision is made and for visa applications in Australia, you must be in Australia when the decision is made. If you make a visa application in Australia, you must ensure that you have a visa to return *before* leaving the country, otherwise if you're application is refused you may have no right of review. If you apply for a visa in Australia, you're usually granted a bridging visa to remain within the law if your current visa expires while a decision is being made regarding your application.

**Extensions, Conditions & Expiry:** If you wish to stay longer than your visa allows, you should apply for another visa. If your visa expires while you're in Australia and you haven't applied for an extension, you're committing a criminal offence and can be fined up to $4,000, given a suspended prison sentence of up to six months or even deported. If you're deported, you will usually be barred from entering Australia for one to three years. Persons deported for criminal or security reasons are permanently excluded. If a visa is granted subject to certain conditions, e.g. restrictions on work or study, you must abide by those conditions or your visa may be cancelled. If you wish to change your visa status, e.g. from a visitor to a student, you must leave the country and make a new application while overseas.

**Waiting Period:** Note that it can take a long time to receive a migrant visa. However, if you're really keen to go and you meet the criteria for the category of visa for which you're applying, you'll usually get your visa in the end. You should be prepared for a long wait (e.g. a number of years) and possibly a lot of questions and demands for additional paperwork from immigration officials. If your application is pooled (which applies to visas in categories subject to a 'points test') or if processing of the class of visa is suspended, your application will be delayed indefinitely and may eventually be refused. The processing time for migration applications varies according to the country where you're applying and the number of applicants. Family migrants are given priority. In certain circumstances, e.g. for compassionate reasons, an application can be expedited, although no guarantees are given.

**Visa Validity:** If you're accepted for immigration you'll be asked to send your passport to the embassy or consulate and a visa will be stamped in it. You must usually arrive in Australia within six months of the date stamped in your passport. Note that if you don't enter Australia by the 'initial entry' date of your visa, it will expire and you will need to re-apply for migration. If you enter Australia by the initial entry date you will have used (or validated) your migrant visa and by doing so will have become a permanent resident (if applicable).

# MIGRATION

To be accepted for migration to Australia you must meet the personal and occupational requirements of the category for which you're applying, and be of good health and character. The Australian migration programme is divided into four main visa categories: family; skilled; refugee, humanitarian and special assistance; and interdependent migrants, each of which have their own eligibility requirements, as follows:

- **Family** Migrants must have a relative in Australia who can sponsor them.

- **Skilled Migrants** must have skills or abilities that will benefit Australia.

- **Refugee, Humanitarian and Special Assistance Migrants** – see page 87 and information form 964i (*Refugee and Humanitarian Entry*).

- **Interdependent** Migrants must have an interdependent relationship with an Australian citizen, permanent resident or eligible New Zealand citizen.

The above migration categories are explained in detail in this chapter. In addition to the above, former Australians who have lost their Australian citizenship and former residents who have spent most of their life before the age of 18 in Australia and who have maintained ties with Australia, are also eligible for migration. Dependants of New Zealand citizens who have settled or intend to settle in Australia are also allowed entry into Australia. In general, applicants must apply for residence while outside Australia, although applications can be made while in Australia in exceptional circumstances, e.g. when a visitor's family overseas has died while he's in Australia, when he has met an Australian and plans to marry, or when a return to his country could result in political persecution.

The Department of Immigration and Multicultural Affairs (DIMA) has an enquiry telephone service in Australia (☎ local call rate 13-1881 or 🖳 www.immi.gov.au). In most countries the local Australian embassy or consulate has a recorded message information service (e.g. ☎ 09065-508900 in Britain), although it's usually difficult to get through and numbers are often expensive premium rate lines. The form, *Migrating to Australia – Who can migrate?* (957i), contains general information about migration and the various categories. An *Application for Migration to Australia* form (47) must be completed by all applicants wishing to travel to Australia to live permanently. There's a fee (e.g. £5 in Britain) for this form and the information package. If you wish to inquire about an application it must be made in writing, quoting your DIMA file number, although you may telephone the DIMA and enquire about the progress of your application (but this can delay its processing).

**Never make any firm plans or arrangements (such as travel arrangements, selling your home or resigning your employment) in the expectation that your visa application will be granted. Even when an application appears to be going smoothly it can still be delayed or even rejected at the last minute, e.g. on health grounds.**

## VISA QUOTAS

The Australian migration year runs from 1st July to 30th June (the same as the Australian financial year) and each year the federal government announces the quotas for the coming year. All applications for categories where a quota (or capping) applies are processed on a 'first-come, first-served' basis. When a cap is reached for the current immigration year, the granting of visas is suspended, although processing continues and applicants are granted visas when the new immigration year commences (and a new quota is allocated). The following quotas are for the year 2001/02:

| Category/Component | Quota |
|---|---|
| Family: | |
| Preferential Family | 37,900 |
| **Total Family** | **37,900** |
| Skill: | |
| Skilled-Australian-sponsored | 4,350 |
| Skilled-Australian-sponsored * | 2,000 |
| Employer Nominated (ENS/RSMS) | 6,000 |
| Business Skills | 7,900 |
| Special Talents | 170 |
| Skilled Independents | 25,050 |
| **Total Skill** | **45,470** |
| Special Eligibility | 1,600 |
| **Total 2001/02** | **84,970** |

\* In the 2001/02 programme, the Skilled-Australian-linked (SAL) category was renamed the Skilled-Australian-sponsored category (SAS), but a quota was included for SAL for previous applicants.

Migration planning figures can never be exact because while some categories (e.g. independent and SAS) attract fixed quotas, others are demand-driven. There's no upper limit placed on the number of migrants who can qualify in demand-driven categories, where, if you meet the criteria, you're accepted.

## HEALTH & CHARACTER CHECKS

Applicants for migration visas must pass health and character checks before they're granted a visa.

**Medical Examination:** All applicants (and their family members) for permanent or long-term temporary residence (over 12 months), plus short-term temporary applicants if their health is of 'special significance', are required to undergo a medical examination. This includes an X-ray for those aged 16 or older and an HIV/AIDS test for those aged 15 or over. TB screening is part of the medical examination for all those aged 16 or over (and for those aged under 16 if it's suspected that they have, or have had, TB). Visitors to Australia are required to sign a declaration stating that they 'have never had tuberculosis or any serious condition likely to endanger or be a cost to Australia'. Hepatitis B screening is compulsory if the applicant is pregnant, a child for adoption or an unaccompanied refugee minor. Pregnancy must be declared by prospective migrants. Note that a long-term or serious illness or condition suffered by you or a dependant could void your application, e.g. if you have a child who requires special schooling. Results of the examination are sent to the Department of Health in Australia and can take around six weeks to be assessed. Your case officer will provide you with instructions and forms for your medical examination after you have lodged your application and during its processing.

**Statement of Good Character:** One of the requirements for entry into Australia is that you must be of good character. Applicants aged 16 to 65 who have resided in their present country for over 12 months in the last ten years must obtain a 'police certificate' detailing any criminal convictions. The police certificate can be obtained as soon as you decide to apply for migration to Australia, and if you receive it before making your visa application it should be included with it. The procedure for obtaining a police certificate varies from country to country, e.g. in Britain a 'certificate' can be obtained by visiting your local police station and requesting a 'Personal Record of Prosecution/Criminal History' from the National Identification Service, Subject Access Office, Room 1229, New Scotland Yard, Broadway, London SW1H 0BG. In Australia a certificate of 'no criminal record' (fee $36) can be obtained from the Australian Federal Police, Criminal History Branch, Locked Bag 1, Weston, ACT 2611. Note that if you have a criminal record it may jeopardise your application – stringent efforts have been made in recent years to prevent the entry of convicted criminals and other undesirables. Further information is provided in *Character requirement: police certificates* (form 47P).

Medical and police clearances are valid for only 12 months, and therefore you're required to make your initial entry into Australia within 12 months of your medical or police clearance date, whichever occurs first.

# Documentation & Interviews

All application forms must be completed in English and you must provide originals or certified copies of all documents (as requested).

**Documentation:** You must usually provide certified copies of documents such as educational and trade qualifications, training courses and experience, employer references, and birth and marriage certificates. All documents must be certified by a legal professional, a Justice of the Peace or other person authorised to witness statutory declarations (e.g. a Commissioner for Declarations in Australia), who must state that the photocopy is a true copy of the original. **Original documents mustn't be sent unless specifically requested.** Additional information concerning your application can be provided at any time (and will be taken into account) prior to a decision being made. You must keep the DIMA informed of any change in your circumstances if they relate to information already provided that's no longer correct. Note that if you provide incorrect information or documents, your application or visa can be cancelled.

**Trade & Professional Qualifications:** Assessments of some qualifications can usually be done fairly quickly, although if they must be referred to Australian professional bodies it can take up to six months.

**Interviews:** If you meet the criteria for migration to Australia, you and your family members will be invited to attend an interview with an officer of the Department of Immigration and Ethnic Affairs. If for some reason you fail to attend a scheduled interview your application won't automatically be refused and a decision may be made on the basis of the information already provided. If you're invited to an interview, take care how your answer seemingly innocuous questions such as 'Why do you wish to emigrate to Australia?' It's advisable to always answer positively and rehearse your answers to potential tricky questions.

# FAMILY MIGRATION

There's only one category of family migration called 'preferential family' and there's a strict quota, which in 2001/02 was 37,900. Of these places, 27,800 were reserved for spouses of Australians, 4,600 for fiancé(e)s, 2,150 for children including adopted children, 500 for parents, 2,350 for other dependants and special need relatives, and 500 for interdependent relatives (mainly same sex partners). The allocation for parents has been slashed from 6,000 in the mid '90s to just 500 in 2001/02, which in effect means that the government has virtually stopped the migration of mostly aged people from joining their family members in Australia.

Applicants in the preferential family category need to be sponsored by a relative who must be aged at least 18 and a settled Australian resident (which is generally accepted to be the case after two years continual employment). However, in spouse and parent classes, a minor child can act as a sponsor under certain special circumstances. Your relative in Australia must undertake to assist you financially and with accommodation during your first two years in Australia, plus, if necessary, attendance at English-language classes. Migrants aren't usually eligible to receive unemployment and other welfare benefits for a period of two years or longer, so sponsors must be prepared to accept a possible significant cost. For more information see the form entitled *Sponsorship* (961i).

# Family Migration Classes

You can be sponsored as a family migrant in one of the following visa classes:

- **Partner (class 100):** A husband, wife or *de facto* partner who has been living with the sponsor for at least one year.

- **Dependent Child (101):** A natural or adopted child (usually under 18) of the sponsor who's dependent on the sponsor. A child who's married or engaged to be married isn't eligible.

- **Adoption (102):** A child under 18 coming to Australia for adoption, where the adoption is supported by the appropriate state or territory welfare authorities in Australia, or a child under 18 who was adopted by Australian citizens or permanent residents while they were genuinely resident overseas for at least 12 months at the time of the application.

- **Parent (103):** A parent of the sponsor in Australia. Parents must meet the 'balance of family' criteria outlined in the information *Sponsorship* form (961i). The sponsor must have lived in Australia for at least two years before lodging the application. Note that there's a surfeit of applicants in this visa class and a very low annual quota, and most parents have to wait years before they obtain a visa.

- **Orphan Relative (104):** An orphan under 18 who's unmarried and a relative of the sponsor.

- **Carer (104):** A relative capable of providing substantial and continuing help to an Australian citizen, permanent resident or eligible New Zealand citizen living in Australia, who's in need of permanent or long-term help which cannot be provided by a relative in Australia or be provided by local welfare, hospital, nursing or community services. The carer must be prepared to provide the care for at least two years.

- **Aged Dependent Relative (104):** A single, widowed or divorced relative who's old enough to be granted an old age pension under the Social Security Act 1991, and has been dependent on the sponsor in Australia for at least three years. The sponsor is expected to have lived in Australia for at least two years before lodging the application.

- **Remaining Relative (104):** The sponsor's last brother or sister or non-dependent child outside Australia. You and your spouse must not have a parent or sibling or non-dependent child (or step relative within the same degree of relationship) living in the same country or have more than three relatives outside Australia. You must also have had no ongoing contact with such relatives for a reasonable period. The sponsor is expected to have lived in Australia for at least two year years before lodging the application.

- **Prospective Marriage (300):** A prospective spouse planning to marry a sponsor in Australia receives a temporary visa to stay in Australia for up to nine months. You must marry your sponsor and apply to remain permanently within this period, after which you will be granted a two-year provisional (temporary) visa if all the requirements are met. If the relationship is still ongoing at the end of the two-year period, you will be granted a permanent visa.

# Assurance of Support

An assurance of support is mandatory for some categories of family migration, where the sponsoring relative in Australia must undertake to provide financial support (should it be necessary) for the migrant. It's a legal commitment by the assurer to repay the Australian Government if certain welfare benefits are paid to the migrant during his first two years in Australia. Where applicable, a refundable bond and a migration 'health services' charge is payable (a bond isn't required for orphan relatives). The points test (see page 88) doesn't apply to family applicants. An assurance of support may be requested in other family visa classes, but neither the bond nor the migration health services charge are applicable.

The Assurance of Support bond is $3,500 for the first applicant and $1,500 for each other person over 18 included in the application. The bond now applies to a wide range of family categories, including spouses and fiancés, and is a legally binding guarantee that none of those being sponsored will seek to obtain certain social security benefits within their first two years in Australia. Financial institutions providing the bond service charge a fee of around $200 (a list is available from Australian missions). The bond is refundable after two years together with the accrued interest.

There's also a migration health services charge of around $900 for most applicants who require an assurance of support. This charge offsets the cost to the health budget arising from the health needs of migrants covered by the assurance of support in their first two years residence in Australia. The charge applies to each person included in the application regardless of age and must be paid before the application can be approved. The charge is refunded if the applicant withdraws his application or decides not to travel to Australia after payment has been made.

Under current policy, children sponsoring their parents as immediate family must arrange an assurance of support to care for their parents for ten years. An assurance is sought when the parent is within ten years of retirement (currently age 51 for a woman and 55 for a man). This means that any special benefit paid to the parent becomes a debt payable by the assurer, although assurances aren't currently enforced when the parent becomes a citizen. However, owing to rising welfare costs, the government has revised the scope of the assurances, which remains in force for five years even when the parent becomes a citizen. Any unemployment benefit paid to the parent during this period is also recoverable from the assurer.

An assurance of support is required if you sponsor:

● a parent who meets the balance of family test applying to stay in Australia;

● an aged parent who meets the balance of family test applying to stay in Australia;

● an orphaned unmarried relative under 18;

● a relative who's willing and capable of providing support to an Australian resident who's in special need of assistance on a permanent or long-term basis;

● an aged relative who's dependent on you;

● a last remaining brother or sister or non-dependent child outside Australia;

● a relative assessed by the Department of Immigration as being at risk of becoming a charge on the social welfare budget if approved to settle or remain in Australia.

For more information see the *Assurance of Support* form (960i).

# SKILLED MIGRATION

The skilled migration category is intended to contribute to Australia's economic growth and to be accepted there must be a demand in Australia for your skills, outstanding talent or business skills. The system was extensively reviewed and simplified in 1998-1999. Some states offer financial assistance and other help to migrants. The skilled migration visa classes are skilled-Australian-sponsored (SAS), which replaced the previously called skilled-Australian-linked (SAL) in July 1999, labour agreement, employer nomination, distinguished talent, skilled independent, and business skills, each of which is described in more detail below:

**Skilled-Australian-sponsored:** The SAS migration category provides migration for non-dependent children; parents of working age (who don't meet the 'balance of family' test); brothers and sisters; and nieces and nephews. Those planning to migrate in this visa category must be sponsored by a relative in Australia and meet health and character requirements. There are two subclasses, Skilled-Australian-sponsored (SAS) and regional-sponsored, under which all applicants are assessed.

Applicants in the skilled-Australian-sponsored subclass must be of working age and pass a 'points test' (see page 88). Points are awarded for skill, age, relationship to sponsor, citizenship of the sponsor, the capability of the sponsor to provide settlement support, and the residential location of the sponsor in Australia. Points are awarded for English language ability in the SAS category.

Applicants in the skilled-regional sponsored migration subclass must be aged under 45, have at least functional English and hold a qualification equivalent to an Australian diploma or higher, which is relevant to their usual occupation. In addition, their sponsor must have lived in a designated area (see page 83) of Australia for at least one year and must not have received certain social security benefits for more than two weeks during this period. Further details of both subclasses are provided in forms Skilled–Australian-sponsored (958iS) and Skilled regional sponsored migration (958iR).

If you have relatives who are able to sponsor you under the SAS category, you should ask them to obtain a form *Sponsorship for Migration to Australia* (M40) from their local office of the Department of Immigration, Local Government and Ethnic Affairs in Australia. When they have completed the sponsorship form they should send it to you and you must then obtain a copy of the *Application for Migration* kit from your nearest Australian mission.

**Labour Agreement:** Allows the entry of people with skills, qualifications and experience required by a labour agreement or a regional headquarters agreement. Applicants must be nominated by an employer or organisation with which an agreement exists and the terms and conditions of that agreement must be met.

**Employer Nomination:** Allows the migration of highly skilled people, nominated by employers in Australia who have been unable to find or train workers in Australia. The Employer Nomination Scheme (ENS) allows employers anywhere in Australia to sponsor overseas employees when they cannot find suitable applicants in Australia. Employers must have advertised vacancies both locally and nationally and must have a good training record. Nominations are valid for 12 months only and the scheme is subject to annual quotas (6,000 in 2001/02, including RSMS below).

The Regional Sponsored Migration Scheme (RSMS) was established in 1995 and provides a mechanism for employers in regional Australia to nominate skilled workers for permanent entry to Australia. Note that, even when you're sponsored by an employer, it's important to assess your prospects of future employment in Australia should you need or wish to change jobs. You should also bear in mind that ENS/RSMS applicants are tied by contract to work for an employer for a certain period, so you won't be able to leave after a short period to work for another employer or become self-employed. Applicants should be aged under 45 and must have functional English skills and possess qualifications and/or job training equivalent to at least Australian diploma level.

Skill matching is designed to help migrants find employment in regional Australia if their particular skills and abilities are in demand. Applicants under the independent migration category who intend to settle in a city or area of Australia other than Sydney, Newcastle, Brisbane, Perth, Wollongong, the Gold Coast or the Sunshine Coast, who haven't yet decided where they wish to settle, can apply to have their skills matched with an employer seeking someone with their skills. The core requirements for skill matching are the same as the requirements under RSMS.

The Skill Matching visa, introduced on 1st July 1999, is designed to link skilled migrants with specific skilled vacancies through RSMS. It provides opportunities for skilled people who don't meet the current passmark under the Skilled Independent category to be included in the Skill Matching Database (see below) without having to apply for a visa. The Skill Matching visa isn't points tested but applicants must be aged under 45, have degree, diploma or trade certificate qualifications which are recognised in Australia, have a vocational level of English and have been employed in an occupation listed in the skilled occupations list for at least 6 months in the 12 months immediately before lodging the visa application. Applicants who meet these criteria have their occupational and personal details placed in the Skill Matching Database and, unless they are successfully nominated by either a State or Territory Government or an employer, their details remain in the database for a period of two years. This database (with approximately 1,000 applicants in 2001) is distributed to all State and Territory Governments and a network of regional development authorities, and is also a resource for State and Territory Governments to use in targeted promotional campaigns to encourage skilled migrants to settle in their jurisdiction.

**Distinguished Talent:** Allows the migration of people with outstanding records in an occupation, the arts or sport. Applicants must show they will be an asset to the Australian community.

**Skilled Independent:** This class covers the entry of highly skilled people whose education, skills and employability will contribute to the Australian economy. Applicants must be of working age and pass the 'points test' (see page 88), under which points are awarded for skills, age and English-language ability. Applicants whose job is on the 'occupations requiring English' list must demonstrate a high standard of English language ability. Further details are provided in the information form *Independent skilled migration* (958iI). Applications are made using form 47 (*Application for Migration to Australia*) and additional information is provided in form 47N (*Explanatory notes – Application for migration to Australia*).

The quota for independent migrants in 2001/02 was 25,050, although the category is usually suspended well before the end of the immigration year. This immigration criteria has been tightened in recent years with more rigorous investigation placing greater emphasis on the interviewing of applicants. As a result, successful applicants can expect to wait up to two years for a visa.

**Business Skills:** Provides for migration on the basis of established skills in business and/or investment. Applicants must have recent experience running a successful business or a substantial investment portfolio as an owner or part-owner, or have been a senior executive in a large company. They must be committed to managing a business and/or investment in Australia in which they have substantial ownership. Further information is provided in the *Business Skills Migration – Requirements* form (962i).

## REFUGEE & HUMANITARIAN MIGRANTS

Australia is committed to supporting international humanitarian and refugee programmes, and per capita takes in more refugees than any country in the world. It has become home to some 600,000 refugees since 1945 (over 100,000 from South-east Asia since 1975), including large numbers of Afghans, Cambodians, Chileans, Chinese, Czechs, Hungarians, Lebanese, Soviet Jews, Timorese, Vietnamese, White Russians and Yugoslavs. In the 2000/01 immigration year, 12,000 places were allocated to refugee and humanitarian migrants (4,000 for refugees, 3,100 for the special humanitarian component, 2,800 for the special assistance category and 2,100 for onshore protection visas). These aren't included in the immigration quotas. Note, however, that illegal immigrants (such as boat people) may be 'interned' for years to discourage others and refugees often have a *very* difficult time finding work. Under new laws proposed by the government, humanitarian refugees may be denied social security for up to six years.

The only people who don't need to apply for refugee status on arrival in Australia are those whose status has already been decided overseas under the terms of the United Nations convention. Otherwise you'll be granted refugee status in Australia only if you can prove that you have 'a well-founded fear of persecution in your own country for reasons of race, religion, nationality, or membership of a particular social group or political opinion'.

## INTERDEPENDENT MIGRANTS

Interdependent migrants is a sub-category of the Partner category and is sub-divided into Spouses (married to or in a *de facto* marriage with their partners), Prospective Spouses (planning to marry their sponsors in Australia) and Independency (*de facto* relationships). There was a quota of 500 for this visa category in 2001/02. A *de facto* partner must have been living with the sponsor for at least one year. Dependent members of a family, such as children or aged relatives of the applicant, can be included in the application. Spouses and prospective spouses must be sponsored by an Australian citizen, permanent resident or eligible New Zealand citizen, with whom they have an interdependent relationship. This relationship must be ongoing, involve a mutual commitment to a shared life together and a fiancé must be genuinely known to the sponsor and must not be coming to Australia for an arranged marriage. As with most migrants, prospective partners must be assessed for good health and character (see page 81). An 'assurance of support' isn't required from the sponsor. Applicants must complete form 914 (*Application for Entry for Temporary Residence in Australia on the Grounds of Interdependency*) and the sponsor is required to complete the 'sponsorship' section of this form.

If you're sponsoring a spouse or fiancé, you can sponsor only a total of two people a minimum of two years apart, and if you were sponsored to Australia as a spouse or fiancé, you cannot sponsor a spouse or fiancé yourself for five years after the date you were sponsored. Exceptions are if your previous spouse/partner has died or abandoned the relationship leaving children, or if you have formed a new relationship which is long-standing or which has produced children.

Spouse applications are processed in two stages. In the first stage a prospective spouse receives a temporary visa (subclass 300) to stay in Australia for up to nine months, during which period he must marry his sponsor and apply to remain permanently. After marriage you will be granted a two-year temporary visa (subclass 820) providing all the requirements are met. The second stage begins around two years after the application for a provisional visa, when, providing the relationship is still ongoing, you will be granted a permanent visa. A prospective spouse is permitted to work in Australia.

Note that the DIMA requires declarations from both partners and two other people that a marriage or relationship is genuine and ongoing, evidence to support your claim, and an Australian police clearance if you have lived in Australia for over one year. A non-resident who has a long-term relationship with an Australian resident or citizen and who overstays his visa by more than 28 days can now make an application for residency in Australia (previously he had to leave Australia and apply overseas). Further information is contained in the form *Migrating to Australia as a spouse or prospective spouse* (1093i).

## POINTS TEST

A points test applies to certain categories of migrants, including skilled-Australian-sponsored applicants, independent migrants and business migrants. Some factors apply only to skilled-Australian-sponsored applicants and some just to business migration applicants. The points test aims to ensure that the principal applicant has the skills and other attributes necessary to allow him to quickly enter the Australian workforce, and support himself and his family without relying on the Australian government. Note that only one spouse is assessed and either partner can be considered a principal applicant for the points test, so couples should choose the partner with the best prospects of scoring sufficient points. The principal applicant for **independent migration** (see page 89) is assessed only under the following factors:

- **Skill:** qualifications and experience in his occupation;

- **Age:** at the date the application is lodged;

- **Language Skills:** English skills may be tested before points are allocated.

Applicants for **skilled-Australian-sponsored** migration (see page 85) are assessed under the following factors in addition to the above:

- **Relationship:** relationship of principal applicant to sponsor;

- **Citizenship:** citizenship of sponsor;

- **Location:** location of sponsor in Australia;

- **Settlement:** settlement of sponsor, i.e. whether they're self-supporting.

Business migrants (see page 93) are assessed under a range of factors, including business attributes (turnover, labour cost, assets, sponsorship and investment), age, language and capital.

Information forms for the above categories contain a do-it-yourself points test. However, you shouldn't be too optimistic and unless you're certain that you qualify for a skills category you should err on the conservative side. **Note that your score will depend on whether your trade or professional qualifications are accepted in Australia.** If you have qualifications in a field in which you don't work and have no current experience, they won't be taken into account when assessing your points total. Applicants for trade skills' assessments are classified against the relevant Australian occupations on the basis of their training and employment experience, and the specific duties of individual trades' classifications in Australia. Skilled tradesmen may be given additional points if they're willing to settle in Australia's major regional cities or in the larger outback towns, i.e. outside the country's capital cities. Some two-thirds of migrants currently settle in Sydney or Melbourne.

When you lodge your application at an Australian mission, a provisional score is made, although in many cases the final assessment depends on checking your skills and qualifications in Australia or confirming certain details. This can take some time. Note that if your circumstances change which would increase your score after you have made an application, you cannot make any changes and must make a new application and pay an additional fee. Therefore any imminent changes in your situation should be taken into account before making an application.

In 1992, a 'pool system' was reintroduced, giving prospective migrants a second opportunity to gain acceptance for migration. If you gain insufficient points to pass but attain the pool mark, your application will be held in the pool for 12 months in case a newer, lower pass mark is set. **Note, however, that your likelihood of being accepted for migration after joining the pool are almost non-existent, as pass marks are usually raised rather than lowered.** If your score doesn't reach the pool mark it's automatically refused or your application may be put in the Skill Matching database (see above).

In managing the migration programme, the Australian government periodically changes the pass and pool marks of the points test, and applies limits (caps) on the number of visas granted in certain categories. Changes to pass and pool marks affect applications in the pool as well as applications that have been lodged but not yet assessed. When the cap has been reached, applications continue to be processed in the order in which they are lodged, up to the visa approval stage. However, visas aren't granted until places become available in the next 'immigration' year (when a new quota is allocated). **Note that if a change is made to the points test between the time an application is lodged and before it's assessed, the change applies to that application.**

# Independent Migration

The score required for independent migrants, i.e. migrants who aren't applying for skilled-Australian-linked or business migration, is 110 points to pass and 70 points to join the pool. Your score is calculated on employability, skills, experience, age and language skills criteria as shown below. Note that applicants for independent visas have no right of appeal, even when an obvious error has been made. Only Australians who have been affected by an adverse decision can seek a review of a decision, e.g. when an Australian employer or an individual citizen sponsors someone (in any case, very few applications are approved after a review).

**Employability Factor:** The qualifications and experience listed in this factor relate to the qualifications and experience necessary to work in your usual occupation in Australia. Your usual occupation is a job in which you have worked for a continuous period of at least six months during the two-year period immediately prior to lodging your application. If you have held more than one occupation which fits this description, you will be assessed against each occupation and will be given your best score. If you do a skilled job but don't have the required training or qualifications, you won't get top marks as a skilled tradesman. Note that for several years now, medical practitioners (e.g. doctors) have received no points and therefore aren't eligible to apply under the independent migrant scheme because Australia has a surfeit of medical practitioners.

Points for skills are awarded for your usual occupation and the acceptability of your qualifications, based on what's necessary to follow your occupation in Australia. The requirements may involve a combination of a number of factors such as the possession of formal qualifications, a period of job training and/or work experience, plus membership of a professional association or an industry body. Currently the only occupations which score sufficient points for you to be successful as an independent migrant are those for which the skill level in Australia requires a trade certificate, degree, diploma or an associate diploma. General information about individual occupations and the required skill levels can be obtained from the Australian Standard Classification of Occupations (ASCO) dictionary, available for reference at Australian missions overseas and offices of the Department of Immigration, Local Government and Ethnic Affairs in Australia or via the Internet (🖳 www.abs.gov.au). Graduates who have obtained their qualification in the five years prior to their application are awarded 40 points for their skills and are required to demonstrate that they have worked continuously for at least six months in the last two years.

To achieve the points set out below, your qualifications must be assessed as equivalent to the Australian qualification level listed below and must be relevant to your usual occupation. Note that an applicant in the independent migration category must score at least 50 points for skill to be accepted for the pool.

**Points    Criteria**

60    Occupations that require a degree (or higher) or trade level qualifications where entry to the occupation requires training specific to the occupation *and* that are included on the Skilled Occupation List (SOL);

50    'Generalist' occupations that require degree level qualifications but not necessarily training for a particular occupation;

Occupations that require diploma or advanced diploma level.

Applicants also receive points for experience, occupational targeting, Australian qualifications and for spouse skills as detailed below:

**Experience:** Ten points for applicants nominating an occupation that attracts 60 points under skill factor and have worked in their nominated or a closely-related occupation for three out of the previous four years. Five points for applicants who have been employed in an occupation on the SOL for three out of the previous four years.

**Occupational Targeting:** Five points for applicants whose skills are in short supply (occupations included in the Migration Occupation in Demand List (MODL). Applicants who have a genuine job offer in an occupation included in the MODL receive a further five points.

**Australian Qualifications:** Note that qualifications must be have issued by an Australian educational institution. five points for applicants with a diploma trade qualification or a degree. Ten points for applicants with a PhD (doctorate degree).

**Spouse Skills:** Five points for applicants whose spouse also meets minimum requirements for skills (including work experience), age and English language ability.

You also receive five bonus points if you satisfy one of the following criteria: you have had at least six months associated work experience in a skilled occupation during the previous four years; a commitment to bringing a high level of capital into Australia demonstrated by depositing $100,000 in an approved government investment for a minimum of 12 months; or you have a high level of fluency in a national language of one of Australia's major trading partners or one of Australia's major ethnic communities.

**Age:** Age is one of the most important criteria for gaining acceptance as a migrant and you must be under 45 at the time of application. Note that your age is 'frozen' on application, so it's therefore important to apply before your age puts you into a higher age bracket (providing fewer points), particularly if this would give you too few points to qualify. Points are allocated for age as follows:

| Age | Points |
|-----|--------|
| 18–29 | 30 |
| 30–34 | 25 |
| 35–39 | 15 |
| 40–44 | 10 |

**Language Skills:** Language skills apply to migrants in the independent, skilled-Australian-linked and regional linked categories. The English test applies to most skilled occupations and applicants are encouraged to take a language proficiency test under the International English Language Testing System (IELTS). An Occupations Requiring English (ORE) list is published and prospective migrants whose occupations are listed on the ORE must demonstrate that they have vocational level English (and must score at least 15 points in the 'language skills sub-factor), irrespective of any other attributes they may have.

Families with a spouse or dependants aged 18 or over with less than functional English must pay an 'English Education Charge' (EEC) to cover the cost of English language classes in Australia. Under this scheme, applicants must pay from $2,380 for themselves and $2,380 for their spouse for English lessons, e.g. a primary applicant seeking a visa under the employer nomination scheme who doesn't have functional English must pay $4,080 and a spouse or adult dependant must pay $2,040 in fees (total $6,120), in return for which migrants receive up to 510 hours of tuition.

Applications for residence made in Australia are exempt from the English education charge, although overseas applicants in certain migration categories are liable for the charge if they don't have functional English. For further information see forms *Migrating to Australia: English language assessment* (9661) and *Fees* (990i). The following points are awarded for English language skills:

| Language Skills | Points |
|---|---|
| Able to obtain a score of at least six points in each of the four skills of reading, speaking, understanding and writing in IELTS; | 20 |
| Able to obtain at least five points in each of the four skills of reading, speaking, understanding and writing in IELTS. | 15 |

The maximum 20 points may be awarded:

● Without testing if you hold a degree, higher degree, diploma or trade certificate which required at least three years full-time study and all instruction was conducted in English;

● If you have passed an Occupational English Test as part of an assessment of your qualifications.

15 points may be awarded:

● Without testing if you hold a degree, higher degree, diploma or trade certificate which required at least two years full-time study and all instruction was conducted in English.

# Skilled-Australian-Sponsored (SAS) Migration

The pass mark for skilled-Australian-sponsored (SAS) migration is 110 points and the pool mark is 70 points. Note that a husband and wife can combine their skills and age points to pass the points test under the skilled-Australian-sponsored class. Skilled-Australian-sponsored migration applicants are also assessed under skill (note that if you intend to apply under this category, you must have a nominated occupation that appears on the Skilled Occupations List/SOL when you apply) and age (shown under **Independent Migration** on page 89), but not English language skills, plus family relationship, citizenship of sponsor, location of sponsor and settlement factors, as shown below:

| **Family Relationship:** | **Points** |
|---|---|
| Parent, non-dependent child, brother, sister, aunt or uncle. | 15 |

**Citizenship:**

| **If the sponsor has been an Australian citizen** | **Points** |
|---|---|
| for five years or more | 10 |
| for less than five years | 5 |

**Location Factor:** If your sponsor has lived in a state or territory designated area (i.e. outside the main cities) for the last two years, you can add five points. These include Queensland (except urban Brisbane and the Sunshine and Gold Coasts), Western Australia (except the Perth Metropolitan area), South Australia, the Northern Territory, Tasmania, the Australia Capital Territory or Victoria (except the Melbourne region). Note that nowhere in NSW is a designated area. A list of post codes of designated areas is provided. There's an increased allocation for the skilled–Australian-sponsored category for regional migration. A bond (e.g. $10,000 to $30,000) may be payable by migrants who settle in regional areas and is forfeited if they move to a state capital city.

**Settlement:** If your sponsor has been resident in Australia for the last two years and he (or the sponsor's spouse) has been in employment (including self-employment) or is financially independent (such as a self-supporting retiree) in Australia for the last two years, you can add ten points. Note, however, that no points will be awarded if the sponsor has received jobsearch allowance, newstart allowance or special benefit for more than four weeks in total in the last two years, or if they are currently receiving any form of social security benefit, allowance or pension, other than an age or war veterans' pension, family allowance and family allowance supplement.

# Business Migrants

The Business Migration Program (BMP) seeks to attract successful business people planning to establish a new business venture in Australia or to become an owner or part-owner of an existing business in Australia and actively participate in the enterprise. Note that the application fee is high ($3,250 in 2001) and therefore you must ensure that you qualify under the current rules before making an application. Business migrants who pass the points test and establish a business in Australia are closely monitored for the first three years of business operation. Under the Business Migration Points Test, applicants must pass a similar points test to other migrant categories and score at least 105 points from the factors of business attributes, age, language and capital, outlined below:

## Business Attributes

**Owner/Part-owner (subclass 840):** An owner/part-owner business is defined as one in which you (or you and your spouse) have had at least a 10 per cent shareholding equity in not less than two of the four years preceding the application, plus a day-to-day management role responsible for overall direction and performance. In addition, you must have employed not less than five full-time or equivalent employees. A maximum of two businesses may be combined for the purpose of calculating points under this factor and some part-time employees, consultants and contractors may be counted pro-rata as employees.

● **Turnover:** Business attributes relate to the turnover of an existing principal business in not less than two of the four years preceding the application, for which points are awarded as shown below:

| Turnover | Points |
| --- | --- |
| $5,000,000 | 60 |
| $3,000,000 | 55 |
| $1,500,000 | 50 |
| $750,000 | 40 |
| $500,000 | 35 |

- **Labour Costs:** Additional points are awarded for annual labour costs and/or total assets. If the main business had annual labour costs in two of the four financial years preceding the application of not less than $250,000 or $500,000, the following points are awarded:

| Amount | Points |
|--------|--------|
| $500,000 | 10 |
| $250,000 | 5 |

- **Assets:** If the main business had total assets in two of the four financial years before application of not less than $750,000 or $1.5 million, the following points are awarded:

| Amount | Points |
|--------|--------|
| $1,500,000 | 10 |
| $750,000 | 5 |

- **Sponsorship:** If you've been offered sponsorship by a state or territory government, you receive an additional 15 points, which are awarded in addition to any gained as an owner/part owner. State or territory sponsored owner/part owner applicants apply under visa subclass 842.

**Senior Executive in a Major Business (subclass 841):** A major business is defined as one which had an annual turnover of at least $50 million in two of the four years preceding the application and receives 65 points. Sponsorship by a state or territory government has the effect of redefining a major business as one which has had an annual turnover of at least $10 million in two of the four years preceding the application. State-sponsored senior executive applicants apply under visa subclass 843, which earns 65 points.

**Established business in Australia (subclass 845):** If the following conditions applied for the 12 months prior to the application, 60 points are awarded:

- the main business employed three legal permanent residents (who weren't members of your family) in direct full-time employment or its equivalent AND
- had a minimum turnover of at least $200,000 a year OR had exports with a minimum value of $100,000 a year.

**Investment-linked migration (subclass 844):** The following points are awarded when an applicant has deposited the sums listed below for a minimum three-year term in a designated investment:

| Amount | Points |
|--------|--------|
| $2,000,000 | 80 |
| $1,500,000 | 70 |
| $1,000,000 | 65 |
| $750,000 | 60 |

Points scored from factor four (net assets) aren't applicable to this visa class.

# Age

The following points are awarded to business migrants for age:

| Age | Points |
|---|---|
| under 20 | 0 |
| 20–29 | 20 |
| 30–44 | 30 |
| 45–49 | 25 |
| 50–54 | 10 |
| over 54 | 0 |

# Language

The following points are awarded to business migrants for English language ability:

| Standard | Points |
|---|---|
| Better than functional | 30 |
| Functional | 20 |
| Less than functional but bilingual in two or more other languages | 10 |
| Limited | 5 |
| None | 0 |

These point scores apply to all visas apart from Investment-Linked Migration, for which all levels of language ability attract an additional five points. The exception is 'no ability in English' which scores no points.

# Capital

The following points are awarded to business migrants for the capital factor, which includes the net assets of the applicant and spouse:

| Amount | Points |
|---|---|
| $2,500,000 or more | 15 |
| $1,500,000 to $2,500,000 | 10 |
| $500,000 to $1,500,000 | 5 |
| Less than $500,000 | 0 |

You may include personal and business assets, but only if these assets are available for transfer to Australia within two years. Note that this isn't applicable to Investment-Linked Migration.

## Appeals

DIMA has a Migration Review Triburnal (MRT) for applicants whose visa application is turned down and who wish to lodge an appeal. There are strict time limits for lodging appeals and it is very expensive ($1,400 in 2001). If you feel you have grounds for an appeal then you should contact the MRT (GPO Box 3001, Canberra City, ACT 2601, ☎ local call rate 1300-361969 or 02-6245 9999, 💻 www. mrt.au).

## VISA FEES

There are fees (which have remained more or less static in recent years) for all visas other than a three-month visitor's visa. Application fees for migrant visas are particularly high ($1,125) and aren't refundable, so you should ensure that you have a *very* good chance of being accepted before making an application. Fees are supposedly intended to cover the costs incurred by the Australian government and aren't refunded if your application is unsuccessful (although many applications must be rejected in minutes, particularly those where the points test applies). Applicants adversely affected by a change of rules prior to an application being assessed, such as an increase in the number of points required under the points test, aren't entitled to a refund of fees.

Fees can be paid in cash or by cheque or postal order payable to the 'Commonwealth of Australia'. The temporary business entry (TBE) visa may be paid by credit card (e.g. American Express, Diners Club, Mastercard or Visa). In Australia, applicants can pay by electronic funds transfer (EFTPOS) or by credit card. Applications for visitors' visas can be made by post, in person or through an authorised travel agent. The fees shown below are those applicable on 1st April 2001. For country specific charges you should contact your nearest Australian mission.

| Type of Application | Fee |
| --- | --- |
| Migration Australia Forms Package | $10 |
| Sponsorship for entry for Temporary Residence | $225 |
| Resident return Visa – Lodged Overseas | $90 |
| Migration to Australia | $1,125 |
| Declaratory Certificate of Australian Citizenship | $55 |
| Registration of Australian Citizenship by descent | $110 |
| Additional children registered at the same time | $110 |
| Grant of Australian Citizenship | $120 |
| Evidentiary certificate of Australian Citizenship | $55 |
| Resumption of Australian Citizenship | $65 |
| Temporary Resident | $155 |
| Working Holidaymaker | $155 |
| Occupational Trainee | $155 |
| Student | $290 |

| | |
|---|---|
| Visitor Visa (maximum six months, valid four years) years) | $60 |
| Re-Evidencing of Resident return visa | $65/80 |
| Business Migration Program | $3,240 |
| Temporary Business Sponsorship | $3,250 |
| Temporary Business Nomination | $225 |
| Declaratory visa (adult) | $225 |
| Declaratory visa (under 18) | $200 |
| Temporary Business Entry (short stay) | $60 |
| Temporary Business Entry (long stay) | $155 |

## TEMPORARY RESIDENCE

Temporary residence includes people coming to live or work in Australia for periods of from three months to four years. Applicants are expected to stay for the full period of their planned stay. There are no set quotas for visas for most temporary workers, which are open to a wide range of occupations, including: executive, technical and professional people; academic staff; medical practitioners; foreign government officials; sportsmen/women; entertainers; media and film staff; working holidaymakers; religious personnel; domestic staff; retirees; and occupational trainees (a full list is given below). In the period 1999–2000, over 150,000 temporary visas were issued. Applications for temporary residence visas are made using form 147 '*Application for a temporary residence visa (non-business)*'. Applicants may be required to have a medical examination and chest X-ray before a visa is granted, although this isn't usual when the intended stay is 12 months or less. In most cases, temporary residents are granted a multiple entry visa for the period of their approved stay. Note that temporary visa holders have no access to social welfare benefits or national public health cover while they are in Australia.

**Sponsors:** Many temporary residents must be sponsored (or require a nomination, written invitation or a sponsor's undertaking to support an application), e.g. by a prospective employer or organisation, as shown in the table below. Sponsoring employers must have a satisfactory record of training staff and show that there's no resident person available with the required skills. The sponsor must be willing to accept financial and legal responsibility for the temporary resident and is responsible for his welfare and accommodation. If the sponsor is an employer, any salary paid must be guaranteed and must fall within the industry pay awards for the job. Temporary residence subclass visa groups include the following:

| Number | Visa Type | Fee | Sponsorship |
|---|---|---|---|
| 410 | Retirement | Yes | No |
| 411 | Exchange | No | No |
| 415 | Foreign Government Agency | Yes | Yes* |
| 416 | Special Program | Yes | No |
| 417 | Working Holiday | Yes | No |
| 418 | Educational/Research | Yes | Yes* |

| 419 | Visiting Academic | Yes | No |
|---|---|---|---|
| 420 | Entertainment | Yes | Yes |
| 421 | Sport | Yes** | Yes* |
| 422 | Medical Practitioner | Yes | Yes |
| 423 | Media and Film Staff | Yes | Yes* |
| 424 | Public Lecturer | Yes | Yes* |
| 425 | Family Relationship | No | No |
| 426 | Domestic Worker (Diplomatic/Consular) | Yes | No |
| 427 | Domestic Worker (Overseas Executive) | Yes | Yes*** |
| 428 | Religious Worker | Yes | Yes |
| 430 | Supported Dependant | Yes | No |
| 432 | Expatriate | Yes | No |
| 442 | Occupational Trainee | Yes | No |
| 456 | Business (Short Stay) | Yes | No |
| 457 | Business (Long Stay) | Yes | Yes |
| 956/977 | Business (Short Stay) ETA | Yes | No |

\*   Formal sponsorship is required if the stay in Australia exceeds three months.

\*\*  Fee applies only to professional sports persons.

\*\*\* Must have been included in sponsorship of an overseas executive.

**Temporary Workers:** Certain categories of skilled workers and professionals are permitted to enter Australia for a fixed period (e.g. the duration of a contract) to take up employment where it can be shown that a job cannot be filled by a resident. Temporary workers seeking to work in Australia for longer than four months must be sponsored by their prospective employer. The sponsor must lodge a *Sponsorship for Entry to Australia for Temporary Residents* form. Applications for temporary residence for employees are granted for a period of up to four years providing:

● the prospective employer will provide sponsorship and pay the fees;

● the required skills are shown to be unavailable in Australia;

● the job is full-time;

● the pay and conditions aren't less than the normal pay and conditions for such a job in Australia;

● the employment of a temporary resident isn't a substitute for training Australian or permanent residents for such a position;

● the position isn't for an unskilled or semi-skilled job;

● the normal health and character requirements are met.

If you receive a temporary resident visa permitting you to work in Australia and your spouse is named on the application as your dependant, he or she will also be permitted to work in Australia. A temporary residence visa isn't automatically renewable and no change of job or sponsor is allowed after entry into Australia. Note that anyone in Australia for less than six months must have private health insurance unless their country of citizenship has a reciprocal health agreement with Australia. Information about non-business temporary residence visas is provided in *Temporary residence in Australia - non-business – general guide* (form 986i).

## Temporary Business Visa

Temporary business people can work in Australia for from three months to four years and there's no market testing for personnel coming to undertake key activities. Regular employers of overseas personnel can seek ongoing sponsorship status as pre-qualified sponsors and don't need to establish their sponsorship credentials each time they wish to sponsor personnel from overseas. Standard sponsorship status is available to employers wishing to sponsor a fixed number of personnel on a one-off basis. Most visas don't allow workers to change their employer or occupation without prior permission. Note that it's no longer possible to obtain a temporary business visa in Australia when you arrived as a tourist, because many people with temporary business visas granted in Australia were found to be working illegally. The temporary business class visa includes the following subclasses:

**Exchange:** Skilled people wishing to come to Australia to broaden their work experience and skills under reciprocal arrangements that allow Australian residents similar opportunities overseas. It includes people seeking entry under certain bilateral exchange agreements or a Fulbright scholar. The stay is for a maximum of two years.

**Independent Executive:** People wishing to establish a business in Australia using their own capital (usually a minimum of $250,000).

**Executive (Overseas):** Senior management personnel and staff for executive positions covered by a Regional Headquarters (RHQ) agreement.

**Specialist:** Workers with trade, technical or professional skills who have been recruited by an Australian employer for a limited period. It also applies to staff for a specialist position covered by a Regional Headquarters (RHQ) agreement.

**Medical Practitioner:** Suitably qualified foreign medical practitioners where the relevant state or territory health authority endorses the need to meet specific requirements from overseas. You cannot change your employer without prior permission.

**Information and Communications Technology Experts:** In January 2001, the Australian government announced new measures to facilitate entry of workers with Information and Communication Technology (ICT) skills in an attempt to cover acute shortages in this field. All ICT occupations are regarded as key occupations and applicants for this visa type are given immediate visa processing priority.

## Cultural & Social Visa

The cultural and social class visa includes the following subclasses:

**Special Program:** People coming to Australia under approved programmes to broaden their work experience and skills (generally youth exchanges or a GAP year between secondary and higher education). It includes young people coming to Australia under a Churchill Fellowship to broaden their experience and understanding of the country, generally in the context of a youth exchange programme or to take part in a community-based programme of cultural enrichment or community benefit. You may not change your employer or occupation without prior permission and are permitted to stay in Australia for a maximum of 12 months.

**Entertainment:** People involved in a wide range of social and cultural events and activities, taking into account the need to protect the employment of Australians in the industry. You may not change your employer or change the times or places of engagements in Australia without prior permission.

**Sport:** Amateur or professional sports people coming to Australia to engage in competition with Australian residents and to improve general sporting standards through high calibre competition and training. Sponsorship or letters of invitation may be necessary depending on the activity and length of stay in Australia. They must sign a declaration that on arrival in Australia they will have a return or onward ticket and sufficient funds to support themselves (and any family members accompanying them) for the duration of their stay. You cannot change your employer without prior permission.

**Media and Film Staff:** Correspondents and other professional media staff members posted to Australia by overseas news organisations, and photographers and film and TV crews making documentaries or commercials for overseas consumption. You cannot change your employer without prior permission.

**Public Lecturer:** Professional lecturers or subject experts invited to make public presentations. You cannot change your employer without prior permission.

**Religious Workers:** Religious workers, including ministers, priests and spiritual leaders to serve the spiritual needs of people of their faith in Australia.

# Domestic Workers Visa

The domestic workers class visa includes the following subclasses:

**Domestic Workers (Diplomatic/Consular):** Domestic staff for diplomats and consular staff posted to Australia. Written approval is required from the Department of Foreign Affairs and Trade (DFAT).

**Domestic Workers (Overseas Executive):** Domestic staff of certain holders of visas in subclass 457 (Long Stay Temporary Business Entry). A visa in this class may be granted only if it can be shown that the entry of domestic staff is necessary for the proper discharge of the executive's representational duties. Domestic workers may not change employers or remain in Australia after the permanent departure of their employer.

# Educational Visa

The educational class visa includes the following subclasses:

**Foreign Government Agency:** Foreign government officials to conduct official business on behalf of their government for up to three months when the officials don't have diplomatic or official status in Australia.

**Educational:** Full-time staff for educational and research institutions or organisations to fill academic, teaching and research positions unable to be filled from within the Australian labour market. You cannot change your employer without prior permission.

**Visiting Academic:** People whose presence in Australia will contribute to the sharing of research knowledge. They may not receive a salary from the host institution in Australia.

**Occupational Trainee:** Persons undergoing training in Australia compatible with their employment history. The training should be to upgrade existing skills and be readily usable on return to the applicant's home country. They may not work in Australia other than in relation to their course of training.

# Expatriate Visa

The expatriate class visa allows for the temporary stay of certain spouses or dependants of persons employed by international companies in remote locations in Southeast Asia, the South Pacific or Papua New Guinea. They may not perform any work in Australia.

# Family Relationship Visa

The family relationship class visa allows the temporary stay of unmarried young people under the age of 18 for an extended holiday with relatives or close family friends who are Australian citizens or residents. They may not perform any work in Australia.

# Retirement Visa

The retirement class visa provides an extended temporary stay (up to four years) for those wishing to retire to Australia. Note, however, that it allows only 'temporary' residence, albeit indefinitely (although it can be revoked at any time), and there's no provision for retirees to apply for permanent residence at a later date. Retirees who apply to enter Australia under this visa category can be either single people or couples (either married or in a *de facto* relationship), who must:

- be at least 55 years of age (your spouse may be any age);
- have no dependants other than their spouse;
- satisfy the funds transfer requirements (see below);
- have no intention of entering the workforce;
- take out comprehensive private medical insurance with an Australian provider before your visa can be granted (retirees aren't covered by Medicare, Australia's national health care system);
- meet health and character requirements.

At the date that you apply to settle in Australia, you must have sufficient funds to maintain yourself while in the country, which should consist of either a capital transfer of at least $650,000 or a capital transfer of at least $200,000 plus a pension or income, or further capital providing an annual income of at least $45,000. The income can come from any source, a pension or dividends from investments. If you receive a British state pension you should be aware that the amount you receive will be frozen when you leave Britain and you won't be entitled to annual cost of living increases (see page 310). For more information see *Summary of Funds Available for Transfer*.

Note that you must be able to meet the funds criteria on the day that you lodge your application. If you need to sell a house or other assets to meet these requirements, the sale must be completed within 12 months of the date of your application. Once accepted, you will receive a visa allowing you to make multiple entries during the first six months after the date when the visa was issued. When you arrive during this six-month period, you will receive an entry permit allowing you to stay in Australia for four years. The multiple entry visa expires six months after your visa is issued. If you then need to leave Australia for a temporary period, you *must* obtain another visa to allow you to return to Australia. Once in Australia you can apply for an extension of stay after four years and, providing you still meet the criteria for a retirement visa, you will be granted a further stay of two years.

Note that, if you have relatives in Australia who can sponsor you (see pages 79 and 82), you may be able to retire to Australia under the family migrant scheme.

## Supported Dependant Visa

The supported dependant class visa allows the temporary stay of certain dependants of persons entitled to remain permanently in Australia. The supporter must complete a *Declaration of Support* with documentary evidence of the family relationship.

## Working Holiday Visa

The working holiday class visa includes just one subclass: Working Holiday, which is the largest visa category for temporary residents and accounts for over 45 per cent of the total. Concerns have been voiced in Australia over jobs being taken from Australians by working holidaymakers; however, the farming industry, particularly fruit and vegetable picking, relies to a large extent on working holidaymakers to harvest their crops. In 1997, a parliamentary committee decided that visitors on working holiday visas do take jobs from young Australians, despite evidence to the contrary showing that they take jobs where Australians either lack the necessary skills, are unwilling to take jobs or local labour isn't available. Statistics also show that those on working holiday visas inject almost $500 million a year into the economy and many businesses in the tourist industry would be hard hit without them (creating yet more unemployment). There's no cap on the number of working holiday visas issued.

**Eligibility:** Working holiday visas are available to single people and childless couples between the ages of 18 and 30. The purpose of the working holiday visa is to allow young people the opportunity to visit Australia and supplement their travels through casual employment. Those eligible for a working holiday visa include (summer 2001) nationals of Canada, Denmark, Germany, Ireland, Italy, Japan, South Korea, Malta, the Netherlands, Sweden and the UK (Norway is expected to be added to the list in late 2001). Negotiations are under way for additional countries to be added – check the latest list with an Australian mission in your home country. If you hold a British, Canadian, Dutch or Irish passport you may apply in any country; others must apply in the country of their nationality. Note that you can obtain a working holiday visa only once. Applicants must satisfy the following criteria:

- the prime purpose of the visit is a temporary stay in Australia and permanent residence isn't intended;
- employment is incidental to the holiday and is to be used to supplement the money that you bring with you;
- employment hasn't been arranged in advance except on a private basis and on your own initiative;
- there is a reasonable prospect of your obtaining temporary employment to supplement your funds;
- you can show that you have reasonable funds to support yourself for some of your time in Australia and pay for your return air fare. The minimum amount required is £2,000 in Britain, although it isn't necessary to have a return ticket at the time of your entry into Australia. It helps to have relatives or friends in Australia who can provide extra funds if necessary;
- you meet normal character requirements and health standards, where necessary;
- full-time employment isn't taken for more than three months with one employer;
- you leave Australia when your working holiday visa has expired;
- you do not remain in Australia longer than 12 months;
- you sign a declaration not to undertake any studies in Australia apart from an English language course of a maximum of ten weeks.

Applications must be made to an Australian mission in your home country (or the country where you're resident) with the following:

- a completed application form 1150 (If your application form isn't completed correctly, it will be returned);
- evidence of funds for the duration of your stay, which must be confirmed by a bank statement or other evidence (If you don't have sufficient funds at the time of your application you could borrow some and repay them after obtaining a bank statement. However, it isn't wise to arrive in Australia with insufficient funds, as you may need to prove you have access to funds on arrival and if you don't you could be refused entry);
- a valid passport, which should be valid for three months *after* your proposed departure date from Australia (If your passport doesn't comply with this, you must obtain a new one);
- a cheque payable to the 'Commonwealth of Australia' for the sum of $155;
- a stamped addressed envelope for the return of your passport.

Applications can be made in person or by post (preferred). You should apply for a working holiday visa at least four to five weeks before your intended departure date, and, if you're applying by post you should send documents by recorded delivery. If your application is approved, your visa will be valid for 13 months from the date of issue. If your first arrival date in Australia won't allow you to have your full 12 months there, you can apply for an extension, although there's a hefty fee. If you plan to apply for an extension, you should apply around two months before the expiry of your temporary entry permit. An extension of stay beyond 12 months after your first entry isn't possible.

# VISITORS

A visitor's visa is valid for stays of up to three months (visa valid 12 months) or for stays of up to six months (visa valid for 12 months). A visitor's visa is also required by those coming to Australia to conduct business of a short-term nature and for someone visiting Australia for medical treatment (see below), although a different form must be completed. Visas can be obtained on-the-spot from travel agents (for nationals of selected countries – see ETA below) and at Australian missions (if you're applying by post you should allow a minimum of three weeks in most countries). Many travel agents and companies provide a visa service for visitors, although there's usually a fee in addition to any visa fee levied by the Australian government.

There's no fee for a visitor's visa valid for stays of up to three months, but a fee ($60) applies to a visitor's visa valid for stays of up to six months (or for a visa valid for four years for short stays of up to three months). If applicable, ensure that your visa allows multiple entries within its period of validity, when it should be marked 'multiple travel'. If you're applying for a six-month visa, you must be able to show that you have access to adequate funds (e.g. £3,000 in Britain), although the amount will be lower if you will be staying with friends or family in Australia. The retired parents of an Australian citizen can obtain a visitor's visa valid for 12 months. It isn't necessary to make a separate application for a child who's included on a parent's passport. Note that your passport must be valid for the period of your proposed stay in Australia.

Australia has one of the most efficient visa processing systems in the world for visitors planning to spend up to three months there, called Electronic Travel Authority (ETA). Under the ETA system travellers can be pre-cleared for travel at the same time as they make their travel arrangements. Travel agents using the ETA system simply enter your passport number into a computer system linked to the Australian immigration database and receive a confirmation within seconds. No stamp is placed in your passport. Note that to qualify you must travel to Australia on a participating airline (includes most major airlines) or a cruise ship. ETA is eventually intended to replace visa application forms and labels or stamps in passports, although if you require a passport stamp you must complete an *Application to visit Australia for tourism* (form 48). An ETA visa is issued free of charge (although agents may levy a fee) and is valid for a single entry into Australia within one year. Citizens of the following countries are eligible for an ETA visa: Andorra, Austria, Belgium, Brunei, Canada, Denmark, Finland, France, Germany, Greece, Hong Kong, Iceland, Ireland, Italy, Japan, Liechtenstein, Luxembourg, Malaysia, Malta, Monaco, the Netherlands, Norway, Singapore, South Korea, Spain, Sweden, Switzerland, the United Kingdom, the USA and the Vatican City.

The ETA system builds on the Advanced Passenger Clearance (APC) system whereby Qantas passengers arriving at Sydney airport can be cleared in as little as 20 seconds! It's designed to fast-track passengers at airports through immigration and customs processing, and has substantially reduced the time taken to process passengers. It also allows passengers on certain flights to Australia to complete their immigration and customs processing while in the air. On arrival, electronic cards containing passenger details are simply 'swiped' through an immigration card reader. In mid-2001, the Australian government introduced an online ETA application (💻 www.eta.immi.gov.au) whereby for a fee of A$20 payable by credit card only, you can be issued with an ETA visa online. Your application will be processed while you're on-line and you are informed of the result of your application before leaving the Internet ETA system. As part of the application and approval process, you will be issued with a reference number and you can check the status of your application and approval at any time on the site.

It's possible to obtain an extension for a visitor's visa under certain circumstances, although you must apply before your visa expires and must have a good reason. However, a stay totalling more than six months in a calendar year isn't usually permitted. Note that it's expensive (currently $120) to extend a three-month visitor's visa to a six-month visa in Australia, therefore if there's any likelihood of you wishing to stay longer than three months you should obtain a six-month visa in advance. Note that visitors extending their stay in Australia must produce evidence of health insurance.

There are plans to scrap tourist visas for visitors from 'low risk' countries, i.e. rich countries such as Canada, Japan and the USA, whose nationals have little intention of overstaying their permitted period in Australia. **Note that visitors aren't permitted to engage in any type of employment or formal study.** They may, however, undertake non-formal study involving short-term courses of up to three months which are recreational or 'personal-enrichment' in nature and aren't subsidised by any government.

## Business Visitors

A visitor's visa is also required by someone coming to Australia to conduct business of a short-term nature, i.e. business agreed to by the Australian Government Office. A business visa allows you to visit Australia to look for business opportunities, assess business conditions, act as a consultant, attend meetings and sign contracts. Nationals of eligible countries (see the list above) can obtain a business ETA valid for the life of your passport, otherwise you must complete form 456, *Application for a temporary business entry visa (for a stay of up to three months)*. A visa allowing a stay of up to one month with a single entry valid for one month from the date of issue is issued free of charge. A temporary business entry (TBE) visa valid for stays of up to three months (with multiple entries valid for five years or the life of your passport, i.e. up to ten years) costs $60 in Britain and a long stay visa valid for four years and stays of up to six months costs $155.

## Medical Treatment

A visitor's visa is also required by someone coming to Australia for medical treatment, when form 48ME (*Application to Visit Australia for Medical Treatment*) must be completed. Medical treatment includes either elective or emergency treatment for either a short or a long stay. The treatment must not be available in your home country and you must:

- provide documentary evidence that you can pay for medical treatment;
- make arrangements for hospital accommodation and treatment in advance;
- receive significant benefit from such treatment in Australia;
- not pose a public health risk, e.g. because of a contagious disease.

If you're applying for an extension of stay for medical treatment, you will need to meet the above criteria and present evidence that:

- arrangements have been made with a doctor and/or hospital to provide you with medical and/or hospital care, i.e. a firm date for treatment has been made;
- arrangements have been made to pay the full unsubsidised cost of treatment and you can demonstrate you have the means to pay;
- if treatment is in a public hospital, the state or territory medical authorities have agreed to your admission and treatment.

If you're providing comfort and support to a person seeking medical treatment and that's the purpose of your stay in Australia, then you should also apply for a medical treatment visa.

## STUDENTS

Foreign students require a student visa (costing around $290), which is issued after acceptance on a course and payment of at least half the first year's annual fees. There are seven types of student visa:

- **Independent ELICOS:** for overseas students studying English for Overseas Students.
- **Schools:** for students at primary or secondary school.
- **Vocation Education and Training:** for certificate and diploma students.
- **Higher Education:** for students studying for a bachelor degree or a graduate certificate or diploma.
- **Masters and Doctorate.**
- **Non-award Foundation Studies/Other** for students on courses that don't lead to a degree or other formal award.
- **AusAID or Defence Sponsored.**

Students must have the financial resources to meet tuition fees (scholarships are available), return fares to Australia and day-to-day living expenses for the duration of their course – estimated in 2001 to be from $8,500 to $15,500 or more for a single person annually depending on where you are studying. Students should also have Overseas Student Health Cover (OSCH) or alternative private health cover. Courses that qualify for a student visa include tertiary level studies at universities or colleges; courses at Technical and Further Education (TAFE) colleges; English-language courses; occupational or religious training; business study or training, e.g. secretarial and business courses; short courses at universities or colleges of advanced education; and study exchange arrangements between Australian and overseas educational establishments. Secondary-level applicants for non-government schools must first obtain an offer of a place, which must be confirmed by a letter from the school. Full fee-paying students from so called 'gazetted' countries (with a lower risk of students overstaying their visas) should lodge their application for a visa *after* they have enrolled and obtained an *Acceptance Advice Form* (AAF). Full fee-paying students from non-gazetted countries should lodge their application for a visa *before* paying tuition fees, confirming enrolment and obtaining an AAF.

Students must usually be attending full-time courses, but are permitted to take part-time jobs of up to 20 hours a week to help cover their living costs, plus a full-time job during the summer break. The spouse of a post-graduate student may be permitted to work full-time and other dependants up to 20 hours a week. However, if you wish to work you should apply for a work visa. In order to retain a student visa, you must have a satisfactory attendance and academic results' record. On completion of your course you must leave Australia when your visa expires, for which an undertaking must be given in writing. Note that it isn't possible to switch from a visitor's visa to a student visa while in Australia.

Information about student visas is provided in *Student entry to Australia* (form 1160i) and *Application for a Student (Temporary) Visa* (forms 157a).

# 4.

# ARRIVAL

On arrival in Australia, your first task will be to negotiate immigration and customs, which fortunately for most people presents no problems. Australian customs and immigration officials are usually polite and efficient, although they may occasionally be a 'trifle overzealous' in their attempts to deter smugglers and those planning to stay or work illegally. If you arrive in Australia by ship, customs and immigration officials may board the vessel to carry out their checks. Small boats must dock at a 'proclaimed point of entry' (which includes various ports throughout Australia) and you should notify officials a few hours in advance of your arrival. Note that, with the exception of New Zealanders, everyone wishing to enter Australia requires a visa (see **Chapter 3**). **If you arrive in Australia without one, you'll be refused entry.** You may find it more convenient to arrive in Australia on a weekday than at the weekend, when offices and banks are closed.

There are also a number of tasks that should be completed on arrival, which are described in this chapter, plus suggestions for finding local help and information.

## IMMIGRATION

All arrivals must complete an Incoming Passenger Card (IPC), distributed by airlines and shipping companies (one per family), before their arrival in Australia. The IPC contains your personal details such as name, address in Australia and passport number, and is used by immigration officials to record the reason for your visit. The card is also for customs and quarantine purposes and contains questions concerning plants and animals and whether you have exceeded the duty-free allowances. A married couple and their children under 18 years need complete only one statement. Note that, if you (or anyone over 12 months of age who is travelling with you) have visited a yellow fever infected country or area (e.g. Africa or South America) in the 14 days prior to your arrival in Australia, a yellow fever vaccination certificate is required.

When you disembark, you proceed to the Entry Control Point where you present your passport and IPC. You may be asked to verify the reason for your visit and provide evidence that you have sufficient funds for your trip and a return or onward ticket. Your IPC is returned to you and must be presented when you arrive at the customs checkpoint (see below). Australia operates an Advanced Passenger Processing (APP) system at major airports (e.g. Sydney) where passengers can be cleared in the 'express' lane in as little as 20 seconds. It also allows passengers on certain flights (Qantas, Air New Zealand, Cathay Pacific and Japan Airlines) to complete their immigration and customs processing at check-in and be issued with an Express card, which is simply passed through an immigration card reader on arrival.

When you receive your visa from an Australian mission overseas, you usually get a stamp in your passport stating that the visa is valid 'subject to an entry permit on arrival'. This means that you must satisfy the immigration official that you won't infringe the terms of your visa. If you have a visitor's visa, you should present it along with evidence that you have sufficient funds (or access to funds) to last you throughout your stay (e.g. $1,000 per month) and enable you to leave Australia when your visa expires. Cash, travellers' cheques, credit cards, bank statements and an airline ticket will all help convince immigration officials. If you have friends or relatives in Australia with whom you'll be staying, you'll usually require fewer funds. Note, however, that the immigration officer may check with them to verify your statement. Generally, the onus is on you to *prove* that you're a genuine visitor and won't infringe the immigration laws. The immigration authorities aren't required to establish that you'll violate the immigration laws, and in cases where they believe that you plan to work illegally or will overstay your visa, they can refuse you entry or restrict your entry to a shorter period than that permitted by your visa.

The treatment of foreigners by immigration officers varies, but young people in particular may be liable to close scrutiny, especially those travelling light and 'scruffily' dressed or coming from notorious drug areas such as Asia or South America. Like any other visitor, you should carry evidence of your funds (or access to funds) and proof of why you're entering Australia and why you'll need to leave (e.g. to return to work or study overseas). Take care how you answer seemingly innocent questions (immigration officials *never* ask innocent questions) from immigration officials, as you could find yourself being refused entry if you give incriminating answers. Whatever the question, never imply that you may remain in Australia longer than the period permitted or for a purpose other than that for which you've been granted permission. For example, if you aren't permitted to work in Australia, you could be asked, "Would you like to work in Australia?" If you reply, "Yes", even if you have no intention of doing so, you could be refused entry.

When all is in order and the immigration official is satisfied, he will stamp your passport with the official entry permit stating the period that you're permitted to remain in the country. If you decide that this isn't long enough, some visas (e.g. visitor's visas) can be extended, but it's an expensive procedure and you'll need to convince the authorities that you should be granted an extension. You may find that it's easier to leave the country, e.g. by travelling to New Zealand or Indonesia, and re-applying for a new visa from there.

## CUSTOMS

After you've cleared immigration, you proceed to the baggage claim area to collect your bags. When you have all your bags, you go to the customs checkpoint, where you hand your Traveller's Statement to a customs officer. All airports in Australia use a system of red and green 'channels'. Red means you have something to declare and green means you have nothing to declare, i.e. no more than the duty or tax-free allowances, no goods to sell, and no prohibited or restricted goods. **If you're *certain* that you have nothing to declare, go through the 'green channel', otherwise go through the red channel.** Customs officers make random checks on people going through both red and green channels and there are stiff penalties for smuggling.

When you enter Australia to take up temporary or permanent residence, you can usually import your belongings duty and tax-free. Personal and household goods that you've owned and used overseas for over 12 months can be imported free of duty and sales tax, although proof of length of ownership may be required and this concession doesn't apply to motor vehicles, alcohol or tobacco products. Any goods not owned and used overseas for over 12 months may be subject to duty and tax at varying rates, depending on where you've come from, where you purchased the goods, how long you've owned them, and whether duty and tax have already been paid in another country. If you need to pay duty or tax, it must be paid at the time goods are brought into the country. Payment may be made in cash, by travellers' cheque in Australian currency or by American Express, Bankcard, Diners Club, Mastercard or Visa card.

There's no limit to the amount of Australian or foreign currency (banknotes and coins, not travellers' cheques or other monetary instruments) that can be brought into Australia, but amounts of $10,000 or more (or the equivalent in foreign currency) must be declared on arrival. **Note that, if you're caught trying to smuggle any goods into Australia, they can be confiscated and, if you attempt to import prohibited items (see page 113), you may be liable to criminal charges and/or deportation.**

Australian Customs publish a variety of information for travellers, including a booklet entitled *Customs Information for Travellers*, available from Australian customs offices (see **Appendix A** for a list). General enquiries should be directed to the Australian Customs Service, GPO Box 148, Fyshwick, ACT 2609 (☎ within Australia 1300-363 263 and from outside Australia 02-6275 5041, 💻 www.customs. gov.au). For information regarding:

● duty-free allowances (e.g. alcohol and tobacco), see page 441;

● the importation of motor vehicles, see page 240;

● the importation of yachts and leisure craft, see page 415;

● the importation of pets, see page 461.

## Temporary Residents & Visitors

In addition to the usual duty-free concessions (see page 441), temporary residents and visitors coming to Australia for a limited period may bring most articles into the country duty and tax free, provided customs is satisfied that they're for your personal use and will be taken out of Australia on your departure. However, you may be required to lodge a cash or bank security with customs to the value of the duty and tax otherwise payable. Customs will determine the form of security acceptable in each case and, if you don't take the articles with you when you leave Australia, you'll need to pay the duty and tax assessed. Before shipping any articles to Australia which you think will qualify for this concession, you should contact a customs office for advice (see **Appendix A**). This concession isn't available if you're migrating to Australia or a returning resident.

Tourists and temporary residents may bring a motor vehicle, caravan, trailer, yacht or other craft to Australia for up to 12 months (or longer under certain circumstances) without paying duty or tax on it. However, you may be required to lodge a cash or bank security with customs equal to the amount of duty or tax otherwise payable.

## Migrants & Returning Residents

If you're coming to Australia to take up permanent residence for the first time or returning to resume permanent residence, you may import duty and tax free belongings, furniture and household articles that you have owned and used overseas for at least 12 months before your departure for Australia. Migrants may also bring machinery, plant and other equipment to Australia duty and tax free provided certain conditions are met. Commercial equipment imported tax and duty free mustn't be sold, hired, mortgaged or otherwise disposed of during your first two years in Australia.

**Unaccompanied Effects:** The Australian customs service is responsible for the clearance of all unaccompanied effects from overseas. Unaccompanied personal effects can be cleared by the owner, a nominee appointed by the owner or a customs broker (a list of brokers, who charge a fee for their services, is published in the yellow pages). If you don't use a broker, you'll need to contact the local state or territory customs office to arrange clearance and must produce your passport and complete an *Unaccompanied Effects Statement* (form B534). Your effects can be cleared through customs prior to your arrival, provided you'll be arriving in Australia within six months of the arrival of your belongings. If you employ an international company (see page 140), they'll handle the associated paperwork and customs clearance for you. Household effects are inspected on arrival in Australia for possible illegal and quarantine risk items. A list of all the items you're importing is required if you pack the goods yourself. Note that duty-free concessions don't apply to goods arriving in Australia as unaccompanied effects. Australian customs publish an *Unaccompanied Effects* leaflet.

# Prohibited & Restricted Goods

There are strict laws prohibiting or restricting the entry of drugs, steroids, weapons, firearms and certain articles subject to quarantine into Australia. If you're carrying any goods which you think may fall into any of the following categories, you must declare them to customs on your arrival in Australia.

**Drugs of Dependence:** If you're carrying any prescribed drugs of dependence, including medicines containing narcotics, hallucinogens, amphetamines, barbiturates, tranquillisers or vaccines, you must declare them to customs on arrival. It's wise to carry a doctor's prescription with you, and Australian customs recommend that you declare all medicinal products when you arrive. If you're uncertain about any drugs or medicines that you're carrying, check with the customs officer on your arrival. **Note that penalties for drug offences in Australia are severe and can result in imprisonment** (see **Crime** on page 451).

**Other Substances:** The importation of anabolic steroids, androgenic substances, natural and manufactured growth hormones, and certain other pharmaceutical substances is prohibited unless prior written approval has been obtained from the Department of Health and Aged Care, Therapeutic Goods Administration, Canberra (☎ within Australia 1800-020 653 or from outside Australia 02-6232 8610, 🖳 www. health.gov.au/tga).

**Weapons/Firearms:** Many weapons and firearms are prohibited in Australia, while others require a permit and safety testing to import them. You should contact Australian customs before you travel if you intend to import any weapons or firearms. Note that there are strict rules about carrying firearms and dangerous goods such as fireworks and flammable liquids in aircraft. If you wish to do so, contact your airline for advice before you travel.

**Quarantine:** Australia is free from many of the world's worst animal and vegetable diseases and from pests that afflict many other regions of the world, and it has strict quarantine regulations to ensure that it remains that way. **All food or goods of plant or animal origin must be declared on your Traveller's Statement.** This includes gifts and souvenirs that are made from plants or animals, or that contain plant or animal material (such as seeds, skin or feathers). If you have prohibited or unwanted items that you don't wish to declare, you can drop them in the quarantine bin on the way to collect your baggage. Food includes any fresh or cooked, dried, packaged, bottled or tinned food products, e.g. meat and meat products, milk and dairy products, eggs and egg products, honey and bee products, beans, nuts, confectionery, herbs and spices, jams, sauces, herbal medicines, teas and beverages. Any food from meals you were served on the aircraft or ship must be left on board or put in the quarantine bin. Animal products include rawhide, bee products, skins and hides, feathers, bones, wool and animal hair, shells and hunting trophies. Plants and plant products include wood carvings, bamboo, cane and rattan items, straw objects such as corn dollies, fresh and dried flowers, potpourri, seeds, pine cones and ornamental wreaths. Live animals can be imported only with prior permission and a valid import permit (see page 461). Note that there are also restrictions on taking fruit and vegetables (produced in Australia) between certain states.

Declared goods won't automatically be confiscated and in most cases they're simply inspected by a quarantine officer and returned to you, although some items may require treatment (e.g. fumigation). Quarantine inspections have been strengthened in recent years and on-the-spot fines of up to $250 are imposed for minor offences. For further information contact the Australian Quarantine Inspection Service (AQIS), GPO Box 858, Canberra, ACT 2601 (☎ within Australia freecall 1800-020 504 or from outside Australia 02-6272 3933, 🖳 www.aquis.gov.au). AQIS publish an information leaflet, *What Can I Take Into Australia? – A quarantine guide for people entering Australia.*

**Protected Wildlife:** Australia has laws which strictly regulate the import and export of wildlife and products made from the skins, feathers, bones, shells, etc. of protected species. Wildlife or any clothing, accessories, handbags, shoes, trophies, ornaments, souvenirs, etc. made from protected species will be seized by customs on arrival. Travellers are particularly warned of restrictions on items made from hard corals (including black coral), giant clam shells, orchids (including live orchids), turtles, alligators and crocodiles (including gavials and caiman), cats (leopards, tigers, jaguars, etc.), elephants (especially ivory and hide products), snakes, lizards and monitors (goannas), rhinoceros, whales, and zebras. Some overseas retailers provide certificates and other guarantees stating that their products are made from protected animals specially bred in captivity and legally farmed for by-products, such as their skins. Such certificates aren't recognised by Australia and the only document recognised by customs is an import permit from Environment Australia (EA), GPO Box 787, Canberra, ACT 2601 (☎ 02-6274 1111, 🖳 www.ea.gov.au). Import permits may be issued by EA, provided that export approval has been obtained from the relevant wildlife authority in the country where you made the purchase and where Australian wildlife import requirements have been met.

**Telephones & CB Radios:** The importation of cordless telephones and citizenband (CB) radios is prohibited unless they're approved by the Australian Spectrum Management Agency (SMA). Only importers authorised by the SMA and the Australian Telecommunications Authority (AUSTEL) who comply with strict conditions may bring cordless telephones into Australia. Approved cordless telephones must display an approval number and an AUSTEL 'permit to connect' authorisation number. Cellular mobile telephones and facsimile machines can be imported.

# EMBASSY REGISTRATION

Nationals of some countries are required to register with their local embassy or consulate as soon as possible after arrival in Australia. Registration isn't usually compulsory, although most embassies like to keep a record of their nationals resident in Australia (if only to help justify their existence) and it may help to expedite passport renewal or replacement.

# FINDING HELP

One of the biggest difficulties facing new arrivals in Australia is how and where to obtain help with day-to-day problems. For example, finding a home, schools, insurance requirements and so on. This book was written in response to this need. However, in addition to the comprehensive information provided here, you'll also require detailed local information. How successful you are in finding help will depend on your employer, the town or area where you live (e.g. those who live and work in a major city are much better served than those living in rural areas), your nationality and English proficiency, even your sex. Many people find their first few weeks or months in Australia stressful, so it helps if you're prepared for a turbulent time. The British newspaper, *Australian News* (see **Appendix A**), has a pen-pals page through which prospective migrants can make contact with recent migrants already in Australia, which helps ease the culture shock.

Obtaining information isn't a problem, as there's a wealth of information available in Australia on every conceivable subject (from astronomy to zoology). The problem is sorting the truths from the half-truths, comparing the options available and making the right decisions. Much information isn't intended for foreigners and their particular needs. You may find that your friends, colleagues and acquaintances can help, as they are often able to proffer advice based on their own experiences and mistakes. **But beware!** Although they mean well, you're likely to receive as much false and conflicting information as accurate data (not always wrong, but possibly invalid for your particular area or situation).

The Department of Immigration, Local Government and Ethnic Affairs provides some basic post-arrival facilities and there's a wealth of settlement programmes for migrants in Australia. A limited number of hostels (in Melbourne and Sydney) and self-contained apartments are provided for immigrants with nowhere to stay on arrival, although they're drab, depressing places mostly used nowadays by refugees. Some states offer extra help to immigrants; for example, South Australia provides skilled migrants with financial assistance for up to two years after their arrival, and employer groups also take part in this scheme. Government programmes for immigrants include migrant resource centres, telephone interpreter services, translation services, an adult migrant English programme, welfare assistance and a grant-in-aid scheme (mainly for refugees). Migrant resource centres (over 30) are located in all major cities and towns and provide newcomers with counselling and contacts to help them overcome initial problems.

Telephone interpreter services are available 24 hours a day throughout the country for the cost of a local phone call (☎ 13-1450). Operators speak several languages and can provide information on accommodation, education, health, insurance, legal and police matters, social welfare and a wide range of other topics. There are also translation units in Sydney, Melbourne and Canberra, and translations can be obtained via the telephone interpreter service (a fee may be charged for documents other than migrant settlement documents).

Local council offices, libraries, tourist offices and Citizens' Advice Bureaux (CABs) are excellent sources of reliable information on a wide range of subjects. Some companies may have a department or staff whose job is to help new arrivals, or they may contract this job out to a local company. If a woman lives in or near a major town, she's able to turn to many women's clubs and organisations for help (single men aren't so well served). There are numerous expatriate associations, clubs and organisations in Australia's major cities and large towns (including 'settlers' or 'friendship' associations) for immigrants from most countries, providing detailed local information regarding all aspects of life in Australia, including housing costs, schools, health services, shopping and much more. Many organisations produce data sheets, booklets and newsletters, operate libraries, and organise a variety of social events, which may include day and evening classes ranging from cooking to English classes. For a list of local clubs, look under 'Clubs and Associations' in the yellow pages. The Department of Immigration can put you in touch with clubs and societies in the city or area where you plan to live in Australia.

Most embassies and consulates provide information bulletin boards (jobs, accommodation, travel, etc.) and keep lists of social clubs and societies for their nationals, and many businesses (e.g. banks and building societies) produce books and leaflets containing useful information for newcomers. Libraries and bookshops usually have books about the local area (see also **Appendix B**).

## CHECKLISTS

## Before Arrival

The following list contains a summary of the tasks that should (if possible) be completed before your arrival in Australia:

- Obtain a visa (if applicable) for all your family members (see **Chapter 3**). Obviously this *must* be done before arrival in Australia.

- If possible, visit Australia prior to your move to find a job, compare communities and arrange schooling for your children (see **Chapter 9**).

- Arrange temporary or permanent accommodation (see **Chapter 5**).

- Arrange for the shipment of your personal effects to Australia (see page 140).

- Arrange health insurance for your family (see page 312). This is essential if you won't be covered by Medicare on your arrival in Australia (see page 283).

- Open a bank account in Australia and transfer some funds (you can open an account with most Australian banks from overseas). You should also obtain some Australian currency before your arrival in Australia, which will save you having to change money immediately on arrival.

- Obtain an international driving licence, if necessary.

- Obtain an international credit card (or two), which will prove invaluable during your first few months in Australia.

- Collect and update your records, including those relating to your family's medical, dental, educational, insurance (e.g. car insurance), professional and employment (including job references) history.

Don't forget to bring all the above documents with you, including birth certificates, driving licenses, marriage certificate, divorce papers, death certificate (if a widow or widower), educational diplomas and professional certificates, employment references, student ID cards, medical and dental records, bank account and credit card details, insurance policies, and receipts for any valuables you're bringing with you. You'll also need any documents which were necessary to obtain your visa (see **Chapter 3**), plus numerous passport-size photographs.

# After Arrival

The following list contains a summary of tasks to be completed after your arrival in Australia (if not done before arrival):

- On arrival at an Australian airport or port, have your visa cancelled and passport stamped, as applicable.

- If you don't own a car, you may wish to rent one for a week or two until you buy one locally (see page 244). Note that it's difficult or impossible to get around in rural areas without a car.

- Register with your local embassy or consulate (see page 115).

- If you plan to work in Australia, obtain a tax file number as soon as possible (see page 327). This is necessary to open a bank account and before (or soon after) starting work.

- Open a bank account at a local bank and give the details to your employer (see page 333). This should be done within six weeks of arrival, during which period your passport is sufficient identification (after six weeks other proof of identification is necessary). If you don't have a permanent address, you can pay to use a 'travellers' contact point', which provides mail holding and e-mail services.

- Do the following within the next few weeks:
  - Apply for a Medicare Card at a Medicare office. This also applies to temporary residents if their country of nationality has a reciprocal agreement with Australia.
  - Arrange schooling for your children (see **Chapter 9**).
  - Find a local doctor and dentist (see **Chapter 12**).
  - Arrange whatever insurance is necessary (see **Chapter 13**), including health insurance (see page 312), car insurance (see page 323), home contents insurance (see page 319) and personal liability insurance (see page 321).

# 5.

# ACCOMMODATION

In most cities and regions of Australia there's a wealth of property for sale, although finding good rental accommodation isn't so easy, particularly in major cities such as Sydney and Melbourne. In Sydney, property at affordable prices is in high demand and short supply, and rents are high particularly after the Olympics in the year 2000. Particularly hard hit are those on low incomes, students and the young, the unemployed, pensioners and single parents, some of whom spend half their wages on rent. Accommodation accounts for around 30 per cent of the average Australian family's budget, but can rise to as much as 50 per cent for tenants and those buying in major cities (renters generally pay a higher proportion of their income in rent than homebuyers do in mortgage payments). Around 18 per cent of Australians move house every year and the average person has 11 addresses during his lifetime.

Home ownership in Australia is, at around 70 per cent (40 per cent owned outright), one of the highest rates in the world and higher than both Britain and the USA. Most Australians expect to be buying their own homes by the time they reach their 30s, although in recent years more people have been renting and many people under 35 have dropped out of the homeownership market altogether. In an attempt to reverse this trend, the government has introduced housing grants for first-time home buyers. Australia is a highly urbanised society with over 70 per cent of the population living in the main cities situated on or near the coast, including Adelaide, Brisbane, Canberra, Darwin, Melbourne, Perth and Sydney, all of which have particular characters and attractions. Only some 15 per cent of Australians live in rural areas. The vast majority of Australians live in detached bungalows on individual plots of land, although apartments (called 'units' or 'home units') are common in inner cities and coastal areas, and townhouses are popular in the suburbs.

Oversupply generated by a building boom in the '80s followed by a severe recession in the early '90s, which led to a slump in house prices and the worst housing market for 20 years, leaving many people in negative equity (where their mortgage was more than the value of their homes). In the mid-'90s, prices recovered in most regions and 1999–2000 saw a major property boom. However, the introduction of a goods and services tax (GST) in July 2000 hit the market hard, prompting a property crisis, particularly in New South Wales and Victoria where prices reached record highs in 1999. By mid-2001, the market had stabilised somewhat and property prices were rising once more, the average house price in Australia being around $190,000, although it was much higher in the major cities, particularly anywhere within easy travelling distance of the central business district (CBD).

Homelessness is a huge problem in Australia, where soaring rents and a critical shortage of public housing have led to tens of thousands of people being forced to live in cars, caravans, private hotels, rooming houses and Salvation Army hostels. In major cities, people with mental health, drug and alcohol problems make up most of the homeless, although an increasing number of families and unemployed people find themselves in the same predicament. Public housing is provided by state governments and is available to those on low and moderate incomes (applicants are means tested), although there are long waiting lists – over 200,000 people nationwide, who usually have to wait a number of years. Homelessness is set to worsen as a consequence of government cutbacks in public housing in recent years.

# TEMPORARY ACCOMMODATION

On arrival in Australia, you may find it necessary to stay in temporary accommodation for a few weeks (or even a few months) before moving into permanent accommodation or while waiting for your personal effects and furniture to arrive from overseas. In most large towns and cities, apartments or holiday flats are available, which are usually self-contained and fully furnished with their own bathrooms and kitchens. They're cheaper than hotels (e.g. 25 to 50 per cent less than a standard hotel double room), have over twice the space and are more convenient, particularly for families. Serviced apartments are usually rented on a weekly basis. Single people and married couples (without children) may be able to find temporary accommodation in hostels (see page 373). There are a limited number of government hostels (e.g. in Melbourne and Sydney) and self-contained apartments for migrants with nowhere to stay on arrival, although these are usually drab, depressing places and are mostly used by refugees. For information about hotels, bed and breakfast, self-catering and hostels, see **Chapter 15**.

# RELOCATION COMPANIES

If you're fortunate enough to have your move to (or within) Australia paid for by your employer, he may arrange for a relocation company to handle the details. Relocation companies in Australia generally deal with corporate relocations rather than acting for individuals. In addition to providing housing, education and employment services, many relocation companies will also find business premises in Australia and relocate complete companies, including plant and machinery. There are relocation companies in all major cities in Australia, most of which provide the following services:

**House Hunting:** This is usually the main service provided by relocation companies and includes both rented and bought properties. Services usually include locating a number of properties matching your requirements and specifications and arranging a visit to Australia to view them. You should allow at least two months between your initial visit and moving into a purchased property. Rental properties can usually be found in two to four weeks, depending on the location and your requirements.

**Negotiations:** Companies usually help and advise you on all aspects of house rental or purchase and may conduct negotiations on your behalf, organise finance (including bridging loans), arrange surveys and insurance, organise your removal to Australia and even arrange quarantine for your pets (see page 461).

**Schools:** Consultants usually provide a report on local schools (both state and private) for families with children. If required, the report can also include private boarding schools.

**Local Information:** Most companies provide a comprehensive information package for a chosen area, including details of employment prospects, state and private health services, local schools (state and private), estate agents, shopping facilities, public transport, amenities and services, sports and social facilities, and communications.

**Miscellaneous Services:** Companies may provide advice and support (particularly for non-working spouses) both before and after a move, orientation visits for spouses, counselling for domestic and personal problems, help in finding jobs for spouses, and even marriage counselling (moving to another country puts a lot of strain on relationships). A relocation company may also find you a suitable car if one isn't provided by your employer.

Although you may consider a relocation company's services expensive, particularly if you're footing the bill yourself, most companies and individuals consider it money well spent. You can find a relocation company through the Relocation Group in Australia and the International Relocation Association (TIRA) or look in your local yellow pages under 'Relocators'. One relocation company with offices throughout Australia is Australiawide Relocations, PO Box 111, 19-23 Bridge Street, Pymble, NSW 2073 (☎ 02-9488 9444, ✉ austrelo@bigpond.com).

If you wish to look at properties for rent or sale in a particular area, you can make appointments to view properties through estate agents in the area where you plan to live and arrange your own trip to Australia. However, you must make *absolutely certain* that estate agents (see page 133) know exactly what you're looking for. It's also possible to view properties over the Internet, e.g. via the Real Estate Display Centre (🖳 www.realestatecentre.com.au). Most agents will also send you details of properties by fax or e-mail.

## BUYING PROPERTY

Buying a house or apartment in Australia has traditionally been a good long-term investment, although this was severely tested during the recession in the early '90s. However, most people still find buying preferable to renting, depending of course on how long you're planning to stay in Australia and where you're planning to live. If you're staying only short term, say less than three years, you may be better off renting. For those staying longer than three years, buying is the better option, particularly as buying a house or apartment is generally no more expensive (and often cheaper) than renting – and you could make a profit. Market analysts generally agree that property prices in Australia's major cities (particularly Sydney and Melbourne) will continue to rise in the immediate future. It's also more difficult to rent than buy a good property in most cities. See also **Mortgages** on page 341.

Nevertheless, if you're a migrant, you should seriously consider renting for a period before buying, particularly if you're unsure of where you want to live or work, there's a possibility that you may change jobs or states within your first year or two in Australia; you may even decide, as many people do, that Australia isn't for you and return home within a few years.

The secret of successfully buying a home in Australia (or anywhere else for that matter) is research, research and more research, preferably before you even set foot there. You may be fortunate and buy the first property you see without doing any homework and live happily ever after. However, a successful purchase is much more likely if you thoroughly investigate the towns and suburbs in your chosen area, compare the range and prices of properties and their relative values, and study the procedure for buying property. It's a wise or lucky person who gets his choice absolutely right first time, and there's a much better chance if you do your homework thoroughly. There's a huge choice of homes in Australia, including apartments, townhouses and a wide range of 'standard' and individually-designed, detached homes. Apartments (called 'units' or 'home units') are common in inner cities and coastal areas, and townhouses (or row houses) are also common in cities and their suburbs. Villa units are low-rise properties separated by a garage or small courtyard (garden) and similar to a townhouse. Outside the major cities, most people have a home built to a standard or individual design on their own plot of land, although package deals, including a plot of land and a house are also common.

**Information:** Magazines are published by local property associations in major cities and states. Most banks, building societies and credit unions publish free booklets for homebuyers, which generally contain excellent (usually unbiased) advice, and the Home Purchase Assistance Authority (☎ freecall 1800-806 653, 🖳 www.hpaa.nsw.gov.au) publishes a free booklet, *The A-Z of Home Purchase*. The Saturday editions of major newspapers are the best for home advertisements, and most of them have a property section. Note, however, that sometimes the advertised price is only for the plot of land and the building is extra. The measurements of rooms are usually stated in feet and inches (not metres or square metres) and aren't usually included in ads. The size of a plot may be stated in square metres or acres and the size of a house in 'squares', where one square equals 100ft$^2$ (9.3m$^2$).

**Non-residents:** All proposed acquisitions of urban real estate by non-resident foreigners must be approved by the Australian authorities. Retirees and other 'temporary' residents must obtain permission from the Foreign Investment Board, Department of the Treasury, Parkes Place, ACT 2600 (☎ 02-6263 3795, 🖳 www.firb. gov.au) in order to buy property in Australia.

## Australian Homes

Don't be in too much of a hurry to buy a home in Australia until you've had a good look around, have a clear idea of the relative prices and types of properties available, *and* know exactly what you're looking for. For example, do you want a house with a garden or an apartment, with perhaps higher security and lower heating bills? Do you want an older house with character and space or a modern townhouse or apartment with all mod cons? There's a huge variety of homes to choose from, including modern detached homes, apartments, townhouses, period homes and mobile homes.

**Modern Homes:** Over three-quarters of Australia's eight million homes are detached houses, some 15 per cent are apartments, and around 10 per cent are townhouses, semi-detached, row or terrace homes. The most common Australian family home is a detached, single-storey bungalow (ranch style) on a quarter or third of an acre plot. It has three or four bedrooms, a combined lounge/dining room, kitchen (possibly eat-in), bathroom (or two), separate toilet, laundry room, possibly a family or rumpus room (which may be an extension of the kitchen), and a garage or car port. Bathrooms usually include a bath and separate shower, and there may also be a shower room. Larger houses, e.g. from four bedrooms, have two or more bathrooms, with the master bedroom having an en suite bathroom or shower. Larger homes may also have a study and other rooms. The mild climate allows year-round, outdoor living, and most detached homes have terraces or patios with a barbecue, and around half have a swimming pool (which must be completely fenced off and childproof).

The quality of modern Australian homes is generally excellent. Construction may be brick (the most expensive and generally reserved for luxury homes), brick veneer (the most popular), or weatherboard and fibre cement known as fibro (the cheapest but no longer common). Brick veneer has the outward appearance of a full brick construction, except that the inner frame is made of timber and the inside is lined with plaster board or similar material. It costs less than a full brick home and is particularly suited to Australia's climate. A fibro house is basically a timber frame covered with fibre cement on the outside and plasterboard on the inside. Roofs are generally made of terracotta or cement tiles, although galvanised steel decking or fibre cement sheeting is often used in contemporary style homes. In remote country areas (e.g. the outback and the bush), running water, sewerage, mains electricity and telephone lines are a luxury, and septic tanks, rain water tanks, generators and dirt roads are common. Houses are raised on stilts in some tropical areas or those subject to flooding, where the garage may be located below the living area.

When you buy a new home, kitchen and bathroom fittings, fitted carpets, curtains and light fittings are usually included in the price. Bedrooms have built-in wardrobes, and kitchens are fully fitted with a cooker and possibly even a dishwasher. Fly screens are common on external doors and all windows and allow you to leave the doors and windows open without inviting insects in. Good insulation helps keep homes cool in summer and warm in winter; in the southern states, homes may have a fireplace or a heating unit in the lounge. Air-conditioning may be fitted as standard in up-market homes. Wallpaper is rare in Australia, where interior walls are generally painted. Most semi-detached and detached houses have single or double garages included in the price. In major cities, there are home display villages where you can view the latest designs from Australia's largest builders. New properties have a builder's warranty.

**Apartments:** Apartments (flats), called units or home units in Australia, are common in inner city and beachside areas because of the high cost of land, although they aren't as widespread as in European cities. Apartment blocks are usually purpose-built with up to 20 storeys and are rarely conversions of old large houses. Blocks may contain split-level apartments and penthouses (which traditionally occupy the whole top floor of a high-rise building) and usually have underground parking. Many modern apartment blocks have communal pools and other facilities such as tennis courts, saunas and gymnasiums. Queensland's Gold Coast is popular among retirees, who buy apartments in retirement villages which include swimming pools, bowling greens, tennis courts, croquet lawns and billiards rooms and are served by village buses. Units in Australia are sold freehold under the Strata Titles Act. Note that apartments, particularly older apartments, aren't usually built or designed to the high standards found in North America or many European countries. Many older apartments are tiny, with poor storage and inadequate parking, and are lacking in quality fixtures and fittings.

**Period & Older Homes:** There are many period homes in the inner suburbs of the major cities, most of which have been modernised and are now relatively (or very) expensive. Terraced housing is found in some older inner-city suburbs, e.g. in Sydney, where decorative wrought ironwork is a feature of early homes, particularly in suburbs such as Paddington and Darlinghurst. Federation (early 19th century) houses made of wood and sandstone are also attractive and highly prized. In Queensland ,there are elevated timber and iron houses with balustrades and verandas (known appropriately as 'Queenslanders'), which allow cooling breezes to permeate the house. However, there's also a vast amount of housing stock with no architectural merit or heritage value. Many homes built in the '50s and '60s building boom reflect the less sophisticated and enlightened ideas of that era and are entirely unsuited to today's lifestyle. In many cases, the plots they occupy are worth much more than the properties built on them.

If you need to modernise or renovate a property, you should expect to pay at least 20 per cent more than your original budget. Note also that many old homes have problems such as damp, electricity faults and insect infestations.

**Mobile Homes:** Mobile homes (also called transportable or manufactured homes because they're factory built in two or more sections and erected on site, usually in around six weeks) are popular in Australia, particularly among retirees. Many mobile homes look like conventional homes and include features such as bay windows, skylights, verandas, built-in wardrobes and even brick finishes. They cost between $60,000 and $120,000 and, at the top end of the market, aren't much cheaper than conventional homes. Note also that mobile homes are likely to depreciate over the years, rather than appreciate like a conventional home.

Mobile homes are usually sited in caravan parks or specially built estates. Sites must usually be leased, e.g. on a weekly or monthly basis, and you should beware of spiralling rents, which are an issue in most states (although some parks have rent controls). There are also a number of restrictions in parks, e.g. overnight fees for guests, and in some states owners even require the permission of park owners to sell. For further information contact the Manufactured Housing Industry Association, PO Box H114, Harris Park, NSW 2150 (☎ 02-9637 0599), which publishes an information booklet. The Queenslands Consumers Association publishes an online *Guide to Mobile Home Living* (🖳 www.consumer.qld.gov.au).

# Cost

Property prices vary considerably throughout the country and in the various suburbs of the major cities. Not surprisingly, the further you are from a town or city, the lower the cost of land and property. Two-bedroom apartments (of around 75m$^2$) start at around $100,000 in outer city suburbs and rise to over double this in a central or popular beach location. For many buyers it's a choice between a small apartment in an inner city and a large detached family home in the outer suburbs – in recent years the average Aussie battler (commuter) has had to move further and further into the outer suburbs of major cities in order to find affordable accommodation.

A two or three-bedroom, single-storey home in most city outer suburbs costs between $60,000 and $100,000; four-bedroom, two-storey homes cost from around $80,000 to $200,000. On the other hand, waterfront properties in Sydney are astronomically expensive and a reasonable two-bedroom apartment in an attractive building with water views costs more than $500,000 (million dollar homes are commonplace in Sydney, in Melbourne and on the White Sunshine Coast). There's a high demand everywhere for waterfront properties, which are generally an excellent investment, particularly in NSW where the government plans to preserve the coastline from further development (canal developments are already banned).

Average house prices in the capital cities in mid 2001 were around $310,000 in Sydney, $250,000 in Melbourne, $185,000 in Darwin, $180,000 in Canberra, $160,000 in Perth, $140,000 in Brisbane, $135,000 in Adelaide and in Hobart. Units and townhouses are some 20 to 30 per cent cheaper than detached houses. Average prices for apartments in Adelaide, Brisbane and Hobart have remained stagnant in recent years, while prices have been escalating in Canberra, Melbourne and Sydney. The average cost of a Sydney house increased by around 33 per cent between 1998 and 2000, with the biggest price rises among homes valued at over $500,000. South

Australia is the cheapest state for homes for first-time buyers, while Sydney has Australia's most expensive property, although a recent survey of the world's most affordable cities for young couples buying a first home ranked Sydney 11th out of 31 cities in 17 countries.

In mid-2001, the Australian property market was generally good for sellers, except in the Northern Territory, Victoria and Western Australia, where sales were slow. Continued interest rate cuts in the last few years have also helped the property market. However, it's feared that many people will find themselves in severe financial difficulties if interest rates rise sharply. In 2001, buyers were more interested in housing in the suburbs or in purpose built 'satellite cities' outside the main cities (e.g. Palmerston near Darwin), where accommodation is substantially cheaper yet home owners are still near enough to benefit from the advantages of city life. 'Rural residential' allotments are also becoming increasingly popular.

Not surprisingly, selling at auction is popular, particularly when prices are rising. Around 25 to 30 per cent of homes in Melbourne are sold at auction compared with around 20 per cent in Sydney, around 15 per cent in Brisbane and 10 to 15 per cent in Adelaide. High demand in 2001 led to houses in the inner suburbs of Melbourne and Sydney selling at auction for well above their guide prices.

Note that a few kilometres can make a huge difference to the price of a property, with apartments in central areas costing up to $2,000 per square metre more than those in harbour-side developments a few kilometres further out. Land prices also reduce considerably from around 15km/9mi outside a city and are at their lowest around 25km/16mi from cities. The cost of land varies from as little as $25,000 for an average size suburban house at least 25km/16mi from cities such as Adelaide, Hobart and Perth to over $200,000 for a similar plot within 15km/9mi of central Sydney (if you can find one). The cost of building a home varies according to the location and the quality of materials used. Brick veneer costs from around $400 to $700 per m2, depending on the location. Note, however, that the cost of building a home increased considerably after the introduction of GST in July 2000. For up-to-date prices, obtain a free copy of the *Cost of Living and Housing Survey Book* published by the Commonwealth Bank of Australia.

There are few bargains when it comes to buying property and, although you may be able to negotiate a reduction of 5 or possibly 10 per cent (particularly if a seller is looking for a quick sale in a buyers' market), there's usually a good reason when a property is substantially cheaper than other similar properties. Although it's sometimes unwise to look a gift horse in the mouth, you should generally be suspicious of a bargain. On the other hand, most sellers and estate agents price properties higher than the market price or the price they expect to receive, knowing that buyers will try to drive the price down, so always haggle over the price asked (even if you think it's a bargain). This is, in fact, one of the few occasions in Australia when you're expected to bargain, although you should try to avoid insulting an owner by offering a derisory price.

If you're buying a home for a limited period or as an investment, you should buy one that you hope will sell quickly and at a profit. Homes that sell best are exceptional period houses of character with lots of original features, and water and beach-front homes (particularly in Queensland), which are in high demand and can be let for most of the year to holidaymakers if required. Luxury units in central Brisbane, Melbourne and Sydney are also a good investment. Note, however, that buying property in Australia is usually a long-term investment and isn't recommended to those seeking a short-term gain. You must pay capital gains tax on the profit made on the sale of an investment property (see page 359).

You can find out the price of homes in any Sydney suburb through the *Sydney Morning Herald Home Price Guide*, which lists all the sales results (both auction and private treaty) in Sydney suburbs for the last 12 months (it can be ordered via the Internet from 💻 www.apm.com.au). A similar service is provided by newspapers in other major cities, and you can also peruse property ads in a number of publications via the Internet (e.g. 💻 www.sydneyproperty.com.au).

# Fees

The fees associated with buying a home in Australia usually total 4 to 5 per cent of the purchase price, which is lower than in many other countries. Most fees are calculated as a percentage of the value of the property you're buying, so the more expensive the property, the higher the fees. Even removal costs will be higher if you have a large house (unless you have a lot of empty rooms). If you're buying *and* selling, you must consider the cost of both transactions. The main fees are as follows:

● **Stamp Duty:** Stamp duty varies considerably according to the state or territory and averages around $1,000 (on a $50,000 property), $2,300 ($100,000 property) and $7,230 ($200,000 property). Stamp duty is lowest in New South Wales and highest in the Northern Territory, Tasmania and Victoria. In some states, it's lower for first-time buyers or is waived altogether. Some states, e.g. Victoria, are campaigning for stamp duty to be adjusted to the same levels in all states, and stamp duty rates are expected to be reviewed in 2003/04.

● **Land Transfer Registration:** This fee is for recording a change of owner at the Land Titles Office and is payable each time a property is sold. It's either a flat fee (ACT, NSW, NT, QLD and TAS) or a variable fee based on the price paid (SA, VIC and WA). The fee on a $100,000 property varies between $58 in New South Wales (fixed fee) and $432 in South Australia (variable fee – $902 on a $200,000 property).

● **Legal Fees:** Legal fees are usually between 1 and 2 per cent of the purchase price, but may vary according to the work involved. Legal fees vary considerably from state to state, e.g. from $500 in Adelaide, Perth and Hobart to around $1,500 in Brisbane for a property costing over $100,000. The fees in most states are within the $500 to $1,000 range.

● **Solicitor's or Conveyancer's Fees:** These are the fees for the documentation necessary for a property purchase (see **Conveyance** on page 132). There isn't a fixed charge and the cost of conveyance can range from around $400 to $1,500.

● **Government Taxes:** There are federal and state taxes on financial transactions that vary according the state or territory.

● **Mortgage Fees:** A range of fees is associated with mortgages, including a mortgage application or establishment fee, a valuation fee, legal fees, maintenance fees and a loan registration fee (for information see page 344).

● **Termite & Pest Inspection:** This is compulsory in some states, while in others it's sufficient to certify that a property is free of termites and pests. However, a termite inspection is always recommended, whether required by law or not. The inspection costs from $140 to $220 and may be paid by the vendor or buyer or shared.

● **Strata Inspection:** When you're buying an apartment (unit), it's wise to have a strata inspection (relating to the Strata Titles Act – see **Apartments** on page 124 and **Title** on page 130), which will tell you whether there have been any administrative or structural problems with the building. Strata inspections cost from $165 to $220.

● **Inspection or Survey Fee:** Although it isn't compulsory to have a building inspection or a structural survey carried out, it's often wise, particularly when you're buying an old detached house. You should allow from $275 to $440 for a structural survey.

● **Building Insurance:** It's a condition of lenders that properties are fully insured against structural and other damage (see page 318). Note that it may be necessary to insure a property from the day you sign the purchase contract.

● **Miscellaneous Costs:** If you're buying a new home, you may need to pay an architect and other fees. You will also usually need to pay utility connection, reconnection, registration or transfer fees for gas, electricity, water and telephone. Although not a fee as such, removal costs must also be taken into account. In addition to the fees associated with buying a property, you must also consider the running costs, which include local property taxes (rates) and possibly land tax (see page 345), contents insurance (see page 319), standing charges for utilities (electricity, gas, telephone, water), community fees for a unit or other communal property, garden and pool maintenance, and a caretaker's or management fees if you leave a home empty or let it. Annual running costs usually average around 2 to 3 per cent of the cost of a property.

# Building Your Own Home

Building a new home or having a new home built is common in Australia and usually takes from four to 12 months. It's generally cheaper and better to have a new home built than to buy and renovate an older home, as you don't need to make compromises for old building standards and the existing dimensions or plot restrictions. You also don't need to match new work to old or make good any damage to existing structures. New homes are generally built to a much higher standard that older homes. Note, however, that new regulations for insurance, building code performances and the introduction of GST in 2000 have led to a sharp increase in the price of building materials and therefore the cost of a new home. Many Australians design and even build their own homes and, if you're up to it, you can do much of the work yourself, although plumbing and electrical work can be done only by qualified tradesmen. **Note, that building a home isn't for the faint-hearted, as it's fraught with problems.** Alternatively, you can buy a plot and hire a builder or purchase a plot from a builder/developer with exclusive rights to develop a particular estate (called project or estate homes). Builders' project homes are extremely popular and are cheaper than building a home to your own design or having it designed and built by an architect, and land plus house packages are cost effective. All builders maintain show homes which can usually be visited without an appointment at weekends. The cost per square metre of building a home depends on the type of construction and the location; the following costs are for homes in an average location:

| Construction Type | Project Home Cost (per m²) | Architect Built Home Cost (per m²) |
|---|---|---|
| Full brick | $1,200–1,300 | $1,600–2,200 |
| Brick veneer | $550–650 | $1,400–1,500 |
| Weatherboard | $650–750 | $1,200–1,300 |

Fibre cement prices are subject to demand. Brick veneer is the most popular, while full brick is reserved for luxury homes; weatherboard and fibre cement are rarely used nowadays. Timber cladding is popular in some cities, e.g. Brisbane. Note that the quality of fixtures and fittings used make a huge difference to the price.

**Land:** The cost of land varies considerably according to the city or region and the distance from a city centre. For example, a plot around 8 to 15km/5 to 9mi from Sydney centre costs at least $250,000, while a similar plot in Perth costs from around $60,000. Plots over 30km/19mi from city centres range from a high of around $80,000 in Sydney to around $30,000 in Adelaide and Perth. Most land and property in Australia is owned freehold, the only exception being the Australian Capital Territory (ACT), where land is sold on a 99-year lease (after 99 years, leases have to be re-applied for). Residential blocks are released by the government and sold at public auction, and any unsold sites are available for sale at the Land Sales Office. Plots up to 30km/19mi from a city cost from around $50,000 to $150,000. Reserve prices (average $60,000) are set at 80 per cent of the assessed market value and lessees must start work on building within 12 months and complete properties within two years. All sites are provided with services such as water, electricity, sewerage and sealed roads.

New properties built by a professional builder are always covered by a warranty, and most lenders won't make a loan on a new house without one. A standard contract for a new home usually provides that the builder rectifies any defects notified by the purchaser for a limited period, e.g. three months. Note that it's important to choose your builder carefully, as building disputes are common and it can be expensive if you need to seek legal redress.

# Retirement Homes & Sheltered Housing

For those who are retired or nearing retirement age (e.g. over 55), purpose-built retirement homes and sheltered housing are available in most areas of Australia, where there are over 2,300 retirement villages. Villages vary in size and offer differing levels of accommodation, from self-contained independent living apartments, townhouses or cottages, to serviced apartments, hostels and nursing homes. Most villages offer a luxurious lifestyle, a supportive environment, safety and security, and some are more like country estates or luxury hotels with prices starting at well over $300,000. Before buying a retirement home, you should visit a number of villages and talk to residents, as they vary enormously in the quality and variety of housing, amenities and cost. There's a huge demand for homes in retirement developments and villages and they usually sell quickly.

Retirement homes offer special features, facilities and convenience for the elderly and retired (most residents are in their late 60s or older), including guest suites that can be booked for visitors. Facilities may include a heated outdoor or indoor swimming pool (or both), spa complex, bowling green, tennis courts, croquet lawn, landscaped gardens, restaurant, lounge/dining area, open fire, billiards room, craft room, library service, sun room, private bar, lifts, garage and private gardens. In some villages, all home cleaning is included and meals may also be provided (called 'assisted living'). One of the most important features of retirement homes is that help is on hand 24 hours a day, either from a live-in warden or caretaker or via an alarm system linked to a control centre. A nurse and maintenance man are usually on call and there are visiting doctors and dentists. Many villages provide 24-hour, seven days a week emergency care and some also have their own nursing homes.

**Funding:** Most villages are resident funded, where each resident purchases a unit through a tenancy arrangement; some are donor funded, i.e. run by a charitable or non-profit organisation and operated on a loan and licence basis (see below), with places reserved for retirees who are unable to make a donation.

**Title:** In some villages, you purchase a strata or unit title, which is the same as buying a unit in the normal way. Strata title arrangements usually include a management agreement for the provision of services and facilities tailored to the needs of residents, as well as a possible deferred management fee. Strata title provides the highest level of security of tenure, the ability to borrow against the equity in your home, and retention of any appreciation in its value.

Under leasehold title, you purchase a long lease, which is a common tenancy arrangement in retirement villages. Leases are usually for 99 or 199 years, and a leasehold title is cheaper than a strata title, although stamp duty is still quite high. Note that leases are transferable, but there's no capital appreciation if the lease is transferred.

A company-share title is effectively a share in the company that owns the village which includes the right to tenancy, although shares can be difficult to resell.

A loan and licence arrangement usually applies to donor funded villages (see above), where you pay the sponsor/developer a sum (donation) plus an interest-free loan, which buys you the right to occupy a unit and use the facilities of a village.

**Costs:** Initial (ingoing) costs of buying a retirement home include the purchase of a unit or lease, fees such as stamp duty and legal fees, and costs associated with agreements or contracts. Running (ongoing) costs include weekly/monthly fees for maintenance, insurance, rates, services and facilities. A deferred management fee may be payable on leaving a retirement village, which is usually a percentage of the original purchase price. Note that, when a unit or lease is put up for sale, fees must usually be paid until it's sold. This leaves owners (or their families) open to abuse, and some retirement villages deliberately allow units to remain empty so that they can charge fees (of up to $1,000 a month!) without providing any services. Other common problems include financial disputes, access to services, quality of management, and compliance with codes of practice.

State governments oversee the retirement village industry and most have a code of practice that aims to regulate the promotion, development and operation of villages. Check with the state authorities and the state retirement Village Residents Association. All states also have a Council of the Aging (COTA) that provides information and advice about retirement villages (go to 💻 www.cota.org.au).

# Contracts

Once a suitable property has been found and a price has been agreed, the estate agent will complete a Contract of Sale, which is signed by both parties. Contracts are published in standard form by the Law Society and the Real Estate Institute. From July 2001, the front of all contracts carries a government statement bringing to your attention important matters such as the recommendation to seek legal advice and information on cooling-off periods and the payment of deposits. The client as well as the estate agent must sign this statement in front of a witness. **Note, however, that you should never sign a contract without having it checked by a legal adviser.** It's important to check that a property's particulars are complete in every detail and have been entered correctly and that the terms of sale are correct, including any changes made to the standard terms. A deposit (typically 10 per cent of the purchase price) is paid by the buyer to the agent and deposited in the agent's escrow (trust) account until completion, which is usually around a month later. **Note that the deposit is forfeited if you pull out of a purchase after signing a contract and aren't covered by a clause in the contract.** However, a holding deposit paid before signing a contract (as a sign of 'good faith') is refundable if you change your mind. Only after the contract has been signed do the searches and checks (see **Conveyance** below) take place and, when all searches have been satisfactorily completed, the sale is completed.

After signing and exchanging contracts, called simply 'exchange', both parties are legally obliged to go through with the deal, subject to cooling-off rights in NSW, the NT, SA and Victoria of two to five working days. For example, buyers in NSW have a cooling-off period from the day of exchange until 5pm on the fifth working day following, during which they can withdraw from the purchase without penalty other than forfeiting 0.25 per cent of the purchase price. Note that cooling-off rights don't apply when buying at public auction. Any conditions attached to a sale must either be dealt with before the exchange or during the cooling-off period, otherwise they *must* be included as a specific provision (conditional clause) in the contract. Vendors sometimes refuse to sell unless a certificate waiving the cooling-off period is signed.

**Conditional Clauses:** Contracts often contain conditional clauses, such as the sale being conditional on a clear survey or smoke test. Conditions usually apply to events out of control of the vendor or buyer, although almost anything agreed between the buyer and vendor can be included in a contract. If any conditions aren't met, the contract can be suspended or declared null and void and the deposit returned. However, if you fail to go through with a purchase and aren't covered by a clause in the contract, you'll forfeit your deposit or even be compelled to complete a purchase. Note that, if you're buying anything from the vendor such as carpets, curtains or furniture which are included in the purchase price, you should have them listed and attached as an addendum to the contract. Any fixtures and fittings present in a property when you view it (and agree to buy it) should still be there when you take possession, unless otherwise stated in the contract.

When signing a contract to buy a home or land on which you require a loan, you should complete the clause regarding your ability to obtain finance. This makes the contract 'subject to finance'; if you cannot obtain finance within the time specified in the contract, e.g. 7 to 14 days, it will then become null and void and you won't have to proceed. Without a finance clause, you could be sued by the vendor for failing to buy the property. If you cannot arrange finance in the specified time, you can ask for an extension to the settlement date.

Most properties in Australia are owned freehold, where the owner receives a copy of the certificate of title (deeds) or the strata title in the case of a retirement village property. A certificate of title is usually issued by the state lands title office (land registry), where land and property ownership is recorded. Mortgages are also recorded at the lands title office.

# Conveyance

Conveyance (often improperly called conveyancing) is the legal term for the process of buying and selling properties and transferring the deeds of ownership. A conveyance is a deed (legal document) that conveys a house from the vendor to the buyer, thereby transferring ownership. There are two main stages when your conveyancer will become involved. The first stage will take you up to the exchange of contracts and the second will lead to the completion of the sale, when you become the new owner.

Conveyance includes ensuring that proper title is obtained, arranging the necessary registration of the title, checking whether the land has been registered and the existence of any restrictive covenants, enquiring about any planned developments that may affect the value of the property (like a new airport runway or motorway at the bottom of your garden), and drawing up a contract of sale. Note, however, that conveyance duties and laws in Australia vary according to the state or territory where the property is situated. Searches should include an identifications survey (to identify the rightful owner), zoning certificate, drainage or sewerage service diagram, property certificate, building inspection report, pest certificate, technical report, strata records search (for a strata title unit – see page 128), and enquiries with the local council and utility companies as to whether the property is clear of any debts. Note that land tax, council and water rates are a charge on the property and, if they haven't been paid by the previous owner, the new owner must pay them.

Property conveyance in Australia is usually done by a solicitor (lawyer) or a conveyancer (also called settlement agents, land brokers and land agents), although you can also do it yourself. In the ACT, Queensland and Tasmania, solicitors have a monopoly on conveyance and in Victoria a conveyancer must work with a solicitor, but in other states you can engage a conveyancer. In some states (such as South Australia and Western Australia), the majority of settlements are handled by conveyancers, which helps reduce costs. Some lenders carry out conveyance as a free service to borrowers. Separate conveyance fees are usually paid by both the buyer and the vendor (in some states the buyer's costs are higher, as there's more work involved).

There isn't a fixed fee for conveyance, which can range from around $400 to $1,500. Shop around for the lowest rate, as some solicitors and conveyancers will negotiate. Conveyance companies are generally cheaper than solicitors and usually levy fixed fees with no hidden charges. Always check what is included in the fees and whether a quoted fee is 'full and binding' or just an estimate. A low basic rate may be supplemented by much more expensive 'extras' (called disbursements). Ask your friends, neighbours and colleagues if they can recommend a solicitor or conveyancer and try to obtain a binding quotation in writing. **It isn't wise to use a solicitor or conveyancer who is acting for both the borrower and the lender, as conflicts of interest could arise.**

It's possible and perfectly legal to do your own conveyance, and there are a number of DIY kits available. However, you'll need to do at least ten hours' work and you require a good grasp of details plus a good measure of patience. **Conveyance isn't recommended for most people, as it's complex, time-consuming and risky.** If you miss a mistake in the lease, you could be left with an unsalable property – if a solicitor or licensed conveyancer is at fault, you can at least sue him!

## ESTATE AGENTS

Most property in Australia is bought and sold through estate agents, who sell property on commission for owners. When buying property in Australia, always use a licensed agent. The Real Estate and Business Agents Act imposes obligations and requirements on licensed agents, which protect both buyers and sellers by creating a source of legal redress in the event of error, negligence, misrepresentation or loss. The act protects deposits paid by purchasers and prevents conduct which could be misleading or prejudicial to buyers, and is backed by disciplinary procedures and a Fidelity Guarantee Fund. However, the act doesn't apply to private sales where no agent is involved.

The Real Estate Institute of Australia (Level 1, 16 Thesiger Court (PO Box 234), Deakin West, ACT 2600, ☎ 02-6282 4277, 💻 www.reiaustralia.com.au) is the umbrella organisation for state real estate organisations, e.g. the Real Estate Institute of New South Wales, and you should check with them that an agent is a member. In July 2000, the Property Agents and Motor Dealers Act came into force, whereby estate agents are obliged to adhere to a code of conduct and incur harsher penalties for false or misleading representations. Estate agents must adhere to a code of ethics (of which you can request a copy) and must have professional indemnity. Clients also have access to a Tribunal and Complaints Fund.

There's a multi-listing service in all states, whereby homes are advertised in real estate offices throughout the state, which costs vendors nothing until their home is sold. However, some agents may only show you, or at least try to push, properties for which they have an exclusive listing (when they don't need to share the commission with anyone else).

Estate agents usually act for the seller and it's their job to obtain the highest price they can for a property, so don't expect impartial advice if you're a buyer. If they offer to make a considerable reduction on the advertised price, it probably means that it's overpriced and has been on their books for a long time. An estate agent will usually try to get you to view as many properties as possible (irrespective of whether they fit your requirements or price range), as this shows sellers that he's doing a good job. You should try to sort out the possibles from the improbables before making any appointments to view and, if you're shown properties that don't meet your specifications, tell the agent immediately. You can also help the agent narrow the field by telling him exactly what's wrong with the properties you reject.

Don't see too many properties in one day, however anxious you are to find somewhere, as it's easy to become confused as to the merits of each property. Many homes for sale hold an 'open house' at weekends (possibly with a 'home open' sign outside), although the total inspection period may be as little as an hour. Otherwise, it's essential to make an appointment with an owner or agent to inspect a property. Note that it's possible to inspect Australian properties via the Internet from anywhere in the world, as all large estate agents, builders and developers now have websites.

**Auctions:** An alternative to buying from an agent is to buy at auction, although this method generally applies to properties at the upper end of the market. Auctions have become ncreasingly popular in the last few years, as sellers can sell quickly and buyers can usually save money (it's most common in Melbourne and Sydney). Note, however, that it's absolutely vital to do your homework before buying at auction, particularly regarding the market value of properties. Many agents will quote a price 10 or 20 per cent below a property's expected sale price in order to attract more interest at auctions, although in a sellers' market many properties sell for much more than their reserve price. Property auctions are advertised in local newspapers and may be held on site.

You can engage a buyer's representative to find a house, bid for it at auction and negotiate the sale. Agents may charge as little as a few hundred dollars to bid at an auction or up to 3 per cent of the price if they conduct a search and secure a property. However, this can save you a lot of time, trouble and money. It isn't wise to bid yourself unless you know the ropes and are confident of what you're doing. It's necessary to have your finance in place in advance when buying at auction, as you will be required to pay the deposit on the spot (usually 10 per cent) and close within a reasonable period. **Note that cooling-off rights (see page 131) don't apply when buying at auction.**

**Publications:** Many estate agents produce free newspapers and magazines containing details of both old and new houses and colour prospectuses for new property developments. There are a number of free real estate magazines in Australia, including *The Homebuyer* (Published by the Real Estate Institute of Western Australia, ⌨ www.reiwa.com.au), *Australian Property Investor* (available at newsagents or by subscription from ⌨ www.apimagazine.com.au).

## RENTED ACCOMMODATION

Renting rather than buying a home is usually the better choice for anyone who's staying in Australia for a few years or less, when buying isn't usually practical, and for those who don't want the expense and restrictions involved in buying and owning a home. If you're a migrant, it's also sensible to rent for a period before buying, particularly if you're unsure of where you'll be living or working. There's also a likelihood that you will change jobs or states within your first few years in Australia (a common occurrence) or even decide to return home. Renting also allows you to become familiar with the weather, the people and the neighbourhood, before deciding whether you want to live there permanently.

There's isn't a strong rental market in Australia (although it's becoming more popular in the major cities), where most people own their own homes and renters are often made to feel like second-class citizens. Rented accommodation is scarce in most major cities, particularly in Sydney and Melbourne, where houses in the inner suburbs are rare and you may have to settle for an apartment or a house in an unpopular outer suburb. Furnished accommodation is more expensive than unfurnished and is even more difficult to find, which can be a problem if you're waiting for your furniture to arrive from overseas. Short-term (see page 372) can usually be arranged before arrival, but you shouldn't rent a property long term without inspecting it first. If you're planning to rent for more than a few weeks, it's wise to investigate the rental market in your chosen area before arriving in Australia, e.g. by studying the advertisements in Australian newspapers (which can be done via the Internet) and contacting agents. Note that some landlords don't allow pets or smokers, so check whether any restrictions apply in advance.

# Finding a Rental Property

Your success or failure in finding a suitable rental property depends on many factors, not least the type of property you're looking for (a one-bedroom apartment is easier to find than a four-bedroom detached house), how much you want to pay and the area where you wish to live. Good rental accommodation is in short supply in major cities, particularly Sydney and Melbourne, with the possible exception of luxury homes with astronomical rents. There are often 20 to 30 applicants for each vacant property in popular suburbs, particularly homes with three or more bedrooms, and you may have to take what you can get. Most people settle for something in the outer suburbs and commute to work. Note, however, that if you need to travel into a city centre (particularly Sydney) each day, you should be prepared to spend at least an hour or longer travelling each way from the outer suburbs. There are a number of ways to find a rental property, including the following:

● Ask your friends, relatives and acquaintances to help spread the word, particularly if you're looking in the area where you already live. A lot of rental properties are found by word of mouth, particularly in Sydney and Melbourne, where it's almost impossible to find somewhere with a reasonable rent unless you have connections (many rental properties change tenants without coming onto the market).

● Check the advertisements in local newspapers and magazines (see below). The best days for advertisements are Saturdays.

● Visit estate agents and letting agents. All cities and large towns have estate agents who also act as letting agents for owners (look under 'Real Estate Agents' in the yellow pages). Obtain rental lists from agents during the week or have them faxed to you at your place of work.

● Look for advertisements in shop windows and on notice boards in shopping centres, supermarkets, universities and colleges, and company offices.

● Check newsletters published by churches, clubs and expatriate organisations, and their notice boards.

To find accommodation through advertisements in local newspapers, you must be quick off the mark, particularly in the cities. Buy the newspapers as soon as they're published, if possible the night before, and start phoning 'at the crack of dawn' – even then you're likely to find a queue when you arrive to view a property in Sydney or Melbourne. You must be available to inspect properties immediately or at any time. Finding a property to rent in Sydney is like trying to find one in London or New York, where the best properties are usually found through personal contacts. Some people will go to any length to rent a property, including offering to pay above the asking price (bidding wars sometimes break out), pay six months' rent in advance and sign a contract for two or three years.

Most properties in Australian cities are let through agents, whose main task is to vet prospective tenants. Always dress smartly when visiting agents in order to create a good impression. When registering with an agent, you need two forms of identification (e.g. driving licence and passport), written references from your employer and/or previous landlord, and character references. Agents usually contact all referees and may ask why you left your previous accommodation. If you have a pet, you may need a reference from your previous landlord stating that it was clean and well-behaved, but note that animals aren't usually permitted in rental apartments. You'll need to complete a registration form and should ensure that it's complete and correct in every detail, or you will jeopardise your chances. Young people, students, the unemployed and single parents have a tough time finding anywhere at an affordable rent and, if you're on a low income or are unemployed, you'll need to prove that you can pay the rent. If you're acceptable, you may be given the keys to view a property in return for a $50 deposit and proof of identity.

## Rental Costs

Rental costs vary considerably according to the size (number of bedrooms) and quality of a property, its age and the facilities provided. Not least, rents depend on the region, city and neighbourhood. Rents are also lower in rural than urban areas. As a general rule, the further a property is from a large city or town, public transport or other facilities, the cheaper it will be. The average renter spends around $180 per week on accommodation, although in recent years rents have increased at a much faster rate than house prices in most major cities. A typical three-bedroom house costs between around $160 and $300 per week in most cities with the exception of Sydney and Melbourne, where you'll pay over $320 per week. Rental rates in Darwin can be almost as high. Approximate weekly rents for unfurnished properties are shown below:

| Type of Property | Weekly Rent ($) |
| --- | --- |
| Studio/bedsit | 90–120 |
| 1-bedroom apartment | 80–160 |
| 2-bedroom apartment | 130–230 |
| 3-bedroom apartment | 150–300 |
| 2-bedroom house | 130–300 |
| 3-bedroom house | 160–320 |

The lower rents quoted above apply to modest homes in the less expensive outer suburbs of cities such as Adelaide and Perth. The upper prices apply to outer suburbs in more expensive cities such as Sydney, Melbourne, Brisbane and Darwin. They don't include properties located in the central business district (CBD) of major cities or in exclusive residential areas, for which the sky's the limit. It may be possible to find cheaper, older apartments and houses for rent, but they're rare, generally small, and don't contain the standard fixtures and fittings of a modern home.

Most letting agencies and estate agents charge tenants a fee of two weeks' rent for a one-year lease and one week's rent for a six-month lease, which are legal maximums. Usually, you're expected to pay one month's rent in advance, depending on the type of property and the rental agreement, plus a bond (see below) which is held against damages. Tenants must also pay a fee for the lease document, plus a deposit for electricity and gas. Beware of hidden extras such as a fee for connecting the gas, electricity or telephone (or a refundable deposit).

**Bond:** When renting property in Australia, a bond (deposit) must be paid in advance. The bond is usually equal to four weeks' rent but is normally higher for furnished than unfurnished properties and can be as much as eight months' rent for a luxury furnished property (the bond is unlimited in NSW on fully furnished properties costing over $250 a week). It's lodged with the Rental Bond Board together with a copy of the inspection (condition) report which details the condition of the home plus an inventory. The inspection and inventory must usually be done within seven days of taking possession and tenants receive a copy signed by both the tenant and the agent. The property is re-inspected when you leave and, if necessary, deductions are made for cleaning and repairs, although there's no deduction for ordinary wear and tear. Information regarding rental bonds can be obtained from ☎ freecall 1800-422 021.

It's best to pay your rent by cheque or standing order, for which you should (by law) receive a receipt from your landlord. Rents are controlled in some states, although this doesn't usually extend to new properties or tenancies after a certain date. Your contract may include details of when your rent will be reviewed or increased, if applicable (the rent for a fixed-term tenancy can be increased only when provision for an increase is included in the lease contract). You must be given notice in writing of any rent increases and a rent tribunal can review excessive rent increases and the existing rent if services are reduced.

# Rental Contracts

When you find a suitable house or apartment to rent, you should insist on a written contract with the owner or agent, which is called a tenancy agreement. In some states such as NSW and Victoria, a standard form must be used by law and in others there are usually minimum conditions which cannot be reduced by landlords. The Agreement for Tenancy states the responsibilities of both parties and provides a fair balance between the landlord and tenant, although you should read it carefully before signing it. Apart from self-catering holiday accommodation (see page 372), renting a house or apartment usually requires a commitment of six or 12 months with an option to renew.

The owner is responsible for property rates (taxes) and unit service charges, and the tenant for utility costs, unless otherwise agreed. Tenants must take good care of the property, although the landlord is required to maintain it in a habitable condition and ensure that basic services such as water and sewerage are in order. If the landlord refuses to carry out urgent and necessary repairs within a reasonable period of time, you can arrange to have them done and send him the bill, although you mustn't deduct the cost from the rent. If you rent a house, garden and swimming pool, maintenance costs may be included in the rent.

If you wish to vacate a property before your lease expires, you're liable to pay the rent up to the end of your lease period, although you may be able to find someone to take over the lease and repay your bond (check whether this is possible with your agent or landlord). If you give the landlord adequate notice of termination (usually 21 days), he should try to minimise his loss by advertising and re-letting the property. If you have a verbal contract (termed a periodic tenancy) on a weekly or monthly basis, a week's or a month's notice is sufficient. If you're a tenant with a verbal or written agreement, you cannot be evicted or be forced to leave unless your landlord obtains an eviction order. In order to be evicted you must be in breach of your lease, e.g. by failing to pay the rent, damaging the property, sub-letting, renovating without permission or refusing the landlord entry. A landlord cannot evict you by removing your belongings and changing the locks, or forcing you to leave by cutting off services. At the end of a fixed-term residential tenancy agreement, the landlord can terminate the agreement by giving 60 days' notice before the end of the agreement. The landlord may repossess a property for his own use or to sell it with vacant possession. He isn't required to his reason for terminating the contract, although there may be grounds for a tenant to appeal to the local Residential Tenancy Tribunal, e.g. age, poor health or lack of alternative accommodation.

A renting guide is available from estate agents explaining the rights and responsibilities of tenants and landlords. Some people (e.g. Asians, coloureds and students) may encounter discrimination, although it's illegal under the Federal Discrimination Act. Most states have a Residential Tenancy Tribunal to investigate complaints by landlords and tenants, disputes over bonds, excessive rents, repairs and evictions. You can also obtain advice at a tenants' advice centre, community legal centre, consumer affairs office, Citizens' Advice Bureau or from the Legal Aid Commission. Most large cities also have a tenants' union hotline. The local Office of Fair Trading in many states publishes a *Renting Guide* or *Tenants' Rights Manual* (in NSW see 🖳 www.fairtrading.nsw.gov.au).

## Single Accommodation

Finding accommodation that doesn't break the bank is a huge problem for young single people and students (and anyone not earning a small fortune). For many, the solution is a bedsit, lodgings or shared accommodation. If you're seeking inexpensive accommodation, you may find it more difficult in cities when the new term starts and students are looking for housing. Single accommodation covers a broad spectrum, including hostels, guest houses, lodgings, bed and breakfast and inexpensive hotels, although these usually provide only temporary accommodation. Don't expect any luxuries in inexpensive single accommodation, as the standard is generally poor and is usually at its worst in areas with high demand. You must be over 18 to hold a tenancy agreement and young people usually find it harder to find a rental property than mature people, because of the prejudice that the young are unreliable, noisy, poor, itinerant and untidy (etc.).

There's a huge demand for student accommodation (often from overseas students) in the major cities, particularly in Sydney and Melbourne. In some cities, students have saturated the rental market and foreign students who are prepared to pay more for accommodation than Australian students have helped drive up rents and exacerbate the problem.

**Bedsits:** If you prefer to live on your own but don't want to pay a lot of rent (who does?), the solution may be a bedsit or studio apartment. A bedsit usually consists of a furnished room in an old house, where you live, eat, sleep and in some cases also cook. If separate cooking facilities are provided, you must usually share them with someone else (or a number of people). You must also usually share a bathroom and toilet, provide your own linen (sheets, blankets and towels), and do your own laundry and cleaning. Bedsits offer privacy but can be lonely and depressing. A bedsit costs from around $85 a week for singles and from $110 a week for doubles. Slightly up-market from a bedsit is a flatlet or studio, which may have its own bath or shower and toilet, and sometimes a separate kitchen or kitchenette (a tiny kitchen). The rent for a studio apartment is around 50 per cent more than for a bedsit.

**Lodgings:** Another possibility is to find lodgings in a private home, which is becoming increasingly common as many people have been forced to take in lodgers to pay their mortgages. This is similar to bed and breakfast accommodation (see page 371) except that you're usually treated as a member of the family and your rent normally includes half-board (breakfast and an evening meal). In lodgings you have less freedom than in a bedsit or studio and are required to eat at fixed times but will at least have some company. Lodgings are often arranged by schools and colleges for foreign students.

A boarding house is similar to lodgings, where the owner takes in a number of lodgers and may provide half-board or cooking facilities. The rent is around the same as for bedsits. Note that a boarder, paying guest or lodger is termed a 'licensee' in law and has fewer rights than a tenant, although it's often difficult to make a distinction. This applies to anyone lodging with the owner and sharing the bathroom and kitchen. If you're a 'licensee', your landlord cannot increase your rent without your consent, although he can ask you to leave at any time (but must give you adequate time to pack and remove your belongings).

**Shared Accommodation:** Sharing is another answer to high rents, particularly in major towns and cities, and is popular among students and the young. It usually involves sharing the kitchen, bathroom, living room and dining room, but may include sharing a bedroom. All bills are usually also shared (in addition to the rent), including electricity, gas and telephone, and in some cases food bills. Some landlords may include electricity, gas and water in the rent. The cleaning and general upkeep of the house or apartment (and the cooking) are also usually shared. As always when living with others, there are advantages and disadvantages to shared accommodation, and its success depends on the participants' ability to live together.

If you rent a property with the intention of sharing, make sure that it's permitted in your contract. The law regarding flat-sharing is complicated and it's simpler when one person is the tenant and sub-lets to the others, which must be permitted by the tenant's agreement. It's possible for all sharers to be joint tenants with one tenancy agreement or individual tenants with individual tenancy agreements. Whatever the arrangement, you should have a single rent book and pay the rent in a lump sum. It's usually the occupants' responsibility to replace flatmates who leave during the tenancy. If you're seeking long-term accommodation, check the duration of the lease.

The cost of sharing a furnished apartment varies considerably according to its size, location and amenities. A rough guide is from $85 (single) to $110 (double) per week with your own bedroom, or up to $210 with your own bathroom. Often you'll be sharing with the owners, which can sometimes be a bit inhibiting, as many couples buy a three-bedroom house and let one or two bedrooms to help pay the mortgage. Flat-sharing is particularly common in major cities, where many newspapers and magazines contain advertisements for flat-sharers, e.g. the *Sydney Morning Herald* and the *Melbourne Age*. Note, however, that 'broad-minded girl/guy' is usually code for 'we are lesbian or homosexual'. There are also agents in major cities where you pay a registration fee of $100 to $150 and sharers are matched with others with similar interests.

# GARAGE OR PARKING SPACE

A garage or parking space may not be provided when you rent or buy an apartment, although most modern houses have a single or double garage and sometimes room for further parking in the driveway. New houses and blocks of apartments are likely to have adequate parking for both residents and visitors. Note that, when buying a property, the cost will almost always include the garage or garage space if a property has one, i.e. it won't be sold separately as in some other countries. If you live in a town or city, it's often difficult to find an apartment or house with a garage or parking space, although it may be possible to rent a parking space in a private car park or a lock-up garage locally. A garage is useful, particularly in areas with a high incidence of car theft (anywhere in most cities).

Free on-street parking is often difficult or impossible to find in cities and large towns, although you may be able to obtain a resident's parking permit for on-street parking. In general, off-street parking in Australia is in short supply, particularly in cities and older residential areas, where houses and units were built without garages or off-street parking areas.

# MOVING HOUSE

Shipping your belongings to Australia takes just a few weeks from Europe or North America, although it can be two to three months from the time your belongings are collected to the time they arrive at your new home in Australia. Unless you plan well in advance, you'll almost certainly arrive in Australia before your belongings. Obtain at least three written quotes before choosing a shipper and check what the extra cost will be if you need to increase the load later, as it isn't unknown for original estimates to spiral wildly. Note that some companies routinely increase the price after everything has been packed, ostensibly because more was included than was stated in the estimate. A removal company (called a removalist in Australia) will usually send a representative to carry out an inspection and provide an estimate. There are numerous advertisements from shipping companies in newspapers published specifically for migrants such as *Australian News* and *Australian Outlook* in the UK (see **Appendix A**).

If possible, always use an international removal company that's a member of an association such as the International Federation of Furniture Removers (FIDI), the Overseas Moving Network International (OMNI) or the Association of International Removers (AIR). Members usually subscribe to a payment guarantee scheme, whereby if a member company fails to fulfil its commitments to a customer, the removal will be completed at the agreed cost by another company or you'll receive a full refund. Removal companies will also pack your belongings and provide packing cases and special containers, although this is naturally more expensive than doing it yourself (ask how they pack fragile and valuable items). Check whether the cost of packing cases, materials and insurance are included in a quote.

You can send your effects by full container load (FCL) or part load (groupage), which is cheaper but usually takes longer. FCL shipments are loaded into an individual container holding around 1,000ft$\Delta$ (28m$\Delta$). A shipment of around 800ft$\Delta$ (22.5m$\Delta$) is cheaper to send as groupage. Obtain a separate quotation for excess items that won't fit into the container. If the destination in Australia isn't within 30 miles

(48km) of the port of arrival, you may need to pay an extra charge for door to door delivery. There may also be extra charges in Australia such as storage and quarantine (if necessary). Ask about possible extra charges in advance. Note that most international removers expect to be paid before your household goods are shipped, although some allow you to pay when you take delivery. The cost of moving your house contents from your previous country of residence to Australia may be paid for by your Australian employer.

Before shipping any household articles to Australia, check whether they're worth taking, e.g. many people take electrical apparatus that's incompatible and furniture which is unsuitable or simply isn't needed in their new home. It isn't worthwhile taking TVs (see page 140), refrigerators (which are usually too small), cookers (provided) and wardrobes (which are built-in in most homes). If you're moving from a country with a cold climate, bear in mind that furniture and furnishings must be suitable for a hot climate (unless you're heading for Tasmania). You should carefully consider the cost of packing and shipping large items to Australia, as it may be cheaper to sell them and buy new items on arrival. Generally, you should take possessions with you if it's cheaper than buying them in Australia, taking into account the cost of shipping large items. Good quality furniture and antiques are worth taking, as are small electrical appliance if the voltage is the same as Australia (240V).

If you pack your belongings yourself, you'll need to provide an inventory for Australian customs. If you do your own packing, don't use straw but wood, wool or paper, and don't include any prohibited or illegal items (see page 113), as customs and quarantine checks can be rigorous and penalties severe. On the day of the move, make sure there's room for the removal van or truck to park, if necessary by asking the police to cordon off an area outside your home. Give the shipping company a telephone number and an address in Australia through which you can be contacted, and try to get a relative or friend to handle any problems in the country from which your belongings are being shipped.

**Be sure to fully insure your household contents during removal with a well established insurance company** – you aren't required to use the one recommended by the removal company, but it may be sensible to avoid a dispute between the remover and insurer. You should have an all-risks marine insurance policy from domicile to domicile, which is underwritten by an established and solid insurance company. It's wise to make a photographic or video record of any valuables for insurance purposes. If you need to make a claim, be sure to read the small print, as all companies require you to make claims within a limited period. Note also that your insurance cover may differ according to whether items were packed by you or by the shipper. Send a claim by registered mail. **If you need to put your household effects into storage, it's imperative to have them fully insured, as warehouses have been known to burn down.** Don't forget to insure your home contents from the day you move in (see page 319).

Although most people wouldn't consider doing their own house move, if you have only personal effects to transport locally within Australia, you can hire a van by the hour, half-day or day (small local rental companies are cheapest). Many removal companies sell packing boxes in various sizes and hire or sell removal equipment (trolleys, straps, etc.) for those who feel up to doing their own house move. See also the checklists contained in **Chapter 20**.

# INVENTORY

When moving into a property that you've purchased, you should check that the previous owners haven't absconded with anything that was included in the purchase as a fixture or fitting or anything which you specifically paid for, e.g. carpets, light fittings, curtains, fitted cupboards, kitchen appliances or doors. One of the most important tasks on moving into a rented house or apartment is to complete an inventory of the contents and an inspection report on its condition. This includes the condition of fixtures and fittings, the state of furniture and carpets (if furnished), the cleanliness and state of the decoration, and anything missing or in need of repair. A rental property should be spotless when you move in, as this is what your landlord will expect when you move out.

An inventory is provided by your landlord or a letting agent and may include every single item in a furnished property (down to the number of teaspoons). The inspection and inventory must usually be done within seven days of taking possession and you'll receive a copy signed by both you and the agent or landlord. A copy is also lodged with the Rental Bond Board (see page 137). The property is re-inspected when you leave and, if necessary, deductions are made from the bond for cleaning and repairs, although there's no deduction for ordinary wear and tear.

Note the reading on your meters (electricity, gas, water) and check that you aren't overcharged on your first bill. Meters should be read by the relevant authorities before you move in, which you may need to organise yourself.

# HOME SECURITY

House-breaking and burglary are endemic in Australia's major cities, where many homes are broken into a number of times a year, often within a short time. When moving into a new home, it's sensible to replace locks (or lock barrels), as you have no idea how many keys are in circulation for the existing locks. Note that, if you want to change the locks in a rented property, you may need to obtain approval from your landlord or agent, and you must also give him a copy of all keys. In addition to new door locks, you may wish to install an alarm, window locks, shutters, grilles, security lights and other deterrents. According to crime statistics, entry in around 40 per cent of home burglaries is via an unlocked door or window, so always ensure they're locked, even when vacating your home for a short period (doors should be locked even when your home is occupied). Don't let anyone into your home unless you're certain who they are, particularly at night. External doors can be fitted with a spy-hole, so that you can check a visitor's identity before opening the door. **Remember, prevention is better than cure, as people who are burgled rarely recover their property.**

A good alarm system is probably the best way to scare off thieves and it may also reduce your home contents insurance (see page 319). Some security companies provide home security systems connected to a Central Monitoring Station (CMS). When a sensor (e.g. smoke or forced entry) detects an emergency or a panic button is pushed, a signal is sent automatically to the CMS which is manned 24 hours a day. Always choose a system that suits your house and requirements.

Some properties are fitted with high security door locks, which are individually numbered and for which extra keys cannot be cut at a local store. Make sure you have full details from the previous owner or your landlord so that you can get additional keys cut or change the lock barrels. No matter how good your door and window locks, a thief can usually break in if he's determined enough, often by simply breaking a window (although you can fit steel security blinds) or by punching a hole in a wall or the roof in remote areas. Try to deter thieves by ensuring that your house is always well lit, particularly when nobody is at home, when it's also sensible to leave a TV or radio on (a timer switch can be used to switch radios, TVs and lights on and off at random). **It's always wise to give the impression that a house is occupied, particularly when it isn't!** Some people keep a large dog (a miniature poodle isn't much good as a deterrent) to guard their homes when they're out. The Australian Consumers Association (see page 443) publishes an excellent book entitled *Safe and Secure – A Guide to Household and Car Security* by Richard Upton.

**Smoke Alarms:** An important aspect of home security is making sure that you have early warning of a fire, which is done by installing smoke detectors. A battery-operated smoke detector costs from around $10. One should be fitted on each floor, but not in kitchens or bathrooms (where they will go off every time you switch on the cooker or shower). All new and renovated buildings in Australia must have a smoke alarm installed but this isn't compulsory for existing buildings, where only a small percentage are fitted with smoke detectors, although it has been estimated that the death toll from fires would be reduced by half (plus a drastic reduction in the number of injuries) if all homes had them. Smoke alarms should be tested weekly to ensure that the batteries aren't exhausted. You can also install a gas detector, which activates an alarm when a gas leak is detected. Note that, from January 2000, all South Australian home owners must install smoke detectors or face a $750 fine.

# UTILITIES

Utilities is the collective name given to electricity, gas and water supplies. Electricity and gas are used for cooking and heating in cities and towns throughout Australia, and it's common for homes to have both electricity and gas. Each state and territory has its own Energy Commission, which have traditionally been owned and administered by local governments. However, ACT, NSW, Queensland and Victoria will deregulate and privatise their electricity industry from 1 January 2002, and South Australia and Western Australia will follow suit a year later. Privatisation has enabled business users to shop around for electricity (and save $millions a year), even from distributors in neighbouring states connected to the same grid system (Tasmania, Western Australia and the Northern Territory *aren't* linked in a grid with the rest of the country or neighbouring states). There are a number of electricity generating and distribution companies in most states. Australia has a non-nuclear policy and has no nuclear power stations, despite being a major producer of uranium.

# Electricity

The electricity supply in Australia is 240/250 volts AC, with a frequency of 50 Hertz (cycles). If you move into a new home in Australia, the electricity supply may have been turned off by the local electricity company. To have the electricity reconnected and the meter read, for which you should allow at least two days, you must contact your local electricity company and complete a registration form. There's usually a charge for connection and a security deposit, e.g. $100. You need to contact your electricity company to get a final reading when you vacate your home. Power cuts are rare in most parts of Australia, although fairly frequent in some areas.

**Power Rating:** Electrical equipment rated at 110 volts (for example, from the USA) requires a converter or a step-down transformer to convert it to 240 volts, although some electrical appliances (e.g. electric razors and hair dryers) are fitted with a 110/240 volt switch. Check for the switch, which may be located inside the casing, and make sure it's switched to 240 volts *before* connecting it to the power supply. Converters can be used for heating appliances but transformers, which are available from most electrical retailers, are required for motorised appliances (they can also be purchased secondhand). Add the wattage of the devices you intend to connect to a transformer and make sure that its power rating *exceeds* this sum.

Generally, all small, high-wattage, electrical appliances such as kettles, toasters, heaters and irons, need large transformers. Motors in large appliances such as cookers, refrigerators, washing machines, dryers and dishwashers will need replacing or fitting with a large transformer. In most cases, it's simpler to buy new appliances in Australia, which are of good quality and reasonably priced. Note also that the dimensions of Australian cookers, microwave ovens, refrigerators, washing machines, dryers and dishwashers, differ from those in some other countries. All electrical goods sold in Australia must conform to Australian safety standards. If you wish to buy electrical appliances such as a cooker or refrigerator, you should shop around, as prices vary considerably (choose those that have a high energy efficiency rating, which are cheaper to run). Refrigerators/freezers in Australia are normally 'tropicised' or fan assisted to cope with the high average temperatures, which is why it isn't usually worthwhile bringing one with you.

**Frequency Rating:** A problem with some electrical equipment is the frequency rating, which in some countries, e.g. the USA, is designed to run at 60 Hertz and not Australia's 50 Hertz. Electrical equipment *without* a motor is generally unaffected by the drop in frequency to 50Hertz (except TVs, see page 182). Equipment with a motor may run with a 20 per cent drop in speed, but washing machines, cookers, clocks, record players and tape recorders are unusable in Australia if they aren't designed for 50 cycle operation. To find out, look at the label on the back of the equipment. If it says 50/60 Hertz, it should be okay. If it says 60Hertz, you can try it anyway, **but first ensure that the voltage is correct as outlined above.** If the equipment runs too slowly, seek advice from the manufacturer or the retailer. For example, you may be able to obtain a special pulley for a tape deck or turntable to compensate for the drop in speed. Bear in mind that the transformers and motors of electrical devices designed to run at 60Hertz will run hotter at 50Hertz, so make sure that equipment has sufficient space around it for cooling.

**Fuses:** Most apartments and all houses have their own fuse boxes, which are usually of the circuit breaker type in modern homes. When a circuit is overloaded, the circuit breaker trips to the OFF position. When replacing or repairing fuses of any kind, if the same fuse continues to blow, contact an electrician and **never fit a fuse of a higher rating than specified, even as a temporary measure.** When replacing fuses, don't rely on the blown fuse as a guide, as it may have been wrong. If you use an electric lawnmower or power tools outside your home or in your garage, you should have a Residual Current Device (RCD) installed. This can detect current changes of as little as a thousandth of an amp and in the event of a fault (or the cable being cut) will switch off the power in around 0.04 seconds.

**Plugs:** Unless you've come from New Zealand, all your plugs will require changing, or a lot of expensive adapters will be required. Australian (and New Zealand) plugs have three pins: two diagonally slanting flat pins above one straight (earth) pin. Plugs aren't fused. Some electrical appliances are earthed and have a three-core flex – you must *never* use a two-pin plug with a three-core flex. **Always make sure that a plug is correctly and securely wired, as bad wiring can prove fatal.** For maximum safety, electrical appliances should be turned off at the main wall point when not in use.

**Bulbs:** Electric light bulbs (called globes in Australia) are of the Edison type with a bayonet, not a screw fitting. To insert a bulb, push it in and turn it clockwise approximately 5mm. Low-energy light bulbs are also available and are more expensive than ordinary bulbs, although they save money by their longer life and reduced energy consumption. Bulbs for non-standard electrical appliances (i.e. appliances not made for the Australian market) such as refrigerators, lamps and sewing machines may not be available in Australia, so bring extras with you. Plug adapters for imported lamps and other electrical items can be difficult to find in Australia, so you should bring a number of adapters and extension cords with you, which can be fitted with Australian plugs.

**Safety:** Only a qualified electrician should install electrical wiring and fittings, particularly in connection with fuse boxes. Always ask for a quotation for any work in advance and check the identity of anyone claiming to be an electricity company employee (or any kind of 'serviceman') by asking to see an identity card and checking with his office. Special controls can be fitted to many appliances to make their use easier for the disabled and the blind or partially sighted (e.g. studded or Braille controls).

**Cost & Bills:** Electricity charges vary considerably according to the state and local competition, e.g. Energy Australia (Sydney) charge 10.32¢ per kilowatt hour (kWh), plus a standard service charge (e.g. $18 to $19 per quarter). Some companies offer a range of tariffs which may include peak, off-peak and weekend rates (some tariffs require a special meter to be installed). The biggest savings can be made when using a night rate with electric storage water heaters. Many metropolitan households use gas for cooking and heating and some 5 per cent (300,000) Australian homes use solar energy (see page 148) for heating water. Bills usually show meter readings, the kWh used, charges and a daily energy/cost comparison. There's no tax on electricity bills. Customers are billed quarterly and payment can be made at post offices, certain banks, by phone (with a credit/EFTPOS card) and by mail (by cheque).

# Gas

Australia has vast natural gas reserves and it's available in all of Australia's major cities from companies such as Australian Gas Limited (AGL). The gas industry was deregulated in July 2001 in ACT, New South Wales, Queensland, South Australia and Victoria, and Western Australia will follow suit in July 2002. Gas is popular for cooking (it costs less than electricity), although it's less commonly used to provide heating and hot water (although gas heaters are becoming more popular). Note that there may be no gas supply in older homes and modern houses may also be all electric. If you're looking for a rental property and want to cook by gas, make sure it already has a gas supply (some houses have an unused gas service pipe). In country areas without piped gas, you can buy a cooker that uses bottled gas. If you buy a house without a gas supply, you can arrange with your local gas company to install a line between your home and a nearby gas main (provided there's one within a reasonable distance, or the cost will be prohibitive).

If a home already has a gas supply, simply contact your local gas company to have the gas supply reconnected or transferred to your name (there's a connection charge). Usually a security deposit (e.g. $100) is payable and there may also be a payment to establish an account (e.g. $20). You must contact your local gas company to get a final reading when vacating a property. If you need to purchase gas appliances, such as a gas cooker or fire, you should shop around as prices vary considerably. Note that special controls can be fitted to many appliances to make them easier to use by the disabled and the blind or partially sighted (studded or Braille controls). Gas tariffs vary but are around 1.3¢ per megajoule and there's a quarterly supply maintenance fee of $27.27. Rates vary from city to city (or even its suburbs) and region to region and are more expensive in remote areas. There's no tax on gas bills. Customers are billed quarterly and payment can be made at post offices, certain banks, by phone (with a credit/EFTPOS card) and by mail (by cheque).

Gas central heating boilers, water heaters and fires should be checked annually. Always ask for a quotation for any work and check the identity of anyone claiming to be a gas company employee (or any kind of 'serviceman') by asking to see an identity card and checking with his office. **Note that gas installations and appliances can leak and cause explosions or kill you while you sleep. If you suspect a gas leak, first check to see if a gas tap has been left on or a pilot light has gone out.** If not, there's probably a leak, either in your home or in a nearby gas pipeline. Ring your local gas service centre immediately and **vacate your home as quickly as possible.** Gas leaks are extremely rare and explosions caused by leaks even rarer (although often spectacular and therefore widely reported). Nevertheless, it pays to be careful. You can buy an electric-powered gas detector which activates an alarm when a gas leak is detected.

# Water

Each city and major region in Australia has a water board operated by the local government. Water, or rather the lack of it, is a major concern in Australia and the price paid for all those sunny days. Australia is the world's driest country, and country areas are hit by frequent droughts. Many country homes have a bore (well) that comes in handy when there are water restrictions, which may restrict homeowners to watering their gardens once every three days before dawn or after dusk (to reduce evaporation). Many homes also have rain water tanks that can be used to water gardens and for baths and showers. In some states there are frequent water restrictions such as sprinkler bans during the day, e.g. between 9am and 6pm or from 8am until 8pm in Western Australia, although there may be no restriction on hand held hoses. To reduce water consumption, many people plant mainly native Australian plants requiring little water and use wood chips or gravel as an alternative to lawns. **In Australia, water is a precious resource and not something simply to pour down the drain!**

When moving into a new home, you should enquire where the main stopcock is, so that you can turn off the water supply in an emergency. If the water stops running for any reason, you should turn off the supply to prevent flooding from an open tap when the supply starts again. Contact your local water company if you have a problem reconnecting your water supply, as it could have been turned off by them. If you need a plumber, e.g. as a result of a burst pipe, you may be able to get a recommendation or a list of names from your local water company. Before calling a plumber, always ask the minimum call-out charge. Note that in some states (e.g. Victoria), water companies no longer inspect work carried out by plumbers, who certify their own work. Plumbers must be licensed and have indemnity, and work valued at over $500 must have a certificate of compliance. New sewerage systems have been installed in many areas, the bulk of the cost being paid for by residents, irrespective of whether they want or need the improvements.

**Charges & Bills:** There was traditionally a fixed charge for water in Australia based on the gross rental or rateable value of a property. However, water is now metered in metropolitan areas, and most households pay for their actual consumption rather than a flat fee. When consumption is metered, you may be charged around 95¢ per 1,000 litres (kl). Bills also contain a water service charge, e.g. $20 per quarter. Water bills may include water, sewerage and drainage and may show your average daily use in litres. Note, however, that in some areas, e.g. Sydney and coastal districts, sewerage and drainage are charged separately, and quarterly charges can be high, e.g. $99. Bills can usually be paid in a number of instalments, e.g. two or four per year, and can be paid at post offices and certain banks (in cash or by cheque), by phone (with a credit/EFTPOS card) and by mail (by cheque).

**Quality:** Although Australian drinking water is among the cleanest and safest in the world, the quality varies and it can taste terrible in areas with high mineral deposits. It's possible to have a water purifier fitted to a drinking water tap to improve the taste. Fluoride is added to water in some cities. Australian water doesn't usually contain limescale, so it isn't necessary to use a decalcification liquid to keep your kettle, iron and other apparatus and utensils clean. Contaminated water in garden hoses and domestic swimming pools can cause amoebic meningitis, so it's important to clean pools and hoses thoroughly and frequently.

# HEATING & AIR-CONDITIONING

Central heating isn't common in northern, eastern and western Australia, as the climate doesn't usually warrant it. In these regions, a portable electric fan heater, an electric fire or radiator/column heater, or a gas fire is sufficient to heat most rooms during the wet or winter seasons. Both gas and electric heaters and hot water systems have an energy efficiency rating. Central heating, double glazing and good insulation are more common in new homes in southern states, where many people consider them essential. Central heating systems may be powered by oil, gas, electricity or solid fuel, and luxury homes may have a combined, thermostatically controlled heating and cooling (air-conditioning) system. Many homes have storage heaters, which store heat from electricity supplied at a cheaper, off-peak rate overnight and release it to heat the home during the day. In country and remote areas, where open fires and stoves are fairly common, solid fuels such as coal and wood are often used (and may also provide hot water). Whatever form of heating you use, you should ensure that your home has good insulation, without which up to 60 per cent of heat is lost through the walls and roof.

**Solar Heating:** Solar heating is popular in Australia and is most commonly used to provide hot water, although dual solar hot water and heating systems (with a hot-air solar radiator) are available. These are usually combined with an electric booster or gas heating system, as solar energy cannot be relied upon year-round for hot water and heating requirements, e.g. on overcast days. The use of solar energy is most common in remote areas. Some 5 per cent of Australian homes (300,000) use solar energy for heating water, including around 25 per cent of homes in WA and 60 per cent in the Northern Territory (average savings are around $200 a year compared with electricity). Although currently relatively expensive to install, breakthroughs in solar cell technology are set to increase its efficiency and reduce the cost dramatically in the next decade. Solar energy can meet up to 90 per cent of normal household heating needs.

**Humidity:** Note that central heating dries the air and may cause your family to develop coughs and other ailments. Those who find dry air unpleasant can increase the humidity by adding moisture to the air with a humidifier, vaporiser, steam generator or even a water container made of porous ceramic. These range from simple water containers hung from radiators to electric or battery-operated devices. Humidifiers that don't generate steam should be disinfected occasionally with a special liquid available from pharmacies (to prevent nasty diseases). In regions where high humidity is a problem, you can buy a dehumidifier to re-circulate room air and reduce humidity.

**Air-conditioning:** In most regions of Australia, air-conditioning is a blessed relief in summer, while in northern and western Australia it's considered essential at almost any time of the year (also in cars). It's still considered something of a luxury in southern states such as Victoria and New South Wales, where it's usually confined to luxury properties, although you won't consider it a luxury when the temperature soars above 40°C (104°F)! Most business premises are air-conditioned throughout Australia. Modern homes in tropical areas often have a ducted air-conditioning system powered by electricity. You can choose between a huge variety of air-conditioners, fixed or moveable, indoor and outdoor installations, with high or low power. An air-conditioning system with a heat pump provides cooling in summer and heating in winter.

Most window-mounted air-conditioning units have a choice of fan speeds and the fan can usually be switched on separately from the cooling system. The cooling system can be adjusted for temperature and units often have a vent that can be opened to allow air into the room when they aren't in use. When using air-conditioning, all windows and outside doors should obviously be closed. Note that, if you suffer from asthma or respiratory problems, air-conditioning can exacerbate your condition. Many homes have electric pedestal and/or ceiling fans to provide cooling during the summer.

You can have a study made of your home's heating and cooling requirements and the cost, taking into account the climate and the current insulation and equipment installed. An engineer will produce a report detailing the most-effective means of insulating, heating and cooling your home, and provide a number of cost estimates. The Australian Consumers Association (see page 443) publish an excellent book entitled *Warm House Cool House* by Nick Hollo.

# 6.

# POST OFFICE SERVICES

Australia Post (AP) handles over 4 billion articles of mail per year (11 million per day, a large percentage of which is junk mail) and provides one of the best postal services in the world in terms of cost, speed and reliability. AP underwent deregulation in 1994, when parts of the mail business were opened to private competitors. However, it has since gone from strength to strength and is a highly profitable and well-run business. Although there are plans to completely deregulate AP in the future, a date has yet to be fixed.

There's a post office in most main towns in Australia (a total of over 4,000), offering a wide range of services, most of which are described in this chapter. In country and outback towns, postal services are provided by an Australia Post agency (e.g. a general store, petrol station or café/restaurant) licensed to provide most of the services offered by a main post office.

The post office provides a wide range of services, which, in addition to the usual services provided in most countries, include a number of unique services. Services include stamps, poste restante mail, telegrams, faxpost, money orders, giroPost, bill payment, passport applications, and gifts (e.g. at Christmas from AP shops or by mail order). Australia Post also sells stationery and office products (they publish a catalogue), and orders with a minimum value of $50 are delivered free of charge almost anywhere in the country. It also operates the country's largest over-the-counter bill payment service (Telstra, income tax, gas, electricity, council rates, water rates, Medibank and insurance) and some 20 per cent of consumer bills are paid at AP's retail outlets. AP handles over 130 million financial transactions a year through its electronic retail network and provides one of the country's largest banking services (giroPost). Credit cards can be used to pay for purchases costing over $10.

Post boxes in Australia are red with a white stripe and modern mailboxes look like litter bins, although there are still some Victorian 'receiving pillars' around. In cities and large towns, there are express 'gold' post boxes (see page 154). However, post boxes are scarce in rural areas and you may need to take your post to a post office or agency. In major towns and metropolitan areas, there are mail deliveries once a day, Mondays to Fridays, while in remote areas deliveries may be restricted to just once a week (although a twice-weekly service has been introduced in some areas) and deliveries can be affected by the weather, as mail is usually delivered by air. In the outback, mail must usually be collected from a local post office or agency. There are no weekend deliveries anywhere in Australia.

The post office parcel delivery and courier services have been privatised in recent years, although AP maintains a monopoly on letters weighing up to 250g. Private operators must charge a minimum of $1.80, which is four times the AP rate for a standard letter. There's a thriving courier business in Australia, particularly in the major cities, where 24-hour domestic and international courier services are provided by many companies, including Allied Express, Ansett Courier, DHL, FedEx, Mayne Nickless and TNT. AP also operates a domestic courier service, Australia Air Express, with Qantas. Many more companies (such as Salmat and Streetfile) just deliver locally, e.g. within a particular city. In major cities, there are companies such as Mail Boxes Etc. which provide a wide range of mail services (e.g. mail boxes) as well as courier, fax, telephone and business services.

The post office produces a wealth of free brochures concerning postal rates and special services, most of which are available from any post office. A general *Post Charges* booklet contains details of most services and rates, and a comprehensive

*Post Guide* ($50) is available for businesses. Information about Australia Post's services is also available via the Internet (⌨ www.auspost.com.au).

## BUSINESS HOURS

Post office business hours in Australia are usually from 9am to 5pm, Mondays to Fridays, and from 9am to 12am on Saturdays. In major cities, general post offices may have slightly longer business hours, e.g. Sydney general post office is open from 8.15am to 5.30pm Mondays to Fridays and from 8.30am to noon on Saturdays. Post offices in major towns don't close at lunchtime. In country and outback areas, Australia Post agencies generally keep the same hours as post offices, but may close for an hour during lunch or shut earlier in the afternoon. They usually open on Saturday mornings and have extended opening hours on some evenings.

## LETTER POST

AP provides a single domestic mail service, and there has been a price freeze at 45¢ for standard (small) letters since January 1992. Domestic mail charges also apply to Christmas Island (Indian Ocean), Cocos (Keeling) Islands, the Australian Antarctic Territories and Norfolk Island. Domestic mail is sent by air between states or to remote areas within Australia. Domestic Christmas greeting cards posted in November and December are charged at a reduced rate of 40¢.

Australia Post delivers over 93 per cent of metropolitan letters the next day and a further 5 per cent one day later. Local mail is usually delivered the next day and interstate mail to major towns and cities in one to two days. However, the post office has a worse record for deliveries to country locations, which officially take two days in the same state and up to four days interstate. The airmail service is fast and reliable, airmail letters taking a maximum of eight days to most destinations (three to five days to Britain and six to seven days to the USA), depending on where they're posted and the destination. Compensation (at AP's discretion) up to $50 is paid for the loss or damage of mail upon production of a receipt or other proof of posting.

## Domestic Mail

There are two sets of rates for domestic mail, depending on whether a letter is 'small' or 'large'. Small letters must be rectangular with the length at least 1.414 times the width (AP likes to be precise!), a maximum size of 122mm x 237mm, a maximum thickness of 5mm and a maximum weight of 250g. Large letters sent by ordinary post must be rectangular, a maximum size of 260mm x 360mm, a maximum thickness of 20mm and a maximum weight of 500g. Domestic mail rates are as follows:

|  |  |
|---|---|
| Small letters (up to 250g) | 45¢ |
| Large letters: | |
| from 50 to 125g | 98¢ |
| from 125 to 250g | $1.47 |
| from 250 to 500g | $2.36 |

Over 500g, parcel post rates apply (see page 157).

The following points apply to domestic mail services:

- As well as at post offices, stamps can be purchased at hotels, motels, stores, newsagents and from vending machines. Most machines issue fixed-value stamps, although new electronic machines print gummed postage 'labels' to the exact value required. Peel and stick stamps (no licking) at 45¢, for standard letters sent by ordinary post, are available in booklets of 10 ($4.50), 100 ($45) and 200 ($90). No surcharge is levied by private stamp vendors in Australia.

- Pre-paid envelopes are available in various sizes: DL and C6 (maximum 5mm thick) cost 54¢ each or $5.13 for a pack of 10, C5 (max. 20mm thick) $1.19 ($11.31 for 10), C4 (20mm) $2.37 ($22.52 for 10) and B4 (20mm) $2.70 ($25.65 for 10). The maximum weight for DL and C6 envelopes is 250g and for all other sizes 500g.

- AP provides an express domestic post service with guaranteed next day delivery. No paperwork or forms need be completed, as items are sent in pre-paid envelopes or 'satchels'. There are three sizes of pre-paid envelope: C5 ($3.50), B4 ($4.60) and DL (only available with window envelopes in business packs of 50), which can be used for letters and documents up to 500g and 20mm thick. In addition, express post satchels are available in two sizes (items can be any thickness): up to 500g ($5.80) and up to 3kg ($8.75). Items weighing from 3kg to 20kg or too large for an express post satchel must be sent as express post parcels (see page 156). All types of envelopes and satchels are available in packs of 10.

- Pre-paid envelopes and satchels can be handed in at post offices or posted in express 'gold' post boxes in cities and major towns. Items must be presented at a post office before close of business or the mail closing time in some provincial centres. Items posted by 6pm (earlier in Perth and some provincial centres) Mondays to Fridays are guaranteed next day delivery to Australia's capital cities and some provincial centres. The express service also operates within states between the capital city and provincial centres. Outside these areas, the fastest possible delivery is provided, but there are no guarantees. The cost is refunded if items aren't delivered the next working day (where applicable). Express post must not be used to send cash, gold, jewellery, precious stones, negotiable securities or other valuables, which should be sent by registered post (see page 159).

- Domestic mail, including parcels and registered packets, can be sent cash on delivery (COD), where the addressee pays a specified amount to the postman on delivery. The fee is $5.45 in addition to postage and includes insurance cover up to $100 (additional insurance is available for $1 per $100 insured).

- There are reduced rates for bulk local deliveries of a minimum of 50 letters (10 in a small community). The post office also provides a 'print post' service for periodicals sent within Australia.

- If you send a letter with insufficient postage, it will usually be delivered, although the addressee will be charged $1 plus the deficient postage (also applies to parcels). If the post office is unable to deliver a letter, it's returned to the sender with a note stating the reason it couldn't be delivered.

● Most mail in Australia is sorted by machine, which is facilitated by the use of full and correct postal addresses (omitting all punctuation). All items of mail should have a four-digit postcode (zip code) after the town and state or territory. In major cities, codes indicate whether the town is a suburb of a major city, e.g. 2000 is the central business district (CBD) of Sydney and postcodes from 2001 to 2999 are suburbs. A locked or private bag is the same as a post office box number (written as 'PO Box' or 'GPO Box'). All addresses must contain the name of the state or territory, which are abbreviated as follows:

| State/Territory | Abbr. | First Digit |
| --- | --- | --- |
| Australian Capital Territory | ACT | 2 |
| New South Wales | NSW | 2 |
| Northern Territory | NT | 5 |
| Queensland | QLD | 4 |
| South Australia | SA | 5 |
| Tasmania | TAS | 7 |
| Victoria | VIC | 3 |
| Western Australia | WA | 6 |

Postcodes are listed at the back of the white pages or you can phone 13-1317 for postcode information. You can buy envelopes with pre-printed squares for the postcode. A typical Australian address is shown below:

> Bruce & Sheila Kelly
> 99A Waltzing Matilda Street
> Wooloowollongong
> Sydney
> NSW 2005
> Australia

Note that you should always put your address on the back of mail so that it can be returned if it cannot be delivered.

● Domestic mail and international sea mail for the blind weighing up to 7kg is delivered free of charge. Air mail up to 7kg costs 9¢ per 50g or part thereof. Items must have the official blind symbol on the address side or 'MATERIALS FOR THE USE OF THE BLIND' or similar words.

● You can receive mail via post offices throughout Australia through the international poste restante service, where mail is addressed to a main post office. Mail sent to a poste restante address is returned to the sender if it's unclaimed after 14 days (a month if sent from overseas). Identification is necessary for collection, e.g. a passport. Mail should be addressed as follows: Your Name, c/o Poste Restante, Chief Post Office, Sydney, NSW 2000. Note that some poste restante desks in main cities are hectic and it's often better to send mail to a smaller town or a suburb (where you may be able to check whether you have any mail by phone). Some general post offices (e.g. Martin Place in Sydney) provide a list of addressees of poste restante mail on a computer. Poste restante mail can be redirected to a suburban post office from a main office for $5 a month.

Most hostels and hotels hold mail for guests, and there are also private mail and message holding and forwarding services in Australia, e.g. travel agencies, which charge a monthly or annual fee. When using a mail holding service, you can telephone from anywhere in Australia to see if there's any mail for you and have it redirected. If you have an American Express card or use American Express travellers' cheques, you can have mail sent to any American Express office in Australia. Standard letters are held free of charge, but registered letters and packages aren't accepted. Mail, which should be marked 'client mail service', is kept for 30 days before being returned to the sender. Mail can be forwarded to another office or address, for which there's a charge. Other companies also provide mail holding services for customers, e.g. Thomas Cook and Western Union.

● Like many countries, Australia provides a range of special services for philatelists. In addition to Australia, AP produces stamps for the Australian Antarctic Territory, Christmas Island and the Cocos (Keeling) Islands. AP publishes *Stamp Bulletin* magazine (five issues a year) which is available free to Australian residents from Reply Paid 64, Australian Stamp Bulletin, Locked Bag 8, South Melbourne VIC 3205. AP also operates a Stamp Explorers Club for children aged 6 to 13 years, who receive a membership card entitling them to special discounts and benefits and the *Stamp Explorer* magazine (four issues a year). To join the Stamp Explorers Club, write to Reply Paid 14, Australian Stamp Bulletin, PO Box 511, South Melbourne VIC 3205 or you can subscribe via the Internet (🖳 www.auspost.com.au).

**Finally, carefully check all your mail and don't throw anything away unless you're certain that it's junk mail.** It isn't unknown for newcomers to throw away important correspondence during their first few weeks in Australia (with luck, a few bills will be included!). Look for 'real' letters among your junk mail.

# International Mail

AP provides four services for international mail: express post international, air mail, economy air mail and sea mail.

**Express Post:** AP provides an express post international service to over 140 countries. The service offers two sizes of pre-paid envelope, C5 ($9.70) and B4 ($14.65), which can be used to send letters and documents weighing up to 500g. Envelopes are also available in discount packs of ten. As with domestic express mail, items can be posted in express mail 'gold' posting boxes. Air despatch from Australia is guaranteed the next day from capital cities and other specified areas subject to the availability of flights (otherwise your envelope will be replaced free of charge).

**Air Mail:** AP divides international letter mail into two zones only, as follows:

|  | Asia Pacific (AP) | Rest of the World (RW) |
|---|---|---|
| Letter up to 50g | $1 | $1.50 |
| Letter 50 to 125g | $2 | $3.00 |
| Letter 125 to 250g | $3 | $4.50 |
| Letter 250 to 500g | $6 | $9.00 |
| Postcard | $1 | $1.00 |

All airmail letters (including letters for European destinations) should have a blue air mail label affixed to the top left hand corner, available from post offices, or 'PAR AVION – BY AIR MAIL' written or stamped on the front. Aerogrammes (pre-printed air mail letters) are available and cost 78¢ to all destinations. They're also sold in packs of ten ($7.30). International pre-paid envelopes are available in three sizes: DL ($1.58), C5 ($3.17) and B4 ($4.75), and can be purchased in packs of ten at a small discount. Air mail letters, documents and parcels are limited to 20kg for most countries (some countries have a lower limit, e.g. 10kg).

**Economy Air:** For non-urgent international mail, AP provides an economy air mail service, where the main part of the journey is made by air. Mail takes between 10 and 28 days to most destinations (10 to 14 days to Britain and 14 to 21 days to the USA). Note, however, that for most mail it's hardly worthwhile, as the savings are insignificant unless you're sending a heavy parcel (see page 157).

**Sea Mail:** Sea mail is the cheapest service and allows delivery to almost any country. It's ideal for heavier items when speed is not critical. Average sea mail delivery times are: zones 1 and 2, one to two months; zones 3, 4 and 5 (including Britain and the USA), up to three months or longer (much, much, longer to some countries).

Leaflets are published in September listing the latest posting dates for Christmas for surface and airmail, which are some time between the beginning of October (e.g. 6th October for the UK and 8th October for the USA by sea mail) and the end of November, depending on the country.

The fastest way to send mail overseas via a post office is by EMS international courier (see below), AP's premium door-to-door express courier service.

If you want to increase your chances of receiving a reply or simply wish to save a correspondent money, you can send them an international reply coupon ($2). These are exchangeable at post offices overseas for stamps equivalent to the basic air mail rate anywhere in the world for a letter weighing up to 20g.

# PARCEL POST

Standard parcels are usually delivered the next working day within the metropolitan area of capital cities and certain large country towns in the same state, and within two working days to other locations in the same state. Interstate parcels are delivered within two to six working days, depending on the destination. Note, however, that AP has a poor reputation for deliveries to country locations. AP provides five services for international parcels (in order of speed and cost): EMS international courier, express, air mail, economy air mail, and sea mail.

**Domestic Parcels:** The cost of domestic parcels varies considerably according to where they're sent from and the destination (based on the postcode). A parcel weighing up to 250g costs up to $2.74 anywhere in Australia outside the local area; between 250g and 500g the price is from $3.73; for parcels over 500g there's a basic charge of $5.10 (same state) or $6.70 (interstate) plus a charge per kg, which ranges from 27¢ to a maximum of $4.25. Local parcels weighing up to 500g cost $2.10 and parcels weighing from 500g to 2kg $3.25. Note that large letters (see page 153) weighing up to 500g can be sent by letter mail. Important parcels can be sent by registered post, which provides a signature on delivery and insurance of up to $100. Parcels can also be sent cash on delivery. AP provides special satchels for sending articles anywhere in Australia in two sizes: up to 500g ($3.80) and up to 3kg ($7.10).

Local parcels cost $1.35 up to 500g and $3 from 500g up to the maximum weight of 20kg (there's also a flat rate of $10 for air mail parcels). AP also operates a nationwide small parcel service costing $2.10 for parcels weighing up to 250g and $3.10 for parcels weighing from 250g to 500g. Regular parcels weighing over 500g cost $4.60 for deliveries within 50km/31mi.

**EMS International Courier Service:** The fastest way to send international parcels is via the EMS international courier service (serving over 180 countries). International parcel rates are calculated according to a four-zone system plus New Zealand. A parcel weighing up to 500g costs from $29 to $39 ($37 to the USA and Canada and $39 to Europe) and between $46 and $62 for parcels weighing between 1.5 and 2kg. Above 2kg, each additional 500g costs between $5 and $10 depending on the zone, up to a maximum of 20kg. Although relatively expensive, EMS rates are generally lower than those of other international courier services. EMS parcels are guaranteed to arrive within a certain number of days, e.g. two to four days to Britain and four to five days to the USA. Parcels sent by EMS must include a completed EMS 001 customs form (see below).

**Express Parcels:** AP provides domestic and international express parcel services. For domestic express parcels, there's guaranteed next day delivery between Australia's capital cities (except Darwin) and some other major towns (you can claim a refund if a parcel isn't delivered the next day). The service also operates within states between the capital city and provincial centres. Outside these areas, the fastest possible delivery is provided, but there are no delivery guarantees. The maximum permitted weight is 20kg, maximum length 105cm and maximum girth 140cm. Parcels must be presented at a post office before close of business or mail closing time in some provincial centres. There's a standard charge of $5.95 for parcels weighing up to 500g and $8.75 for parcels weighing from 500g to 20kg, plus a distance charge per kilo (or part) calculated using the origin and destination zones: e.g. for a parcel going from Sydney (zone 2000) to Adelaide (zone 5000) the charge is $2.90 per kg. For parcels over 1kg, the distance charge may be calculated on the parcel's measurements rather than its weight.

**Air Mail:** The air mail service is fast and reliable, parcels taking a maximum of seven or eight days to most destinations (three to five days to Britain and six to seven days to the USA), depending on where they're posted and the destination.

**Economy Air Mail:** For non-urgent international parcels, AP provides an economy air mail service. The main part of the journey is made by air and items take between 10 and 28 days to most destinations (10 to 14 days to Britain and 14 to 21 days to the USA). Note that, while the maximum weight for economy air mail is 20kg to Britain and the USA, to many countries it's just 500g. The saving over regular air mail is insignificant unless you're sending a parcel weighing over 1kg.

**Sea Mail:** Sea mail is the cheapest way to send parcels and allows delivery to almost any country. It's ideal for heavier items when speed is of no importance (and when delivery is also unimportant – mail may not arrive at all when sent to some countries!). Average sea mail delivery times are one to two months to zones 1 and 2 and two to three months (or longer) to zones 3, 4 and 5 (which include Britain and the USA).

**Customs Declaration:** Parcels and small packets sent to international addresses must be accompanied by a customs declaration form available from post offices. No customs form is required for small and large letters and express post international. A *Customs/Douane* form CN22 must be completed for items weighing up to 2kg and up to $500 in value, and an *International Post – Customs Declaration* (form C231) for items weighing above 2kg and over $500 in value. Note that items over $2,000 in value must be registered with customs. Insured items other than EMS parcels (see above) require a form C233. Press firmly when completing forms, some of which have six copies! Gifts posted to Australia up to the value of $200 are duty-free, except for alcohol and tobacco products. For gifts exceeding $200, duty is calculated on the value in excess of $200. The value of packages that are part of a larger consignment will be added for customs purposes. Note that there are restrictions on the sort of goods that can be posted to Australia (see below). Dangerous goods must not be sent through the mail, and senders of all overseas parcels and satchels must sign a Dangerous Goods Declaration.

**Wrapping Parcels:** A leaflet entitled *Packaging Hints* is available from post offices, describing how to pack goods for sending through the mail. When sending drawings, large photographs, paintings, or anything which will be damaged if bent, **always sandwich them between stiff cardboard.** 'Postpak' packaging products, including boxes (plus gift boxes), padded bags, tough bags, mailing tubes and accessories are available from Australia Post Shops and stationery stores. You can send quite large objects by parcel post, but it's wise to enquire before packaging your mother-in-law for shipment to Outer Mongolia (just to make sure she arrives safely and *isn't* returned). All parcels must be securely wrapped and clearly addressed; if they aren't, you may be asked to wrap them again. **Note that international parcels *must* be *very* securely wrapped, or they will be shredded in transit to some countries.**

**Restricted Articles:** A dangerous goods brochure, *Some Things Were Never Meant To Be Posted*, is available from post offices and lists what *cannot* be sent through the mail. This includes anything that's radioactive, flammable, explosive, corrosive, oxidising, alive or likely to deteriorate during its journey through the post (e.g. a cake). Many overseas countries have restrictions on certain items such as medicines and alcohol.

## IMPORTANT DOCUMENTS & VALUABLES

The post office provides a number of services for the delivery of important documents and valuables:

**Registered Mail:** If you're sending money, jewellery or valuable documents, you should use registered mail, which costs $1.96 in addition to the standard postage charge. Domestic pre-paid envelopes which include postage and the registered mail fee are available in two sizes: small or DLE (130 x 240mm, 5mm thick) costing $2.38 each ($22.61 for ten) and large or B4 (353mm x 250mm, 20mm thick) costing $3.45 each ($32.78 for ten). Domestic registered mail labels are also available in boxes of 50 ($84.50). International registered mail is available only for letters and documents and costs $7.91 for DLE size (130 x 240mm) and $13.82 for B4 size (353 x 240mm). You receive a receipt for registered mail, which must be signed for on delivery (although the signatory doesn't need to be the addressee). Delivery of domestic registered mail can be confirmed (fee $1.53) by completing a delivery confirmation card and sending it with your registered mail article. There's also a person-to-person option (fee $4.35 per article) where a registered article must be signed for by the person to whom it's addressed.

**Insurance:** International insurance is available for EMS international courier (see page 158) letter and parcel post articles. The basic fee is $3 plus $2 for each $100 (or part thereof) insured up to a maximum of $5,000 (a lower limit applies to some countries). Domestic and international registered mail is 'insured' for $100 against loss or damage, and additional insurance up to $5,000 is available for domestic registered mail for $1.05 per $100 insured. Additional insurance cannot be purchased for international registered mail.

**Delivery Confirmation:** Delivery confirmation is available with registered mail, insured articles and, for some countries, parcel post. International delivery confirmation costs $2 per article plus postage. Delivery confirmation costs an additional $1.53 per article for registered post and $4.35 for person-to-person deliveries. Proof of delivery must be requested at the time of posting. Signed evidence of delivery is returned to the sender, but not from a named individual.

## MISCELLANEOUS SERVICES

The following miscellaneous services are provided by Australia Post:

**Payment of Bills:** AP provides a bill payment service from all post offices and post agencies. A total of some 160 organisations offer their customers the option of paying their bills at post offices, including telephone bills, tax payments, credit card bills, electricity, gas, council rates, water rates and insurance premiums. Simply present your account slip and invoice with payment by cash or cheque. A receipt is provided.

**Money Orders:** Money orders offer a convenient, safe and economical way to pay bills, transfer cash and pay for mail-order purchases if you or the recipient doesn't have a cheque account. Money orders can be purchased for 5¢ amounts up to $1,000 and cost $2.50, so they aren't cost effective for small amounts. Express money orders up to the value of $10,000 cost $20 and can be transferred across Australia from post office to post office within one business hour. There's an additional 10¢ stamp duty in Western Australia. Money orders can be cashed at post offices (identification is required for values above $20) or paid into a bank account. Information regarding money orders can be obtained by calling freephone ☎ 13-1318.

**Western Union International Money Orders:** AP is the Australian agent for Western Union International Money Orders. These US$ money orders are recognised and accepted in over 120 countries and sold at main post offices throughout Australia. They can be purchased for values up to US$1,000 for a fixed fee of A$8.65 (plus 10¢ stamp duty in Western Australia), irrespective of their value. They must be cashed at an American Express bank or travel service office or paid into a bank account.

## CHANGE OF ADDRESS

When moving house within Australia, you should obtain a Change of Address Kit from a post office containing a *Change of Address Request* form, a brochure describing the service, a moving home checklist, and six postcards to inform your relatives and friends about your move. The change can be permanent or temporary and mail can also be held at your local post office or be collected from a nominated post office. Proof of identity must be provided when lodging the form and a minimum of three working days' notice is required. There's a monthly fee of $35 for business and government, and $5.50 for others (there's no charge for certain pensioners and sickness beneficiaries). There's an additional charge for the redirection of parcels.

AP provides a 'priority address notification' service which saves time and effort in informing organisations of your address. Upon receipt of your *Change of Address* form, AP will send you a list of companies which you may wish to notify of your new address. If you're a customer of any of the companies listed on the form, simply tick the box beside the company's name and AP will inform them of your change of address free of charge.

If you receive mail for the previous occupants of your home or any mail that isn't addressed to you, there are two things you can do with it (the third is to throw it away, which is illegal!). You can send it on to the addressee by crossing out the address, writing the new or correct address and dropping it in a post box without a stamp. If you don't know the addressee's new address, you can cross out the address and write 'Address Unknown' and drop it in a post box.

# 7.

# TELEPHONE

Almost all Australian homes (some 97 per cent) have a telephone, and Australia also has one of the highest (per capita) numbers of mobile phones in the world. Because of its huge size, communications in Australia have always been a priority and today it has one of the highest standards of communications in the world, employing the latest digital technology, broadband cable, fibre optics and satellite systems. Wireless and radio-based communication is used in rural and remote areas, where in future residents with receive their telecommunications services via satellite links and enjoy the same services that are available in metropolitan centres. There are also solar-powered public phone boxes in outback areas requiring no mains electricity. The Australian telecommunications market was deregulated in 1997 and consumers are now able to choose from a number of companies in most regions and major cities. Thanks to recent technological advances, it's now possible to have a single number for your home, office and mobile phones (for more information call Onenumber on ☎ 18-500).

The telecommunications industry in Australia is regulated by the Australian Communications Authority (Austel), PO Box 7443, St. Kilda Road, Melbourne, VIC 3004 (☎ 02-6243 1111, 💻 www.aca.gov.au) and has its own ombudsman (☎ freecall 1800-062058, 💻 www.tio.com.au). The ombudsman attempts to resolve complaints concerning telecommunications issues, but only after consumers have attempted to settle them with the company or carrier concerned. Austel has numerous leaflets available by post or online with consumer information and advice.

From November 1998, all telephone numbers have had an eight-digit subscriber number following a two-digit area code. **The general emergency telephone number throughout Australia is 000.**

## TELEPHONE COMPANIES

The Australian telecommunications market was deregulated on 1st July 1997 and some twenty-five companies now operate in the country, although the market is still dominated by Telstra (formerly Telecom Australia and two-thirds government-owned), which has an overall market share of around 75 per cent (9 million customers), including 60 per cent of long-distance business. Its main rival Optus (established in 1992 and owned by Cable & Wireless) has around 15 per cent of the market (over 2.5 million customers, including fixed and mobile phones). AAPT and Primus are other large communications companies. Not surprisingly, the lack of competition (prior to deregulation) led to Australians paying some of the highest telephone charges in the world, with Telstra and Optus charging customers an average of five times the actual cost of providing international call services.

However, since deregulation many new companies have entered the market, including BT Australasia, GlobalOne, Primus/Axicorp, Satellite Cowboys and WorldxChange, and users can now choose from a number of companies when making long-distance and international calls. Long-distance phone charges have been slashed by up to 70 per cent and the price of mobile phone calls has fallen by 50 per cent and that of local calls by 12 per cent in the last three years. In the first six months of deregulation, there were tens of thousands of defections from Telstra and Optus. However, despite the increased competition, deregulation has failed to deliver the expected benefits to consumers, although it's generally agreed that the situation has vastly improved in recent years.

In 1998, Telstra lost its monopoly on local calls worth $4 billion per year, and most other telephone companies now offer local calls. However, Telstra still has around 90 per cent of the local call market and some companies such as Optus offer only local calls for small businesses. Local number portability (LNP), which allows users to switch between phone companies without changing their number, has been introduced, although if you sign up with a company you might have a prefix assigned to your telephone number and your calls automatically go through your selected company when you dial.

Before signing up with a telephone company, check the competition and compare rates. If you make a lot of long-distance and international calls, you can save a lot of money by using one of the new companies whose call rates are usually well below those charged by Telstra and Optus. However, you should continually monitor the market, as new deals are constantly being introduced and what was the best offer last month (or week) is unlikely to remain so for long. Many companies offer a range of services, which may include local and long-distance telephone services, pay TV, and high speed access to on-line and interactive services such as the Internet. This may be beneficial, as many companies offer attractive package deals if you buy two or more services, such as telephone and pay TV.

## INSTALLATION & REGISTRATION

Before moving into a new home, check whether there's a telephone line and that the number of lines or telephone points is adequate (most homes already have phone lines and points in a number of rooms). If a property has a cable system or other phone network, you don't require a Telstra phone line. However, if you move into a house or apartment where you aren't the first resident, a telephone line will almost certainly already be installed, although there will usually be no phone. If you're moving into a house or apartment without a phone connection, e.g. a new house, you must usually apply to Telstra for a line to be installed or connected.

To have a telephone line installed or re-connected, call at any Telstra shop or dial the Telstra Customer Service Centre (☎ local call rate 13-2200) between 8am and 5pm, Mondays to Fridays. Telstra will arrange a suitable date and time with you to connect your phone service. If you live in a metropolitan area, your phone should be connected within seven days at the latest. Connection often takes longer if you live in a rural or remote area, e.g. from two weeks to two months. If you simply need an existing Telstra service reconnected, this can usually be done on the day and time requested or at least within three working days. If you're moving home within the same exchange area and call-charging zone, you may retain your old number; otherwise your old number is typically re-allocated to the incoming customer at your old address. You may request an unlisted number ('silent line') for which an unlisted number fee applies.

Line installation costs $190.30, although this depends on the amount of work involved, and you're required to pay an advance of $300 from which the fee is deducted. If a line already exists, connection costs $55, which is deducted from an advance payment of $150. Credit assessments are made for all customers and your billing period may depend on your credit assessment. Payment of a security bond may be required or you may be given only restricted access, e.g. no international calls. Interest is paid on a bond, which is generally repaid after 12 months when you've established a satisfactory payment record. Generally, a $250 bond is necessary if you wish to make interstate calls and a $500 bond if you want to make international calls.

If your phone or line has a fault, you must report it to Telstra on ☎ local call rate 13-2203. If your life, health, safety or shelter may be at risk without a phone, you can register for a priority repair service (24 hours, seven days a week). You can take out a maintenance contract with Telstra to maintain equipment and cabling. Telstra publish a booklet, *Guide to Using Telstra's Telephone Services for Residential & Business Customers*, available from Telstra shops or by calling ☎ local call rate 13-1800. If you need help in using a Telstra product or service, dial ☎ local call rate 13-2200.

## CHOOSING A PHONE

You aren't required to rent a phone from Telstra and can purchase a phone from a wide range offered by Telstra and other retailers. Note that renting a phone from Telstra doesn't pay, as in one year you'll have paid for the price of a basic (but adequate) telephone. The only advantage of renting a Telstra phone is that they'll fix it free of charge if it's faulty and you can change phones as often as you wish. On the other hand, if an inexpensive private phone has a fault, it may be cheaper to throw it away than have it repaired. **Before buying a phone, be careful to check prices and features, which vary considerably.**

The price of a phone usually depends on its quality, country of origin and not least its features. A basic, one-piece phone (with the keys on the handset) costs around $25, while an all-singing, all-dancing model costs from $90. Typical features include a built-in loudspeaker (so you can talk and listen without using the handset), on-hook dialling, number memory facility, last number re-dial, mute button, LCD display (so you can check the digits entered),- timer or call cost counter, lock and an intercom system. You can even buy a videophone, which allows two callers using them to see each other on a small screen.

Cordless phones are popular and can be operated at between 50 and 150 metres from their base station (the batteries last from a few days to around 60 days). If you're thinking of buying a cordless phone, note that they usually rely solely on mains power and therefore are useless if there's a power failure. The latest cordless phones have a battery backup and should prevent calls being overheard and calls being made on your number with another handset (via a security code). Despite the battery backup of some phones, it's unwise to rely solely on a cordless phone. Other features may include a battery low indicator, paging and intercom facilities. Note that all cordless phones sold in Australia must have an Austel permit (shown by a sticker), and the import of cordless phones and citizenband radios without it is prohibited. Most cordless phones cost between $100 and $250.

You might also consider a telephone with a built-in answering machine. Answering machines (like all electronic equipment) are becoming increasingly sophisticated and the latest machines offer a variety of features, including fast erase, monitoring/screening, two-way conversation recording, cue and review, answer only, paging, logging of time and date, digital talking diary, call screening, music, memo facility; and remote message retrieval (which allows you to listen to your messages from almost anywhere in the world, simply by ringing your home or business number and dialling a code).

For those with special needs, a variety of special phones and attachments are available. If you live or work in a noisy environment, a headset can be purchased allowing hands-free operation. Special handsets are available for the blind and extra large key pads for the partially blind. Phones fitted with a flashing light, loud ring, a built-in amplifier or magnetic coupling (for use with hearing aids) are available for the hard of hearing (e.g. politicians).

You can try the latest Telstra phones at your local Telstra shop (see your phone book), where advice and demonstrations are available. Telstra publish a wide range of booklets and leaflets, including a catalogue of their products and services (for information ☎ freecall 1800-038000). There are over 80 Telstra shops in Australia for general enquiries, information about Telstra's products and services, product demonstrations and sales, and telephone bill payments. Shops are open from 9am to 4.30pm Mondays to Fridays or longer in many locations. Telstra also has telephone Customer Service Centres in all major cities and towns, open from 8am to 5pm, Mondays to Fridays. However, you should also compare phones and other equipment from high street shops and, if possible, test them before buying. See also **Mobile Telephones** on page 174.

## USING THE TELEPHONE

Using the telephone in Australia is much the same as in any other country, with a few local eccentricities thrown in for good measure. When dialling a number within your own exchange area, dial only the number, e.g. if you live in Sydney and wish to dial another subscriber in Sydney. When dialling anywhere else, the area code must be dialled before the subscriber's number. When telephone numbers are printed, the area code is usually shown in brackets, e.g. (02) 1234 5678. When dialling a number in Australia from overseas, you dial the international access code of the country from which you're calling (e.g. 00), followed by Australia's international code (61), the area code *without* the first 0 (e.g. 2 for Sydney) and the subscriber's number. For example, to call Sydney 1234 5678 from the UK, you would dial 00-61-2-1234 5678. Note that, because of the huge time difference between Australia and many other countries, you should always check the local time when making international calls to Australia. For operator assistance dial 1234.

In some remote areas, there are manual exchanges where you must call the local operator to make a call. Some outback areas in Western Australia and the Northern Territory have radio telephones, where numbers are prefixed by R/T. Calls to R/T numbers can be made via the national network and radio telephone exchanges, although they're expensive. A radio telephone is like using a two-way radio and only one person can speak at a time (you need to say over when you finish speaking and cannot interrupt the other person). Party lines (shared by two or more homes) are common in the outback.

**Codes & Numbers:** Australia introduced a new numbering system in November 1998 and subscriber numbers now have eight digits. If you have a problem obtaining a number, check that it's correct in the white pages or by calling directory enquiries on 1223 (local and national) or 1225 (international). The area codes for states and their capital cities are listed on the next page:

| State/Territory | Capital | Code |
| --- | --- | --- |
| Australian Capital Territory | Canberra | 02 |
| New South Wales | Sydney | 02 |
| Northern Territory | Darwin | 08 |
| Queensland | Brisbane | 07 |
| South Australia | Adelaide | 08 |
| Tasmania | Hobart | 03 |
| Victoria | Melbourne | 03 |
| Western Australia | Perth | 08 |

**Free Numbers:** Toll-free numbers, called freecall in Australia, have a prefix of 1800 and are usually provided by businesses who are trying to sell you something or, having sold you something, provide a free telephone support service. Note that mobile phone carriers may charge for 1800 calls. As in most countries, freecall numbers leave you on hold for ages during which time you have to suffer the torment of muzak. You can obtain a personal freecall number called Homelink 1800, which allows your family and friends to phone your home free of charge (so don't give it to telephone salesmen!). There's a 33¢ surcharge for each domestic Homelink call (for information on Homelink call ☎ freecall 1800-061222).

**Reduced Rate Numbers:** Numbers with the prefix 13 or 1300 are usually charged at the local call rate from anywhere in Australia, although some 13 or 1300 numbers are restricted to callers within a city or state.

# Operator Assisted Calls

There's an extra charge for operator assisted calls, and the minimum charge period is three minutes. You can use Telstra Call Connect (dial 12456) when you don't know the number for a local or national call. For operator-assisted domestic calls, dial 1234. The following operator-connected services are available:

**Ring Back Price:** A call can be timed and the charge given at the end of the call. If you want to know the cost of a national or international call, dial 1222 before the number and the cost is given (for a fee) at the end of your call. Although useful when you aren't using your own phone and must pay for a call, using 'ring back price' is expensive.

**Particular Person Call:** You can make an international particular person call (called a personal or person-to-person call in most other countries), where you start paying for the call only when the person required comes on the line. Note that it may be cheaper to make a brief call to find out whether the person you wish to speak to is available.

**Reverse Charge & Third Party Charge Call:** A reverse charge, transferred or collect call, is where the person called agrees to pay for the call. Useful when you've no change, the payphone won't accept your coins or when you're calling your mother-in-law. Note that making a reverse charge call from overseas to Australia is *very* expensive, as it's charged at the operator connected call rate. For reverse charge and third party charge calls, dial 12550. These calls cannot be made to mobile phones.

**Wake-Up Calls:** To book a wake up or reminder call, dial 12454 (booking and call charge cost $2.15).

**Line Faults:** You can report line faults 24 hours a day to Telstra on 13-2203 (for residential lines), 13-2999 (for business lines) or 018-018111 (for mobile phones). Telstra aims to repair telephone services within one working day in urban areas, two days in rural areas and three days in remote areas. If you suspect that your phone is faulty, test the line with another phone if you have one or test your phone on another line, e.g. that of a friend or neighbour. A priority repair service is provided for non-commercial emergency and essential service organisations, and to individuals whose life, health, safety or shelter would be at risk without a telephone.

**Telstra Telecard:** IDD and non-IDD calls (via the international operator) can be made with a free Telstra Telecard to over 200 countries and to Australia from over 65 countries using the Australia Direct service. Direct-dialled Telecard calls are 5 per cent cheaper than payphone rates, although if you call via the operator there's an additional service charge. Calls from payphones are charged at payphone rates (see page 172). Telecards can be used to dial direct from any tone phone, which includes all payphones and most private phones, although they cannot be used from mobile phones. When using a Telecard overseas, you may be charged an astronomical sum. If Telecard calls need to be made via the operator, they-'re always more expensive than direct-dialled calls. Telecards are also open to abuse, both in Australia and overseas. Although they offer convenience, it comes at a high price, which is fine provided someone else picks up the bill!

# INFORMATION & ENTERTAINMENT NUMBERS

The use of premium rate information and entertainment numbers has increased considerably in recent years; the majority have the prefix 190 (known as infocall numbers) and provide recorded information. Infocall numbers are charged at premium rates ranging from 60¢ to $5 or more per minute or incur a fixed charge (up to $7) irrespective of how long you stay on the line. Rates are set by the service provider. Most 'bulletins' last around three minutes. The same tariffs apply throughout Australia irrespective of the time of day or the day of the week.

Infocall numbers offer a wide range of recorded information on practically any subject, including astrology/horoscopes, comedy/entertainment, cricket, lotteries, keno and pools, news, sport, the stock market, tides, time, weather, snow conditions, soccer results, racing, international flights, as well as offering games, computer help, dating services, chat and sex, legal and medical advice. You can also obtain personal (live) advice on finance, computers, study, legal matters and gardening. Most information service companies provide a free directory of their services (you can obtain a list by calling ☎ 1800-035055 – and that call is free!). Information and entertainment numbers are huge money-spinners for the companies and are beloved by TV and radio competitions. **Note that, if you use these numbers frequently, you can go bankrupt!** Some people have received huge telephone bills, which include calls to national and international sex lines that they haven't made. It's extremely difficult to prove that you (or a family member) didn't make these calls, even if you can show that you were out of the country at the time! To prevent this happening, you can instruct Telstra (☎ freecall 1800-038000) to install 190 Restricted Access on your line. To access 190 numbers under this scheme, you need to enter a four-digit PIN before dialling the number.

A new information line, called Easy Info, will provide you with up to five information searches, e.g. phone numbers, addresses and time zones for a single call costing $2.50. Easy Info is available on ☎ 12452.

## DOMESTIC CALL RATES

In most towns and cities in Australia, local calls can be made only through Telstra, as other telephone companies don't have access to Telstra's local network, although some such as Optus are (very slowly) building their own local network. However, most users have a choice of companies for domestic long-distance calls. Telstra charges for all local calls (users don't receive a certain number of free calls per billing period as in some other countries) and levies a quarterly service and equipment charge, which is around $40 to $50 for a residential line.

**Local Calls:** Local calls (within a given distance of any city or region) between standard (fixed line) telephones cost 22¢ (40¢ from payphones) regardless of the length of the call. Other local calls (e.g. from a standard phone to a mobile phone) are charged in 3 minute blocks from 8am to 8pm Mondays to Fridays and in 4.5 minute blocks at other times. The boundaries for local calls are shown on a map in your white pages directory.- Note that calls within the same area code aren't all classed as local calls, e.g. all numbers in the Northern Territory have the code 08, but calls from Darwin to Alice Springs (a distance of 2,103km/1,307mi!) are charged at long-distance rates. In March 2000 Telstra introduced a 'neighbourhood' call rate of 15¢ for business and residential calls made between numbers on the same exchange. The concept of a neighbourhood call has been criticised as unnecessarily complex since the only way to find out which calls are neighbourhood calls is to look up the complicated local prefix index in the back of the phone book!

**Long-distance Calls:** You can use Telstra or another carrier or service provider (e.g. Optus) for your long-distance (or subscriber trunk dialling/STD) calls. Customers with a choice of carriers need to dial a code before the area code, e.g. to choose Telstra you must dial 1411 before the area or country code.- You can check your current long-distance telephone company by calling 12711 for a pre-recorded message that gives the name of the selected company. You can find out the cost of Telstra national and international calls by dialling 1222 before dialling the number (see **Ring Back Price** on page 168).

Long-distance calls are timed and charged according to the distance, time of day and the day of the week; they're charged by the second and are itemised on your telephone bill. Note that long-distance call rates vary considerably and, if you make a lot of calls, you should shop around for the lowest rate. So-called 'telephone plans' are very popular with telephone companies in Australia for long-distance calls. Under these plans, the consumer pays a fixed rate per call, irrespective of the time of day or the day of the week. For example, in mid-2001 Telstra were offering the EveryDay STD plan, under which you can phone anywhere long-distance at any time of the day and talk for up to three hours for $2.97. Optus were offering a FreeTime plan with similar conditions and rates. Other Optus long-distance rates were 24¢ per minute for calls made between midnight Sunday and midnight Friday, and 11¢ for calls between midnight Friday and midnight Sunday.

# INTERNATIONAL CALLS

International telephone, fax and telex links are provided by the Overseas Telecommunications Commission (OTC) using undersea cables and satellites (Australia has telephone connections with around 200 countries via Intelsat). All private telephones in Australia are on International Direct Dialling (IDD), allowing calls to be dialled direct to some 200 countries. To make an international call, dial 0011, the country code, the area code without the first zero, and the subscriber's number. Dial 0101 for the international operator (0107 from payphones) to make non-IDD calls, credit card calls, person-to-person and reverse charge calls (which aren't accepted by all countries). Dial 1225 for international directory enquiries. The international code for most countries is listed at the back of the white pages under 'Telstra 0011 International and Telstra Faxstream 0015 International' and includes the time difference (one sure way to upset most people is to wake them at 3am). You can also obtain dialling codes, world time information and a time converter for over 220 countries via the Internet.

**Choosing the Carrier:** As with all types of telephone calls, customers in most regions and major cities can choose the carrier they use for international calls. Since deregulation, there has been a huge reduction in the cost of international calls and it's now possible to telephone Britain and New Zealand for 21¢ a minute, with no connection fee (around one-quarter of the cost before deregulation). Note, however, that if you make a lot of international calls it may be beneficial to sign up with a number of companies and 'cherry pick', using the one that offers the lowest rate to the country you're calling. To use a particular carrier, you must open an account with them and may either pre-select that company or dial an access code before an STD or overseas number.

Telstra in mid-2001 offered two schemes for international calls: 0011 Easy Minutes with international call prices charged per minute at a greatly reduced rate (e.g. 31¢ to the US and 37¢ to Britain); and 0018 Easy Half Hours with international call prices charged in half hour blocks at reduced rates (e.g. $3.30 per half-hour to the US and Britain). Both schemes offer a flat rate 24 hours a day, seven days a week. You can find out the cost of Telstra international calls by dialling 1222 before dialling the number (see Ring Back Price on page 168). Optus offered a FreeTime scheme, under which you can call Britain, Canada, Ireland and the US at any time of the day, any day of the week and talk for up to three hours for $6.50.

**Country or Australia Direct:** Australia subscribes to a Country Direct service, which allows you to make reverse charge (collect) or credit card (e.g. Telstra Telecard) calls to around 50 countries, including Britain and the USA. Codes are listed under the 'Operator Assisted Calls' section at the back of the white pages directory, and further information can be obtained by dialling freecall 1800-801800. You can also make reverse charge and credit card calls to Australia from over 50 countries using the Australia Direct service, which gives you direct and free access to an operator in Australia. Note, however, that using Country or Australia Direct is an expensive way to make a call.

# TELEPHONE BILLS

Most residential customers in Australia are billed quarterly or bi-monthly for line rental, phone rental (if applicable) and calls. Business customers usually receive their bills monthly, although both business and residential customers may be able to choose to be billed monthly, bi-monthly or quarterly. Telstra also provides a payment card which allows you to pay your account in advance instalments. Where applicable, the telephone connection fee is included in your first bill.

Telstra's billing is spread over a number of different systems and has been widely criticised. Itemised billing is being introduced and includes local calls, STD calls, international calls, telephone information services, operator-connected calls, calls to mobile phones, telecard calls, Homelink 1800 calls, and line and equipment charges, all of which are itemised separately. Telstra also provides e-mail delivery of customer bills and a website where customers can check the status of their account. Optus has an all-in-one billing service with a single bill for all services, including local and long-distance calls, mobile phones, pay TV and Internet services.

Telstra bills can be paid at any post office, by mail to Telstra, GPO Box 9901 in all capital cities, at Telstra shops (cash, cheques, credit/charge/EFTPOS cards), with a Telstra payment card, by electronic telephone banking and by phone (with a credit/EFTPOS card). Telstra accepts American Express, Bankcard, Mastercard, Redicard, Diners Club and Visa credit cards. If you have any queries about your Telstra telephone bill, call the Telstra Customer Service Centre (☎ local call rate 13-2200 for residential services) between 8am and 5pm, Mondays to Fridays.

If you believe that your bill is wrong, Telstra will monitor your line and equipment for faults and, if you dispute the amount owed, you need only pay the amount that isn't in dispute while your query is being investigated. If you fail to pay your bill, a reminder or a disconnection notice will be issued. If you still fail to pay, your service will be disconnected and reconnection will take place only after payment of the account in full plus a reconnection fee has been received.

# PUBLIC TELEPHONES

Public telephones (or payphones) are provided in all cities and towns in Australia in public streets, inside and outside post offices, at airports, bus and railway stations, in hotels, pubs, restaurants, service stations, shopping centres, and other private and public buildings. Note that making non-local calls from hotels is expensive, although free local calls can often be made from phones in a hotel lobby. Payphones accept a range of payment options, including coins, Phonecards, PhoneAway cards, Homelink services, Telstra Telecards, Optus Calling Cards, credit cards, and reverse charge and third party charge calls. A Telstra Telecard or Optus Calling Card allows you to make calls from virtually any phone and have them charged automatically to your home or business account. Locals calls cost 40¢ from a payphone for an unlimited period, although users are requested to limit calls to three minutes when there are people waiting. Modern pushbutton payphones accept 10¢, 20¢, 50¢ and $1 coins. Some 30,000 payphones also accept phone cards and a few also accept credit cards. Telstra are installing new payphones that accept microchip smart cards. Calls to the 000 emergency service are free from payphones.

All payphones in Australia (some 85,000) are operated by Telstra (including around 300 solar-powered satellite payphones in remote outback areas), an estimated 95 per cent of which are claimed to be in working order at any given time, although it isn't uncommon to find vandalised or out-of-order payphones in some areas. Most are modern, digital tone phones, although there are antiquated payphones in country and remote areas. In addition to these, there are 40,000 payphones operated by private businesses. Around 1,000 multi-access payphones have been modified so that they can be used by the disabled, including those in wheelchairs and the visually impaired. Some payphones also have hearing aid couplers, special volume controls and hands-free operation. There are also teletypewriter payphones at Telstra Payphone Centres in major cities and regional payphone centres for those with speech and hearing impediments (☎ freecall 1800-068424 for information). Telstra Payphone Centres in major cities are usually open from around 9am to 6pm, Mondays to Fridays, and from 10am to 4pm on Saturdays.

**Phonecards:** Telstra phonecards are available in denominations of $5, $10, $20 and $50 and are available from over 15,000 retail outlets nationally (displaying a 'Phonecard Sold Here' sign), including newsagents, stores, pharmacies and kiosks. An audible signal is given when a phonecard is nearing the end of its value. Note that, when making an international call, you should insert at least $3 in coins or a phonecard with a minimum of $3 credit. Phonecards can store and automatically dial telephone numbers through the use of Autocall features. They're produced in a number of designs on topical themes and (as in other countries) have become collectibles – since their introduction in 1990, many are already fetching high prices among collectors, and Telstra issues a bi-monthly newsletter and catalogue.

**International Calls:** Not all payphones in Australia can be used to make international calls. Payphones allowing international calls are marked ISD (International Subscriber Dialling), or IDD (International Direct Dialling). These include all gold phones. You can check by dialling 0011 (free). If it's an ISD phone, you'll hear the message 'congratulations, you're connected to ISD'; if not, there will be no reply. International calls can also be made from Telstra telephone centres in the major cities and public telephone booths at major post offices. Calls made from a payphone are more expensive than from a private phone, and payphones don't accept incoming calls.

When using a payphone, partly used coins are lost but wholly unused coins are returned when you hang up the receiver. Payphones also have a 'follow on call' button – if you still have unused coins in credit, you can press this button and make another call using the remaining credit. If the display flashes, insert more coins until the flashing stops. It's best to insert relatively small coins unless you're calling long-distance. Instructions for using modern pushbutton payphones are as follows:

● Lift the handset and wait for the dialling tone. If you don't hear a dialling tone, the telephone is out of order.

● Insert the minimum call charge of 40¢ (or more for long-distance calls), a phonecard or a credit card. When you have inserted at least 40¢, the credit display will show how much you have in credit. If you're using a phonecard or credit card, you'll be instructed when to dial.

● Dial the number required.

● When your credit is almost exhausted, there's an audible warning (a short burst of pips on the line) and a visible warning (a flashing red light) ten seconds before your time is about to expire. **Immediately insert more coins (or a new phonecard) or the call will be disconnected.**

- Replace the handset; any completely unused coins will be returned. If you still have credit for partly used coins, you can press the 'follow on call' button and make another call using the remaining credit. Otherwise any credit will be lost, so it pays not to insert too many $1 coins. If you're using a phonecard or a credit card, **don't forget to take it with you.**

If you have difficulties, phone the operator on 1234.

**Credit Card Payphones:** Some phones accept only credit cards (e.g. American Express, Diners Club, Mastercard and Visa), Telstra and Optus account cards, and EFTPOS cards. Credit card phones are predominantly located in major airports and other transport hubs, and large shopping centres. To use a credit card phone, swipe the magnetic strip of your card through the phone's card reader, enter your PIN number and dial when you hear the dialling tone. Note that there's usually a high minimum charge when using a credit card payphone, so they should be used only in an 'emergency'.

# MOBILE TELEPHONES

Mobile phones were introduced in Australia in 1987 and by 1997 it had the fourth-highest number of mobile phones per capita in the world after Sweden, Finland and Denmark. By 2000, over 8 million Australians had a mobile phone (over 40 per cent of the population) and the booming market shows no signs of slowing. **Before buying or using a mobile phone, you should be aware that health fears have been raised in some countries over the effects of the electromagnetic fields generated by them.** On the other hand, a mobile phone could save your life in an emergency!

Mobile phone services are operated by Telstra (over 50 per cent of the market), Optus (over 30 per cent), Vodaphone (less than 5 per cent), and other smaller companies. One-Tel, a very large and relatively new competitor in the mobile phone market, went out of business in mid-2001. The analogue network was phased out in 2000 and Australia now has an all-digital network, although phones in some rural areas without a digital service still have access to the analogue service. The digital network covers some 90 per cent of the population, including all the major population centres and corridors (all operators provide coverage maps).

In addition to services in the major metropolitan areas, Telstra mobile satellite and radio services provide mobile communications to the marine, remote land area and aeronautical markets. MobileSat allows you to plug a computer, fax machine or satellite navigation equipment into a terminal in a car, boat or aircraft and receive crystal clear communication wherever you are in Australia or up to 200km/124mi off the coast. Australia subscribes to the GSM digital network, which allows the same phone to be used in over 20 countries worldwide, including most of western Europe, Asia, the Pacific, central and South Africa, and the Middle East (referred to as international roaming).

Buying a mobile phone is a mine-field, as not only are there three networks from which to choose but numerous tariffs, connection fees, monthly subscriptions, insurance and call charges. Before buying a mobile, shop around and compare phone prices and features, installation and connection charges, rental charges and charge rates. **Most importantly, if you live or work in a remote area, make sure that a company's coverage includes that area.** Phones are sold by Telstra shops, specialist dealers, and department and chain stores which have arrangements with service providers or networks to sell airtime contracts (along with phones). Don't rely on getting good or impartial advice from retail staff, some of whom know little or nothing about phones and networks (it's said that the difference between Clint Eastwood and a mobile phone seller is that Clint isn't a real cowboy). Retailers advertise in magazines and newspapers, where a wide range of special offers is promoted. There are dozens of mobile phones on the market priced from around $250 for an average phone to over $700 for a top model. Some car manufacturers fit car phones as standard equipment, particularly to attract women drivers (some of whom are born with phones attached to their ears).

Before buying a phone, compare battery life, memory number capacity, weight (now down to around 100g or less for the lightest models), size and features, which may include alphanumeric store, automatic call back, unanswered call store, call timer, minute minder, lock facility, call barring, mailbox, messaging services, Internet web-surfing and e-mail.- Note that, when you sign up with a service provider, the cost of a phone is subsidised (and remains the property of the service provider) and retailers and network providers recoup the cost through line rentals and call charges. You can sign up for as little as $44, although the minimum cost over 18 months is usually several times this.

The most important point is where you're going to use a phone, followed by when, how often, and whether you'll make mostly local, long-distance or international calls. Don't be influenced by an inexpensive phone when the real costs lie in high call and line rental charges. Generally, the higher the connection and line rental charges, the lower the cost of calls. If you make a lot of calls, select a tariff with low call charges. Conversely, if you make few calls or need a phone mostly for incoming calls, choose a tariff with low monthly costs. Note that calls to and from mobile phones, including calls made from a fixed-line phone, are much more expensive than calls between fixed-line phones, and calls to 1800 numbers aren't free from mobile phones. Telephone numbers with the prefixes 014, 015, 017 and 018 are analogue mobile numbers, which are gradually being phased out. Digital mobile telephones have the prefix 04. You can obtain pre-paid cards (e.g. $25, $60 or $100, available from post offices), which avoid the need to sign a long-term contract or produce a credit card. If you have a phone with a pre-paid card, there's no charge for receiving calls; it's an ideal solution for someone who wants a phone mostly for incoming calls. You can buy 'top-up' cards for as little as $10.

**Security:** Theft of mobile phones is a huge problem and stolen mobiles are usually reprogrammed (cloned) to make free calls overseas. Mobile phones should never be left in cars. You should insure a phone for its real value – if a rented phone is stolen, you'll be billed for its replacement cost, not what you paid for it. All phones are provided with a unique serial number which allows their use to be blocked if they're stolen, and digital phones can be programmed to stop users making certain calls, e.g. international calls. New clone-proof digital mobile phones are being introduced, and all mobile phones are expected to be digital within five years.

Free booklets, *Hold the phone – read this before you buy a mobile* and *Mobile phone etiquette for Australia*, are available from the office of the telecommunications industry ombudsman (☎ freecall 1800-062058).

One spin-off of the mobile phone explosion is that they've created a new breed of 'cellular Samaritans' who report emergencies, accidents, crimes, traffic jams and other problems.

# DIRECTORIES

Australian telephone subscribers, both business and private, are listed in directories (also called phone books) which may be subdivided into white and yellow pages. In most areas, white and yellow pages are contained in the same volume, while in major cities such as Sydney there are separate volumes. White pages contain a list of subscribers in alphabetical order and yellow pages a list of businesses listed by business type. If you don't have the latest local phone book when you move into a new home, you can get one free from your local post office. You can order other directories (☎ freecall 1800-810211), for which there's a $6.80 delivery charge plus $4.18 for each directory in each consignment. You can also buy a CD-ROM for $19.95 containing all 55 Australian directories with over 7.5 million names and phone numbers. White and yellow pages are also available on the Internet (🖳 www. whitepages.com.au and 🖳 www.yellowpages.com.au), including versions of the white pages in German, Indonesian and Italian. New editions of phone books are delivered free to subscribers' homes. Directories can also be viewed at post offices, international telephone directory reference libraries and public libraries. Telstra recommend that you recycle your old telephone books (special bins are provided in major cities when new books are issued).

An entry containing your name, address and telephone number is automatically listed in the white pages directory covering your area. You may also purchase an extra entry, e.g. when two people share a telephone, or enhance your listing by having it printed in bold type. Business customers may also list an occupation. You can request an unlisted or ex-directory number (called a 'silent number'), for which there's a fee of $2.93 monthly. In this case, your name and number won't appear in any directories and won't be made available by directory enquiries (1223). Elements of your address such as your street and house number can also be suppressed (e.g. just your name and suburb is listed), for which there's an annual fee of $30. Around 10 per cent of Australians have silent numbers. If you are bothered by nuisance calls, Telstra run a National Unwelcome Call Service offering advice and solutions (☎ 1899-805996).

A wealth of information is contained in the white pages, including 24-hour emergency numbers, Telstra information and services, a translation and interpreting service (TIS), services for the disabled and aged, community help and welfare services, abbreviations of place names (used in directories), telephone prefixes and place names, and telephone information services (190 numbers).

**Yellow Pages:** In addition to subscriber phone books, business directories called yellow pages are published for all regions of Australia. Yellow pages include emergency and useful local numbers, local government numbers, a calendar of events, an entertainment seating guide, public transport information, inner city and surroundings maps. Subscribers are listed under a business or service heading (in alphabetical order) for the area covered. If you don't have the latest yellow pages when you move into a new home, you can obtain a free copy from your local post office. New editions of yellow pages are delivered to subscribers' homes. All phone books and yellow pages are available in public reference libraries and public telephone booths may also contain local directories. There are separate business directories in the major cities such as the Business Information Guide (BIG) in Melbourne.

**Directory Enquiries:** There are various numbers for directory enquiries (called 'directory assistance' in Australia). Usually you dial 1223 for local and national directory assistance and 1225 for overseas directory enquiries. All directory assistance calls are usually free except from mobile phones. If you want directory enquiries to find a number for you, you must know the town or city of the person or business whose number you require. Telephone numbers for most subscribers in major international cities can be obtained from directories in central reference libraries in major towns and cities.

## EMERGENCY NUMBERS

There's only one national emergency number in Australia, the 000 service, which is for police, fire, ambulance, coastguard, cave and mountain rescue services. Emergency calls are free from all telephones, including payphones. When you dial 000, the operator will ask you which emergency service you require ("Emergency, which service please?") and you'll immediately be put through to that service. You must state clearly your name and location and give a brief description of the emergency.

Lists of other '24-hour Emergency Numbers' and 'Personal Emergency & Help Services' is included at the front of the white pages telephone directory and inside the front cover of the yellow pages. These include maritime rescue, aviation search and rescue, chemist emergency prescriptions, child abuse, child protection, crime stoppers, crisis centre, customs coastwatch, dentists, distress call, doctors, domestic violence, drug intelligence, electricity, gas, water, hospitals, kids' helpline, lifeline, Mindwise (mental health), poison information, rape line, youth line, city missions, state emergency service, translating and interpreting service, veterinary surgeons and counselling for victims of crime. Lifeline (☎ local call rate 13-1114) provides a confidential, 24-hour counselling service in times of personal crisis throughout Australia for the cost of a local call. There is also a Women's Information Service (☎ freecall 1800-817227). See also **Emergencies** on page 282 and **Counselling** on page 295.

## INTERNET

Australia has the highest number of Internet users per capita outside the USA (around 42 per cent of households and 56 per cent of small businesses) and enjoys the world's second lowest (after the USA) Internet access charges thanks largely to Telstra's untimed local calls. This means that for a one-time charge of 22¢ subscribers can stay on the Internet for as long as they wish. The speed of access is expected to increase dramatically in future, as high speed lines and cable modems are introduced, although broad band access has so far been very limited. There are Internet service providers in all capital cities and also in many regional cities, where the most popular providers are OzEmail, Access One and Bigpond (Telstra). Competition has driven down fees in recent years and you should shop around for the best deal. There are also many ISPs who provide a free service.

If you have correspondents or friends who are connected to the Internet, you can also make long-distance and international 'calls' for the price of a local phone call. Internet users can buy software from companies such as Quarterdeck and Vodaltec (costing around $100) that effectively turns their personal computer into a voice-based telephone (both parties must have compatible software). You also need a sound card, speakers, a microphone and a modem, and access to a local Internet provider. While the quality of communication isn't as good as using a telephone (it's similar to using a CB radio) and you need to arrange call times in advance (e.g. by e-mail), making international 'calls' costs virtually nothing. All you pay is the cost of a local call to your Internet provider. Even this call is free in some areas where cable phone companies provide free local calls. Once on the Internet there are no other charges, no matter how much distance is covered or time is spent online.

# TELEGRAMS, TELEX & FAX

Telegrams (cables) can be sent by phone or from any post office in Australia. There are three rates: urgent (two to four hour delivery), ordinary (four to six hours) and letter (24 hours), although in some remote areas of Australia deliveries are made just once a week by air. The cost depends on where a telegram being sent from, the destination and the speed required.

Telex is the largest dedicated text message network in the world, with over 2 million subscribers worldwide in over 200 countries. There are public telex bureaux at all capital city chief telegraph offices and at Telstra offices in many towns.

**Fax:** When sending an international fax, dial 0015 (FaxStream) instead of 0011, followed by the country code, area code and fax number. FaxStream is a network of specially selected lines which provide optimum quality for international fax calls. Line rental costs $31.95 per month. Australia Post provides a public fax and delivery service (FaxPost), which allows faxes to be sent to virtually anyone in Australia or overseas, irrespective of whether you or the recipient has a fax machine. FaxPost allows delivery of faxed documents to all major centres in Australia within two hours (or the same day) plus fast delivery overseas.

To fax a document via FaxPost to someone in Australia without a fax machine, you fax the document to the Fax Centre Post Office nearest the addressee (there are around 2,000 throughout Australia); it's then delivered within two hours, the same day or by mail, depending on your instructions. If you don't have a fax machine but the addressee does, you must deliver your document to the nearest Fax Centre, from where it will be faxed to the addressee. A document can also be sent to someone when neither party has a fax machine, in which case the document is delivered to the nearest Fax Centre and faxed to the Fax Centre Post Office nearest the addressee, from where it's delivered.

International faxes can be transmitted to over 90 countries and to any fax machine in the world, provided IDD phone access is available. Messages can be delivered to overseas addressees without a fax machine by courier messenger, often on the same day, or can be delivered next day by mail. The cost for domestic faxes is $4 for the first page and $1 for additional pages, and for international faxes $8 for the first page and $2 for additional pages. Faxes can also be sent from hotels, business offices, and Telstra phone centres in major towns and cities.

Mobile phone and portable computer users can use a portable fax, which allows fax transmissions to be made from virtually anywhere in Australia and overseas. ISDN (integrated services digital network) lines allow you to send large computer files at high speed and virtually error free, e.g. file of several hundred megabytes takes just a few seconds to send compared with many minutes by e-mail.

# 8.

# TELEVISION & RADIO

Australian television (the 'electric goldfish bowl') is among the best in the world and much better than the rubbish dished up in many other countries, e.g. the USA, but not as good as British TV. However, over half the programmes are purchased from Britain and the USA, most local content consisting of sport, soaps, current affairs and game shows. Free-to-air (or terrestrial) TV includes both government-owned and commercial stations. In addition, pay (cable) TV is provided in most major cities, and satellite TV is also available in country and outback areas. WebTV was introduced in 1998, where customers can purchase a set-top box (for around $200) with a built-in modem for Internet access (no computer is required), a pay-TV decoder and a CD-ROM drive for games. Digital TV is also available in metropolitan areas and will be available in regional areas by 1st January 2004. Digital TV allows hundreds of channels to be transmitted by satellite and cable. Australian radio includes both state-owned ABC and commercial stations and is generally excellent.

Australians are avid TV viewers and almost all homes have a colour TV (over half have two or more) and 80 per cent have a VCR, which has spawned a nation of couch potatoes. As in most western countries, Australian children spend up to a third of their leisure time watching TV, which has been criticised for providing a mixture of mindless junk, violence and sex, detrimental to the education of children. In households where TV reigns supreme, the 'idiot box' is far more influential with children than parents. The poor quality of some programmes in Australia is offset by some of the best and funniest advertisements in the world (which they should be, considering they cost more to produce than many programmes). There's no TV or radio licence (which were abolished in 1974), so at least the rubbish is 'free'!

TV programmes are listed in daily newspapers (Saturday newspapers also include Sunday programmes) and weekly guides such as *TV Week*, which is produced in separate editions for each state or territory (because of local time differences). Many Saturday and Sunday newspapers also provide free weekly TV and radio guides. However, few if any pay TV programmes are listed in most publications. Programmes can also be displayed via TV teletext or on the Internet e.g. on 🖳 www.sofcom.com. au. Note that the time difference between the states (see page 468) means that nationwide programmes are broadcast at different times according to where you live in Australia.

## STANDARDS & EQUIPMENT

The standards for TV reception in Australia aren't the same as in many other countries. TVs and video recorders manufactured for use in North America (NTSC Standard) and for the European PAL B/G or PAL-I systems won't function in Australia. Some foreign TVs can be converted to operate under Australia's PAL-D system, although it usually isn't worth the trouble and expense of shipping a TV (or VCR) to Australia.

The cost of a TV varies considerably according to its make, screen size, features and, not least, the retailer (shop around). The cost of a quality TV ranges from around $300 for a 34cm (14in) portable TV to $2,000 for a state-of-the-art 63cm (24in) TV. Video recorders start at around $200 and DVDs at around $500. TVs are becoming ever more sophisticated and many offer a wide array of features, including on-screen displays of volume and picture controls, and picture-in-picture, which allows you to superimpose on the screen a small picture of what's showing on other channels by pressing a button on the remote control. TV addicts can add Dolby surround sound (using a Dolby pro logic amplifier with decoder and separate speakers) and create cinema sound effects. Other recent innovations include LaserDisc, Digital Video Disc (DVD) and Video CD systems, although these are still expensive when compared with VHS video.

When buying a TV in Australia, you'll find it advantageous to choose one with teletext, which apart from allowing you to display programme listings also provides a wealth of useful and interesting information, including news, weather, sport, travel, finance, shopping and entertainment. Teletext also provides subtitles for selected programmes for people with hearing problems, which are usually indicated in programme listings. Pay TV and satellite stations also provide teletext services. Note that, whatever you buy, in a year's time (or less) it will be superseded by a new, 'improved' model.

There's an active market in secondhand TVs and videos (and most other things) in Australia so, should you wish to sell your old TV to buy one with the latest bells and whistles (or because you're leaving Australia), you'll have no problem. Secondhand colour TVs can be purchased from retailers, rental companies and through advertisements in local newspapers from as little as $100. Some retailers offer to part exchange your old TV for a new one, although they may offer you less than its market value.

TV rental is fairly common in Australia and is mostly offered by specialist national rental companies (such as Rentlo), although some local TV and radio shops also rent. It's always cheaper to buy than rent a TV or video, particularly over a long period. Some people are tempted to rent by the ever-changing technology, although you should bear in mind that rental TVs are rarely the latest models and the minimum rental period is usually 12 or 18 months. Renting a TV is a habit carried over from the '50s and '60s when few people could afford to buy a TV outright. Today, renting hardly ever makes economic sense.

# FREE-TO-AIR STATIONS

There are five national terrestrial or free-to-air (FTA) networks in Australia: ABC, Seven, Nine, Ten and SBS. ABC (Australian Broadcasting Corporation) and SBS (Special Broadcasting Service) are government owned, while Seven, Nine and Ten are commercial networks. There are also a number of regional commercial stations (including Capital, NBN, Northern, Prime, Seven Queensland, Southern Cross and Win), Imparja Television (an Aboriginal commercial station), plus local, community and student TV. Not all areas receive all the national networks: most state capitals can receive between three and five, while in some remote areas ABC may be the only free-to-air station you can receive. The regional stations are affiliated to the national commercial networks, e.g. Prime, Seven Queensland and Southern Cross are affiliated to Seven, NBN and WIN to Nine, and Capital Television to Ten. Overall control of Australia's TV and radio services is exercised by the Australian Broadcasting Authority (ABA).

**Programmes:** Australian TV is famous for its soaps, although some have terrible scripts and even worse 'acting'. The most popular Australian soaps include Neighbours, Home and Away, and Flying Doctor, which are sold worldwide and are particularly popular in Britain. British comedy, drama and soaps are also popular in Australia, as are the 'better' American programmes. The choice of films on FTA TV is usually terrible and you need to subscribe to pay TV to see the latest films. Australian TV isn't as paranoid about nudity as American TV, but you're unlikely to see any explicit sex (except perhaps on pay or satellite TV). News and current affairs programmes are popular, although news tends to be parochial and doesn't include much world news. There are good weather forecasts on all channels.

There's little good quality Australian produced drama and comedy, mainly because of lack of funds or because ratings are too low. The best Australian production seems to run to are the so-called 'infotainment' shows, which show you how to update your home, garden, etc. for next to nothing (the show also costs the producer next to nothing!).

Australian TV, particularly commercial stations, shows a surfeit of live sport, particularly at weekends. Coverage includes both local and international events, including tennis, soccer, cricket, rugby, Australian rules football, American football, baseball, basketball, motor racing and athletics. To protect significant sporting and cultural events from being bought by pay TV, the government introduced an 'anti-siphoning' list of events (11 sports plus the Olympic and Commonwealth Games) which should be televised free to the general public. However, over half the events on the anti-siphoning list have never been shown at all on FTA TV and less than a third have been shown live on FTA. Pay TV operators are pushing to have the list reduced or to be permitted to show live sports and events that have been rejected by the FTA stations. In mid-2001 there was no sign of compromise on the matter, and every sporting event was treated as an individual case.

**Commercial TV:** Australia has three commercial networks, Seven, Nine and Ten, which are available in major cities and offer 24-hour programming. Nine Network has been the leading station for over ten years, although it's closely rivalled by Seven Network. Nine is unashamedly populist and produces good lifestyle programmes, game shows, and news and current affairs programmes but isn't so good at comedy and drama, although its imported American programmes such as *ER* and *Friends* rank at the top of the viewing ratings. Its other forte is sport, which dominates programming. Seven Network is the second-highest rated network (by viewing figures) after Nine and is strong on comedy and drama and more likely to show non-commercial programmes. Its most popular programmes include *The Weakest Link* and recent movies. Seven Network has weaker news and current affairs than the Nine Network. Ten Network has given up trying to compete with Nine and Seven for the mainstream market and concentrates on screening popular American shows (*The Simpsons*, *X-Files*) for the under 40s. It isn't strong on local programmes, although it did come up with *Neighbours* and *Heartbreak High*. Breakfast TV is popular on all commercial stations.

The quality of programmes on commercial TV varies from terrible to excellent. The competition to buy foreign (e.g. British and American) programmes and exclusive rights to sporting events is fierce, particularly with the increased competition from pay TV. It's hoped that this will result in the networks producing more of their own programmes, which, apart from being superior to a lot of the imported drivel, are also a lucrative export product. Commercial TV networks currently produce just over half their programmes.

Advertisements on commercial TV are frequent and irritating, particularly when you're trying to watch a film or sport. Some sports events are ruined by commercial breaks, and ads are sometimes even screened during play at the bottom of the screen. Breaks tend to be more frequent and last longer than in many other countries and even exceed some American stations (where the ads seem to last longer than the programmes). The maximum permitted advertising quota is 13 minutes per hour but, when promotional slots and trailers are included, it's much longer. Commercial stations are huge money-spinners and regularly change owners.**Imparja:** Imparja Television is an Aboriginal owned and run commercial TV station operating out of Alice Springs. It covers a third of the country, mainly in the Northern Territory, South Australia and western NSW. Broadcasts range from soap operas to programmes made especially for Aboriginal people.

**ABC:** The Australian Broadcasting Corporation (ABC), affectionately known as 'Aunty' after the British Broadcasting Corporation (BBC) on which it's modelled, is government owned and operates both TV and radio (see page 188) stations throughout Australia. Being financed by the government, it carries no advertising. The name of the local ABC station varies according to the state, e.g. it's called ABN in NSW (the N is for NSW) and ABV in Victoria, although it's usually found on channel two. Being non-commercial, it holds the moral high ground with regard to quality programming (almost nothing American is aired!) and its output contains a large percentage of locally produced programmes with the emphasis on comedy, drama, natural history (mostly about Australia), news and current affairs. Comedy and drama programmes are often imported from Britain. The ABC also operates Australia Television, an international satellite TV service broadcasting to over 30 countries and territories in Asia and the Pacific.

**SBS:** The Special Broadcasting Service (SBS) is a government sponsored, multicultural TV station, established in 1978 to provide multi-lingual radio and TV services that inform, educate and entertain all Australians, and reflect Australia's multicultural society. SBS is available in all major cities and a number of regional areas, reaching around 16 million people. It's similar to PBS in America, although it screens a large percentage of programmes in foreign languages with sub-titles, in addition to English-language programmes. It's mainly funded by the government but carries advertising. It's usually found on channel eight, although you need a special receiver in some areas. SBS has its critics, although most viewers appreciate that it provides foreign 'culture' unavailable on other channels and excellent world news coverage which is far superior to the more parochial output of the ABC and commercial stations. It also shows foreign sport (e.g. European soccer) that isn't found on commercial TV and is the traditional host channel of the (soccer) World Cup. It's sometimes criticised, however, as being insensitive to community needs and, although it exports its few home-produced programmes, it also shows a lot of 'trashy' foreign films. SBS has a relatively small but dedicated following.

**Community or Local TV:** There are five or six community or local TV stations in all major cities. Community TV stations include ACE-TV (Adelaide), Briz31 (Brisbane), CATV (Canberra), MCT-31 (Melbourne), LINC TV (NSW), CTVP 31 (Perth) and CTS (Sydney). There's also student TV in some cities, such as RMITV in Melbourne.

# PAY TELEVISION

Pay TV was introduced in Australia in 1995 and shouldn't be confused with pay-per-view, where subscribers pay on a per programme basis (e.g. for a live concert or sports event). With pay TV, viewers pay a monthly fee for a package of stations, delivered via cable or satellite. There are two major pay TV operators in Australia, Foxtel and Optus Vision, plus a few smaller operators.

The installation of cables for pay TV in Australia was one of the largest and fastest cable installation programmes undertaken anywhere in the world. Both Telstra and Optus laid their cables in the same streets in Sydney, Melbourne and Brisbane, afraid that their rivals would steal a march on them (Optus laid its cables above ground, to the revulsion of residents, rather than burying then as Telstra did). Cable currently reaches around three million homes (40 per cent of the total), mostly in major cities. Most homes in Brisbane, the Gold Coast, Melbourne and Sydney are cabled, plus parts of Adelaide and Perth. The broadband cable is used to deliver pay TV, FM radio, telephone, high-speed Internet access, and other interactive services such as community information systems. It also enables operators to offer pay-per-view films and other broadcasts on demand.

Some 15 per cent of households in Melbourne and Sydney subscribe to pay TV, although the biggest fans are children; many families have tried it and quit. Unlike satellite and cable TV in Europe and North America, pay TV in Australia doesn't have sufficient big exclusive sports or entertainment specials to attract the average viewer (Australia's climate also means that many people have better things to do than watch TV). Foxtel provides some 30 channels, including world news, the cartoon network, the world movie channel, Fox Sports, Fox Children's Network, Sky and BBC World. Optus Vision provides around 25 channels, including Disney and Warner Bros, news, general entertainment, education, sport, films, music and community broadcasts. However, critics claim that most output consists of old films, minor sports, boring documentaries and banal local news. Pay TV operators have been allowed to broadcast advertisements since 1997.

As with the rest of the media business in Australia, pay TV is a battle between the press moguls Kerry Packer (aligned with Optus Vision) and Rupert Murdoch (Foxtel in partnership with Telstra), with (so far) both coming out losers. Initially, pay TV was a financial disaster, with combined losses for Optus Vision and Foxtel totalling over $3 billion in less than four years, although both companies are now firmly established in the market. Foxtel claims to be the more popular with some 725,000 homes subscribing to its cable and satellite services (around half the market). Optus doesn't publish subscriber figures and has the disadvantage of not having satellite services; its emissions are therefore limited to the cable network in Brisbane, Melbourne and Sydney.

Foxtel and Optus both charge an installation fee of around $40 (which may be much higher for homes with difficult access) and a monthly subscription of between around $40 and $80 or more depending on the programme package (you can choose from a range of packages depending on your preferred viewing, e.g. sport or films). Subscriptions can be paid by direct debit, cash (at an ANZ branch or post office), cheque, money order or credit card. Some cable companies offer inexpensive phone services, in some cases including free local off-peak calls, and it's possible to save enough money on your phone bill to pay for your cable TV. Optus offers customers who use its pay TV and long-distance telephone services a discount on their monthly TV bill, or an equal discount on their long-distance phone bill.

Although Melbourne, Sydney and Brisbane have been 'cornered' by Optus and Telstra, the rest of the country is wide open and being exploited by small companies (such as Northgate Cable in Ballarat and Neighbourhood Cable in Mildura (VIC)) who have encroached on Telstra's market share by offering telephone, TV and Internet services at lower prices. For example, Northgate Cable provides a 27-channel pay TV service in Ballarat for $27.50 per month, and Neighbourhood Cable charge $30 per month. Subscribers usually receive free monthly programme guides, which are also available from newsagents. However, most Australian newspapers and TV guides virtually ignore pay TV and don't list any programmes, while some list only selected channels (e.g. Showtime and Foxtel highlights). The Australian PayTV website (🖥 www.auspaytv.com) offers comprehensive information on the current state of the market as well as links to all pay TV companies.

## VIDEOS

In the last decade or so, there has been an explosion in the number of video rental outlets in Australia, which reached saturation point some years ago (they total over 3,000 with an annual turnover of more than $600 million). Some 80 per cent of households (over 5 million) have at least one VCR and around 60 per cent of households rent at least one video per month. There's also a thriving video sales market. Many video shops are open until 8pm or 10pm, seven days a week. To rent a video you must usually be a member, for which shops insist on proof of address and verification of your signature. A parent is required to stand as a guarantor for those under 18. Some video shops have a children's membership scheme with special deals for kids and cheap rental rates for children's films (although most kids are more interested in video nasties than *The Jungle Book*!). The latest releases can be rented for around $7 per night and older films can be rented for up to a week for as little as $3. Rental outlets usually have special offers for film buffs such as a free old movie with each new release rented or seven old movies for a week for $10.

Members are issued with a membership card, which must be shown when hiring videos. Usually, you can take out up to three or four films at any time and must return them up to two hours before closing time the following day. If you're late returning a film, you're charged an extra day's rental for each day overdue. Note that, if you lose or damage a film, you'll be expected to pay for a replacement at retail price. Videos can also be rented from some public libraries. Most video shops also sell secondhand videos at reduced prices as well as older videos which are on general sale.

## RADIO

Radio reception in Australia is excellent in most parts of the country, including stereo radio, which is clear in all but the most remote or 'mountainous' areas (not that Australia has many mountains). Radio is very popular, particularly among the young – three out of four teenagers listen daily. Local stations broadcast on the FM wave band in stereo or on the medium wave (MW) band. High-quality FM radio can also be received via cable or satellite, which provides dozens of stations. The short wave (SW) band is useful for receiving foreign radio stations. Digital radio was introduced in 2001 and allows stations to transmit several channels of sound simultaneously, as well as text and pictures to a small screen attached to receivers. Australian radio is regulated by the Australian Broadcasting Authority (ABA) and there are no radio licence fees in Australia.

There are literally hundreds of radio stations in Australia, including ABC, commercial, ethnic, community and university-based stations (operated on a shoe-string and run by volunteers). In the last few decades, dozens of public (community) radio stations have sprung up around Australia, supported by the government and various educational institutions. They often have a limited transmission range and cater for specific community groups within their areas, e.g. there are some 16 public radio stations in Sydney, which although amateurish are diverse and original.

**Commercial Radio:** Commercial radio is hugely popular in Australia and includes large city stations with vast budgets and hundreds of thousands of listeners. Stations provide a comprehensive service of music and other entertainment, local news and information, education, consumer advice, traffic information and local events. There are also 'talk-back' stations (such as Melbourne's top-rated 3AW) which intersperse music with phone-in discussions that provide listeners with the opportunity to air their views. Many stations have 'star' presenters whose 'fame' (infamy) is often due to their outrageous and insulting behaviour towards their listeners (sports commentators can also be extremely rude about players' performances). The location of a station can be determined by its call sign, the first number of which is the same as a state or territory's postcode, e.g. 2UE is a Sydney station and 3CR is in Melbourne.

Stations cater for every musical taste (e.g. pop/rock, easy listening, classical, jazz), although pop stations are the most popular and cater mostly for mainstream tastes. Some stations even change their output (e.g. from easy listening to hard rock or vice versa) at the drop of a hat if their audience figures fall dramatically. Music is usually blended with news updates, traffic and weather reports, although some stations have taken to playing less music and telling jokes, which apparently receive a higher rating than music. Radio stations employ real 'comedians', not just DJs trying to raise a chuckle (termed comedy jocks), with a down-to-earth sense of humour where anything goes and nothing is sacred.

As their name implies, commercial radio stations in Australia carry advertising, which is their main source of income. There's an overheated market for commercial FM stations (which change hands for huge sums) and a pent-up demand for licences in the major cities. The largest radio station networks in Australia are owned by DMG Radio Australia, Austereo and the Australian Radio Network.

**ABC:** The Australian Broadcasting Corporation (ABC) is government funded and operates both TV (see page 185) and radio stations throughout Australia. It runs metropolitan radio stations in nine cities and 36 regional stations, including Radio National, ABC Classic FM and the Triple-J (JJJ) youth radio network. ABC metropolitan radio includes 702 Sydney and 774 Melbourne. It also operates the 24-hour Parliamentary & News Network, a parliamentary radio service broadcast to all capital cities except Darwin (lucky them!) and to Newcastle. The ABC is also responsible for Radio Australia, an international radio service broadcast via short wave and satellite (in English and eight other languages) to the Asia-Pacific regions and world wide, although services have been reduced in recent years and remain under threat from budget cuts.

ABC Radio National provides excellent news coverage (international news is sent by satellite from the BBC in London) and is broadcast nationwide on both AM and FM. However, in general, ABC stations aren't as popular as commercial stations (Triple-J is one exception) and are regarded as the thinking person's radio stations.

Triple-J, the ABC's youth FM radio station, is a good place to hear new music outside the main pop stream and plug into Australia's youth culture. There's no advertising on ABC radio stations.

**Ethnic Radio:** Australians can tune in to local radio broadcasts in over 50 languages, including Aboriginal radio in outback regions. The Special Broadcasting Service (SBS) was established in 1994 and like SBS TV (see page 185) broadcasts in many languages. It's available in all state and territory capital cities plus some other cities.

**BBC World Service:** The BBC World Service (the insomniac's station) broadcasts world wide, in English and around 35 other languages, with a total output of over 750 hours per week (a *very* long week). The BBC World Service is the most famous and highly respected international radio service in the world, with regular listeners estimated at some 120 million (give or take a few). Its main aims are to provide unbiased news, project British opinion, and reflect British life, culture, and developments in science and industry. News bulletins, current affairs, political commentaries and topical magazine programmes form the bulk of its output, supported by a comprehensive sports service, music, drama and general entertainment. The BBC publishes a monthly magazine, *BBC On Air*, containing comprehensive information about BBC World Service radio and TV programmes. For a free copy and frequency information, write to BBC On Air, Room 205 NW, Bush House, Strand, London WC2B 4PH, UK (an annual subscription costs GB£24).

# 9.

# EDUCATION

Australian educational institutions generally have a good international reputation, particularly universities and tertiary-level colleges, which enrol over 50,000 foreign students each year from all corners of the globe (further 100,000 foreign students are enrolled in vocational institutions, English-language colleges and other schools). Australian schools have a high standard of teaching and good academic results, and the country has a proud record of academic and scientific achievement. In international surveys, Australian students score highly in mathematics and science (ahead of most other western countries but behind some Asian countries).

Full-time education was introduced in West Australia in 1871, other states following suit shortly afterwards, and is compulsory from the ages of 6 to 15 (16 in Tasmania). Around 75 per cent of pupils complete 12 years of schooling, although this varies with the state or territory. Primary education lasts for six or seven years up to the age of 12 or 13 and secondary schooling for a further five or six years. Students are encouraged to remain at school until the completion of their 12th year (around the age of 18), although this may depend on the local job market. The government has cut unemployment benefits for young people in recent years to encourage them to stay on at school or take up training, rather than leave school and search for non-existent jobs. This has led to overcrowding in many high schools, where classes are bulging with students who don't want to be there.

Education in Australia is mainly the responsibility of state and territory governments, each of which has its own education system. Australia has around 9,600 primary and secondary schools, some 30 per cent of which are private (mostly Catholic church schools with some Church of England and other parochial schools). Most public (i.e. state) schools are co-educational (mixed) day schools, with the exception of a few secondary schools that accept boarders. Education at public schools is free, although parents must pay for books, uniforms, outings, caps and special programmes. Independent (private) schools are partially government funded but charge fees, some of which are very high. Private schools include both day and boarding schools, many of which are single-sex, particularly at secondary level. It's generally considered that private schools are superior to public institutions, although there's little difference between the best public and private schools. However, it's true that the worst-performing private schools are generally streets ahead of the worst public schools, and school-leavers from the public system are much more likely to end up on the dole than those educated at private school.

There's no legal obligation for parents to educate their children at school and they may educate them themselves or employ private tutors (with the advent of the Internet it's possible for children to be educated almost exclusively at home). In Victoria, parents aren't even required to inform the Education Department of their decision. Parents educating their children at home don't require a teaching qualification, although they must satisfy the local education authority that a child is receiving full-time education appropriate to his age, abilities and aptitudes (they will check and may test your child). Information can be obtained from the Alternative Education Resources Group in most states.

**Literacy:** A national literacy survey in 1997 found that a third of students in primary years three and five cannot read or write adequately, branded a 'national disgrace' by the federal schools minister. A national goal was set for each child starting school from 1998 to achieve an acceptable level of literacy and numeracy within four years. Pupils are tested for literacy skills every two years, in school years 3, 5, 7 and 9 or 10. A National Literacy and Numeracy Week is celebrated annually in early September to help publicise the literacy work in schools, and awards are made to schools and pupils who have made the most impressive progress. The problem of illiteracy is exacerbated by the thousands of migrant families who don't speak English or where English isn't spoken at home. Aboriginal children also have a low rate of literacy, generally three to four years behind other students. It's estimated that half of all Australians aged 15 to 74 (over six million people) have poor or very poor literacy skills, just two million people (15 per cent) having good literacy skills and a mere 300,000 very good skills. Adults with the poorest skills are (not surprisingly) mostly from non-English speaking backgrounds. The federal government also plans to introduce national standards and testing in numeracy.

**Further Information:** There are many books and magazines for parents faced with choosing a primary or secondary school, including *Choosing a School* magazine (published in separate editions for the Sydney, Melbourne and Canberra areas), available from Universal Magazines, Private Bag 154, North Ryde, NSW 2113 (☎ 02-9887 0339).

## PUBLIC OR PRIVATE SCHOOL?

Your choice between public and private schools will vary considerably according to where you live. Admission to a public school for foreign children is dependent on the type and duration of the visa (see **Chapter 3**) granted to their parents, and attendance may not be possible. Only nationals of Papua New Guinea and certain South Pacific states may apply for entry to junior secondary public schools in Australia. Senior secondary students of any nationality may attend public schools but must pay full fees (called the Overseas Students' Charge), which vary from $5,000 to $10,000 annually.

If you're able to choose between public and private education, the following checklist will help you decide:

● How long are you planning to stay in Australia? If you're uncertain, it's probably better to assume a long stay. Due to language and other integration problems, enrolling a child in an Australian school (public or private) with an Australian syllabus is recommended only for a minimum of a year, particularly for teenage children.

● Bear in mind that the area in which you choose to live will affect your choice of public school(s). Although it isn't always necessary to send your children to the public school nearest your home, you may have difficulty obtaining admission to a public school if you don't live within its catchment area.

● If your stay in Australia will be only for a short period, do you know where you're going after leaving Australia? This may be an important consideration with regard to your children's schooling in Australia. How old are your children and what age will they be when you plan to leave Australia? What plans do you have for their subsequent education and in which country?

● What age are your children and how will they fit into a private school or the Australian public school system? The younger they are, the easier it will be to place them in a suitable school.

- If your children aren't English-speaking, how do they view the thought of studying in English? Is teaching available in Australia in their mother tongue, and, more importantly, is that the best option?

- Will your children require your help with their studies? Will you be able to help them, particularly with the English language if it isn't their mother tongue? Is extra English tuition available at local schools?

- What are the school hours? What are the school holiday periods? How will the school hours and holidays influence your and your spouse's work and leisure activities?

- Is religion an important consideration in your choice of school? In public schools, religion isn't taught as a compulsory subject. However, most private schools are church-sponsored (e.g. Catholic) and religion is an important part of the curriculum.

- How large are the classes? What is the teacher-pupil ratio? Note that public school classes number between 30 and 35 pupils in metropolitan areas, less in rural areas, and are slowly being reduced in most states; classes in private schools can be as small as 15.

- What specialist staff does the school employ?

- Do you want your children to go to a co-educational (mixed) school? Public schools are usually co-educational, while private schools are often single-sex.

- Should you send your children to a boarding school? If so, should it be in Australia or in another country?

- What are the secondary and further education prospects for your children in Australia or another country? Are Australian examinations recognised in your home country or the country where you plan to live after leaving Australia?

- Does a school have a good academic record? All schools can provide exam pass rate statistics (e.g. HSC) and a prospectus, which they may mail to you. Note, however, that public schools in some states aren't permitted to publish their university entrance ranking results.

- Do students participate in decision-making?

- How much homework and what kind is expected at the various age levels?

- How are students selected? Is there a waiting list?

- Are uniforms worn and, if so, are they compulsory?

- What are the facilities for art and science subjects – for example, arts and crafts, music, computer studies (how many computers?), science, hobbies, drama, cookery and photography? Does the school have an extensive library of up-to-date books (a good library is usually an excellent sign)? Obtain a school's prospectus or handbook, where this information should be listed.

- What is the consensus in the local community about a school? Why do people feel the way they do? What are a school's aims and philosophies (a school's charter describes its educational philosophy and core purpose)?

- Are parents actively involved in the school? Do you have the time or enthusiasm to get involved?

- Do the children and teachers seem happy? Is there a genuine warmth between pupils and teachers? Is there a sense of achievement, challenge and purpose?

Obtain the opinions and advice of others who have been faced with the same decisions and problems as you, and collect as much information from as many different sources as possible before making a decision. If possible, attend a school open day and speak to teachers, parents and students. Most parents find it helpful to discuss the alternatives with their children before making a decision (if it isn't already too late, you could always decide against children and save yourself a lot of trouble!).

Many schools have special programmes for children with learning difficulties and for gifted children, and there are also special hospital schools, schools for children with learning difficulties, schools for gifted children, and schools for blind and deaf children. However, whenever possible, children with disabilities attend regular schools in which support is provided for them. Parents can obtain information from the Australian Remedial Education Association (AREA) and the Special Learning Difficulties Association (SPELD).

## PUBLIC SCHOOLS

The term 'public school' (or government school) refers to a non fee-paying school funded wholly from state and federal government budgets. State and territorial governments have the major responsibility for education and provide most funding, supported by the federal government. States administer their own primary and secondary schools and are also responsible for technical and further education. The federal government is responsible for tertiary education and provides supplementary funding for schools and for technical and further education. It's also responsible for education in the Australian territories of Norfolk Island, Christmas Island and the Cocos Islands. In the period 1999–2000, the federal government spent over $10 billion on education, which accounted for around 7 per cent of the total federal budget (less than half the health expenditure and only fractionally more than defence). The government is keen to foster links between schools – particularly technology high schools and TAFE colleges – and industry. Local businesses also provide sponsorship and extra funding for schools, plus practical work experience, share resources such as computers and other equipment, and help in creating specialised science courses. In recent years, however, many primary schools have been forced to cut back on computer classes by lack of resources.

Spending on public schools varies from state to state and is a hotly debated subject. A large number of public schools are modern institutions, having been built in the last decade, particularly in the outer suburbs of capital cities. Nevertheless, budget restrictions have resulted in school closures and have driven more families to send their children to private schools. In the mid-'90s, there was an unprecedented exodus of students from public to private schools, making it difficult for governments to provide quality public education in some areas (a number of public schools were forced to close by falling enrolments). In recent years, some public schools have been increasingly turning to voluntary levies to raise funds (usually to pay for additional materials) as state and federal funding has been cut. In some states, 'free' public education is fast becoming a misnomer, with many parents being forced to pay $1,000 to $2,000 per year (see **P&C Committees** below and **Uniforms & Expenses** on page 198).

Most students attend schools near their homes, although in country areas a long journey may be involved, particularly to secondary school. Usually, primary and secondary schools are separate institutions, but in some country areas there are combined primary and secondary (area or central) schools. School buses may be provided for children in rural areas, while in remote outback regions children do their lessons by correspondence or via the 'school of the air', where lessons are given over the Flying Doctor radio network throughout Australia (both public and private schools participate in programmes). Correspondence lessons use video and audio tapes and are usually supervised by a member of the family and administered by a correspondence school in a state capital. Public schools don't have canteens or restaurants, although school 'tuckshops' sell snacks, sandwiches and soft drinks at break and lunchtimes.

**P&C Committees:** Parents play a vital role in education in Australia, where each school has a committee comprising teachers, parents and student representatives, called a Parents and Citizens (P&C) committee. Parents can influence decisions such as the design and wearing of uniforms, discipline, homework and the curriculum. P&C committees (a third of which are made up of parents) also raise funds for school outings and equipment and assist in running certain aspects of the school such as administration, classroom assistance and school shops. An enthusiastic and flourishing P&C committee is usually a sign of a good school.

**Curriculum & Homework:** The curriculum contains eight key learning areas: English; mathematics; science; technology; human society and the environment; creative and practical arts; health and physical education; and foreign languages. Although states have a measure of autonomy in setting their own curricula, they must follow guidelines laid down by the federal government, and the curriculum is broadly similar in all states, so children generally experience few problems when moving from one state to another. Individual schools also have a degree of autonomy and can determine their own teaching and learning approaches within the guidelines provided and offer options within the resources available. Some schools specialise in languages and place greater emphasis on foreign language study, with special programmes and innovative teaching methods. Where necessary, students from non-English speaking countries are given extra English classes, and English as a Second Language (ESL) programmes are provided in schools with significant numbers of children from non-English speaking backgrounds.

Computer technology is an increasingly important aspect of teaching in Australian schools at all levels right across the curriculum, where computers are used in language development, to access databases, in student-centred learning, and in distance learning. Some schools excel in their use of computers, although the ratio of computers to students is low in most public schools, many of which buy computers (and other equipment) with money raised by parents and sponsors.

Extra-curricular activities are common in Australia and include sports (an important feature of Australian school life), arts and crafts, camps, excursions and social events such as discos and barbecues. School bands, orchestras, choirs, dance troupes and dramatic societies are also common.

School homework varies considerably, some children doing too little and others doing more than is healthy; only around a quarter of schools/pupils strike a healthy balance between study and recreation. A maximum of two or three hours each school day is recommended for students in their 11th and 12th years of secondary school, although many do over 20 hours a week.

**Choosing a School:** The quality of public schools, their teaching staff and the education they provide, varies considerably according to the state or territory, region, town, city, suburb and individual school. If you want your children to have a good education, it's absolutely essential to get them into a good school, even if it means moving house and changing your job. Children have the right to attend their local public school, although they may attend any other public school (in the state or territory where they live) where there's a vacancy. However, priority at any school goes to local children (see **Admissions** below). It's important to research the best schools in a given area and to ensure that your child will be accepted at your chosen school **before buying or renting a home**. There's an education 'underclass' in some deprived areas, particularly those with high unemployment and a large percentage of families living on income support. Some high schools (usually in the poorer and more disadvantaged areas) have discipline, drug and violence problems, and have installed video cameras and taken other measures to identify offenders. Obviously, these schools are best avoided if at all possible.

**Problems:** The public school system has been in a state of almost constant flux in recent years, when there has been criticism of the quality of teacher selection and of training and teaching methods (added to which there's an acute shortage of teachers). Many teachers in public schools are demoralised and, according to some reports, around half would give up teaching if they could. Their complaints include falling pay compared with other professionals (although teachers are generally well paid), long teaching hours, a lack of resources, low professional standing, an overcrowded curriculum, overcrowded classes, violence and discipline problems (corporal punishment is forbidden in public schools), children with little or no English and poor working conditions, e.g. teaching in portable classrooms in temperatures over 40°C (104°F)!

# Admissions

You should address enquiries about admission to a public school (enrolment) to the headmaster or principal of the school of your choice. Enquiries should be made well in advance of taking up residence in a new area. Most children go to the school nearest their home, particularly at primary level. All children are guaranteed a place at their local public high school, but parents have the option of applying to up to four non-local high schools. Placement outside the local area depends on the availability of places and, if daily travel isn't feasible, accommodation at the school. Buses are provided for children who have a long journey to school. When visiting a school, you should take your child's reports, references and certificates from previous schools. New pupils are assessed and admitted to the appropriate class for their age and educational level, and it's unusual for a child to be placed with children of more than one year's age difference.

Starting ages for primary and secondary schools vary with the state or territory and there are at least six different school entry ages across Australia, although the terms are similar (see below). In South Australia and the Northern Territory there's a continuous intake and children may begin school when they turn five years of age.

However, in Western Australia children born after 30th June aren't able to start school until the year they turn seven, and in Victoria they must be aged five by 30th April of the year of enrolment. Such differences can cause problems when children move to a new state, and the federal government has proposed a plan which would ensure that children start school at the same age in all states. All schools prefer children to start at the beginning of a new term if possible, and most schools like parents to apply in October for children starting school the following year. The normal intake is in January/February, although some states operate a mid-year intake as well.

## School Holidays & Hours

Australia's academic year follows the calendar year from January to December. All states have four terms of around ten weeks per year except Tasmania, which has three. Terms are separated by holidays, usually lasting two weeks, except the summer break, which is five or six weeks. There may also be breaks for public holidays. The length and dates of school holidays vary considerably with the state or territory. Public primary and secondary (high) schools in NSW had the following holidays in 2002/03 (all dates are inclusive):

| Holiday | Dates |
|---------|-------|
| Autumn | 13th to 28th April |
| Winter | 6th to 21st July |
| Spring | 28th September to 13th October |
| Summer | 21st December to 27th January |

Holiday dates are published by schools well in advance, thus allowing you plenty of time to schedule family holidays during official school holidays. Normally parents aren't permitted to withdraw children from classes during the school term, except for visits to a doctor or dentist, when the teacher should be informed in advance (if possible).

Classes start at around 9am and continue until 4pm, with a break for lunch and mid-morning and mid-afternoon recesses. Some children may need to work longer hours if they need extra tuition, for example in English. The maximum classroom teaching hours are around 20 hours in secondary schools and 22.5 in primary schools. Exam stress is a problem at secondary schools and universities. Many schools provide care and recreational facilities outside school hours for children whose parents are working, seeking work or studying, for which a fee is levied. Supervision may include before and after-school care and care during school holidays. Children being looked after may spend up to 25 hours a week in care, in addition to normal school hours. Fees vary from almost nothing to $60 per week for before and after-school care, rising to $75 for two children and $90 for three.

## Uniforms & Expenses

Most schools encourage pupils to wear school uniform and they're compulsory at some state and most private schools (although tracksuits or jeans may be permitted during winter). Uniforms are usually optional in primary schools. Uniforms can be expensive (with different uniforms for summer and winter), as each school usually has its own embroidered jumpers, socks, caps and blazers, which means that they must be specially made in small quantities. Uniforms can sometimes be purchased secondhand from school shops. Hats are an integral part of school uniforms and are designed to protect pupils from the sun. High protection sunscreen is also provided free to pre-school and primary year one pupils in many states, and most schools have a 'hot weather' policy where all children must wear sun hats (with a peak and 'legionnaire' flap to protect the back of the neck) and sun cream at playtime. Students at some colleges are being encouraged to wear sunglasses with UV400 polycarbonate lenses to protect against eye cancer and other eye problems caused by the sun. In addition to uniforms, parents can expect to pay for some or all of the following:

- additional clothing items such as sportswear and gym shoes, and bags or satchels in which to carry them;

- transportation to and from school (local transport authorities may provide concessionary or free travel in some areas);

- textbooks, notebooks, writing paper, pens, pencils, calculators, etc., and arts, crafts and manual work materials. Some states provide free books for primary school students; their cost may be subsidised for secondary school students. Many secondary schools operate a text book loan or rental scheme, whereby a refundable deposit is paid by each student at the beginning of secondary schooling. Text books can also be purchased secondhand.

- library books, sports facilities and team matches, and excursions.

The estimated minimum cost of equipping a child is around $500 per year in primary school and up to $2,000 per year in senior secondary school. Parents of children in the last two years (11 and 12) of secondary school can apply for a means-tested grant from Austudy (see page 207).

# Pre-School & Kindergarten

Attendance at a pre-school for children under five years of age isn't compulsory in Australia. However, for most of the 30 per cent or more of Australian working mothers who have children aged four or below, finding a day care centre or pre-school is essential, and it can be particularly difficult in cities and urban areas. Attendance fees aren't usually charged in states where pre-schools are government run (although there may be a 'voluntary' levy). However, federal government cuts have resulted in the closure of many non-profit, community-based, child-minding centres in recent years, and those that have remained open have begun to charge for attendance. Fees are around $20 per day at a public day care centre but may depend on the parents' income, with better-off parents asked to contribute more and low income parents exempt. Public pre-schools, also called child-parent centres (or kindergarten for the year prior to primary school), are often located at primary schools and open during school hours. In commercially run centres, fees are payable to private or voluntary organisations and, in city areas, can amount to $200 or more per child per week.

Most pre-schools are conducted on a session basis, with sessions of two to three hours for two to five days a week. Children can usually attend from 9am to noon or from 1pm to 3pm Mondays to Fridays. Many children attend public pre-school centres on around four half-days per week during the year preceding primary school. Programmes usually follow the free play approach, with the emphasis on social and emotional development through creative activities. Pre-school doesn't generally provide education (just educational games), although research has shown that children who attend pre-school are generally brighter and usually progress at a faster rate than those who don't (it's a moot point whether this is cause and effect!). Pre-school is highly recommended, particularly if your mother-tongue isn't English. After one or two years in pre-school, a child is integrated into the local community and is well prepared for primary school.

# Primary School

Primary education in Australia begins at five or six years of age, depending on the state or territory (see **Admissions** on page 197), and is almost always co-educational (mixed). Some primary schools also provide nursery or pre-school classes for children under five (see above), and some states (such as Queensland) are operating a trial programme under which certain children can start primary school at four years of age at selected schools (pupils are evaluated to see whether they're 'suitable' for early enrolment). Primary education isn't, however, compulsory until age six and lasts for six or seven years (school years 1 to 6 or 7) up to the age of 12 or 13, depending on the state or territory.

All primary schools must meet broad curriculum and standards guidelines developed by the Board of Studies. The emphasis is on the development of basic language and literacy skills, simple arithmetic, moral and social education, health training and some creative activities. In the higher primary years, lessons include English, mathematics, science, technology and computer studies, social studies (e.g. studies of society and environment), music, art and craft, health and physical education. Optional subjects may include religious instruction, community and foreign languages (called a 'language other than English' or LOTE), and instruction on a musical instrument. Note that in some states (e.g. Victoria) foreign languages are compulsory. Schools can also develop their own programmes to suit local needs and priorities within government guidelines. Swimming lessons are provided, usually at public swimming pools, as public schools don't usually have their own pools. Sex education is also taught.

Parent-teacher interviews are conducted once or twice a year and provide an opportunity for parents to discuss their child's progress. Children are continually assessed and parents periodically receive written reports, e.g. twice a year in Victoria. Under the state-wide literacy and numeracy standards initiative, pupils are assessed in years 3, 5 and 7. Assessment results are usually confidential and are used to identify pupils' special needs, such as those who need extra help with their English.

The school day is generally divided into three or four sessions, with daily instruction lasting for around five hours and consisting of 20 or 30-minute lessons. Pupils in primary schools usually have one teacher for most (if not all) subjects and are promoted each year on the basis of completing the previous year, rather than achievement. In large schools, pupils are graded according to age, while in country areas a primary 'school' may consist of no more than a couple of portable classrooms and two teachers teaching 15 to 30 pupils of various ages in all subjects. Many new primary schools are also designed on the 'open plan' concept, which allows two or more teachers to supervise up to 70 pupils (team teaching), although pupils are divided into small groups for separate activities, including individual study. Children progress to a secondary (high) school at school year 7 or 8 (aged 12 or 13).

# Secondary School

Secondary school (called high school in Australia) is for children aged from 12 or 13 to 17 or 18 (from school years 7 or 8 to year 12). High school lasts for a maximum of five or six years, depending on the state or territory. All secondary students complete year 10 (age 16) and the majority stay on at school until year 12 (age 18). Completion of year 12 is usually necessary to attend an institution of higher education, such as a university or college of advanced education.

The most common state secondary school is the comprehensive or multi-purpose high school. High schools are usually co-educational, although there are some single-sex schools in capital cities. In some states there are separate high schools for technical, agricultural and commercial subjects, where general academic subjects are combined with practical training, and selective high and grammar schools which provide a more challenging environment for academically-gifted students (competition for places is stiff). Some high schools are further classified as technology or language high schools, or as centres of excellence in certain subjects. Most states and territories also provide schools for academically gifted children, where admission is subject to test and school reports. The fifth and sixth years (11 and 12) are usually taken at separate colleges offering a range of subjects studied by adults as well as senior students. Agricultural high schools usually cater for boarders, and some country state schools have hostels for children who are unable to travel to and from school daily. Technology high schools are generally for the less-academically gifted and put the emphasis on science and technology. Most secondary schools have modern facilities for teaching commercial subjects, home economics, manual crafts and other technical disciplines.

Students in secondary schools generally have a different teacher for each subject, although variations may occur where open plan or more flexible teaching methods have been adopted. Promotion to the next year is generally automatic on completion of the previous year, although students may be grouped according to ability (streamed) in some subjects after an initial period in unstreamed classes. However, classes aren't streamed in academic or technically oriented subjects. In most states, the first one or two years consist of a general programme followed by all students, although there may be some choice of lessons (electives). In the last two years, a basic core of subjects is retained and students are able to select additional optional subjects, although in some states students select optional subjects from the start of high school.

The core subjects in all schools comprise the eight key learning areas of English, mathematics, science, technology, studies of society and the environment, the arts, health, and foreign languages. Optional subjects may include an additional foreign language, history, geography, a further humanities or social science subject, computer studies, commerce, art, crafts, music, theatre, home economics, a manual arts subject, agriculture and physical education. Some schools also offer optional courses in subjects such as consumer education, conversational foreign languages, word processing, commerce, driver education, drama and leisure studies. Note that in some schools, all students (regardless of their sex) may be required to study subjects such as cooking, sewing, woodwork and metalwork. Distance education (correspondence) courses may be available to students wishing to study a subject not generally offered (or which may clash with other subjects on the timetable), and Saturday schools may offer language studies that aren't available in a student's own school. A wider range of options is usually available in larger schools and there's an increasing trend towards encouraging individual schools to develop courses suited to the needs and interests of their students. Victoria has a 'Schools of the Future' programme, where secondary schools are self-managing and control their own finances and develop their own teaching programmes to reflect the aspirations of the school community, the interests and abilities of students, and the knowledge and skills of teachers.

One of the national goals for schooling in the 21st century is an increase in vocational education and training in schools and, in recent years, there has been more emphasis on the incorporation of vocational training into the senior secondary curriculum. Under the Australian Vocational Training System, students may obtain vocational education and training sector certificates as part of their senior study, and undertake some of their programmes in the workplace.

Students attaining the minimum school leaving age of 15 (16 in Tasmania) may leave school and seek employment or enrol in a vocational course at a TAFE institution (see page 213) or a private business college. Completion of year 10 of secondary school is the minimum entry requirement for many TAFE courses. Those who continue to year 12 have a choice of options for further study in TAFE institutions, higher education and other tertiary-level establishments. A student's eligibility for entry to higher education is assessed during or at the end of his final two years in secondary schooling. Most states use various combinations of school assessment and public examinations (see below).

# Examinations

Individual states and territories set their own examinations, although in most states students take the School Certificate (SC) at age 16 (at the end of year 10) and the Higher School Certificate (HSC) at age 18 (the end of year 12). Most states issue students with certificates after they've completed their compulsory education at age 15, and the majority of students who leave at this age go on to do an apprenticeship or other trade training. The school certificate (replaced by a junior or achievement certificate in some states) is based on school assessment as well as state-wide reference tests in English and mathematics. The HSC (replaced by a senior certificate, matriculation certificate or the tertiary admission examination/certificate of education in some states) is necessary in order to gain entrance to an Australian university. However, a few universities (in NSW) have waived the HSC requirement if families can afford fees of at least $8,000 for a year at a private college undergoing a 'foundation' course. Some schools also offer the international baccalaureate (IB) plus additional courses with state or TAFE accreditation. Senior high schools offer tertiary courses such as Open University or TAFE off-campus.

The HSC is based on an external examination held in October or November of school year 12 in addition to school assessment based on a student's last two years' work. In order not to disadvantage children who suffer from exam nerves and to reduce cramming and stress, more emphasis is placed on course work and continuous assessment than on the final examinations. In NSW, HSC students are assessed against a set of standards, rather than against each other, as part of a radical change in measuring performance in the final years of schooling. Students now receive detailed information about their performance in each subject, detailing the skills they've mastered.

## PRIVATE SCHOOLS

Around 27 per cent (over 35 per cent in years 11 and 12) of Australian children attend private non-government schools (officially referred to as independent schools), of which there are some 2,600 in Australia. These range from nursery (kindergarten) schools to secondary schools, from traditional-style schools to those offering 'alternative' methods of education such as Montessori and Rudolf Steiner schools. They include schools sponsored by churches and religious groups (parochial schools), schools for students with learning or physical disabilities, and schools for gifted children. In addition to mainstream parochial schools, there are also schools for religious and ethnic minorities (e.g. Muslim schools, where there's a strict code regarding the segregation of boys and girls). Most private schools are single-sex, although some have become co-educational in recent years. There are also boarding schools in Australia, although few schools accept boarders only. Children who board usually do so because they live too far from school to travel every day or because their parents work overseas.

Many private schools are modelled on English 'public schools' and generally use the same terminology as them. For example, years are called forms, the first form at high school being equivalent to the public school year 7 or 8 at age 12 or 13, while final year students are referred to as sixth formers. Some private primary schools are called preparatory (prep) schools. However, there's no snobbery attached to attending a private school in Australia – what's important is a school's academic standing and how well your children perform. Some parents switch their children from a public to a private school when they progress to secondary school. The quality of secondary education is crucial in gaining access to a good university course and a child's subsequent career.

**Parochial Schools:** The Catholic church operates by far the largest number of private schools in Australia, and there are relatively few other parochial schools (e.g. Anglican, Uniting Church and Christian community). A total of over 630,000 children attend some 1,700 Catholic schools or two-thirds of all private school students and 20 per cent of all school children. Most Catholic schools are part of a system administered by the Catholic Education Office, and their fees are usually much lower than for other independent schools (see below), as 75 per cent of their operating costs are met by federal and state governments. Clergy account for almost all teachers in Catholic schools, which (not surprisingly) devote an above average amount of time to religious subjects. Catholic high schools accept children from other religious backgrounds, but priority is given to Catholics.

**Fees:** Fees vary considerably according to a variety of factors, including the age of students, the reputation and quality of the school and its location (schools in major cities are usually the most expensive). Day school fees vary from as little as $1,500 to $2,000 per year for a parochial primary school and $3,000 to $6,000 per year for a high school. However, fees at non-denominational schools are up to $8,000 per year for primary and over $11,000 per year for 'elite' high schools (fees have risen considerably in recent years). Tuition fees at boarding schools can top $20,000 per year, with boarding charges of $6,000 to $10,000 on top. Note that some schools publish fees per term (usually four a year), particularly if they're high, while others are per school year. Some schools offer reduced fees to parents with two or more children attending the school. To the fees must be added another $2,000 or so per year for uniforms, books, building levies, special equipment (e.g. for sports), excursion charges, computers and assorted surcharges.

Independent schools are subsidised by the federal government on a 12-point sliding scale: wealthy schools are subsidised at the lowest level (1) and poor schools at the highest level (12). Students at most private schools receive more public funding than those in public schools and there's controversy over the public funding of elite and wealthy private schools, where affluent parents are subsidised from the public purse. Most private schools provide scholarships for bright or talented pupils, which vary in value from full fees to a small percentage. Scholarships are awarded as a result of competitive examination, individual talents or skills, and need.

**Curriculum:** Most private schools provide a similar curriculum to public schools and set the same examinations. However, some private schools offer the international baccalaureate (IB) examination, an internationally recognised university entrance qualification, which may be an important consideration if you plan to stay in Australia only for a short period. The advantages of private schools are manifold, not least their excellent academic record, which is generally much better than public schools. Don't, however, send your child to a school with high academic standards unless you're sure that he will be able to handle the pressure. Many private schools have resolutely embraced new technology, and the use of computers and the Internet to teach pupils is widespread. Private schools place the emphasis on traditional teaching, including hard work, good manners, consideration for others, responsibility, and not least, a sense of discipline (values which are sadly lacking in some public schools). They provide a broad-based education (aimed at developing a pupil's character) and generally provide a more varied approach to sport, music, drama, art and a wider choice of academic subjects than public schools. Their aim is more the development of the child as an individual and the encouragement of his unique talents than imparting knowledge and skills on a 'production-line' basis. This is made possible by small classes (an average of around 15 to 20 pupils or as little as half that of many public schools), which allow teachers to provide pupils with individually tailored tuition. Private schools are also able to cater for special needs, including gifted children, slow learners or those who suffer from dyslexia, those who benefit from a single-sex school, those requiring boarding facilities, and children whose parents want them to be educated in the customs of a particular religious belief. **Don't, however, assume that all private schools are excellent or that they all offer a better education than public schools, which isn't true.**

**Admissions:** Once you know you're going to live in Australia and have decided to send your children to a private school there, you should apply immediately, if possible at least one or two years in advance, which is generally considered to be the best time to book a place. The best and most popular schools have a demanding selection procedure and long waiting lists (perhaps many years), and parents register a child for entry at birth (or even at conception!) at some schools. Don't rely on enrolling your child in a particular school and neglect the alternatives, particularly if the chosen school has a rigorous entrance examination. When applying, you're usually requested to send previous school reports, exam results and records.

Before enrolling your child in a private school, make sure that you understand the withdrawal conditions in the school contract.

# HIGHER & FURTHER EDUCATION

Post-school education in Australia is generally divided into higher and further education. Higher education, called tertiary education in Australia, is usually defined as courses of an equivalent or standard higher than HSC (see page 202) and usually refers only to first degree courses; further education generally embraces everything except first degree courses, although the distinction is often blurred.

Higher education courses may be full-time, part-time or sandwich courses, which have nothing to do with food but are courses that combine periods of full-time study with periods of full-time training and paid work in industry and commerce. Australian universities are both teaching and research institutions, and many have world-renowned research programmes funded by industry in the applied science and technology fields. The states and territories are responsible for administering higher education, but the federal government provides the funding. Australia has one of the highest ratios of universities to population in the world, and the number of students in higher education has increased considerably in the last decade, totalling some 600,000.

Degree level courses are offered by around 40 universities ('unis'), including former Colleges of Advanced Education (CAE) and Institutes of Technology (IT), which became universities in the late '80s. The oldest universities are Sydney and Melbourne (established in the 1850s), which, with the universities of Adelaide, Queensland, Tasmania and Western Australia, form the traditional 'sandstone' universities (the Australian equivalent of America's Ivy League). Note that degrees from 'new' universities aren't rated as highly as those from the sandstone universities, 'corporate' universities (UNSW and Monash) and universities of technology (UTs).

Australia also has a number of specialist higher education establishments which include the Australian College of Physical Education (Sydney), the Australian Defence Force Academy (Canberra), the Australian Film, TV and Radio School, the Australian Institute of Music (Sydney), the Australian International Hotel School (Canberra), the Australian Maritime College (Cooranbong, NSW), the Christian Heritage College (Brisbane), Engineering Education Australia (distance education), the International College of Hotel Management (Adelaide), KvB College of Visual Communication (Sydney), Macleay College (Sydney) and the National Institute of Dramatic Art (Sydney).

The age of admission to university is usually 18 (although most admit exceptional students at a younger age) and courses are usually for three years, although some last for four. This is seen as a big advantage for foreign students from countries where courses often last much longer and helps Australian universities attract a large number of overseas students. Most Australian universities have between 8,000 and 30,000 students, and the largest (Monash) over 40,000, although they're usually dispersed over a number of campuses. Around a quarter of university students are 'mature' students aged over 30, two-thirds of whom are women. Most older universities follow British or American traditions and offer a wide range of courses. Many have a multi-campus structure, each campus specialising in a particular discipline, e.g. an agricultural science college linked to the main campus.

Australia rates highly in the percentage of students accepted at its higher education establishments and its number of graduates (which are highest in natural sciences but low in engineering). However, disadvantaged students (which include those from non English-speaking backgrounds, Aboriginals and Torres Strait Islanders, rural dwellers, the disabled and the poor) are under-represented at universities, particularly in the elite institutions. Many prospective students cannot afford the high fees, which have led to student protests in the form of occupations and sit-ins of university buildings in recent years. Universities have been struggling with funding cuts and many have been forced to axe places, cut research budgets and reduce numbers of postgraduate courses.

Competition for students is fierce, and universities have resorted to innovative advertising to lure school-leavers; some have even lowered their entrance requirements to attract more students. Many universities deliberately over-enrol, partly in order to receive higher government grants, which has lead to an increase in student-staff ratios and fears of a reduction in the quality of teaching. In order to compete with private colleges and other degree-level public institutions, many universities have introduced associate degree courses in fields such as management, dance, applied science, dental therapy, and electrical and electronic engineering.

**Overseas Students:** All Australian universities accept overseas students and many spend $millions on overseas marketing and student recruitment (Australia's top eight sandstone universities established their own overseas marketing arm in 1997). There are no quotas for foreign students, but all non-resident students must pay full fees (although grants are available – see page 206). Overseas students, mostly from Asia, are a major source of income for universities, contributing over $3 billion to the Australian economy. Many universities also have thousands of 'offshore' students at facilities in Asian countries and in New Zealand. Australian universities enrolled around 95,000 foreign students in 2000 and the number is expected to increase steadily in the next few years. When students at secondary schools and private colleges are included, the total number of foreign students studying in Australia reaches around 200,000.

Overseas students require a student visa (see page 106), which is issued after acceptance on a course and payment of at least half the first year's fees. Students must have the financial resources to meet tuition fees, return fares to Australia, and day-to-day living expenses for the duration of their course. Foreign students must have an adequate knowledge of English (unless studying English!). If English isn't your mother tongue or the language in which you gained your previous qualifications, you must take the Short Selection Test (SST). Private health insurance is required by all students, e.g. Medibank Private Overseas Student Health Cover (see page 316). Students must be attending full-time courses but are permitted to take part-time jobs of up to 20 hours per week to help cover their living costs. In order to retain their visas, students must have satisfactory attendance and academic results records. On completion of their courses, overseas students must leave Australia when their visas expire (an undertaking must be given in writing). Note that it isn't possible to switch from a visitor's visa to a student visa while in Australia.

# Grants & Fees

Annual living costs for students (excluding course fees) in 2001 were estimated to be a minimum of $10,000 per year plus a further $5,000 for a spouse and $3,000 for each child (possibly less outside major cities). Many students find it difficult to survive and some are forced to choose a university according to where they can more easily survive on meagre resources (or where they can find part-time work), rather than according to the courses it offers. Many students work part-time during terms and holidays to supplement their income, and around half live with their parents to save costs.

**Youth Allowance & Austudy Grants:** Resident students enrolled on an approved course at an approved educational establishment may be eligible for a government grant, called a Youth Allowance or Austudy grant, which are forms of income support. A booklet explaining eligibility for Youth Allowance and Austudy grants is sent to all Australian applicants who are offered a place at university. Note that migrants aren't eligible for Austudy grants for two years after their arrival in Australia, and students who have been permanent residents for over three years but don't have Australian citizenship no longer qualify for Austudy grants and are required to pay HECS fees (see page 208) in advance.

Youth Allowance is for full-time students aged 16 to 24 and Austudy is for students over 24 who are starting their studies (note that, if you're following a masters or doctorate course, you're not eligible for either grant) Whether you receive a grant depends on your income and assets (and those of your parents and spouse), and your age and living circumstances. The rules are complicated (the application contains a questionnaire with over 300 questions!). If your family's assets are worth more than $438,250, you aren't eligible for a payment. If you're independent, assets are assessed according to whether you're a home owner. Liquid assets are also taken into account, and payments may be deferred if liquid assets are over $2,500 for a single person or over $5,000 for a couple. Students granted Youth Allowance or Austudy grants may earn up to $6,136 per year.

When applying, you need your original birth certificate or passport, your tax file number, taxation notice of assessment and the tax file number of your parents or spouse (if applicable), plus other documents depending on your personal situation. Full details of the documentation required is listed on the application form. Applications should be made within 28 days of starting a course of 30 weeks or less. Note that, if you apply late, you'll receive your grant only from the date your application is filed. Once your form is received, you'll receive your Notice of Assessment (usually within 21 days) detailing your eligibility and payments. Payments are made directly into a bank, building society or credit union account every two weeks. In 2001, the following fortnightly Youth Allowance grants were available:

| Age/ Status | Living at Home | Living away from Home |
| --- | --- | --- |
| Under 18 | $158.80 | $290.10 |
| Over 18 | $190.90 | $290.10 |
| Special Groups* | $234.50 | $352.30 |

*Special Groups usually refer to the long-term unemployed starting study.

In 2001, the following fortnightly Austudy grants were available:

| Status | Amount |
| --- | --- |
| Single or partnered without children | $290.10 |
| Partnered with children | $318.60 |

Rent assistance is also available to single students without children receiving the away from home rate of Youth Allowance. If students have to live away from their permanent home, fare allowances may be paid but not daily travel costs. An Austudy supplement is available, offering students the option of 'trading in' part of their Austudy grant in order to receive double the amount in the form of an interest-free loan. Repayment is required when income exceeds a certain level (the same as for HECS – see page 208).

**Other Grants:** Special grants (awards) are available for those undertaking a masters degree by or a PhD. For details write to individual universities. There are special programmes (e.g. Abstudy) for Aboriginal students from low-income families, which provide extra student places, living allowances and other support. A range of scholarships is also available, and students may receive scholarship payments of up to $10,000 per year tax-free. Full information is provided in *Scholarships Australia: the Directory of Scholarships and Grants for Study in Australia and Overseas* (New Hobsons Press) or on the Department of Education, Training and Youth Affairs website (🖳 www.detya.gov.au) under the Scholarships link.

**Course Fees:** University tuition fees for Australian students were introduced in 1990 (prior to which tuition was free) under the Higher Education Contribution Scheme (HECS). The fees payable depend on the subject(s) being studied, as follows:

● **Band 1 ($3,521 per year):** Arts, humanities, justice, legal studies, social studies/behavioural science, visual/performing arts, education and nursing – some 35 per cent of students study these subjects.

● **Band 2 ($5,015 per year):** Mathematics, computing, certain health sciences, agriculture, renewable resources, built environment/architecture, engineering, processing and administration, business and economics.

● **Band 3 ($5,870 per year):** Law, medicine, medical science, dentistry, dental services and veterinary sciences.

If the units taken for a degree course fall into different fee bands, the student pays a proportion of each band, according to the number of units in each band. Students can choose to pay the HECS fee before graduation in a lump sum, in which case they qualify for a reduction of 25 per cent. For example, the cost of an arts degree is reduced from $3,521 to $2,641 a year if paid up front, a saving of around $2,600 over the three years of an undergraduate course. Paying in advance has an even bigger impact for students enrolled in Band 3 courses which normally cost $5,870 a year, where a 25 per cent reduction saves around $7,300 over five or six years. The 25 per cent discount also applies to partial payments, although only one payment per semester attracts the discount.

Only around a fifth of students are able to take advantage of the lump sum payment option. (Note that, if you're not an Australian citizen and don't fulfil the residency requirements, you probably won't qualify for an HECS discount and must pay the fees up front every semester.) The vast majority take the deferred payment option, whereby the HECS charge is effectively an interest-free loan, which is repaid weekly when a graduate's income exceeds $22,346 per year. Repayments are made on a sliding scale as follows:

|  |  |
|---|---|
| **Salary** | **Per Cent** |

| below $22,346 | 0.0 |
| $22,346–$23,565 | 3.0 |
| $23,566–$25,393 | 3.5 |
| $25,394–$29,456 | 4.0 |
| $29,457–$35,551 | 4.5 |
| $35,552–$37,420 | 5.0 |
| $37,421–$40,223 | 5.5 |
| over $40,223 | 6.0 |

If you make additional 'voluntary' payments of $500 or more in respect of a deferred HECS liability, you're entitled to a 15 per cent discount (i.e. for evey $500 payment, your liability is reduced by $588). Students who choose to complete an honours year or a higher degree may be exempted from paying HECS fees for that year through an HECS scholarship, or government or university funding.

In addition to tuition fees, students can expect to pay between $500 and $1,000 on text books, which are sold at an 8 per cent discount to students who have proof that they're studying at an Australian educational institution. This discount is known as the Educational Textbook Subsidy Scheme and was introduced as a compensating measure by the government shortly after GST was applied to most goods including books, which went up by 10 per cent! Books must be bought at a registered bookseller and you must take your current textbook list with you when you go to buy them. Textbooks can be purchased secondhand; most universities run secondhand book shops, and books can even be bought secondhand via the Internet (🖳 www.book exchange.com.au).

More information about HECS can be obtained from ☎ freecall 1800-020108 or via the Internet (🖳 www.hecs.gov.au).

**Overseas Students' Fees:** Overseas students must pay full tuition fees, which are higher than those for Australian students and vary with the course and university. The government sets minimum fees, but individual institutions can (and often do) charge higher fees. The minimum fees in 2001 were $8,670 per year for arts, law and business courses, $12,950 per year for engineering, law and science courses, and $17,840 per year for dentistry, medicine and veterinary science. Various scholarships are available which cover tuition fees and living costs or only tuition fees. These are administered by the Australian International Development Assistance Bureau (AIDAB) and the Department of Education, Training and Youth Affairs (DETYA). Information can be obtained from Australian embassies and high commissions overseas.

# Admissions

Admission to Australian universities for Australian students is usually based on their exam results in the Higher School Certificate (HSC) or the equivalent taken in their final year of high school. However, some universities in NSW have waived the HSC requirement if families can afford fees of at least $8,000 for a year at a private college doing a 'foundation' course. This option has been available to overseas students for years, but is now also offered to local students.

University admission systems vary considerably, and each state has its own method of ranking students for entry to universities within the state. For year 12 students the following systems are used:

**NSW, ACT, Victoria & WA:** In these states, all students are given a numerical 'score' called a Tertiary Entrance Rank (TER), which is based on exam results compared with a set of standards. TERs are generated by the Tertiary Admissions Centre and determine whether a student will gain acceptance to a particular university or course.

**Queensland & SA:** Queensland uses an Overall Position (OP) system, which ranks students on a scale of 1 to 25 (out-of-state students are ranked from 1 to 100), while South Australia uses a ranking system of 0 to 90.

**NT & Tasmania:** The Northern Territory and Tasmania (which have just one university each) work on an institution basis.

All Australian universities accept students from other states, when a complicated system of converting marks is used. There are plans to introduce a nationwide system of university entrance marks, although it's expected to be some years before this is instituted (as with many things in Australia, most states think that their way of doing things is best). Note that entrance requirements for mature students are usually different from those mentioned above, and most universities operate special adult entry admission schemes, which allow applicants over a certain age admission on the basis of work experience and qualifications other than academic.

Generally, the better the university (or the better its reputation) and the more popular the course, the higher the entrance qualifications necessary. The minimum entrance requirements are set by individual universities and colleges and vary considerably. Some universities have been forced to lower entrance requirements in recent years owing to falling student numbers. Note that no university excels in all subjects, and it's important to choose a university on the strength of its teaching excellence in your particular subject. Obtain a prospectus from the universities on your shortlist. There are also a number of excellent guides available to help you make your choice (see below).

**Overseas Students:** Generally, overseas students' qualifications which would admit them to a university in their own country are taken into consideration. Whatever your qualifications, each application is considered on its merits. All foreign students require a thorough knowledge of English, which will usually be examined unless a certificate is provided. Australian universities accept the international baccalaureate (IB) certificate as an entrance qualification, but an American high school diploma isn't usually sufficient. Contact individual universities for detailed information or, for general information, the Overseas Students Branch of the Department of Education, Training and Youth Affairs, GPO Box 9880, Canberra, ACT 2601 (☎ 02-6240 8111, 🖳 www.aei.detya.gov.au).

**Applications:** To apply for a place at university, you should begin by writing to the Tertiary Admissions Centre (TAC) in the state of your choice. There's now a common deadline for applications at the end of September. Each state TAC allows you to make one application, on which you list a number of preferences. Acceptance depends on your qualifications (see above) and how many places are available. You should make sure that you spread your preferences to include some courses on which you're almost certain to gain acceptance. It's possible to change preferences once you know your score, e.g. if you score considerably higher or lower than anticipated. Alternatively, you can re-sit your exams or take a year off and re-apply the following year.

# Semesters & Courses

The university academic year follows the calendar year, courses taking place from February until November or December. The year commences with an orientation week (O-week), during which enrolment takes place for new students. The year is usually divided into two semesters of around 14 weeks, with a recess of around two weeks in mid-semester and a six to eight-week summer break, with examinations in November or December. However, most universities now offer summer semesters which allow students to catch up on failed or missed subjects. Students take a main subject plus one or two subsidiary subjects, concentrating on their main subject for the first one or two years. In some universities, it's possible for students to design their own degree courses. Many students choose a sandwich course, which includes a period spent working in industry or commerce. Timetables may be flexible and usually include less than ten hours of classes a week in order to maximise individual reading and research time. Class sizes are usually very large, some lectures attracting as many as 500 students. Most courses are taught through lectures and tutorials, students being assessed on their work in essays, assignments, practicals and examinations (annual and final).

# Degrees

A diploma is bestowed on students who successfully complete a course of at least two years, either full-time or the equivalent period part-time. The most common degrees awarded in Australia are a Bachelor of Arts (BA) and a Bachelor of Science (BSc). Bachelor's degrees are given a classification, the highest of which is an 'honours' degree, which is granted to students who have undertaken an extra year of specialised study after a three-year pass degree or awarded to students who perform outstandingly in a four-year degree course. The highest pass is a first class degree, which is quite rare. Second class degrees are average, while a third class degree is poor. The lowest classification is a 'pass'. Students can request special consideration and be given a second chance by sitting another exam; in some cases they're granted a conceded pass.

Second (postgraduate) degrees are usually a Master of Arts (MA) or a Master of Science (MSc), which are awarded to Bachelors for a one-year course in a subject other than their undergraduate subjects. Students who do postgraduate work in the same subject(s) as their undergraduate work usually undertake a three-year Doctor of Philosophy (PhD) research programme.

Under the Australia Qualifications Framework, a national system for the recognition of qualifications established in 1995, students can move more easily between TAFE colleges (see page 213), private colleges and universities, and have their studies and experience classified. The new qualifications consist of diploma, advanced diploma, bachelor's degree, graduate certificate, graduate diploma, masters degree and doctorate.

# Accommodation & Facilities

After acceptance at university, students are usually advised to apply for a place in a hall of residence or other college accommodation, such as self-catering houses and apartments. However, such accommodation is limited and in high demand, and many universities don't provide student accommodation at all. You should write as soon as possible after acceptance to the accommodation or housing officer, whose job is to help students find suitable accommodation (both college and private). There's a huge (largely unfilled) demand for student accommodation (often from overseas students) in the major cities, particularly Sydney and Melbourne, and many universities are looking at ways of providing more student accommodation. The cost of accommodation in halls of residence range from around $80 per week for self-catering to around $250 for full board. Overseas students are usually given priority for housing, although you should investigate the availability and cost of local accommodation before accepting a place at a university. The Coordinating Committee for Overseas Students helps overseas students find accommodation.

A large number of students rent privately owned apartments or houses, which are often shared with other students, although in many areas this kind of accommodation is difficult to find and expensive (from around $100 per week for a single room and $150 for a double). Sharing a room with a fellow student costs from around $70 per week. Another alternative is to find lodgings where you rent a room in a private house with meals included (see also **Single Accommodation** on page 138). It's generally recognised that students shouldn't spend more than 30 per cent of their income on accommodation.

**Facilities:** All universities have a huge variety of clubs, societies and organisations, many run by the students' association or union, which is the centre of social activities. Most campuses are members of the National Union of Students (NUS), which represents students at state and national levels. Most universities also have excellent sports facilities, and all have bars and canteens. Most clubs fall into the categories of cultural, sporting, recreational, political and department-based. During orientation week, most clubs and societies are represented and compete to sign up new members. Fees are payable, although there are a large number of benefits and facilities, many specifically for overseas students. All universities levy a student amenities or general service fee (anything from $100 to $400 per year), which helps to finance sports associations, the student union and the representative council.

**Further Information:** Numerous books are published for university students, including *Study and Travel in Australia* (also available on CD-ROM) and *A Guide to Australian Universities*, both published by Magabook, PO Box 444, Rockdale, NSW 2216 (☎ 02-9567 5300, 🖳 www.magabook.comau). New Hobsons Press (Level 4, 2 Elizabeth Plaza, North Sydney, NSW 2060, ☎ 02-9936 8630, 🖳 www.nhpress.com.au) publishes a wide range of books for students, including *Australian Study Opportunities*, *The Directory of Higher Education Courses* and *Uni Survival Guide*, a guide to Australian university life containing university profiles. The *Good Universities Guide* by Dean Ashenden and Sandra Milligan (available from Reply Paid 95, Good Universities Guide, 19-21 Olive Street, Subiaco, WA 6008 (☎ freecall 1800-682133, 🖳 www.thegoodguides.com.au) also makes interesting reading, although it has been criticised by some universities. A higher education supplement is published in the Wednesday edition of *The Australian* newspaper.

# Further Education

Further education generally embraces everything except first degree courses taken at universities and colleges of higher education, although the distinction between further and higher education (see page 205) is often blurred. Further education courses may be full or part-time and are provided by universities, technical and further education (TAFE) colleges, technical colleges, evening colleges, the Adult Migrant Education Service, the Council of Adult Education, the Workers' Education Association and by numerous 'open learning' institutions such as the Open Training and Education Network (OTEN). Qualifications that can be earned through further education include the school certificate (SC), the higher school certificate (HSC), the international baccalaureate (IB), trade certificates, bachelor's and masters degrees, MBA degrees, and a range of internationally recognised certificates and diplomas. Around 80 per cent of Australians take a further education course at some time during their lives.

**TAFE Colleges:** By far the largest organisation offering further education courses in Australia is Technical and Further Education (TAFE) colleges, which have over 1 million students studying at some 200 colleges, many with a number of campuses and training centres (including some universities). Many courses have a strong vocational focus and are noted for their practical, hands-on emphasis. The majority of TAFE courses are at the certificate, diploma and advanced diploma levels, although some degree level courses are offered, and courses can be used as entry to a full-time degree course at university. TAFE courses include pre-apprenticeships and apprenticeships, trade, post-trade and technician courses, plus commercial and general courses to certificate level. Some states have technical schools where high school students learn a trade and go on to a TAFE college. TAFE courses are also used to supplement apprenticeships and on-the-job training. Most courses last for around two years and can be undertaken on a part-time or full-time basis or combined with a job when the employer allows time off to attend classes.

TAFE colleges offer hundreds of courses, including all major skills in a wide range of industrial, commercial, artistic and domestic occupations. Many courses are specifically designed for school-leavers to upgrade their skills and for adults wishing to get back into the workforce. Courses range from semi-skilled trade training to professional subjects and include correspondence courses and special programmes for disadvantaged groups. Courses for apprentices cover dozens of different trades, including building, metal, electrical, automotive, electronics, plumbing, printing, food, gardening, farming, fashion, hairdressing, textiles, jewellery and watchmaking industries, to name but a few. Pre-apprenticeship courses allow young people to undertake a substantial part of a trade course before taking up an apprenticeship with advanced standing.

Fees vary with the state or territory, each of which sets its own fees. The average cost of a full-time course is $250 and for a diploma course around $350 per year, although some states waive fees for school-leavers who enrol directly in TAFE courses on leaving school. Fees, due to rise in 2002, can be paid in instalments, and there are concessionary rates (or no fees) for low-income earners. Students are also eligible for Austudy grants (see page 207).

**Open Learning:** Open (or distance) learning, which means studying at a time and place that suits you, is co-ordinated by Open Learning Australia (OLA) and offered by around 30 universities and TAFE colleges. OLA schedules four 13-week study periods per year, students being able to choose the study period in which they start and how many periods they study each year. Students can also choose how many units to complete within a study period. Anyone can enrol and there are no quotas or residential requirements. In 2000, there were some 6,700 students enrolled on OLA courses, including secondary students who were unable to gain a suitable university place or are unable to study full-time because of work or other commitments. OLA is also ideal for anyone wishing to study one or more university subjects without enrolling for a degree. Qualifications gained via OLA can be used to gain admission to a university as a full-time student. Most units are broadcast twice a year on ABC TV and are supplemented by radio broadcasts, telephone tutorials, handbooks and audio tapes. Fees are modest, and some students can pay via a similar scheme to the HECS (see page 208). For information contact Open Learning Australia, Level 6, 30 Collins Street, Melbourne, VIC 3000 (☎ local call rate 1300-363652, 💻 www.ola. edu.au).

**Private Colleges:** Vocational training is offered by private colleges, which are closely aligned to the industries for which they prepare students. Many private colleges offer training in courses such as hospitality, secretarial, business and computer studies. Prospective students should check whether a course has been accredited by contacting the Australian Council for Private Education and Training (☎ 02-9660 6455, 💻 www.acpet.edu.au), which is the regulating body of private colleges and assures the quality of the tuition provided. Some institutions offer distance learning Master of Business Administration (MBA) courses for those who cannot (or don't wish to) study on a full or part-time, locally taught basis. Around 40 universities, business schools and professional organisations offer MBA courses in subjects such as banking, business administration, communications, economics, European languages, information systems, management, marketing, public relations, and social and political studies.

# LANGUAGE SCHOOLS

If you don't speak English fluently (or you wish to learn another language) you can enrol in a language course offered by numerous language schools in Australia. Some 140 languages are spoken in Australia, so there's plenty of opportunity to learn and practise foreign languages. Obtaining a working knowledge or becoming fluent in English (or 'strine') while living in Australia is relatively easy, as you'll be constantly immersed in the English language and will have the maximum opportunity to practise. However, if you wish to speak or write English fluently, you'll probably need to attend a language school or find a private tutor. Many thousands of foreign students (mostly from Asian countries) come to Australia each year to learn English, thus ensuring that English-language schools are big business. Note that it's usually necessary to have a recognised qualification in English to be accepted at a college of higher or further education in Australia.

English-language courses are offered at all levels by universities, language schools, migrant education colleges, foreign and international organisations, local associations and clubs, private colleges, technical and further education (TAFE) colleges, open learning institutions and private teachers. Classes range from language courses for complete beginners, through specialised business or cultural courses, to university-level seminars leading to recognised diplomas. The Department of Multicultural Affairs supports Settlement English courses for some migrants, and the cost may be funded by the department. There are English-language schools in all cities and large towns in Australia, most equipped with computers, language laboratories, video studios, libraries and bookshops.

Most language schools offer a variety of classes according to your current language ability, how many hours you wish to study per week, how much money you want to spend and how quickly you wish to learn. Full-time, part-time and evening courses are offered by most schools, and many also offer residential courses or accommodation with local families (highly recommended to accelerate learning). Courses that include accommodation (often half board, consisting of breakfast and an evening meal) usually represent good value. Bear in mind that, if you need to find your own accommodation, particularly in Sydney or Melbourne, it can be difficult and expensive. Language classes generally fall into the following categories:

| Category | Hours per Week |
| --- | --- |
| Compact | 10–20 |
| Intensive | 20–30 |
| Total immersion | 30–40+ |

Most schools offer compact or intensive courses and also provide special English courses for businessmen and professionals (among others), leading to a wide variety of examinations, most of which are recognised internationally.

Course fees vary considerably and are usually calculated on a weekly basis. Fees depend on the number of hours tuition per week, the type of course, and the location and reputation of the school. Expect to pay up to $500 pre week for an intensive course and around $300 per week for a compact course. Total immersion or executive courses, which are provided by many schools, can cost $2,000 or more per week, and not everyone is suited to learning at such a fast rate (or has the financial resources).

# 10.

# PUBLIC TRANSPORT

Public transport in Australia varies from region to region and town to town. In most cities and large towns services are good to excellent and relatively inexpensive, although some suburbs and areas are poorly served. Most Australian cities have a relatively small suburban rail network and many regions aren't served by trains at all, which is one of the reasons most Australians are so attached to their cars (only Americans are more devoted to their cars than Australians). However, it isn't *always* essential to own a car in Australia, particularly if you live in a city (where parking is often impossible). On the other hand, if you live in the country or a suburb off the main rail and bus routes, it's usually essential to have your own transport. Bus and rail services in most areas are also severely curtailed on Sundays and in some cases on Saturdays as well.

Bear in mind when travelling interstate that Australia is a huge country (nearly as big as Europe or the USA and over 30 times the size of Britain) with vast distances between capital cities. Flying will save you a lot of time and the loss of sleep associated with long-distance bus and train journeys, although you'll see little of Australia when flying around the country. Book early if you plan to travel long distance on public holidays or at the beginning or end of school holidays (see page 198). Despite the vast distances involved in travelling in Australia, most Australians prefer to travel by private car.

In cities, trains are much faster than buses, particularly during rush hours, even where new faster roads have been built. Most cities have an integrated public transport system, and tickets usually allow transfers between buses, trains, trams and ferries (as applicable), fares being calculated on a zone system, e.g. travelpasses in Sydney. Buses and trams carry around 65 per cent of passengers in the major cities, where there's a range of daily, weekly, monthly, quarterly and annual tickets, plus discounted books of ten tickets offering savings on single fares. Many cities have free downtown shuttle buses. Note that passengers caught travelling without tickets can be fined up to $200.

**Sydney:** Australia's largest city has an integrated service that includes buses, ferries, suburban trains and City Rail's 'underground' system (actually a conventional railway that runs underground in the city centre). Sydney also has a monorail and light railway, although both are expensive and mainly a novelty for tourists rather than a serious mode of public transport. Sydney has the most expensive public transport of any Australian city, but it's still relatively cheap by international standards. In 2000, Sydney received some much-needed transport improvements including expanded rail and ferry lines and a new underground railway linking the airport to the city centre. A New South Wales state transit directory and a comprehensive Sydney Public Transport Directory available from the Roads Traffic Authority (RTA) for $3 (☎ local call rate 13-1500).

**Melbourne:** Melbourne has an inexpensive and efficient public transport network consisting of buses, trains and trams, which has recently been privatised. Trams form the backbone of the public transport system and the city's network is the most extensive in the world and the only one remaining in Australia (unlike Sydney, Melbourne was wise enough to retain its trams). The network covers 325km/202mi and is served by some 750 trams (only St Petersberg has more) operating up to 20km/12mi outside the city centre. The Melbourne public transport system is called the 'Met', which is the collective name for bus, rail and tram services (a free 'Get around on the Met' map is available – ☎ local call rate 13-1638). Tickets can be purchased at train stations, on board buses and trams, and from retail outlets such as newsagents and cafés. An unpopular automated 'Metcard' ticketing system has recently been introduced.

Other Australian cities also have an adequate or good public transport service consisting mainly of buses and a limited suburban rail network, supported by a few ferries and, in Adelaide, a single tram line. Apart from New South Wales, few states have an extensive rail network.

Students visiting or living in Australia should obtain an International Student Identity Card (ISIC), which offers a range of travel discounts. STA Travel is the biggest nationwide travel agency and can provide tickets for all domestic and international travel. A number of guides are available for handicapped passengers, including the *Accessing City Rail* from City Rail, a guide to access for wheelchairs on trains, and *Easy Access Australia*, which is available from 🖳 www.easyaccess australia. com.au.

## TRAINS

In the mid-19th century when the first Australian railways were built, the states were independent colonies and governed from London; consequently, Australia's rail network grew piecemeal without any consultation between states. When the Australian federation was formed in 1901, the six colonies all had different gauge lines from their neighbours! This resulted in passengers having to change trains at state borders, often in the middle of the night, a situation which stifled the development of rail travel until the early '60s, when a standard gauge (1,435mm) was introduced on some main lines. However, Australia still has three different railway gauges – 1,067mm, 1,435mm and 1,600mm – and, although the main interstate lines now use the standard gauge, it's only in the last few years that much thought has been given to expanding and updating the local rail network, which by European standards is antiquated and severely limited. Most Australian cities have only a sparse suburban rail network and many areas of the country aren't served by trains at all. As in the USA, the main task of Australian railways is to haul long-distance freight, bulk minerals (particularly coal in NSW and Queensland), grain and petroleum products.

Australian trains are more comfortable, leisurely and sociable than buses, but slower (Australian long-distance trains are God's way of telling you to slow down!), more expensive and sometimes difficult to book. You need to reserve well in advance for the most popular long-distance trains, particularly during the peak holiday season. Some trains have wheelchair access, including the V/Line Sprinter trains in Victoria and the Countrylink XPT (an abbreviation for Express Passenger Train) and Xplorer trains operating in NSW, Queensland and between Sydney and Melbourne (at speeds of up to 160kph/100mph).

Rail Australia consists of four state-owned rail companies (Countrylink, Queensland Rail, V/Line and Westrail) and the Great Southern Railway (GSR), which was created when the *Ghan*, *Indian Pacific* and *Overland* services were sold by the federal government in 1997. Some states (such as Victoria) have also since privatised their railways.

## Interstate Trains

Australia offers some of the most spectacular long-distance rail journeys in the world, although the unchanging scenery in some regions can begin to pall after a few hours.

Interstate rail travel has been overtaken by the age of air travel and (apart from suburban services in the major cities) is mainly of interest to tourists and travellers with plenty of time on their hands (the average speed of Australian trains is around 65kph/40mph). There's an interstate railway service serving all states except Tasmania and the Northern Territory. Trains don't stop at all intermediate stations, e.g. those within a few hours of major terminals.

Long-distance trains have evocative names such as the *Indian Pacific* (Sydney-Adelaide-Perth) and the *Great South Pacific Express* (Sydney-Brisbane-Cairns), the *Spirit of the Outback* (Brisbane-Longreach), the *Ghan* (Adelaide-Melbourne-Sydney-Alice Springs) and the *Prospector* (Perth-Kalgoorlie). The *Indian Pacific* crosses Australia and takes its name from its route from the Pacific Ocean (Sydney) to the Indian Ocean (Perth), a journey of 4,348km/2,700mi taking around 65 hours. It includes the longest stretch of straight track (478km/300mi) in the world across the Nullabor Plain in Western Australia. The *Indian Pacific* is one of the world's longest trains with up to 25 carriages, plus an observation lounge, restaurant, bar and music room with piano. The *Great South Pacific Express* is 'the first five-star hotel on wheels' in Australia and the country's answer to Europe's Orient Express. Cars are carried on the *Queenslander*, the *Spirit of the Outback* and between Adelaide and Alice Springs, Melbourne and Perth, and on the Melbourne-Mildura goods line. The *Prospector* (Perth-Kalgoorlie) provides only first-class, air-conditioned accommodation and maintains the fastest average speed (around 110kph/68mph) of any train in Australia, taking 7.5 hours for the 655km/407mi journey.

**Accommodation:** Long-distance trains offer a range of accommodation which may include de luxe, first, holiday and economy class sleeping berths, and first and economy class seats. Sleeping berths are available on overnight services (for a surcharge) and are well worth the extra charge on long journeys. In first class there are twinette cabins, which have seats that fold into two sleeping berths and share facilities with adjacent cabins. First class single roomettes have a private toilet and wash basin, and first class cabins a shower, toilet, wash basin, hot and cold water, and a socket for an electric shaver. Deluxe cabins and family units are available on the *Ghan* and *Indian Pacific* trains, where meals are included with first class sleeping berths. In Queensland, economy class sleepers have three sleeping berths, and each carriage has communal showers and toilets. Where sleeping berths are unavailable, there are reclining seats. Two-berth 'holiday class' cabins are available on *The Ghan* and the *Indian Pacific* trains. Coach class cars have reclining seats and, on trains to Perth, Alice Springs and Cairns, coach and economy class sitting cars include showers. All long-distance trains are air-conditioned.

# City Services

**Sydney/NSW:** Sydney has the most extensive suburban rail network in Australia, although even here many suburbs have no rail services. Most routes are served by old, mostly double-decker, trains (Sydney was the first city in the world to introduce double-decker electric trains), on which seats can usually be reversed to face in either direction (these are being replaced by ultra-modern Tangara trains). Yellow stripes on platforms indicate where half-length, four-carriage trains stop (you must stand behind the yellow line). Doors open and close automatically, although the doors on old trains are rarely closed during hot weather, so keep clear of the doorways (or hold on tight).

Trains operate from around 5am until midnight – violence, although rare, has caused the cancellation of trains after midnight on some suburban routes. After dark there are special 'Night Safe' areas (marked on the platform in blue) where you can wait for trains. After 8pm, only two carriages are in use (next to the guard's compartment, indicated by a blue light), and a help button is positioned near the door which can be used to alert the guard or driver.

The NSW Countrylink network operates the most comprehensive state rail service in Australia using Xplorer trains, on which seats must be booked in advance. There are commuter trains between Sydney and Wollongong, Katoomba, Lithgow, Newcastle and Goulburn. For information ☎ 13-2242 between 6.30am and 10pm any day.

**Canberra:** Australia's capital city is served by the main Sydney-Melbourne line, which passes through Wodonga to the north-east of Canberra; from there you must take a bus, which takes around nine hours. It's usually better to fly when travelling to Canberra. Canberra's main railway station is on Wentworth Avenue in the suburb of Kingston.

**Melbourne:** The Victorian State Railway, the V/Line, was recently privatised and is now on lease to the British travel company National Express. V/Line operates all rail and associated coach routes within Victoria, including day and overnight, high-speed (XPT) services to Sydney (Melbourne-Sydney during the day and Sydney-Melbourne overnight) taking 13 hours. V/Line supersaver fares offer a 30 per cent discount when travelling off-peak, i.e. on Tuesdays, Wednesdays and Thursdays arriving in Melbourne after 9.30am and leaving Melbourne at any time except between 4pm and 6pm. In recent years, new, air-conditioned, 'high-speed' Sprinter trains have been introduced on some routes. The Canberra Link involves taking a train to Wodonga on the border with NSW and a bus from there to Canberra. There are *Overland* daily night services to Adelaide taking 12 hours (change to the *Indian Pacific* in Adelaide for Perth). The city centre 'City Loop' forms an underground railway around the centre.

**Adelaide:** Long-distance trains stop at the Adelaide Rail Passenger Terminal in Keswick, 2km south-west of the city centre. There's an overnight service to Melbourne taking around 12 hours and a day coach/train service taking 11 hours. The *Ghan* to Alice Springs (19 hours) leaves at 2pm on Thursdays with an additional service on Mondays in winter. There are five weekly trains to Perth (none on Tuesdays and Thursdays) taking around 36 hours, possibly requiring a change of train at Port Pirie. There's a small network of suburban trains in Adelaide operated by the State Transport Authority. Note that tickets must be purchased before entering platforms or mounting trains.

**Perth/Western Australia:** *Indian Pacific* takes 65 hours to travel from Perth to Sydney and runs three times a week on Sundays, Mondays and Thursdays. The cheapest fare is around $424. The *Trans-Australian*, from Perth to Adelaide, takes 38 hours and departs on Wednesdays and Saturdays (fare from around $262). There are also suburban lines (operated by Westrail) between Perth and Armadale, Fremantle, Joondalup and Midland. The only other rail services in Western Australia are the Perth-Bunbury line and the Perth-Kalgoorlie route operated by the *Prospector*. Note that tickets should be purchased from vending machines at train stations before boarding. Multi-ride tickets can be validated at stations. Seven-day advance purchase fares are available in the low season offering a 30 per cent discount. A car train service is available between Adelaide and Perth.

**Brisbane/Queensland:** There's a fast Citytrain service in Brisbane with seven lines, and the Airtrain, connecting the airport to the city and the Gold Coast, has recently been opened. The 640km/398mi stretch between Brisbane and Rockhampton is electrified and served by modern 'tilt' trains (fast trains which run along narrow-gauge lines – hence the name!).

Queensland has the most extensive rail network of any Australian state, covering over 10,000km/6,200mi of lines on narrow gauge tracks (trains in Queensland are slower than buses due to the narrow gauge). All trains are operated by Queensland Rail (☎ local call rate 13-2232), whose 'flagship' train (all passengers travel first class with sleeping berths) is the *Queenslander*, taking a leisurely 30 hours between Brisbane and Cairns. The *Westlander* operates from Brisbane to Charlesville (777km/482mi), taking 16 hours, and the *Inlander* links Townsville with Mount Isa. The only rail link from outside the state is from NSW (served by XPT trains), on which northbound trains run overnight and southbound trains during the day. Seat or sleeper reservations are compulsory on long-distance trains, known as 'Traveltrains'. Most services are air-conditioned and provide sleeping cars and sitting cars with bar and meal services. Note than many trains stop at small stations on request and some trains are mixed freight and passenger trains (usually mainly freight with one passenger car). Vehicles can be transported on the *Queenslander* and the *Spirit of the Outback* (Brisbane-Longreach) services. Cars can be transported by rail between Adelaide and Alice Springs, Melbourne, Perth and Sydney, and on the Melbourne-Mildura line.

Local 'tourist' trains include the Kuranda Scenic Railway and the *Spirit of the Tropics*, designed for budget travellers and incorporating a non-stop disco car (Club Loco)! The vintage *Gulflander* train operates between Normanton and Croydon in the west of the state. There are 'plans' for a regional rail line on the Sunshine Coast (the existing track is sited 20km/12mi inland from the heavily-populated coastal area).

'Sunshine' rail passes offer unlimited economy class travel on most routes (including the Brisbane suburban network). Ordinary one-way tickets allow unlimited stopovers and 14 days to reach your destination, while return tickets are valid for two months. Stop-offs must be stated when buying tickets and reservations made for all journeys. You can change your travel plans, but a re-booking fee may be charged. Day rover tickets in Brisbane cost $8 and are valid after 9am and at weekends.

**Alice Springs/Northern Territory:** Alice is served by the *Ghan*, which departs from Adelaide at 2pm on Mondays and Thursdays and arrives in Alice at 12.30pm the following day. The return leaves Alice at 5.10pm and arrives in Adelaide at 4.30pm the next day (although it's often early). The fare is from $182 one-way. The station in Alice is a 15-minute walk from the edge of the town (taxis meet trains). Otherwise, the Northern Territory (including Darwin) has no rail services, although there are plans to extend the line from Alice Springs to Darwin by 2004.

**Other Services:** There are no regular passenger railways in Tasmania, although there's a freight rail service throughout the island and several steam railways for tourists (e.g. Ida Bay to Deep Hole). Elsewhere in Australia a few small private railways serve mainly agricultural and industrial areas, e.g. the iron-ore mining developments in the north-west of Western Australia and an extensive tram network in Queensland connecting the sugar cane fields to the mills in sugar-producing areas.

**Vintage Trains:** There are a number of 'vintage' trains in Australia, e.g. from Cairns to Kuranda, which takes 90 minutes to cover the 33km/20mi, and there are also vintage and tramway museums in all states where you can enjoy excursions on restored steam trains. These include the Puffing Billy in the Dandenongs Ranges in Victoria, the Ida Bay Railway in Tasmania and the New South Wales Railway Museum (at Thirlmere near Picton). On the first Sunday of the month from March to November, a steam train leaves Sydney Central station for Thirlmere. The Hotham Valley Tourist Railway in WA operates Xplorer trains to various destinations, and restored locomotives operate on short excursions from Alice Springs. The Barossa Wine Train runs from Adelaide to the Barossa wine region on a day trip taking in three wineries and extensive wine tasting.

# General Information

● Interstate train passengers are permitted up to 50kg/110lbs of luggage (two items not exceeding 25kg/55lbs each and within a maximum of 180cm/71in in circumference). Medium-size suitcases and hand baggage can be carried in compartments, but larger luggage should be booked in at the luggage desk not less than 30 minutes prior to departure. Note that booked luggage is carried in the baggage car and isn't accessible during the journey. There are also luggage storage spaces at the ends of passenger compartments.

● Luggage can be sent unaccompanied and can be insured. Many stations and airports have luggage lockers (from $2 for up to 24 hours), left luggage offices and luggage trolleys. When using a luggage locker, insert the correct money to release the key. Note the number of the locker in case you lose the key.

● Snacks are served on long-distance, in-state trains (such as XPT and Xplorer trains), and all interstate trains have dining cars offering both à la carte dining and light meals. There are also lounge and club cars on most services. Railway food is generally good and can be excellent on 'tourist' trains such as the Ghan, Indian Pacific and Queenslander. Note that there are no bar facilities for economy passengers on some long-distance services (e.g. from Adelaide to Melbourne) and there may be a large fine (e.g. $100) for consuming your own alcohol! Taking your own picnic onto a train isn't prohibited, but may be frowned upon. There are restaurants and snack bars at main stations, and food and drink machines are provided at many smaller stations.

● Public payphones (which accept Telecards) are available on long-distance train services.

● There's generally no smoking on Countrylink, Queensland Rail, V/Line and Westrail trains. There are designated smoking areas on national long-distance trains. You can be fined for smoking in a non-smoking carriage or area.

● Toilets are provided on trains on all but the shortest distance services but shouldn't be used when a train is in a station.

● In most cities, bicycles can be transported on suburban trains free of charge or for a small fee during off-peak times, although it may not be permitted during peak periods (e.g. 6 to 9am and 3 to 6pm on weekdays) or a permit may be required.

● Banks or autobanks (ATMs) are located at main railway stations in Brisbane and Melbourne (but surprisingly not in Adelaide, Perth or Sydney).

- Note that state capital cities have more than one railway station, although long-distance trains always arrive and depart from the main interstate station, e.g. Central Station in Sydney and Spencer Street Station in Melbourne. There are rail enquiry numbers in all states which can usually be reached by calling ☎ local call rate 13-2232, although it's often difficult to get through. It's usually easier to visit a rail information office or a station to obtain train information

- For further information about Australian railways contact Rail Australia, GSR Building, Burbridge Road, Mile End, SA 5031 (☎ 08-8217 4321, 💻 www. railaustralia.com.au). Rail Australia has agents in many countries, including Canada, Denmark, France, Germany, Hong Kong, Japan, Korea, the Netherlands, New Zealand, Singapore, South Africa, Sweden, the United Kingdom and the USA. They publish a brochure, *Australia By Rail*, which describes the long-distance routes and trains, or you can consult them on the website. An indispensable book for train buffs is ***Australia & New Zealand by Rail*** by Colin Taylor (Bradt Publications).

# Tickets

Rail tickets in Australia can be purchased from station ticket offices, automatic ticket machines and newsagents (in major cities). Most long-distance and main line trains have both first class and standard (economy) seating, although there's little difference between seats on some trains, e.g. XPT trains operating in NSW, Queensland and Victoria. The Perth-Bunbury line in Western Australia, most trains in outback Queensland, and all suburban lines have no first class accommodation. Children under the age of four travel free, unless they're occupying a separate seat or a sleeping berth on an interstate train (when the under 16 fare applies). Those aged from four to 15 travel at a discount (usually half-fare), as generally do students and pensioners, depending on on the state where you're resident. Low season is from 1st February to 30th June and the normal season from 1st July to 31st January. Low season and normal fares are the same when travelling in economy class seats or for travel on *Overland* trains between Adelaide and Melbourne.

Many ticket offices in Sydney and other NSW towns are open only for a few hours per day during rush hours, although passengers can buy tickets from automatic ticket machines at other times. Many stations are unmanned for at least half the day during the week and all day at weekends. Tickets can be paid for with major credit cards (e.g. Mastercard and Visa) subject to a $10 minimum charge. Fare evasion is endemic in Australia, particularly in the major cities, where an estimated 3 per cent of passengers travel without tickets (over 5,000 culprits were discovered in a three-week blitz on Sydney's city loop). Fare evaders face fines of up to $100 and Sydneysiders may soon have to pay up to $200.

**Ticket Machines:** Automatic ticket machines have been introduced in recent years, although there have been a 'few' teething troubles, particularly in Melbourne (where the first machines ate your money, chewed up your tickets and stole your change). You usually select your destination, choose the type of ticket (e.g. single or return), insert the fare (machines accept both coins and notes) and, if you're lucky, a ticket will be ejected with your change. You must get a ticket validated (stamped with the date and time) in a separate machine, without which it's invalid; you must validate a multiple-ride ticket each time you travel. In some cities you must insert your ticket in a ticket barrier with a green arrow (not a red cross) in the direction of the arrow shown on your ticket when leaving a station; a return ticket or multi-day pass will be returned if you're on the outward journey, otherwise the ticket will be retained.

**Reservations:** Reservations are recommended (at least two months in advance) on all long-distance trains, many of which are fully booked months in advance in the summer season and during school holidays. There's no reservation fee on major routes, on which bookings are accepted up to nine months in advance (six months on other long-distance routes). However, if a booking is altered or cancelled, there's a fee of: $5 if you make the alteration or cancellation at least 30 days prior to travel; 10 per cent of the fare if you make it 30 days prior to travel; 20 per cent of the fare if within seven days of travel. There are no refunds for unused tickets after the departure time and date shown on the ticket. For reservations ☎ local call rate 13-2232.

Bookings can be made via Rail Australia's website (🖳 www.railaustralia.com.au). Tickets can be booked for any journey throughout the country (apart from local suburban routes) and must be made and paid for at least seven days in advance. The outward journey must start on the date stamped on tickets, and journeys must be completed within the validity of the ticket. Journeys can usually be broken, except with discount fares. Bookings can be made through Thomas Cook offices in many countries, and Austrailpasses can be purchased from Qantas and offices of Jetabout Tours world wide.

**Discount & Commuter Tickets:** On some main routes there are discounts of up to 40 per cent for advance purchase tickets (e.g. seven days), although these aren't applied to the cheapest regular fares (and therefore may not be the cheapest travel option). Note that only a limited number of discounted seats may be available. Standby fares are available on some routes. In major cities, off-peak suburban fares are available after 9am on weekdays and any time at weekends, offering savings of up to 60 per cent on return journeys. In Sydney you can buy a Sydney Pass for three, five or seven days ($85, $115and $135 respectively) which is valid for suburban trains, city buses and ferries. There's also a range of season tickets (weekly, quarterly and annual) for commuters, providing large discounts over standard fares, which may include travel on suburban trains/trams, buses and ferries (e.g. in Sydney). Weekly passes usually cost around eight times the single fare. A photograph is normally required for a season ticket.

# BUSES & TRAMS

There are comprehensive bus services in Australia's major cities and an extensive network of long-distance interstate buses, usually referred to as coaches. Bus services in rural areas are less frequent, and it may be necessary to have your own transport if you live in the country. Melbourne is the only Australian city with an extensive tram network, although other cities are also planning new tram lines.

Buses are the cheapest form of public transport in Australia, both within cities and long distance, and provide a far more comprehensive network than the railways, encompassing almost every corner of Australia. Each city and region of Australia has its own bus companies providing town and country services. In large towns and cities, most bus services start and terminate at a central bus station, which is generally modern and clean. Most are equipped with toilets, showers, luggage lockers or a left luggage office, shops, and a snack bar or restaurant. They have little in common with the seedy places inhabited by drunks, drug addicts and assorted derelicts found in many other countries. Smoking is prohibited on all buses and trams in Australia.

If you need assistance, ask at the bus station information office. Most bus companies provide free timetables and route maps, and in some cities comprehensive timetables and maps are available which include all bus services operating within their boundaries. A night bus service operates in the major cities. See also **Timetables & Maps** on page 230.

# City & Country Buses

In most cities in Australia there are a number of local bus companies, sometimes operated by the local railway company or the state or city authorities. There's a comprehensive bus network in all Australian cities, and services are frequent, including a night bus service in the major cities. Buses are slow but fairly frequent in most cities, where they're often the only option for getting to most suburbs. Major cities usually have an integrated public transport system, the same ticket being valid on buses, suburban trains, trams (Melbourne) and ferries (Sydney). In stark contrast to the cities, in country areas there's usually only one bus company and services are sparse and infrequent. In remote areas there may be only school buses, which usually carry other passengers but aren't obliged to.

Buses on most routes operate from around 6am until 11pm or midnight (but possibly only until 7pm on Sundays). Buses run frequently during the weekday rush hours, e.g. every 10 or 15 minutes on the main routes. Outside rush hours there's usually a half hour service on most routes during weekdays, although services are often severely restricted at weekends and on public holidays (there may be no service at all on some routes on Sundays and public holidays). In major cities there's usually an express bus service (called 'rockets' in some cities) operating between the outer suburbs and the major centres on routes to city centres (express bus numbers are usually prefixed with an X). Night services operate in the major cities from around midnight until 6am, some of which have radio links with taxi operators, so that you can arrange to have a taxi meet you at your destination (very civilised). There are free buses in most major cities covering a circular (loop) route within the city centre.

It's usual to board a bus via the front door and disembark from the centre doors. You must normally ring a bell to inform the driver that you want him to stop at the next stop (a buzzer sounds in the cab) and stand by the centre door. When the bus stops, a green light is illuminated which signals that you must push the handle or press a button to open the door, which doesn't usually open automatically. In most cities, bus stops have numbers, which are often quoted by people when giving directions, and they may be colour-coded. Buses also display their route number, although in some cities numbers may vary according to whether they're running to or from the city centre. All bus companies publish route maps, and there are comprehensive city travel guides in most cities and state bus directories in some states.

**Tickets:** In the major cities, journeys are based on a zone system whereby the bus network is divided into a number of conentric areas (the central business district and inner suburbs are usually designated zone one). Tickets are valid for travel within a single zone or a number of zones, and may be colour coded corresponding to the zones (and modes of transport) for which they're valid. Tickets are usually valid for up to two hours with unlimited transfers during this time, and 'single' tickets usually allow a return trip if it's completed within two hours. You must validate your ticket for your final journey before the two-hour period has elapsed. Tickets may be valid for longer at certain times of day, for example in Melbourne tickets are valid for six hours after 7pm.

Tickets can be purchased from bus stations, on board buses and trams, and from retail outlets such as newsagents and cafés in some cities. Automatic ticket machines are also provided in some cities, but they may gobble your money and refuse to give you a ticket. You can usually buy a ticket from the driver or conductor on boarding a bus, which must then be validated in a machine (to the right of the driver) which stamps your ticket with the date and time of boarding plus the time of expiry of the ticket. If you have a multi-ride ticket, you must validate it each time you travel.

All bus companies offer day passes and weekly, monthly and annual tickets for commuters. A monthly ticket may allow you to take an additional adult with you free of charge at weekends. There are also off-peak, reduced fare tickets that allow you to travel outside rush hours (e.g. between 9am and 3pm or 3.30pm Mondays to Fridays) and at weekends. In most cities you can buy a book of ten tickets (e.g. a TravelTen in Sydney) at a saving of up to 40 per cent compared with buying single tickets. There are concessionary fares for children and pensioners, which are usually half the adult fare. A day 'rover' ticket is available for around $5 in most cities and allows unlimited bus travel for a whole day; it may also include travel on other modes of city transport. Fares may be higher for travel during rush hours, at night and at weekends. Note that there are fines of up to $100 for anyone discovered travelling without a ticket.

## Long-Distance Buses

Long-distance interstate buses are generally cheaper, faster and easier to book than trains, and there's a more comprehensive network. However, they'also less comfortable and more restrictive than trains, and time consuming due to the vast distances involved. Long-distance buses are particularly popular among independent travellers (e.g. backpackers), 80 per cent of whom use them almost exclusively. Travelling by bus is around one-third of the cost of travelling by air. There are numerous daily departures on the most popular routes, although some services operate only a few times per week and, in the Northern Territory, northern Queensland and northern parts of Western Australia some routes are interrupted for weeks at a time during the wet season (November to May). Note that there are unsociable arrival hours on some long-distance routes.

**Companies:** The company in Australia with the most extensive national route network (some 900 destinations daily) is Greyhound Pioneer Australia. The other major national bus operator is McCafferty's, which covers most areas except Western Australia and Tasmania and has over 1,000 scheduled services per week. The main operator in the southern part of Western Australia is the state rail company, Westrail, while Tasmanian Redline Coaches provides express services throughout Tasmania.

**Reservations:** Reservations can be made through travel agents or direct with bus companies: ☎ local call rate 13-2030 or 💻 www.greyhound.com.au for Greyhound Pioneer and ☎ 13-1499 or 💻 www.mccaffertys.com.au for McCafferty's. There are also many booking agents in major cities, including YHA travel offices, some of which allow you to book tickets by phone and pay with a credit card. Long-distance bus tickets are similar to airline tickets, with destinations shown by a code such as

SYD for Sydney and MEL for Melbourne. When checking your baggage, make sure that the baggage code matches that of your destination (otherwise you may end up in Cairns and your baggage in Perth!).

**Buses:** Buses are usually equipped with air-conditioning, reclining seats, toilets, TV and videos with stereo sound, individual reading lights, panoramic windows and water fountains. It's wise to get a seat near the front away from the toilet and on the left-hand side away from the lights of approaching traffic at night. Long-distance journeys are tiring and you shouldn't expect to get much (if any) sleep if you're travelling overnight. Frequent stops are made for food, drinks, toilets and showers. There are strict rules concerning what you can eat and drink on buses. Note that no alcohol may be consumed (maximum fine $500) and smoking is prohibited on all services. Interstate buses don't cater for those in wheelchairs.

**Fares:** There's lively competition between the major long-distance bus companies and many independent and inter-state operators, which helps reduce fares. Discounts abound and you should always shop around for the best deal (generally, the more popular the route, the lower the fares). Some companies offer discounts to backpackers on certain services and there are also discounts for students, although the biggest discounts are usually offered on last-minute bookings. Visitors can purchase bus passes overseas in many countries, although you may get a better deal in Australia. Note that bus passes aren't valid on some local services and a surcharge is usually payable on routes in remote areas.

It's always cheaper to buy a through-ticket for a long journey, rather than separate tickets for short stretches, and most tickets allow unlimited stopovers. You can cancel tickets provided you give 24 hours' notice, but there's a cancellation fee of around $10. A 25 per cent discount is provided for students and children on most services. There's fierce competition on the most popular routes, e.g. Melbourne-Sydney, where fares are around $50, although off the main inter-city routes fares can be high. The main express routes served by Greyhound Pioneer Australia include the following (times and prices are approximate):

| Route | Journey Time (hours) | Approx. Fare One Way ($) |
|---|---|---|
| Sydney-Adelaide | 22 | 95 |
| Sydney-Canberra | 4 | 28 |
| Sydney-Melbourne (inland) | 13 | 50 |
| Canberra-Melbourne | 10 | 45 |
| Melbourne-Adelaide | 11 | 45 |
| Adelaide-Alice Springs | 20 | 135 |
| Adelaide-Perth | 34 | 200 |
| Adelaide-Brisbane | 31 | 150 |
| Darwin-Alice Springs | 20 | 145 |
| Darwin-Kakadu | 4 | 70 |
| Alice Springs-Ayers Rock | 6 | 60 |
| Cairns-Brisbane | 24 | 145 |
| Cairns-Darwin | 40 | 300 |

| Brisbane-Sydney | 16 | 70 |
| Brisbane-Melbourne | 24 | 130 |
| Perth-Darwin | 55 | 436 |

**Tours:** Numerous coach companies offer tours which include accommodation (e.g. hotel, motel, bungalow, cabin or camping) and most meals, ranging in duration from a few days to several months. On camping tours, meals are usually cooked by a travelling cook and prices include meals, tents, sleeping bags and other equipment. Passengers aren't required to erect tents. Some tour companies cater for backpackers and, although they usually offer a more 'rough and ready' service, provide good value.

## SHIPS & FERRIES

Until the '60s, the traditional method of travel to Australia was by ship. Although most people now arrive by air, it's still possible to travel to Australia by ship (e.g. from Britain and the west coast of the USA) if you have lots of time (around five weeks from Britain) and money. Many container ships and freighters carry a limited number of fare-paying passengers, costing from around £2,000 one way (which isn't so expensive when you consider that it includes accommodation and all meals). Many round-the-world cruise ships stop in Australia, departing from Europe in January or February and arriving in Australia in March or April. Cruise companies include CTC Lines, Cunard Lines and P&O Cruises. Contact your travel agent for information. For information about ships from Britain contact the Strand Cruise and Travel Centre (UK ☎ 020-7836 6363) or P&O Containers, Fleet Operations (UK ☎ 020-7441 1472).

**Tasmania:** The only regular maritime passenger service in Australia is the car ferry operating between Melbourne and Devonport on the north coast of Tasmania. It's served by the *Spirit of Tasmania*, a luxury 467-cabin ship of 31,356 tonnes with a capacity of around 1,300 passengers plus vehicles. The trip is often rough, so poor sailors should take seasickness pills (or a plane). In fact, the ferry isn't much cheaper than flying and takes around 14 hours compared with less than an hour by air from Melbourne to Hobart. Ferries run three times weekly in either direction on Mondays, Wednesdays and Fridays from Melbourne's Station Pier, and on Tuesdays, Thursdays and Saturdays from Devonport (although there are seasonal variations). Departures are at 6pm or 7.30pm to Tasmania and at 4pm or 6pm in the other direction. Cabins and hostel-style accommodation are available.

Fares vary with the season (touring or holiday) from around $100 single, including an evening buffet dinner and continental breakfast. There are three fare rates depending on the time of year: bargain (late April to mid-September), holiday (Christmas to March) and shoulder (the rest of the year). There's a 25 per cent discount for students in cabin accommodation and occasional mid-week discounts also. Vehicle transportation is heavily subsidised by the Tasmanian government and costs between $30 and $40 (depending on the season) one way.

There's also a *Devil Cat* service between George Town (east of Devonport) and Melbourne. The journey takes just six hours, but passengers are more liable to seasickness than on the ferry service. For information about ferries contact the TT Line, Station Pier, Port Melbourne, VIC 3207 (☎ local call rate 13-2010, 🖳 www.tt-line.com.au).

**Sydney:** Travelling by ferry is one of the joys of living in Sydney, where many people use it to commute to work. The city has eight main ferry routes and 33 ferry wharves, all served from the main Circular Quay ferry terminal. In addition to regular (slow) ferries, there's also a catamaran (RiverCat) service from Circular Quay to Parramatta (via the Parramatta River) and a JetCat service to Manly. Most ferries run from around 6am until midnight, although times vary with the route, and services are restricted at weekends, when ferries may not stop at all wharves. Most services run every 50 minutes during the day and more frequently during rush hours, e.g. every 15 or 20 minutes. Regular commuters can buy a book of ten tickets (called a 'Ferry Ten') and weekly, quarterly and annual commuter tickets, which offer even greater savings, and can be combined with other modes of public transport such as buses and suburban trains.

Special tickets are available for trips to major attractions (such as Taronga Zoo), which include the return ferry trip from Circular Quay and the entrance fee and are cheaper than buying separate tickets. Special ferries are also available to follow sailing races such as the famous Sydney-Hobart race, which starts on Boxing Day (26th December).

**Other Ferries:** There are ferries in Victoria operating between Cowes on Philip Island and Stony Point on the Mornington Peninsula, from Stony Point to Tankerton on French Island, and from Sorrento to Queenscliff. Brisbane has a fast and efficient ferry service along and across the Brisbane river operating every 20 minutes from dawn until around 11pm, Mondays to Saturdays (operating hours are reduced on Sundays). In Perth there's a ferry service across the Swan River from the Barrack Street jetty to the Mends Street jetty. Ferries also operate from Fremantle to Rottnest Island. Darwin harbour ferries make daily crossings to Mandorah on the Cox peninsula. A ferry service also operates from Woodbridge on the south-east coast of Tasmania to Roberts Point on Bruny Island.

**Cruises:** All major cities offer sightseeing trips and cruises on local waterways, which may include coffee, lunch and dinner cruises (often including a show). Longer cruises are also available, including trips to the Great Barrier Reef from ports in northern Queensland, many of which use glass-bottomed boats to allow a view of the marine life. There are paddle-wheelers at Echuca-Moama in Victoria and paddle-steamers in Mildura in north-western Victoria.

Note that one of the first things you should do after boarding a ferry or ship is to study the safety procedures, i.e. what to do if it sinks!

# TIMETABLES & MAPS

All public transport companies in Australia produce comprehensive timetables, route maps and guides, and many councils publish excellent guides and maps (available from libraries, tourist centres, newsagents and council offices), which include all bus, rail and ferry transport services operating within a city or region. At major airports and railway stations, arrivals and departures are shown on electronic boards and computer screens. Note that most transport companies use am (before noon) and pm (after noon) in timetables, rather than the 24-hour clock used in many countries. When am and pm isn't indicated, the general practice is that times printed in light type are before noon and times printed in bold type are after noon. When travelling from east to west (or vice versa), bear in mind that there may be local time differences, which are usually announced by the conductor. For example, there's a 30-minute time zone change between the eastern states and South Australia (see **Time Difference** on page 468).

**Rail:** Always check and double check the departure (and arrival) time of a train (particularly in the outback when the next train may be a week next Thursday and be fully booked), especially when you need to make a flight connection. You may have to undertake part of your jouney by air or bus to link with a connecting train. Note that schedules are liable to change at short notice, particularly at weekends and during holiday periods. Most long-distance trains operate throughout the year, but local and in-state trains may not run on public holidays (note also that these vary with the state – see page 65), e.g. many don't operate on holidays such as Christmas Day, Good Friday and ANZAC Day (25th April). It's also important to check that a train actually stops where you want to go, as long-distance trains usually make few stops.

The state rail authorities and the Great Southern Railway all publish free timetables, and Rail Australia also publishes a summary of major long-distance services (also available online). Suburban timetables are published separately, and leaflets are available concerning particular services from stations. The *Thomas Cook Overseas Timetable* is the nearest thing Australia has to an Australia-wide rail timetable. On long-distance timetables +1, +2 and +3 indicates that the train arrives one, two or three days after departure. **However, bear in mind that rail timetables in Australia are usually works of fiction and bear little relation to 'real' time.**

**Bus:** Bus timetables may be for individual routes, all routes operated by a particular company, or all routes serving a city, town or region. Timetables including all local bus company services are often published by local councils and are available free (or for a nominal price) from bus companies, libraries and tourist information centres.

# TAXIS

There are two kinds of taxi in Australia: licensed taxis or cabs (short for 'cabriolet') and private radio taxis. The main difference from the passenger's point of view is that licensed taxis (which are usually white or yellow) can be hailed in the street and radio taxis can only be booked by phone. Taxis can be 'officially' shared in some states, e.g. in Darwin there are shared 'multi-ride' taxis with 12 seats which pick up passengers en route. Wheelchair accessible taxis are available in most major cities. There are also water taxis in Sydney operating from Circular Quay to most areas on the harbour, which are a novel (but expensive) way of getting around the harbour. The fare depends on the time of day and the number of passengers.

Licensed taxis can ply for hire anywhere within their fare area and can be hailed on the street, hired from taxi ranks, railway stations, airports and hotels, or ordered by telephone. There are free courtesy phones outside main hotels. Taxis for hire display a 'Vacant' or 'For Hire' sign or light on the roof. It's usually fairly easy to get a taxi in a city late at night, as there are many 'night' taxis, although they can be difficult to find just after the pubs close because of the strict drink-driving laws in Australia (and between midnight and 6am on Sundays in major cities). Taxi drivers run a high risk of being mugged in some areas of major cities (e.g. Sydney), which has led to some suburbs being officially classified as 'no-go' areas (and not only for taxi drivers!). Since 1997, taxis in Sydney have been fitted with a protection screen between the passenger compartment and the driver, and a satellite tracking system is installed in taxis to monitor their position and speed (taxis in Melbourne are being fitted with video cameras).

Taxis are relatively inexpensive in Australia, and rates vary little from city to city. In Sydney there's a standing charge (flagfall) of $2.35 plus $1.15 per km. There are a number of surcharges, including a charge of $1 when a taxi is called by telephone and an extra $2.20 when a bridge toll (e.g. Sydney Harbour Bridge) is included in the journey. There's usually a surcharge for journeys at night and at weekends (in some cities there are three daytime rates). There's usually also a small charge for luggage carried in the boot (trunk). Outside city limits you must pay a higher 'country' rate and possibly a surcharge (befouling fee) of $15 if the taxi gets dirty! Many taxis accept credit cards for fares over $5.

Tipping isn't necessary and, although most people round the fare up to the nearest dollar, drivers may actually round the fare down rather than give change and may even refuse tips (Americans will be horrified at this 'anti-tipping' attitude, which is obviously a plot to undermine the free world!). Australian taxi drivers are generally honest and helpful (unlike those in many others countries) and are a blot on the taxi driver's bad name! Complaints about service or hire charges can be made to the local taxi licensing office. Make a note of the taxi's registration number and the date and time of the incident and, if you think you've been overcharged, obtain a receipt.

In addition to taxi services, many taxi companies operate private hire (e.g. weddings, sightseeing), chauffeur and courier services, and provide contract and account services, e.g. to take children to and from school. A two-passenger bicycle taxi (pedi-cab) can be hired in Adelaide at Elder Park for $10 an hour.

# AIRLINE SERVICES

Air travel is the fastest way to get around Australia, and 80 per cent of domestic long-distance trips (15 million journeys per year) are made by air. Australian airlines are strict about safety, and it's one of the safest places in the world to fly (Qantas has been rated the safest airline in the world by IATA, who in 2000 also named Airservices Australia the world's best provider of air traffic control services). Australia is served by around 50 international airlines operating scheduled passenger services. Australia's national airline is Qantas (Queensland and Northern Territory Aerial Service), formed in 1920 (only KLM is older) and privatised in 1995. It's one of the best (noted for the excellence of its food and wines) and most profitable airlines in the world. Qantas has a fleet of around 145 aircraft and carries more than 20 million passengers per year (over 13 million on domestic routes) to 120 destinations in 45 countries. It has partnership agreements with seven other international airlines, including American Airlines and British Airways, whereby partners can buy seats on Qantas flights and vice versa. There are Qantas Club lounges at all major airports in Australia and shared lounges in many other countries.

Australia's second airline is Ansett, which serves over 70 towns and cities in Australia and also operates flights to New Zealand and a number of Asian destinations, including Bali, Hong Kong and Malaysia. Ansett has 12 international partners, including Singapore Airlines and Air New Zealand, and provides an extensive network of domestic flights through its subsidiaries Ansett Express, Ansett Airlines of South Australia, Ansett WA, Ansett NT, East-West and Air Queensland.

Both Ansett and Qantas have their own terminals at Australia's major airports and both cater for disabled passengers and passengers in wheelchairs. Note that smoking is prohibited on all flights operated by Australian airlines, both domestic and international, with a maximum $500 fine for offenders (so don't try smoking in the toilet!).

Flying times between Sydney and other state capitals are: Canberra (236km/ 147mi) 30 minutes; Brisbane (746km/464mi) and Melbourne (708km/440mi) around one hour 15 minutes; Adelaide (1,166km/725mi) and Hobart (1,039km/646mi) around two hours; and Perth (3,284km/2,041mi) around five. As with international flights, the major domestic airlines are Qantas (50 destinations) and Ansett Australia (all major cities plus the most popular tourist destinations). There are also five regional airlines and around 25 smaller commuter airlines in Australia (many owned by or linked with Ansett or Qantas), which mainly fly in-state routes and provide access to remote areas, islands and tourist destinations.

There are many flights each day between Australia's major cities (although some journeys require a number of stops), but on less travelled routes there are just one or two flights a week. You should always book a domestic flight as far in advance as possible, particularly during holiday periods (this will also allow you to take maximum advantage of reduced fares). Many regional and local airlines operate small aircraft, which are generally booked well in advance and consequently don't offer discounts or low fares. Many domestic airlines also offer a variety of air tours lasting from two to 14 days.

**Baggage:** The baggage allowance in economy (tourist) class on flights from Europe depends on whether you travel east or west. On easterly flights (via Asia) the baggage allowance is 20kg/44lbs (one piece) and on westerly flights (via North America) it's two pieces. The maximum permitted weight of any single item is 32kg (70lbs) in both directions. Never pack electronic equipment such as personal computers and transistorised music systems in your hold baggage, but keep them in your hand baggage. If you have a portable computer, it's wise to have it checked by hand, as data could be erased or corrupted by powerful X-ray machines. Passengers are requested not to leave baggage unattended at any time at airports, as it may be stolen or taken away by security staff. Always obtain a check-in stub for your baggage, as without it you cannot claim for compensation if it's lost or stolen. **Keep any valuables in your hand baggage and ensure that they're fully insured.**

Passengers are limited to one piece of hand baggage per person such as a briefcase measuring up to 34cm x 23cm x 48cm or a soft frame garment bag measuring up to 60cm x 114cm x 11cm, plus a handbag and personal belongings such as a coat or camera. Hand baggage rules are strictly enforced, and if you try to take too many items or too large an item on board it may be confiscated and put on a later flight.

The baggage allowance on Qantas domestic flights is three bags for first class passengers, two bags for business class passengers and one for economy class passengers. The economy baggage allowance is 30kg (66lbs), but frequent flyers (Ansett and Qantas) and Qantas Club members receive an additional 10kg (22lbs) allowance.

Check-in time is 90 minutes before departure for international flights and one hour for domestic flights (sometimes less for first and business class passengers). Most airports have 24-hour luggage lockers, although you should note that after 24 hours, lockers may be sealed to ensure that you pay the excess due. Some airline baggage enquiry offices allow passengers to leave bags free of charge for up to 24 hours.

# Airports

The main airports in Australia are Adelaide, Brisbane, Cairns, Darwin, Melbourne, Perth, Port Hedland, Sydney and Townsville. Sydney and Melbourne are Australia's two largest international airports; Adelaide, Brisbane, Cairns, Darwin, Hobart, Perth and Townsville also have international airports. The capital, Canberra, doesn't have an international airport and is served by domestic flights from other Australian cities (Sydney is only half an hour away by air). Most of Australia's major airports are owned and controlled by the Federal Airports Corporation (FAC), although they're gradually being privatised. When minor airports and country landing strips are included, Australia has a total of over 400 'airports'. Most Australian airports are deserted much of the time and come to life for only a few hours a day, when international flights arrive and depart. Terminals may open for only a few hours before arrivals or departures and close for the day after the last flight has arrived or left. International terminals are usually separate from domestic buildings and the two may be located some distance apart. There are bus and taxi services from all major airports to local city centres.

**Sydney:** Sydney's international airport is named Kingsford-Smith (after Australia's pioneering aviator) and is located in the suburb of Mascot, 10km/6mi south of the city centre. The international and domestic terminals are located 4km/2.5mi apart on either side of the runway. It's Australia's busiest airport and handles around 6 million passengers a year (three times the number of Melbourne and Brisbane airports). It was refurbished and modernised in 1998 in time for the 2000 Olympics, including an underground railway link to the city centre. A second Sydney airport is planned, although the state government is finding it difficult to find a suitable site owing to concerns over aircraft noise (the 'anywhere but in my back yard' problem).

**Melbourne:** Melbourne's Tullamarine airport is located 23km/14mi north-west of the city centre and is Australia's second-largest airport (after Sydney), although third in terms of international traffic after Sydney and Brisbane. It's the only airport in Australia operating 24 hours a day. Melbourne has tried (with some success) to attract airlines by reducing airport charges and now serves many more international destinations than previously. The Airtrain rail link from the airport to the city and to the Gold Coast was recently opened. Melbourne has a second airport at Essendon between the city and Tullamarine, which operates local flights within Victoria and to Tasmania.

**Adelaide:** Adelaide airport is just 6km/4mi south-west of the city centre and has both international and domestic terminals, five minutes' walk apart. Only two airlines, Qantas and Singapore International, have direct international flights to Adelaide, although many airlines provide free connecting flights to Melbourne, Sydney and even Singapore in order to attract passengers.

**Brisbane:** Brisbane airport is 10km/6mi from the city centre and has separate international and domestic terminals some 12 minutes apart by road. There are international flights to New Zealand, Europe, North America, Japan, Singapore and Papua New Guinea.

**Darwin:** Darwin airport (located 8km/5mi south of the city centre) has the longest runway in the country and operates international flights to Singapore, Kuala Lumpur, Bali, Kupang, Timor and Borneo. There are domestic flights (from the same terminal as international flights) to most major cities once a day or less frequently.

**Perth:** Perth airport (21km/13mi east of the city centre) is a gateway for services from Asia and Europe. It has international and domestic terminals located on opposite sides of the runway some 10km/6mi apart by road. Changing flights can be a chore, although many international flights arrive after midnight when there are no connecting domestic flights anyway. Fares to Europe are lower from Perth than elsewhere in Australia and there's a lively market in international tickets.

**Other Airports:** Alice Springs airport is 7km/4mi south of the town centre, from where most flights are to Darwin or Adelaide. Cairns and Townsville have international airports which are also connected to Brisbane and other major cities by regular domestic flights. Tasmania has three main airports: Hobart, Launceston, and Devonport, and Wynyard (or Burnie), served by domestic flights from the mainland. The only international flights are from Hobart to New Zealand (Christchurch).

# Fares

The Australian airline industry was deregulated in 1990, prior to which there was a duopoly operated by Qantas and Ansett, who charged the same (very high) fares and offered virtually the same services. Deregulation heralded the arrival of a number of new domestic carriers who quickly forced Qantas and Ansett to reduce fares, e.g. the cost of a Sydney-Perth ticket was immediately halved! Random discounting is now common on domestic flights, although there are often conditions such as advance booking, flying at weekends only or between fixed dates. A variety of discount fares are available when flying to Australia from some countries (e.g. Britain), although Australia's isolated position in the world means that international travel is invariably expensive. Domestic air travel is also relatively expensive because of the long distances involved. **If you're migrating to Australia, you should book as far ahead as possible (but never before you've received your visa!).**

**International Fares:** Air fares are high from most countries to Australia, as there's a relatively low volume of traffic on most routes and little competition. The main exception is between Britain and Australia (the 'kangaroo route'), which is one of the most competitive routes in the world. In mid-2001 various airlines started a price war offering cut-price tickets on selected flights. The low season return fare is around GB£550 from London to Sydney (GB£335 single) between April and June, rising to GB£900 during the high season of December to January (when fares vary little between airlines). Fares during the shoulder season of July to November and February to March are usually between GB£500 and GB£600. Fares from London to Melbourne or Brisbane are usually more expensive than to Sydney. From Europe, fares vary according to whether you're flying east via Asia or west via North America. It's usually cheaper to fly via America between November and February.

Note that flights in the weeks immediately prior to Christmas are usually fully booked months in advance, and delaying your flight a few days until after the Christmas period can mean a considerable saving. Expect to pay GB£100 to GB£200 or more for return flights with British Airways, Qantas or Singapore Airlines, which may be worthwhile if you take advantage of their domestic fare deals. Fares are higher if you break the journey, although most travellers find that it's worthwhile taking advantage of stopover deals and it also helps avoid or reduce jet lag.

Fares from the USA aren't as good value as from Europe, although excursion and promotional fares are available which are much lower than full-fares, e.g. apex and promotional return fares from Los Angeles to Sydney/Melbourne are around US$845 in the low season and US$1,265 in the high season. Regular tickets are valid for 12 months, so it may pay to buy your ticket well in advance of your trip. There's not a lot of choice from the USA, from where just five airlines fly non-stop to Australia: Air New Zealand, Canadian Airlines, Continental, Qantas and United Airlines. Most other airlines stop at Honolulu, Papeete or Auckland, or a combination of these. When flying from Sydney to Los Angeles, you leave Sydney in the afternoon and arrive in LA in the morning of the same day! An 'open-jaw' ticket (flying into one airport and out of another) is usually no more expensive than an ordinary return.

Major airlines offer economy, business and first class fares. Full fare tickets allow you to change the date and time of travel at a moment's notice and offer a full refund should you decide not to travel. When buying apex and other discounted tickets, always make sure that you fully understand any ticket restrictions. Return fares from Australia to Europe are higher than when travelling in the opposite direction. The best deals are from Sydney, although bargains can be found from Melbourne and Perth (discount fares are advertised in the major daily newspapers). A 'departure tax' of $30 is incorporated into the ticket price for passengers aged 12 or over. Departing passengers must also complete an *Outgoing Passenger Card*.

Charter flights are also available from Britain to Australia (with Britannia Airways and Airtours) between November and April. Flights cost from around GB£400 return. Note, however, that charter flights have severe restrictions, including no stopovers, a minimum stay of two weeks and a maximum of eight.

**Stopovers & Round-the-World (RTW) Tickets:** When travelling to Australia, you can travel one-stop or take advantage of a number of stopovers, e.g. in Asia, the Pacific and North America. Most return tickets from Europe include 'free' stopover options on outward and return journeys, usually in Asia or the Pacific. Round-the-world tickets to Australia from London via Asia and North America start at around GB£800 for four stops, depending on the season. From Europe you can also fly via South Africa or South America, although these options are more expensive than the usual Asian or North American routes.

# 11.

# MOTORING

Australians are devoted to their cars and (like Americans) rarely go anywhere without them. A survey in 2000 found that 75 per cent of Australians consider their car to be extremely or very important. It's essential to have your own transport in Australia if you live anywhere other than in one of the main cities. Travelling interstate involves vast distances (on the North American scale) and driving in the outback is reminiscent of driving in North Africa. Australians are used to driving long distances and think nothing of driving hundreds of miles to visit relatives or friends for a few days or even a day out. Almost 80 per cent of all goods in Australia are transported by road, and passenger travel is also dominated by road transport, with almost 12 million passenger vehicles on the road.

Australian cities are often sprawling (particularly Sydney), so people are inclined to use their cars rather than public transport. However, Australians haven't learnt how to co-exist with the motor car in their cities, where traffic jams, parking problems and vehicle pollution are endemic. Traffic congestion and pollution is chronic in Sydney (where it's estimated it will get six times worse in the next 20 years) and Melbourne, where rush hours should be avoided if at all possible. There are 'park and ride' facilities in cities to encourage commuters to use public transport, although they aren't widely used (encouraging car pooling is also a hard slog).

Australia has a relatively high accident rate and around 1,800 people are killed and 16,000 injured on Australian roads each year, although the numbers are falling, partly as a result of the widespread introduction of random breath testing and speed cameras, and a reduction in legal alcohol/blood levels. However, the prevalence of alcohol (and drugs) among fatal accident victims remains a major problem. The risk of young males aged 17 to 25 dying on the roads is around three times that of other age groups, and they're five times more likely to die in a car accident than women of the same age. Public holiday periods are the most dangerous times to be on the roads.

The individual states and territories have jurisdiction over the registration of motor vehicles, driving licences and traffic rules, which therefore vary with the state or territory. For specific information, obtain a copy of a state or territory's 'highway code' (it has various names such as the *Road Users' Handbook* in New South Wales). If you're going to Australia for a short period, don't forget to take your foreign licence, international driving permit (if applicable), car insurance policy, no-claims discount certificate, and records of membership of motoring organisations.

# VEHICLE IMPORT

If you plan to import a motor vehicle or motorcycle into Australia, either temporarily or permanently, first ensure that you're aware of the latest regulations. Any vehicle imported into Australia must meet the registration requirements of the state or territory where it's going to be registered (or it must be modified). If you're in doubt, check with the relevant motor vehicle registration authorities (see **Appendix A**). The current conditions governing the importation of vehicles are provided in various publications produced by the Australian Customs Service, including *Customs Information for Travellers* and *Importing a Motor Vehicle or Motorcycle*. These are available from Australian embassies and high commissions overseas or from the Controller-General, Australian Customs Service, Customs House, 5 Constitution Avenue, Canberra ACT 2601 (☎ local call 1300-363263 or 02-6275 5041, ▯ www. customs.gov.au).

Exporting a car to Australia can save you a considerable amount of money, particularly if you own a luxury or sports car and have owned it for a number of years. European cars usually cost around twice as much in Australia. However, you must take into account shipping costs, insurance, port/unpacking and steam cleaning charges in Australia, and Australian customs duty and sales tax. It costs around GB£1,000 to ship a small family car (e.g. a Ford Escort or VW Golf) from the UK to Sydney plus around GB£500 in other fees. Before deciding to import a car, it's worthwhile checking that spare parts and servicing will be available and what they'll cost. Note also that Australian insurance companies may refuse to provide cover on vehicles that aren't sold in Australia because of the high cost of accident repairs.

**Vehicle Standards:** All imported vehicles must meet Australia's safety, emissions and anti-theft standards and must comply with safety requirements relating to lighting, seat belts, child restraint anchorages and glazing. The standards are contained in a booklet (*Importing Vehicles to Australia*) available from the Vehicle Safety Standards Office (GPO Box 594, Canberra ACT 2602 (☎ freecall 1800-815272 or 02-6274 7444, ✉ vimports@dotrs.gov.au). It's illegal to import a new or secondhand vehicle unless it meets Australian emission standards or arrangements have been made to modify the vehicle to meet these requirements after its arrival. Before importing any vehicle, it's essential to ensure that it will meet the required standards, which can be done by contacting the Vehicle Safety Standards Office.

**Permanent Import:** Australian citizens and migrants with permanent Australian residence may import one vehicle in any 12 month period. A vehicle must have been owned and used overseas for at least 12 consecutive months (unless it's over 15 years old) and must be right-hand drive. Although a left-hand drive vehicle can be converted to right-hand drive, it's expensive and usually isn't worthwhile (and the conversion may not be accepted by the Australian authorities). Vehicles can be imported without proof that they meet Australian Design Rules (see page 243), but are expected to provide a level of safety similar to Australian vehicles and must pass a roadworthiness inspection. Any vehicle imported into Australia must also meet the registration requirements of the state or territory where it's going to be registered. If in doubt, check with the relevant motor vehicle registration authorities (see **Appendix A**).

**Temporary Import:** Vehicles can be imported for up to one year by overseas visitors from certain countries, who must submit an application or present a valid *Carnet de Passage en Douane* at the port of entry. In order to obtain the *carnet*, you must provide security in the form of a Banker's Letter of Indemnity, a Cash Bond or a special indemnity insurance policy such as one issued by the Australian Automobile Association (AAA, GPO Box 1555, Canberra ACT 2601, 🖳 www.aaa. asn.au). The security payable in Australia is equal to the amount of duty and GST otherwise payable (see below) and is refunded when you return the *carnet* to the automobile association you obtained it from. You're permitted to import a left-hand drive vehicle temporarily, but it must display a 'Caution Left-Hand Drive' sign on its rear.

In most states and territories, it's necessary to present the vehicle for inspection at the nearest motor vehicle registration authority as soon as possible after importation. You'll need the following documents:

● evidence that a security has been paid to the customs authorities (*Carnet de Passage*);
● evidence that the vehicle has Australian third party insurance;

- your home driving licence or an international driving permit;
- the vehicle's current registration certificate.

After the vehicle has passed the mechanical and safety inspection and the documentation has been checked, a temporary permit (known as an *Unregistered Vehicle Permit*) is issued allowing it to be driven in Australia until the expiry date of your *carnet*.

**Shipment:** Most international shippers serving Australia can arrange for the shipment of vehicles, and there are also specialist vehicle shipping companies in some countries. Shippers usually offer a range of services, including shared containers, 'sole use' containers and roll on/roll off (where vehicles are driven onto and off a ship). Shop around and obtain a few quotations. Containerisation is the best but also the most expensive option.

**Import Application:** An *Application for Vehicle Import Approval* form must be submitted to the customs authority at the intended port of entry at least four weeks prior to the planned arrival of a vehicle in Australia (the fee of $50 must accompany the application). An application form is contained in the booklet, *Importing Vehicles to Australia*, mentioned above. Note that the application form is available online. To avoid delay in clearing the vehicle through customs, you should also present your passport, driver's licence, purchase and transportation documents, bill of sale, registration and insurance papers, service records and log book.

**Quarantine Clearance:** Quarantine clearance is required from the Australian Quarantine and Inspection Service after a vehicle arrives at the port of entry. A car should be steam cleaned before shipment, as it will need to undergo a quarantine inspection on arrival in Australia. When a vehicle arrives in Australia, it's inspected internally and externally for soil, seeds, insect and disease-bearing organisms. If any suspect traces are found (which is usually the case), the car must be thoroughly cleaned inside and out, and the engine and undercarriage steam cleaned (at your expense).

**Duty & Tax:** Customs clearance is performed at the port of entry. Customs clearance includes the payment of duty and GST, and completion of the form *Entry for Home Consumption* in triplicate. The duty and tax payable is revised from time to time and you should confirm the rates prior to shipment. In July 2000 the following duty rates applied:

| Vehicle Type | Vehicle Age | Customs Duty (%) |
| --- | --- | --- |
| Passenger (including 4WD) | Up to 30 years | 15 |
| Passenger (including 4WD) | Over 30 years | 0 |
| Campervans and mobile homes | Any | 15 |
| Commercial | Any | 5 |
| Motorcycle | Any | 0 |
| Other (including 'off-road' 4WD) | Any | 5 |

All imported vehicles are also subject to Goods and Services Tax (GST) levied at 10 per cent of the value of 'taxable importation value' (VoTI). VoTI is the sum of the duty, customs value, and international insurance and transportation costs. A vehicle's customs value is calculated as follows:

● **Vehicles purchased after 2nd March 1998:** Purchase price plus the cost of any modifications or improvements;

● **Vehicles purchased before 2nd March 1998:** Purchase price plus the cost of any modifications or improvements (but not normal wear and tear maintenance), less a depreciation allowance of 5 per cent for the first month of ownership, plus 1 per cent for each subsequent month of ownership up to a maximum of 76 per cent (equal to six years' ownership).

If there's insufficient evidence of the purchase price paid or a vehicle's purchase price was unrealistic, the customs value is determined as 40 per cent of the current Australian market value of the vehicle. To claim depreciation, you must present your passport and all purchase documents, bill of sale, registration papers, service records and the shipping bill of lading, together with any other documents that may assist customs in determining its 'customs value'. Ownership is determined by documentation in the importer's name and extends from the date of purchase or delivery (whichever is the later) until the date the owner or the vehicle left the foreign country (whichever is the earlier). The value is calculated in Australian dollars on the date the vehicle was exported to Australia. Australian manufactured vehicles aren't subject to customs duty and may be re-imported into Australia free of GST, provided tax was paid prior to export and no refund was obtained. Note also that Australia is pledged to reduce or abolish import duty and tax on imported foreign cars (see **New Cars** on page 245). In addition to duty and GST, Luxury Car Tax (LCT) at 25 per cent is levied on all vehicles except motorcycles and commercial vehicles valued at over $55,134 (2001).

Details of duty rates, customs values, depreciation allowances and personal import approvals are available from Australian Customs and Registration Departments and shipping agents.

# VEHICLE REGISTRATION

Vehicle registration (referred to as 'rego') in Australia must be renewed annually and includes road tax, stamp duty (between 2 and 5 per cent of the vehicle's 'market' value depending on the state) and (except in the case of imported vehicles) third party liability insurance. Registration is the responsibility of the states and territories and fees vary, but are usually $400 to $600 for an average vehicle (Western Australia is cheapest and the ACT is the most expensive). In some states, such as NSW, registration costs vary from $180 to $315 according to the tare (unladen) weight of the car. Registration of a vehicle is made with the local state traffic authority, e.g. the Road and Traffic Authority (RTA) in New South Wales (see addresses in **Appendix A**). Payment of vehicle registration can be made at any post office, and a current registration label must be displayed behind your car windscreen; if you lose it, a replacement costs around $20. Motorists who don't pay their rego within a few weeks of it falling due face fines (tens of thousands of motorists drive without rego).

**Compliance Plate:** Before a vehicle can be registered in Australia, it must be fitted with an Australian compliance plate which indicates that it complies with Australian Design Rules (ADR). A compliance plate is fitted automatically to a car manufactured in Australia; imported vehicles must be inspected by a state government motor vehicle registration authority. Before a vehicle can be tested, evidence must be shown that import duty and GST have been paid, as applicable (see page 346).

**CTP:** It's necessary to have proof of compulsory third party (CTP) insurance (shown by a 'green slip' issued by the insurance company) to register a vehicle in Australia (see also **Change of Ownership** below).

**Number Plates:** Registration (number) plates are issued by state and territory authorities and must be displayed at the front and rear of cars and at the rear of motorcycles. The registration numbers must be those that are recorded on the vehicle's registration papers. A vehicle may not be parked or driven on a public road without registration, and plates must be returned to the issuing authority when they expire. Each state or territory has different coloured plates as shown below:

| State/Territory | Colour |
| --- | --- |
| ACT | blue on white |
| NSW | black on yellow |
| NT | red on white |
| QLD | green on white |
| SA | green on yellow |
| TAS | blue on white |
| VIC | dark blue or white |
| WA | black on yellow |

There are also commercial, official, diplomatic and personalised registration plates with different colours. Note that it is illegal to drive with one state's colours while permanently living in another state.

**Change of Ownership:** If you buy a secondhand car, the previous owner must sign the back of the registration paper, which you must take with the test certificate, if applicable (see page 248) to the motor registry. The change of ownership must be registered with the state authority and a registration transfer fee paid (between $14 and $25 depending on the state), plus stamp duty of 2 to 5 per cent depending on the state. When a vehicle is bought or sold, the CTP insurance (see above) transfers to the new owner until the registration expires.

# BUYING A CAR

Cars are relatively expensive in Australia and generally cost slightly more than in most European countries and up to twice as much as cars in the USA, particularly imported cars (on which there's a hefty import tariff). The Commonwealth Bank Australia quotes new and used car prices in its free annual *Cost of Living and Housing Survey Book*. Information regarding the purchase of both new and used cars is published by Australian motoring organisations (see page 275), e.g. in NSW the National Roads & Motoring Association (NRMA) publishes a booklet entitled the *Worry-Free Guide to Buying a Car*. New and used car guides are also available, including the *New Car Buyer's Guide*, the *Used Car Buyer's Guide* and Universal's *New 4WD Guide*.

# New Cars

A number of foreign manufacturers make or assemble cars in Australia, including Ford, Holden (General Motors), Mitsubishi, Nissan and Toyota, which comprise over 75 per cent of the new car market, although other Asian manufacturers are starting to establish a foothold. In 2000, the Subaru Impreza was Australian 'car of the year'. Ford and Holden models are the most popular and consequently the cheapest for spares and repairs. The Holden Commodore is rated as one of Australia's best family cars, followed by the Ford Falcon, Mitsubishi Magna and Toyota Camry. Note that local models are often different from those available in other countries, as manufacturers style their cars according to what the local market demands (Australians are proud of their 'unique' cars, particularly old Holden models).

Australians are fond of big gas-guzzling, six-cylinder cars, although their fuel consumption has fallen considerably in recent years and their engines last longer and aren't as likely to overheat as four-cylinder engines on long runs. Four-wheel-drive (4WD) cars are especially popular in country areas, although the running costs (fuel and maintenance) are around 30 per cent higher than two-wheel-drive cars. They do, however, keep their value well. Station wagons or estate cars are also popular and are often chosen in preference to a 4WD in suburban areas.

Although comparisons between new car prices in different countries are often difficult, e.g. due to fluctuating exchange rates and the different levels of standard equipment, prices in Australia are generally high, although they have remained more or less static for the last few years. A small five-door, four-cylinder saloon costs from around $15,000 and a six-cylinder model from around $30,000. There's a high tariff on imports to protect local manufacturers, although Australia is pledged to reduce or abolish import duty and tax. The tariff was to have fallen to 5 per cent by 2005 and be abolished altogether by the year 2010. However, after much debate (and fierce opposition from local car manufacturers) it was decided to reduce the tariff by 2.5 per cent per year until the year 2000, when it was frozen at 15 per cent for private cars and 5 per cent for commercial vehicles until 2005.

The cost of labour and parts for even the least expensive family cars can be very high in Australia, so it may pay to buy a car with a long or extended warranty. Popular, local-manufactured cars are best if you don't want high repair bills (spares and servicing for some German and Japanese cars are astronomical).

Air-conditioning is standard on most cars in Australia and is essential for anyone who spends much time behind the wheel. It certainly isn't a luxury when you're stuck in a traffic jam in summer or on long-distance trips in the outback. A basic air-conditioning unit costs from around $2,000 (installed) for a small family car. Note, however, that air-conditioning decreases power and increases fuel consumption. Not that fuel consumption is considered very important in Australia, where petrol is much cheaper than in many other countries.

# Used Cars

Used cars can be excellent value for money in Australia, particularly low mileage cars less than a year old, where the savings on the new price can be as high as 25 per cent (the minute a new car leaves the showroom, it's usually worth 10 per cent less than the purchase price). Some models (e.g. luxury models) depreciate much more quickly than others and many are excellent secondhand buys. Australians tend to keep their cars longer than people in many other countries, the average age being over ten years.

**Dealers:** Like most countries, Australia has its share of dodgy used car dealers, who employ every underhand trick in the book when selling to unsuspecting buyers. It isn't unknown for salesmen to add details to an agreement after you've signed it, so make sure that everything is completed before signing and obtain a copy. Never sign a form with some details left blank (such as the price, repayment period and payments), which is like signing a blank cheque! Avoid signing a purchase form that's subject to a 'satisfactory' mechanical inspection, as this may mean that, unless a vehicle is found to have major faults, you're stuck with it.

A new law, the Property Agents and Motor Dealers Act, 2000, came into effect on 1st July 2001, establishing trading standards for used car dealers, who are now required to adhere to a code of conduct. All cars sold by licensed dealers must display a 'statutory warranty', which guarantees that the cars are free from defects and that any defects occuring during the warranty period will be repaired free of charge. Warranty periods are three months or 5,000km for cars under 10 years old or with under 160,000km on the clock, and one month or 1,000km for cars over 10 years old or with more than 160,000km on the clock. Under the new law, buyers have a 'cooling-off' period (until 5pm of the next working day), may take the car for a test drive and have it independently inspected. They also have the option of a 'complaint resolution process'. Note, however, that if you decide to use the 'cooling-off' period you must pay a deposit of up to $100, which you'll lose if you decide not to buy.

It's always best to buy a used car from a licensed dealer who's bound by the Auctioneers and Agents Act (and who may be a member of a Motor Traders Association); if there's any question about a car's history (e.g. it's stolen, still under finance or not as it appears), a licensed dealer must rectify the problem. When you buy from a car dealer, he will usually help you with the paperwork and provide a roadworthiness certificate and warranty, which is compulsory in most states. A dealer may also include free membership of a local motoring organisation. Always carefully check what's included or excluded from a used car warranty, as many contain a number of conditions, which, if you don't adhere to them, will void the warranty. Note, however, that if you buy a car in Sydney and break down in Perth the warranty won't be of much use! You may as well save money by buying privately.

**Buying Privately:** To sell a car legally in Australia, the seller must have the car inspected within one month of the sale and present the inspection certificate to the buyer. If you're buying privately, you should therefore only buy a car that carries a valid 'pink slip' confirming that it meets safety and roadworthiness criteria. The car must also have a sign stating that it has 'no statutory warranty'. It's best to buy a car with around 9 to 10 months' registration (rego), which means that you avoid the cost of registration and need only pay the rego transfer fee plus stamp duty on the declared value of the vehicle (see **Registration** on page 243). Note that many people understate the price when buying privately, as stamp duty is payable as a percentage (between two and five depending on the state) of the declared value of a car. It's estimated that some 60 per cent of declared values are low.

**Visitors & Travellers:** Short-term residents such as long-stay tourists, backpackers and working holidaymakers may wish to consider the flexibility of having their own transport, which can be economical when split between a number of people. If you want an old reliable car, it's best to buy a Ford Falcon or Holden Commodore, which are engineered to survive Australia's rough outback roads, and have strong six-cylinder engines and relatively inexpensive parts that are easy to obtain. Secondhand parts for most older Australian-made cars can be picked up cheaply from car breakers' yards throughout the country. Station wagons and panel vans are popular among travellers, as you can put a mattress in the back for sleeping. Note, however, that imported cars (e.g. German and Japanese) are generally considered more reliable than Australian-built cars, although they're also much more expensive. Expect to pay from $1,000 for an old 'banger' (which should, however, be mechanically reliable) and from around $5,000 for a decent secondhand car that will last a number of years.

**Cheap Cars:** Cheap cars can be purchased through car markets in most cities, where owners gather to sell their vehicles. For example, in Sydney you can buy or sell a vehicle at the Kings Cross Car Market, which is dedicated to travellers buying and selling cars and campervans. Note, however, that there are no guarantees, so you need to know what you're buying. One of the advantages of buying from travellers is that they may include camping equipment, spares and other useful items in the price. You can also pick up cars registered in a state other than the one where it's being sold, which can be good buys, particularly if you plan to sell in the state where the vehicle is registered. It's also possible to buy at auction, although this isn't recommended unless you're an expert mechanic. The main disadvantage of buying a cheap car is that it will have high mileage and may be in poor mechanical condition.

A number of dealers (car yards) in the major cities specialise in selling cars to travellers, and most are honest, as their reputation depends upon it. Many offer to buy vehicles back at an agreed price (provided you don't wreck them), which is usually 50 per cent of the price paid. Note, however, that dealers may try to knock down the buy-back price by finding fault with the car, even when it has been agreed in writing. If this happens, you may get a better deal selling it privately (you should get around two-thirds of the price paid after six to nine months, provided you didn't pay too much). Obviously a buy-back deal is feasible only if you're returning to your starting point.

**Mechanical & Other Checks:** Australian motoring organisations (see page 275) will check a car before you buy it for a fee of around $125 (around $145 if you're not a member). Alternatively a 'mobile' mechanic will do it for around $40. It's important to contact the state Registry of Encumbered Vehicles (☎ freecall 1800-814762), which will tell you if a car is under finance or has been stolen or if there are any outstanding fines (e.g. parking) against it (when you buy a car you assume responsibility for any outstanding fines). The small fee levied could save you $thousands.

**Publications:** The best days for car advertisements in local newspapers are Wednesdays and Saturdays. There are also advertisements in publications such as the *Trading Post* (Sydney) and car magazines. You can also buy interstate newspapers, although it's rarely worth travelling far to inspect a car unless it's a rare model or exceptional value for money (you can travel a very long way to find a 'lemon' which wasn't worth walking around the block to see). Note that deciphering used car ads can be difficult unless you speak 'Australian', e.g. a panel van is a van with no rear windows and only front seats, and a ute is a utility or pick-up truck (an open-backed van).

# TEST CERTIFICATE

In most states and territories, vehicles must pass a periodic technical inspection. For example, in New South Wales a vehicle over three years old must pass an inspection every year (fee around $20) before its registration can be renewed. In order to sell a car in Australia, you must have the car inspected within one month of the sale and present the inspection certificate to the buyer. The technical inspection is carried out by authorised garages and includes checking all lights (i.e. headlights, brake lights and indicator lights), brakes, steering, windscreen wipers and washers, horn, tyres (which must have at least 1.5mm of tread across the whole surface) and seat belts. If your car passes, you're given an inspection report ('pink slip') which must be displayed behind the windscreen. If your car fails the test, you're given a defect notice ('black slip') listing the points on which it has failed. Note that you can get a defect notice if your car is too noisy, drips oil or blows too much smoke; a car can even be failed if the inspector thinks it's too dirty to test! If you get a defect notice, you may be permitted to drive home or to a garage for repair, depending on why it failed.

The police can stop and test your vehicle at any time and, if you get a defect notice, it must be repaired and officially cleared before you may drive it again. The police will affix a yellow sticker (called a 'canary') to your windscreen, which allows you to drive your car home or to a garage for repair (they may also do this to a stationary car, which means that they wish to inspect it). If a red sticker is attached to a vehicle, it means that it's considered to be unroadworthy and may not be driven until it's repaired on the spot or towed away for repair.

# SELLING A CAR

The main points to note when selling a car are:

- A potential buyer shouldn't test drive your car unless he's covered by your or his own insurance. You're responsible if someone drives your car with your permission and has an accident.

- If you're planning to sell your car, you must usually have it safety inspected one month before the sale and give the test certificate ('pink slip') to the prospective buyer. It's illegal to sell a car in an unroadworthy condition, unless you're selling it as a non-runner without a test certificate. Never describe a car as being in a better condition than it is. If it's subsequently found to have faults, you could be liable to reimburse the buyer or pay for repairs.

- You must sign the back of the registration paper and give it to the buyer. When a vehicle is sold, the compulsory third party (CTP) insurance transfers to the new owner with the registration until it expires.

- Inform your insurance company. Either cancel your insurance or transfer it to a new car. Note that, if you cancel your insurance, even for a short period, this may affect your no-claims discount when you take out insurance on a new car. When you sell a car, you're required to notify the motor vehicle registration office by completing the appropriate part of the vehicle registration papers. The new owner of the car must also register his ownership with them (this is intended as a cross check of ownership).

● If you're selling your car privately, you should insist on cash. It's usually a formality for the buyer to accompany you to your bank and make a cash transfer on the spot. There are confidence tricksters (crooks) who will, given half a chance, happily give you a dud cheque and drive off with your car. If someone insists on paying by cheque, you should *never* allow them to take your car until the cheque has cleared. Don't allow a dealer or car auctioneer to take your car until a cheque has cleared, as cheques sometimes bounce after companies have ceased trading.

● Include in the receipt that you're selling the car in its present condition (as seen) without a guarantee, the price paid and the car's kilometre reading. The new owner may ask for a declaration in writing that the car is accident free, which applies to major accidents that have caused structural damage and not slight bumps.

● The buyer must pay stamp duty, which is based on the declared value of the vehicle, i.e. the price at which you sell it.

You can advertise a car for sale in local newspapers, on free local notice boards, in local or national newspapers (Wednesdays and Saturdays are best), and in motoring magazines. The best place to advertise a car depends on its make and value. Cheap cars are probably best sold in local newspapers, while expensive vehicles and collectors' cars are often better advertised in the motoring press or in national newspapers such as *The Australian*. Buyers will travel a long way to view a car that appears good value (if nobody phones, you'll know why). Note that it's usually difficult to sell a vehicle outside its 'home' state (i.e. where it's registered), as it must undergo a new inspection and receive new registration plates and papers. For this reason, if you sell a car in a state other than where it's registered, you will normally receive less than its market value.

# DRIVING LICENCE

The minimum age for driving in Australia is 17 or 18 for a car or motorcycle, depending on the state or territory. A young driver may obtain a licence before he reaches the required age after passing a written road knowledge test, e.g. at age 16 in NSW. There are special licence classes for heavy goods vehicles, buses, taxis, tow trucks and driving instructors. If you're a resident of Australia, you must have a licence issued by the state or territory where you're resident, and if you move state or territory you must obtain (not just apply for) a new licence and return your old licence within three months. The same applies to foreign licence holders coming to Australia as permanent residents.

Previously, states issued their own vehicle licences, but in November 1988 nationally agreed common licence classes were introduced. The basic licence (category C) permits you to drive a motor car or vehicle with a maximum of 12 seats (including the driver) weighing less than 4.5 tonnes. A category LR licence is required to drive heavy goods vehicles and vehicles with more than 12 seats. You must be aged 17 or over to hold a C licence and must have held a C licence for at least one year to qualify for an LR licence. A category R-Date licence is required to ride a motorcycle of up to 250cc, and an R licence for any motorcycle. The various levels of licences are usually distinguished by their colour: learner's licence (green), provisional licence (red), unrestricted licence (silver or gold). A silver unrestricted licence is issued for one or three years after you first pass your test; after five years, you qualify for a gold licence which is valid for a further five years. An NSW driving licence costs $22 per year plus a $10 administration fee (prices are similar in most states).

To obtain a driving licence in New South Wales, you must:

● provide your foreign licence (with a translation if necessary), which is photocopied and returned;

● prove your identity, e.g. with a passport and another document such as a credit card or an account card from a bank, building society or credit union;

● pass an eyesight test;

● pass a road knowledge test;

● pass a driving test;

● pay the fee.

If you fail the road knowledge test, you can take it again (e.g. on the next working day) and you'll only be asked the questions that you got wrong. It's necessary in most states to undergo an eyesight test and in certain cases a medical examination, e.g. sufferers from diabetes and epilepsy.

If a person holding a foreign licence fails the driving test, he can no longer drive in Australia until he passes it. He must first obtain a learner's licence, which allows him to drive while supervised by a licensed driver with a clean licence (no demerit points) who has held a licence for at least seven years. If you've held a foreign driving licence for less than a year, you'll be eligible only for a provisional licence (a licence issued to NSW drivers for one year after they pass their driving test). This means that you must display a 'P' plate (front and rear) on your vehicle at all times and are restricted to lower speeds (maximum 80kph/50mph), a reduced alcohol/blood level (0.02g per 100ml) and are permitted to accumulate a maximum of three demerit points (see below) during the term of your licence.

In some states, learner drivers must keep a logbook (teenagers are supervised by their parents) to prove that they've gained experience driving in a range of conditions and that their L-plate training period has extended to a year. A three-month L-plate period applies in many states. The Roads and Traffic Authority (RTA) in NSW publishes a booklet, *Licence to Drive*, and a *Guide to DART* (Driving Ability Road Test), both of which are available from local motor registries. If your last licence expired over five years ago or you're over 85 years of age and fail a driving test, you may be required to return to a learner's licence. Learners must take a written road knowledge test before taking a practical driving test (cost $20). A driving test costs $35 or around an extra $60 if you use a driving school vehicle (check in advance as fees can be excessive).

**Demerit Points:** Fines as well as demerit points are issued for traffic and driving infringements, depending on the severity of an offence. Demerit points range from one (e.g. failing to dip your headlamps) to six points (exceeding the speed limit by over 45kph/28mph), although most offences carry three demerit points. A list of the infringements and consequent demerit points is provided in a state's *Road User's Handbook*. If you accumulate a certain number of demerit points within a limited period (usually two years), your licence may be revoked. The number you need to accrue in order to be banned from driving depends on the type of licence you carry. If you accumulate 12 points, your licence will usually be cancelled for a minimum of three months. You should check with the RTA for the point limit of the type of licence you carry. Your licence can also be cancelled for up to five years (and you can be imprisoned) for serious offences such as failing or refusing to take a breath test (see page 268), failing to stop after an accident in which someone has been injured or killed, and exceeding the speed limit by over 45kph/28mph.

**Visitors:** Most foreign licences are valid for a year in Australia, although it's usually worthwhile obtaining an international driving permit, particularly if your national licence doesn't contain your photograph (e.g. an old British driving licence). If a foreign licence isn't written in English, an official translation must be obtained. This can be done in Australia by the local state Ethnic Affairs Commission or the Translating and Interpreting Service of the Commonwealth Department of Immigration and Ethnic Affairs. Your driving licence, translation and passport must be carried when driving.

Note that there are heavy penalties in Australia for driving without a licence (or with an expired licence), including fines of up to $2,000, a prison term of up to six months and a ban from driving for a period.

# CAR INSURANCE

For personally imported vehicles the following categories of car insurance are available in Australia:

**Third Party:** The minimum insurance cover required by law is third party, usually referred to as compulsory third party (CTP) or 'greenslip', which is required in all states and territories. CTP covers only bodily injury (plus injuries to third parties caused by passengers) and doesn't cover damage done to third party property, for which third party property insurance is required (see below). Under common law, compensation is paid for both economic loss (medical costs and loss of earnings) and non-economic loss (e.g. pain and suffering), if applicable. You 'green slip' must be produced when registering a vehicle. When a vehicle is bought or sold, the CTP insurance transfers to the new owner until the registration expires. CTP is included in a car's annual registration fees, but in the case of imported vehicles (which are exempt from the first year's rego insurance) it must be independently arranged. Note that it can be difficult to insure some imported vehicles that aren't sold in Australia. Foreign insurance policies aren't valid in Australia, and all vehicles operated there must be insured with an Australian company. **CTP insurance isn't recommended, as you could be faced with a huge bill if you damage someone else's property.**

**Third Party Property (TPP):** TPP cover protects you against liabilities for damage caused to other third party property in an accident, e.g. if you damage another car or knock down a fence. TPP usually includes a provision of up to $3,000 for your own car if it's damaged by an uninsured driver (but you must be able to identify the driver).

**Third Party, Fire and Theft (TPF&T):** Known in some countries as part comprehensive, TPF&T cover includes (in addition to third party cover) loss of or damage to your car and anything fitted to it caused by fire, lightning, explosion, theft or attempted theft. It usually covers breakage of glass. Note that the amount you can claim may be limited, e.g. to $5,000, unless otherwise agreed when you take out a policy. Bear in mind that it isn't unusual for a car to overheat and catch fire in Australia so, unless you're driving a worthless heap, it will pay you to have TPF&T insurance (and carry a fire extinguisher!). It's also important to insure your belongings, particularly if you're travelling around Australia in a camper van and are carrying all your 'worldly possessions' with you. Check the small print of your insurance policy and note that travel insurance (see page 321) isn't intended for those who are taking everything with them and won't usually cover all your belongings. **Note that TPF&T insurance is offered by only a few insurance companies in Australia.**

**Comprehensive:** Comprehensive insurance covers you for all the risks listed under the CTP and TPP above, plus damage to your car, theft of contents, breakage of glass (e.g. windscreen replacement), personal accident benefits and medical expenses. It also usually includes damage due to natural hazards, e.g. storm damage, but *not* loss or damage due to fire and theft, which are subject to an additional premium. Extra cover may be included free or for an additional fee, e.g. the cost of hiring a car if yours is involved in an accident or stolen, legal assistance, no-claims discount protection, and extra cover for a car stereo or phone. Comprehensive insurance may also cover you against loss when your car is in a garage for service or repair. Check a policy for any restrictions: for example you may not be covered against theft if your car isn't garaged and locked overnight. Personal accident, medical expenses, clothing and personal effects cover, are usually included in comprehensive policies. Comprehensive insurance can be extended to include other vehicles not belonging to or hired to the policyholder. Note that comprehensive insurance generally covers you for third party risk when you're driving a car that doesn't belong to you. Most lenders insist on comprehensive insurance for leasing, contract hire and hire purchase agreements.

Note that any insurance policy can include other people to drive your car (either named or unnamed). Separate passenger insurance is usually unnecessary, as passengers are automatically covered by all Australian motor insurance policies.

If you've temporarily imported your vehicle into Australia, you should ensure that you have insurance cover from your country of origin, as accident, fire and theft insurance is generally not available for imported vehicles. The only alternative is a 'tourist insurance policy' issued by some automobile associations such RACWA, but this may have a high excess (e.g. $750).

# Premiums

The most important factor influencing premiums is a car's insurance class (although not all insurers place cars in the same class), which is calculated according to the new cost, the cost of spare parts and labour, repair times, and the car's performance. In addition to the car's insurance class, other factors affecting the premium include:

● the type of insurance cover required;

● the make and type of car;

● the age and value of the car;

● your driving experience and driving record (demerit points or loss of licence);

- your age, sex (women drivers usually pay lower premiums as they have fewer accidents) and occupation;
- what you use your car for, e.g. business or pleasure;
- your accident record and no-claims discount;
- who will drive the car besides the owner;
- your health (you may be required to pay an excess if you suffer from epilepsy or diabetes);
- where you live and whether your car is garaged overnight;
- the number of miles you do per year (some policies offer reduced rates for those who do low mileage);
- any extras you require, such as a protected no-claims discount.

Australian cities and states are divided into zones, and premiums are much higher for those living in inner cities than for those in outer suburbs and small country towns. Driving conditions are more hazardous in cities (owing to the high volume of traffic), where there's also usually a high risk of theft. Some insurers insist that a car (particularly a high-risk car) has an engine immobiliser.

Note that the cost of CTP insurance is fixed in most states and varies from around $205 in South Australia (over 40km/25mi from Adelaide) to around $370 in ACT. The exception is NSW, where the cost can vary considerably (so shop around). With comprehensive insurance, you must usually pay a standard excess of $100 to $400 when you make a claim. You must ensure that you state any previous accidents or driving offences when applying for car insurance, otherwise your insurer can refuse to pay out in the event of a claim. Drivers under 25, inexperienced drivers (holders of a licence for less than two years) and drivers with a bad accident record must usually pay a larger compulsory excess. You're usually also required to pay an excess, e.g. $50, if you make a claim on your windscreen cover (which normally covers all glass), but this doesn't affect your no-claims discount. Drivers who have lost their licence for drunken or dangerous driving must usually pay a much higher premium for a number of years.

For a small extra premium, most insurance companies provide cover for legal costs arising from road accidents (this is also available separately from Australian motoring organisations, but is more expensive). If you cannot live without a car, ensure that your policy will pay for car hire in the event of an accident or your car being stolen (or that you have separate 'uninsured loss' insurance to cover this). Special 'mobility' insurance is available to pay for the cost of alternative transport after losing your licence for a motoring offence, medical revocation of your licence or being unable to drive owing to injury.

Motor insurance policies are valid for a year from the date you're first insured. You must usually pay in advance, although some companies allow you to pay in instalments either monthly, quarterly or half-yearly by direct debit from a bank account, possibly without incurring an additional charge (if there's an extra charge, check the interest rate). Initially you'll receive a 'cover note' to prove that you're insured until your insurance certificate is issued. Check that the details in the cover note are correct, particularly the type of cover required and the date and time it commences. Towards the end of your insurance period, you'll receive a renewal notice from your insurance company.

You can change your insurance company and policy whenever you like in Australia, for example by giving seven days' notice and returning the certificate, whereupon you'll receive a portion of your premium back, provided you've made no claims. **Note, however, that if you don't renew your motor insurance by the due date your cover will cease automatically.** If you're staying in Australia for a short period, you can usually take out a fixed period policy, e.g. for three or six months, although this may be much more expensive than cancelling an annual policy and obtaining a refund. It's important to shop around and obtain quotations from a number of insurance companies when obtaining or renewing insurance (including direct insurance companies who sell policies over the phone), as quotes can differ by $hundreds!

## No-Claims Discount

A foreign no-claims discount (or bonus) is usually valid in Australia, although some Australian insurance companies won't accept a no-claims discount earned overseas with a foreign insurance company. You must provide written evidence from your present or previous insurance company, not simply an insurance renewal notice. Some insurance companies offer an introductory discount. The no-claims discount offered by insurance companies is typically 20 per cent (one year), 30 per cent (two years), 44 per cent (three years), 50 per cent (four years) and 60 per cent (five years), which is usually the maximum.

Normally, when you make a claim you lose two years' no-claims discount, even if the claim is for fire or theft, so it's sometimes cheaper to pay for minor damage yourself. Damage to glass doesn't affect your no-claims discount, but you're usually required to pay the first $50 or $100 of a claim. Most insurance policies offer a protected no-claims discount policy or allow you to insure your no-claims discount. This means that you can usually make one 'at-fault' claim within a certain period (e.g. three years, or two claims within five years) without losing any of your no-claims discount.

Some companies provide an extra no-claims discount or lower premiums for experienced motorists with a clean licence and an accident-free driving record. If you insure two or more vehicles, you can claim a no-claims discount on only one vehicle, although you may be given a discount on the premium for the other vehicles. Note that if you're uninsured (e.g. don't drive) for longer than two years, you usually lose your entire no-claims discount.

## GENERAL ROAD RULES

Each state and territory has its own driving laws, but in general the variations are minor. However, it's essential to familiarise yourself with the local idiosyncrasies in the law by obtaining a copy of a state or territory's 'highway code' (such as the *Road Users' Handbook* in New South Wales) from the relevant local authority (e.g. the Roads and Traffic Authority in NSW) or motoring organisation. Handbooks contain advice for all road users, including motorists, motorcyclists and pedestrians. The NSW handbook is available in English, Arabic, Chinese, Croatian, Greek, Korean, Japanese, Serbian, Spanish, Turkish and Vietnamese (they may also be available on audio cassette). A *Heavy Vehicle Drivers' Handbook* and a *Motorcycle Riders'*

*Handbook* are also published in NSW. The Australian Automobile Association (AAA) publishes a free booklet, *Motoring in Australia*, which contains sections in English, French, German, Japanese and Spanish.

The following general road rules are taken from the NSW *Road Users' Handbook* (unless otherwise noted) and may help you adjust to driving in Australia and avoid an accident:

● Among the many strange habits of the Australians is that of driving on the left-hand side of the road, which they inherited from the British. You may find this a bit strange if you come from a country where people on the right; however, it saves a lot of confusion if you do likewise. It may be helpful to have a reminder (e.g. 'think left!') on your car's dashboard. Take extra care when pulling out of junctions and one-way streets and at roundabouts. Remember to look first to the *right* when crossing the road on foot. If you're unused to driving on the left, you should be prepared for some disorientation or even terror, although most people have few problems adjusting to it.

● At crossroads and junctions in Australia where no right of way is assigned, traffic coming from the right has priority (as in the continent of Europe). At major junctions, right of way is always indicated by a 'GIVE WAY' (yield) sign or a 'STOP' sign. There are also usually road markings. When faced with a stop sign, you must stop completely (all four wheels must come to rest) before pulling away, even if you can see that no traffic is approaching. At a give way sign, you aren't required to stop, but must give priority to traffic already on the road you're joining. You must also give way to traffic on your right when joining a highway (motorway) or dual carriageway from a slip road.

● Apart from the international octagonal 'STOP' sign (white on red) and the triangular 'GIVE WAY' sign (black on white with a red border), most Australian road signs don't follow international standards, but the different types of signs can usually be distinguished as follows:

  – Warning signs tell you that there may be dangers ahead and are usually diamond shaped with black diagrams (sometimes accompanied by red) and symbols (such as a kangaroo) on a yellow background.

  – Regulatory signs give instructions (in words) that must be obeyed and are usually rectangular with black letters on a white background (some also have red markings). Some parking signs are green on white.

  – Highway signs give information about the start, end and exits from highways.

  Other types of sign include those are used in rural areas to indicate where livestock can be expected on or near roads (you must slow or stop as required and can be fined for disobeying signs) and temporary signs used at roadworks. The most important signs are shown in a state or territory's 'road users' handbook'. Signs may be emphasised by painted warnings on the road.

● On roundabouts (traffic circles), vehicles on the roundabout (coming from your right) have priority over those entering it. Traffic flows clockwise round round-abouts and not anti-clockwise, as in countries where traffic drives on the right. Some roundabouts have a filter lane which is reserved for traffic turning left. You should stay in the lane in which you entered the roundabout, follow the lane markings to leave and signal as you approach the exit you wish to take. There are many roundabouts in Australia, which, although sometimes rather a free-for-all, speed up traffic considerably and are usually preferable to traffic lights, particularly outside rush hours (although some busy roundabouts also have traffic lights).

● Australia was one of the first countries to make seatbelts compulsory. They must be worn by all front and rear seat passengers when fitted, and children must be properly restrained by an approved child restraint or adult seatbelt if fitted; in the absence of an approved restraint or seatbelt, they must travel in the back seat. In Victoria, a child under the age of one year isn't permitted to be carried without being properly restrained in any vehicle required to have child restraint anchorages. The exceptions are taxi cabs, vehicles registered in another state or territory, and cases when there isn't an unoccupied seat. Children aged one to 13 must use an approved child seat that meets the relevant Australian standard or a firmly adjusted adult seatbelt when available. A child must *never* travel in the front seat without using a child restraint or seatbelt, even when the back seat is full. Seatbelts or restraints must be approved (to the requisite Australian standard) and be appropriate for the age and weight of a child, as follows:

- under six months (weighing less than 9kg/20lb): a rear-facing baby seat with built-in harness in either the front (but not when the front seat is fitted with an air bag) or rear of a car;
- from around six months to five years (from 8kg/18lb to 18kg/40lb): a rear-facing seat or, if there's insufficient space, a front-facing restraint with built-in harness;
- from around three to ten years (14kg/31lb to 32kg/71lb): a child safety harness, which should be used where only a lap belt is available.

A booster seat or cushion can be used in the front or rear seats with an adult three-point (sash) seatbelt or in a rear seat with a child harness. Special harnesses and belts are also available for the handicapped. **Note that all belts, seats, harnesses and restraints must be correctly fitted and adjusted, or they may be useless (many child seats are wrongly fitted).** Some child seats have fatal flaws, and many cars have seatbelt straps that are too short for rear-facing baby seats. If all available restraints in a car are in use, children may travel unrestrained (although this is *extremely* unwise).

One in five drivers killed in accidents since 1994 wasn't using a seatbelt, and drivers not using seatbelts are three times more likely to be killed than those using them. It's estimated that seatbelts would prevent around 75 per cent of deaths and 90 per cent of injuries suffered by those involved in accidents not wearing seat belts. Note, however, that lap belts fitted in the centre rear seat of many cars are dangerous and should be replaced. In addition to the risk of death or injury, you can receive a $75 or $100 fine for ignoring the seatbelt laws (and will also lose three points on your licence) and for each unrestrained child under 14. Note that it's the driver's responsibility to ensure that children are properly restrained. If you're exempt from using a seatbelt for medical reasons, a safety belt exemption certificate is required from your doctor. More information can be obtained from motoring organisations and 'Motor Vehicle' authorities.

● Railway level crossings can be dangerous places, especially where there are no gates, booms or flashing lights. Always approach a level crossing slowly, look and listen for trains, and be prepared to stop. There are usually warning signs ahead of crossings. Where there are gates, booms or flashing lights, start to cross only when the signals have stopped flashing and the gates or booms are fully open. You must stop at a crossing when:

- there's a stop sign;
- there's a gate or boom across the road;
- red lights are flashing;
- a railway employee signals you to do so;
- you're carrying flammable, explosive or dangerous goods.

Crossings without gates (e.g. in country areas) must be approached with extreme caution, including pedestrian railway crossings. Even a car that's built like a tank won't look so smart after a scrap with a 70-tonne locomotive.

● Be particularly wary of cyclists, moped riders and motorcyclists. It isn't always easy to see them, particularly when they're hidden by the blind spots of a car or when cyclists are riding at night without lights. **When overtaking, ALWAYS give them a wide . . . WIDE berth.** If you knock them off their bikes, you may have a difficult time convincing the police that it wasn't your fault; far better to avoid them (and the police).

● When loading and unloading children, school buses flash orange lights at the front and rear, and may also display a 'GIVE WAY' sign at the rear. You must drive slowly near school buses and give way to children crossing the road. Lights remain flashing for around 30 seconds, after which the doors close and the bus moves off.

● If you needed spectacles or contact lenses to pass your sight test, you must always wear them when driving. It's wise to carry a spare pair of glasses or contact lenses in your car.

● White or yellow markings are painted on the road surface in towns and cities, e.g. arrows to indicate the direction traffic must go in a particular lane. You should stay in the centre of the lane in which you're driving and, where there are no lane markings, keep to the left side of the road. In many cities, there are transit lanes in operation during rush hours, e.g. 6am to 10am Mondays to Fridays, which may be used by buses, taxis, motorcycles, bicycles and emergency vehicles. A passenger vehicle may use these lanes *only* if it's carrying one or two passengers (real passengers, not dummies!), e.g. in NSW a passenger vehicle in a T2 lane must have at least one passenger and in a T3 lane at least two passengers. Otherwise these lanes may be used only if you intend to make a turn within 100 metres. There are also 'BUS ONLY' lanes in cities.

● In cities such as Melbourne, tram lines are delineated by solid yellow lines, which you should remain clear of unless you want a close encounter with a tram (continuous yellow lines may not be crossed, but broken lines may be crossed if you don't obstruct a tram). When a tram has started to cross an intersection, it has right of way over all other vehicles. There are special rules concerning the overtaking of trams, and you must not pass a tram when it stops to pick up or drop off passengers (unless there's a central island). Note that tram tracks can be slippery when wet; cyclists and motorcyclists should take care.

- White lines mark the separation of traffic lanes. A solid single line or two solid lines means no overtaking in either direction. A solid line to the left of the centre line, i.e. on your side of the road, means that overtaking is prohibited in your direction. You may overtake only when there's a single broken line in the middle of the road or double lines with a broken line on your side of the road. Note that double lines may be crossed when making a right turn in some states, but not in others, and U-turns are usually prohibited across any unbroken centre line even if associated with a broken line.

  It's usually illegal to overtake on an inside lane unless traffic is being channelled in a different direction. However, overtaking on the inside ('undertaking') is permitted in some states on a highway with three or more lanes in each direction. In Australia, the right-hand lane isn't usually just for overtaking and, although you should keep to the left, it isn't obligatory. Motorists must indicate before overtaking *and* when moving back into an inside lane after overtaking, e.g. on a dual carriageway or highway.

- Headlights must be used when driving between sunset and sunrise or at any time when there's insufficient daylight to be able to see a person wearing dark clothing at a distance of 100 metres (so keep an eye out for people in dark clothing). It's illegal to drive on side (parking) lights in Australia, and headlights must usually be dipped (low beam) when driving in built-up areas where there's street lighting. Headlamps must also be dipped within 200 metres of an approaching vehicle, immediately an oncoming vehicle has dipped its headlights and when travelling within 200 metres behind another vehicle. If you happen to be riding a camel on a road at night in Broome (WA), you must have a rear light!

- Headlight flashing has a different meaning in different countries. In some countries it means "after you", while in others it means "get out of my way". It can even mean "I'm driving a new car and haven't yet worked out what all the switches are for". **In Australia headlamp flashing has only one legal use – to warn another vehicle of your presence**, although most people use it to give priority to another vehicle, e.g. when someone is waiting to pull out of a side road. Note that it's illegal in some states to warn other vehicles that they're approaching a speed trap or police road block by flashing your lights (although many drivers do it). Hazard warning lights (all indicators operating simultaneously) are used to warn other drivers of an obstruction, e.g. an accident or a traffic jam on a main road.

- The sequence of Australian traffic lights is red, yellow, green, yellow and back to red. Yellow is a warning to get ready to go, but you must not start moving until the light changes to green. Yellow (after green) means stop at the stop line; you may continue only if the yellow light appears after you've crossed the stop line or when stopping might cause an accident. A green filter light may be shown in addition to the full lamp signals, which means you may go in the direction shown by the arrow, irrespective of other lights showing. Cameras are often installed at busy traffic lights to detect motorists driving through red lights (a favourite pastime of many Australian motorists).

In some cities (e.g. Adelaide) there are flashing 'NO RIGHT TURN' signs at some junctions during business hours. In Melbourne, to accommodate the city's trams, a special rule applies at intersections where there's a 'RIGHT TURN FROM LEFT ONLY' sign (known locally as the 'hook turn') accompanied by curved broken lines on the road surface. At these intersections you must keep to the left lane and wait until you get a green light to make a right turn. At traffic lights in some states there are 'TURN LEFT AT ANY TIME WITH CARE' or 'LEFT TURN ON RED PERMITTED AFTER STOPPING' signs, permitting vehicles to turn left even when faced with a red light (as in most of the USA – although there it's a right turn). However, drivers must first stop if indicated and only proceed when they can do so safely.

Flashing yellow lights and stop signs with three large black dots are used at some intersections to mean that you must stop and give way to all traffic. A sign of a white 'B' on a black background indicates traffic lights for buses in bus lanes, marked 'BUSES ONLY' (you should never drive in bus lanes – unless you're driving a bus). In Queensland, motorists must give way to buses pulling out into traffic in towns (i.e. in a 60kph/37mph zone).

● Always approach pedestrian crossings with caution and don't park or overtake another vehicle on the approach to a crossing (usually shown by zigzag lines or a large white diamond). At some crossings, a flashing amber light follows the red light, to warn you to give way to pedestrians before proceeding. **Note that pedestrians have the legal right of way once they've stepped onto a crossing without traffic lights, and you must stop. Motorists who don't stop are liable to heavy penalties.** Where a road crosses a public footpath, e.g. at the entrance to a property or car park, motorists *must* give way to pedestrians.

● Tail-gating (driving too close to the vehicle in front) is commonplace in Australia and most other countries, where few drivers have any idea of safe stopping distances (including thinking distance, i.e. the time it takes a driver to react). In good conditions, you should leave a gap equal to three seconds between your vehicle and the one in front in order to be able to stop in an emergency. Note that the three-second rule applies to cars with good brakes and tyres, on dry roads, in good visibility and with an *alert driver*. If you're half asleep and driving an old banger on a wet or icy road, you had better not exceed 20kph/12mph, otherwise you'll never stop in an emergency! As a safety precaution, always try to leave a large gap between you and the vehicle in front. This isn't just to allow you more time to stop, should the vehicles in front decide to get together, but also to give the 'tail-gater' behind you more time to stop. **The closer the car is behind you, the further you should be from the vehicle in front.**

● A conviction for most motoring offences results in a fine and demerit points on your licence, which, if you collect enough, will result in the suspension of your licence for a period (see page 272). Some fines are imposed on-the-spot, e.g. for marginal speeding and other 'minor' offences. Serious offences such as dangerous or drunken driving involving injury or death to third parties can result in a prison sentence.

# AUSTRALIAN DRIVERS

Like motorists in all countries, Australians have their idiosyncrasies and customs. Although they aren't considered to be among the best in the world, most Australians are good and careful drivers, who take their driving seriously. On the other hand, Australia has its fair share of seriously crazy drivers, added to which (according to a specialist's report in 1997) there are some 80,000 drivers with dementia on Australian roads (you may be forgiven for thinking that they're ALL driving on the same roads as you or that perhaps they made a mistake and there are *only* 80,000 drivers *without* dementia). Northern Territorians are reckoned to be Australia's worst drivers, particularly in traffic, and are scornfully referred to as bush motorists (who tend not to bother with the niceties of driving, such as indicating, stopping at stop signs and red lights, keeping to lanes, etc.). Running red lights is commonplace in Australian cities and the all-red period (when all vehicles are required to stop) has been increased to help combat this problem.

Australian drivers tend to be aggressive, particularly truck drivers, and it's usually every man for himself, particularly in Sydney. On the outback roads of central and northern Australia, you're likely to come across road trains, which are multi-trailer, articulated lorries up to 50 metres in length and weighing over 100 tonnes, driven by maniacs who don't move over for anyone (except perhaps another road train). It's best to pull over and let them pass (allow at least a kilometre if you plan to overtake one). Most Australian men have a cavalier attitude to driving and believe they're wonderful drivers (it's a macho thing), although the accident statistics tell another story. Drinking and driving is still fairly commonplace, despite regular spot checks. The macho attitude among young male drivers is a killer and the risk of young people aged 17 to 25 dying on the roads is around three times that of other age groups. However, the once appalling accident rate has fallen in recent years through improved roads, random breath testing, stricter laws, safer vehicles, and better driver training and education. Women generally drive as well as men, have far fewer accidents (particularly the under 25s), and are much less likely to drink and drive. However, young women drivers are increasingly showing aggressive driving behaviour normally associated only with men.

Beware of kangaroos and other animals which stray onto country roads, particularly at night (attempts to teach them the 'blue cross' code have failed miserably). An encounter with a big boomer can seriously damage your vehicle, which is why most car and truck owners who regularly use country roads fit their vehicles with 'roo bars' (the steel bars you commonly see on 4-wheel-drive vehicles in countries without kangaroos). Some cars are fitted with an alarm ('shu-roo') which emits a high-pitched noise to frighten kangaroos. Many Australians try to avoid travelling when it's dark because of the danger posed by animals (most are nocturnal and feed at night). Note that you should swerve to avoid a kangaroo only when it's safe to do so, as many people kill themselves trying to avoid them. Water buffalo are a problem in some northern parts of the country, and grazing cattle can also be a menace in country areas.

Take it easy when driving in inclement weather. Ice and snow are rare in most areas except the mountainous regions of New South Wales, Victoria and Tasmania (which, being farthest south, experiences the worst winter weather). Fog can also make driving extremely hazardous in winter in some regions.

Tempers are rising on Australia's overcrowded streets and road rage ('invented' in California – where else?), where drivers blow their tops and attack or drive into other motorists, is becoming more common. It's often provoked by tailgating, headlight flashing, obscene gestures, obstruction and verbal abuse, so take care how you behave when driving in Australia.

However, despite their idiosyncrasies, Australian drivers are usually above average (average is bad) and not as belligerent as those in many other countries. Don't be discouraged by the tail-gaters and road hogs, as driving in Australia is less stressful than in many other countries and can even be enjoyable in country areas (provided you avoid dirt tracks). Most people who come from countries where traffic drives on the right quickly become used to driving on the 'wrong' side of the road. Just take it easy at first and bear in mind that there may be other motorists around just as confused (and frightened) as you are.

# AUSTRALIAN ROADS

There are some 813,000km (over 500,000mi) of roads in Australia, varying in quality from eight-lane highways to rutted dirt tracks which are impossible to negotiate in anything less than a four-wheel-drive (4WD) vehicle. Only some 40 per cent of roads are sealed, including nearly 19,000km (12,000mi) of the National Highway System linking the capital cities plus Brisbane and Cairns in Queensland, and Hobart and Burnie in Tasmania. Roads are usually classified as primary or secondary routes. Primary routes are the major roads that link the states and territories, together with those serving the principal centres of population and industry within them. Secondary routes include those which facilitate the carriage of produce from farms and mines, forest roads serving tourist resorts, and most streets in towns and cities. Lighting is good on major urban roads and usually adequate on other urban roads.

Generally, the roads between major cities and state capitals are excellent with dual carriageways (divided highways) in metropolitan areas, particularly in the eastern coastal areas of Sydney, Newcastle and Brisbane, although it's generally felt that investment in roads has not kept pace with the continued growth of traffic, especially in metropolitan areas. In rural areas, where traffic density isn't high and there are vast distances between towns, roads may have only two lanes, and in the outback dirt roads are common. In general, the quality of Australian roads is excellent, although some main roads are in a poor condition from being constantly chewed up by juggernauts and the heavy volume of traffic.

**Urban Roads:** There are wide roads in most cities, particularly in the suburbs, where they're usually laid out on a grid system (except in Canberra and Sydney). Victoria's roads are the most crowded, followed by urban roads in New South Wales. Driving in Sydney is to be avoided if at all possible (finding somewhere to park can be a nightmare), while Melbourne isn't much better in spite of the new Citylink. Most major cities are choked during rush hours, e.g. 6am to 10pm, and Sydney is congested at almost any time although new roads built for the 2000 Olympic Games and the Eastern Distributor and M5 have helped. Sydney Harbour bridge is an infamous bottleneck (a toll is charged when travelling south), although the harbour tunnel (included in the bridge toll) has relieved some of the congestion.

Sydney has a 'Metroad' system, which helps make travel into, through and out of the city (a tiny bit) easier. Driving in Adelaide, Brisbane (with its new Gateway

Bridge) and Perth is relatively easy, although rush hours should be avoided. Tasmanian roads are fairly traffic free (a few cars tail-to-tail represents a traffic jam) and driving there is relatively easy (except in winter). Note that many cities have tortuous one-way systems. Signposting in cities can be confusing and street names are often difficult to find. Signposting is virtually non-existent in the outback and can be a bit of a joke (e.g. 'Darwin 2,000km'). Note that distances are shown in kilometres (km) in Australia and not miles.

**Highways, Expressways & Freeways:** Major roads in Australia are variously described as highways, expressways and freeways. The distinctions between these types of road are sometimes blurred, but in general freeways (as their name suggests) are toll-free roads, whereas tolls ($2.50 to $3) are payable at intervals on highways and expressways. Expressways usually have fewer junctions and traffic lights than highways, and neither expressways nor freeways allow bicycles. Highway and expressway numbers are sometimes prefixed with an M or an F (which does not indicate a freeway!). Toll roads are unpopular with Australians, and the M2 in Sydney has been shunned by many motorists; it carries only around half the number of vehicles forecast. However, despite this setback, more toll roads have been built, including the Melbourne Citylink and the Eastern Distributor in Sydney. All major roads are sealed and many have three or four lanes in each direction.

Highway 1 runs right around Australia, mostly hugging the coast, and is Australia's most dramatic road. Note that road numbers are rarely used in Australia and most people refer to roads by their names. Highway 1 is known by various names in various parts of Australia, such as the Princes Highway between Sydney and Adelaide. Some stretches are extremely picturesque, and it passes through many interesting towns. The most direct route between Sydney and Melbourne is via the more busy inland Hume Highway (number 31). The most direct route between Melbourne and Adelaide is the Western Highway (number 8), but the Princes Highway (1) offers better views. The main roads between Sydney and Brisbane are the coastal Pacific Highway (1) and the inland New England Highway (15). The quickest route from Sydney to Adelaide is via the Great Western (32), Mid Western (24) and Stuart Highways (20). (Actually, it's by air!) In NSW a Western Sydney orbital is planned linking the national highways north and south of the city at a cost of $920 million.

On national highways there are route markers (small shields by the roadside) every 5km/3mi bearing the initial letter of the last or next major town above the distance in kilometres. There are emergency telephones every kilometre on Australian highways for use in the event of accidents and breakdowns. Some highways have a 'crawler' lane or hard-shoulder (for slow-moving vehicles) and uphill speed ramps are common on steep downhill stretches to slow vehicles if their brakes fail. National highways are a federal government responsibility and have been funded from an excise levied on fuel since the early '80s, although it's claimed that far more fuel tax has been collected than spent on the roads.

Note that the vast distances and the hot sun induce drowsiness in drivers and you should make frequent stops for refreshment and rests on a long journey. There are frequent roadside rest areas on main highways, and free coffee is provided at stops on some highways to help reduce driver fatigue. Drivers falling asleep at the wheel are a major cause of accidents on highways, particularly at night (as the sign says, 'Drowsy Drivers Die'!). It's always sensible to have company on long journeys.

**Outback Roads:** In some sparsely populated country areas ('back of Bourke') there are long stretches of road with only one lane paved and wide unsealed shoulders. Even main highways such as the Western Australia coastal road (highway 1) have stretches consisting of a single lane with dirt shoulders. Many outback roads are dirt and in varying stages of neglect. In country and outback areas off the main highways, minor roads can be terrible, consisting mainly of dirt tracks. In some outback areas in Western Australia, there are sealed roads built privately by mining companies, and visitors may be allowed to use them with a permit.

There has, however, been a vast improvement in the outback road network in recent years, making it possible for the average motorist to explore the country by car (on main highways) without the need of a 4WD vehicle. However, high ground clearance is necessary on unsealed outback roads and 4WD is often essential if you don't want to get stuck (although it isn't failsafe). Outback driving can be hazardous for the inexperienced driver, and thorough preparation is essential, as conditions vary from area to area and season to season. The best time to travel is during the cooler winter months between April and October. Many outback roads are deeply rutted and can be washed away by flash floods and remain impassable for weeks on end during the wet season (some roads in northern Australia are impassable from December until May). Dust can also be a problem during the heat of summer in central Australia (when air-conditioning is practically essential). Note that you should keep a close eye on the temperature gauge in hot weather.

When travelling in the outback, road conditions and routes must be checked with the local authorities, in addition to weather forecasts and the availability of fuel. On some roads in the outback, motorists are required to complete a police destination card giving their expected time of arrival at the next town. It's sensible to carry a two-way UHF radio tuned to the local Royal Flying Doctor Service. Make sure a vehicle is roadworthy, and carry plenty of spares, including two spare wheels, a plastic windscreen, tools, a week's supply of food and water (20 litres per person in a number of containers), a first-aid kit, spare fuel (keep the tank topped up at all times), a workshop manual and maps.

If you break down, it's imperative to stay with your vehicle. As a last resort, burn a tyre, as property owners in the outback never ignore smoke. Note that a motorist must (by law) aid someone who has broken down in the outback. In bygone days it wasn't unusual to come across a vehicle in the outback containing the skeletons of its occupants, although (despite the horror stories) people rarely die in the outback nowadays. Many books are published for outback travellers, including *Outback Australia* (Lonely Planet), *Explore Australia by 4WD* by Peter and Kim Wherrett (Five Mile Press) and *The Driving Guide Series* (covering most of Australia's regions) by Ian Read (Cimino Publishing). The Flying Doctor also publishes a booklet, *Outback Travelling*, for visitors planning long-distance trips.

**Information:** Information about road conditions is provided by motoring organisations and state government roads departments, e.g. in Queensland the Main Roads Department publishes *Queensland Road Conditions*. Road conditions throughout Australia can be obtained from the NRMA (☎ local call rate 1300-655046, 🖳 www.nrma.com.au), 24 hours a day.

# TRAFFIC POLICE

Police in Australia don't need a reason to stop motorists and can stop you for a spot check at any time. In recent years, random breath testing has increased considerably as police have cracked down on drinking and driving. Australian state police aggressively enforce all traffic regulations and use a variety of equipment and tactics to catch offenders. Roadblocks with mobile breath-testing units are used to check for drink-driving infringements and automatic cameras are installed at intersections to identify drivers running red lights. Radar units and speed cameras are employed to identify speeders, and aeroplanes and helicopters are used to catch speeding vehicles on rural highways. Never antagonise a police officer or make any smart cracks, as this is the fast lane to prosecution; remain courteous and obsequious and you may be let off with a caution. Although you may have read about corrupt Australian police (see page 463), don't even think about trying to bribe an officer unless you wish to be charged with a much more serious offence! Note that, when crossing a state border, your vehicle may be searched for firearms, drugs, pornography, and fresh fruit and vegetables (which may not be transported from one state to another, to prevent the spread of parasites).

You're required by law to carry your car or motorcycle registration papers and your driving licence (including an international driving permit if required) when driving in Australia. You must give a policeman your name and address when requested, although you aren't required to answer questions before obtaining legal advice. Marginal speeding and other minor offences (such as not having your driving licence) are usually dealt with by on-the-spot fines (officially called 'Traffic Infringement Notices'), which have increased considerably in many states in recent years and can be up to $250. Residents can pay an on-the-spot fine within 28 days and aren't required to go to court. If you think you haven't committed an offence, you can contest a fine or prosecution in a court of law, although it isn't usually worthwhile unless you have incontrovertible proof of your innocence.

All states are owed $tens of millions (over $200 million in NSW) in unpaid motoring fines. In Western Australia (since 1995), the licence of a motorist is automatically suspended until a fine is paid and goods can be seized (such as a car or furniture) in lieu of unpaid fines. This move is followed by a community service order, with jail as a last resort (although the system has proved a success, other states have been reluctant to follow suit).

# MOTORCYCLES

The minimum age for riding a motorcycle in Australia varies with the state or territory but is usually 17. A young driver may obtain a licence before he reaches the required age after passing a written road knowledge test, e.g. at 16 years and nine months in NSW. The following information is based on vehicle licences in NSW and is similar to other states. A learner is permitted to ride a motorcycle with a maximum engine capacity of 250cc with a power to weight ratio of no more than 150kw per tonne (whatever that means). An L (learner) plate must be displayed on the back and you mustn't carry a passenger. In some areas of NSW, learners must complete a pre-provisional licence course before taking a road knowledge test. The course can be taken at age 16 years and six months and allows a learner's licence to be issued at 16 years and nine months.

To obtain a provisional motorcycle licence (class R), you must take a riding test between three and six months after you receive your learner's licence. After passing the test, a P (provisional) plate must be displayed on the back of the motorcycle for a period of one year. If you've held a foreign motorcycle licence for less than a year you'll be eligible only for a provisional licence, and if you fail the riding test you may be required to undertake further rider training.

Although Australia has an excellent climate for biking, it has declined in popularity in the last decade, and bikes are more a fashion statement nowadays than a transport option, many over 40s buying them only for leisure riding. There was a massive slump in motorcycle sales in the '90s (due to the Australian dollar's collapse against the Japanese yen), with sales running at around 25,000 a year compared with 80,000 at their peak, and in mid-2001 the motorcycle market was chronically depressed. The average price is around $5,000, top models costing close to $80,000. If you need a bike only for a short period (e.g. a trip around Australia), some dealers offer buy-back options on secondhand bikes. There's a good market in secondhand bikes and you may be able to pick up a bargain from a departing visitor (the best time to buy a bike is at the start of the Australian winter in May). Motorcycles can be rented in Australia, although rates are high and range from $65 to $450 per weekend ($1,000 per week) depending on the engine capacity (there are usually discounts for longer than a week). A deposit of around $1,000 is payable by credit card. One-way rentals are possible with a drop-off fee, although it may be cheaper to buy a secondhand bike and sell it when you no longer need it.

Large capacity bikes are best for long-distance travel. It's essential to take spares and tools when on a long trip as well as plenty of drinking water, and travelling alone in the outback isn't recommended (see page 405). Contact motorcycle clubs and motoring organisations for information about outback road conditions and the availability of fuel.

A helmet must be worn at all times (but remove it when going into a bank or they may think that you're planning to rob it!). In recent years, motorcycle accidents have been greatly reduced thanks to helmets, better bikes and protective riding gear, better training and defensive riding by bikers. In general, laws that apply to cars also apply to motorcycles. Note that motorcyclists aren't popular with motorists in Australia, particularly in the major cities, where lunatic motorcycle couriers have given bikers a bad name. The NSW Roads and Traffic Authority publishes a *Motorcycle Riders' Handbook*.

# ACCIDENTS

If you're involved in (or cause) an accident in Australia, which results in injury to a person or animal, or damage to any third party's vehicle or property, the procedure is as follows:

1. Stop immediately. If possible move your vehicle off the road and keep your passengers and yourself off the road. If you have an accident (or a breakdown) on a major highway, don't stay in your vehicle whatever the weather (even if it's parked on the hard shoulder) as there's a danger that another vehicle will run into it (many accidents on highways occur on the hard shoulder). Wait on the embankment or nearby land (this also applies to stopping on other fast roads).

Note that failing to stop after an accident or failure to give particulars or report the accident to the police is a serious offence.

2. Warn other drivers of any obstruction by switching on your hazard warning lights (particularly on highways) or by placing a warning triangle at the edge of the road at least 50 metres behind your car on secondary roads and 150 metres on a main highway. If necessary, for example when the road is partly or totally blocked, turn on your car's dipped headlights and direct traffic around the hazard. In bad visibility, at night, or in a blind spot, try to warn oncoming traffic of the danger, e.g. with a torch, or by waving a warning triangle up and down.

3. If anyone is injured, immediately phone for an ambulance, the fire brigade (if someone is trapped or oil or chemicals are spilled) or the police (dial 000). Emergency telephones are provided on main highways. Give first-aid only if you're qualified to do so. Don't move an injured person unless absolutely necessary to save him from further injury and don't leave him alone except to phone for an ambulance. If necessary, cover him with a blanket or coat to keep him warm.

4. The police may attend and investigate an accident where someone is killed or injured, damage is caused to property, animals or vehicles in excess of $500, a person fails to stop and exchange information, or a driver is believed to be under the influence of alcohol or drugs. If you think someone else involved in an accident is drunk or has otherwise broken the law (e.g. his vehicle is unroadworthy), you should call the police. The police normally breathalyse everyone involved in an accident as a matter of routine. Note that calling the police to the scene of an accident may result in someone being fined or charged for a driving offence. In all cases, you mustn't say anything which could be interpreted as an admission of guilt, even if you're as guilty as hell. **Admitting responsibility for an accident, either verbally or in writing, may release your insurance company from responsibility under your policy and could also result in a criminal charge**. In other words you must say nothing (not even 'sorry') or only that your insurance company will deal with any claims. Let the police and insurance companies decide who was at fault.

5. If either you or any other driver(s) involved decide to call the police, don't move your vehicle or allow other vehicles to be moved unless it's necessary to unblock the road, in which case you should mark the positions of their wheels with chalk and measure the distance between vehicles. Take photographs of the accident scene if a camera is available (you can keep a disposable camera in your car) or make a drawing showing the positions of all vehicles involved before moving them.

6. Check immediately whether there are any witnesses to the accident and take their names and addresses, particularly noting those who support *your* version of what happened. Write down the registration numbers of all vehicles involved (or those of witnesses) and their drivers' and owners' names, addresses and insurance details. Note also the identification numbers of any police present. You must (by law) give anyone having reasonable grounds for requiring them (e.g. the owner of damaged property) your name, address and insurance details and the vehicle owner's name and address (if different).

7. If you're involved in an accident where damage over $500 or $1,000 (depending on the state) is caused to property, animals or vehicles, the nearest police station must be notified within 24 hours (if the police don't attend the scene). If you've caused material damage, you must inform the owner of the damaged property as soon as possible. If you cannot reach him, report the accident to a police station within 24 hours (this also applies to damage caused to other vehicles when parking). It's often wise to report any accident involving another vehicle within 24 hours to avoid any repercussions later. Make sure your visit is officially recorded by the police officer on duty and that you receive signed verification of your report.

8. If you have an accident involving a domestic animal and are unable to find the owner, it must also be reported to the police or the RSPCA. If a domestic animal is injured, it should be taken to the nearest vet or animal shelter. If you injure a wild animal, you should try to lessen any suffering it may experience and remove it from the road (care should be taken, as many Australian mammals carry their young in pouches), and notify the local Wildlife and Information Rescue Service (WIRES).

8. You may be asked questions or asked to make a statement by the police, although you aren't obliged to say anything (apart from giving your name and address). If you do make a statement, it should be short and unambiguous. However, it may be preferable *not* to make a statement until you've spoken with a solicitor, particularly if you're involved in a serious accident. **When you do make a statement, don't sign it unless you're certain that you understand and agree with every word.**

9. Lastly, you should report all accidents to your insurance company in writing as soon as possible, even if you don't intend to make a claim (but reserve your right to make a claim later). If you're injured and plan to make an insurance claim, you must obtain a doctor's report as soon as possible after the accident to verify your injuries (this will obviously be done automatically if you're admitted to hospital). Your insurance company will ask you to complete an accident report form, which you should return as soon as possible (don't forget to sign it). It's possible to avoid delays in insurance claims by completing a collision report at the nearest police station to where the accident occurred.

# DRINKING & DRIVING

As you're no doubt well aware, drinking and driving make a dangerous cocktail. In Australia you're no longer considered fit to drive when your blood contains between 0.02g and 0.08g of alcohol (depending on the state and other factors) per 100ml of blood. The limit for experienced drivers is 0.05g in the ACT, NSW, Queensland, Tasmania and Victoria (some states are considering lowering it to 0.02g), while in the Northern Territory, South Australia and Western Australia it's 0.08g. In most states, the limit is 0.02g for drivers with a learner's or provisional licence, drivers under 25 who have held a licence for less than three years, anyone driving a bus, taxi or car for hire or reward, and drivers of heavy goods vehicles or anyone carrying a dangerous load. In some states, drivers with a learner's or provisional licence must not drive with any alcohol in their blood.

For a male of average body weight, the maximum he can drink and remain under the 0.05g limit is around two standard glasses of beer or wine (or 30ml of spirits) in one hour (it's usually just one glass for a woman). One standard drink can put anyone over the 0.02g limit. Some pubs have machines where you can test your own blood/alcohol level, although they aren't failsafe. Note that you can still be over the legal limit the morning after a heavy night's drinking. If you're planning a business or social engagement where you know you'll be drinking, you should leave your car at home and use public transport, a taxi or go with another driver who won't be drinking.

Random breath testing (RBT) is permitted in Australia (it started in Victoria in 1976) and the police frequently set up road blocks and breathalyse all drivers, particularly late at night on Thursdays, Fridays and Saturdays. Often the police employ mobile testing stations (known as 'booze buses'), although in some states (e.g. Victoria) all traffic police carry breath testing equipment and every motorist stopped (regardless of the reason) is breathalysed. RBT usually involves simply blowing or speaking into a meter. If you fail the breathalyser test, you'll be taken to a police station and be given a further test on a breath analysis unit. If you're still over the limit, you'll be charged and your licence can be immediately suspended. If you refuse to take a breath test, the penalty is the same as for a high range drink-drive charge, so you have nothing to gain and everything to lose by refusing a test.

In NSW, fines for driving over the legal alcohol limit are usually a maximum of between $500 and $1,500 and the disqualification period varies from less than three months to life. Those who are well above the limit and repeat offenders can be jailed for up to one year in NSW (longer in some other states). If you have a blood-alcohol level of 0.15 or more and are involved in an accident that causes injury or death, the penalties can be severe, e.g. up to ten years' imprisonment in NSW. Drivers must pay much higher insurance premiums after being disqualified for drunken driving, and visitors who are apprehended for drunken driving in Australia are reported to their home country's traffic authorities.

If you have an accident while under the influence of alcohol, it can be very expensive. Your car, accident and health insurance can all be nullified. This means you must pay your own (and any third party's) car repairs, medical expenses and other damages.

You can also be disqualified for driving while under the influence of drugs in Australia. If, after passing a breath test for alcohol, you're considered by the police to be under the influence of another drug, you can be arrested and taken to a hospital for further testing of your blood or urine (instant drug tests aren't yet in use in Australia). Samples may be tested for drugs such as marijuana, heroin, morphine, cocaine, barbiturates, tranquillisers and sleeping tablets.

# CAR THEFT

Car theft is rife and on the increase in Australia, where a car is stolen every five minutes, costing over $1 billion a year. Many stolen cars are broken up and sold for spares, while the rest are given a false identity and sold. If you regularly park your car in a city street, you have a high chance of having it or its contents stolen, although the favourite spot for thieves (particularly on Fridays and Saturdays) is suburban shopping mall car parks. Having your car stolen means more than just taking a taxi home. It may mean weeks of delay sorting out insurance, extra time and expense travelling to work, loss of (sometimes irreplaceable) possessions, and loss of your insurance no-claims discount. It may also involve hiring a solicitor or going to court to re-claim your car after it has been sold by the thief (if a car is stolen and sold, it can be a nightmare getting it back). For complete peace of mind, particularly in Sydney or Melbourne, you're better off using public transport!

If you drive a new or valuable car, it's wise to have it fitted with an alarm, an engine immobiliser (preferably of the rolling code variety with a transponder arming key) or other anti-theft device, and to use a visible deterrent such as a steering or gear change lock. This is particularly important if you own a car that's particularly desirable to car thieves, which includes all imported sports and executive cars, which are often stolen by professional crooks to order. A reflection of the high number of stolen cars in Australia is that most new cars are fitted with dead locks and sophisticated alarm systems as standard equipment.

Don't take unnecessary risks and always lock your car, engage your steering lock and completely close all windows (but don't leave pets in an unventilated car). Never leave your keys in the ignition (which is illegal in a public place in Queensland), not even when filling up at a petrol station or in your driveway. Put any valuables (including clothes) in the boot or out of sight and don't leave your vehicle registration papers or any form of identification in the car. If possible, avoid parking in commuter (e.g. at railway stations) and long-term car parks (e.g. at airports or malls), which are favourite hunting grounds for car thieves. When parking overnight or when it's dark, always park in a well-lit area, which helps deter car thieves.

Car theft has spawned a huge car security business in the (losing) battle to prevent or deter car thieves. These include a multitude of car alarms, engine immobilisers, steering and gear stick locks, personal wheel clamps, window etching with the car registration number, locking wheel nuts and petrol caps, and removable/coded stereo systems (a favourite target of thieves). If you plan to buy an expensive stereo system, you should choose one with a removable unit or control panel/fascia (which you can pop in a pocket), but *never* forget to remove it, even when stopping for a few minutes (although thieves sometimes steal the 'back box', leaving you with a useless facia).

A good security system won't prevent someone breaking into your car (which usually takes a professional a matter of seconds) or prevent it being stolen. What it will do is make it more difficult and may prompt a thief to look for an easier target. However, thanks to new tracking systems, most owners of valuable cars can be virtually assured that a stolen car will be recovered (usually within around four hours of it being reported stolen). Tracking systems such as Mobiletrack have an almost 100 per cent recovery rate in recovering stolen vehicles (so far thieves have been unable to find a way around them).

If your car is stolen, report it to the police and your insurance company as soon as possible. Don't, however, expect the police to find it or even take much interest in your loss. The Australian Consumers Association (see page 443) publishes an excellent book entitled *Safe and Secure - A Guide to Household and Car Security* by Richard Upton.

# PETROL

Three grades of petrol are available in Australia: regular unleaded (92 octane), premium unleaded (96 octane) and leaded (97 octane), which will be available until 2002. Premium unleaded isn't sold at all petrol stations, although it's becoming more widely available. Specially treated petrol is sold in Sydney during the summer months in order to reduce pollution. Diesel is also available at most petrol stations (the price is similar to unleaded), and two-stroke petrol is available for mopeds, boats, lawn-mowers, etc. Prices vary from area to area, even within cities; in outback areas (where petrol stations are few and far between) and Tasmania, prices are around 15¢ higher than in cities. Prices are usually between 95¢ and $1 per litre (or around $4.30 to $4.50 per imperial gallon). Premium unleaded is usually only a few cents more than regular unleaded petrol. Petrol is usually cheapest at supermarkets, which sometimes prompts a price war (discounting has become commonplace in recent years). Petrol prices in Australia are similar to those in the USA and around half European prices. In recent years, there have been claims of price fixing by the major oil companies, but the big four companies, Mobil, Shell, BP and Ampol, are permitted to own and operate only 4 per cent of the stations carrying their name, where they can fix the prices. The remaining outlets are franchises, who buy petrol from the oil company at a wholesale price and fix their own prices.

Many cars in Australia have been converted to run on liquid petroleum gas (LPG) or low propane gas, including most taxis. Most petrol engines can be converted to use both petrol and LPG (they can be switched between them), although you'll lose around a third of your boot space to accommodate the gas tank. The advantage is that LPG costs from around 50¢ a litre, although there's a loss of power of around 15 per cent. All urban areas and most large country towns have LPG outlets. However, a word of warning: LPG tanks occasionally explode, often with fatal results!

All new cars registered in Australia are fitted with a catalytic converter and run on unleaded fuel, although a surprisingly high percentage of older cars still run on leaded (nearly 40 per cent). Most cars that aren't fitted with catalytic converters can also run quite safely on unleaded petrol without any engine adjustments and without affecting their performance. However, tests in recent years have shown that using unleaded petrol in non-catalysed cars causes more pollution than using leaded fuel. **A car fitted with a catalytic converter must never be filled with leaded petrol.** To do so will damage the catalytic converter, which is expensive to replace. To prevent errors, unleaded petrol pump pipes are usually coloured green and the nozzles of leaded petrol pumps are larger than those of unleaded pumps and won't usually fit the petrol filler hole of a car fitted with a catalytic converter. Nevertheless, pay attention, particularly when a garage attendant is filling your car.

The trading hours of petrol stations vary considerably. Most open from 7.30am to 6.30pm Mondays to Saturdays and on Sunday mornings. Many petrol stations are open 24 hours a day in cities and on major highways. However, they run a high risk of robbery and even assaults on staff at night in some cities, and the number of 24-hour stations is expected to be reduced drastically in future. Some stations also have automatic pumps accepting $5 and $10 bills, and possibly credit and debit cards (however, don't rely on finding any outside major towns). Most petrol stations accept major credit and charge cards and local debit (EFTPOS) cards. Most petrol stations provide additional services such as checking oil, water and tyre pressure, and cleaning windscreens. Some also have a car wash and most have a shop selling a wide range of motoring accessories and other goods. In fact, the main business of many petrol stations isn't selling petrol, on which profit margins are minimal. Today's petrol stations are more like convenience stores and sell a wide range of souvenirs, ice cubes, ice cream, confectionery, snacks, soft drinks, newspapers and magazines. Many petrol stations also have workshops and can usually handle minor repairs on-the-spot.

# SPEED LIMITS

Needless to say, excessive speed is one of the major causes of accidents in Australia, and on country roads (where limits are widely ignored) one in three serious injuries is caused by speeding. Despite prosecutions and large fines, speeding is widespread in Australia, and many motorists have a complete disregard for speed limits. In general, roads are posted with signs showing the maximum legal speed (in kilometres per hour and not miles per hour), e.g. in NSW white rectangular signs indicate the speed limit in black numerals within a red circle. Note that in addition to mandatory speed limits, there are square yellow signs indicating advised limits, e.g. when approaching a sharp bend, which aren't compulsory. The following speed limits are in force for cars and motorcycles throughout Australia, unless indicated otherwise by a sign:

| Type of Road | Speed Limit |
| --- | --- |
| lit | 60kph/37mph |
| unlit | 100kph/62mph |

In some urban areas (e.g. in Sydney) there's a 50kph/31mph limit, introduced in an attempt to reduce accidents, particularly those involving pedestrians. In Western Australia the speed limit is 110kph/68mph on country roads and highways, and in the Northern Territory there's no speed limit outside built-up areas, although speeds are severely limited by potholes and ruts on most roads.

In some urban areas, there are zones with lower speed limits, including local traffic zones (40kph/25mph), shared traffic zones, where pedestrians, bicycle riders and other vehicles all use the road (10kph/6mph), and school zones, which have reduced speed limits on school days during school hours (e.g. 40kph/25mph or 25kph/15mph). However, after a court case and intervention by the federal Transport Minister, state governments were declared not to have the power to impose fines for speeders in a temporary 25kph/15mph speed limit school zone (after thousands had already been fined). Note that in some residential areas there are speed humps (known as 'sleeping policemen' or 'traffic calmers' – although they certainly don't calm drivers!), designed to slow traffic. They're sometimes indicated by warning signs and, if you fail to slow down, it's possible to damage your suspension or even turn your car over. Learners and provisional licence holders are limited to a maximum speed of 80kph/50mph, even when a higher limit is in force. If you're towing a caravan, trailer or another vehicle you're also limited to 80kph/50mph.

Speed limits are rigorously enforced in Australia and police employ radar units and speed cameras to identify speeders. Light planes and helicopters are used to spot speeding vehicles on interstate highways, where white lines may be painted on the road surface to help aerial police calculate speeds (by timing a vehicle between lines). Radar detectors are illegal in all states except Western Australia and the Northern Territory, and you can be fined up to $700 for using one (it will also be confiscated). However, they're in widespread use throughout Australia. If an oncoming vehicle flashes his headlights at you, it may be that he has spotted a radar trap and is trying to warn you. If this happens, it's wise to slow down if you're exceeding the speed limit.

Marginal offences are usually dealt with by on-the-spot fines, which can run into $hundreds. You can also 'earn' demerit points on your licence and be disqualified from driving for a period. In NSW the number of demerit points you receive depends on the amount by which you were exceeding the speed limit, as follows:

| Amount Over Limit | Demerit Points |
|---|---|
| Less than 15kph/9mph | 1 |
| Between 15kph/9mph and 25 kph/15mph | 2 |
| Between 25kph/15mph and 30kph/18mph | 3 |
| Between 30kph/18mph and 45kph/28mph | 4 |
| More than 45kph/28mph | 6 |

Driving more than 45kph/28mph above the speed limit is considered dangerous driving and you'll also have your licence cancelled for at least three months; if it results in an accident causing injury or death, the penalties can be severe (e.g. up to ten years' imprisonment in NSW).

# GARAGES & SERVICING

When buying a car in Australia or importing one, you should bear in mind the local service facilities, as not all cars can be easily serviced. All the major European and Japanese manufacturers are well represented, but garages servicing American and exotic European cars are few and far between. If you drive a 'rare' car, it's wise to carry a basic selection of spare parts, as service stations in Australia may not stock them and you may need to wait several weeks for them to be sent from overseas. Most garages are open from around 7.30am to 6.30pm, Mondays to Fridays. Small garages and workshops are cheaper, although the quality of work is variable and it's best to choose one which has been personally recommended. Ask your friends and colleagues if they can recommend a garage close to your home or workplace. Note, however, that if anything goes wrong (and it often does) you'll have a better chance of redress with a main dealer or a garage that's a member of a trade association or approved by a motoring organisation. When a car is under warranty, it must usually be regularly serviced (at the recommended service intervals) by an approved dealer in order not to invalidate the warranty. Servicing and repairs at main dealers is expensive, particularly for imported cars.

Always obtain a number of quotations for major mechanical work or body repairs and tell the garage if an accident repair is to be paid for privately, as they may increase the price when an insurance company is paying. Quotations for accident repairs usually vary wildly, and some garages include the replacement of unnecessary parts. Always get a second opinion if you're quoted a high price for a repair, e.g. by simply ringing an approved dealer. Poor workmanship and overcharging by garages are the biggest concerns for motorists in Australia and generate the most consumer complaints. Always instruct a garage what to do in writing and, for anything other than a standard service, get a written estimate that includes labour and parts. Ask the garage to contact you (give them a phone number) to obtain approval before doing anything that isn't listed or if the cost is likely to exceed the original estimate.

Many garages, including most main dealers, will provide a replacement 'rental' car while yours is being serviced, although you must book in advance and arrange comprehensive insurance. Some garages will collect your car from your home or office and deliver it after the service or will drop you at a railway station or local town and pick you up there when your car is ready for collection.

## ROAD MAPS

Among the best road maps available in Australia are those produced by the major oil companies and sold at petrol stations. Good maps are also published by local Roads and Traffic Authorities and automobile associations such as the NRMA in NSW (see page 275), which may be free or discounted for members. These are usually cheaper and sometimes better than the oil company maps. One of the best 'commercial' maps available is the *Australian Road Atlas* (George Ohip/O'Neil). Free maps of Australia are available from tourist information centres, libraries and car rental companies. A good road map distinguishes between national and state highways and shows the distances between towns and cities and approximate driving times. It should also indicate the state of roads, i.e. whether they're sealed or dirt. Because of the vast distances between towns, a map should also indicate rest points and the distances between them. Street directories (e.g. Gregory's) are published for major cities and are available from bookshops and newsagents. Local town maps are also available from libraries and tourist offices.

## CAR RENTAL

The car rental business is extremely competitive in Australia, where there are five nationwide companies (Avis, Budget, Hertz, National and Thrifty) and a plethora of smaller companies. The major companies have offices in cities and towns throughout the country and at most major airports. These provide one-way rental, which means you can rent a car at one branch and leave it at another. Note, however, that there are a number of conditions, Western Australia and the Northern Territory aren't usually included, and it's expensive (around $200 extra). Cars can be rented from garages and local car rental companies in most towns, which often have much lower rates than the nationals. Look in local newspapers and under 'Car Rentals' in the yellow pages. Shop around for the best rate. Airlines offer fly-drive deals on flights to or within Australia, which must be booked in advance and don't necessary represent good value.

There's a wealth of companies in Australia renting old cars such as 'Rent a Ruffy' and 'Rent a Wreck', typically from around $30 per day. You should beware of cowboy rental companies offering 'rental cars from hell'. Be particularly careful when hiring older cars (cars from major rental companies aren't more than three years old and are usually less than a year old), as they could be in a dangerous condition. If you rent a car in an unroadworthy condition, you're responsible if you're stopped by the police or cause an accident. If you need a vehicle for a few months or longer, you may be better off buying one and selling it when you no longer need it.

Rental cars from major companies can often be ordered with a portable telephone, child restraints or a roof rack, for which some charge a fee. All rental cars from national companies are covered for roadside breakdown assistance from a motoring organisation (see page 275). You can also rent a 4WD vehicle, campervan, motorhome, station wagon, minibus, prestige luxury car or a sports car, and a choice of manual or automatic gearbox is often available. Performance cars can be rented from a number of specialist rental companies, although if you want to test drive a car for a few days with a view to buying one, you may get a better deal from a garage. Some companies also rent cars with hand controls for registered disabled drivers. In addition to self-drive car rentals, in many cities you can rent a luxury car with a chauffeur.

The rates charged by the national rental companies in major cities are almost identical, daily rates averaging $50 to $60 for a small family car, $75 for a medium-size car and $100 for a large car. Four-wheel-drive vehicles cost from around $100 a day. Smaller local companies are usually cheaper, although you shouldn't automatically assume that this is so, as the major companies offer special deals, including standby, weekend (e.g. three days for the price of two), weekly and monthly rates. You may also be able to negotiate a lower rate if business is slow. In some areas where competition is fierce (such as Tasmania), rates are usually lower, particularly in the off-season. Compulsory third party insurance and a collision damage waiver (CDW) are usually included in rates, but check the small print, as even with CDW you may be liable in certain circumstances. If CDW isn't paid, you must pay an excess, e.g. $300 to $1,500 (up to $4,000 in the Northern Territory) if you have an accident. Personal accident insurance is available for an extra charge of around $2.50 per day. Stamp duty of 1 or 1.5 per cent is payable on all car rentals.

When comparing prices, take into account all the costs, taxes and surcharges, as what initially looks a bargain may not be when you include all the extras. Unlimited mileage is usually standard in cities, but not always. When travelling in the outback, there's a flat daily charge plus a charge per kilometre. Note that rental car insurance doesn't usually cover travel on dirt roads, with the exception of 4WD vehicles; even then insurance doesn't usually cover off-road travel, i.e. anything that isn't a maintained (sealed or dirt) road. Most rental companies expect you to have experience of driving 4WD vehicles before they'll rent one to you. If you're planning to travel in rural areas or interstate, you should make sure that the rental includes membership of a local motoring organisation.

You should always check the kilometre restrictions, which may be only 100km to 300km (62 to 186mi) 'free' per day, after which you pay a charge (e.g. 25¢) per km. Most companies restrict travel to sealed roads within 100km to 200km (62 to 124mi) of the rental outlet or within the state or territory where the car is rented (although ACT rentals usually cover the whole of New South Wales). If you breach the rules regarding the operating area, your insurance is automatically cancelled. Major companies usually quote different rates for metro (city), country and 'remote' driving.

To hire a vehicle in Australia, you require a full national or international driving licence, which must have been held for a minimum of two or three years. You must usually be aged over 21, although some companies set the minimum age at 23 or 25 (which usually applies only to certain vehicles, such as 4WDs). A major credit card is usually necessary for identification and the estimated costs (including petrol) must be paid in advance. The petrol bond is refunded when a vehicle is returned with a full tank. Without a credit card, the estimated rental charge must be paid in advance plus a bond of around $200, which is returned, less any legitimate deductions.

**Campervans & Motorhomes:** Campervans can be rented for around $1,100 per week (2/3 berth), and motorhomes between $1,300 (4 berth) and $1,500 per week (6 berth). Rates vary according to the season, the period, and the state or territory. Rentals are usually for a minimum of seven days (although four-day rentals are available). The above rates are for peak periods for rentals of less than three weeks and are reduced considerably for off-peak periods and for rentals of three weeks or longer. Rentals must be paid in advance, and a bond of around $700 is also payable but is reduced if comprehensive damage insurance is purchased (daily rate around $30). A CDW costs around $12 per day, and there are also government taxes to pay. Some companies offer older vehicles (e.g. over three years old) at lower rates. There's a surcharge of $10 to $15 per day during December and January (school holidays) for campervans and motorhomes.

Vehicles are usually equipped with air-conditioning, refrigerator, sink, gas stove/grill, wardrobe, convertible beds and a water tank, and some deluxe vehicles also have a shower and toilet. Essential items such as blankets, linen, crockery and cooking utensils are also usually provided. Note that rented campervans and motorhomes may not be used north of Mossman in Queensland or north of Geraldton in Western Australia, and vehicles aren't permitted to travel on unsealed roads, which voids the insurance cover. One-way rentals are possible with some companies, usually between major cities.

Vans and utility vehicles (pick-ups) are available from major rental companies by the hour, half-day or day, and from smaller local companies (which once again, are usually cheaper). You can also rent a caravan or trailer from a number of companies (prices vary with the season).

# MOTORING ORGANISATIONS

There are motoring organisation in all Australian states and territories. The Australian Automobile Association (AAA) is the only national motoring organisation in Australia, operating as an umbrella organisation for motoring organisations in individual states and territories. It provides no services to individual motorists and any requests must be directed to local organisations. The AAA publishes a booklet entitled *Motoring in Australia*. Some 75 per cent of Australian motorists are members of a motoring organisation, one of the highest rates in the world. The largest is the National Roads and Motoring Association (NRMA) in New South Wales, with almost two million members.

There are few essential differences between the basic services provided by Australian motoring organisations, although membership costs vary. The primary service of motoring organisations is to provide emergency assistance in the event of an accident or breakdown. Most organisations offer various membership levels providing different levels of service, which usually include towing and vehicle recovery, free public transport or a rental car, home start and legal advice. Motoring organisations provide a fast and efficient service, usually arriving within one hour of notification of a breakdown. Note that it's the vehicle that is covered (irrespective of the driver) and not the individual. The larger organisations offer both national and international accident or breakdown cover for no extra charge.

All organisations charge a joining fee and an annual membership fee, for example the NRMA (NSW) has a $44 joining fee and a standard membership fee of $70 per year or more for the expanded NRMA plus service. Fees are similar in other states and territories. The NRMA Plus package provides additional services, including emergency accommodation, passenger transport, replacement rental car, vehicle transport and extended towing service (up to a maximum cost of $2,000). In this case, you must be more than 100km (62mi) from your home, and the breakdown or accident damage must take at least 24 hours to repair.

All organisations offer additional services, which may include free publications, international driving permits, international camping cards, travel services, crash repair centres, driving schools, holiday centres, road maps and itineraries, advice on weather and road conditions, accommodation guides, car and household insurance (motoring organisations are among Australia's largest insurers), vehicle inspection and technical advice, legal advice, and emergency accommodation. Some motoring organisations (e.g. the NRMA) are expanding into financial services, ranging from home loans to cheque books and superannuation to cash management accounts.

If you break down, call the local motoring organisation by phoning a 24-hour telephone number for assistance. Keep your membership card in your car and quote your membership number when calling for help. There are emergency telephones every kilometre on Australian highways for calling for assistance from local motoring organisations. Non-members can also get assistance, but it can be expensive. Members of foreign motoring organisations (affiliated to the AAA) who break down anywhere in Australia can obtain free breakdown assistance from Australian organisations, plus free maps and accommodation directories at members' rates (on production of a membership card). Most Australian organisations also have reciprocal arrangements with motoring organisations in other countries (for when you're driving overseas).

# 12.

# HEALTH

Australia is among the most advanced countries in the field of medicine and is noted for its highly-trained medical staff and modern hospitals equipped with the latest high-tech apparatus. Health care services in Australia are provided by both government (including Commonwealth, state, territory and local governments) and private organisations. The country spends around 8 per cent of its GDP on health care (compared with some 15 per cent in the USA), which is about average for OECD countries. Despite the rising cost of modern medicine, with its astronomically expensive equipment to diagnose and treat illnesses such as cancer and heart disease, costs have largely been contained in the last 15 years. Recently, there has been a growing emphasis on preventive medicine and community care, including education programmes to promote a healthy lifestyle. Two yardsticks widely used to measure the quality of health care are the infant mortality rate (around six deaths for every 1,000 live births) and life expectancy (81 years for women and 75 for men), both of which rate Australia among the 'best' in the world.

Australia has a national health system called Medicare, which provides free or subsidised medical care and free hospital treatment in public hospitals for all permanent residents (plus certain visitors) irrespective of their age, income or health status. The public health system is supplemented by a wide variety of private practitioners, hospitals and clinics, plus a range of voluntary agencies and non-profit organisations. Alternative medicine and natural remedies are popular in Australia, where acupuncture, homeopathy, chiropractic, osteopathy, physiotherapy and naturopathy thrive. Health facilities and doctors are unevenly distributed in Australia, the major cities and urban areas having a huge surplus of GPs, while in most country areas there's a shortage, particularly in the Northern Territory and Western Australia. Trying to encourage doctors to relocate from the cities to remote country and outback areas is a major problem, which the government is trying to address by importing doctors specifically to work in country areas. The Royal Flying Doctor Service provides medical services in remote country areas and evacuates urgent cases to hospital.

**The Nation's Health:** Australians are generally healthier than they were 20 years ago, owing to a decrease in smoking and drinking and an improved diet (although Australia's love affair with junk food and red meat is largely undiminished). Nevertheless, the amount of exercise Australians take is generally low, and over half the adult population is either obese or overweight; many children have eating disorders and anorexia, and a quarter are classified as obese. Stress-related problems (often due to over-work or lack of sleep) are on the increase in Australia's cities, and the country has a relatively high suicide rate, particularly among the young and the over 65s. Voluntary euthanasia is a topical subject in Australia, particularly since the world's first voluntary euthanasia law was passed in 1995 in the Northern Territory. This was subsequently overturned in 1997 by the federal government after four people had been medically assisted to die. In most states, patients can refuse life-sustaining treatment, but doctors cannot assist them to die (although in reality many doctors do 'assist' terminally-ill patients).

The biggest killers in Australia are cancer (the cause of some 30 per cent of deaths), heart disease and stroke, and smoking-related illnesses. Alcoholism is fairly widespread, as is drug addiction, which is a serious and increasing problem. The country has an unusually high level of diabetes: in 2000, there were some 800,000 sufferers (over 4 per cent of the population). There are special health programmes in Australia for Aborigines and Torres Strait Islanders, many of whom have acute health problems (often related to alcohol abuse and poor diet) and a much lower life expectancy than other Australians. Virulent flu (influenza) strains are a widespread problem and directly or indirectly kill some 1,500 people a year and affect as many as 30 per cent of the population (flu vaccinations are recommended for those aged over 65). Miscellaneous health problems in recent years have included outbreaks of salmonella poisoning (from cooked meat), hepatitis C (a life-threatening infection transmitted mostly by intravenous drug users), legionnaire's disease, dengue fever and meningococcal disease. Air pollution caused by high smog levels is an increasing problem in Australia's cities, particularly Sydney (where pollution is higher than London, New York or Tokyo) and Melbourne, where asthmatics, bronchitis sufferers and the elderly are particularly at risk. Sydney is reportedly the allergy capital of the world on account of the numerous plants that send out pollens on breezy spring days.

**Skin Cancer:** Australia has the highest rate of melanoma in the world: although cases are reducing as people take heed of warnings, some 850 people die each year from skin cancer. If you aren't used to Australia's fierce sun, you should limit your exposure and avoid it altogether during the hottest part of the day (between around 10am and 3pm), wear protective clothing (including a hat) and use sunscreen. Those with fair skin should take extra care, as you can become burnt in just 15 minutes on a hot summer day. The government's slogan in the battle against skin cancer is 'Slip, Slop, Slap', i.e. slip on a shirt, slop on sunscreen and slap on a hat. This is backed by a 'SunSmart' campaign begun in 1987, which is particularly targeted at teenagers. It's important to use a sunscreen with a high protection factor, e.g. a pH 15+ broad-spectrum, water-resistant sunscreen (sunscreens with a protection factor of 30+ are now available). In 2000, the largest skin cancer research project in the world was started in Australia with the results expected in 2002.

Too much sun and too little protection dries your skin and causes premature aging, so care should be taken to replace the skin's natural oils (many Australian women in their 20s and 30s have the skin of people 20 or 30 years older). Medical experts recommend the wearing of good quality sunglasses, e.g. with UV400 polycarbonate lenses, to protect against eye cancer and other eye problems caused by the sun. Hikers should wear legionnaire or Arab style hats with neck flaps. Children are particularly vulnerable and should wear wide-brimmed hats in the sun and a T-shirt when swimming. Those who live the outdoor life (such as sportsmen and women) are also especially at risk and should follow the example of Australian cricketers by wearing total block-out zinc cream on exposed areas when spending a long time in the sun. Drink plenty of water when in the sun to prevent dehydration (in extreme heat you should drink a litre every hour), and avoid excess alcohol and over-exertion, particularly if you're elderly. Other problems associated with too much sun include sunstroke, sunburn, heat exhaustion, prickly heat and fungal infections.

**Wildlife:** Australia has some of the deadliest creatures in the world, including a plethora of poisonous snakes (e.g. the brown, black, yellow whip, tiger, death adder and western taipan), venomous spiders (e.g. red-back, trap-door and funnel-web), scorpions, crocodiles, sharks, jellyfish, sea snakes, stonefish, catfish and other unpleasant marine life, many of which can deliver a fatal sting. Note that, although you're unlikely to have a close encounter with most of Australia's wildlife (unless you venture into the bush or the sea on unprotected beaches), many poisonous snakes can be found in suburban parks and gardens and near water courses. You should avoid undergrowth and country areas unless you're wearing protective clothing, i.e. not thongs (flip flops) or shorts, and try to avoid disturbing wildlife. Insects (e.g.

mosquitoes, ticks and wasps) are also a problem in many areas, although they're unlikely to kill you. Children are taught at school to recognise dangerous wildlife.

**Immunisation:** Child immunisation is a problem in Australia, where a large percentage of older children aren't fully immunised against diseases such as whooping cough, tetanus and diphtheria, resulting in many unnecessary deaths. Many parents are concerned about the side effects, although these are insignificant compared to the effects of the diseases themselves. In an attempt to 'encourage' parents to immunise their children, the government has introduced measures such as the requirement to have children immunised in order to receive family payments such as child care benefit (see page 306). There's also a maternity immunisation allowance given as a one-off payment ($208 in 2001) when the child is 19 months old and is fully immunised. As a result of an intense campaign for child immunisation, in 2001 nearly 90 per cent of children under 18 months were fully immunised (in some states such as NSW the figure is nearer 100 per cent).

Children should have six sets of injections between the age of two months and four years in order to be fully immunised against diphtheria, tetanus, whooping cough, poliomyelitis, hib, hepatitis B, measles, mumps and rubella. Children aged between 10 and 19 years also need booster shots for most of these diseases. Immunisations can be provided by your family doctor, an immunisation clinic, local authorities and some public hospitals. There's an Australian Child Immunisation Register (ACIR) where all immunisation details are recorded and which can be accessed by parents and authorities (☎ freecall 1800-653809).

**The Disabled:** Australia provides better than average facilities for the disabled. Note, however, that accommodation and support services for the disabled are relatively poor. All capital cities and most regional centres produce maps showing accessible paths, parking and toilets for those with mobility difficulties, and nationwide facilities are listed in *Easy Access Australia* (available from 🖳 www.easy accessaustralia.com.au). Many councils provide a directory of services for people with disabilities and for older residents. General information is available from the National Information Communication Awareness Network (NICAN), PO Box 407, Curtin, ACT 2605 (☎ 02-6285 3713).

**Water:** You can safely drink the tap water in Australia, although the wine tastes much better and, taken in moderation, even does you good (if you believe the winegrowers!). Water supplies are fluoridated in most parts of Australia in order to help prevent dental decay.

# EMERGENCIES

The action to take in a medical 'emergency' depends on the degree of urgency. If you're unsure who to call, ask the telephone operator (☎ 1234) or call your local police station (N.B. a mobile phone can be a lifesaver in a remote area or when you need help and are alone). They'll tell you who to contact or even call the appropriate service for you. Whoever you call, you should give the approximate age of the patient and, if possible, specify the type of emergency. **Keep a record of the telephone numbers of your doctor, local hospitals and clinics, ambulance service, dentist and other emergency services, next to your telephone.**

Dial 000 for an ambulance without a doctor (but usually with a paramedic) **only in an emergency.** Many ambulances are equipped with cardiac, oxygen and other emergency equipment (called intensive care ambulances). Ambulance services aren't covered by Medicare, although in most cities you can become a member of the St John's Ambulance Association for around $15 per year, which entitles you to free ambulance services. Private health insurance may include ambulance costs.

There are air ambulances (helicopters) in some cities, and remote outback areas are served by the Royal Flying Doctor service, established as a non-profit organisation in 1927 and funded by the federal government and voluntary contributions. The service covers some 80 per cent of outback areas from 21 main bases, ensuring that most patients are less than two hours from medical help. Services include regular clinic visits to remote communities, visits by specialists and, in some areas, dental treatment. The service also offers advice on touring and emergency procedures (travellers in remote areas can rent a transceiver with emergency call buttons). For more information contact the Royal Flying Doctor Service of Australia, Federal Office, Level 5, 15-17 Young Street, Sydney, NSW 2000 (☎ 02-9241 2411, 🖥 www.rfds.org.au).

In minor 'emergencies' or for medical advice, you should phone your family doctor if you have one. Failing this you can ask the operator (☎ 1234) for the telephone number of a local doctor or hospital (or consult your phone book). Police stations keep a list of doctors' and chemists' private telephone numbers in case of emergency. In some cities and regions, there are private, 24-hour doctor services that make house calls (but check the cost before using them).

If you're physically able, you can go to the Accident, Casualty or Emergency department of a public hospital, many of which provide a 24-hour service. Check in advance which local hospitals are equipped to deal with emergencies and the quickest route from your home. This information may be of vital importance in the event of an emergency, when a delay could mean the difference between life and death. Emergency cases, irrespective of nationality and the ability to pay, are *never* turned away in Australia, and treatment may be free if you're a national of a country with a reciprocal health agreement with Australia.

If you have an emergency dental problem outside normal surgery hours, call a dentist providing an emergency service (listed in the yellow pages).

# MEDICARE

Medicare is the name of the national health service in Australia, established in 1984 and administered by the Health Insurance Commission (HIC). It provides free treatment in public hospitals and free or subsidised treatment by doctors (including specialists), optometrists and dentists in certain cases. All permanent residents of Australia are eligible to join Medicare, and restricted access is also granted to citizens of certain countries with which Australia has a reciprocal health care agreement. If you're working in Australia, you're automatically covered for injury and illness as a result of an accident by compulsory workers' compensation insurance (see page 63).

Medicare provides benefits for the following:

- doctor's consultation fees, including treatment by specialists (when referred by a GP);

- most surgical and other therapeutic procedures performed by doctors;

- X-rays, pathology tests, other medical tests, examinations and certain surgical procedures (listed in the Medicare Benefits Schedule);

- eye tests performed by an optometrist;
- some surgical procedures performed by dentists registered with Medicare;
- specified items under the Cleft Lip and Palate Scheme;
- all associated treatment costs when you're treated as a public (Medicare) patient in a public hospital.

Medicare *doesn't* cover the following:

- dental examinations and treatment (although certain essential dental surgery is covered);
- ambulance services;
- home nursing;
- physiotherapy, occupational therapy, speech and eye therapy, chiropody, podiatry, and psychology;
- acupuncture (unless treatment is provided by a doctor);
- spectacles and contact lenses;
- hearing aids, prostheses and other appliances;
- medicines;
- medical and hospital costs incurred overseas;
- medical treatment that isn't immediately necessary;
- elective or cosmetic surgery or hospital treatment that isn't of an essential nature;
- treatment arranged before arriving in Australia;
- accommodation and medical treatment in a private hospital;
- accommodation and medical treatment as a private patient in a public hospital;
- medical repatriation or funeral costs;
- examinations for life insurance, superannuation or membership of a friendly society.

Medicare also doesn't cover situations where someone else is responsible for medical costs (e.g. a compensation insurer, an employer or a government authority). If you receive treatment under Medicare for an injury or accident which is subject to compensation by a third party, such as an insurance company or workers' compensation, the insurer must reimburse Medicare for any benefits related to the injury before making any payments to you. You're usually required to indicate whether this is the position when making a claim.

**Contributions:** Medicare is partly funded (less than 20 per cent) by a 1.5 per cent levy on taxable income (above $13,807) and by general taxation. In an effort to 'encourage' high earners to take out private health insurance, the levy was increased in 1996 by 1 per cent for single people earning over $50,000 per year and couples earning over $100,000 per year. If you're self-employed, the levy is included in your annual income tax charge. Certain people are exempt from paying the levy, including pensioners with a pensioner concession card or a Commonwealth seniors health card, war veterans and widows, and defence force personnel without dependants, as well as single people on incomes below $13,807. Couples and sole parents who earn less than $28,200 are entitled to a reduction in their Medicare levy. The unemployed and dependants have automatic deductions made from their unemployment benefits or other allowances.

**Enrolment:** You should enrol in Medicare as soon as possible after your arrival in Australia, although it isn't necessary until you use the system, as you can join retrospectively, i.e. claim a refund of previous medical expenses after joining Medicare. You can apply in person at a Medicare office or you can call ☎ 13-2011 (local call rate) and have an application form sent to you. Medicare produces a comprehensive booklet *Welcome to Medicare* in a number of languages. You're required to show proof of eligibility, e.g. your passport with a residence stamp if you're a permanent resident. Applicants must also provide details of their residence, income and assets.

You receive a plastic Medicare card (green and gold) by post around two to three weeks after applying, which shows your Medicare membership number, the names of all dependants entitled to use the service and the expiry date of the card. Cards are valid for five years, although you must obtain a replacement card if you change your address or other details on the card change (e.g. your family increases in size). The card has a signature strip on the back and must be signed immediately. If you receive treatment before you obtain your card, you must pay in full and claim a refund or delay payment until you receive your card. There's a three-month waiting period before claims are met for new members. You must quote your Medicare number when making enquiries or a claim and use your Medicare card to:

● receive a cash benefit at a Medicare customer service centre;

● receive treatment (without payment) from a doctor or optometrist who bulk bills Medicare (see below);

● obtain free treatment in a public hospital;

● obtain prescriptions.

**Schedule Fee:** The benefits provided by Medicare are based on a schedule of fees, the Medicare Benefits Schedule (MBS) set by the Commonwealth government, which are increased annually (on 1st November) at half the rate of inflation. When a doctor charges more than the schedule fee, patients must meet the additional cost. Medicare pays 85 per cent of the schedule fee or the schedule fee less $52.50 (2001 figure), whichever is the larger amount. The shortfall is called the 'gap' amount, which can be covered by private health insurance (see page 312).

**Safety Net:** Those who require frequent treatment are protected from high gap costs by a 'safety net'. When you (or your family members) have made gap payments amounting to a total of $302.30 (adjusted annually on 1st January) in a Medicare financial year (from 1st July to 30th June), benefits are increased to 100 per cent. Note that, if your GP charges more than the schedule fee, the extra amount doesn't count towards the safety net total (gap amounts for in-hospital services also doesn't count). It isn't necessary for individuals to register for the safety net, as Medicare keeps a record of gap payments and the higher (100 per cent) benefits apply automatically as soon as the limit is reached. However, families (even when all members are listed on a Medicare card) need to complete a *Medicare Safety Net Registration Form* and take or send it to a Medicare customer service centre. A family includes a spouse (or *de* *facto* spouse), children under 16 in your care and dependent full-time students aged under 25. It's important to register your family as soon as possible, as you receive 100 per cent of the schedule fee for a service only after you've registered for the safety net, i.e. refunds aren't paid retrospectively.

**Bulk Billing:** Bulk billing (also called direct billing) is where a doctor (or optometrist) doesn't charge the patient, but the patient assigns his right to benefits to the doctor, who bills Medicare directly. If your doctor bulk bills, you'll be asked to complete a form after treatment, of which you receive a copy. You don't need to pay anything and aren't required to make a claim to Medicare. Most doctors bulk bill at least some of their patients, particularly pensioners and Commonwealth Seniors Health Card holders (see **Retirees** below). A 15-minute GP consultation is valued at around $27 by Medicare, who reimburse doctors $22.95 (85 per cent). However, GPs aren't happy with the schedule and want increased rebates, which have fallen in real terms in recent years. Independent surveys have shown that the real value of a consultation is at least $44, and recent research in Sydney revealed that over 90 per cent of GPs were spending time with patients on an unpaid basis. As a result, fewer doctors are bulk billing and even fewer are expected to in the future. In 2001, there was intense debate between the government, reluctant to increase the health budget and thus inject funds into the payment of GP consultations, and the Australian Medical Assocation (AMA), whose members (not surprisingly) wish to be paid for all the time they spend with patients.

**Claims:** If your doctor or optometrist doesn't bulk bill, he will give you a bill for his services. You can either pay the bill and claim a refund from Medicare or submit the bill to your local Medicare office with a claim form. Bills can be submitted by mail (addressed to Medicare, GPO Box 9822 in your state's capital city) or in person with a completed claim form and the original bills or receipts for payments. You'll thn receive a cheque made out to the practitioner, which you give to him plus the balance (gap), if any, payable by you.

If you've already paid for treatment and make a claim in person, you'll receive a cash refund (a cash limit applies). Always take your Medicare card with you when attending a Medicare office. Claims made by mail are paid by cheque (you can also drop your claim's form in the box provided at Medicare offices, in which case you'll be refunded by cheque or by direct payment into your bank account). Electronic lodgement of Medicare claims was introduced in 1997 in an attempt to reduce delays in payments and improve access to Medicare for those living in rural and remote areas. The system enables members to use their Medicare cards in EFTPOS-style machines (like bank ATMs). Telephone claims (☎ local call rate 1300-360460) can by made by anyone living outside Adelaide, Brisbane, Melbourne, Perth and Sydney. These can be made at any time and do not require a form; you simply endorse your Medicare receipt with the information the telephone operator gives you and send the it to Medicare.

**Retirees:** Retirees who aren't in receipt of a social security or veterans' pension and whose income is below the pension cut-off point may qualify for a range of free and concessionary health services. Retirees can apply for a Commonwealth Seniors Health Card (contact the Welfare Teleservice ☎ local call rate 13-2468) and receive prescriptions at $3.50 each for medicines and drugs listed on the Pharmaceuticals Benefits Scheme (PBS – see **Drugs & Medicines** on page 289) and (from September 2001) a telephone allowance.

**Restrictions/Ineligibility:** Note that foreign retirees with a temporary visa (see page 97) aren't covered by Medicare and must take out private health insurance. Foreign diplomats and their families also aren't covered by Medicare. Medical expenses incurred by men aged over 55 and women aged over 51 who have been sponsored in the family reunion migration category are the responsibility of their sponsor for ten years or until they reach retirement age.

**The Future:** As in many other countries, the rising cost of health care and health insurance has created severe problems for Medicare, which is over-worked, under-resourced and facing a funding crisis. It's also burdened by the increasing life expectancy of Australians (around 12 per cent of the population is aged 65 or older, a figure which is expected to double by the year 2050). In recent years, the cost of private health insurance, which usually supplements rather than replaces Medicare, has increased sharply and many people have cancelled their policies (thus adding to the burden on Medicare). Before Medicare was introduced in 1984, some two-thirds of Australians had private cover; this has since fallen to less than a third. Many people believe that Australia now has a two-tier health system: a costly private health sector with all the 'bells and whistles' for those who can afford it and a neglected second-rate public system for those who cannot.

Many public hospitals are cash-starved and cannot cope with the demand; many have a shortage of nursing staff and doctors as well as lack of new medical technology. Although most urgent cases are admitted within 30 days, there are long waiting lists for elective surgery under Medicare, and non-urgent cases may have to wait up to a year for treatment. In early 2001, there was graphic media coverage of patients sitting on trolleys waiting for a bed. It's generally agreed that vastly increased health expenditure is necessary if Medicare is to continue.

General information about Medicare in English is available from the Medicare Information Service (☎ local call rate 13-2011) and information in other languages is available from the Medicare Multilingual Telephone Information Service (☎ 13-1202).

# PRIVATE HEALTH SERVICES

Private health treatment functions both within Medicare and independently of it, and most public hospitals admit private patients. In addition to specialist appointments and hospital treatment, people most commonly use private health services to obtain second opinions, private health checks or screening, and for complementary medicine such as acupuncture, chiropractic, homeopathy, naturopathy, osteopathy and physiotherapy (which aren't usually covered by Medicare or private health insurance). Private patients are usually free to choose their own doctor and hospital, and may be accommodated in a single, hotel-style room with a radio, telephone, colour TV, en suite bathroom and room service, depending on their policy.

With the deterioration of Medicare services and lengthening waiting lists, you're strongly advised to consider taking out private health insurance, which will ensure you always receive the medical treatment you need, when you need it. For information about private health insurance see page 312.

# DOCTORS

There are excellent family doctors throughout Australia, who are generally referred to as general practitioners (GPs). The best way to find a doctor, whether as a Medicare or private patient, is to ask your colleagues, friends or neighbours if they can recommend someone. There's a glut of doctors in most cities and metropolitan areas and an acute shortage (totalling around 1,000 GPs) in rural areas, where the ratio of doctors to population is less than half the national average. Therefore in rural areas or the outback, where you're also served by the Royal Flying Doctor Service, you may need to travel some distance to visit a doctor. The shortage has led the government to introduce a scheme to attract foreign doctors to practise in rural areas (around half are from Britain and Ireland). In general, doctors are discouraged from migrating to Australia and receive a points penalty when being assessed, but the new scheme allows them to obtain temporary work visas for contracts of up to three years in remote areas.

Your GP can provide advice and information on all aspects of health and medical care, including preventive medicine, blood donations, home medical equipment and special counselling. If you're a Medicare patient, he should also be able to advise you about the range of benefits provided under Medicare, including immunisation, maternity care, contraceptive help and psychiatric treatment. Note that patients in Australia have no legal right to see their medical records, as they do in many other countries.

**Fees:** It isn't necessary to be registered with a doctor in Australia, where you can choose to visit any doctor, either as a Medicare patient (provided the doctor is registered with Medicare) or a private patient. If you wish to be treated as a Medicare patient, you must check whether a doctor charges the schedule fee ($22.95) for consultations and bulk bills Medicare or whether he levies an extra charge (which may be $15 or more for a consultation) – see **Bulk Billing** on page 286. Note that many doctors now levy an additional fee, and in some areas you may have difficulty finding a doctor who doesn't, although pensioners and Commonwealth Seniors Health Card holders are usually exempt. Some doctors levy a 'co-operative charge' (e.g. $2.50) to discourage frivolous visits. The low remuneration paid to doctors by Medicare encourages doctors to rush consultations (referred to as 'six-minute' or 'stop-watch' medicine). If you're concerned that your doctor doesn't allow sufficient time for a thorough examination, you should change doctors, although you may need to choose one who charges an additional fee. If you wish to see a GP privately, you (or your insurance company) must pay the full fee, which is at the doctor's discretion but is usually at least $36 for a routine consultation.

**Choosing a Doctor:** You should enquire in advance (e.g. by asking the receptionist) whether a doctor has the 'qualifications' you require, for example:

● Is he or she of the 'right' sex?

● Is he easily reached by public transport, if necessary?

● Is it a group practice? This may be preferable to an individual practice, where you may be required to see a locum (replacement) doctor when your doctor is absent (in a group practice doctors cover for each other outside surgery hours).

● What are the surgery hours (Saturday and evening surgeries may be held)?

- What is the procedure for home visits?
- Does the doctor practise preventive or complementary medicine (e.g. acupuncture)?
- Does the doctor prescribe contraception?
- Does the doctor bulk bill or levy an extra charge?
- If you're a private patient, what does a consultation cost?

Many doctors in the suburbs of major cities work at public clinics and medical centres, where a number of doctors have a group practice, at least one of whom will usually be female (there's a relatively large percentage of women doctors in Australia). Clinics and medical centres usually have an in-house pharmacy, and medical tests, such as X-rays and blood and urine analysis, may also be conducted in-house.

**Surgery Hours:** Surgery hours vary, but are typically from 8.30am to 6 or 7pm, Mondays to Fridays, with early closing one day per week, e.g. 5 or 5.30pm on Fridays. Evening surgeries may also be held one or two evenings per week. Emergency surgeries may be held on Saturday mornings, e.g. from 8.30am to 11.30am or noon. Most doctors' surgeries have answering machines outside surgery hours, when a recorded message informs you of the name and telephone number of the doctor on call (or deputising service).

**Appointments:** An appointment must be made to see a GP, usually one or two days in advance. If you're an urgent case (but not an emergency), your doctor will usually see you immediately, but you should still phone in advance if possible. Note, however, that surgeries often overrun and you may need to wait well past your appointment time to see a doctor. Australian doctors make house calls, although these can be expensive for private patients.

**Specialists:** Medicare patients must always be referred by a GP to a specialist, e.g. an eye specialist, gynaecologist or orthopaedic surgeon. If you want a second opinion on any health matter, you may ask to see a specialist, although unless it's a serious matter your doctor may refuse to refer you. You may, however, be able to convince another doctor to refer you or you can consult a specialist as a private patient. Patients with private health insurance may be free to make appointments directly with specialists, although most insurance companies prefer patients to be referred by GPs. Note that most specialists have long waiting lists for Medicare patients.

# DRUGS & MEDICINES

Medicines and drugs are obtained from chemists (pharmacies), which also provide free advice concerning minor ailments and recommend appropriate medicines. Many drugs and medicines in Australia can be prescribed only by a doctor via an official form called a prescription, which is written in a secret language decipherable only by doctors and pharmacists. Some drugs and medicines sold freely in other countries require a doctor's prescription in Australia, while certain drugs are available over the counter in Australia that are controlled in other countries. Over 175 million prescriptions are dispensed each year in Australia and around a quarter of household health expenditure is on medicines. Most chemists also sell non-prescription medicines and drugs, toiletries, cosmetics, health foods and cleaning supplies. A health food shop sells diet foods, homeopathic medicines and eternal-life/virility/ youth pills and elixirs, which are quite popular in Australia (even though their claims are often in the realms of fantasy). **Always use, store and dispose of unwanted medicines and drugs safely, e.g. by returning them to a pharmacist or dispensing doctor, and never leave them where children can get their hands on them.**

At least one chemist is open in most towns during the evenings and on Sundays for the emergency dispensing of medicines and drugs, and there are 24-hour pharmacies in some cities. A roster is posted on the doors of chemists and published in local newspapers and guides. If you require medicine urgently when chemists are closed, you should contact your GP or a police station. To obtain medicines prescribed by a doctor, simply take your prescription to any chemist. Your prescription may be filled immediately if it's available off the shelf, or you may be asked to wait or come back later.

The Pharmaceutical Benefits Scheme (PBS) subsidises the cost of around 1,700 necessary and life-saving medicines. Most medicines available on prescription are subsidised under the PBS, so just by having a prescription filled you receive the benefit of the subsidy. PBS medicines are available to all Australian residents and to visitors from countries with which Australia has a reciprocal health care agreement. Proof of residence or nationality may be necessary. If you're eligible but unable to provide proof, you may be charged the full price for medicines, although you can obtain a refund at a Medicare customer service centre or by posting your claim (plus the receipt and your Medicare card or proof of eligibility) to Medicare, GPO Box 9822 in a state or territory's capital city. If you qualify for concessions (see below), you should pay a maximum of $20 towards the cost of each PBS medicine. Note that the cost of non-prescription medicines can vary considerably and, if you need a medication regularly, it's worth shopping around. It's possible to buy prescription (and other) medicines by post (post free) at savings of up to 50 per cent from Pharmacy Direct, 3 Coal Street, Silverwater, NSW 2128 (☎ local call rate 1300-656245 or 02-9648 8888, 💻 www.pharmacydirect.com.au).

In recent years, the government has restricted the prescription of expensive drugs in order to control the escalating cost of pharmaceuticals. GPs must now prescribe the cheapest of a particular group of drugs, and patients wishing to use a more expensive drug must pay a 'therapeutic premium' (the difference between the government subsidy and the cost of the drug). If a medication isn't available under PBS (i.e. is non-prescription), you must pay the entire cost. If you have private health insurance, you may be able to reclaim the cost of prescriptions from your insurance company.

**Concessions:** Once you or your family (spouse or *de facto* spouse, children aged under 16 and dependent full-time students under 25) have spent $669.70 (adjusted annually on 1st January) on prescription medicines in a calendar year, you're entitled to receive all additional prescription medicines at the concession rate of $3.50 per item for the remainder of the calendar year. All purchases must be recorded on a *Prescription Record* form by your pharmacist.

If you have an approved concession card (issued to pensioners, the unemployed, low-income families, war widows and their dependants), you pay $3.50 per prescription until you've spent a total of $182.00, after which there's no charge for the remainder of the year.

**Foreign Prescriptions:** If you're visiting Australia, you may bring a maximum of four weeks' prescription medicines with you. You should also have a doctor's prescription which, after it has been endorsed by an Australian-registered doctor, will allow you to obtain medication in Australia. Note that the brand names for the same drugs and medicines vary considerably from country to country so, if you regularly take medication overseas, you should ask your doctor for the generic name. If you wish to match medication prescribed overseas in Australia, you need a current prescription with the medication's trade name, the manufacturer's name, the chemical name and the dosage. Most foreign drugs have an equivalent in Australia, although particular brands may be difficult or impossible to obtain.

## HOSPITALS & CLINICS

Most Australian towns have a hospital or clinic, signposted by the international hospital sign of a white H on a blue background. Australia has a variety of public and private hospitals and clinics, and there are various kinds of public hospitals, including district hospitals, teaching hospitals, general hospitals, children's hospitals, veterans' hospitals, dental hospitals, psychiatric hospitals and day hospitals. Major hospitals are called general hospitals and provide treatment and diagnosis for in-patients, day-patients and out-patients. They may have a maternity department, infectious diseases unit, psychiatric and geriatric facilities, rehabilitation and convalescent units, and cater for most forms of specialised treatment. Australia's public hospitals are funded jointly by the federal government and state and territory governments, and administered by state and territory health departments. There's also an increasing number of private hospital operators in Australia (such as Australian Hospital Care), and some public hospitals are operated by private companies under a contract.

**Public Hospital Treatment:** Medicare pays for the full cost of accommodation and medical treatment performed by hospital appointed doctors for Medicare patients in public hospitals. Hospital bills for treatment under Medicare are always paid directly by Medicare. Note, however, that you'll have no choice of doctors or hospital, nor of when you'll be admitted for treatment or surgery. Medicare patients also receive free X-rays and pathology tests in public hospitals and free out-patient services in some public hospitals. Patients are usually accommodated in general wards or twin rooms. If you want a TV or a telephone, you must pay extra for them. When you visit a public hospital, you should take your Medicare card with you (if applicable). The staff may ask whether you wish to be treated under Medicare or as a private patient.

In recent years, there has been a funding crisis in public hospitals in many states, some of which have a chronic shortages of basic medical supplies, including bed linen, bandages, swabs, sterile dressings, syringes and drugs. Some public hospitals also have a lack of diagnostic equipment, e.g. for brain scans. In some over-worked public hospitals, patients are left lying for hours in emergency departments and in corridors waiting for ward beds. Some public hospitals also suffer from a shortage of doctors and nurses and are forced to recruit casual staff from locum and nursing agencies. Note, however, that there's usually no shortage of equipment or drugs that would put patients' lives at risk.

**Private Treatment:** If you're a private patient in a public or private hospital, Medicare will pay 75 per cent of the schedule fee for medical services and the remaining 25 per cent will be paid by your private health insurer, if you have one. If your doctor bulk bills (which means that he charges only 75 per cent of the schedule fee), you won't need to pay anything. You'll also be charged for hospital accommodation and items such as theatre fees and medicines (as applicable). These costs may be recovered from your private health insurance, although you should check with your insurer prior to admission. If you don't have private health insurance, you'll be asked to pay the estimated costs at the time of admission. The average charge for a private bed is around $225 per day in a public hospital and almost $600 per day in a private hospital, where prices have increased greatly in recent years.

Private patients are usually provided with single rooms equipped with all the comforts of home, including radio, TV, telephone, en suite bathroom and room service. If you're a private patient, you can choose the hospital and your attending doctor and surgeon, although if you want your own doctor to treat you in a public hospital there's a daily 'accommodation' charge. Note that doctors treating patients in private hospitals bill them independently. When you leave hospital, you'll generally be asked to pay the difference (if any) between your health insurer's refund and the hospital fees. Since mid-1998, patients in private hospitals have been given a quotation for the cost of surgery and out-of-pocket expenses and generally receive one or two bills for the total cost although some hospitals still prefer to charge separately for different treatments and care.

# CHILDBIRTH

Childbirth in Australia usually takes place in a hospital labour ward or birth centre (a small unit normally located in the grounds of a hospital), where a stay of up to five days is usual (although many women leave hospital within three days of giving birth). Public hospitals are under pressure to discharge mothers earlier, and even privately insured mothers are being encouraged to cut their hospital stay in exchange for lower maternity (e.g. obstetrician) bills. If you wish to have a child at home, you must find a doctor or midwife (see below) who's willing to attend you. Some doctors are opposed to home births, particularly in cases where there could be complications (many births in Australia are induced) and when specialists and special facilities (e.g. incubators) may be required. You can hire a private midwife to attend you at home throughout and after your pregnancy. Few people in Australia choose to give birth at home.

Medicare patients are usually unable to choose the hospital where they have their baby, nor their obstetrician. Note that, if you have private health insurance, your insurer will generally cover around 75 per cent of costs and fees. The remaining 25 per cent is made up by Medicare and the individual. If you have a choice, find out as much as possible about local hospital methods and policies concerning childbirth, either directly or from friends or neighbours, before booking a bed. The policy regarding a father's attendance at a birth varies with the hospital. A husband doesn't have the right to be present with his wife during labour or childbirth, which is at the consultant's discretion. If the presence of your husband or partner is important to you, you should check that it's permitted at the hospital where you plan to have your baby and any other rules that may be in force. Women who don't speak English often have problems and are generally dissatisfied with their hospital treatment during pregnancy; interpreters are rarely provided, and information isn't usually published in foreign languages.

Midwives (nurses with specialist training) are responsible for educating and supporting women and their families during the childbearing period. They can advise women before they become pregnant, in addition to providing moral, physical and emotional support throughout a pregnancy and after the birth. Your midwife may also advise on parent education and antenatal classes for mothers. Note that antenatal classes, which used to be free, now have to be paid for, although this is usually covered under private insurance. There are Maternal and Child Health Centres in some states (e.g. Victoria), funded by the state government or local councils. However, there's a dearth of services for new mothers in many areas and post-natal care may be patchy or even non-existent, new mothers being left to their own devices.

**Further Information:** Family planning associations provide free teaching, counselling and related services. There are many publications for mothers, including *New Mother's Handbook* published for Melbourne and Sydney (Universal Magazines, Unit 56-8, Byfield Street, North Ryde, NSW 2113) and *The New Good Birth Guide* by Sheila Kitzinger (Penguin).

# BIRTHS & DEATHS

Births in Australia must be registered with the Registrar of Births, Deaths and Marriages within 60 days (even when a child is stillborn). When birth takes place in a hospital, parents are given the relevant form to register the birth. In the case of home births, a form can be obtained from a hospital or from the Registrar of Births. A child born to an unmarried mother is usually registered in her name but can be registered in the father's name if both parents agree. The birth of a child to foreign parents or the death of a foreigner in Australia may need to be reported to a consulate or embassy, e.g. to obtain a national birth certificate and passport for a child or to register a death in the deceased's home country. If you need to obtain a copy of a birth, marriage or death certificate, the cheapest way is to apply to the registrar in the state or territory where it was registered.

**Deaths:** When someone dies in Australia, it must be reported to the Registrar of Births, Deaths and Marriages within a certain period, which is usually 21 days. The registrar is normally notified directly by the hospital authorities when a death occurs in a hospital. He decides whether to issue a death certificate after obtaining a medical certificate and other details concerning the deceased. If someone dies suddenly, accidentally, during an operation, in unusual circumstances, or the cause of death is unknown, the registrar will notify the police and/or a coroner, who will decide whether an autopsy is necessary to determine the cause of death.

The registrar will need to know the personal details of the deceased, including his date and place of birth and death, marriage details (if applicable) and whether he was receiving a state pension or any welfare benefits. The registrar then issues a death certificate, which authorises the funeral to take place. The certificate must be given to a funeral director (or undertaker) to organise the burial or cremation, or you can arrange for the body to be shipped to another country for burial. You may wish to announce a death in a local or national newspaper, giving the date, time and place of the funeral and your wishes concerning flowers or contributions to a charity.

In the event of the death of a resident of Australia, all interested parties must be notified (see **Chapter 20**). You'll need a number of copies of the death certificate, e.g. for the proving of the will (probate), pension claims, insurance companies and financial institutions. A brochure, *What To Do When Someone Dies*, is available from Centrelink (☎ local call rate 13-2850).

**Funeral Costs:** Traditional funerals are expensive in Australia, where cremation costs an average of around $3,500 and burial around $4,000 (undertakers only get one bite of the cherry and have to make the most of it!). A grave plot (which are in short supply in some cities) can cost anything from $400 to $3,000 plus digging fees of around $400 to $900. Note that the tenure on a plot may be indefinite or limited, e.g. from 25 to 99 years, after which you must make an additional payment if you wish to retain the plot. You can pay in advance for your funeral through a variety of 'pay-now-die-later' schemes, with price and service guaranteed, although there are no legal safeguards and the prepaid funeral trade is rife with fraud, mismanagement and over-selling. If you want to have a body buried overseas or have someone who died overseas buried in Australia, the body will probably need to be transported by air, which can be *very* expensive.

# DENTISTS

There are excellent dentists in cities and towns throughout Australia, although they're thin on the ground in country areas. There's no need to register with a dentist in Australia, and the best way to find a good one is to ask your colleagues, friends or neighbours (particularly those with perfect teeth) if they can recommend someone. Dentists are listed under 'Dental Surgeons' in the yellow pages and are permitted to advertise any special services they provide such as emergency or 24-hour answering services, a dental hygienist, and evening or weekend surgeries. There are mobile dentists in some country regions, and in remote areas emergency dental services are provided via the flying doctor service. Many family dentists in Australia are qualified to perform treatment such as endodontics or periodontics, carried out by specialists in many other countries.

General dental services aren't funded by Medicare, although it pays for 75 per cent of in-hospital medical procedures performed by an oral surgeon. The cost of dental treatment has risen considerably in recent years, and charges, which vary with the area and the dentist, can be very high. Most dentists accept payment by credit card (plus gold, diamonds, bearer bonds, etc.). Dental teaching hospitals in the major cities treat patients for less than private dentists, although you may be something of a guinea pig. Pensioners and the unemployed with a Medicare concession card are entitled to free general and emergency dental treatment under the Commonwealth Dental Health Program, although there are waiting times of up to two years for treatment! Children in some states receive free school dental care. Note that, if you miss a dental appointment without giving 24 hours' notice, your dentist may charge you a standard fee. Information about dental fees can be obtained from the Australian Dental Association, PO Box 520, St Leonards, NSW 1590 (🖥 www.ada.org.au). For information about **Dental Insurance** see page 317.

# OPTOMETRISTS

As with dentists, there's no need to register with an optometrist or optician. You simply make an appointment with anyone of your choice, although it's sensible to ask your colleagues, friends or neighbours if they can recommend someone. Opticians and optometrists are listed in the yellow pages, where they may advertise their services.

There are three kinds of professionals providing eye care in Australia. The most highly qualified is an ophthalmologist, who's a specialist physician trained in diagnosing and treating disorders of the eye. In addition to performing eye surgery and prescribing drugs, he may also perform sight tests and prescribe spectacles and contact lenses. You may be referred to an ophthalmologist by an optometrist or your GP. Optometrists are licensed to examine eyes, prescribe corrective lenses, and dispense spectacles and contact lenses. They're also trained to detect eye diseases and may prescribe drugs and treatment. An optician is not the same as an optometrist (as in some other countries) and may not examine eyes or prescribe lenses; opticians are licensed to fill prescriptions written by optometrists and ophthalmologists and to fit and adjust spectacles. There are also optical retail chain stores in Australia, where you can have spectacles made within an hour. Note that you aren't required to buy your spectacles or contact lenses from the optometrist who tests your sight, and he must give you your prescription at no extra charge.

The eye care business is very competitive in Australia and, unless someone is highly recommended, you should shop around for the best deal. Prices for both spectacles and contact lenses vary considerably, so it's wise to compare costs (although make sure you're comparing like with like) before committing yourself to a large bill. Special offers are common such as 'buy a new pair of spectacles and receive a spare pair free'. Note, however, that the lowest prices and special deals aren't necessarily the best value. Always ask about extra charges for eye examinations, fittings, adjustments, lens-care kits, follow-up visits and the cost of replacement lenses (if they're expensive, it may be worthwhile taking out insurance). Many opticians offer insurance against the accidental damage of spectacles for a nominal fee. Medicare pays for 85 per cent of the cost of eye tests by optometrists.

Many Australians wears contact lenses. Disposable (one-day) and extended-wear (e.g. one or three months) contact lenses are widely available, although most medical experts believe that extended-wear lenses should be approached with extreme caution, as they greatly increase the risk of potentially blinding eye infections. **Obtain advice from a doctor or eye specialist before buying them.** Soft contact lenses or spectacles (frames and lenses) can be purchased in Australia from around $150 to 200 (usually inclusive of an eye examination).

It's best to have your eyes tested before your arrival in Australia and to bring a spare pair of spectacles or contact lenses with you (also bring a copy of your prescription in case you need to obtain replacements in a hurry).

# COUNSELLING

Counselling and assistance for health and social problems is available under Medicare and from many community groups and volunteer organisations, ranging from national associations to small local groups (including self-help groups). Local authorities provide social workers to advise and support those requiring help within their community. If you need to find help locally, you can contact your local council, local voluntary services or a citizens' advice bureau. A list of 24-hour emergency services (including many counselling services) is included at the front of both white and yellow pages, as are community help and welfare services, and help for young people.

Many colleges and educational establishments provide a counselling service for students, and general hospitals have a psychiatrist on call 24 hours a day. Problems for which help is available are numerous and include drug rehabilitation, alcoholism (e.g. Alcoholics Anonymous), gambling, dieting (e.g. Weight Watchers), smoking, attempted suicide and psychiatric problems, homosexuality-related problems, youth problems, rape and battering, marriage and relationship counselling, and rape.

Trained counsellors provide advice and help for sufferers from various diseases (e.g. multiple sclerosis and muscular dystrophy) and the disabled (e.g. the blind and deaf). They also help very sick and terminally ill patients (e.g. cancer, leukaemia and AIDS sufferers) and their families come to terms with their situation. A number of voluntary organisations and local authorities run refuges for battered wives (and their children) or maltreated children, whose conditions have become intolerable (some provide 24-hour emergency phone numbers). If you or a member of your family are the victims of a violent crime, the police will usually put you in touch with a local victim support scheme.

In times of need there's nearly always someone to turn to, and all services are strictly confidential. In major towns, counselling may be available in your own language if you don't speak English. If you need help desperately, someone speaking your language will usually be found. Lifeline (☎ 13-1114) provides a confidential, 24-hour counselling service in periods of personal crisis (e.g. for the lonely, desperate and suicidal) throughout Australia for the cost of a local call. There's also a freecall Women's Information Service (☎ 1800-817227). Many councils publish a directory of children's and family services.

# DRUG & ALCOHOL ABUSE

Drug abuse is an increasingly serious problem in Australia, where it's estimated that heroin users alone spend around $3 billion per year on the drug (it also costs the country around $1.66 billion per year to deal with the problem). The average beginner is just 14 and the average time between take-up and death is around ten years (some 1,000 people die each year from drug abuse). Cannabis is the most widely taken drug, followed by amphetamines, ectasy and hallucinogens. The use of so-called hard drugs is less, although heroin overdoses account for three-quarters of drug-related deaths. Cannabis (pot) and marijuana are widely grown and smoked throughout Australia, where each state has its own laws regarding the use (or abuse) of these drugs (see **Crime** on page 451).

The National Campaign Against Drug Abuse (NCADA) was established in 1985 to reduce the use of both legal and illegal drugs through community education, drug education programmes for parents and children, and professional training. The campaign had a budget of $27.5 million in 2001 and was particularly aimed at schools. However, despite the NCADA campaign and increased vigilance by police and customs officers to reduce the supply of drugs from overseas (particularly heroin), large amounts of drugs are still being imported into Australia (mostly via Sydney).

Many people believe that the authorities are fighting a losing battle against the drug barons and that universal prohibition has actually increased consumption. Some experts would like to relax Australia's tough prohibitionist drug policies, although it's impossible without the USA's approval (and it has the opposite opinion, even though its uncompromising measures have proved an abject failure). Some people in the judiciary and police believe that punishing drug-users via the criminal justice system is debasing the legal system, and that they should be treated in hospitals. Plans to give free drugs to addicts in a controlled programme (as pioneered in Switzerland) have been strongly opposed by the USA.

Many government and voluntary organisations provide drug advice and rehabilitation services, including residential facilities. There are government-run detoxification units in the major cities, where there are also voluntary groups providing counselling and support for drug users, their relatives and friends (see your local white or yellow pages). There's also a national Children's Help Line (☎ freecall 1800-551800). If you can afford to pay for private treatment, a number of private clinics and hospitals specialise in treating people for drug, alcohol and substance abuse, and other health problems.

**Alcohol:** Drunkenness and alcoholism are rife in Australia, where it's estimated that more than 6,000 Australians die each year from alcohol-related causes (including some 30 per cent of road deaths). Apart from the direct or indirect loss of life, alcohol abuse costs Australian industry $millions per year in lost production through absenteeism, and it's also a serious problem among children. The government has instituted a national alcohol programme to warn people of the dangers of excessive drinking. Alcoholics Anonymous has self-help groups throughout Australia (see your telephone book).

# SMOKING

As in most countries, smoking contributes to a huge loss of life and working days in Australia, although the number of smokers has steadily decreased over the last few decades to around 20 per cent of men and women and it's thought that by 2002 Australia will be the first country in the world with a smoking rate of less than 20 per cent. The dramatic reduction is due in part to the massive uptake of the anti-smoking drug Zyban, subsidised by the government from February 2001. In the first three months of its listing on the Pharmaceutical Benefits Scheme, some 165,000 prescriptions were written costing the taxpayer $40 million. Nevertheless, some 20,000 people die annually in Australia from smoking-related illnesses, costing the state around $13 billion per year in health care, which has prompted some two-thirds of Australians (presumably all non-smokers) to think that smokers should pay a higher Medicare levy. However, although smokers place a higher burden on Medicare, they also die younger and it has been calculated that the life-long health costs of smokers are actually less than those for non-smokers in some countries!

It's estimated that some 20 per cent of pregnant women continue to smoke throughout their pregnancies, despite the dangers to their unborn child. An anti-smoking campaign ('Smoking, Who Needs It?') launched in 1990 aims to reduce smoking among young women in particular. In fact, smokers are under siege on all fronts in Australia, and the Australian Medical Association has called on federal and state governments to sue tobacco companies to recoup the health costs of smoking. As in many other countries, tobacco companies face huge bills as a result of court cases brought by smokers for smoking-induced illnesses such as cancer. Over three-quarters of Australia's top companies restrict smoking (and the consumption of alcohol) in the workplace, around half enforcing a total ban on smoking at work and a third having restricted areas where employees are permitted to smoke. It's legal for employers to specify in job advertisements whether they will hire smokers (employers are fearful of law suits from non-smokers).

In recent years, there has been increasing concern about passive smoking (known as 'environmental tobacco smoke'), where non-smokers involuntarily inhale the smoke created by smokers, although it hasn't generated the paranoia seen in the USA (where anyone who smokes in a public place is liable to be summarily executed). The National Health and Medical Research Council has recommended a statutory ban in all enclosed public spaces outside the home. However, the anti-smoking lobby is gaining ground fast: in September 2000, smoking was banned in dining areas in all clubs and hotels, and many restaurants and pubs already have smoking and non-smoking sections; in 2001, legal history was made when a barmaid in NSW who contracted throat cancer as a result of passive smoking in the bar where she worked for eight years, was awarded more than $300,000 in damages. There's a smoking ban on Australia's international airlines and on all domestic flights, and in some states smoking is prohibited on all public transport. The attitude towards smoking varies from state to state: Queensland is the most lenient, while the ACT is the toughest and has introduced laws against smoking in all enclosed public places, including shopping malls, hotels, restaurants, cafés, bars, pubs, clubs and sports stadiums. This policy is likely to be adopted by other states, although in mid-2001 many had failed to commit themselves to a timetable for its introduction.

Action on Smoking and Health (ASH) provides advice on giving up smoking and information on the rights of non-smokers, and the anti-smoking group QUIT produces leaflets in 13 languages (National Quit Line ☎ local call rate 13-1848). There are also non-smoking clinics and self-help groups throughout Australia to assist those wishing to stop smoking. Contact your local health authority for information.

# SEXUALLY TRANSMITTED DISEASES

Like most western countries, Australia has its fair share of sexually transmitted diseases (STDs), including the deadly Acquired Immune Deficiency Syndrome (AIDS). The furore over AIDS has died down in the past few years, which many fear may cause those most at risk to be lulled into a false sense of security (many Australian teenagers still practise unsafe sex). The explosion of AIDS predicted by many 'experts' hasn't materialised, particularly among the heterosexual population, although the number of heterosexual cases is increasing. There are around 660 deaths from AIDS annually in Australia. **AIDS is always fatal and to date there's no cure.** All blood used in transfusions in Australia is screened for the human immunodeficiency virus (HIV), which usually leads to AIDS. A total of around 17,600 cases of HIV had been officially recorded in Australia up to the end of 1998, mostly among homosexual men (Sydney, Melbourne and Adelaide have thriving gay communities), around a third of whom were later diagnosed as having AIDS. In recent years, there has been a major education campaign to warn people of the risks of AIDS (the fourth campaign was launched in 2001), during which the number of HIV cases has fallen.

The spread of AIDS is accelerated by the sharing of syringes by drug addicts, among whom AIDS is rampant (many of Australia's heroin addicts are infected with HIV). In an effort to reduce syringe sharing among HIV-positive drug addicts, free needles (and condoms) are distributed to drug addicts. The spread of AIDS is also accelerated by prostitutes, many of whom are also drug addicts, although the vast majority of people diagnosed with AIDS and HIV infection in Australia are men with a history of homosexual contact. The best protection against AIDS (and other STDs) is a condom, although they're not failsafe (against AIDS or pregnancy) and the only guaranteed protection is abstinence (or 'NO!'). Condoms are on sale at chemists, some supermarkets, men's hairdressers, and vending machines in public toilets in pubs and other places.

Public hospitals and clinics provide free tests, treatment and advice for STDs and AIDS. All cases of AIDS and HIV-positive blood tests in Australia must be reported to the local health authorities (patients remain anonymous). If you wish to talk to someone in confidence about AIDS, there are many organisations and self-help groups providing information, advice and support in all areas (see your local telephone book).

# 13.

# INSURANCE

The Australian government and Australian law stipulate various obligatory state and employer insurance and benefit schemes. These include health, sickness, work injuries and disability insurance, state and private (superannuation) pensions, maternity and unemployment benefit. Australia is a nation of gamblers, which is reflected in the relatively low level of insurance, even for basic contingencies, e.g. loss of income insurance, life assurance, and comprehensive insurance for cars, buildings and home contents. Many people tend to (or have to) rely on state insurance and benefits (social security), including sickness allowance, unemployment benefit, state pensions, additional family payments, income support, and maternity allowance. Note, however, that social security provides only for the most basic needs.

Most Australians and foreign residents and their families receive health treatment under Medicare (see page 283), the public health system. If you don't qualify for Medicare, it's essential to have private health insurance, which is obligatory for some temporary residents. If you're coming to Australia from overseas, you'd be wise to ensure that your family has comprehensive health insurance during the period between leaving your last country of residence and arriving in Australia. This is particularly important if a private health insurance in your home country doesn't cover you overseas. One way is to take out a travel insurance policy. However, it's usually better to extend your present health insurance policy, if possible, particularly if you have existing health problems which may not be covered by a new policy.

There are only a few cases in Australia when insurance for individuals is compulsory, including building insurance if you have a mortgage (because your lender will insist on it) and third party motor insurance (CTP), which is required by law. If you're an employee you must also belong to a superannuation fund. You may also need third party and accident insurance for high-risk sports. Voluntary insurance includes accident, income protection, private health, home contents, personal liability, legal expenses, dental, travel, motor breakdown and life insurance.

It isn't necessary to spend half your income insuring yourself against every eventuality from the common cold to being sued for your last cent, but it's important to be covered for any event which could precipitate a major financial disaster (such as a serious accident or your house falling down). **As with everything to do with finance, it's imperative to shop around when buying insurance.** Just picking up a few brochures from insurance agents and making a few phone calls could save you a lot of money (enough to pay for this book many times over). Regrettably, you cannot insure yourself against being uninsured or sue your insurance broker for giving you bad advice! It's your responsibility to ensure that your family is legally insured in Australia. **Note that Australian law may be very different from that in your home country or your previous country of residence, and you should never assume that it's the same.**

If you want to make a claim against a third party or a third party is claiming against you, you'd be wise to seek legal advice for anything other than a minor claim. Bear in mind that if you wish to make a claim on an insurance policy, you may be required (in some cases by law) to report an incident to the police within 24 hours.

Note that information in this chapter is intended only as a guide, as the rules regarding insurance matters are constantly changing, particularly social security, superannuation and health insurance. You should therefore obtain the latest information from the appropriate authorities or an insurance company in Australia. See also **Car Insurance** on page 251 and **Motor Breakdown Insurance** on page 275.

# INSURANCE COMPANIES

There are numerous insurance companies in Australia, providing either a range of insurance services or specialising in certain fields. You can buy insurance from many sources, including traditional insurance companies selling through their own salesmen or independent brokers, direct insurance companies (selling direct to the public), banks and other financial institutions, and motoring organisations. The major insurance companies have offices or agents (brokers) throughout Australia, including most large towns, and most of them will provide a free analysis of your family or business insurance needs.

**Brokers:** If you choose a broker, you should use one who is independent and sells policies from a wide range of insurance companies. Some brokers or agents and most banks are tied to a particular insurance company and sell policies only from that company. An independent broker should research the whole market and take into account your particular requirements, why you're investing (if applicable), the various companies' financial performance, what you can afford, and the type of policy that's best for you. He mustn't offer you a policy because it pays him the highest commission, which incidentally you should ask him about (particularly regarding life assurance).

**Direct Insurance:** In recent years, direct marketing and direct response insurance companies (bypassing brokers) have resulted in huge savings for consumers, particularly for car, building and home contents insurance. Direct marketing companies give quotations over the phone; often you aren't even required to complete a proposal form. Compare premiums from a number of direct sales insurance companies with the best deals from brokers before choosing a policy.

**Shop Around:** When buying insurance, you should shop 'til you drop and then shop around some more! Premiums vary considerably (e.g. by up to 100 or 200 per cent), although you must ensure that you're comparing similar policies and that important benefits haven't been omitted. Bear in mind that the cheapest policy isn't necessarily the best, particularly regarding the prompt payment of claims. Many analysts believe that it's better to pay for independent insurance advice rather than accept 'free' advice, which may be more expensive in the long run. You should obtain a number of quotations for each insurance need and shouldn't assume that your existing insurance company is the best choice for a new insurance requirement. Buy only the insurance that you *want* and *need* and ensure that you can afford the payments (and that your cover is protected if you're sick or unemployed).

# INSURANCE CONTRACTS

Read all insurance contracts carefully before signing them. If you don't understand everything, ask a friend or colleague to 'translate' it or obtain professional advice. Policies often contain traps and legal loopholes in the small print. If a policy has pages of legal jargon and gobbledegook in *very* small print, you have a right to be suspicious, particularly as it's common practice nowadays to be as brief as possible and write clearly and concisely in language which doesn't require a doctorate in law. Take care how you answer questions on an insurance proposal form; even if you unintentionally provide false information, an insurance company can refuse to pay out when you make a claim.

Most insurance policies run for a calendar year from the date on which you take out a policy. All insurance policy premiums should be paid punctually, as late payment can affect your benefits or a claim, although if this is so it should be noted in your policy. Before signing an insurance policy, you should shop around and take a day or two to think it over (never sign on the spot, as you may regret it later). With some insurance contracts, you may have a 'cooling off' period during which you can cancel a policy without penalty.

**Claims:** Although insurance companies are keen to take your money, many aren't nearly so happy to settle claims. Like insurance companies everywhere, some Australian insurance companies will do almost anything to avoid paying out in the event of a claim and will use any available loophole. Fraud is estimated to cost the insurance industry $millions a year (particularly motor insurance fraud), and staff may be trained to automatically assume that claims are fraudulent. If you wish to make a claim, you must usually inform your insurance company in writing by registered letter within a number of days of the incident (possibly within 24 hours in the case of theft). **Failure to do so will render your claim void!** Don't send original bills or documents regarding a claim to your insurance company unless it's absolutely necessary (you can send a certified copy). Keep a copy of all bills, documents and correspondence, and always send letters by registered mail so that your insurance company cannot deny receipt.

Don't bank a cheque received in settlement of a claim if you think it's insufficient, as you may be deemed to have accepted it as full and final settlement. Don't accept the first offer made, as many insurance companies try to get away with making a low settlement (if an insurer pays what you have claimed without a quibble, you probably claimed too little!). When dealing with insurance companies, perseverance often pays. Insurers are increasingly refusing to pay up on the flimsiest of pretexts, as they know that many people won't pursue their cases, even when they have a valid claim. Don't give up on a claim if you're sure you have a good case, but persist until you have exhausted every avenue. If you cannot reach agreement, you can contact Insurance Enquiries and Complaints (☎ local call rate 1300-363683, 💻 www. iec.ltd.com.au) for independent arbitration or take legal action.

# SOCIAL SECURITY

Social security (welfare) is the name given to state benefits paid to residents in Australia. Social security is non-contributory and is financed from general taxation (although there's a taxation levy for Medicare), and comprises around 25 per cent of GDP. Australia has one of the most comprehensive social security systems in the world, which has engendered widespread welfare dependency, around a third of all Australians relying on welfare payments as their main source of income (half of whom are pensioners). In the period 1998–99, social security payments totalled around $53 billion. Nevertheless, many people fail to apply for allowances and pensions to which they're entitled. If you apply and your application is rejected, you can ask for the decision to be reviewed by an Authorised Review Officer (ARO); if it's turned down again, you can appeal to the Social Security Appeals Tribunal and finally to the Administrative Appeals Tribunal.

**Fraud:** Social security fraud is huge, although the government has cracked down in recent years, during which many people have lost their benefits or had them reduced (many have also been prosecuted). More than 2,000 people are convicted of cheating the welfare system every year at huge cost to taxpayers. Many people are found to be receiving too much in payments as well as many receiving too little. The most common form of welfare fraud is people claiming unemployment benefit while working. Many cheats are discovered through tip-offs from the public under the government's confidential 'dob in a dole bludger' initiative. Another method used to detect fraudsters is data-matching between Centrelink and the Australian Tax Office.

**Income & Means Tests:** Eligibility for most social security benefits is subject to an income and/or means test. The poorest 10 per cent of Australians receive some 600 per cent more in government payments than the richest 10 per cent over their lifetime. If you're found to have sufficient income or assets after a means test, your social security payments will be reduced or terminated. Assets which are means tested include most investments but not belongings such as your principal home, cars, holiday homes, antiques and superannuation pensions. Financial investments are deemed to earn a certain income (adjusted annually).

**New Migrants:** Since 4th March 1997, migrants have had to wait 104 weeks (any time spent in Australia as an Australian resident can be counted towards this period) before they can claim most social security payments, although refugees and humanitarian entrants are exempt from the waiting period. Migrants can, however, claim Special Benefit or Widow's Allowance in exceptional circumstances and are eligible for the minimum rate of Family Payment (see below) during the two-year waiting period. Migrants also have access to Medicare during their first two years in Australia. Note that some sponsors of migrants need to provide an Assurance of Support (see page 84), which makes them liable to repay the government if certain welfare benefits are paid to the migrant during his first two years (ten years for children sponsoring a parent who's within ten years of retirement).

According to the Welfare Rights Centre, the two-year waiting period for welfare has caused some migrants to become destitute and homeless, and there have been calls to have it suspended or cancelled, although these have so far been unsuccessful. A NSW Ethnic Communities Council survey discovered that more than two-thirds of newly arrived migrants were unaware that they couldn't claim benefits for two years. Migrant service units monitor and review services to migrants and refugees and liaise with ethnic and voluntary groups, and there are also migrant resource centres in the major towns and cities. Settlement support is provided for migrants with genuine financial problems.

**Benefits:** The main beneficiaries are the aged and disabled, single parents, those who are unemployed, sick or in special need, and families with children. Benefits include a disability support pension, double orphan pension, carer pension, child disability allowance, sheltered employment and rehabilitation allowances, parenting or guardian allowance (if a single parent), newstart allowance, youth training allowance, sickness allowance, mobility allowance, multiple birth payment (triplets or more), pharmaceutical allowance, rent assistance, parenting allowance, partner allowance, widow allowance, bereavement allowance, family tax payment, maternity allowance and a health care card. A discretionary payment (called a special benefit) may be paid to those who aren't eligible for other forms of assistance but are unable to support themselves.

The federal and state governments jointly fund a wide range of welfare services relating to home care for the elderly and disabled and their families. Some 1,500 nursing homes (around a fifth are state run) and around 1,000 hostels receive federal support to provide residential care for elderly people. A federal government disability services programme funds organisations to provide services that help people with disabilities maintain their independence and achieve their potential. The Commonwealth Rehabilitation Service employs a number of specialists to work with disabled people to help them return to economic and social independence.

**Information:** A range of publications detailing social security allowances, benefits and pensions are available from Social Security offices and community organisations. The Department of Social Security provides a telephone enquiry service on ☎ 13-2468 or 13-1202 for languages other than English. Calls are charged at local call rates from anywhere in Australia. For more information contact the Department of Family and Community Services (FaCS), PO Box 7788, Canberra Mail Centre, ACT 2610 (☎ local call rate 1300-654227, 🖳 www.facs.gov.au).

# Family Payments

All family payments were transferred in 2000 from Centrelink to a new government department, called Family Assistance. Family payments are available to parents or guardians with dependent children, including those who are full-time students but aren't in receipt of an Austudy or Abstudy allowance. The amount paid depends on the age and number of children in the family and the family's total income. Payments are usually made fortnightly into the mother's bank account, although if you have large expenses such as school uniforms it's possible to receive part of the payment in a lump sum in advance twice a year (January and July). Families with low incomes may also receive a supplement. Under the Family Tax Benefit A scheme, the maximum family payment per fortnight in 2001 was $116.20 for each child under 13, $147.28 for each child aged 13 to 15, $37.38 for each child aged 16 to 17 and $50.12 for each full-time student under 24. Under Family Tax Benefit Scheme B the maximum family payment per fortnight in 2001 was $99.82 for each child under 5 and $69.58 for each child under 15 or aged 16 to 18 if a full-time student. The base rate of Family Tax Benefit is $37.38 for each child under 18 and $50.12 for each full-time student aged 18 to 24. There's also a Large Family Supplement under which you receive $7.98 extra per fortnight for the fourth and each subsequent child.

Family Tax Benefits are subject to an income test (unless your taxable income is less than $28,200 a year) whereby, if your annual income is over $28,200 per year, your payments are reduced by 30 per cent for every dollar over this amount until they reach the base rate. Your payments remain at the base rate until your income is over $73,000 per year, when payments are reduced further by 30¢ for every dollar over this amount. Family payment and other payments for children aren't taxable. Note that one-parent families receive the maximum amount of Family Tax Benefit B regardless of income.

**Child Care Benefit:** Child Care Benefit is available for parents whose children are in registered or approved care while the parents are working, actively looking for work or studying. Benefit is also available for school children in after-school care, although you receive a maximum of 85 per cent of the full amount. Depending on the type of care your child is in, you can receive Child Care Benefit from 20 to 50 hours a week. If your annual income is under $28,856, you receive full benefit; otherwise the benefit is subject to an income test.

**Maternity Allowance:** A Maternity Allowance is now available in respect of all new babies and all adopted babies aged under 26 weeks. To qualify for this allowance you must also qualify for Family Tax Benefit A (see above) before 13 weeks after the birth or adoption. The income tested allowance is paid as a lump sum of $780 (2001) and is usually paid at the same time as the first installment of Family Tax Benefit A.

For full information on family benefits you should contact the Family Assistance office (☎ local rate call 13-6150, 🖳 www.familyassist.gov.au).

# Unemployment Benefits

Australia has no unemployment benefit or 'dole' as such, but payments are made under the Jobsearch or Newstart schemes. If you're unemployed, you must register with the Department of Social Security where, provided you qualify, you'll be given a form to complete and lodge within 14 days. You must provide proof of identity and your tax file number. If you've been terminated (sacked, retrenched, etc.) from a previous position, you'll need your Employment Separation Certificate, which states the reason you left work and your wages. For new immigrants there's a two-year waiting period before payments start. If you remain unemployed for more than a year, you must apply for the Newstart Allowance. Rates of payment depend on individual circumstances, including your age, marital status and number of children. In 2001, payments ranged from $357.80 per fortnight for a single person over 21 with no dependent children to $645.60 per fortnight for a couple aged over 21 with children. Payments are subject to asset and income tests. Note that neither jobsearch nor newstart allowances aren paid during an absence from Australia.

**Jobsearch Allowance:** To qualify you must either be aged under 18 or have been registered with the DSS for a year or less, have permanent residence status and be actively looking for work. You must also convince the DSS that you're looking for work or that you're improving your job prospects by attending training or educational classes. To receive payments you must report in writing to the DSS every two weeks on your job searching activities. This is called the 'activity test' and, if you don't have good reason for not meeting the requirements, your allowance will be stopped.

**Newstart Allowance:** To qualify you must be aged over 21, a permanent resident, unemployed and have been registered with the DSS for over a year. You must also be actively searching for work. In your initial interview with the DSS you must sign an undertaking agreeing to a plan of action to improve your employment prospects. Refusal to sign the agreement will limit or nullify your chances of qualifying for the allowance. You must also report to the DSS every two weeks. The newstart allowance is usually paid from the day the jobsearch allowance (see above) stops, if applicable. The income and assets tests for jobsearch and newstart allowances are the same, as are the rates.

**Work Experience:** In an attempt to improve employment prospects, unemployed people aged 18 to 34 years who have been receiving a newstart allowance for six to 12 months can be obliged to do work experience, mainly on local projects or in community service. They receive an extra $20.80 per fortnight. In July 2002, an Australians Working Together package will come into effect, under which unemployed people will be encouraged to take up jobs by allowing them to keep more of their income support payments when they start work. There will be new requirements for income support benefits, and beneficiaries will be obliged to take up opportunities to help them become 'job-ready'.

# State Pensions

State pensions are paid to men at 65 years of age and women at 62, although the pensionable age for women is gradually being increased to 65. The qualifying age was first raised from 60 to 60.5 years on 1st July 1995, and it will be further increased by six months at two-year intervals until 1st July 2013, when it will reach 65 (in fact, it will be 65 for anyone born on 1st January 1949 or later). A full Australian pension is payable after 25 years' residence during a person's working life, which is reckoned to be between the ages of 16 and 65 for men and 16 and 60+ for women. You generally need to have lived continuously in Australia for ten years to qualify for a state retirement pension. However, Australia has reciprocal social security agreements with some countries (including Austria, Canada, Cyprus, Denmark, Ireland, Italy, Malta, the Netherlands, Portugal and Spain), which may enable newcomers to receive a pension as soon as they reach pensionable age, irrespective of their residence period. Note that Britain no longer has a reciprocal social security agreement with Australia (see **UK Pensioners** below).

In addition to the basic retirement pension, various other pensions are paid in Australia, including pensions for wives, widows, single parents, double orphans (i.e. both of whose parents are deceased), carers, people with disabilities, and people who have been bereaved. All pensions are paid at the same rates (listed below) and most are subject to an income and assets test. Other social security payments may be paid in addition to the retirement pension. There are also occasionally one-off payments such as the $300 received by eligible low income pensioners in 2001.

Unlike state pensions in most countries, which are paid irrespective of a person's wealth or income, most Australian pensions are subject to income and assets tests (the test which produces the lower rate of pension applies!). This is the case for all pensions except invalid pensions for permanently blind persons and pensions for war and defence widows. Around 30 per cent of Australians are considered too wealthy to receive a state pension. In 2001, a full retirement pension was $402 per fortnight for a single person and $335.50 each for a married couple.

**Income Test:** Under the income test, a full pension is paid if your gross income doesn't exceed $106 per fortnight for a single person or $188 per fortnight for a couple, plus an additional $24.60 for each child. For each dollar earned above these amounts, the fortnightly pension payment is reduced by 40¢ for single people and 20¢ each for couples. Therefore, no payment is made if your fortnightly income exceeds $1,111 (single without children) or $1,193 (couple without children). A private pension (whether in Australia or from overseas) counts as income and may therefore reduce your state pension.

**Assets Test:** Under the assets test, the pension you receive depends on your status and on the market value of your assessable assets (which are indexed annually) as shown below:

| Status | Maximum Asset Value For Full Pension | For Part Pension |
|---|---|---|
| single homeowner | $133,250 | $267,250 |
| single non-homeowner | $228,750 | $362,750 |
| married homeowner couple | $189,500 | $413,166 |
| married non-homeowner couple | $285,000 | $508,666 |

Your pension is reduced by $3 per fortnight for every $1,000 of assets above the 'full pension' limits listed above, so that you receive no pension if your assets are above the 'part pension' amounts (i.e. $134,000 above the maximum value for a full pension in the case of single people and $223,666 for couples). There's no assets test for those aged over 70. The assets test doesn't include your principal family home or the land on which it's built up to two hectares (provided it's used for domestic purposes). Prepaid funeral expenses and aids for the disabled such as wheelchairs are also excluded (what generosity!). The retirement pension is taxable but on its own is below the tax threshold. State pensions are indexed twice a year in line with changes in the Consumer Price Index (CPI). Pensions are pegged at 25 per cent of average male earnings to ensure that the rates keep pace with the rest of the community.

In order to claim a pension, you require at least three original documents which prove your identity, details of all bank, building society and credit union accounts, and any other money you have invested, and your latest rent receipts, rent book or other proof of the amount paid if you're paying private rent. The documentation should be brought with you when lodging a claim, although it can be provided later. If you're married (or have a *de facto* partner), you should bring your partner with you and he must also complete a form, prove his identity and provide details of his assets.

You can choose the day on which you want your pension paid in order to eliminate peak times at DSS offices and banks. Pensions are usually paid into a bank, building society or credit union account. Australian pensions can be paid overseas, although pensioners going overseas for longer than six months must obtain a pre-departure certificate from social security. If the period overseas is expected to be a year or more, pension payments may be sent to an overseas address. Under reciprocal agreements with other countries, a full Australian pension is payable after 25 years' residence during a person's working life, reckoned to be between the ages of 16 and 65 for men and 16 and 60+ for women. If you've lived in Australia for less than 25 years and then go to live overseas, you'll receive an Australian pension proportionate to the number of years spent there, e.g. if you've spent 12.5 years in Australia, you'll receive half of the full retirement pension. Pensioners who delay their retirement become eligible for a cash bonus equal to 9.4 per cent of their pension entitlement for each year they continue working.

There's a worsening crisis in state pension funding in Australia (and most western countries), where fewer and fewer workers must support an increasing number of pensioners. Most countries expect to at least double their over 65 population in the next 50 years. In 2000, 12 per cent of Australians were over the age of 65; by 2051, the figure is expected to be 25 per cent. As in many countries, there are plans to transfer the burden from the public to the private sector, which is why the mandatory Superannuation Guarantee Scheme was created in 1992 (see below). However, despite the introduction of superannuation, some 75 per cent of people are expected to be eligible for a full or part state pension for at least the next 25 years. The Commonwealth government spends around $20 billion per year on retirement benefits (around 3 per cent of the country's GDP) and this figure is expected to increase to 4.5 per cent by 2050.

Australian pensioners are entitled to concessional dental treatment, prescriptions and optometrist services, concessions on public transport fares in most states and territories, and various other benefits (which vary from state to state) that may include reduced council rates and utility costs (e.g. telephone rental, water rates), free mail redirection and reduced registration fees for dogs.

**Pensioners:** British state pensions are frozen at the prevailing rate with no annual adjustments for inflation when they move to certain Commonwealth countries, including Australia, Canada, New Zealand and South Africa. This affects over 350,000 British pensioners. There are some 150,000 British state pensioners in Australia with frozen British state pensions (which may be equivalent to just a few A$); around 100,000 of these receive social security 'top-up' payments totalling some $80 million per year from the Australian government. Note that from 1st March 2001 Australia and Britain ceased their reciprocal social security agreement. However, if you were receiving benefits under the agreement on 1st March 2001, you'll continue to receive those payments, and if you migrated to Australia on or before 1st March 2000, the date on which Australia served notice of termination of the agreement on the UK, you'll continue to have your UK contributions recognised for grants of Australian Age Pension.

**Information:** For further information about retirement pensions in Australia, contact Centrelink or the Department of Family and Community Services (☎ local call rate 1300-653227, 🖳 www.facs.gov.au).

# SUPERANNUATION

Superannuation (usually referred to simply as 'super') is the term commonly used in Australia for a private pension fund. As the number of retired workers has increased and the number of young workers to take their place has declined (partly because of higher unemployment), the pressure on government funds to pay state pensions has also increased. In order to reduce the burden, the federal government introduced compulsory employer superannuation funds in 1992 under the Superannuation Guarantee Scheme. Superannuation doesn't, however, replace the state pension (which continues to be available to those who need it), but is intended to supplement it and provide a higher income in retirement. Super rules have been extended to include part-time and casual workers and those who leave the workforce for up to two years. Self-employed, non-resident employees paid for work undertaken outside Australia aren't required to belong to a super fund, and resident employees employed by non-resident employers and paid for work undertaken outside Australia also needn't be covered.

Generally, if you earn over $450 per month (whether as a full or part-time employee or a casual worker), your employer must pay super for you; some awards require employers also to pay super for employees earning less than $450 per month. Employees earning between $450 and $900 per month can choose to receive their super as additional salary. Funds are non-contributory for employees, although voluntary contributions can be made. Employer contributions must be at least the minimum level laid down by the government, termed the Superannuation Guarantee (SG). The following table shows the fixed percentage of an employee's gross earnings that must be paid into a superannuation scheme under the Superannuation Guarantee:

| Financial Year | Superannuation Guarantee |
|---|---|
| 2000/01 | 8% |
| 2001/02 | 8% |
| 2002/03 and beyond | 9% |

The amount paid has been phased in gradually (starting with 3 per cent for companies with a payroll of $1 million or less in 1992) and will reach 9 per cent in the financial year 2002/03, as shown in the above table. However, this is generally considered to be too low, as this amount produces an annual income of just $20,000 a year. It's thought that a savings level of 12 to 15 per cent is necessary if retirement expectations are to be met.

There are around 7 million super fund members (some 90 per cent of the workforce) with over $440 billion in superannuation assets. There are various types of super funds, including employer-sponsored funds, industry funds, financial institution funds and do-it-yourself funds (which hold an increasing share of super assets). Banks, building societies, credit unions and life assurance companies can all provide superannuation funds in the form of Retirement Savings Accounts (RSAs). Repayment of all RSA deposits is guaranteed, but investment earnings are usually modest, e.g. 4 per cent a year, and many believe they're a waste of time (some employers have been trying to push workers into RSAs that leave them worse off than superannuation funds). If you're self-employed or aren't part of a recognised superannuation scheme, you can contribute to an independent private or public scheme (or a number of schemes). Many people begin with small contributions, particularly part-time, casual and seasonal workers. To help amounts under $1,000 grow, super fund managers are required to protect them against fees and charges.

You aren't obliged to join your employer's fund and employees can choose their own fund (they must choose within 28 days). There's a huge difference between the best and worst performing super funds, so it's wise to shop around and compare fund performance over a five or ten-year period and the level of fees (smaller industry funds don't do as well as the larger ones). Note, however, that in most cases, you'd be foolish to turn down the opportunity to join an employer's fund if it's a good one, as it usually provides extra benefits. These may include higher employer contributions, free life and disability insurance and insurance against loss of earnings due to injury or illness. Some funds offer members discounted home and personal loans and private health insurance. It's possible that in future employees will be able to use part of their superannuation funds to buy a home. Your super payout may be related to your final salary, which is the best option. If it isn't, you should ensure that the fund is invested safely, as you could lose out if the share market or property prices collapse in the years just before retirement. Note that when you join a fund, you have a 14-day 'cooling-off' period, during which you may withdraw your membership. If you change employers or professions, your superannuation benefits can be transferred into another fund.

**Tax & Surcharge:** Superannuation is taxed at 15 per cent. This applies to both the super contributions and the income from super funds, although tax relief can be claimed against superannuation payments. In order to avoid being taxed at the top rate of 47 per cent, some employees pay higher superannuation contributions and reduce their salary (called 'salary sacrifice' arrangements). Since 20th August 1996, however, contributions to superannuation for high income earners have attracted a surcharge of up to 15 per cent. The surcharge applies on contributions made by those earning $81,493 (2000/01 figure) per year or more (for both employees and the self-employed). The surcharge is phased in at 1 per cent for every $1,000 (or part thereof) earned above $81,493, e.g. if you earn $82,000 you must pay a 1 per cent surcharge, on $83,000 there's a 2 per cent surcharge, and so on up to a maximum surcharge of 15 per cent for those earning more than $94,493. The surcharge also applies to anyone who fails to provide his tax file number to his super fund, so many people pay the surcharge even though their income is below the $81,493 threshold (but it can be reclaimed). This means that super savings are taxed three times: when contributions are made, when there are earnings and when benefits are paid out! In total almost 2 per cent is siphoned off by the government, which reaps some $3 billion per year in taxes (and rising) and the government is loath to kill the golden goose. Since the surcharge was announced, many wealthy people have quit super and taken out private pensions (over 1.5 million super accounts have been closed). Nevertheless, super remains an attractive tax shelter, as high-earners can choose to pay 30 per cent on income directed into superannuation rather than paying 47 per cent income tax. PAYG taxpayers can also reduce their tax by paying more into their superannuation funds up to a specified amount.

Since compulsory employer superannuation was introduced in 1992, a number of problems have surfaced and it has become increasingly complicated and difficult for the layman (or anyone) to understand. Although successive governments have tinkered at the edges (some 2,000 changes have been made), many analysts believe that it needs a complete overhaul. The Association of Superannuation Funds of Australia (PO Box 1485, Sydney, NSW 1005, ☎ 02-9264 9300, 🖳 www.super annuation.asn.au) publishes a number of useful factsheets including *What Information You Should Receive from Your Superannuation Fund*.

**Withdrawals:** Undeducted contributions (those made out of after-tax salary) may be withdrawn at the age of 55 up to the year 2025, after which superannuation will be accessible only at the age of 60. In other words, if you were born after 1st July 1960, you'll have to wait until you're 60 – a measure designed to prevent 'double dipping', i.e. taking super benefits early, spending the money and then applying for a state pension at 65. However, under special circumstances such as permanent disability, severe financial hardship or change of employer the preserved component of superannuation can be claimed prior to the age of 55. Similarly, those over 55 are obliged to exhaust their superannuation funds before being entitled to unemployment benefit. If you leave Australia permanently, your super benefits won't be released until you reach the preservation age. The maximum age for contributing to a super fund is 70, provided you work a minimum of ten hours a week (if you work beyond the age of 65, you should check whether you're still eligible for superannuation – and seek psychiatric help).

Benefits can be taken in a lump sum, an annuity or a regular monthly income (e.g. an allocated or lifetime pension), or a combination of these.

# PRIVATE HEALTH INSURANCE

The Australian Medicare (see page 283) system provides free or subsidised medical treatment for all permanent residents. Anyone living or working in Australia (even temporarily) who isn't eligible for Medicare treatment and who doesn't like living dangerously should have private health insurance. Private health insurance in Australia is usually complementary insurance, so called because it complements (rather than replaces) Medicare. It's commonly used to pay the difference ('gap') between the Medicare schedule fee and what Medicare actually pays (see page 285). The main reason most people have private health insurance in Australia is to circumvent Medicare waiting lists for specialist appointments and non-emergency hospital treatment (e.g. elective surgery). Patients are also usually free to choose their own doctor and hospital. **Private insurance ensures that you receive the medical treatment you need, when you need it.** Note, however, that (despite what insurance companies might say) the quality of private treatment isn't better than that provided by Medicare, and you shouldn't assume that because a doctor (or any other medical practitioner) is in private practice, he's more competent than his Medicare counterpart. In fact, you're likely to see the same specialist or be treated by the same surgeon under Medicare as privately (but a few years earlier).

Most private health insurance in Australia is provided by health funds, which are regulated by the Commonwealth government and follow the principle of 'community rating' to determine premiums, i.e. premiums don't vary according to age, sex or your state of health. This ensures that high-risk members such as the elderly and the chronically sick aren't required to pay astronomical premiums as in some other countries. However, most health funds are eroding this principle and in recent years have introduced a variety of conditions to exclude expensive treatment (called exclusion policies) and surgery such as joint replacements; there may also be financial limits. Many analysts believe this could be the thin end of the wedge and that insurance companies will abandon 'community rating' by stealth.

Changes to private health insurance have been proposed by the government, although they're strongly contested by the Australian Medical Association, which fears that health funds will dictate clinical practices, i.e. the insurer rather than the doctor will decide the treatment.

Private health insurers are allowed to offer four categories of membership as follows:

- single person;

- couple;

- family, consisting of at least two adults and one or more other, which may include children or grandparents;

- single-parent, consisting of at least one adult (who's the contributor) and one or more dependent children.

When taking out family or single-parent membership, always carefully check what constitutes a dependent child, as your children may not be covered.

Each state has its own private health insurers, the largest of which include Medibank Private, the Medical Benefit Funds (MBF), National Mutual Health Insurance and the Hospital Contribution Fund (HCF). By far the largest insurer is Medibank Private, a non-profit health benefits organisation (established in 1976) operated by the state-run Health Insurance Commission, covering some 3 million people (two-thirds of all those with private health insurance), with some 275 customer service centres throughout the country. **Medibank Private also provides overseas visitors cover for temporary residents of Australia who aren't eligible for Medicare benefits.** It's possible to obtain health insurance from some banks (e.g. NAB), although they may insure only high earners. Compare the benefits and costs provided by a number of health insurers. Most provide a choice of basic, intermediate and comprehensive cover, with intermediate and comprehensive levels usually providing private rooms in private hospitals and ancillary cover.

**Types of Insurance:** Health insurers offer two basic types of insurance: hospital and ancillary. Hospital cover contributes to the cost of in-hospital treatment and accommodation as a private patient in a private or public hospital. Ancillary cover contributes to the cost of out-patient medical services that aren't covered by Medicare, such as dental treatment, spectacles or contact lenses, physiotherapy, acupuncture, chiropractic and other alternative therapies. Ancillary insurance may also include ambulance cover, home nursing and other services, although there's usually no refund for X-rays or prescriptions. There are payment limits for ancillary cover, both per visit limits and annual limits. Some funds (e.g. HCF) have a 'fit and well' policy which pays for gym membership or sports equipment such as running shoes.

**Premiums:** In mid-2001, the average costs of 100 per cent hospital cover for a family was around $1,400 and the average cost of 100 per cent ancillary cover around $1,000. Premiums vary considerably according to the state or territory and are highest in Victoria and South Australia and lowest in the Northern Territory and Western Australia. The average cost of private health insurance per year for a single person is: basic (private hospital expenses, including choice of doctor) $700, comprehensive (covers 100 per cent private hospital expenses) $800, and ancillary (non-hospital expenses such as dental, optical, physiotherapy and chiropractic treatment) $500. Premiums vary little between couples, families and single-parent families, who all pay around double the single premium. Premiums can usually be paid monthly, quarterly or annually, and a discount may be given for prompt or annual payment. Alternatively, you can pay on a weekly or fortnightly basis through deductions from your pay packet.

Medicare automatically pays 85 per cent of the Medicare Benefits Schedule (MBS) fee for a doctor's services, accommodation in a private hospital or for a private bed in a public hospital, and the insurer pays the balance (see page 285). Health insurers have contracts with hospitals and doctors in order to assert some control over costs and therefore reduce their premiums. You may need to choose a hospital and doctor contracted to your health insurer; otherwise you must pay the 'gap' between what the insurer will pay and what your doctor or hospital charges. Note that some insurers have agreements with relatively few private hospitals, outside which you're limited to a private bed in a public hospital, and you may not be covered outside your home state. You should receive a written quotation for non-emergency hospital treatment, including all costs and out-of-pocket expenses.

**Extra Costs & Excess Charges:** Note that the benefits (rebates) provided by health insurers aren't usually 100 per cent and you normally need to make a contribution (an excess or co-payment) towards fees, called 'out-of-pocket' costs. These can be very high and can run into $hundreds or even $thousands (and can increase at short notice). If you want your own doctor to treat you in a public hospital, you must pay a daily accommodation charge, and some insurers levy a fee per night (e.g. $80) for private hospital patients. In addition to out-of-pocket costs, there's also usually an annual excess charge, which can be up to $2,000 for a family and may be applied per person for a couple. When you leave hospital, you're generally asked to pay the difference (if any) between your health insurer's refund and the hospital's fees. **High out-of-pocket expenses are the main reason people have abandoned private health insurance in recent years.**

People have been deserting private health insurance in their thousands as premiums and surcharges ('gap' fees) have soared. Before Medicare was introduced

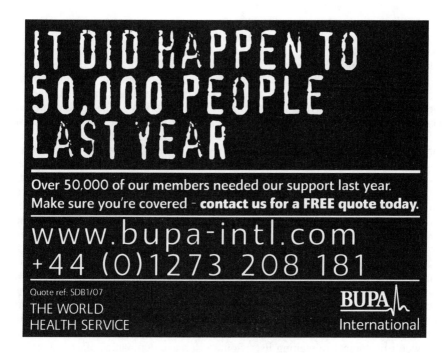
in 1984, over 50 per cent of Australians had private cover; this has since fallen to below a third (some 6 million people) – the system ceases to be viable at 30 per cent! After increasing premiums by 10 to 20 per cent in the last year, insurers were losing around 1,000 members a day in 1997. The government is desperate to encourage people to return to (or remain in) private health cover, as Medicare is facing a funding crisis and its survival in its present form relies heavily on a strong private health sector. **If things go on this way, there could be a collapse of health funds AND Medicare (maybe you'd better insure with a foreign company).**

Private health insurance premiums increased vastly from 1990 to 1997 (14 per cent in 1996/97 alone), although since then premiums have stabilised somewhat. However, despite the high premiums, health insurers are making very little (or no) money owing to the spiralling costs of hospital accommodation and operations; some are even on the verge of bankruptcy. The number of people cancelling their policies simply adds to the vicious circle of increasing premiums and the pressure on Medicare.

**Incentives:** In 2000, the federal government introduced a 30 per cent rebate on private health insurance premiums. Under the scheme, anyone who pays hospital and/or ancillary premiums to a registered health fund can obtain a 30 per cent reduction on the cost of their health insurance. The rebate is not means tested but the private health insurance policy must cover people eligible for Medicare. The rebate can be claimed in three ways: from your health fund as a premium reduction, thereby reducing your premium costs; from a Medicare office, which will reimbourse you the 30 per cent; or from the Taxation Office on your annual income tax form.

**Medicare Levy Surcharge:** In an effort to encourage high earners to take out private health insurance, the government obliges those who don't have private health insurance that at least covers doctor's fees and accommodation in hospital to pay an increased Medicare levy (see page 284). From 1st July 1997, the Medicare levy was increased by 1 per cent for single people earning over $50,000 per year and families earning over $100,000 per year who don't have private health insurance (the increase applies pro rata if you have insurance for less than a full year). The taxable threshold increases by $1,500 for each child, excluding the first. This means that a single person with a taxable income of $50,000 must pay a surcharge of $500 per year and a couple with three children earning $110,000 a surcharge of $800. It may be cheaper to buy insurance with a large excess (which reduces the premium), even if you never intend to use it, than pay the increased levy. The government may have created the worst of both worlds, whereby it subsidises private health insurers without relieving the burden on Medicare.

**Waiting Periods:** Note that all funds have waiting periods before new members are eligible to make a claim, e.g. a general two-month wait for all treatment, nine months for obstetrics (i.e. you cannot join when pregnant and claim for the costs against your insurance) and one year for existing conditions. This is to prevent you from making a claim directly after joining and then dropping your membership. However, accidents are covered from the day you join. Before changing funds, always check the waiting times for treatment, particularly if you have existing health problems. If you already belong to a private health insurance scheme (such as BUPA in Britain), you may be able to transfer your membership to Australia, in which case you won't be subject to waiting lists. Some insurance companies offer a short-term scheme for people staying in Australia for a limited period.

**Students:** Overseas Student Health Cover (OSHC) is obligatory for foreign students and their families in Australia and must cover them for the duration of their visa (or the first 12 months). It's provided by a number of insurance companies, including Medibank Private. Your premium, which must be paid before you arrive in Australia, will depend on the length of your student visa, up to a maximum 12 months' cover. If your student visa is for more than 12 months, a further premium is payable after 12 months. If you're a private student, your premium will be paid on your behalf by the school, college or university at which you'll be studying. If you're a government-sponsored student (e.g. by the Australian Agency for International Development/AusAID), the agency or department of the Australian government which is sponsoring you will pay your premium to Medibank Private.

OSHC includes cover for doctors (including specialists) at a surgery, your home or in hospital, and pathology services such as blood tests and X-rays. Payments are the same as for Medicare members, i.e. 85 per cent of the government schedule fee for outpatient treatment and 100 per cent of the schedule fee for hospital in-patient services (see page 285). If a doctor charges more than the schedule fee, you must pay the difference. OSHC provides full cover in a general (shared) ward in a public hospital, including all charges for out-patient treatment. If you choose to be treated in a private hospital, Medibank Private will contribute towards the cost of treatment and accommodation, but you'll be responsible for paying the difference between the schedule fee and the actual fee charged. The services that aren't covered by OSHC are much the same as for Medicare (see page 283). If you wish to be covered for excluded services, you'll need additional private health insurance.

**International Health Policies:** It's also possible to take out an international health insurance policy, which may be of particular interest to people living in Australia temporarily, or those whose work involves a lot of travel or who work part of the time overseas. Some policies offer members a range of premiums from budget to comprehensive cover. All policies offer at least two fee scales, one covering the whole world, including North America (and possible other high cost areas), the other excluding North America. Most policies include a full refund of hospital, ambulance, home nursing (usually for a limited period), out patient, emergency dental treatment and repatriation charges. All policies include an annual overall claims limit, usually from $200,000 to $2,000,000 (the higher the better, particularly for North America).

Some comprehensive policies provide a fixed amount for general medical costs (including routine doctors' visits) and elective dental, optical and maternity expenses. Premiums range from around $1,500 to over $5,000 per year, depending on your age, level of cover and the areas covered (if North America is covered, premiums are much higher). If you don't require permanent international health insurance, you should consider a policy which provides limited or optional cover when you're overseas. Note that all bills, particularly those received for treatment outside Australia, must include precise details of treatment received. Terms such as 'dental treatment' or 'consultation' are usually insufficient.

If you're living or working in Australia and aren't covered by Medicare, it's risky or even foolhardy not to have private health insurance for you and your family. Whether you're covered by an Australian or foreign health insurance policy makes little difference (except perhaps in cost), provided you have the required level of cover, including international cover if necessary. (Note that, if you can afford private insurance, it's generally considered foolish not to have it.) If you aren't adequately insured, you could be faced with some extremely high medical bills. When deciding on the type of policy, ensure that the insurance scheme covers *all* your family's health requirements. If your stay in Australia is short, you may be covered by a reciprocal agreement between your home country and Australia, or by a private health insurance scheme. **Make sure you're fully covered in Australia *before* you receive a large bill.**

When changing employers or leaving Australia, you should make sure that you have continuous medical insurance. For example, if you and your family are covered by a company health fund, your insurance will probably cease after your last official day of employment. **If you're planning to change your health insurance company, ensure that no important benefits are lost. When changing health insurance companies, you should inform your old insurance company if you have any outstanding bills for which they're liable.**

**Complaints:** If you're unable to resolve a complaint with your health insurer, you can contact the Private Health Insurance Complaints Commissioner, Suite 1201, Level 12, St. Martins Tower, 131 Market Street, Sydney 2000 (☎ local call rate 1300-640695 or 02-9261 5944). See also **Chapter 12.**

# DENTAL INSURANCE

It's unusual to have full dental insurance in Australia, as the cost is prohibitive. Routine dental services aren't funded by Medicare, although it pays for 75 per cent of in-hospital medical procedures performed by an oral surgeon, and pensioners qualify for free general and emergency dental treatment under the Commonwealth Dental Health Program. Basic dental treatment is usually provided under a health insurer's ancillary policy, and most international health insurance policies offer optional dental cover or extra dental cover for an additional premium, although there are many restrictions, and cosmetic treatment is excluded. Where applicable, the amount payable by a health insurance policy for a particular item of dental treatment is fixed and depends on your level of dental insurance. A list of specific refunds is available from insurance companies.

Some dentists also offer a dental insurance scheme. Patients must be 'dentally fit' (so if you have 'bad' teeth, you won't be accepted) and are graded according to the condition of their teeth. Insurance doesn't cover expensive items such as crowns, bridges and dentures. **Note that if you have healthy teeth and rarely pay for more than an annual check-up and a visit to a hygienist, dental insurance provides poor value.** See also **Dentists** on page 294.

## BUILDING INSURANCE

For most people, buying a home is the biggest financial investment they'll ever make. When buying a home, you're usually responsible for insuring it before you even move in. If you take out a mortgage to buy a property, your lender will usually insist that your home (including most permanent structures on your property) has building insurance from the time you sign the contract and legally become the owner. Even when it isn't required by a lender, you'd be extremely unwise not to have building insurance.

Building insurance usually includes loss or damage caused by fire, theft, riot or malicious damage, water leakage from pipes or tanks, oil leakage from central heating systems, flood, storm and lightning, explosion or aircraft impact, vehicles or animals, earthquake, subsidence or landslide, and falling trees or aerials, and may also include cover for temporary homelessness. Some insurance companies also provide optional cover to include trees and shrubs damaged maliciously or by storms. Building insurance must be renewed each year, and insurance companies are continually updating their policies, so you must take care that a policy still provides the cover you require when you receive a renewal notice.

Lenders fix the initial level of cover when you first apply for a mortgage and usually offer to arrange the insurance for you, but you're usually free to make your own arrangements. If you arrange your own building insurance, your lender will insist that the level of cover is sufficient. Most people take the easy option and arrange insurance through their mortgage lender, which is generally the most expensive option, e.g. some direct insurance companies guarantee to cut building insurance costs for the majority of homeowners insured through banks and building societies.

Most lenders provide index-linked building insurance, where premiums are linked to inflation and building costs (premiums are usually added to your monthly mortgage payments). It's your responsibility, however, to ensure that your level of cover is adequate, particularly if you carry out improvements or extensions which substantially increase the value of your home. All lenders provide information and free advice. If your level of cover is too low, an insurance company is within its rights to reduce the amount it pays when a claim is made, in which case you may find you cannot afford to have your house rebuilt or repaired should disaster strike.

The amount for which your home must be insured isn't the current market value but the cost of rebuilding it if it's totally destroyed. This varies according to the type of property and the area and is calculated per $1,000 of insurance, e.g. from around $3 to $4 per $1,000 of cover (per year) in an inexpensive area to $10 per $1,000 in the most expensive high-risk areas. Therefore insurance on a property costing $150,000 to rebuild costs from around $450 to $1,500 per year. There's usually no deduction for wear and tear and the cost of redecoration is usually met in full. Note that building insurance doesn't cover structural faults that existed when you took out the policy, which is why it's important to have a full structural survey carried out when you buy a property.

In recent years, increased competition (particularly from direct insurers) has reduced premiums. The National Roads and Motoring Association (NRMA) in New South Wales is the nation's biggest insurer and insures around 1.4 million homes. Insurance for 'non-standard' homes such as those with thatched roofs or timber construction is usually higher. The highest level of cover usually includes damage to glass (e.g. windows and patio doors) and porcelain (e.g. baths, washbasins and WCs), although you may have to pay extra for accidental damage, e.g. when your son blasts a cricket ball through the patio window. Always ask your insurer what *isn't* covered and what it will cost to include it (if required).

Premiums can usually be paid monthly (although there may be an extra charge) or annually. Note that there may be an excess, e.g. $50 or $100, for some claims, which is intended to deter policyholders from making small claims. Some policies have an excess only for certain claims, e.g. subsidence or landslip (when your house disappears into a hole in the ground or over a cliff), which is usually $2,000 or $4,000. Owners of houses vulnerable to subsidence and those living in flood-prone areas are likely to pay higher premiums.

Many insurance companies provide emergency telephone numbers for policyholders requiring urgent advice. Should you need to make emergency repairs, e.g. to weather-proof a roof after a storm or other natural disaster, most insurance companies allow work up to a certain limit (e.g. $2,000) to be carried out without an estimate or approval from the insurance company, but check first. Building insurance is often combined with home contents insurance (see below), when it's called home or household insurance, which is usually cheaper than taking out separate policies.

## HOME CONTENTS INSURANCE

Home contents insurance is recommended for anyone who doesn't live in an empty house. Burglary and house-breaking is a major problem in Australia, particularly in the major cities. Although there's a lot you can do to prevent someone breaking into your home (see **Home Security** on page 142), it's usually impossible or prohibitively expensive to make your home completely burglar proof without turning it into a fortress. However, you can ensure you have adequate contents insurance and that your most precious possessions are locked in a safe or safety deposit box.

**Types of Policy:** A basic home contents policy covers your belongings against the same sort of 'natural disasters' as building insurance (see above). You can optionally insure against accidental damage and all risks. A basic contents policy doesn't usually include such items as credit cards (and their fraudulent use), cash, musical instruments, jewellery, valuables, sports equipment and bicycles, for which you may need to take out extra cover. You can usually insure your property for its secondhand value (indemnity) or its full replacement value (new for old), which covers everything except clothes and linen (for which wear and tear is assessed) at the new cost price. The most popular form of contents insurance in Australia is replacement value, and it's best to take out an index-linked policy, where the level of cover is automatically increased by a percentage or fixed amount each year. Most policies have a maximum amount they'll pay per item and/or a maximum amount per claim, e.g. $1,500 for each item of jewellery or work of art or a total claim of $7,500.

A basic policy doesn't usually include accidental damage caused by your family to your own property (e.g. putting your foot through the TV during a political party broadcast) or your home freezer contents (in the event of a breakdown or power failure). A basic policy may include replacement locks, garden contents, personal liability insurance (see below), loss of oil and metered water, and temporary accommodation. If they aren't included, these items can usually be covered for an additional premium. Some policies include legal expenses cover (e.g. up to $100,000) for disputes with neighbours, shops, suppliers, employers and anyone who provides you with a service (e.g. a plumber or builder). Most contents policies include public liability cover, e.g. up to $2 million. Items such as computers and mobile phones may need to be listed individually on your policy, and computers and other equipment used for business aren't usually covered (or may be covered only for a prohibitive extra payment). If you have friends or lodgers living in your home, their personal property won't be covered by your policy.

**Premiums:** Your premium will depend largely on where you live and your insurer. All insurance companies assess the risk by location based on your postcode. **Check before buying a home, as the difference between low and high-risk areas can be considerable.** Annual premiums, which start at around $350 to $400 per annum in low-risk areas, can be several times this amount in high-risk areas. Many homeowners in high-risk areas would be willing to forego theft insurance, although insurance companies are reluctant to offer this option, as theft is a convenient excuse to load premiums.

As with building insurance, it's important to shop around for the lowest premium, as premiums vary considerably with the insurer. If you're already insured, you may find that you can save money by changing insurers. However, watch out for penalties when switching insurers. Combining your home contents insurance with your building insurance (see above) is a common practice and is usually cheaper than insuring each separately. Having your building and contents insurance with the same insurer also avoids disputes over which company should pay what, which can arise if you have a fire or flood affecting both your home and its contents. Those aged over 50 or 55 (and possibly first-time homeowners) may be offered a discount, and some companies provide special policies for students in college accommodation or lodgings (ask an insurance broker).

**Security:** Most insurers offer a no-claims discount or a discount (e.g. 5 or 10 per cent) for homes with burglar alarms and other high security features. In high-risk areas, good security is usually a condition of insurance. Beware of the small print in policies, particularly those regarding security, which insurers often use to avoid paying claims. You'll forfeit all rights under your policy if you leave doors or windows open (or the keys under a mat or flower pot), particularly if you've claimed a discount for impregnability. If there are no signs of forced entry, e.g. a broken window, you may be unable to claim for a theft (so break a window!). If you plan to leave your house empty for a long period, e.g. a month or longer, you may need to inform your insurer.

**Sum Insured:** Take care that you don't under-insure your house contents (including anything rented such as a TV or video recorder) and that you periodically reassess their value and adjust your premium accordingly. Your contents should include everything that isn't part of the fixtures and fittings and which you could take with you if you were moving house. If you under-insure your contents, your claim may be reduced by the percentage by which you're under-insured. Some insurance companies offer policies called 'no-sum' or 'fixed-sum', where you aren't required to value all your possessions but are covered for a fixed amount depending on the number of bedrooms in your home. With this type of policy the insurance company cannot scale down a claim because of under-insurance. However, you're usually better off calculating the value of the contents to be insured. You can take out a special policy if you have high-value contents, which may be cheaper than a standard contents policy. **Always list all previous burglaries on the proposal form, even if nothing was stolen.**

**Claims:** Some insurers provide a 24-hour emergency helpline for policyholders and assistance for repairs for domestic emergencies, such as a blocked drain or electrical failure, up to a maximum amount for each claim. Take care when completing a claims form, as insurers have tightened up on claims and few people receive a full settlement. Many insurers have an excess of $50 to $100 per claim (see above). Bear in mind that, if you make a claim, you may need to wait months for it to be settled. Generally, the larger the claim, the longer you have to wait for your money, although in an emergency a company may make an interim payment. If you aren't satisfied with the final amount offered, don't accept it and try to negotiate a higher figure. If you still cannot reach agreement, you can contact the Insurance Enquiries and Complaints (☎ local call rate 1300-363683, 🖳 www.iec.ltd.com.au) for independent arbitration or take legal action.

# PERSONAL LIABILITY INSURANCE

Personal liability insurance provides personal insurance for individuals and members of their families against compensation for accidental damage, injury or death caused to third parties or their property. It usually covers anything from spilling wine on your neighbour's Persian carpet (if you pour white wine on a red wine stain, it will disappear) to your dog or child biting someone. Although common in Europe and North America (where people sue each other for $millions at the drop of a hat), personal (or legal) liability insurance is unusual in Australia. However, home contents policies (see above) usually include personal liability insurance up to $2 million and it's also included in travel policies (see below).

# HOLIDAY & TRAVEL INSURANCE

Holiday and travel insurance is recommended for all who don't wish to risk having their holiday or travel spoilt by financial problems or to arrive home broke. As you know, anything can and often does go wrong with a holiday, sometimes before you even get on the plane (particularly if you *don't* have insurance). Travel insurance is available from many sources, including travel agents, insurance brokers, tour operators, banks, airlines and motoring organisations.

**Level of Cover:** Before taking out travel insurance, carefully consider the level of cover required and compare policies. Most policies include cover for loss of deposit or holiday cancellation, missed flight, departure delay at both the start *and* end of a holiday (a common occurrence), delayed baggage, personal effects, lost baggage (e.g. $3,000), medical expenses (up to $4 million) and accidents (including evacuation home if necessary), money (e.g. $500 to $1,000), personal liability ($2 million or $4 million), legal expenses, and a tour operator going bust. You should also insure against missing your flight after an accident or transport breakdown, as almost half of travel insurance claims are for cancellation (you should also be covered for transport delays at the end of your holiday, e.g. the flight home). With some policies, the amount you can claim for belongings may be limited to around $400 per item, which will be insufficient to cover your Rolex watch or Leica camera. Some home contents policies include cover for belongings worldwide. Note, however, that your insurance company won't pay out if you're negligent, e.g. you leave your camera in a taxi or on a beach.

**Medical Expenses:** Medical expenses are an important aspect of travel insurancem and you shouldn't rely on reciprocal health agreements, cover provided by charge and credit card companies, house contents policies, or private medical insurance, none of which usually provide the necessary cover. The minimum medical insurance recommended by experts is $500,000 for Europe and $2 million for North America and the rest of the world. Personal liability should be at least $2 million for Europe and $4 million for the rest of the world. **Note that many travel and holiday insurance policies don't provide the level of cover that most people need.** Always check any exclusion clauses in contracts by obtaining a copy of the full policy document, as all relevant information won't be contained in insurance leaflets.

**Exclusions:** Health or accident insurance included in travel insurance policies usually contains exclusions, e.g. dangerous sports such as white-water rafting, mountaineering, skiing, hang-gliding, scuba-diving, crocodile wrestling and kangaroo boxing, and even riding a motorbike in some countries. Check the small print and find out exactly what terms such as 'hazardous pursuits' include or exclude. Skiing and other winter sports should be specifically covered and *listed* in a travel insurance policy. Special winter sports policies are available, which are usually more expensive than normal holiday insurance.

**Cost:** The cost of travel insurance varies considerably according to your destination. Many companies have different rates for different areas, e.g. Australia, Europe, North America and worldwide (excluding North America). Premiums for travel within Australia are around $26 to $35 per person for two weeks, European destinations are usually from $135 for two weeks, and North America (where medical treatment costs an arm and a leg) and a few other destinations costs from $185 for three weeks. The cheapest policies offer reduced cover, but may not be adequate for most people. Premiums may be higher for those aged over 65 or 70. Generally, the longer the period covered, the cheaper the daily cost, although the maximum period may be limited, e.g. six months. With some policies an excess (e.g. $50) must be paid for each claim.

**Annual Policies:** For people who travel overseas frequently, whether for business or pleasure, an annual travel policy is often an excellent idea, costing around $200 to $300 per year for worldwide cover for an unlimited number of trips. However, always carefully check exactly what is included and read the small print (some insist that travel is by air). Most annual policies don't cover you for travel within Australia and there's a limit on the length of a trip, e.g. one to six months. Some companies offer 'tailor-made' insurance for independent travellers (e.g. backpackers) for any period from a few days to a year.

**Claims:** Although travel insurance companies will quickly and gladly take your money, they aren't so keen to pay claims, and you may need to persevere before they pay up. Fraudulent claims against travel insurance are common, so unless you can produce evidence to support your claim, insurers may think that you're trying to cheat them. Always be persistent and make a claim irrespective of any small print, as this may be unreasonable and therefore invalid in law. **Insurance companies usually require you to report any loss (or any incident for which you intend to make a claim) to the local police or carriers within 24 hours and to obtain a report. Failure to do this will usually mean that a claim won't be considered.**

Flight insurance and comprehensive travel insurance is available from insurance desks at most airports, including travel accident, personal accident, worldwide medical expenses and in-transit baggage. When you pay for your travel costs with some credit cards, your family (possibly including children under the age of 25) are provided with free travel accident insurance up to a specified amount, e.g. $300,000. **Don't rely on this insurance, as it usually covers only death and serious injury.**

# MOTOR BREAKDOWN INSURANCE

Breakdown insurance for cars and motorcycles is available from Australian motoring organisations (see page 275), which also offer travel insurance for motoring holidays.

# CAR INSURANCE

Car insurance is available from numerous Australian insurance companies (see page 251). Third party (bodily injury) insurance (CTP) is compulsory in Australia.

# 14.

# FINANCE

Competition for your money is fierce in Australia, where financial services are provided not only by many Australian and foreign banks, but also by building societies, credit unions, investment brokers, insurance companies, mortgage originators/providers, Australia Post, and even supermarkets and service organisations (such as motoring organisations). Banks are facing increasing competition from a shake-up of the country's financial services industry, which it's estimated will eventually save consumers $billions per year (although it's happening very slowly). Sydney is Australia's most important financial market, although it's relatively small in international terms. The country has a sophisticated financial system and in recent years has had a strong growth rate and low inflation (around 2 per cent) with falling unemployment. In 1999, Australia's gross domestic product (GDP) was around US$22,000 per head and the 'average' Australian's wealth over $100,000, although it's far from evenly distributed.

Australia is a credit-financed society, and banks and finance companies queue up to lend you money or provide credit (interest rates on credit cards are high). Levels of personal debt are over 40 per cent of spending (similar to the UK and USA) and in 1999 average household debt was almost $26,500, Australians owing unprecedented amounts on credit cards (an average of around $3,000 per person) and personal overdrafts. Conversely, personal savings in Australia are among the lowest in the western world. There are fears that, if interest rates (which remained low in 2001) rise rapidly, many people will be unable to service their debts; even with low interest rates, bankruptcies have been running at record levels in the last few years. Credit and assorted other cards have largely replaced cash and now account for the vast majority of retail purchases. Your financial standing in Australia is usually decided by the number of cards you have, including credit cards, cash cards, EFTPOS (debit) cards, charge cards, store cards and assorted specialist cards. Australia, like many western countries, is fast becoming a cashless society.

Taxes in Australia vary considerably with the state or territory: overall per capita taxation is lowest in Queensland and highest in Victoria and NSW. Taxes are levied at Commonwealth (federal), state and local government levels. There are no wealth, inheritance or gift taxes in Australia (it's the only one of the OECD countries not to have some form of inheritance tax). States and territories don't currently levy income tax, but receive their income from stamp duty on commercial and legal documents (cheques, receipts, transfers of land, insurance policies and mortgage transactions), payroll tax (a state tax imposed on an employer's payroll and the biggest source of income for state governments), taxes on motor vehicles, land and liquor, and miscellaneous licence fees. Since the high court's decision to outlaw state taxes on alcohol, petrol and tobacco, there has been a continuous taxation war between state and federal governments. The main form of local government tax is property tax, augmented by charges for services such as sewerage and water.

The total of direct and indirect taxation in Australia is relatively low by international standards, although the government is continually inventing new ways of taxing people, including various taxes on superannuation (pension) funds, a special tax to pay for the public health service, a tax for not having private health insurance, and fringe benefits tax. Australia went through a major reform of the tax system in 2000 (although many argue that it's still unfair, contradictory and inefficient, as well as unnecessarily complicated) and introduced a goods and services tax (GST – a form of value added tax) in July 2000, which has been an administrative nightmare for virtually every Australian business.

Personal finance in Australia is a jungle, and there are plenty of predators about just waiting to get their hands on your loot. Always shop around for financial services, and never sign a contract unless you know exactly what the costs and implications are. Although bankers, financiers and brokers don't like to make too fine a point of it, they aren't doing business with you because they like you, but simply to get their hands on your pile of chips. It's up to you to make sure that their share is kept to a minimum and that you receive the best possible value for your money. **When dealing with 'experts', bear in mind that, while making mistakes is easy, fouling up completely requires professional help!** A new Consumer Credit Code was introduced in 1997 and is detailed in the Department of Fair Trading booklet, *Walking the Credit Tightrope is Now a Lot Less Risky* (don't you believe it!).

When you arrive in Australia to take up residence, ensure that you have sufficient cash, travellers' cheques, credit cards, luncheon vouchers, coffee machine tokens, silver dollars, gold nuggets and precious stones, to last at least until your first pay day, which may be some time after your arrival. Don't, however, carry a lot of cash. During this period you'll find that a credit card (or two) is useful. Note that among the various Australian eccentricities is the government's financial year, which runs from 1st July to 30th June.

There are numerous books and magazines to help you manage your finances. Centrelink gives free financial advice (☎ local call rate 13-2850, 💻 www.centrelink. gov.au). Personal finance information is published in the financial pages of the Saturday and Sunday editions of major newspapers. Good general information on many aspects of finance is available on the Money Manager Internet site (💻 www. moneymanager.com.au). For information regarding pensions (including super-annuation) and life assurance, see **Chapter 13**.

# TAX FILE NUMBER

Your tax file number (TFN), consisting of nine digits, is probably the most important number you'll receive in Australia. Without one, you'll be taxed at the maximum rate (47 per cent) on all your wages. You also need a TFN to claim unemployment and sickness benefits, to make any investment, and to enrol in a fee-free course of higher education. It's also required when completing your annual income tax return and when you start work or change jobs (there are both personal and business tax file numbers). You can obtain an application form to apply for a TFN from your local Australian Tax Office (ATO). You must produce identification such as your passport with a valid visa, birth certificate or driving licence and should receive your TFN around two weeks after making an application. The ATO publishes a brochure, *Applying for Your Tax File Number*, which explains the application procedure.

**Withholding Tax:** When you earn interest income of $120 or more per year or receive dividends from shares or distributions from unit trust investments, Australian banks are required to deduct 'withholding' tax if you don't provide a TFN (although it isn't compulsory to give your bank your TFN). Your bank is also required to report annually to the ATO the details of interest/dividend income earned, any withholding tax deducted and the TFN quoted. Withholding tax is calculated at 30 per cent on dividends and royalties and at 47 per cent on other interest income. As you may be entitled to a tax refund, you need to include details of withholding tax deductions on your tax form.

Those exempt from withholding tax include pensioners, children aged under 18 who aren't working (although a TFN should be obtained if investment income is likely to be above $643 per year), religious and voluntary organisations, government bodies and local authorities, and customers with special accounts where the interest doesn't accrue to the person named as the account holder. Under double-taxation agreements, withholding tax is usually limited to 15 per cent on dividends and 10 per cent on royalties.

## AUSTRALIAN CURRENCY

The Australian unit of currency is the Australian dollar (A$). Although the Australian economy has been fairly strong in recent years thanks to steady growth and low inflation (around 2 per cent in 2000), the A$ fell to an 11-year low against the US$ owing to the turmoil in Asian money markets and collapsing Asian currencies in 1997 and hasn't recovered since. In mid-2001, the A$ was generally weak, particularly against the US$, but some experts were predicting that it would appreciate in the second half of 2001.

The Australian dollar is divided into 100 cents, and coins are minted in values of 5¢, 10¢, 20¢, 50¢ (all silver-coloured cupronickel coins), and $1 and $2 (gold-coloured bronze coins with irregular milling on the edge). Note that $1 and $2 coins are smaller than the 20¢ coin, which can cause confusion. Keep a supply of 20¢ and 50¢ coins handy for parking meters and other machines. Although the smallest coin is 5¢, prices are still shown in single cents and rounded up or down to the nearest 5¢. Australian banknotes have lurid designs and are printed in values of $5 (orange/mauve), $10 (turquoise/yellow), $20 (red/khaki), $50 (gold/green) and $100 (blue/grey). The $50 and $100 bills are treated with suspicion by many people and may not be accepted by small businesses, tax drivers, etc. Gold 'Australian nuggets' with a face value of $15 to $100 (their actual value is many times the face value) are available from banks and are a popular investment (except when the value of gold plummets, as it did in 1997).

Forgery is a problem in Australia, where there are a 'significant number' of forged $20, $50 and $100 notes in circulation, so be on your guard if someone insists on paying a large bill in banknotes. You should also check that you don't receive New Zealand coins in your change, which are worth less than Australian coins. New plastic $5 and $10 notes (made of polymer) have been introduced in recent years, which it was claimed were impossible to counterfeit (counterfeiters have already cracked them – back to the drawing board!). They last longer than paper notes and can be recycled when they're withdrawn (which is just as well).

It's sensible to obtain some Australian coins and banknotes before arriving in Australia and to familiarise yourself and your family with them. You should have some dollars in cash, e.g. $50 to $100 in small bills, when you arrive, but should avoid carrying a lot of cash. This will save you having to queue to change money on arrival at an Australian airport (where exchange rates are usually poor and there are often long queues). It's best to avoid $50 and $100 notes (unless you receive them as a gift!). There's no limit on the amount of Australian or foreign currency that can be brought into Australia, but amounts of $10,000 or more (or the equivalent in foreign currency) must be declared on arrival (see **Foreign Currency** below).

# FOREIGN CURRENCY

Australia has no currency restrictions and you may import or export as much money as you wish, in practically any currency. Currency refers to notes and foreign currency and doesn't include travellers' cheques or other monetary instruments. However, amounts of $10,000 or more in Australian or foreign currency must be declared to customs on arrival. This is to combat tax evasion and organised crime. Forms for reporting currency transfers are available from customs officers at ports and airports. Forms should be addressed to the Cash Transaction Reports Agency, c/o The Treasury, Langton Crescent, Parkes, ACT 2600, ☎ 02-6263 2111, 🖥 www. treasury.gov.au). For further information contact the Australian Transaction Reports and Analysis Centre, GPO Box 5516, West Chatswood, NSW 1515 (☎ freecall 1800-021037, 🖥 www.austrac.gov.au).

**Buying & Selling Currency:** Major Australian banks will change most foreign banknotes (but not coins), but offer a better exchange rate for travellers' cheques (see below). When buying or selling foreign currency in Australia, beware of excessive charges. Apart from the difference in exchange rates, which are posted by all banks and *bureaux de change*, there may be a significant difference in charges. Most banks and building societies buy and sell foreign currency, although you usually need to order it a few days in advance, as only the major branches in capital cities keep foreign currency in stock. It pays to shop around for the best exchange rates, particularly when changing a lot of money (it's possible to barter over rates in some establishments). Most banks have a wide spread (e.g. 5 to 10 per cent) between their buying and selling rates for foreign currencies. The A$ exchange rate against major international currencies is listed in banks and in the major daily newspapers.

**Travellers' Cheques:** Travellers' cheques are widely accepted in Australia in all major international currencies. The commission for cashing travellers' cheques varies with the bank, e.g. of the big four banks, ANZ charges $7 for cheques under $3,000 in foreign currency, WBC charges $7.50 for all foreign currency cheques, and the National charges $5 and the Commonwealth $7 per transaction (irrespective of the number of cheques cashed or their value). No fee is charged when cashing American Express or Thomas Cook travellers' cheques at their own branches. Australia Post charges a 1 per cent fee, and other banks and travel agents 1.5 to 2 per cent or a flat fee of $5 to $10 (plus a stamp duty of 20¢ per cheque). Banks in rural areas (if you can find any) usually levy the highest fees for cashing travellers' cheques. You can also cash travellers' cheques at luxury hotels and some businesses, although exchange rates are usually poor. Note that you need your passport to cash cheques.

Most banks charge a commission of 1 per cent of the face value when you're buying travellers' cheques. If you're planning to take up residence or spend some months in Australia, it's worthwhile buying A$ travellers' cheques, as you'll avoid exchange rate fluctuations and save on commission and fees. When travelling outside Australia, it's best to buy travellers' cheques in £sterling or US$, which are the most widely accepted (US$ cheques should always be used when visiting the USA). Lost or stolen travellers' cheques can be replaced in Australia and most countries overseas (the easiest to replace are American Express ☎ freecall 1800-251902 and Thomas Cook ☎ freecall 1800-127495) and you should always keep a record of your cheque numbers separate from your cheques.

**Cash Transfers:** If you have money transferred to Australia by banker's draft or a letter of credit, bear in mind that it can take up to two weeks to be cleared. You can also have money sent to you by international money order (via a post office), a cashier's cheque or telegraphic transfer, e.g. via Western Union (the quickest, safest and *most expensive* method). You usually need your passport to collect money transferred from overseas or to cash a banker's draft or other credit note.

Postal orders can be sent to Commonwealth countries and a giro post office transfer can be made to most countries. If you're sending money overseas, it's best to send it in the local currency, so that the recipient won't need to pay conversion charges. Note that some countries have foreign exchange controls limiting the amount of money that can be sent overseas. Insured mail is the only safe way to send cash, as the insured value is refunded if it's lost or stolen.

You can send money direct from your bank to another bank via an interbank transfer. Most banks have a minimum charge for international transfers, which makes it expensive for small sums. Overseas banks may also take a percentage (e.g. 1 or 2 per cent) of the amount transferred (everybody wants a cut!).

**Footnote:** There isn't much difference in cost between buying Australian currency by exchanging cash, buying travellers' cheques or using a credit card in Australia. However, many people simply take cash when travelling overseas, which is asking for trouble, particularly if you have no way of obtaining more cash in Australia, e.g. with travellers' cheques or a credit card. **One thing to bear in mind when travelling anywhere, is <u>never</u> to rely only on one source of funds!**

# CREDIT RATING

Whether you're able to get credit (or how much) in Australia usually depends on your credit rating, which is becoming increasingly important in today's hazardous financial world. Most financial institutions use credit scoring and a credit reference agency report to find out whether you're credit worthy. You may need to give signed consent on an application form or sign a special authority. Your credit score will depend on many factors such as your age and occupation, marital status, how long you've held your current job, whether you're a homeowner; where you live, whether you're on the electoral roll, whether you have a telephone and your credit track record. If you're refused credit because of a credit report, you'll be told and can ask to see the report and challenge anything which is incorrect. If you're a new arrival in Australia, a lender may use an agency in your previous country of residence. Individuals can also check the credit rating of a company or person with whom they're planning to do business. Australian credit ratings are held by the Credit Reference Association of Australia (CRAA). If you require access to your CRAA file, contact the Public Access Division, CRAA, PO Box 966, North Sydney, NSW 2059 (☎ 02-9464 6000, ⌨ www.credref.com.au).

If you have a bad credit rating, it's almost impossible to obtain credit in Australia. However, if you're able to provide collateral (i.e. security such as a property), for example for a bank loan, people will fall over themselves to lend you money, particularly those who charge extortionate interest rates. A life assurance policy can also be used to provide collateral for a loan. Finally, if you're refused credit, try looking on the bright side: without credit you cannot run up any debts!

# BANKS & BUILDING SOCIETIES

The major Australian banks with branches in cities and large towns throughout Australia are the Commonwealth Bank of Australia, (majority owned by the Australian government), National Australia Bank, Australia & New Zealand (ANZ) Bank and WBC, collectively referred to as the big four. These banks also have the widest representation overseas. In addition to the national banks, there are also many regional, city and state banks (including drive-in banks).

The major banks offer over 200 products ranging from current and savings accounts to personal superannuation schemes and home insurance. If you do a lot of travelling overseas, you may find the comprehensive range of travel and other services provided by the major banks advantageous. Note that many services provided by Australian banks are also offered by Building Societies (see below). Banks are keen to attract migrants as customers and offer a range of special services to newcomers. The major banks (e.g. the Commonwealth Bank of Australia) provide financial advice and assistance to migrants in a number of countries, and also operate a network of Migrant Service Centres in Australia's capital cities.

Australian banking made huge losses in the '80s, and the first half of the '90s was spent cost cutting and recovering. The second half of the '90s saw strong growth and a stable credit environment leading to high profit margins. Australian banks are now highly profitable, the big four alone making record profits in 2000 (up 18 per cent on 1999). Nevertheless, many regional (bush or country) banks have closed in recent years (over 2,000 branches have closed in the last decade) as banks have slimmed their branch networks. The proliferation of electronic banking (see below) has meant that banks require a much smaller workforce, and they've shed thousands of jobs (bank is a four-letter word with many people in Australia, where they're generally held in low esteem). Consequently, many communities have been left without a local bank, although some towns have successfully fought closures by threatening to withdraw $millions in assets from a bank. In some areas, building societies and credit unions have stepped in to fill the void, but in a small rural town or village, there's likely to be a post office agency, but no bank. A post office account is handy for travellers in rural areas or an account with one of the banks that allow withdrawals to be made from post offices.

The major banks have also established low-cost 'kiosk' branches in supermarkets and shopping centres operated by just one or two people and open seven days a week. After initial indifference, supermarket bank kiosks have proved popular and increased in number to over 500.

**Electronic Banking:** Australian banks are in the forefront of electronic banking and over half of all bank transactions are made through electronic banking methods, some banks recording three-quarters of their transactions electronically. Electronic banking includes automatic teller machines (ATMs and EFTPOS), of which there are some 275,000 in Australia, electronic funds transfer, telephone banking, smart cards, stored debt cards, automated bill payment (BPAY), touch-screen customer service terminals, automated computer banking through dial-up services and Internet banking (although the last is still in its infancy). In future, banks will have even fewer branches and it's expected that almost all banking transactions will be done via a computer or telephone. Video telephone banking will soon allow customers to do business through video contact with centralised bank staff.

Telephone banking (or telebanking) and Internet banking are offered by most Australian banks as well as by building societies and credit unions, usually 24 hours a day, seven days a week. Calls may be answered by a recorded message rather than a real person. Services provided include obtaining account balances, transferring funds between accounts, paying bills, providing details of the last five (or more) cheques cleared or the last five transactions, ordering statements and cheque books, obtaining interest rates earned/charged and obtaining mortgages and other loans.

**Complaints:** Most Australian banks are members of the Australian Bankers' Association (ABA) which has its own Code of Banking Practice that seeks to foster good relations between banks and their customers (provided it doesn't cost the banks any money). A banking ombudsman was established in 1989 by the ABA to mediate in disputes between banks and their customers. Complaints run into thousands every year, particularly with regard to excessive fees and charges. If you have a dispute with your bank which you're unable to resolve with them, you can take the matter to the Australian Banking Ombudsman (56 Pitt Street, Sydney, NSW 2000, ☎ 02-8298 0417, 🖳 www.bankers.asn.au). ABA members agree to abide by the decision of the Australian Banking Ombudsman, although if customers disagree with a ruling they aren't obliged to accept it and are free to take it up with a consumer affairs department or office of fair trading or take legal action.

Note that there's no government or industry-funded deposit protection system for deposits in Australia, as exists in many other countries. Deposit protection in Australia varies between banks, building societies and credit unions, none of which provide an explicit guarantee of deposits. This matter is currently under review by the Commonwealth government and new regulations may be forthcoming.

# Building Societies & Credit Unions

Building societies (or permanent building societies to give them their full name) were established in the 19th century to cater for people saving to buy a home. Customers saved a deposit of 5 or 10 per cent of the cost of a home with the building society, who then lent them the balance. A building society would rarely lend to anyone who wasn't a regular saver, although this policy changed some years ago. Today, Australian building societies have some 3 million members and over $10 billion in assets, although this represents just 5 per cent of the national financial services market. Added competition in the financial sector in recent years (particularly from mortgage originators) has made life difficult for building societies, many of which are struggling to survive in their present form. Like banks, building societies have also been raising their fees to offset smaller margins on home loans.

Building societies and credit unions can now compete with banks on a more even footing and, after a long battle, they recently won the right to issue cheques in their own name (previously all cheques had to be issued by and cleared through banks). Nowadays, building societies offer many of the services provided by banks, including current and savings accounts, cash cards, personal loans, credit cards, insurance and travel services. However, building societies don't all offer the same services, types of accounts or rates of interest. If you're looking for a long-term investment, the number of branches may not be of importance, as members of most building societies are linked with the major banks and customers can use their ATM networks. Building societies don't have an independent dispute scheme, but follow a recommended procedure in the event of complaints.

# Business Hours

Normal bank and building society opening hours are from 9am or 9.30am until 4pm, Mondays to Thursdays, and from 9.30am until 5pm on Fridays, with no closure over the lunch period in cities and most towns. Some city branches open from 8am until 6pm, Mondays to Thursdays, and until 8pm on Fridays, while in rural areas banks may open on only one or two days a week. Some banks and building societies open on Saturday mornings, e.g. from 9am until noon. There are bank branches with extended opening hours at international airports and in an increasing number of supermarkets and shopping centres (some open seven days a week). All banks are closed on public holidays. Most banks, building societies and main post offices in Australia have 24-hour Automatic Teller Machines (ATMs) at branches for cash withdrawals, deposits and checking account balances (see page 336). *Bureaux de change* have longer opening hours, including Saturdays and Sundays in tourist areas and large cities, but should be used sparingly, as they don't offer the best exchange rates and often charge a large commission.

# Cheque Accounts

If you're planning to work in Australia and will be paid fortnightly or monthly, one of your first acts should be to open an account with a bank, building society or credit union, like most of the Australian working population. Your salary will usually be paid directly into your account by your employer, and your salary statement will be either sent to your home address or given to you at work. Employees who are paid weekly or fortnightly are often paid in cash, in which case it's up to you whether you open an account (although it's difficult to survive without one nowadays).

The most common account for day-to-day money management is a transaction (current or cheque) account, which provides a cheque book, ATM access, EFTPOS availability, telephone banking and the facility to pay your regular bills by direct debit. Many people have at least two accounts: a transaction (current) account for their out-of-pocket expenses and regular transactions, and a savings account for long-term savings (or 'rainy day' money) – see page 335. Many people have both bank and building society/credit union accounts. Before opening an account, compare banks' charges and fees (see below), interest rates (e.g. on credit cards and deposits) and the services offered by a particular financial institution or account.

An account can be opened overseas, either in person or by post. When opening an account by post, attach a certified photocopy of the pages of your passport showing its number, expiry date, your specimen signature, photograph and visa (if available). You may also need your driving licence. If a copy of your passport is sent by mail, it must be certified by a professional person (such as a doctor, lawyer or teacher) or a person of similar standing with a public position such as a member of parliament, councillor, civil servant or police officer. Banks and other financial institutions are required by law (under the Financial Transaction Report Act, 1988) to verify the identity of each signatory to an account. To meet this requirement, you must provide either a reference from a reputable person or specific identification documents. Under the 100 point identification system, each acceptable document is given a points rating and a total of 100 points is required to establish your identity. **Note that new arrivals can open an account during their first six weeks in Australia with just a passport.**

Most people pay their bills from their transaction accounts, either by standing order or by cheque. Bills can also usually be paid by phone by simply quoting your account details. Bank statements are usually issued monthly (optionally quarterly), interest is normally calculated daily and paid quarterly, and an overdraft facility may be provided. Note that transaction accounts pay *very* little interest on account balances, e.g. from 0.1 to 0.5 per cent, and Australians lose $billions per year by leaving excess cash in these accounts when they could be earning 2 to 5 per cent in savings accounts. If you regularly have $1,000 or more on deposit, you should consider keeping it an account that pays a 'reasonable' interest rate. The minimum opening balance may be as low as $1, although you should bear in mind that you usually need to maintain a much higher balance in order to avoid bank fees and charges.

**Fees & Charges:** Australian banks have increased charges on transactions by as much as 100 per cent (to $4 in some cases) in recent years in an attempt to lure customers away from branches, as electronic banking costs them a fraction of branch transactions (although the customer still has to pay bank charges!) and to recoup their reduced margins on mortgages and other loans. This caused a public outcry, and in early 2001 a Parliamentary Commission was set up to investigate bank charges (which amounted to almost $2 billion in 1999). It was found that customer have little idea what fees are charged, and recommendations from the Commission included greater transparency from banks over fees and a breakdown of all fees and charges on monthly statements.

An account-keeping fee is introduced when the balance in an account falls below a certain level, e.g. $300 or $500. Those who maintain their account balance above this level or who have loans and deposits of $20,000 or more usually incur no fees, which includes up to 80 per cent of customers. Most banks also charge a monthly 'account keeping' fee, e.g. from $2 to $7. Some accounts offer a certain number of free transactions (e.g. 5 to 35) each month, after which a fee is levied. In order to reduce transaction fees, you should make fewer cash withdrawals and pay cash instead of using an EFTPOS card. There are also one-off fees (e.g. $10 to $35) for a range of services such as overdrawing an account, buying a bank cheque, stopping a cheque, obtaining a replacement statement and writing a rubber (bounced) cheque. The ABA and Centrelink have produced a joint brochure on how to minimise banking fees.

Banks are trying to introduce a 'user-pays' system, where fees are related to the amount of work involved in processing transactions, which means that there are lower fees for electronic banking than over-the-counter branch transactions. Some accounts are exclusively for those who use the electronic banking network to make withdrawals and levy no fees (although there's a penalty rate for over-the-counter withdrawals). Some banks have fee exemptions for customers under the age of 18 or 21, tertiary students and pensioners. Always shop around for the lowest fees. **Note that few building societies and credit unions impose account-keeping fees.**

**Government Taxes:** These are levied on transaction accounts by state and territory governments and in many cases exceed the cost of bank charges. Debits Tax (or bank account debit tax, known as BAD!) is paid on all withdrawals from accounts with a cheque facility, in all states and territories. It's levied on a sliding scale which penalises those who make regular small withdrawals rather than a few large amounts each month. In most states, debits tax is 30¢ on withdrawals of $1 to $99, 70¢ on $100 to $499, $1.50 on $500 to $4,999, $3 on $5,000 to $9,999, and $4 on $10,000 or more.

Debits tax is due be abolished between 1st January 2002 and 1st July 2005 depending on the state (financial institutions duty (FID) was abolished on 1st July 2001). Stamp duty is payable on cheques in South Australia, Western Australia and Norfolk Island, and is deducted from your account when a cheque book is issued.

**Cheques:** Personal cheques aren't usually accepted in payment in retail outlets in Australia, as they cannot be guaranteed (Australian banks don't issue cheque guarantee cards). Where cheques are accepted, you must usually produce identification in the form of a bank card or driving licence. Cheques aren't usually crossed, although you can cross your own cheques by drawing two parallel lines across the face. This theoretically provides additional security, because a crossed cheque can be paid only into a bank account and cannot be cashed. There are a number of ways to further safeguard your cheques, one of which is to write 'not negotiable' between the two parallel lines, which means that the cheque cannot be cashed by a third party. Alternatively, you can write 'account payee only' between the lines, which means that the cheque must be paid into the account of the named payee. For extra security, you can add both 'not negotiable' and 'account payee only' to a cheque. If you cross out the words 'or bearer' on a cheque, this prevents anyone except the named person from cashing it. You can also arrange with your bank that no cash cheques can be drawn on your account and print on cheques the $ limit that can be drawn on any one cheque. Australian cheques are valid for 15 months after the date written on them. **Note that a post-dated cheque can be honoured by your bank before the date written on it.**

To obtain cash from a bank, write the cheque in your own name or write 'cash' alongside 'Pay to' and don't cross it (but never send a cheque made out to cash through the post). Take great care when sending cheques by post, particularly for large amounts, as it isn't unknown for cheques to be stolen and paid into another account.

Some 4 million cheques (around $23 billion) are cleared via the Australian Payments Clearing Association system each day. Clearing takes around two to three days, which is painfully slow in the age of electronic banking, when cheques could easily be cleared the same day they're paid into a bank (if you make a cash withdrawal or payment, you can bet your life it's debited immediately!). The reason is simple: banks invest the money on the overnight short-term money market and would lose $millions if they paid money out as quickly they received it.

# Savings Accounts

All banks, building societies and credit unions provide a range of savings accounts, usually referred to as deposit or investment accounts in Australia, many of which are intended for short or medium term savings, rather than long-term growth. Other types of savings accounts include deeming accounts, cash management trusts, mortgage offset accounts, and savings investment bonus accounts. Retirement Savings Accounts (RSAs) are aimed at capturing the superannuation payments of casual and itinerant workers.

When choosing an account, the most important considerations are how much money you wish to save (which may be a lump sum or a monthly amount), how quickly you need access to it in an emergency and whether you require additional services such as those provided by transaction accounts (see above). For example, you may wish to have instant access to your cash via ATMs with no limit on withdrawals.

You may find a high interest cheque account (often given a fancy name such as a 'cash management call account') useful, as it provides all the usual facilities of a transaction account, plus high interest depending on the account balance (which must usually be a minimum of around $5,000).

Before committing your money to a long-term savings account or investment, you should shop around for the best deal, as interest rates, conditions and fees can vary considerably. Banks, building societies and credit unions frequently introduce new accounts paying increased rates of interest, **but they don't usually notify existing customers of this (they aren't in the habit of giving money away unnecessarily).** Some banks automatically deposit your cash in a standard-rate term deposit when a super-rate term deposit ends. One thing you should *never* do is keep a large amount, say more than $1,000, in a transaction account, which pays a derisory interest rate. Note that interest rates are forever changing in Australia (increasing or decreasing in line with the official bank lending rate) and it may not pay you to tie your up money for a long period.

Most banks and building societies have two basic types of savings accounts: instant access and term deposit accounts. Instant access accounts, as the name says, allow you instant access to your money. There's usually a minimum balance, which may be as low as $50 or as high as $5,000. With some high balance accounts, all deposits and withdrawals must be over $1,000. Interest rates usually depend on the account balance, e.g. $500, $1,000, $5,000 or $10,000.

With a term deposit account, you're required to give notice before you make a withdrawal, which can be anything from 30 days to five years. Note that term deposits can usually only be repaid earlier in exceptional circumstances, when a sharply-reduced rate of interest applies. Interest is usually calculated daily and paid monthly, quarterly, six-monthly, annually and/or at maturity. Not surprisingly, term deposit accounts pay higher rates of interest than instant access. However, if there's any possibility that you will need immediate access to your money, you should keep it in an instant access account (in any case, the interest rate on short-term deposit accounts varies little from that of the best instant access accounts).

Note that non-residents are subject to a withholding tax of 10 per cent on the income earned on bank deposits in Australia, which is deducted at source when interest is paid.

# Cash & Debit Cards

One of the most important innovations in banking in the last decade or so has been the introduction of cash and debit cards, known as Electronic Funds Transfer at Point Of Sale (EFTPOS) cards, which are routinely issued to all transaction account holders in Australia.

**Cash Cards:** A cash card allows you to withdraw money from Automatic Teller Machines (ATMs), commonly known as cash machines, 24 hours a day, seven days a week (provided they don't run out of money). The freedom from bank queues, banking hours and bank tellers provided by cash cards is very convenient, and you should think twice before opening an account which doesn't provide ATMs locally (although most small financial institutions have arrangements with larger banks or building societies). Most people would rather use cash machines than deal with a bank clerk; apart from being time-consuming, it can be *very* expensive. Cash cards can also be used at service stations, supermarkets and other retail outlets throughout

Australia. You can also pay for telephone calls in certain public call boxes, although there are very few of these left.

Cash cards can be used to withdraw a maximum of around $500 per day from any of the participating bank's or building society's ATMs or those belonging to the same network. The big four banks' ATM networks are: Night & Day (ANZ), Autobank (Commonwealth), Flexiteller (National) and Handybank (WBC). Some networks are linked so that you can use your cash or EFTPOS (and credit) cards in ATMs belonging to different banks, e.g. Commonwealth Bank/WBC and ANZ/National Bank, where customers have access to some 5,500 ATMs. Customers of regional banks, building societies and credit unions also have access through reciprocal arrangements. Most banks and building societies allow a certain number of free withdrawals per month (e.g. eight) from machines belonging to their own network, but there's a charge (usually $1) for using an ATM belonging to another bank or network.

Other services provided by banks and building societies via ATMs include mini-statements (usually the last five transactions), account balances, the paying of bills (via a bank giro) and credit card payments, deposits (cash and cheques), transfers between accounts, cheque book and statement ordering, and the facility to change your Personal Identification Number (PIN). Note that these services are usually available only via cash machines at branches of your own bank.

When your application for a card is approved, your card and PIN are sent under separate cover (for security reasons). If you don't have a secure mail box (i.e. a private address or personal mail box), you should collect your PIN from your bank. For extra security, some banks activate cards only after customers have reported their safe arrival. **If you receive an unwanted, unsolicited card, you should cut it up and return it to your bank or building society with instructions to cancel it.** For security reasons, you should **destroy your PIN as soon as you've remembered it and you should never write it down (not even coded).**

The procedure for withdrawing money from ATMs varies from bank to bank and even between ATMs at different branches of the same bank, but is roughly as follows:

1. Check that the ATM is in service, which may be shown by an 'OPEN' sign, a light or a display on the screen. If the machine is out of service, a message to this effect is usually displayed. This it usually means that the machine has run out of cash (common at weekends) or that the bank's computer is out of order. Sometimes an ATM will be unable to dispense cash, but will allow you to do other things such as check your account balance.

2. Insert your card as shown in the illustration on the machine. Most ATMs have a (usually transparent) protective cover which opens automatically. A screen message asks you to enter your PIN on the keyboard. As a security measure, if you enter the wrong PIN a number of times (e.g. three), your card will be retained by the machine and you must contact your bank for its return. You may need to press a 'proceed' key (usually coloured green) to continue after entering your PIN.

3. After you've entered your PIN, the display will ask you which service you require, e.g. cash withdrawal (with or without a receipt). Press the button corresponding to the service required (usually indicated by arrows at the edge of the screen).

4. If you're withdrawing cash, you must now enter the amount required (up to your card's limit) in multiples of $10, e.g. $20, $50 or $100, usually dispensed in $10 or $20 notes. Sometimes you'll need to press the proceed key to continue.

5. At this point your card will be returned and your cash and receipt dispensed. Don't forget to take them all with you!

A 'cancel' or 'error' button (usually coloured red) is provided to terminate a transaction at any point. Your card will be returned and you can start again, if required.

Although it's rare, ATMs do go wrong and occasionally give too little cash (too much if you're luck is in), make mistakes on receipts. Sometimes, 'phantom withdrawals' turn up on your bank statement. You should therefore always obtain receipts for withdrawals and check them against your statement. If you have a problem with a machine, make a note of its location, the date and time, and exactly what happened. Notify your bank as soon as possible. Note, however, that you have only a slim chance of convincing your bank that their 'infallible' machine has made a mistake. Don't keep a lot of money in an account for which you have a cash card and *never* have a cash card for a savings account with a large balance. Beware of using ATMs in 'high risk' areas at night, as muggings occasionally occur. If you lose your cash card, you must notify the issuing bank immediately by telephone and confirm it in writing.

**EFTPOS (Debit) Cards:** Most cash cards are also EFTPOS cards, which are accepted by most retailers and mail-order businesses in Australia and have largely replaced cheques. Over half of all card transactions in Australia are made with EFTPOS cards. There's no limit to the amount you can pay with an EFTPOS card, but you must have the money in your account (or have an authorised overdraft). Many retailers, e.g. supermarkets, allow customers to obtain cash (known as 'cash-back') when buying goods with an EFTPOS card. Many cards can also be used overseas, e.g. Visa or Mastercard 'EFTPOS' cards, to obtain cash and buy goods and services, although there's a charge for obtaining cash.

**Recent Innovations:** Australian banks have invested $millions in creating their networks of ATMs, which some believe will become white elephants as 'smart card' technology is introduced over the next few years. Smart cards contain computer chips (rather than a magnetic strip) and can be used to store a wide range of financial and personal information. New chip technology in smart cards will also combat credit card fraud, which is relatively low in Australia (compared, for example, with Europe) at just 5¢ for every $100 spent. Some ATMs already accept smart cards. Reloadable 'electronic cash' cards with a stored-value (also known as stored value cards or SVCs) are also being introduced in Australia, as are PC-linked credit cards compatible with computers and the Internet. These allow you to order and pay for goods and services via your home or business computer. Both Mastercard and Visa have created 'virtual' credit cards to allow secure payments to be made over the Internet.

# Credit & Charge Cards

Australia is one of the most credit-oriented societies in the world, and in 2001 the average Australian owed around $3,000 on credit and charge cards. Most Australians have a number of credit and charge cards (with a credit limit of up to $10,000 on each), which are accepted by most retail outlets, whatever their size (although you may have a problem using a credit card in remote areas and small towns or in small shops and restaurants). Cards can be used to purchase goods by mail or over the telephone, both in Australia and overseas, although goods should only be sent to the cardholder's address. It's sometimes wise to ask for the carbon paper when you purchase goods in person, as it can be used to obtain your credit card number and a copy of your signature. Always check that a credit card slip is made out for the correct amount before signing it.

The most commonly accepted credit cards in Australia are Bankcard (Australia's own credit card organisation), Mastercard and Visa (and affiliates). Most outlets that accept Bankcard also accept Mastercard and Visa. American Express, Diners Club and Carte Blanche charge cards are also widely accepted. All banks, building societies, and many credit unions and major retailers offer their own credit cards in Australia. Many major department and chain stores in Australia issue their own account credit cards (store cards) and some don't accept any cards other than their own. Interest rates are quoted monthly and are usually *very* high, e.g. up to double what you pay with Visa or Mastercard. It isn't always necessary to have an account with a financial institution to obtain a credit card.

The main difference between the two types of card is that with a charge card you can defer paying the bill for a few weeks or months but must pay the total balance outstanding when it's due (otherwise a penalty payment is payable), whereas a credit card allows you to defer payment for an indefinite period provided you repay a minimum amount (usually aroud 2 to 3 per cent of the outstanding balance) each month and don't exceed your credit limit. Not surprisingly, credit cards are much more popular than charge cards, both with cardholders and businesses. One of the major advantages of international charge cards (e.g. Amex and Diners Club) is that, if they're lost or stolen, they can usually be replaced at short notice when you're travelling, e.g. within 24 hours in some countries. Charge cards also generally offer more benefits than credit cards, particularly for international travellers. Otherwise, you may find that charge cards offer few advantages over credit cards, some of which, e.g. Visa or Mastercard, are more widely accepted, both in Australia and worldwide. Credit cards are also cheaper and more convenient to use.

Both credit and charge cards are issued as ordinary, gold and platinum cards, with different credit and benefit levels. Gold card holders must usually have an annual income of over $50,000 per year and net assets of over $100,000. Even if you don't like plastic money and shun any form of credit, credit cards do have their uses. For example, no deposits on rental cars, no pre-paying hotel bills, safety and security, and above all, convenience. However, in the wrong hands they're a disaster and should be shunned by spendthrifts.

**Costs:** Banks compete fiercely for credit card customers, both on interest rates and the supplementary services attached to cards. The annual fee varies from $30 upwards for a standard card and up to $100 for a gold card. The lowest rates are usually charged by credit unions, some of which charge no annual fee, although they may not give you any interest-free credit days. If you spend over a certain sum on your card, e.g. $1,500, the annual fee may be waived. A number of cards can be issued for a single account (a second card is usually issued free). When choosing a card, bear in mind that a free card with no annual fee may have a high interest rate (which is fine if you plan to pay off the balance each month).

**Interest:** The interest rates charged on credit card balances in mid-2001 were between around 12.5 and 17 per cent. Most cards offer 15 to 55 days' interest-free credit, although there are no free credit days on some cards. Note that banks rarely pass on interest rate cuts to credit card holders. Card issuers use various methods to calculate the interest on cash advances and outstanding balances. (Interest is always charged on cash advances immediately and the interest-free period doesn't apply.) Note also that, if the amount owing isn't paid in full, interest is charged from the date of purchase and the interest-free period is lost altogether. Some cards allow an interest-free period on new purchases only if the balance at the start is zero. A higher interest rate is usually charged on cards offering an interest-free period and there's also usually an annual fee. If you intend to pay off the amount owed in full each month, choose a card with no fee (or a low fee) and the longest interest-free period. Otherwise choose a card with a low interest rate. The best cards are obviously those with no annual or a low annual fee *and* a low interest rate, which are usually restricted to homeowners and/or those with an excellent credit rating.

Credit cards are definitely not for long-term borrowers, although if you borrow less than $1,000 and pay it off within one year it may be cheaper than a loan. Interest is usually paid when your credit card account has a positive balance, i.e. you pay more money to your bank than is owed on a card (you may wish to do this when you plan to overspend your usual credit limit but want the security of using a credit card).

**Benefits:** You should also compare the benefits offered by card issuers, which may include travel and holiday discounts, foreign currency ordering, helplines, special offers on new cars, air miles and other points schemes (see below), reduced hotel and car rental rates, free travel insurance, commission-free travellers' cheques, and free insurance on goods purchased with the card. Some cards, called affinity cards, have ties with registered charities, where a charity (or a number of charities) benefits each time a card is used, although the amount that goes to the charity is minuscule.

Loyalty points are a big attraction for cardholders, where you receive reward points for each transaction (usually one point for each $1 spent). Benefits include free travel, discounted goods and other freebies. Cards are offered by banks in conjunction with companies such as Telstra, General Motors-Holden, Qantas and Ansett. Frequent flyer points can be earned when using credit cards. Card issuers sometimes offer promotions such as 1,000 bonus points for new customers and free prize draws. However, whatever the benefits on offer, you should always check a card's fees and interest rates.

**Credit Limit:** The credit limit for most card holders is around $2,000, although some card issuers allow you to choose your spending limit up to $10,000. Gold and platinum cards have higher credit limits than ordinary cards (or no limit at all). Increasing your credit limit is usually a formality, provided your credit rating is good and you always pay your bills on time. When changing card companies, check that you'll be able to keep your previous credit limit and that you don't lose any important benefits. Many card companies allow existing card holders to transfer their card balance when switching cards and offer a lower rate of interest (for a limited period).

**Cash Withdrawals:** Credit cards can be used to obtain cash from ATMs in Australia and overseas. To do so, you need to enter a personal identification number (PIN). Most banks allow customers to choose their own PIN, although if you use your birth date or telephone number as your PIN you may not be compensated if a card is stolen and used. The PIN must be reasonably disguised and mustn't be written down or contained in documents carried with a card. When you use your card to obtain cash, there's a handling charge and/or commission and a daily limit, e.g. $500 or $1,000. Interest is levied on cash withdrawals from the date of the withdrawal.

**Bills:** Most credit cards require you to repay a minimum of $10 or 2 to 3 per cent of the balance each month, whichever is the greater. If you pay the full amount outstanding, you won't be charged interest and will receive up to seven weeks' free credit. Some credit card issuers offer protection insurance which covers payments in case of sickness, accident or unemployment (check exactly what's covered), which is worth considering. Protection insurance premiums are calculated according to your account balance and are added to your monthly card payment.

**Lost or Stolen Cards:** If you lose a credit card or it's stolen, report it immediately to the police and the issuing office and confirm the loss in writing as soon as possible. Credit card fraud costs $millions a year, although much of it could be eliminated by the use of cards incorporating the holder's photograph and using a PIN number (which must be entered via a keypad each time a card is used), as is the case in some other countries. Most retailers don't bother to check signatures, many of which are illegible anyway.

# MORTGAGES

Mortgages (home loans) in Australia are available from over 110 sources, including banks, building societies, credit unions, mortgage originators/providers, mortgage managers, finance and insurance companies, motoring organisations and state housing authorities. The Commonwealth Bank is the largest lender (around $10 billion annually) followed by the Westpac Banking Corporation. Competition to lend you money is fierce, and homebuyers in Australia have a wider variety of home loan finance than is available in many other countries. However, despite the increased competition, banks still handle over 80 per cent of new home loans. The usual home loan period is 25 years, although it can be anything from 5 to 30 years (or up to the age at which a state pension is paid), while the maximum term for land loans is usually 20 years. The number of mortages taken out in 1999–2000 was up 12 per cent on the previous year, and nearly half of homeowners have a mortgage, the average loan being $136,500. Many lenders offer additional benefits such as free home insurance and life assurance.

**Government Loans:** The Commonwealth and state governments provide funds for housing loans through the Commonwealth/State Housing Agreement, with loan repayments linked to the borrower's income. Interest subsidies provided during the early years of the loan are generally recovered when the borrower's income permits. In most states, the loans are made through co-operative building societies, a list of which is maintained by the state Registrar of Co-operative Societies. Housing commissions and state banks in some states also provide loans, although eligibility is restricted to low and moderate-income families and there are often long waiting lists.

**Interest Rates:** Since March 1996, when the Liberal-National coalition government came to power, the mortgage interest rate has been cut by almost 5 per cent, and, despite several marginal increases made by the Reserve Bank during 2000 and 2001, the interest rate for variable-rate mortgages in mid-2001 was only 6 per cent. In recent years, loans have also been cheaper thanks to increased competition between the banks and other lenders. The major banks have been savaged by smaller, non-bank rivals offering better deals, which has resulted in some excellent offers for borrowers. Banks have been forced to cut their margins (the difference between what they pay on deposits and the home loan rate) from 4 or 5 per cent to around 3 per cent in order to compete with mortgage originators such as Aussie Home Loans, who charge borrowers only some 1.7 per cent above the cost of obtaining funds. In 2001, banks were offering lower interest rates to selected customers such as professionals and other 'high net-worth' individuals.

However, low rates also have their down side, as they encourage people to borrow more than they can afford, and according to surveys a high percentage of Australian families are burdened by their loan repayments. The average size of a home loan has risen by 60 per cent since 1990 to twice disposable income, and home loan defaults have increased, owing partly to a decline in the quality of lending, particularly by mortgage providers, who tend to market loans more aggressively and lend to people that banks reject. There are fears that the number of defaulters will soar if interest rates increase again.

You shouldn't rush into taking out a mortgage, particularly if your income isn't secure. Many people are denied mortgages because of bad credit ratings or insecure employment, which may include the self-employed, who usually need to produce a number of years' tax returns (usually two). It's possible to take out a mortgage protection policy in case you fall ill, have an accident or are made redundant and are unable to pay your mortgage, although it can be expensive and there are many loopholes. Most lenders offer a 'home loan protection plan' which guarantees repayments in case of death or permanent disability.

**Repayments:** Using the table below, it's easy to calculate your monthly and total mortgage repayments. For example, if you borrow $100,000 at 7 per cent over 25 years, your monthly payments will be 100 x $7.07 = $707. Multiply that figure by 12 to arrive at your annual repayments and the result by the number of years of the mortgage term to find out your total repayments.

| Interest Rate | Term of Loan (Years) | | | | | |
|---|---|---|---|---|---|---|
| | 5 | 10 | 15 | 20 | 25 | 30 |
| **Monthly Payments per $1,000 Borrowed ($)** | | | | | | |
| 6% | 19.33 | 11.10 | 8.44 | 7.16 | 6.44 | 6.00 |
| 7% | 19.80 | 11.61 | 8.99 | 7.75 | 7.07 | 6.65 |
| 8% | 20.28 | 12.13 | 9.56 | 8.36 | 7.72 | 7.34 |
| 9% | 20.76 | 12.67 | 10.14 | 9.00 | 8.39 | 8.05 |
| 10% | 21.25 | 13.22 | 10.75 | 9.65 | 9.09 | 8.78 |
| 11% | 21.74 | 13.78 | 11.37 | 10.32 | 9.80 | 9.52 |
| 12% | 22.24 | 14.35 | 12.00 | 11.01 | 10.53 | 10.29 |

Your monthly mortgage repayments mustn't usually be more than 30 per cent of your gross basic income – a couple's incomes are combined (some 60 per cent of families paying off a home loan in Australia have two or more wage earners). The average home loan repayments are around 25 per cent of family earnings (down from around 35 per cent in the late '80s), with the average home loan $136,500 and average repayments around $950 a month. Sydney owner-occupiers are generally more highly geared than Melbourne families. Note that it's usually necessary to have a high income and a secure job to get into and remain in homeownership in Australia, and only some 40 per cent of buyers pay over 30 per cent of their wages towards a mortgage. Interest is calculated on the daily loan balance and charged monthly. Repayments can be paid fortnightly (which can save a considerable amount over the term of a loan) or monthly. Some lenders allow you to reduce your payments by up to 50 per cent for up to six months when taking maternity or paternity leave.

**Deposit:** Although it's possible to obtain a loan for the whole cost of a property (a 100 per cent mortgage) from some developers, particularly if you're a first-time buyer, most lenders expect borrowers to pay a deposit of 5 to 25 per cent of the purchase price. The average deposit paid is around a third of the value of a property in Sydney and some 40 per cent in Melbourne. Housing loan insurance is payable when a loan is greater than 75 or 80 per cent of the value of a property. The insurance premium is usually between $250 and $500 or 1 per cent of the loan value, and is normally added to the loan amount. Expensive 'captive' mortgage insurance is offered by some lenders, when you pay around 20 per cent above the market rate (shop around for independent mortgage insurance). Note that mortgage insurance contracts cover the lender and not the borrower.

**Fixed-Rate or Variable-Rate:** You can usually choose between a fixed-rate and a variable-rate mortgage. With the latter, the interest rate goes up and down in accordance with fluctuations in the bank base rate. Those who cannot afford an increase in their mortgage repayments are usually better off with a fixed-rate mortgage, where the interest rate is fixed for the term of the loan or a number of years (e.g. one to ten), irrespective of what happens to bank lending rates in the meantime. The longer the fixed-rate period, the lower the interest rate offered. If interest rates go down, you may find yourself paying more than the current mortgage rate, but at least you'll know exactly what you must pay each month. To judge whether a fixed-rate mortgage is worthwhile, you must estimate in which direction interest rates are heading (a difficult feat). Most variable-rate loans offer borrowers the option to fix the rate at any time, e.g. when interest rates are rising, and some mortgages combine fixed and variable-rate loans (split fixed/variable rate), which some analysts recommend as the best compromise. Note, however, that this means taking out two loans and incurring higher fees. Homebuyers have shunned fixed-rate loans in recent years as rates have tumbled, although the number is now increasing sharply ahead of fears of interest rate rises.

**Types of Loans:** There are few different types of home loans in Australia, where most are repayment mortgages (endowment, pension and other types of mortgages are rare). Standard home loans often include extra flexibility, including additional payments, offset accounts, redraw facilities, variations to payment frequency and fixed-variable splits. However, many lenders offer basic variable-rate loans with fewer features than standard loans (such as no offset account or redraw facility). Most lenders offer low-start (honeymoon-rate) loans, which reduce your mortgage payments for a number of years (usually one or two). Note that around a third of all complaints against banks concern home loans, in particular honeymoon-rate loans, on which banks levy high fees.

A new type of loan introduced in recent years is an equity overdraft loan (called current account mortgages in Britain). It works like a standard overdraft bank account where the more money you pay into your account the lower the amount owed (and hence less interest is payable), and you can borrow money whenever you wish (usually up to your original mortgage limit) at the same rate of interest as your mortgage (it isn't recommended for spendthrifts).

**Reducing the Term:** Variable-rate mortgages usually allow extra payments to be made. Note that paying an extra 10 per cent each month can knock five or six years off the repayment term of a 25-year mortgage. One of the advantages of standard bank loans is that they usually have greater flexibility than other loans and offer additional features, such as redraw facilities and offset accounts. If you make extra payments, a redraw facility allows you to 're-borrow' the money later if the need arises. An offset account enables you to deposit money in a special account and receive interest in the form of a reduction in the interest payable on your loan. This means that a larger part of your repayments goes towards reducing the principal, resulting in significant interest savings and the loan being paid off quicker. An example of an offset account is the Commonwealth Bank's 'mortgage interest saver account' (MISA). Money lodged in a MISA is available on call, and you don't pay bank fees on deposits and withdrawals (each of which must be a minimum of $1,000), although no interest is paid. A minimum balance of $2,000 must be maintained. Making payments fortnightly instead of monthly will also help you pay off a loan quicker.

**Fees & Charges:** Various fees are associated with mortgages, including a mortgage application or establishment fee, a valuation fee, legal fees, maintenance fees and a loan registration fee. The mortgage establishment fee is usually between $300 and $800, although some banks (e.g. the Commonwealth Bank and WBC) have cut or eliminated fees for setting up mortgages, although they may be clawed back by administrative or maintenance fees. Most lenders don't charge a valuation fee, although it can be up to $275. Legal fees are usually waived. Some mortgages have a maintenance fee, e.g. $60 to $100, which may apply only to certain types of loans. Loan registration costs vary from $58 (NSW) to $90 (NT). Stamp duty is also payable on mortgages in all states except the ACT and Northern Territory (the average is around $425 on a $100,000 mortgage and $850 on a $200,000 mortgage).

Some mortgages carry crippling discharge (redemption) or exit fees if they're repaid early, although most now charge $100 to $650 plus a state fee ranging from $50 (NSW) to $107.10 (Tasmania). While most borrowers never change their lenders, some homeowners re-mortgage every two or three years after shopping around for the best deal available. However, you must do your sums carefully, as changing lenders can be expensive. Some banks offer lower 'loyalty rates' of interest for customers who have maintained a loan for five years or more. While mortgage interest rates have fallen in recent years, fees have risen. Always make sure that you receive a list of all costs associated with a loan, including discharge fees.

**Foreign Currency Mortgages:** It's possible to obtain a foreign currency mortgage, e.g. in Swiss francs, US dollars, Deutschmarks or Japanese yen, all currencies which, with their historically low interest rates, have provided huge savings for borrowers in recent years. However, you should be cautious about taking out a foreign currency mortgage, as interest rate gains can be wiped out overnight by currency swings. In the '80s many Australians took out Swiss franc loans and were unable to maintain their payments when the value of the A$ plummeted against the Swiss franc in later years. Most mainstream lenders advise against taking out foreign currency home loans unless you're paid in a foreign currency. The conditions are much stricter than for A$ loans, e.g. they're generally granted only to high-rollers (e.g. those earning a minimum of $100,000 a year) and are usually for a minimum of $200,000 and a maximum of 60 per cent of a property's value.

**Advice & Information:** Whatever type of home loan you choose, take time to investigate all the options and bear in mind that mortgage advice offered by lenders is often deliberately misleading and isn't to be trusted. One way of finding the best deal is to contact an independent mortgage broker. One such company is Mortgage Choice in Sydney (☎ freecall 1800-646789, 🖳 www.mortagechoice.com.au), a one-stop shop for those seeking the best mortgage deal and offering hundreds of home loan deals from which to choose. Note, however, that brokers earn their living from fees paid by lenders and therefore may not always be impartial. Solicitors in some states (e.g. NSW) offer homebuyers a free home loan service. This is a one-stop mortgage service managing every part of the home buying process, including conveyancing, mortgage searches and advising on the best lender. However, although solicitors are bound by fiduciary duty to give independent advice, they may receive fees from lenders. MoneyChoice (operated by the Australian Consumers' Association, see page 443) offers a 24-hour automated telephone service which provides a list of the five lowest-cost lenders; you can have a more comprehensive printout faxed or mailed to you (☎ 1900-170088 – $1.95 per minute, a typical call costing $8).

Wherever you obtain advice, always ensure that it's impartial (ask whether an adviser is being paid a commission by a lender). Invaluable independent advice and comparative tables of lenders are published in specialist magazines such as *Your Mortgage* (quarterly). For information about buying property, see **Chapter 5**.

# PROPERTY & LAND TAXES

Property taxes (called council rates in Australia) are levied by councils on homeowners to pay for local services. These include town planning and building control, health inspections, rubbish collection and disposal (which may be charged separately), roads, footpaths, parks and recreational facilities, libraries, and community and welfare services. In some states there's a swimming pool levy to ensure compliance with safety standards. Rates are based on the 'rateable value' of a property, officially called the 'unimproved capital value', which is reassessed every few years by the Valuer General's Department. Rates are levied annually but are usually paid quarterly. Check the current rates before buying a property, as in some areas they can be very high (pensioners may receive a concession). Rates usually also increase when land valuations go up, although there's a limit on what councils can charge.

Land tax is levied on the ownership of land in all states and territories except the Northern Territory. It's based on the unimproved value of land (i.e. excluding the value of any buildings or capital improvements) at a prescribed date, e.g. 31st December in NSW, which is determined by a state's Valuer General. There's usually a threshold, below which no land tax is payable. In NSW, land tax is payable on investment property holdings (not principal residences) whose land content is valued at over $205,000 at a standard rate of 1.7 per cent; there's also a premium property tax for properties valued at over $1,319,000. In Queensland land tax is only payable if the land is worth over $221,665 and if you've been awarded a deduction claim (as most people are); primary residences are exempt. In ACT land tax is levied at 1 per cent on land valued at up to $100,000, at 1.25 per cent plus $1,000 on land valued between $100,000 and $200,000, and at 1.5 per cent plus $2,250 on land valued at over $200,000. Victoria scrapped land tax on family homes on 1st January 1998 and now taxes only business land holdings, investment properties and holiday homes.

# GOODS & SERVICES TAX (GST)

Australia originally levied a wholesale tax, which was applied at varying rates on a limited range of 'new' goods. In July 2000, as part of a major tax reform, a goods and services tax (GST) was introduced. GST is a broad-based tax (similar to VAT in western European countries) and is levied at a flat rate of 10 per cent on most goods and services. GST is included in the price you pay, and an 'easy' way to calculate the amount of GST on goods and services is to divide the price by 11. Some items are exempt from GST, such as basic foods, certain medical aids and appliances, and cars for the disabled.

The introduction of GST has been a logistical and public relations disaster for the government. Large and small businesses have had tremendous problems in the interpretation and implementation of GST rules, which for a single item may run into several paragraphs! The government has also had to introduce compensatory measures such as the Educational Textbook Subsidy (see page 209), which was offered to students when they objected to the ten per cent increase in the price of books.

In mid-2001, on the first anniversary of the introduction of GST, statistics were released showing that bankruptcies were at a record high and consumer spending at an all-time low, although it wasn't clear whether these were caused by GST or other economic factors. Large groups including pensioners and the self-employed claim that GST has made them significantly worse off. On the other hand, some groups such as fresh food retailers and jewellers (unaffected by GST) have seen sales grow strongly. The general impression is that GST is a negative, time-comsuming tax that has generally made Australians poorer and has done little to combat the black market.

Businesses with an annual turnover of $50,000 or more are required to register for GST. Most businesses must lodge a quarterly return to pay or claim GST, although if a company's annual turnover exceeds $20 million a monthly return must be made.

For sales tax on motor vehicles and motorcycles, see **Vehicle Import** on page 240. For information on GST refunds for tourists see **GST Tourist Refund** on page 442.

# INCOME TAX

As in many countries, there's a two-tier tax system in Australia, first class for the self-employed and companies and a second class system, called pay-as-you-go (PAYG), for employees (see page 351. The self-employed pay their tax in arrears, whereas an employee's income tax is deducted at source from his salary by his employer. There's no state income tax in Australia, although it may be introduced under wide-ranging tax reforms currently under consideration. The income tax year in Australia runs from 1st July to 30th June of the following year (for reasons known only to the tax office). Tax is calculated on taxable income derived during the income tax year, although in certain circumstances a substitute accounting year beginning on a different date may be used. Changes in federal taxation are usually announced in the annual budget in May. Australian income tax law recognises the following general types of taxpayer: individuals, companies, partnerships and trusts. Specific provisions apply to minors, superannuation funds, insurance companies, primary producers, mining operations and certain other businesses.

**Domicile:** Residents of Australia are taxed on their worldwide income and non-residents only on Australian income. An individual is resident in Australia for tax purposes if he:

● normally resides in Australia *or*

● is domiciled in Australia and doesn't have a permanent place of abode outside the country *or*

● spends at least 183 days per financial year in Australia (unless he doesn't intend to take up Australian residence and has a usual place of abode outside Australia).

**Double-Taxation Agreements:** Australia has double-taxation agreements with over 38 countries, including Argentina, Austria, Belgium, Canada, China, the Czech Republic, Denmark, Fiji, Finland, France, Germany, Hungary, India, Indonesia, Ireland, Italy, Japan, Kiribati, the Republic of Korea, Malaysia, Malta, the Netherlands, New Zealand, Norway, Papua New Guinea, the Philippines, Poland, Romania, Singapore, Slovak Republic, South Africa, Spain, Sri Lanka, Sweden, Switzerland, Thailand, the United Kingdom, the USA and Vietnam. Despite their name, double-taxation agreements are designed to prevent you paying double taxes and not to ensure that you pay twice! Under double-taxation agreements, certain categories of people are exempt from paying Australian tax. If part of your income is taxed overseas in a country with a double-taxation treaty with Australia, you won't be required to pay Australian tax on that income.

Foreign employees working in Australia for Australian companies or organisations are subject to Australian tax on their earnings. However, if your stay is less than six months, you aren't considered an Australian resident and are subject to Australian tax at the rates applicable to non-residents (see page 351). However, double-taxation agreements contain particular articles dealing with government services, professors, teachers, directors and entertainers, which may alter this position. If you stay in Australia for longer than six months, you may be considered an Australian resident and will then pay tax at the same rates as residents. Salary and wage income earned by residents from services performed overseas is exempt if the taxpayer has been employed outside Australia for a continuous period of at least 91 days, provided the income has been taxed overseas.

In addition to Australian taxes, you may also be liable for taxes in your home country. Citizens of most countries are exempt from paying taxes in their home country when they spend a minimum period overseas, e.g. one year. One exception is citizens of the USA. It's usually your responsibility to familiarise yourself with the tax procedures in your home country or country of domicile. If you're in doubt about your tax liability in your home country, contact your embassy or consulate. American citizens can obtain a copy of a brochure entitled *Tax Guide for US Citizens and Resident Aliens Abroad* from American Embassies.

**Tax Audits:** The number of taxpayers audited (checked up on) has more than doubled since self-assessment was introduced in 1987, to almost 500,000 a year. Some 70 per cent of those audited are found to have made mistakes, usually (not surprisingly) in their own favour. Among the individuals who come under scrutiny are academics with travel claims, those who have received eligible termination payments or rental property deductions, 'hobby' farmers and business people (such as musicians, glass blowers, knitters, candle-makers, photographers, wood-turners), small businesses (especially), the self-employed and contractors, those selling Amway and other home products, and those making claims for motor vehicles, self-education and home offices. An estimated 75,000 people falsely state that they're self-employed, thus claiming extra deductions.

There are heavy penalties if you make mistakes, which can be as high as 90 per cent of the tax owed plus interest. The Australian Taxation Office (ATO) receives information from a variety of sources, including banks, building societies, credit unions, employers and companies paying dividends. The ATO also provides incentives to those who 'dob in' (report) tax cheats and has tightened up its ability to collect tax and catch tax dodgers in recent years. Note, however, that the ATO is bound by privacy legislation and can only give information about a taxpayer to government agencies authorised to receive it. The ATO has a 'taxpayers' charter' to protect the public from 'rogue' tax officers.

**Tax Evasion & Avoidance:** Tax evasion in Australia is a criminal offence, for which you can be heavily fined or even imprisoned. Nevertheless, most Australians don't consider it a crime to cheat the tax office – an attitude that has spawned a nation of tax fiddlers (it's a national sport). Australia has a flourishing black economy, which the ATO estimates costs around $15 billion per year in unpaid tax on undeclared income.

Tax avoidance, i.e. legally paying as little tax as possible, if necessary by finding and exploiting loopholes in the tax laws, is a different matter altogether to tax evasion. It's practised by most companies, wealthy individuals and self-employed people. Unfortunately there are few (legal) ways an individual paying PAYG tax can reduce his income tax bill (dying is one of them), although it's possible to appeal against your tax bill or anything connected with your tax affairs which you believe is incorrect.

If you own a company or are self-employed, you can delay paying your tax for a period by appealing against a tax demand. As in many countries, the wealthiest Australians use elaborate schemes to avoid paying tax and take maximum advantage of low-tax investments (while the ATO targets Aussie battlers!). Many wealthy Australians avoid or minimise their income tax by establishing trusts, which cost the government $millions per year in 'lost' tax. However, the tax office is planning a crackdown on overseas tax shelters and trusts, and legislation is planned for the near future. Almost 2 million Australians are estimated to use trusts in some form. Note that Australian banks and other institutions paying interest and dividends must provide details to the tax office of all payments made (which is why some people invest their money overseas, although not declaring income earned overseas is illegal).

There are many books published annually about how to reduce your income tax bill, including the *Australian Tax Guide* and the *Australian Master Tax Guide* (Longman). Whether you're self-employed or an employee, you should always ensure that you don't pay any more tax than is necessary.

**Company/Corporate Tax:** For taxation purposes, companies include all bodies or associations (corporate and non-corporate), but not partnerships, where partners are taxed individually. From the 2000/01 financial year, companies are liable to pay tax on profits at a flat rate of 30 per cent. Employers are also liable to a fringe benefits tax on non-cash benefits made available to employees (such as company cars and low-interest loans – see page 356). A company has its own tax file number and may also need a sales tax registration number. The date for filing depends on the company's financial year; tax is usually paid in instalments in the year following the year of the tax liability, e.g. tax owed on 2002 income is paid in 2003.

**Accountants:** If your tax affairs are complicated or you're unable to understand your own finances (like many people), you should consider employing an accountant or tax consultant (many banks also provide a personal tax service). This applies to most self-employed people, but very few who are on PAYG. However, don't pick an accountant simply by sticking a pin in the phone book, but ask your friends, colleagues or business associates if they can recommend someone. If you're self-employed, you should choose an accountant who deals with people in your line of business and who knows exactly what you can and cannot claim.

Substantial tax savings can be made with regard to pensions, trusts and other tax-avoidance schemes, although some schemes apply only to the very rich, as the cost of using them is prohibitive to anyone else. As soon as the ATO closes one loophole, tax accountants find another one. Accountant's fees vary from around $100 to $300 per hour, so ask in advance what the rates are (they're highest in the major cities). Avoid 'high-power' accountants, who will cost you the earth. You can reduce your accountant's fees considerably by keeping itemised records of all your business expenses (preferably on a computer), rather than handing your accountant a pile of invoices and receipts. Note, however, that a good accountant will usually save you more than he charges in fees.

Australia has Byzantine tax regulations (the Income Tax Act runs to around 3,300 pages!) and it's possible to receive conflicting information from different tax 'experts' and even from different branches of the tax office. Taxpayers constantly complain of inconsistency in the way the ATO makes its rulings, and you should never trust the ATO to take only what it should or to credit you all your allowances and deductions; although the ATO won't cheat you deliberately, it does occasionally make mistakes. If you pay PAYG tax, make sure that the tax deducted is correct (see page 351) and never hesitate to dispute a tax bill with which you disagree. A tax appeals system was introduced in 1997, and the ATO also has a problem resolution service (☎ local call rate 13-2870).

**Information:** Tax Help is a volunteer service to help certain people complete their tax returns, including those on low incomes (including senior citizens), people from non-English speaking backgrounds, Aborigines and Torres Strait Islanders, and people with disabilities. The translating and interpreting service (TIS) helps non-English speaking people with tax questions by setting up a three-way telephone conversation with an interpreter and the tax office (☎ local call rate 13-1450). The languages covered include Arabic, Chinese, Croatian, Greek, Indonesian, Italian, Japanese, Korean, Macedonian, Polish, Serbian, Spanish, Turkish and Vietnamese.

For general income tax enquiries, contact the Australian Taxation Office (ATO), Head Office, 2 Constitution Avenue, Canberra, ACT 2601 (☎ 13-2861). There's also a 'fax from a tax' information service where you can receive information via fax (☎ 13-2860). The ATO runs a comprehensive (if complicated) website where most information is accessible (🖥 www.ato.gov.au). Australia's tax system was revised on 1st July 2000. The reform included the introduction of GST and a $12 billion cut in personal income tax. Benefits such as family assistance and pensions were also increased – older Australians are also entitled to a one-off bonus. Extensive information on the reforms can be obtained from the ATO (☎ local call rate 13-6140, 🖥 www.taxreform.ato.gov.au). There's also an information number for older

Australians (☎ 13-2862). Most TAFE colleges (see page 213), in conjunction with the ATO, run a course explaining the tax system and how to complete tax returns.

There are various computer tax programs such as QuickTax (Reckon Intuit) and SmartTax (Mysterious Pursuit), although they're mainly for 'experts'. A better option for individuals is to join the Australian Taxpayers' Association, who for an annual fee of $250 provide you with 24 issues of the latest tax information, a telephone helpline and a 900-page booklet on the current year's tax return (🖳 www.taxpayer.com.au).

# Taxable Income & Rates

Taxable income includes income derived directly or indirectly from all sources except where it's specifically exempted. It includes salary or wages, pensions, lump sum payments, termination payments, allowances and benefits, interest, income from partnerships or trusts, capital gains, foreign income, rental income, dividends and bonuses. The tax law makes a basic distinction between income and capital receipts, and generally only income is assessable. However, capital gains made from the sale of assets acquired after 20th September 1985 are included in your assessable income (see page 359).

Some income is tax exempt, including certain pensions, social security allowances and payments, education payments, and defence and United Nations payments. Other income that's exempt from income tax includes family payment, certain scholarships, bursaries and other educational allowances, and the income of certain non-profit organisations. Most government pensions are subject to tax, although a system of rebates ensures that no tax is paid by a pensioner who earns only a small amount of other income. Special provisions deal with other types of income, including lump-sum payments received on retirement, non-cash benefits, irregular income earned by artists, sportsmen and the like, and the income of farmers. There are concessionary tax rates for some residents, e.g. those who work north of the 26th parallel (Tropic of Capricorn) and those who work in the fruit and vegetable industry (who pay only 15 per cent income tax). Those with irregular income are permitted to average their earnings out over five years; the tax payable is calculated according to a complicated formula taking into account 'normal' income and adding this to one-fifth of the your 'abnormal' income over a five-year period. Special tax rules apply to those under the age of 18, when income is generally taxed at a higher rate.

**Tax Rates:** Since the 2000 tax reform, Australia has had four income tax rates, from 17 to 47 per cent (excluding the Medicare levy – see page 284), as shown below:

| Taxable Income | Tax Rate (%) |
| --- | --- |
| Under $6,000 | 0 |
| $6,001–$20,000 | 17 |
| $20,001–$50,000 | 30 |
| $50,001–$60,000 | 42 |
| Over $60,000 | 47 |

The top rate of tax (47 per cent) applied at 14 times average weekly earnings 40 years ago; today it's payable at just one and a half times average earnings. Around 80 per cent of Australian taxpayers pay tax at 30 per cent or below. Anyone who isn't resident in Australia for a whole financial year receives a pro rata portion of the tax-free allowance ($6,000 per year), e.g. if you're resident in Australia for half the tax year, your tax-free allowance is $3,000. Your taxable income is your income after all allowances and deductions have been made from your gross income from all sources.

**Non-residents:** There's no tax-free allowance for non-residents, who are taxed at two different rates on income earned in Australia as shown in the tables below (note that non-residents should have a tax file number and quote it to their employer, or they'll be taxed at the maximum rate of 47 per cent).

Non-resident wage and salary earners are taxed as follows:

| Weekly Earnings | Tax Rate |
| --- | --- |
| Up to $383 | 29¢ per $1 |
| $384–$960 | $111 plus 30¢ for each $1 over $383 |
| $961–$1,152 | $284 plus 42¢ for each $1 over $960 |
| Over $1,152 | $365 plus 47¢ for each $1 over $1,152 |

Non-residents with business and trading income in Australia are taxed at the rates shown below:

| Taxable Income | Tax Rate (%) |
| --- | --- |
| up to $20,000 | 29 |
| $20,001–$50,000 | 30 |
| $50,001–$60,000 | 42 |
| Over $60,000 | 47 |

# Individual Taxation

The joint filing of returns by spouses isn't permitted in Australia, where the same tax rates apply to married and single individuals. There are three main systems of collecting tax from individuals in Australia:

- Pay-As-You-Go (PAYG);
- Prescribed Payments System (PPS);
- PAYG Instalments System.

**PAYG:** PAYG or direct income tax applies to salary and wage earners and includes superannuation and termination payments. Under the PAYG system, an employee's tax is deducted from his gross salary at source by his employer, who forwards it to the tax office. Provided that you have no income apart from your salary or wages, PAYG is designed to cover your tax liability. Any additional income, e.g. part-time employment or income from investments or savings, whether tax is deducted at source or not, must be declared to the ATO. At the end of the financial year (30th June), you must submit a tax return (see page 357) declaring your annual income from all sources. You receive a credit for your PAYG payments, which are offset against any tax payable.

Note that you must give your employer your Tax File Number (see page 327), or you could be taxed at the highest rate. Note also that, if you want to receive your $6,000 tax-free allowance (and who doesn't?), you must lodge an *Employee Declaration Instalment Form* with your employer; otherwise tax will be deducted from *all* you income.

Many companies pay employees as self-employed contractors, thus avoiding PAYG tax, workers' compensation, fringe benefits tax and the superannuation guarantee charge. This is illegal and a risky practice for employers, who are responsible for deducting all their employees' income tax at source unless a person is categorised as self-employed by the tax office. The PAYG scheme is disadvantageous to employees, who in many cases would be entitled to claim larger and more allowances if they were classified as self-employed, whereby they'd also have the benefit of paying their tax in arrears. For this reason, many employees disguise themselves as independent contractors (the practice is estimated to cost the government up to $100 million per year).

**PPS:** The Prescribed Payments System (PPS) is a system for deducting tax from payments for certain work or services in prescribed industries that aren't covered by the PAYG system. For example, payments to sub-contractors in the building and construction industry are covered by PPS. Under PPS, when payments are made to, for example, a sub-contractor, tax is deducted at source and sent to the tax office. This is then credited when the sub-contractor submits his tax return at the end of the tax year. The system also obliges householders to report to the tax office sums over $10,000 paid under private construction contracts.

**PAYG Instalments System:** This has replaced the Provisional Tax System and is paid by taxpayers who (in a particular tax year) earn over $999 of non-salary or wage income, e.g. in interest or other investment/business income, or who don't pay 'sufficient' tax on their salary and wage income through the PAYG system. You need to pay through the PAYG Instalments System if your most recent income tax assessment shows more than $999 of gross investment or business income or if your most recent income tax return resulted in a tax debt of over $249. PAYG Instalments aren't payable if your income is below the relevant threshold, shown below:

| Marital Status | Threshold |
| --- | --- |
| Single | $37,840 |
| Married/*de facto* | $58,244 (combined) |
| Separated | $70,404 (combined) |

PAYG Instalments are payable in advance, based on an estimate of your income in the coming year and are allowed as a credit against your actual tax liability. If the advance payment exceeds $8,000, it's paid in quarterly instalments. However, if the amount paid (based on your previous year's income) is less than the amount assessed by the tax office at the end of the financial year, the balance owed must be paid within 30 days or by 1st February of the following year. Any shortfall between the advance payment and the amount owed must be paid within 30 days of receiving a notice of assessment from the tax office. Note that PAYG Instalments are something of a minefield and it's often worthwhile employing a tax agent to sort it out. If you're unsure whether you should be paying tax under the PPS Instalments System, contact the ATO.

# Individual Tax Calculation

The following is an example of an individual tax calculation for the year 2000/01:

| | |
|---|---|
| Base salary | $50,000 |
| Bonus | $12,000 |
| Company car | $ 6,000 |
| Interest (Australian source) | $ 6,000 |
| Capital gain | $ 8,000 |
| **Gross Income** | **$82,000** |
| Exempt income | ($7,500) |
| **Taxable Income** | **$74,500** |

| Tax on | | |
|---|---|---|
| $ 6,000 at 0% | | $ 0 |
| $14,000 at 17% | | $ 2,380 |
| $30,000 at 30% | | $ 9,000 |
| $10,000 at 42% | | $ 4,200 |
| $14,500 at 47% | | $ 6,815 |
| $74,500 | | $22,395 |
| Medicare levy on $74,500 at 1.5% | | $ 1,117.50 |
| **Income Tax Liability** | | **$23,512.50** |

# Self-Employed

The business structure you choose when establishing a business is vital in ensuring that you pay no more tax than is necessary (most family businesses operate a family trust in order to reduce taxes). Self-employed, as used in Australia, means a 'sole trader' or someone in a partnership, and not a limited company or trust. A company must assess its own tax liability in its tax return, known as 'full self-assessment', which is being extended to all taxpayers. If you have a limited company, you must pay corporate or company tax on your profits and will need the services of an accountant to deal with this (see page 348).

You're generally better off if you're self-employed, as you can claim more in the way of expenses than employees paying PAYG tax. Another advantage for the self-employed is the delay between making profits (if they have any) and paying tax on them, as the self-employed and small businesses usually pay their tax under the PAYG Instalments system (see page 352). An estimated 75,000 people pretend that they're self-employed in order to claim extra deductions. Recent court cases have declared that, under the current tax laws, taxi drivers, bicycle/motorcycle couriers and airline pilots are independent contractors and are therefore entitled to be treated as self-employed. In the light of these decisions, the ATO sidelined proposals that would have re-classified thousands of self-employed contractors as employees subject to PAYG tax.

The self-employed are eligible to claim more deductions in legitimate business expenses such as travel to and from work, phone bills, and work clothes or uniforms. Note, however, that small businesses are frequently targeted by tax inspectors investigating tax evasion. To be classified as self-employed, you must convince the ATO that you're genuinely self-employed and in business for yourself. The 'three-point test' to decide whether you're an employee or a self-employed contractor is as follows:

- **the contract test:** whether your employer can control your activities while the work is being done, as in an employer-employee relationship;

- **the risk test:** whether you own your equipment and are paid only if the work is done (unlike an employee, who is paid even if it isn't);

- **labour versus completion of the job test:** whether you're paid for hours worked, like an employee, or for completing a job, like a contractor.

If the ATO agrees that you're self-employed, you should get them to confirm their decision in writing.

**Expenses:** Expenses are usually fully deductible provided that they're incurred in producing assessable income or necessarily incurred in carrying on a business for that purpose. Expenses of a capital, private or domestic nature and those incurred in the production of exempt income aren't deductible. Separate records must be kept of business travel and motor vehicle expenses. Entertainment expenses aren't tax deductible unless they're incurred for the provision of fringe benefits to employees. Deductions are allowed for salaries and wages paid to employees, interest, rents, maintenance, repairs, commissions and similar business expenses. Expenditure for the acquisition or improvement of assets isn't deductible (other than depreciation, which may constitute an allowable deduction), but it may be added to the cost base of an asset for capital gains tax purposes and will reduce any taxable gain arising from a later disposition. Capital losses can also be offset against capital gains (see **Capital Gains Tax** on page 359). Australian-source losses may be deducted against the same or different sources of income, and excess losses incurred on or after 1st July 1989 may be carried forward indefinitely, as can excess capital losses after 19th September 1985.

You shouldn't hesitate to claim for anything that you believe is a legitimate business expense. The ATO will disallow them if it doesn't agree, but what it won't do is allow you a deduction to which you're entitled but which you've forgotten to claim. The profit earned in the operation of your business is added to any other income and you're taxed on the total. Each partner in a partnership is taxed individually on his own share of partnership income.

**Obtaining Help:** It's important to obtain expert legal advice before establishing a business or starting work as a self-employed person in Australia. Like everything to do with tax law, the regulations applying to the self-employed and small businesses are complicated and time-consuming and are estimated to cost some $7 billion a year in lost time. Not surprisingly, some 90 per cent of the self-employed and small businesses use a tax agent to complete their tax returns.

## Deductions & Rebates

All taxpayers can claim deductions and rebates in addition to credit for tax paid during the relevant financial year. The gross tax payable on taxable income is reduced by relevant deductions, rebates and credits to obtain the net tax payable. There's a difference between a deduction and a rebate. Deductions reduce taxable income, but rebates are subtracted from the tax payable on your taxable income. Rebates are essentially available only to Australian residents whose dependants also live in Australia. There's no unified system of deductions or rebates that apply to all taxpayers. Full details of all deductions and rebates for individual taxpayers are contained in the free *Tax Pack* (see page 358).

**Deductions:** Deductions are subtracted from your gross income to calculate your taxable income. Most deductions are occupation-specific and must be legitimate expenses incurred in earning your assessable income, provided they aren't capital, private or domestic. They're commonly claimed by employees and include work, car, travel and self-education expenses. Deductions are also allowed for certain non-business expenses such as gifts to approved charities. Deductions must usually be substantiated by documentation, and special documentation requirements must be met where employment-related expenses exceed $300 per year. Allowable deductions include:

● Car expenses relating to work;

● Travel expenses relating to work;

● Occupational clothing expenses (e.g. protective clothing and uniforms);

● Work-related self-education expenses;

● Other work-related expenses, including union fees, overtime meals, books, journals, tools, insurance premiums, telephone, computer and office expenses;

● Tax losses carried forward from previous years;

● Australian film industry incentives;

● Personal (non-employer sponsored) superannuation contributions;

● Interest and dividend expenses such as taxes and fees;

● Gifts or donations to recognised charities, funds, organisations and political parties;

● Expenses for managing your tax affairs;

● The deductible amount of the undeducted purchase price (UDP) of an Australian pension or annuity;

● The undeducted purchase price of a foreign pension or annuity;

● Non-employer sponsored superannuation contributions.

**Rebates:** Rebates (also called tax offsets) provide you with tax relief and are subtracted from the tax due on your taxable income. If rebates are greater than the tax due, you don't pay any tax. There are two exceptions to this: the private medical insurance rebate, where the excess is refunded; and the landcare and water facility rebate, where the excess is carried forward and used to reduce future tax liability. Rebates don't, however, reduce your Medicare levy (see page 284). Rebates are made on tax due in repect of:

● savings income at 15 per cent with a maximum rebate of $450;

- private health insurance premiums at 30 per cent as long as the insurance is from a registered health fund (note that you may choose to claim the rebate as a reduction in your insurance premium) – see page 315;
- net medical expenses (including medical, dental and optical aids) over $1,250 that aren't reclaimable from Medicare or private health insurance at 20 per cent.

There are also:

- zone rebates for people living in some remote or isolated areas of Australia (there are also special areas within these zones) – most apply to areas in northern and central Australia;
- rebates for beneficiaries, pensioners, and overseas forces personnel;
- rebates for low-income taxpayers: if the sum of your assessable income and total reportable is less than $30,999, you may be eligible for a tax rebate of up to a maximum of $1,000;
- certain dependants, as follows:

| Dependant | Rebate |
|---|---|
| spouse (including *de facto*) | $1,365 |
| child-housekeeper | $1,365 |
| child-housekeeper (with dependent child/student) | $1,637 |
| invalid relative | $603 |
| parent or parent-in-law | $1,204 |

Whether you can claim a rebate usually has nothing to do with the amount of taxable income you earned. However, some rebates, such as beneficiary and pensioner rebates and the rebate for low-income taxpayers, do depend on your income.

**Family Tax Benefit:** Under the tax reform in 2000, Family Tax Assistance was replaced by Family Tax Benefit. Family tax benefit can be paid either directly by the Family Assistance Office or through the tax system. Family tax benefit is subject to an income test, usually based on your tax return from the previous tax year. For further information contact the Family Assistance Office (☎ local call rate 13-6150, 🖳 www.familyassist.gov.au).

# Fringe Benefits Tax

Fringe benefits tax (FBT) was introduced in 1986 in order to reduce the amount of non-cash, non-taxable benefits (or 'perks') offered to employees by employers as part of their salary package. It includes company cars for employees' private use, private health insurance, children's private education, low interest or interest-free loans, free or subsidised accommodation and free holiday travel. The level of taxation on company cars depends on the business 'mileage' and is from 6 to 24 per cent. However, leases of luxury cars as part of executive salary packages are exempt. FBT also applies to: discounted goods or services provided by an employer in excess of a specified threshold; payment or reimbursement of private expenses on behalf of employees; entertainment expenses; airline transport provided free or at a discount to employees in the airline travel industry; and the waiver of employee loans or debts. A portion of a living-away-from-home allowance paid to employees may also be subject to FBT, although 'reasonable' costs for food and accommodation aren't. Staff canteens, employer superannuation schemes and employee share acquisition schemes are exempt from FBT. Frequent-flyer schemes aren't taxable, even when your employer pays the membership fees, and child care provided on 'business premises' or a building controlled by your employer is also exempt (including employer-sponsored/leased places at childcare centres).

FBT is paid at the rate of 48 per cent. The FBT tax year is different from the financial year (just to confuse you even further) and runs from 1st April to 31st March. Payments are made quarterly by the 28th of July, October, January and April; each payment being equal to 25 per cent of the previous year's liability, the balance being payable when your annual tax return is filed. An employer must usually file an annual fringe benefits tax return by 28th April each year and fringe benefits are recorded on the employee's payment summary.

# Income Tax Returns

You must lodge a tax return in Australia if any of the following applied (with certain exceptions) during the previous financial year:

- You received a government benefit or allowance and had other income.

- You received a government pension or allowance which was reduced because you had other income.

- You received more than $5,400 in taxable income during the financial year.

- You received more than $643 in income other than salary and wages and you were under the age of 18 on 30th June of the financial year in question.

- You're a non-resident and earned more than $1 from which non-resident withholding tax had not been deducted.

- You stopped full-time education, became an Australian resident or stopped being an Australian resident and your income exceeded the part-year threshold amount.

- You paid tax during the previous tax year (with certain exceptions).

- You were liable for child support under the Child Support (Assessment) Act 1989.

- You made a loss or can claim for a loss made in a previous year.

- You carried out business in Australia.

- You were entitled to a distribution from a trust or had an interest in a partnership which carried out a business of primary production.

- You were an Australian tax resident and any of your income came from overseas.

If you don't need to lodge a return for the financial year in question but lodged one for the previous financial year, you must complete a *Non-lodgement Advice* and send it to the ATO (one is provided in the *Tax Pack* – see below).

Returns must be lodged by 31st October for the previous tax year, e.g. the tax return for the 2001/02 tax year ending 30th June 2002 must be lodged by 31st October

2002. If you're expecting a refund, the earlier you lodge your return, the quicker you're likely to receive it. If you're unable to meet the deadline because of circumstances beyond your control, you should request permission to lodge at a later date in writing to the office where you last lodged, **before the deadline**.

**Tax Pack:** The ATO provides a comprehensive free *Tax Pack* (almost 150 pages) for individual taxpayers, which is available from tax offices, post offices and newsagents (it's also available overseas in some countries). A copy is also delivered to all households just before the end of the financial year (30th June). The pack contains two 'long form' tax returns (consisting of six pages) at the back, one of which is to be completed and sent to the ATO (the other is in case you make a mistake or wish to make a copy for your records). A 'short form' tax return is available for those with simple tax affairs and will be sent to you automatically if you answered a relatively small number of questions on your previous tax return. If applicable, attach statements (group certificates or tax stamp sheets) issued by your employer to your tax return. If you don't have them, you should obtain a statement from your employer showing salary and income tax payments; otherwise, you must complete a statutory declaration for missing or lost group certificates or tax stamp sheets.

Don't forget to sign and date the return on the last page before posting it. If you use the *Tax Pack* to complete your return and make a mistake, you won't be subject to any penalties, although you may be required to pay interest on any tax owed unless the mistake was due to misleading information contained in the *Tax Pack*.

The tax office where you lodge your return is determined by your postcode, a list of which is given in the *Tax Pack*. You can post your tax return or lodge it personally in the box provided at a tax office. You can also lodge your tax return electronically by using *Tax Pack Express* at a post office or at the office of a participating registered tax agent. There's a fee of $20 for this service, although you can claim a deduction in your next return. Taxpayers have been able to lodge their returns over the Internet since 1997/98. **Keep a copy of your tax form and anything else you send to the ATO. This is useful if your tax form is lost in the post or there are any queries.** Keep a copy of all documentation (receipts, invoices, statements, etc.) which substantiate claims made in your tax return. Records must be kept for three and a half years for salary and wage earners and five years for the self-employed (seven years for car and travel-related expenses). Selected tax returns are audited (see page 347), and you may be penalised if the information provided is found to be incorrect. As in most countries, the self-employed are *much* more likely to be audited than employees.

**Tax Agents & Accountants:** Although the tax return is relatively easy to follow and understand, only 30 per cent of taxpayers complete their own returns and many use a tax agent or accountant, the cost of which is tax deductible. The agent then has the responsibility for completing the return correctly and is liable for any errors. He will (or should) also ensure that you claim for all the allowances and rebates to which you're entitled. A tax agent usually charges around $75 to complete a tax return for an average taxpayer, although additional fees are charged for extra services (accountants are more expensive). Shop around and obtain a few quotations – some agents offer a free initial consultation.

**Payment:** After around eight weeks, you'll receive a *Notice of Assessment* from the ATO, which is an itemised account of the tax you owe. At the bottom of the assessment will be your tax debt or, if you're due a refund, your refund cheque (lucky you!). Your notice of assessment will tell you when you must pay your tax bill in order to avoid incurring a penalty for late payment. If you don't agree with the ATO's assessment you can lodge an appeal. If the amount owed is over $8,000, you can make the payment in quarterly instalments. Tax can be paid in person at a tax or post office, or by post by cheque or postal order (payable to the Deputy Commissioner of Taxation), which must be sent with the bottom section of your notice of assessment. If you use a tax agent who lodges returns electronically, your tax bill or refund can be paid directly from or into a bank, building society or credit union account. If you're unable to pay your bill on time, contact your tax office and ask for an extension. You'll need to provide a reason why you need the extension (penniless?) and, if it's granted, you'll be charged interest at a daily rate (equal to 20 per cent per annum) on the amount outstanding after the due date.

## CAPITAL GAINS TAX

Australia doesn't have capital gains tax as such, but provides for the inclusion in assessable income of any profits made on certain assets during the financial year. The part of a gain that's subject to income tax, i.e. the proceeds of a sale less the purchase cost after being reduced by indexation and any losses, is treated as ordinary income and subject to the same income tax rates. However, the amount of tax you pay is calculated by adding 20 per cent of the total gain to your other income, calculating the extra tax due on this portion, and then multiplying it by five (the ATO *never* makes anything simple).

Tax is payable on the sale of certain assets, including real estate (other than your principal home), shares, personal use assets, trust distributions, equipment and plant, and goodwill on the sale of a business. What are termed 'listed personal use assets' such as works of art and antiques are also taxable if the purchase price was over $100. Listed personal use assets include money or property received other than as gifts or loans, but doesn't apply to an inheritance arising from the death of an asset-holder. Exemptions from tax include your principal residence and up to two hectares of attached land, motor vehicles (whether acquired for personal or business use), superannuation and insurance policies, debentures, bonds and other loans without a deferred interest element, certain personal use goods with a disposal value of less than $10,000 and any assets acquired before 20th September 1985.

Any realised capital gain from the disposal of assets acquired after 19th September 1985 is taxable. There are two methods of calculating the taxable gain: indexation or the discount system. Under indexation, the excess of the sale price over the indexed cost base is the taxable capital gain, which is added to your other taxable income. The discount system consists of a 50 per cent discount on the amount of capital gain being taxed provided the assets have been owned for at least 12 months by an individual or jointly with others. If the item was purchased after 21st September 1999, the discount system applies. Capital losses can be used to offset gains, either in the current year or in future years without a time limit, but cannot be used to offset other income. New residents are deemed to have acquired non-Australian assets for their fair market value at the time of becoming a resident (except for assets acquired prior to 20th September 1985, which are exempt). Upon ceasing to be a resident, you can choose to treat all non-Australian assets as 'taxable Australian assets', thereby deferring payment of tax until the assets are disposed of or you resume resident status. Overseas employees who become residents during their Australian assignments are subject to complex tax rules that may affect their assets located outside Australia. If you're in this position, you should obtain expert advice regarding capital gains.

Gains made on the sale of your principal residence in Australia are usually exempt from tax. However, tax is payable on capital gains made on the sale of an investment property or a second home. There's a federal government taxation incentive for those who let a property for less than their mortgage repayments, when the loss can be offset against other income. There's a qualifying period of two years for exemption from tax on an inherited home and, if you choose not to live in an inherited home and sell it after two years, no tax is payable.

There are four capital gains tax concessions available for small businesses: a 15-year exemption from capital gains tax; a 50 per cent active asset reduction; a retirement exemption, where you're entitled to a lifetime tax-free amount of $500,000 (note that, if you retire before the age of 55, the amount must be paid into a superannuation or similar fund); and a 'roll-over'. All these concessions are subject to certain conditions and you should seek advice from a professional tax adviser. Note that tax complications can occur when a business undergoes re-organisation or re-structuring, when you should seek advice from an accountant or tax consultant.

The ATO publishes a number of booklets (also available online), including *Capital Gains Tax – What You Need to Know*, *Capital Gains Tax and Your Home*, *Capital Gains Tax and Investments in Shares and Units*, *Capital Gains Tax after Divorce or Involuntary Disposal of Assets*, *Capital Gains Tax and the Assets of a Deceased Estate*, and *Capital Gains Tax and Small Businesses*.

# COST OF LIVING

No doubt you'd like to know how far your dollars will stretch and how much money (if any) you'll have left after paying your bills. The standard of living in Australia has increased considerably for all income levels in the last 20 years, although incomes have increased much faster for the rich than the poor. However, in recent years, many people in 'middle Australia' reckon that life is becoming more expensive. Australia's inflation rate is based on the consumer price index (CPI), which gives an indication of how prices have risen (or fallen) over the past year. The CPI, which sceptics believe stands for 'con people incessantly', is calculated from a basket of basic goods and services. It received a revamp in 1997, when mortgage interest rates were disocunted and computer equipment, financial fees and higher education fees were included.

In stark contrast to Australia's international image of affluence and plenty, poverty is widespread and there's a widening gap between the rich and poor, the richest 20 per cent of the population earning some 13 times as much as the poorest 20 per cent. Over 50 per cent of Australian families struggle to pay their bills, and many people receive assistance from their families. Some 40 per cent of children live in families with very low incomes, including many one-parent families, and some 2 million adults and children are dependent on government allowances (some 2 million Australians also live in households with an income below the poverty line). Many elderly people also struggle on state pensions (or no pensions) – elderly women are among the poorest sections of society. Many immigrants with families strive to live on $300 to $400 per week, low-income families in major cities paying half or more of their weekly wage in rent payments. In recent years, low-income families have been deserting inner-city suburbs in droves for cheaper outer suburbs and rural areas.

In a recent survey conducted by the ***Economist*** magazine, Sydney was rated the most expensive city in the southern hemisphere and ranked 22nd in the world. Perth is the second most expensive Australian city (33rd in the world) and Melbourne the third (world no.38). Sydney shares its position with New York and Helsinki and is more expensive than Brussels, Houston, Los Angeles, Miami, Milan, Rio de Janeiro and San Francisco. Note that, although most surveys agree that Sydney is Australia's most expensive city, most don't agree on the position of other Australian cities. There's little difference in the cost of living between Adelaide, Brisbane and Perth. The cost of living in rural areas is, not surprisingly, lower than in major cities (particularly housing).

It's difficult to calculate an average cost of living, as it depends on an individual's circumstances and lifestyle. What is important to most people is how much money they can save (or spend) each month. Manufactured goods tend to be expensive in Australia, particularly imported goods, including automobiles, clothes and other manufactured items, which are generally more expensive than in Europe or North America. If you do a lot of travelling, transportation costs will be high owing to the large distances involved, although petrol is much cheaper than in Europe.

Your food bill will naturally depend on what you eat and is similar to the USA and around 25 per cent less than most European countries. Approximately $350 should be sufficient to feed two adults for a month in most areas (excluding alcohol, fillet steak and caviar). The prices of staple foods in Australia's capital cities are listed in the monthly British newspaper *Australian Outlook* (see **Appendix A**) and a free *Cost of Living and Housing Survey* is published annually by the Commonwealth Bank of Australia. Even in the most expensive cities (e.g. Sydney), the cost of living needn't be astronomical. If you shop wisely, compare prices and services before buying and don't live too extravagantly, you may be pleasantly surprised at how little you can live on. Note that it's possible to save a considerable sum by shopping for certain items overseas, e.g. via the Internet (see page 440).

The approximate *minimum* monthly major expenses for an average person or family in a typical town or suburb are shown in the table below. **Note that these are necessarily 'ball park' figures only and depend on your lifestyle, extravagance or frugality, and where you live in Australia – almost everyone will agree that they're either too low or too high!** When calculating your cost of living, deduct the appropriate percentage for income tax (see page 346) and other deductions from your gross salary.

### MONTHLY COSTS (A$)

| ITEM | Single | Couple | Couple with 2 children |
|---|---|---|---|
| Housing **(1)** | 400 | 600 | 800 |
| Food | 300 | 350 | 600 |
| Utilities **(2)** | 100 | 150 | 200 |
| Leisure **(3)** | 75 | 150 | 300 |
| Car/travel **(4)** | 200 | 250 | 350 |
| Insurance **(5)** | 50 | 100 | 100 |
| Clothing | 150 | 200 | 300 |
| Rates | 50 | 75 | 100 |
| **TOTAL** | **1,325** | **1,875** | **2,750** |

1. Rental or mortgage on a modern apartment or semi-detached house in an 'average' small town or outer city suburb. The cost for a single person is for a bedsitter or sharing accommodation. Other costs are for a two (couple) or three-bedroom property (couple with two children). They don't include subsidised housing.

2. Includes electricity, gas, water and telephone, plus heating bills.

3. Includes all entertainment, sports and holiday expenses, plus newspapers and magazines (which could of course be much higher than the figure given).

4. Includes running costs for an average family car, plus third party insurance, road tax, petrol and servicing, but not depreciation or credit costs.

5. Includes all 'voluntary' insurance, except for comprehensive car insurance and expensive private health insurance.

# 15.

# LEISURE

The leisure and tourist industry is one of Australia's largest, earning some 7 per cent of GDP and providing direct or indirect employment for over 500,000 people. Australia is one of the world's top tourist destinations and overseas visitors (mostly from Japan, New Zealand, Britain, the USA and South Korea) numbered nearly 4.5 million in 1998/99, accounting for over $15 billion (some 15 per cent) of the country's export earnings (one of Australia's biggest sources of income is from 'frugal' backpackers who spend an average of around $5,000 each). The 2000 Olympics in Sydney gave a further boost to Australia's position as one of the world's leading tourist destinations, and the city itself was voted top tourist destination (outside Europe) in 2001.

Australia is one of the world's most beautiful countries with a wide range of unusual landscapes. It's a country of infinite variety, offering something for everyone: magnificent beaches for sun-worshippers; beautiful and spectacular countryside and parks for nature lovers; numerous mountains, waterways and seas for sporting types; historic towns and bustling cosmopolitan cities for sightseers; a lively night-life and music scene for party-goers; superb wines and cuisine for oenophiles and gourmets; a wealth of art and serious music for culture vultures; and tranquillity for the stressed.

Until the '70s, Australia was (with some justification) considered to be a cultural desert (cultural cringe was a national trait), the only cultural attraction being the country's 40,000-year Aboriginal heritage. However, the arts have flourished in the last few decades and now match or surpass those found in many 'old world' countries. Australia has a rich history of achievement in high arts such as drama, ballet, opera, music, literature, painting, sculpture, architecture and film. However, while not the cultural philistines depicted by their critics, Australians' appreciation of the arts still lags far behind their love of sport, which is the country's most popular leisure activity (whether taking part or spectating).

The most popular leisure activities apart from sport include cinema, botanical gardens, libraries, animal and marine parks, museums, popular music, art galleries, zoos, operas and musicals, theatre and dance. There are modern performing arts centres in the main cities, many of which vie for the title 'arts capital of Australia', while galleries, theatres, concert halls and cinemas abound in the major towns and cities. The main funding (over $50 million a year) for the arts comes from the Australia Council, plus further contributions from state and local governments and corporate sponsorship. In addition to the more formal events, a profusion of free concerts and entertainment is staged in public parks, shopping and entertainment centres, including jazz, folk, rock, opera and classical concerts, plus impromptu shows by an assortment of jugglers, fire-eaters, buskers, acrobats, dancers and mime artists.

A wealth of festivals and carnivals are held in Australia throughout the year and include music, art, folk, food, wine, beer and harvest festivals, surf life-saving carnivals, and agricultural shows. Most states stage a Royal Agricultural Show, usually in September or October (Sydney's Royal Easter Show is a notable exception). They're much more than 'simply' agricultural shows and include a wide range of displays and entertainment. One of the wackiest events is the Todd River Regatta held in Alice Springs in September, when the Todd River is dry!

Australia offers an abundance of leisure and entertainment facilities and beautiful cities, many of which resemble large country towns. Sydney and Melbourne enjoy an intense rivalry for Australia's premier city. Sydney (Australia's most sophisticated and exciting city) usually wins hands down, thanks largely to its peerless setting

('Venice of the 21st century'), although Melbourne is Australia's cultural and gastronomic capital, and its subtle charms tend to grow on you. The capital Canberra is home to the foremost art collections in the country, although many people consider it a boring modern town with little charm. Other major cities include Adelaide, Brisbane, Darwin, Hobart and Perth, all of which have unique attractions.

However, despite the multifarious attraction of its lively cities, Australia's foremost and most enduring appeal is its immense natural beauty, which owes little to man's intervention (except perhaps on the debit side). Getting away from it all isn't difficult in Australia, with its many lakes and rivers, miles of excellent beaches, and areas of wilderness bigger than many countries (the Northern Territory is one of the world's last frontier lands, where you can still imagine that you're an explorer). Australia is a country of endless contrasts and colour, with an amazing variety of environments ranging from bleak, unearthly deserts to lush tropical rain-forests, from palm-fringed sandy beaches and stunning reefs to majestic snowfields, from sparkling blue seas and remote tropical islands to rugged mountains and spectacular rock formations, and from rolling farmlands and vineyards to wild rivers and vast lakes.

Australia boasts an abundance of natural wonders, many of which are World Heritage sites, including the Great Barrier Reef (the world's most magnificent coral reef), Ayers Rock, Kakadu National Park, the Flinders Ranges, the Murray River, the Grampians, the Yarra Valley, the Dandenongs and the Ranges, the Naracoorte Caves, Bool Lagoon, Katherine Gorge, the Snowy Mountains, and the Tasmanian Wilderness, to name but a few. It's home to a plethora of unique and fascinating flora and fauna, including mammals such as kangaroos, possums, wallabies, duck-billed platypus, wombats and koala bears.

If you're spending a short time in Australia, bear in mind that it's a vast country; don't try to see it all in a few weeks or even months, which is impossible. If you rush through the outback by train or car, you'll see little and the country will appear to consist of a vast nothingness. However, if you take your time and do a bit of walking, you'll experience unexpected wonders. Many visitors seek 'soft-adventure' holidays (e.g. crocodile or shark watching, rather than a close encounter with the sharp end) and eco-tourism such as camel safaris in the outback (the most uncomfortable means of transport invented by man).

Tickets for most large entertainment and sporting events can be purchased from BASS, Ticketek and Ticketmaster ticket agencies (they can also be purchased via the Internet), which have outlets in all the main towns and cities (there's a surcharge of around $5 per ticket). Free entertainment guides are published in the major cities (e.g. the *Sydney City Hub*), and many local councils publish a 'Leisure Directory'. Major newspapers publish weekly guides, and there's a variety of commercial entertainment magazines, such as *Entertainment Guide* magazine in Melbourne. A plethora of travel guides are dedicated to Australia, including the excellent Lonely Planet *Australia* travel survival kit, which is the most comprehensive guidebook to Australia containing 1,000 pages. Other leading guide books include *The Rough Guide to Australia, The Michelin Green Guide to Australia, Frommers Australia From $50 A Day* and the *Insight Guide to Australia*. Leisure information is also available via the Internet, e.g. Sydney City Search (🖥 www.sydney.citysearch.com.au).

For information about sports facilities in Australia, see **Chapter 16**.

# TOURIST INFORMATION

There are tourist offices, travel centres, visitors centres and visitors information bureaux in all cities, large towns and resorts, although few organisations maintain information desks at airports or major railway stations. All states have Tourist Commissions which publish a wealth of information and also act as booking agencies for transport companies, hotels and other accommodation. There are state tourist offices in all state capitals, on major highways at state borders, and in some regional centres. Many smaller towns also have tourist offices run by local councils and regional tourist associations. There are no state-run tourist information offices in Queensland, where tourist offices are often privately operated and act as booking agents for hotels and travel and tour companies. State motoring organisations (see page 275) also provide tourist and touring information.

The opening hours of city offices are relatively restricted by international standards, e.g. from 9am until 5pm Mondays to Fridays and from 9am to between 1 and 4pm on Saturdays. Offices in the main cities and resort towns are also open for a reduced period on Sundays, e.g. 10 or 11am until 4pm. Tourist offices provide you with a wealth of information about local attractions, restaurants, accommodation, sporting events, sports facilities, package holidays, tours, public transport, car rental and much more. Offices can provide information on a wide range of leisure activities and sports, so you should mention any special interests when making enquiries. Most cities and regions publish free entertainment magazines and newspapers containing maps and a wealth of useful information about local attractions and events (distributed by tourist offices, hotels, transport companies and information bureaux).

Australia is promoted overseas by the Australian Tourist Commission (ATC), and most Australian states also maintain tourist offices in a number of countries, including the UK and the USA. The ATC has offices in Auckland, Chicago, Frankfurt, Hong Kong, London, Los Angeles, New York, Osaka, Singapore, Tokyo and Toronto. Note that the ATC is strictly an external organisation which promotes Australia overseas; it doesn't maintain any offices in Australia. The ATC publishes an abundance of information, including an excellent annual *Australia Unplugged* (a guide for young people) and *On the Loose* (for backpackers). It also publishes fact sheets on many topics, including disabled travel, camping, skiing, fishing and national parks, plus a good map of Australia (for which there's a small fee).

A lot of information is published specifically for backpackers and budget travellers such as the free magazine *TNT for Backpackers*, available from TNT, Level 4, 46-48 York Street, Sydney, NSW 2000 (☎ 02-9299 4811, 💻 www. tntmag. com.au). TNT publishes four editions: Sydney, NSW and the ACT; Melbourne, Victoria and Tasmania; Queensland and Byron Bay; and the Outback (which includes South Australia, Western Australia and the Northern Territory). The Sydney/NSW/ACT edition is published monthly, the other editions quarterly.

# HOTELS

The quality and standard of Australian hotels and other accommodation varies considerably and includes superb international five-star luxury hotels, resort hotels, boutique hotels, budget hotels, motels, farms, apartments, guesthouses, hostels, and bed and breakfast accommodation. Sydney has a huge range of accommodation, including 13 five-star hotels (the Regent Hotel is rated one of the best in the world).

However, the widest choice of accommodation is to be found in Queensland (where tourism is the main industry), which has a wealth of luxury hotels, motels, apartments and backpacker hostels in all resort areas. On the other hand, in country and remote areas, the choice of accommodation is severely restricted, and it's wise to obtain recommendations unless you're prepared to put up with the most basic of accommodation.

Rates usually vary with the season. The low season is generally from May to November (winter). However, in the centre and tropical north (the 'top end') winter is normally the best time of year to visit and is therefore the high season. In the summer, hotel rates in the top end drop by up to 30 per cent. There's a lack of accommodation in some cities (such as Sydney, where many hotels average over 90 per cent occupancy), particularly budget accommodation, although prices remain reasonable. The busiest period is between November and mid-May, with beds being almost impossible to find from mid-December to late January in cities and resorts if you haven't booked. You can obtain discounts of up to 50 per cent for weekly bookings, stand-bys, weekend and low season stays. Travel agents who buy rooms in bulk may be able to offer you a better rate than you can obtain yourself, and motoring organisations also offer member discounts. Many airlines sell vouchers offering reduced rates at motel chains.

Major hotel groups operating four and five-star hotels in major cities include Accor, ANA, Beaufort, Peppers, Hilton, Hyatt, InterContinental, Holiday Inn, Jewel Hotels and Resorts, Matson, Mirvac, Nikko, Parkroyal, Radisson, Ramada, Regent, Ritz Carlton, Rydges, Select, Sheraton, Southern Pacific Hotels, Tradewinds, Vista, and Waratah Inns. Most top hotel chains have freecall 1800 booking numbers. Three to four-star chains include All Seasons Resorts, Best Western, Centra, Country Comfort, Flag, Metro Inn, Quality Pacific and Travelodge.

The term 'private hotel' is used to denote a hotel which doesn't serve alcohol. Other terms used for an unlicensed hotel are guest house, lodge and inn. You may also come across 'boutique hotels', which are small hotels more like guesthouses. There are old colonial-style hotels in country and outback areas, many of which have been refurbished in recent years. These include National Trust accommodation in pre-1901 buildings, full of character (the bar may also be full of characters) with eccentric owners and bizarre regulations.

The following table is a *rough* guide to per night room prices in Australia:

| Star Rating | Price Range |
| --- | --- |
| hostels | $10–22 (dormitory) |
| 1/budget | $20–50 |
| 2 | $55–85 |
| 3 | $80–150 |
| 4 | $150–250 |
| 5 | $230–400+ |

Prices are usually quoted per room and not per person and generally include all taxes except goods and services tax (GST). A 10 per cent bed tax was introduced in New South Wales in 1997 to help finance the Olympics (which caused an uproar in Sydney), which has since been replaced by GST at ten per cent countrywide. There's also a 5 per cent tax for accommodation in the Northern Territory. Note that some hotels close on Sundays and public holidays, as they cannot afford to pay staff the high penalty rates demanded.

**Facilities:** A double room usually has twin single beds; if you want a double bed, you should ask for one when booking. Hotels other than motels, private hotels and guest houses must provide a public bar to serve alcohol (guest houses don't have permits to serve alcohol). Many hotel rooms have a refrigerator stocked with cold drinks (where you can also keep your own drinks cold), and an honour system operates whereby guests are trusted to pay for what they consume. In some hotels a toaster is provided, in which case you'll be given sliced untoasted bread for breakfast. Note that telephone calls from hotel rooms are expensive and it's best to stock up on 20¢ coins and call from the lobby. When calling from your room, you must usually dial 9 for the hotel operator and 0 to get an outside line. Air-conditioning (or at least ceiling fans) is an important consideration in summer, particularly in Western Australia, Queensland and the Northern Territory.

**Top Class Hotels:** Top class hotels provide air-conditioned rooms with tea and coffee making facilities, room service, radio and colour TV (maybe with an in-house video film service), en suite bathroom or shower, telephone (often direct dial), mini-bar, hair drier and trouser press. Some hotels provide no-smoking rooms and special rooms for the disabled. Many top class hotels have a choice of restaurants and bars, provide secretarial, business and conference facilities, and have health and leisure centres with a gymnasium, solarium, sauna, Jacuzzi, swimming pools and a range of other sports facilities. Top class hotels in major cities also provide theatre booking agencies, hairdressing salons and a range of shops. Breakfast in top class hotels is expensive at around $12 to $15 for a continental buffet breakfast and $15 to $20 for a cooked breakfast. Note that some luxury hotels discourage room service and impose surcharges at weekends.

**Budget Hotels:** Budget hotels are in short supply in Australia and, if you're looking for budget accommodation, your best bet is a hostel (see page 373), bed and breakfast (see page 371) or a pub. If you don't need to be in the middle of town, suburban hotels offer better value for money. Rooms in budget hotels and guest houses are usually from $20 to $50 for a single and $35 to $70 for a double (some also have suites/triples). Rooms are usually significantly cheaper by the week, e.g. $150 for shared rooms and $230 for doubles. Pub hotels in country areas generally charge from around $25 to $35 for a single room, usually with a shared bathroom. Check whether breakfast is included. Breakfasts at private hotels are usually huge and excellent.

**Pub Hotels:** Pubs are called hotels because they originally had to provide accommodation by law, although nowadays many 'pub hotels' don't have any accommodation. Some pubs provide tourist accommodation and may call themselves hotels/motels. Pubs in country areas, which may be called 'commercials' as guests were traditionally commercial travellers (salesmen), are more likely to offer accommodation than those in cities. Pubs are usually basic (so don't expect a trouser press, bidet or a bedtime mint on your pillow) with a bar downstairs and rooms upstairs which can be noisy (it's best to get a room at the top of the building).

**Motels:** There's a wide choice of modern, comfortable motels (also called motor hotels and motor inns) throughout Australia. The major chains are A1, Best Western, Budget, Country Comfort, Flag International, Metro Inns, and Quality Inns. In remote areas there are road stations (similar to freeway rest stops) with motel-type portable units called 'demountables'. All motel chains will book you a room at another motel in the same chain free of charge, although you should note that not all motels are the same standard within a particular chain.

Motel rooms have a private bath or shower, telephone, TV, tea and coffee-making facilities and a refrigerator. Some luxury motels have a swimming pool or spa. At smaller motels you can park outside your door. At most motels you can order room-service breakfast, although most don't have bars, restaurants or dining rooms. Some motels have self-catering facilities (particularly in resort areas), although motel units (apartments) don't usually include cooking facilities but may have small conventional or microwave ovens. Singles usually start from $40 or $45 per night and doubles from $50 (rising to $140 for a luxury motel). Lower rates are usually available if you're planning to stay for more than a few days. Prices in resort areas are around double those in small towns or country locations. Breakfast isn't usually included in the price. Shared rooms in motels can be economical for a family or a group of three or four, and are popular with Australian families.

**Hotel Guides:** Motoring organisations (see page 275) publish guides to hotels, motels and other accommodation. These include the *A-Z Australian Accommodation Guide*, the NRMA *Accommodation Directory* and *Weekends for Two*, an accommodation guide published bi-anually. The NRMA *Accommodation Directory* lists hotels, motels, serviced apartments, guesthouses, and bed and breakfast accommodation throughout Australia. For general information, contact the Australian Hotels Association (☎ 02-6273 4007, 🖳 www.aha.org.au).

**Bookings:** In cities there are hotel booking agencies such as the Countrylink New South Wales Travel Centre in Sydney (☎ 02-9667 6050). Ausres is a one-stop central booking service for accommodation, tours and travel services (☎ local call rate 1300-365858 or 03-9696 0422, 🖳 www.aursres.com.au). There are accommodation information boards at major airports and at rail and bus stations with direct-dial free phones from which you can book rooms, although these are generally only in up-market hotels.

## B&B, HOMESTAYS & GUESTHOUSES

Bed and breakfast (B&B) accommodation consists of a room in a private house, pub, farmhouse or even on a university campus and is found throughout Australia from cities and large towns to small villages and outback stations. B&B accommodation is more informal than a hotel and often provides a friendly place to meet Australians in their own homes. It encompasses a huge variety of abodes, including historic houses, country homesteads, inner city townhouses and conventional family homes. Farmstays are becoming big business (as outback tourism increases in popularity) and range from fairly basic to luxurious, including ranch-style homesteads, small holdings in farming regions, outback cattle and sheep stations, and specialist farms. Most are working properties where guests become one of the family and are accommodated in the homestead or in an adjoining cabin or cottage. B&B is a relatively new concept in Australia but has become popular in the last decade or so, during which an increasing number of Australians have opened their homes to guests (a trend encouraged by the tourist authorities). However, it isn't an inexpensive option (as it is in Europe), single rooms costing from $40 to $100 and doubles from $70 to $100. Most B&Bs don't accept credit cards.

Homestays, which are similar to a B&B except that meals are provided, cost from $40 to well over $100 a night, depending on the meals and activities provided. Prices for full board at an outback farm (station) are from around $70 per day, although some farms offer inexpensive 'backpacker' accommodation in barns from around $7 per night (for those who don't mind sleeping with cows and pigs). Guesthouses are generally cheaper than B&Bs, guests usually staying for a minimum of a week (like homestays, meals are usually provided).

Although it's sensible to book, particularly during busy holiday periods or in major cities, it's usually unnecessary, particularly if you're touring and need a room only for one or two nights. If you're a smoker, you should ask whether smoking is permitted when booking. If you don't book, you'll have more freedom to go where you please, but you should bear in mind that some B&Bs have a minimum stay of two or three nights. When booking, confirm your arrival time to ensure that your hosts will be at home. If you're staying for more than one night, you may be expected to vacate your room for most of the day and to leave by noon (or earlier) on your last day.

**Guide Books:** There are a number of guide books to B&B accommodation in Australia, including *Bed & Breakfast: Australia's Best* by Jane Schonberger (Ten Speed Press), *Guide to Bed & Breakfast in Australia & New Zealand* by Jeannie Fairlie (Periplus Editions) and the *Australian Bed & Breakfast Book* (Moonshine Press).

# SELF-CATERING

There's a wide choice of self-catering accommodation in Australia, usually consisting of apartments (units), although cottages, houses, chalets and mobile homes are also for rent in country and resort areas. An apartment is often a good choice for a family, as it's much cheaper than a hotel room, provides more privacy and freedom, and allows you to prepare your own meals when you please. Standards, while generally high, are variable, and paying a high price doesn't always guarantee a well furnished or well appointed apartment (most look wonderful in the brochure). Holiday apartments are generally found in tourist areas and serviced apartments (units) in cities and large towns. Holiday apartments are usually rented on a weekly basis. Serviced apartments with one to three bedrooms with living area, kitchen, laundry and bathroom cost from around $120 to $200 per night (there may be discounts for stays of a week or more). There's usually no low season in major cities such as Sydney, where rates are constant throughout the year.

Holiday apartments are generally well equipped with cooking utensils, cutlery and crockery. However, small studios may have only an electric frying pan and a microwave oven for cooking, while larger apartments usually also have a stove. Check when booking if you plan to do a lot of cooking. You may need to provide your own linen and towels, although they can usually be hired for an additional fee. Prices vary considerably according to the location and season and are higher during school and public holidays. Before booking self-catering accommodation, check the holiday changeover dates and times, what's included in the rent (e.g. cleaning, linen), whether cots or high chairs are provided and pets allowed, if a garden or parking is provided, access to public transport (if required), and anything you consider essential (such as a TV, heating, air-conditioning).

Self-catering accommodation is listed in guides such as the NRMA *Accommodation Guide* and lists are maintained by tourist offices. If you're seeking long term self-catering accommodation, see **Rented Accommodation** on page 134.

# HOSTELS

One way to stretch limited financial resources is to stay in hostels. Hostels include beach huts and tree houses in Queensland, mountain cabins in Tasmania, historic renovated buildings, disused railway stations and huge purpose-built developments. Some hostels call themselves 'resorts', although rates remain firmly in the budget bracket. Modern hostels generally provide the best facilities, although they lack character and warmth, and many people prefer the more intimate, smaller, owner-operated hostels. Standards vary enormously, even among hostels operated by the same organisation. One way to discover the best hostels is to ask your fellow travellers.

There's fierce competition between hostel groups in resort areas, particularly on the Queensland coast, where many hostels have touts at the main public transport termini. The competition often leads to a range of extra services and perks, although it's sensible to book during the peak season and on public holidays. If you don't book, you may find it difficult to get a bed in cities and at popular tourist spots at any time. Many hostels have a freecall (1800) number which can be dialled anywhere in Australia. Note that some city hostels only admit overseas backpackers, as locals treat them as cheap dosshouses.

**Facilities:** The larger hostels have high standards and good facilities, which may include lockers or safety deposit boxes, free tea and coffee-making facilities, a self-catering kitchen (with allotted cupboard space and a shared refrigerator), a laundry room and ironing facilities, telephones, a travel booking service, luggage storage, fans or air-conditioning, and heating in winter. In larger cities, hostels usually have an inexpensive cafeteria. Resort hostels may offer a swimming pool, spa, sauna, gymnasium, billiard table, tennis court, BBQ, TV lounge, launderette, shop, bar, café, restaurant and a travel shop. Many hostels offer a range of sports equipment on free loan or for rent (e.g. bicycles) and may also provide free tuition (e.g. sailing) and organise day trips and tours. Most hostels provide free transport to and from local towns, airports, railway stations and bus termini.

There are few restrictions at hostels in Australia, which generally have no curfews and allow 24-hour access, although YHA hostels may have more restrictions than private hostels, where the standard of accommodation and facilities may be higher. All hostels provide sheets, pillow slips and blankets (which saves you carrying a sleeping bag and sheet), although they may need to be rented. Note that some hostels are 'party hostels', which stage backpacker party nights, barbecues and other entertainment. If you're looking for a quiet place to stay, these should be avoided!

Security can be a problem in hostels; if you don't have a safe place for your valuables, never let them out of your sight, even when taking a shower (some travellers live off others and will steal *anything*).

**Accommodation & Costs:** Accommodation may include single and double rooms, family rooms and dormitories (sleeping up to 24). Most hostels have dormitories for between 4 and 12 people, either single sex or mixed (some hostels advertise separate dormitories but put men and women together!). Note that dormitories can be noisy and lack privacy. The cost of a hostel is usually from around

$10 per night for a bed in a dormitory to $25 per person per night for a double. Some hostels have two-bedroom, self-contained units where around six people share a lounge, bathroom and kitchen. Many hostels offer discounts of $10 to $25 for stays of at least four or five days, or weekly rates which usually save you a few dollars per night. Note, however, that some hostels have limits on the length of stays during peak periods.

There's a number of hostel 'chains' in Australia, including the Youth Hostel Association (YHA), VIP Backpacker Resorts of Australia (BRA) and Nomads Backpackers International, in addition to many privately-owned independent hostels. In outback areas there are Aboriginal hostels (operated by the Aboriginal Hostels Association) which may also take in non-Aboriginals.

**YHA:** The Youth Hostel Association (YHA) has around 140 hostels in Australia (around a third of the total number) classified as simple, standard and superior, with a grading of one to five 'backpacks'. Guests don't have to be YHA members but, if you aren't a member, there's an extra charge of $3 per night. In 2001, the annual membership fee was $47 (renewals $30) for over 18s and $13 for under 18s. There are discounts for two-year, three-year and life memberships (certain conditions apply). Children under 17 receive free membership when their parents are members (called family membership), and group membership is also available. Introductory membership is also available, where you pay an extra $3 per night and after ten nights receive full membership (stamps are issued and an 'Aussie Starter Card'). Senior Australian members receive two vouchers (worth $8.50 each) towards hostel accommodation in the state of issue. Members can also purchase accommodation 'packs' or vouchers for 10 nights' accommodation for $150 (valid for two months) or 20 nights' accommodation for $280 (valid for six months). A range of over 800 discounts are offered to YHA members in Australia, including 10 per cent off Greyhound Pioneer Australia's coach passes and up to 30 per cent off car rental. It may be cheaper to join the YHA overseas before arriving in Australia. Visitors can purchase a one-year Hostelling International Card (HIC) for $30 (overseas residents don't pay the joining fee) at YHA membership and travel centres in capital cities or at Australian hostels.

There are few restrictions at YHA hostels, although the length of stays may be limited to a maximum of five to seven days. There are no age restrictions and no rules requiring early check-out. Guests must have sleeping sheets or bed linen (these can be purchased at hostels or hired for around $3 per night); sleeping bags alone aren't permitted. Blankets and pillows are provided.

The YHA has an International Booking Network (IBN) through which bookings can be made up to six months in advance (a fee of $2 may apply when booking in Australia). The YHA publishes a free annual *Accommodation and Discounts Guide* plus a free *Australia Visitors Map* showing the location of its hostels. For further information, contact the Australian Youth Hostel Association, Level 3, 10 Mallett Street, Camperdown, NSW 2050 (☎ 02-9565 1699, 🖥 www.yha.com.au).

**BRA & Nomads:** VIP Backpacker Resorts of Australia (BRA) is an association of around 110 hostels throughout Australia. It offers VIP membership costing $25 a year (not compulsory) which provides accommodation, travel, entertainment and equipment discounts. BRA allow guests to use their own sleeping bags, although sheets and blankets are available for hire. Rates are from around $12 to $16 per night and bookings cost $1.50. For information contact BRA, PO Box 600, Cannon Hill, Brisbane, QLD 4170 (☎ 07-3395 6611, 🖥 www.backpackers.com.au).

Nomads Backpackers International (☎ freecall 1800-819883, ▭ www.nomad-backpackers.com) offer a 'dreamtime card' providing a range of accommodation (e.g. the seventh night free at all hostels) and other discounts throughout Australia.

**Other Options:** YMCAs and YWCAs offer casual accommodation, although their prices are around double those charged by hostels. They have single rooms and some dormitories and are mainly located in the major cities. During summer holidays (i.e. from November to February) and other vacation periods, many university colleges let rooms in their halls of residence to travellers for around $12 to $15 per night for a single room or $20 for bed and breakfast. Rooms must be booked in advance and priority is given to students (others pay a surcharge of 50 to 100 per cent). Note that many universities are located outside cities and towns.

**Publications:** There are many publications for independent travellers, including the *Australia and New Zealand Travel Planner* (published by TNT Magazine, 14–15 Child's Place, Earls Court, London SW5 9RX, UK), which provides invaluable advice for backpackers and travellers plus a complete hostel directory. TNT also publish *TNT for Backpackers* magazines. A free monthly magazine, *For Backpackers, By Backpackers*, is available in Sydney and the YHA also publishes a free magazine, *The Hosteller*, available from YHA hostels. The Australian government produces a backpacker hostel guide listing over 300 hostels which have been assessed by the Australian Automobile Association (AAA) and given a one to five 'rucksack' rating. The guide is available from hostels, transit points, hostel booking offices, travel agents and automobile associations in Australia. Books for hostellers include the *Aussie Backpacker Accommodation Guide* (North Australian Publishing, who also maintain a very informative website, PO Box 1264, Townsville, Queensland 4810, ☎ 07-4772 3244, ▭ www.aussiebackpack.com.au) and the *Independent Traveller's Guide to Australia* (STA Travel).

## CARAVANS & CAMPING

Australia is a great country for camping on account of its generally mild climate and the lack of camping restrictions. Most towns have at least one campsite or caravan park. In the outback you can pitch a tent virtually anywhere you please, although permission is required to camp on private property and there are local regulations restricting camping in some areas. For example, in Western Australia you aren't permitted to camp within 16km/10mi of a caravan or campsite; you can try camping on green areas outside the city centre, but should be on your way early to avoid the attention of the local police. In Brisbane it's illegal to camp within a 22km/14mi radius of the city centre, although short-term camping is permitted in roadside rest areas in most of Queensland.

In national parks, camping is permitted only in designated areas, although some also allow bush camping (there's usually a small fee). Special environmental and safety regulations apply and most don't permit open fires (so you'll need a portable stove). Fees vary from park to park but are usually from around $5 per person per night (you may need to book at popular campsites in national parks). When spending an extended period in a national park, you should let the park ranger know your route and when you expect to return. You must observe all fire ban warnings, take your rubbish with you, wash well away from streams, rivers and lakes, stick to existing campsites where available rather than creating new ones, use only fallen dead wood for fires, take no pets with you, take care not to desecrate Aboriginal sites, and must not interfere with the flora and fauna – apart from which you can do what you like! All states publish information about camping in national parks.

Campsites and caravan parks are common and are available in all major towns and tourist centres (many are located on the edge of beaches). Facilities vary but basic amenities usually include electricity hook-ups, hot and cold water, showers, toilets and laundry facilities. At large sites, there's usually a range of indoor recreation areas, shops, restaurants, lock-up storage for valuables, and a wide variety of sports facilities which may include a swimming pool, tennis courts, volleyball, cycling, table-tennis, trampolining, canoeing, fishing and boating. Camp or caravan sites cost from around $10 a night for two people. A 'night' is usually from noon to noon and some sites charge extra to use electricity, showers, sports facilities (such as tennis courts) and other amenities such as ironing facilities or a freezer. Many caravan parks (such as BIG 4) have on-site caravans, cabins, villas and holiday units, which can be rented from around $30 to $35 a night for a caravan and $35 to $45 for a cabin. Linen and blankets can usually be hired, although a portable heater is useful in winter as many caravans and cabins are unheated.

Many campsites in Australia are primarily caravan parks, intended more for caravanners (trailers) and motor homes than for campers. Many have gravel surfaces (or hard ground) rather than turf, so pitching a tent can be hard work. Most campsites near to major cities are well away from the centre, which means that you need your own transport to get the most out of camping. It's important to book if you have a caravan and require an electricity hook-up. Outside peak periods you can usually find a campsite without difficulty on the spot, but don't leave it too late in the day when you're in a popular area (after noon is too late at some sites).

A swag is all you need when camping under the stars in the outback. Many different types are manufactured (e.g. by the Jolly Swag Company of Australia), the best of which include a mattress, sheet, down filled sleeping bag, blanket and pillow inside a sturdy canvas envelope. You can also buy a tarpaulin cover in case of rain. When camping wild, avoid dried-up river beds in the wet season due to the danger of flash floods (when you'll also need a life jacket!).

Camping tours are popular, and many companies offer organised tours in air-conditioned coaches or 4WD vehicles. You can buy or rent (see page 274) a campervan or mobile home throughout Australia (many people purchase a secondhand one from a departing visitor).

Interesting magazines for campers and caravanners include *Outdoor Australia* and *Wild*, both published quarterly. Excellent guide books are available from automobile associations such as the NRMA's *Camping and Caravan Directory*. See also **Australian Roads** on page 261 for information about driving in the outback.

# PARKS, GARDENS & ZOOS

There are some 2,000 national parks and reserves in Australia covering an area of over 40 million hectares (100 million acres – over 5 per cent of Australia's land area), plus a further 38 million hectares (95 million acres) of marine and estuarine protected areas. Australia has 13 World Heritage sites, including the Great Barrier Reef, Eluru-Kata Tjuta (Ayers Rock/Mount Olga), Kakadu National Park (Northern Territory, where *Crocodile Dundee* was filmed), the Queensland (wet tropics) rainforests, Fraser Island and the Tasmanian Wilderness. National parks include every possible habitat, and many are of great scientific interest. Australia was the second country (the first was the USA with Yellowstone Park) to proclaim a national park, the Royal National Park in Sydney in 1879.

Each state has its own national parks authority, most of which publish guides detailing park facilities. Some parks charge an entrance fee, e.g. $9 for a car in NSW (less for motorbikes and pedestrians), although entry to smaller parks is often free and larger parks also provide free entry at weekends. A two-month holiday pass is available in Tasmania for $30 for a vehicle and $12 for motorcyclists, cyclists and bushwalkers, and an annual pass ($42) for vehicles is also available. All national parks and World Heritage sites have information or visitors' centres with maps, leaflets, slide shows and films, and guided tours are organised during peak times. Some parks provide numbered pegs indicating points of interest, natural features and unique habitats which can be cross-referenced with information sheets. For information about national parks contact the Biodiversity Group of Environment Australia, GPO Box 787, Canberra, ACT 2601 (☎ 02-6274 1111, 💻 www.ea.gov.au) or the appropriate organisation in each state.

Australia has many excellent zoos, wildlife parks and aquariums. The most famous is the Royal Melbourne Zoological Gardens (Australia's oldest and the third oldest in the world, dating back to 1857), which houses around 4,000 species of animals and birds in 'natural' habitats. Taronga Zoo in Sydney is home to Australia's largest collection of native and exotic animals and has a peerless setting beside Sydney Harbour (best visited by ferry from Circular Quay) and extensive breeding facilities, some of which are located at its 'sister' zoo (Western Plains Zoo in Dubbo). Other top zoos and wildlife parks include the Alma Park Zoo north of Brisbane (which houses a large collection of Australian wildlife), Perth Zoo (16 hectares/40 acres of exotic and native Australian fauna), Adelaide Zoo, the Tidbinbilla Nature Reserve (west of Canberra) and the Lone Pine Koala Sanctuary (near Brisbane). There are aquariums in many of Australia's major cities (e.g. the Sydney Aquarium and Manly Oceanarium, and the Melbourne Aquarium opened in 2000 and linked with the Yarra river) and tourist resorts (e.g. Sea World on the Gold Coast).

Australia's cities were designed with people in mind and they generally have an abundance of green spaces and wide boulevards, with both formal and informal ('native') parks within them or nearby. All major cities have impressive botanical gardens such as the Royal Botanic Gardens in Melbourne, home to some 12,000 plant species and the finest in Australia, and the City Botanic Gardens in Brisbane (the Mount Coot-tha Botanic Gardens 12km/7mi west of the city are also impressive). Sydney has its own Royal Botanic Gardens, located adjacent to the harbour and the Sydney Opera House, and an exquisite Chinese Garden (Darling Harbour), while Canberra is home to the National Botanic Gardens on Black Mountain, which contain over 6,000 native plants. Some cities, such as Melbourne, publish a *Parks and Gardens* brochure.

The National Trust (2 Light Street, Griffith, ACT 2603, ☎ 02-6239 5222) is dedicated to preserving historic buildings and parks throughout Australia and owns a number of properties that are open to the public. You can join for $49 a year for individuals ($35 concession) and $68 for families ($49 concession). There are local National Trust offices in each state.

Information about national parks, botanical gardens, aquariums and zoos is available from the Australian Tourist Commission or any good guide book. All tourist offices and visitors' centres provide information about local attractions.

# MUSEUMS & GALLERIES

There are over 1,000 museums and galleries in Australia visited by more than 7 million people annually, including federal and state museums, private galleries, regional exhibitions and privately owned collections. The most important national collections are housed in Canberra and include the National Museum of Australia, the National Gallery of Australia, the National Portrait Gallery, the National Library, the Australian War Memorial (which houses one of the best military museums in the world), the National Film and Sound Archive (free admission), the National Science and Technology Centre and the National Aquarium and Wildlife Sanctuary (admission $10).

Elsewhere, major museums and galleries include the Art Gallery of NSW, the Australian Museum, the Powerhouse Museum (science, decorative arts and social history), the National Maritime Museum and the Museum of Contemporary Art (all housed in Sydney), the National Museum of Melbourne, the Victorian Arts Centre (housing the National Gallery of Victoria) and the Australian Gallery of Sport and Olympic Museum in Melbourne, the Art Gallery of South Australia and the South Australian Museum (both in Adelaide), the National Motor Museum (Birdwood, South Australia), the Western Australian Museum and the Art Gallery of Western Australia (Perth), the Queensland Museum and Queensland Art Gallery (Brisbane), the Tasmanian Museum and Art Gallery (Hobart), and the Northern Territory Museum of Arts and Sciences (Darwin), which houses one of the best collections of Aboriginal art in Australia. Two new museums opened in 2001: the National Museum in Canberra and the Museum of Australian Art in Melbourne.

Admission is usually between $5 and $15 and students normally pay half price. Most museums and galleries are open daily from around 9 or 10am until 5pm, although many have reduced opening hours on Sundays.

There's a strong market for contemporary Australian art, particularly Aboriginal art, which has become fashionable in recent years and can be seen in many galleries. It is, however, usually expensive (apart from mass-produced tourist artefacts, which aren't the genuine article). Famous Australian painters include Sidney Nolan, Brett Whiteley and Fred Williams, although they aren't known internationally outside the art world (most Australian artists tend to become famous only after they've died).

All states have National Trusts that work hand-in-hand with the federal Heritage Commission to preserve historic buildings and sites. There are many reminders of Australia's past as a penal colony and many former prisons have been preserved as museums, notably the Old Melbourne Gaol and the Port Arthur penal colony in Tasmania.

# CINEMAS

Cinema is the most popular leisure activity (apart from sport), among Australians, over 60 per cent of whom visit a cinema each year; ticket sales are around 100 million per year. Australian cinemas are split between first run and arthouse (which show old classics, foreign, cult and experimental films). Films are also shown by cultural organisations, the State Film Centre (Melbourne) and film festivals. Major film festivals in Australia include the Melbourne International Film Festival (held in July) and the Sydney Film Festival held in June. Australia is dominated by three cinema chains: Greater Union, Hoyts and Village, which together account for around 50 per cent of screens in Australia and some 60 per cent of tickets sold. Independent operators (indies) control around 30 per cent of Australia's cinemas, although they're being hard hit by the multiplexes, which have as many as 30 screens (but usually two to 10) and are often owned by the film distributors (film distribution rights are a constant battle for indies). At the other extreme, small towns usually have just one single-screen cinema, many of which are ancient. There are private film clubs in the major cities and local film societies in all areas.

Some cinemas (such as Cinema Plus) have giant screens employing IMAX 3-D technology. New centres have extra-wide comfortable seats with ample leg-room, Dolby stereo or THX surround sound, air-conditioned (non-smoking) auditoriums and free parking. Many also have cafés, restaurants, bars and games rooms. There are also open-air, drive-in cinemas throughout Australia, particularly on Saturday evenings (the charge is usually per vehicle rather than per passenger). Most operate only in summer, although some are open also in winter, when you may be able to rent an in-car heater. There's even a Deckchair Cinema in Darwin where you can watch a film while reclining in a deckchair!

All films on general release in Australia are given a classification (shown below), which denotes any age restrictions:

| Classification | Age Restriction |
|---|---|
| G | General release – no age restrictions |
| PG | Parental Guidance for children under 15; not recommended for children under 12 |
| M | Mature – those aged over 15 |
| R | Restricted – those aged over 18 |

Children (or adults) who look younger than their years may be asked for proof of their age (e.g. a school identity card, student card or driving licence) for admission to age-restricted performances.

Tickets cost around $12 ($8 for children aged under 15) in cities, a little less in country areas. There are reduced prices for matinees, Tuesday evenings and sometimes also on Mondays. Most cinemas offer reductions for children, pensioners and students, although you should check in advance, as some reductions apply only to certain performances. Many cinemas (including all new cinemas) have special facilities for the disabled in wheelchairs. Most chains provide passes which offer large discounts. Most cinemas accept telephone and Internet bookings (major credit cards accepted, although some cinemas charge a booking fee for each seat, e.g. $1.50). Cinemas usually have a number of shows a day, including late-night and all-night shows on Friday and Saturday evenings. Smoking is prohibited in all cinemas. Cinema programmes are published in major national and local newspapers.

Australia has a thriving film industry which has produced many international hits in the last few decades, including such classics as *Picnic at Hanging Rock*, *Gallipoli*, *Mad Max*, *Crocodile Dundee*, *Shine*, *Babe*, *The Piano*, *The Year of Living Dangerously* and *Muriel's Wedding*. (The world's first feature film, *Soldiers of the Cross*, was made in Australia in 1900 by the Salvation Army – not many people know that!). In the industry's heyday, around 40 films per year were produced in Australia. The Australian film industry is aided by the Australian Film Commission (AFC) established in 1975 to assist in the development of low budget, innovative film productions. However, in recent years state funding has been reduced and the Australian film industry faces an uncertain future.

Australian film stars include Bruce Beresford, Cate Blanchett, Mel Gibson, Nicole Kidman, Paul Hogan, Jack Thompson and Toni Collette (Errol Flynn and Chips Rafferty were also born in Australia), plus a number of celebrated directors and producers. However, like most countries, Australia loses most of its talent to Hollywood, which is quick to snap up foreign artists in order to cement its dominance of the silver screen.

# THEATRE, OPERA & DANCE

Australian theatre is of a surprisingly high standard (particularly to those who think Australians are philistines) and extremely varied, thanks to the country's cosmopolitan and multicultural cities, particularly Sydney and Melbourne. In addition to mainstream traditional theatre, where classic plays and international musicals are performed to a very high standard. Australia has a thriving contemporary theatre scene where anything goes. Its far-ranging performances include outrageous Australian comedy, image-based theatre, experimental plays, pub and coffee shop theatre, and outdoor performances.

Melbourne has the most dynamic theatre scene in Australia and boasts over 70 theatres, including the State Theatre, Playhouse and the George Fairfax Studio (all of which are housed in the majestic Victorian Arts Centre), plus Her Majesty's, the Comedy Theatre, the Russell Theatre (home of the Melbourne Theatre Company), the Princess Theatre and the Athenaeum Theatre, and various fringe theatres. Sydney's main theatres include the Opera House, the Belvoir Street Theatre, the Griffin Theatre, the York Theatre, the Pilgrim Theatre, the Studio (at the Opera House), the Symour Theatre (at Sydney University) and the Wharf Theatre, home of the Sydney Theatre Company. The oldest surviving theatre company in Australia is the New Theatre in Sydney (over 65 years old). Other major Australian theatres include the Canberra Theatre Centre, the Lyric and Cremorne Theatres in Brisbane (within the Queensland Cultural Centre and Performing Arts Complex), and His Majesty's Theatre and the Subiaco Theatre Centre in Perth (home of the State Theatre Company of Western Australia).

Major international productions such as are regularly staged in Australia's major cities. Most plays performed in Australia have traditionally been written by American and British playwrights. However, Australian theatre has blossomed in the last few decades and plays such as *Stretch of the Imagination* (Jack Hibbert) and *The Removalist* (David Williams) have become Australian classics. The Australians excel in comedy and love to send themselves (and everyone else) up. The most famous Australian comedy actor is Barry Humphries, whose larger-than-life characters include Dame Edna Everage, Barry McKenzie, Sir Les Patterson and Sandy Stone. Melbourne is the comedy capital of Australia and stages the annual International Comedy Festival in April, while Sydney has the Comedy Store with a different show each night. Tickets for most major productions vary considerably in price, but usually cost between $20 and $40, while performances at fringe theatres cost around $15. Half-price theatre tickets can be purchased on the day of a performance in Sydney from the Halifax kiosk in Martin Place (tickets must be purchased in person and be paid for in cash).

**Opera:** The Australian Opera was established in 1970 and is largely dependent on government subsidies and sponsorship (although it and other performing arts companies still run at huge losses). The Victoria State Opera and the Australian Opera (Sydney) were merged in 1996 to form a new integrated company, Opera Australia, which performs at the State Theatre in Melbourne and the Sydney Opera House. The standard of opera, ballet and classical concerts produced at Australia's main venues is among the highest in the world, and international stars regularly perform there. Home-grown stars include Joan Sutherland, Dame Nellie Melba, Joan Hammond, John Brownless, Yvonne Kenny and Peter Dawson. There are small professional opera companies in some states. The opera season usually runs from July to August and from November to December.

The Sydney Opera House is one of the architectural landmarks of the 20th century and it has become the symbol of the city since its completion in 1973 after 14 years at a cost of $102 million – it was scheduled to be completed in five years at a cost of $7 million; an opera, *Eighth Wonder*, was even written and performed about the building process! In addition to the opera house itself, the building houses two auditoriums (the larger for orchestral concerts seating 2,690, the smaller for opera and ballet performances), a drama theatre known as The Studio and a small playhouse, three restaurants and a café. Despite its imperfect acoustics (modernisation is soon to be undertaken), it's often ranked with the world's leading opera houses, including Covent Garden in London, La Scala in Milan and the New York Met. Opera Australia also performs outdoor concerts such as the Opera in the Park in Sydney in January. Most events at the Sydney Opera House are expensive, although tickets start at $28 for some concerts (rising to well over $100) and there's a $4 surcharge for telephone bookings. Information can be obtained from the Opera Centre, 480 Elizabeth Street, Surrey Hills, Sydney, NSW 2000 (☎ 02-9319 6333 for information or 02-9319 1099 for 24-hour bookings, 🖥 www.soh.nsw.gov.au).

**Dance:** Ballet is the most healthy art form in Australia, surviving largely on box-office receipts, and there are hundreds of ballet schools. The world-famous Australian Ballet was founded in 1962 and has its headquarters in Melbourne, although it performs a summer and winter season at the Sydney Opera House and also tours Australia. Tickets cost from around $50. Australia also has a number of contemporary dance companies, the most famous of which is the Sydney Dance Company (which performs at the Sydney Opera House).

**Festivals:** In addition to the extensive concert programme, Australian cities stage a number of prestigious arts festivals, including the biennial Adelaide Festival (2002, 2004, etc.), which is modelled on the Edinburgh Festival and includes theatre, dance and musical performances from around the world. There's also a fringe festival. Other major arts festivals include the National Festival of Australian Theatre (Canberra, October), the Festival of Perth (February), the Melbourne International Festival (October) and the Melbourne International Comedy Festival (April).

**Information:** Theatre, opera and dance performance listings are provided in weekly and monthly entertainment guides, available from tourist offices in major cities, and many daily newspapers publish free guides such as the 'Metro' on Fridays in the *Sydney Morning Herald* (which includes a theatre directory).

# MUSIC

**Classical:** Classical concerts, music festivals and solo concerts are regularly staged throughout Australia by Australian and international musicians and performers. Australia has eight professional orchestras: six symphony orchestras (one in each state capital) run by the Australian Broadcasting Corporation (ABC), the Australian Opera and Ballet Orchestra in Sydney, and the State Orchestra in Victoria (both of which work with Australian Opera and Australian Ballet). Many Australians are enthusiastic about classical music and a number of festivals are staged, including the Sydney International Music Festival (July), the Sydney Festival (January) and the Melbourne Music Festival (February). The Sydney Symphony Orchestra performs outdoor concerts such as the Symphony in the Park season in January. Musica Viva (Sydney) is the best known chamber music society (and the world's largest) and stages a concert series of international groups and artists. Regional companies (supported by state governments) perform in state capitals and provincial centres.

**Pop:** Pop music is an important part of national popular culture and over the last 25 years Australia has produced some of the world's best pop music. Australia also has a thriving band scene, most of them performing in pubs, where the best of real Australian music is found, and clubs (e.g. RSL and working mens' clubs). Many amateur bands are surprisingly good (often performing their own songs), although some are excruciating. Australia is said to be among the hardest training grounds in the world for pop bands, where internationally famous bands such as AC/DC, Air Supply, InXs, Men at Work and Mental as Anything served their apprenticeship. There's usually an admission fee of $5 to $12 to clubs and pubs with live music, although many concerts are free (depending on who's performing).

Major Australian cities, particularly Sydney, Melbourne and Brisbane, are on the itinerary of most international pop stars, many of whom perform in Australia during the Christmas (summer) season. In Sydney, the main venue for pop concerts is the Sydney Entertainment Centre, and the Sydney Town Hall is also an important venue, while in Melbourne it's the Sport and Entertainment Centre on the banks of the Yarra River. Concerts are held in Melbourne at the Myer Music Bowl in Alexandra Gardens, Olympic Park and Kooyong Stadium. The big names also play at the Brisbane Entertainment Centre and the Perth Entertainment Centre. Free pop concerts are held on summer Sundays in some cities (if it's very hot and the band sounds a bit off key, it may be the result of high humidity, which causes instruments to go out of tune – it's certainly an original excuse!). Big Day Out is an all-day, Australia-wide, popular music festival featuring top bands staged in January and February.

Concert and gig guides are available free in local daily newspapers, many of which also publish a weekly entertainment guide (usually on Fridays). There are free music weeklies in most cities, which are distributed via pubs, record stores and bottle shops. These include *Beat* and *Inpress* in Melbourne, *Beat*, *3D World* and *Drum Media* in Sydney, *Rave* and *The Scene* in Brisbane, the *Son of Barfly* in Cairns and *Pulse* in Darwin. Gig guides are also broadcast on local music radio stations.

**Jazz, Folk, Country and Bush Music:** Jazz has a lively following on the pub circuit, particularly in Sydney, where there are many regular venues (bands also perform in a variety of outdoor venues). A number of jazz festivals are staged in Australia, including the Montsalvat Jazz Festival (Eltham, VIC), held on the Australia

Day weekend (January), and the York Jazz Festival in Western Australia in September. Australian country music has strong local themes, and there are clubs in all major cities; many pubs also feature folk and country groups. Folk and bush music is also popular (it has its roots in English, Irish and Scottish folk music), where fiddles, tin whistles and banjos predominate along with a home-grown instrument called the 'lagerphone' (or zob stick), consisting of a wooden frame covered in metal bottle tops which is bashed on the ground, shaken or hit with a stick. The main festivals are the Australasian Country Music Festival in Tamworth (NSW) in January (featuring over 700 events) and the Land of the Beardies Bush Festival (which also includes a long beard competition!) at Glen Innes, NSW in November.

**Aboriginal Music:** Few people will forget the haunting sound of a didgeridoo (made famous by Rolf Harris in his song *Tie Me Kangaroo Down, Sport*) which is used in the bush to accompany tribal dances (called corroborees). Busking (often non-Aboriginal) didgeridoo players are common in the main cities, and performances are staged for tourists in northern regions (although they're a pale imitation of real corroborees). It's possible to hear the real thing at an Aboriginal cultural festival, and there are some contemporary Aboriginal bands such as Yothu Yindi, although few have had any commercial success. Other forms of native music are Koori, a cross between traditional Aboriginal music and country music, and 'gum-leaf', in which Aboriginal performers make 'music' by blowing on gum leaves.

**Other:** There's also a wide variety of amateur music groups in Australia, including orchestras, military bands, choral societies and even barbershop singers, most of which are constantly on the lookout for new talent. Free music is provided by an army of buskers, many of whom are excellent.

# SOCIAL CLUBS

There are numerous social clubs and organisations in Australia catering for both foreigners and Australians, including Ambassador clubs, Apex clubs, business clubs, church clubs and groups, the freemasons, international men's and women's clubs, Kiwani clubs, Lion and Lioness clubs, Rotary clubs, Round Table clubs, ex-servicemen's clubs, sports clubs, women's clubs, working men's clubs and Returned Services League (RSL) clubs. RSL (or leagues) clubs are an institution and constitute the main social centre in country towns. They're run by the Returned Soldiers League/Returned and Services League or local football clubs and associations and are among the most popular social venues in Australia. Many have huge halls where a variety of shows are regularly staged, plus restaurants, bars, pay/satellite TV, gambling (poker machines), discos, live pop music and ballrooms. Although ostensibly just for members (and their guests), many admit overseas visitors.

Expatriates from many countries run a variety of clubs, associations and organisations in major cities (ask at consulates for information). Many clubs organise pastimes such as chess, bridge, whist, art and music classes, sports activities, theatre and cinema outings and local history tours. If you want to become integrated into your local community or Australian society in general, one of the best ways is to join a social club (even better, join a number). There are singles clubs in the major cities that organise a comprehensive range of activities on every day of the week. If you're retired, you may find that your local council publishes a programme of recreational activities for the retired in your area. Most councils publish a calendar of local sports and social events, and most libraries provide information about local clubs, groups, associations and organisations.

## NIGHTLIFE

There are discotheques and nightclubs in all major Australian towns and cities. Nightlife includes nightclubs, discotheques (discos), dance clubs, karaoke clubs, comedy clubs, cabaret bars, gay clubs, pool halls, RSL clubs (see above) and casinos (described under **Gambling** below). Note that the differences between a bar, pub, restaurant and nightclub are often minimal in Australian cities, and some establishments are a combination of all four. There's a huge variety of gay clubs in some cities (such as Sydney), where information is published in the gay press such as the *Sydney Star Observer* and *Capital Q*.

Many clubs and discos play a combination of live and recorded music. Admission to discos varies, but there's usually a $10 to $15 cover charge, which may include a free drink, and venues with live music may charge as much as $20 for entry and $6 or $8 a drink. Some offer free entry for women on certain days (e.g. Wednesdays) and half-price drinks before 9pm (before the real 'action' starts) on some days. Some up-market discos and dance clubs allow admission only to couples. Note that drinks are usually expensive and even water usually costs from $2.50 to $3.50 per glass. The dress code is usually smart casual, which usually excludes jeans, leather, T-shirts and trainers, although in some establishments these may be *de rigueur* (fashion usually dictates, depending on the venue). Dress may also be at the whim of the doorman (bouncer); if he doesn't like the look of you, you're out (or at least not in). Many discos are open until 3am or later, although some have variable closing times.

Some night-clubs are exclusive 'members-only' clubs with strict dress codes and high prices, which attract an older, more well-to-do clientele. Like discos, some nightclubs remain open until dawn. Sydney and Melbourne have the most cosmopolitan nightlife, with venues to suit every taste in music, fashion and atmosphere. Melbourne has some of the liveliest nightlife in Australia and a plethora of clubs, including the Metro, which is the largest nightclub in the southern hemisphere. The main nightlife areas in Sydney are Oxford Street and the sleazy Kings Cross area (British conservative politicians would feel at home here!), where drugs are freely available and violence is never too far away at some venues.

Daily newspapers and free entertainment newspapers and information sheets (e.g. *3D World* and *Beat* in Sydney) in major cities provide a comprehensive lists of entertainment venues and events.

## GAMBLING

Gambling is one of Australia's favourite pastimes (for some people it's an occupation) and includes betting on horse, greyhound and camel races, football pools, lotteries, bingo ('housie'), casinos, poker machines ('pokies'), card games, two-up (see below), raffles and betting on the results of general elections, public appointments, football matches and other sports events. Aussies are compulsive (and impulsive) gamblers (it's estimated that 40 per cent of the population gamble regularly) and will bet on almost anything, even the proverbial two flies climbing a wall; in the outback (where you need to make your own entertainment) there are cane toad, cockroach, lizard and snail races!

Gambling is a $11 billion industry in Australia and accounts for 1.5 per cent of the annual GDP. On average an adult Australian spends (i.e. loses) $760 a year on gambling; the residents of NSW are among the heaviest gamblers, spending over $12 million per day on lotteries alone. Gambling revenue is a favourite target of the tax man (around 30 to 40 per cent of the profit on poker machines alone), and taxation raised from gambling accounts for some 12 per cent of state and federal governments' revenue.

Compulsive gambling is a huge problem in Australia, where an estimated 2.1 per cent of the population has a gambling problem (the percentage is lower than those addicted to nicotine or alcohol but higher than the percentage hard drugs addicts). Like alcoholism, gambling is a disease which can be controlled but never cured. There are a huge number of Gamblers Anonymous groups and meetings in Australia, and also meetings for the relatives of compulsive gamblers to help them cope with their loved one's addiction. There is a National Hotline offering advice and help for compulsive gamblers (☎ freecall 1800-633635). Compulsive gamblers can ban themselves from casinos under the Casino Control Act. However, you can now gamble at cyber space casinos on the Internet without leaving home, a form of gambling which is set to spiral in coming years. Note, however, that it's totally unregulated and there's no guarantee of getting paid by 'casinos' located overseas (often they're 'based' in offshore jurisdictions).

**Casinos:** Most states have one or more casinos and there are now around 13 in Australia, including four in Queensland, two in Sydney, two in Melbourne, two in Tasmania (Hobart and Launceston) and one each in Adelaide, Alice Springs, Canberra, Darwin and Perth. New casinos to be built in recent years have included the Sydney Star City and Sydney Harbour Casinos and the massive Crown Casino in Melbourne (open 24 hours a day). Games on offer include baccarat, roulette, blackjack, craps, poker, two-up, Sic Bo and Pai Gow (Chinese card games) and keno. Keno is similar to bingo except that you mark from one to 15 numbers out of 80 on your card and, if your numbers are among the 20 drawn, you win. Many casinos have a separate TAB area (see below) where you can place bets on horse and greyhound racing.

Dress rules require 'smart casual dress', which usually means a shirt with a collar and no T-shirts, shorts, sports shoes (trainers) or thongs (flip-flops), although jeans are usually acceptable. However, some ban jeans and insist on a tie for men, so check in advance. Many casinos are open 24 hours a day. Games usually have a $2 minimum bet, although bets may start at $10 or more. Usually you must pay for drinks. Most casinos publish a free *Casino Gaming Guide*, but don't expect any insider tips on how to break the bank!

**Pokies:** Poker machines (pokies) have spread like wildfire in recent years and are now seen almost everywhere (except Western Australia, where they're banned outside casinos), as state governments have rushed to cash in on Australia's gambling fever (pokies represent over half of gambling expenditure). There are more than 185,000 pokies in Australia (around 20 per cent of the world's machines!), NSW leading the table with some 97,000 (10 per cent of the world's poker machines and more than Nevada). Pokies aren't restricted to casinos and are common at leagues and other social clubs, where they are blamed for encouraging gambling among the elderly. Many can be played for as little as 20¢ and some boast jackpots of up to $25,000. In some states (e.g. Tasmania) there are limits on the amount that can be spent on video gaming machines, and in others (e.g. Victoria) there has been a backlash against pokies, which have encouraged gambling among the poor in disadvantaged areas.

**Racing:** Betting on animal racing is a popular form of gambling in Australia and includes horse racing, harness-racing (trotting) and greyhound racing. Gambling on horse and greyhound racing operates on the tote system (an Australian invention) operated by state Totaliser Agency Boards (TABs). TABs have outlets in all towns and cities (around 1,000 in Sydney alone) where offices (which also accept bets on the football pools) are open from around 11am until 6pm Mondays to Fridays, and from 10am until 8pm on Saturdays. The TABs' annual turnover exceeds $4 billion, including around $100 million waged on the Melbourne Cup alone (Australia's premier horse race). To place a bet, you simply write the name of your horse(s) or dog(s) and the race number on a betting slip and give it to the clerk with your stake. If you win, you can collect your winnings immediately after the race (provided you haven't lost your receipt). There are no off-course starting price (SP) bookmakers in Australia, although there's on-course SP betting where odds are given by bookmakers for each horse and you're given a fixed price. However, illegal telephone bookies flourish, and betting syndicates are active throughout Australia.

**Lotteries:** The national lottery ('lotto') is also a popular form of gambling in Australia, where you choose six numbers from one to 40. Numbers are drawn once or twice a week and those who select three or more correct numbers win a prize. The minimum stake is $1 and the first prize is usually in the $hundreds of thousands or $millions (the average payout is some 60 per cent of the amount staked). Results are published in the press and are also available via telephone information numbers. In recent years instant lottery tickets, known as 'scratchies', have become the most popular form of lottery.

**Soccer Pools:** Soccer pools were traditionally the most common form of gambling in Australia, although they've been overtaken by lotteries and other forms of gambling in recent years. Operated by Australian Soccerpools, the pools offer huge cash prizes if you correctly forecast the results of football matches (Australian in the winter and British in the summer). The treble chance is the most popular bet, where you must guess which matches will be score draws (i.e. not 0-0). If you don't want to fill out a coupon each week, you can have a standing order using the same numbers.

**Two-Up:** The national game of chance is called 'two-up', invented by soldiers in the first world war. It's illegal outside casinos (except on ANZAC Day) and a few licensed two-up schools (not that this discourages many Aussies). Not exactly the most sophisticated of games, bets are placed on two coins that are tossed into the air together using a stick called a 'kip'. If one lands heads and the other tails, there's no result and all bets are held for the next throw. If both coins show the same, you win or lose depending on whether you chose heads or tails. Coins must spin when tossed or the arbitrator (called the 'spinner') calls the game void. Bets are placed with the 'boxer'. Casinos keep the stakes when there's a sequence of five identical results (unless you bet on this), which is around a 3 per cent chance.

# BARS & PUBS

Australia is famous for its pubs (an abbreviation of 'public house'), which are a tradition inherited from the British and are often referred to as hotels, although nowadays most don't provide accommodation. Australia has a huge variety of drinking establishments, including bustling music pubs, hotel bars, pubs with restaurants and barbies (barbecues), gay and lesbian pubs, trendy downtown lounge bars, luxury hotel cocktail bars, restaurant bars, wine bars (rare), earthy country and outback hotels with sawdust floors (where women aren't made welcome), elegant restored Victorian and Edwardian pubs (many with verandas and balconies), boisterous barn-like drinking dens, and tropical, niche and cabaret bars. Returned Soldiers League/Returned and Services League (RSL) clubs and other private (often ethnic) clubs are popular drinking places and usually have low prices and an inexpensive restaurant. Many RSL clubs are open to all and not just ex-servicemen (of which there's a diminishing number in Australia). There are guides to local pubs published in some cities, e.g. the *Guide to Melbourne's Pubs* (Melbourne is reckoned to have the most various and interesting pubs in Australia). It's hard to imagine it now, but some states such as South Australia actually started life as temperance states!

Drinking is a way of life in Australia ('land of the liquid lunch') and most social activities revolve around a bottle of wine (or three) and a few dozen 'tinnies' (cans of beer). It has even spawned its own language; for example, beer is variously known as amber fluid, amber nectar, neck oil, singing syrup, brewery broth, and a throat charmer, a can of beer as a frosty, tinny, and tube, and being drunk as stinko, inked, off your face, full as a tick (or a goog), drunk as a fowl (or Chloe – who?), on the slops and schicked (a teetotaler is a 'waterbag'). Buying a round of drinks is called a 'shout' and you won't be popular if you don't when your turn comes around. In Australia, you usually buy your drinks at the bar and pay when you're served (you cannot run up a tab as in continental Europe and the USA). However, some trendy lounge bars insist on serving you at your table (and charging extra for the privilege), although you still pay as you go. Beer gardens and courtyards are common throughout Australia, and many pubs have live music (jukeboxes are also common).

Despite their awesome reputation and the plethora of watering holes, most Australians aren't big drinkers, although there's a hardened minority who do their utmost to compensate for this slur on the Australian character. Australians drink less alcohol per head than the inhabitants of most European countries, although more than the average American, Briton or Canadian. Nevertheless, drunkenness and alcoholism are rife in Australia, where it's estimated that more than 6,000 Australians die each year from alcohol-related causes (including some 30 per cent of road deaths). Many pubs have a DIY breathalyser which will tell you when you're over the limit, although it's wise to go to the pub with a teetotal friend or abstain from driving altogether when you're drinking alcohol. In future, pubs may be forced to provide over-the-bar breath tests before serving customers, in order to protect themselves from negligence claims from drunks and drunken drivers.

**Beer:** Australia is traditionally a beer-drinking country (Darwin is reputedly the world's premier beer-drinking city in terms of per capita consumption). The average Australian consumes around 110 litres (almost 200 pints) of beer per year, although this figure has fallen by some 20 per cent in the last decade or so as wine has become more popular. Australia boasts probably the best selection of beers to be found anywhere. Some bars and clubs boast over 100 different types of beer from around the world. The most popular foreign beers include Guinness (brewed in Australia), Sol and Dos Equis from Mexico, Budweiser and Slitz from the USA, and Heineken, Stella Artois and Löwenbräu from Europe.

Australia is also known for its own beers, and brewing has been elevated to an art form. The best known Australian beers include Fosters, Carlton Draught and VB (Victoria Bitter) from Victoria, XXXX (pronounced four-ex, said to be so-named because Queenslanders cannot spell beer) and Powers from Queensland, Toohey's, Tooth's and Reschs from New South Wales, Emu, Swan Lager (derisively called 'black duck' outside WA) and Redback from Western Australia, Cooper's (one of Australia's best beers) and West End Bitter from South Australia (SA), and Boag's and Cascade from Tasmania. Most Australian beers have an alcohol content of around 5 per cent, which is higher than most American and British beers but lower than German and Czech beers. There's also a range of low-alcohol (LA) beers with around 2 to 3.5 per cent alcohol, which include Carlton Cold, Diamond Draught, Fosters Light Ice, Swan Light and Toohey's Blue. The best and strongest beers (as high as 9 per cent alcohol) are often those brewed by pubs with in-house breweries (called 'boutique' or brew pubs), which are extremely popular. These include the Matilda Bay Brewing Co. in Perth and the Redback Brewery in Melbourne, which makes a German-style *weiss* beer that the locals drink with lemon. Note that boutique and imported beers are more expensive than the commercial brands.

Most beer drunk in Australia is of the lager variety, which is generally sweet-tasting, as it's made with sugar. The taste will be familiar to Americans but will taste like dishwater to bitter or ale drinkers. Fortunately for them, 'real ales' have become more popular in Australia in the last decade, and there are now a variety of naturally conditioned (in casks or bottles) beers available from brewers such as Coopers of South Australia. This is the sort of beer generally made by 'boutique' breweries and sold in their in-house pubs for around $5 to $6 per pint. Real ale is served warmer than lager beer but still much colder than similar beer in other countries (e.g. Britain). Australians drink their beer almost ice cold (around 2°C), often in chilled glasses, so that when it hits your stomach on a hot day it freezes your insides. Not surprisingly, cold-filtered ice beers are gaining in popularity.

Beer is usually served in measures ranging from 115ml/4 fl oz ('small') up to 570ml/20fl oz. Both the names and standard sizes of beer glasses vary considerably from state to state. In Sydney the most common size is 285ml/10oz (a 'middy', 'handle' or 'pot'), while in Melbourne it's 225ml/8oz (a 'glass'). Other measures include 170ml/6oz ('beer six'), 200ml/7oz ('seven') and 425ml/15oz ('schooner' – 285ml/10oz in South Australia). Some pubs serve beer in imperial measures of a half-pint (285ml) and a pint (570ml). The easiest way to order is to simply ask for a small or large beer, but take care, as what passes for a small beer in one state may be twice as large in another and a large one may be very large indeed: a large beer in Darwin, known as a 'stubby', weighs in at 2.35 litres or almost five pints! Beer is usually drunk direct from bottles and cans in country areas. In really hot weather, bottles and cans are kept cool in a foam or polystyrene 'stubby holder' or cooler, and Australians transport their cold beer in an insulated cold box called an 'esky' (after a well known brand name).

Beer is around the same price in Australia as in Europe and North America, a 285ml (half-pint) costing around $3.60 in most pubs, although it can easily be double this in a fancy place. Draught beer is also sold by the jug, which is slightly cheaper than by the glass. Low-alcohol beers are generally slightly cheaper than full strength beers. Bottled beer is sold in 375ml or 750ml bottles (many up-market bars don't sell beer on draught). Some bars and pubs have a 'happy hour' (e.g. from 5pm to 7pm) when drinks are sold at half price or even less, and some watering holes even offer half price drinking from 5pm to 9pm. Many pubs also offer special prices or free drinks to women, the idea being that where women congregate hard-drinking men will accumulate in large numbers. Needless to say, beer is much cheaper to buy from bottle shops (around half the price).

**Wine:** Australian wines have become famous world wide in the last few decades. Wine consumption in Australia is steadily rising at the expense of beer and is around 25 litres per head per year – higher than in any other English-speaking country but still well below the major European wine-producing countries. There are few wine bars, which haven't caught on with the public (although the Casino Wine Bar in Adelaide boasts over 300 wines). Wine is usually reserved for drinking with food (pubs that serve good food generally have a good wine list), although some bars and pubs sell wine by the glass (e.g. $2.50) or the bottle (from around $10). Cheap wine, which may be referred to as bombo, lunatic soup or steam, is best avoided. For information about Australian wine, see **Alcohol** on page 431.

**Other Drinks:** Other popular drinks include alcopops such as Two Dogs Lemonade (an alcoholic lemonade), Strongbow White (cider), Razorback Draught (a shandy), XLR8 (alcoholic cola), Sub Zero (alcoholic soda, 5.5 per cent alcohol) and alcoholic spring water such as DNA (containing 5 per cent alcohol). Alcoholic soda is soda mixed with lime, grenadine, midori or cranberry juice to make a long, cool drink. Coke and other colas are drunk in copious quantities in Australia and cost around $2.20 per glass in a pub. Spirits are rarely drunk in pubs, where a shot of whisky (30ml) or other spirits costs around $3.50 to $6. Designer drinks include (wine) coolers, which are blends of inexpensive wine with sugar and fruit juice or fruit flavouring (they taste like punch).

**Licensing Laws:** Pubs aren't obliged to open for any set hours and landlords decide their own opening hours (usually) within state licensing laws. These vary from state to state and even from pub to pub but generally aren't as liberal as in most European countries (a legacy of the British, who cannot be trusted with alcohol). Pubs are usually open from 10am until 10pm or 11am until 11pm, Mondays to Saturdays and from 12pm until between 8pm and 10pm on Sundays. Sunday pub opening is restricted in most states, e.g. to between six and eight hours (the churches still have some clout). In market areas, pubs may open as early as 6 or 6.30am and close at 6 or 6.30pm. In places near the border of two time zones (see page 468), hardened Australian drinkers will cross back and forth in order to benefit from extra hours' drinking time!

There are no licensing restrictions in Canberra, where pubs can stay open as long as they wish, and in Tasmania pubs can open virtually when they like, although most close by midnight. Some pubs stay open until midnight or 1am on Fridays and Saturdays, particularly in tourist areas, and in cities some establishments with a number of bars and a disco manage to serve alcohol for 24 hours. In some cities there are longer opening hours in summer than in winter. Nevertheless, a lot of drinking still takes place after licensing hours, particularly in country areas where the local policeman is likely to be one of the customers, and when the pubs close there are usually other places to get a drink (restaurants, night-clubs, casinos, discos, etc.).

There are some odd local laws in Australia designed to reduce drunkenness: for example, it's illegal to sell alcohol before 10am each day in Darwin (although even here most people don't start drinking so early in the day!) and in Melbourne it's prohibited to drink at the bar after 10pm, when you must occupy a table (which helps prevent you from falling down). Alcohol can be purchased from licensed 'bottle shops' (it isn't sold in food shops or supermarkets) and from pubs and restaurants. The minimum age for drinking in public places is 18 and, if you look under age, you may be asked for ID (which you should always carry if you're under 20 or look under 18). In some outback towns, pubs have doormen (bouncers) to deter undesirables (waterbags and others who don't drink enough?).

Aboriginals have been ravaged by drunkenness and alcoholism for decades, which has led to the possession and consumption of alcohol being restricted or banned in and around some Aboriginal settlements and towns, where offenders face a huge fine (e.g. $1,000), six month's jail or the confiscation of a vehicle used to transport alcohol.

# RESTAURANTS & CAFES

Australians love their food (tucker), and dining out is one of the greatest pleasures of life in Australia (which is why so many Australians are overweight). Many people eat out around three times a week, and Australian households spend over a quarter of their weekly food budget on eating outside the home. The appreciation of good food and wine is universal in Australia and has nothing elitist about it as in some other countries.

The greatest changes in Australia in the last few decades have been in its cuisine, which in the major cities is among the best and most varied in the world. It wasn't always so. Prior to the '70s, the staple diet of most Australians consisted of meat pies and gravy, fish and chips, and steak, egg and chips (or over-boiled vegetables) supplemented by Vegemite (made from yeast slops) sandwiches, chico rolls (a distant cousin of the Chinese spring roll) and burgers, but such unwholesome conservative British tastes meant that were swept away by the culinary revolution led by migrants (Australia's most important gastronomic resource) and a new breed of young Australians who had travelled (and eaten) the world. BYO (see below) and the rapid rise of Australian wines also had a huge impact on the proliferation of good cheap restaurants, and today Australia boasts the most cosmopolitan and diverse menus in the world.

Melbourne is generally recognised as the gastronomic capital of Australia, followed closely by Sydney, both of which can hold their own with most world capital cities and rate alongside Hong Kong, London, New York and Paris for choice and quality (often ahead of them for value). Both cities boast over 2,000 restaurants (so many in fact, that there's a shortage of good chefs). Perth and Adelaide aren't far behind and have more than enough eateries to satisfy a starving gourmet. Brisbane isn't distinguished by its restaurants, although it also has many good places to eat, and even Darwin isn't bereft of decent restaurants, although it's relatively expensive compared to other capital cities. However, there still isn't much choice in small country and outback towns, where you shouldn't expect to find any decent restaurants or anything other than basic 'Australian' cooking or an Australianised Chinese restaurant.

Note that Australians don't usually drink water with their meals and, if you want water, you may need to ask a few times before you get it.

**Ethnic Restaurants:** Australia doesn't have a recognisable national cuisine and borrows heavily from various foreign cuisines, dishes often being given a distinctly Australian flavour. Australian food is noted for the freshness, variety and affordability of its produce (most ingredients are grown, reared or caught locally). Most cities have a proliferation of ethnic restaurants, reflecting the countries from which most immigrants have come. For example, Melbourne is known for its Greek and Italian restaurants, Sydney for its Lebanese and Thai restaurants, Adelaide its German restaurants, while Perth and Darwin have a wealth of Asian restaurants. Ethnic restaurants in the major cities are often clustered in groups in areas or suburbs where large ethnic communities have been established. Today, Australia leads the world in ethnic dining with a huge variety of European, Middle Eastern, South American and Asian restaurants, which include Chinese (many regions are represented), French, Greek, Indian, Indonesian, Italian, Japanese, Korean, Lebanese, Malaysian, Mexican, Mongolian, Polish, Portuguese, Spanish, Russian, Sri Lankan, Thai, Vietnamese and Yugoslavian, to name but a few.

There are bustling 'China towns' in Sydney and Melbourne rivalling those in European and North American cities. In many shopping and entertainment centres there are Southeast Asian 'food halls' (also called food markets or food courts), where you can buy food from the surrounding kiosks and eat it at a central seating area, thus allowing you to mix dishes from various countries. Note, however, that Chinese and other Asian food may be Australianised to such a degree that it's unrecognisable, and some other foreign cuisine is often 'tailored' to suit Australian tastes and may bear little resemblance to authentic dishes.

**Bush Tucker:** Some restaurants specialise in Aboriginal cuisine (bush tucker), which includes witchetty grubs (usually eaten alive!), emu egg omelettes and pies made from native fruits such as quandongs, boabs and billygoat plums. Other common dishes are emu steaks (from farmed birds), kangaroo (a delicious, almost fat-free meat), water buffalo steaks, camel and crocodile (which tastes like a cross between chicken and pork). Damper is Australian bush bread (made with flour, salt and water) baked in hot coals (usually on a camp fire). Note, however, that bush tucker is generally trendy and expensive, e.g. $40 per head plus wine.

**Vegetarian Restaurants:** Australians are ardent carnivores, although not as much as previously when many people would eat steak and chops for breakfast (a habit still common in the outback). Nowadays there's an increasing number of vegetarians, and vegetarian restaurants are fairly common in the main cities (most restaurants also serve some vegetarian dishes).

**Seafood:** Australia is renowned for its excellent seafood (many people reckon it's the best in the world) and each state or city has its specialities. Australia's seas have yet to suffer from widespread over-fishing (although some stocks are threatened) or pollution, so an abundance of fresh fish and seafood is available, although there isn't the choice found in many traditional fishing countries. The best and widest choice of fish comes from the waters surrounding Tasmania which include brown and rainbow trout, sea-run trout, farmed Atlantic salmon, trevally, trevella, orange roughy and stripey trumpeter. Australia is also famous for it crustaceans and molluscs, which include crayfish, abalone, oysters, mussels and scallops. Other Australian specialities include Sydney Rock oysters, Coffin Bay oysters (from South Australia), yabbies (hard-shelled freshwater shrimps), crabs (e.g. sand and mud crabs), Balmain Bugs (slipper lobsters from Sydney) and Moreton Bay Bugs (a type of lobster caught in the mouth of the Brisbane River). Australia's best fish include barramundi (a breed of perch which grows to over a metre in length and is one of the tastiest fishes in Australian waters), snapper (schnapper), shark (called 'flake' when served in fish and chip shops), King George whiting (South Australia), coral cod/coral trout (Great Barrier Reef), John Dory, ocean perch, reef fish (Queensland) and tuna.

**Sweets:** Among the few real Australian dishes are pavlova, a delicious meringue concoction created for the ballerina Anna Pavlova on her Australian tour in 1935. Others include Peach Melba (created for the Australian soprano Dame Nellie Melba), puftaloons (a fried dough scone) and lamingtons, an Australian institution consisting of a sponge cake dipped in raspberry jam, covered in chocolate sauce and then rolled in coconut. Australian ice cream is popular and one of the best is Norgen Vaaz (a take off of the American Haagen Daz).

**Bring Your Own (BYO):** Rather surprisingly, the majority of Australian restaurants don't have alcohol licences (which are expensive), except in Canberra where most are licensed. Restaurants without an alcohol licence are know as BYO ('bring your own') or BYOG ('bring your own grog'), where customers bring their own wine and other drinks. This is an excellent idea that unfortunately hasn't caught on widely in most other countries, mainly because of the huge profit restaurants make on wine. There may be a 'corkage' charge of $1 to $2 (for opening bottles and providing glasses), although many restaurants make no charge. Some up-market restaurants with alcohol licences also allow BYO, but charge around $5 corkage (which still saves you money, unless you choose the cheapest plonk on the wine list). Regular diners (and drinkers) always carry a few (dozen) bottles of wine in their cars (which isn't illegal in Australia) so that they're never caught short when visiting a BYO restaurant (but get a ride or taxi home if you drink more than one or two glasses). Eating at BYO restaurants is excellent value compared with most of Europe and North America; you can have an excellent meal for $10 to $20 per head (plus the cost of your wine).

**Pub Grub:** The quality of pub food in Australia varies enormously. At its worst it's boring and disappointing, but at its best (it's at its most refined and varied in Sydney) it's delicious and excellent value. However, pub grub is rarely exotic and usually consists of grilled or barbecued steaks and chops, fish and seafood plus roasts, curries and salads. Many pubs also serve ethnic food or a combination of traditional Australia food and ethnic specialities. Outdoor eating is popular (although there's a surprising lack of pavement and garden tables in some Australian cities) and often consists of anything and everything barbecued, including steak, burgers, chops, sausages (snags), chicken, fish and seafood. Many pubs have large courtyards or gardens where they operate non-stop, self-service barbies, where you buy a piece of meat and cook it yourself on the BBQ provided (condiments are supplied). You can also buy salad, bread and side dishes. A typical meal costs around $10, although some pubs have special offers and promotions when meals can be had for a little as $3 or $4. Many also have a self-serve salad bar and basic bar meals from $5 to $10. Meals are usually served in a dining room or lounge bar from noon to 2pm and from 6 to 8pm, although some pubs serve meals until late evening.

**Fast Food:** Fast food outlets have proliferated in Australia and, at the bottom end of the market, can be as bad or worse than those found in any country. However, fast or snack food isn't (always) synonymous with junk food, as evidenced by the increasing quality and amazing variety of fast food establishments in Australia. Australians are hooked on fast food and over 80 per cent of the population eats take-away meals at least once every two weeks, spending around $2 billion per year in the process (or some 10 per cent of their food budget). Common snack outlets include sandwich shops, delicatessens and milk bars (shops selling snacks, sandwiches, rolls, meat pies, pasties, milkshakes, soft drinks, etc.). Fast food 'snacks' include sandwiches, hamburgers, sausages, hot dogs, pies, fish and chips, stuffed potatoes, vegetarian snacks, fried or grilled chicken, seafood, crepes and pancakes, and a huge variety of ethnic snacks such as pizza, kosher food, tacos, samosa, calamari, dim sum, focaccia, sushi, gyros, felafel, couscous, tabouleh, doner or shish kebab, pitta bread, tortillas, filled croissants and bagels.

As in all western countries, American fast food outlets abound, and McDonalds, Hungry Jack's (HJ's, trading as Burger King in other countries), Kentucky Fried Chicken and Pizza Hut can be found throughout the country. A popular budget restaurant chain is Sizzlers, an American-style restaurant serving steak, chicken, fish, and a selection of self-serve salads, pasta dishes and desserts. Take-away barbecued chicken chains include Chicken Treat and Red Rooster. Some fast food outlets such as the American-style Fast Eddy's in Melbourne and Perth are open 24 hours a day. Note that authentic Australian hamburgers are often much better than the mass-produced variety served in chain restaurants. Many places also offer more healthy food such as salads, skinless chicken, etc. At most fast food restaurants you should expect to pay around $5 for a filling meal.

The most popular Australian take-away remains the humble meat pie (which could contain anything from beef or pork to camel, buffalo, kangaroo, crocodile or barramundi). It's Australia's national 'dish' (Aussies, mostly male, eat some two million a day!) and is eaten swamped in gravy or tomato ketchup. A 'pie floater' is a meat pie floating in a bowl of pea soup. Meat pies are typically served in milk bars, cafés and from mobile food vans (a common sight in major cities and tourist spots) and are the reason foreign food is so popular in Australia. However, at their best they can be delicious (at their worst dog food is tastier). **Beware of self-serve and other places where food is kept warm for hours on end, which can lead to food poisoning.**

**Cafés:** The Australians take after the British and drink a lot of tea and an increasing amount of coffee. Café society (and caffeine culture) is all the rage in Australian cities, where there's a huge variety of trendy and elegant cafés, the best of which are invariably Italian. All cafés serve food, although it's usually of the snack and fast food variety ('all-day breakfast' is common) rather than *à la carte* meals. Few cafés have table service or printed menus and you must usually check the blackboard and order from the counter, where you also pay. Many people finish their meal in a café with coffee and a sweet (e.g. ice cream or pastries). Cafés in capital cities are often open until midnight or early morning. Note that cafés don't usually serve alcohol.

**Prices:** Eating out is inexpensive in Australia, where a good meal can be had from around $10 per head without wine. Expect to pay between $15 and $25 per head (plus wine) for three courses and coffee in a mid-range restaurant, while for top class restaurants the sky's the limit. If you're on a tight budget, some restaurants offer discounts to 'backpackers' and many employers operate canteens open to the public where food is served buffet style and you can help yourself (not great food, but cheap and filling). Many restaurants offer lunches which are less expensive than the same meals served in the evening. However, you should avoid tourist-trap restaurants in cities and resorts. There are usually no additions for tax or service, although a surcharge may be levied at weekends and on public holidays to pay extra staff costs. Few people tip (see page 468) in inexpensive restaurants, although many people leave 5 to 10 per cent in mid-range and top class restaurants. In a busy establishment, it's customary to leave the correct money on the table and leave rather than pay the waiter/waitress personally. It's common to split the bill when eating with friends, rather than one person paying for a whole group (unless he's celebrating winning the lottery).

In a restaurant with an alcohol licence, wine usually starts at around $10 per bottle, although some restaurants sell wine at bottle shop (retail) prices. In wine-growing areas, there may be a wine tasting room, where you can choose from wines made on the property.

**Meal Times:** Australians are fairly inflexible about their meal times, and many restaurants have limited hours. For example, dinner (often called tea after the British working class habit) is often served as early as 6 or 7pm and last orders in restaurants may be as early as 9pm (the staff will be packing up to go home by around 10pm). In small towns it's usually difficult to find anywhere serving food after 7.30 or 8pm other than a fast food outlet or a fish and chip shop (lunch may also be served for only one hour, e.g. from 12.30 to 1.30 pm). However, in the major cities many restaurants stay open late and usually allow diners to circumvent local licensing laws. In order to drink legally at a restaurant outside official licensing hours, you must plan to dine, although you can order anything and aren't obliged to eat it (some places may provide a plate of free food to encourage drinkers). The most common closing day for restaurants is Monday.

**Bookings:** Most restaurants accept bookings and payment by credit card, although you should check in advance at budget restaurants, or you may have an embarrassing experience. Note that some top restaurants have a 'no-show' penalty of around $10 per head for those who don't bother to turn up or who cancel at short notice after booking a table, although many restaurants over-book to compensate for no-shows. Some restaurants have dress rules (smart casual is usual, even for the most exclusive establishments) and ban thongs (flip-flops) and shorts (unless perhaps when worn with shoes and socks – not a common habit in Australia). Smoking is banned in many restaurants and, if you're a smoker, you should check that it's permitted before booking.

**Guides:** There are many restaurant guides in Australia, including annual *Cheap Eats* guides to budget restaurants in Melbourne and Sydney (each listing over 500 restaurants) and the Lonely Planet *Out to Eat* series including Melbourne and Sydney. There are free magazines in many cities, e.g. the *Adelaide Advertiser*, which feature local restuarants, although these tend to be the more up-market establishments.

# 16.

# SPORTS

A ustralia is a sporting paradise, thanks largely to its generally mild climate. Sport is an integral part of the nation's culture and the favourite topic of conversation (people even call each other 'sport'); to many Aussies it has the status of a religion. It's both a unifying and divisive pastime (competition is fierce between rival teams), although Australians are generally good sports and appreciate plucky opponents (unless they're Poms). Melbourne is the most sports-mad city (Sydney isn't far behind) and is home to Australia's unique brand of football, Australian Rules. Sports centres abound in all towns and cities and offer facilities for a wide range of sports.

Aerobics is Australia's favourite form of exercise among young people, followed by netball, basketball, swimming, cricket, soccer and Australian Rules football (the top spectator sport in the country). Other popular sports are golf, hiking, jogging/running, cycling, tennis, squash, lawn bowls, martial arts, tenpin bowling, horse racing and motor sports (in no particular order). Australia is famous for its beach culture, and water sports are also very popular (80 per cent of Australians live within around 30km/18mi of the coast). Australians like their sports tough (like their he-man image) and love endurance tests such as ironman/ironwoman competitions and triathlons (a 1,500m swim, 40km/25mi bike ride and 10km/6mi run). However, even these aren't tough enough for 'real' men, who have recently come up with the 'eco-challenge race' which consists of 500km/310mi of bushwalking, canoeing, climbing, cycling, rafting, trekking, horse-riding and kayaking in the outback, rainforests and reef in northern Queensland. All in a day's work, sport!

In Australian schools, sports are incorporated into the normal day and aren't extra-curricular activities, as in many other countries. Schools have a wide variety of teams for all sports and participate in inter-school and interstate competitions (Saturdays are the most busy school sports days and parents are called upon to ferry their children around the country to compete). Children come under pressure from parents, teachers and coaches to perform at their highest level, and club scouts scour school sports meetings for talent. Two-thirds of Australian children join a sports club by the age of 11 and almost half the population is registered to participate in sports (some six million Australians take part in organised sport each year). Children who fail at sport can be made outcasts by their fellow pupils.

There's no such thing as just taking part or engaging in sport just for fun in Australia, where (as in America) winning is everything. Only the Americans devote more time, effort and money to sports perfection than Australians, who are consumed by sport (although more often than not it's only as spectators or gamblers). The country has some 15 national leagues involving team sports (remarkable when you consider the vast distances involved). However, despite the popular image of Australians as bronzed, muscular lifesavers and bathing beauties, most Australians are overweight and unfit, and the nearest they ever get to working up a sweat is jumping up and down in joy/anger while hurling abuse at TV sport (soap opera for blokes). Less than a third of Australians participate in any form of physical activity (Sydneysiders are the biggest slobs).

Owing to the seriousness (life and death) with which they approach international sport, Australians have an unfair advantage over most 'amateur' sporting countries. As a nation they excel at numerous sports, including cricket, rugby, swimming, cycling, hockey, tennis, squash, surfing, rowing, lawn bowls, netball, golf, athletics, motor sports, sailing, horse riding, triathlon and many others. Australians also compete successfully at the World and Olympic Games for the disabled. The government provides financial assistance and coaching for the disabled through the Aussie Able

Program. The country received a huge sporting (and economic) boost from hosting the Olympics in the year 2000 in Sydney, where Australian competitors excelled, and Australian spectators will be remembered as among the best and most magnanimous ever. Melbourne will host the Commonwealth games in 2006.

The government and sports bodies promote sport with slogans such as 'sport for all' and 'life be in it'. Sporting talent is nurtured in Australia and given the best possible encouragement through the Australian Institute of Sport (AIS), founded in 1981 in Canberra, and centres of excellence such as the Australian Cricket Academy. There are over 130 national sporting organisations in Australia and thousands of state, regional, city and local club bodies. Sports fans may be interested in visiting the Australian Gallery of Sport and Olympic Museum in Melbourne (open daily from 9.30am until 4.30pm). The Australian Tourist Commission (see pae ?) publishes a wealth of fact sheets on every conceivable sport. Sports results can be obtained in Australia by telephone or internet. Local municipal councils may publish a 'leisure directory' listing local sports centres and clubs. An annual *Sport Yearbook* (Gemkit Publishing) is available for those seeking an introduction to Australian sport. The federal government also runs a comprehensive website on sport (🖳 www. ausport. gov.au).

## AUSTRALIAN RULES FOOTBALL

Australian rules football (called 'Aussie rules' and simply 'footy') is Australia's leading ball game and considered by most people to be Australia's national sport. However, fans and players of other football codes (and cricket) often disagree and disparagingly refer to Aussie rules as aerial ballet or aerial ping-pong. Its rules were invented in 1858 and are unique, although it was based on Gaelic football played in Ireland. Aussie rules is a fast, skilful, athletic and exciting game, in which the score can change quickly and the outcome may hinge on the last kick. It's a gruelling, macho game and players are very fit and tough, most spurning any sort of protection (although some players do wear mouthguards, protective head gear and gloves to give them a better grip). They also wear tight shorts and sleeveless shirts to show off their 'muscles' – not surprisingly, it's popular with women, who make up around half the spectators.

Aussie rules is played by teams of 18 players on an oval field (around three times the size of a soccer pitch) with an oval ball. The ball can be kicked, caught, hit with the hand, or carried and bounced (every 15 paces). If players don't bounce the ball regularly, they're deemed to have 'run too far'. When a player catches a ball on the volley (before it touches the ground) he is said to have made a 'mark', for which he's allowed to stop and take a free kick. Players cannot be sent off during a game and consequently there are often scraps on the field (the game is sometimes called 'an excuse for a punch-up' or an 'organised brawl'). However, disciplinary tribunals are held the following week if a player is deemed to have committed a breach of the rules such as tripping, kicking, fighting or eye-gouging. Three players can be changed at any time (from the 'interchange bench') and players can come back into the game after being exchanged (as in ice hockey). A match lasts for four quarters of 20 minutes each, but can extend to around three hours when breaks between quarters and stoppages for injuries, disputes and punch-ups are included (plus 'time on', i.e. time added by the umpire).

The goal consists of four tall, evenly-spaced posts, the outer pair of which are slightly shorter than the inner pair. Six points are awarded for kicking the ball between the two central posts (a 'goal') and one point for kicking it through the outer posts (a 'behind'). The goal umpire (dressed in a white coat) waves two fingers (the index fingers on each hand) followed by two white flags to signify a goal and one finger and one flag when a behind is scored. A typical point score for each team is between 70 and 120 points. The score (goals and behinds) is shown in newspapers for each quarter with the final points total shown in brackets as follows:

| Collingwood | 4.5 | 6.7 | 7.9  | 10.12 | (72) |
| Essendon    | 3.6 | 5.9 | 8.11 | 11.14 | (80) |

Here, Collingwood scored four goals and five behinds in the first quarter and by the end of the match had scored ten goals and 12 behinds (drawn games are rare).

The national professional league is the Australian Football League (AFL) comprising 16 teams. Melbourne is the centre of Aussie rules and provides ten of the 16 teams in the AFL, the others coming from Adelaide, Brisbane, Fremantle, Perth, Port Adelaide and Sydney. Aussie rules is the number one sport in five states: the Northern Territory, South Australia, Tasmania, Victoria (where it's a religion) and Western Australia. The Sydney Swans were transplanted to Sydney from Melbourne (they were originally named South Melbourne) in the early '80s in a first move to create a national competition. Matches are played on Friday evenings and Saturday and Sunday afternoons throughout the winter and attract millions of spectators every season. Crowds in Melbourne regularly top 30,000 at major games and 80,000 attend finals. Crowds are noisy but peaceful and there's rarely any trouble. Matches are also televised and shown on national TV and in a number of other countries. The grand final is played in September or October at the Melbourne Cricket Ground before 100,000 fans. It rivals the FA Cup Final in England or the American Super Bowl for atmosphere and passion.

An excellent book on the history of Australian rules is *100 Years of Australian Rules Football* by Ross John.

# RUGBY FOOTBALL

There are two separate codes of rugby football (called 'footy') in Australia: rugby union and rugby league. The main difference between the codes is that rugby union (which has always been strictly amateur) has teams of 15 players and rugby league 13 players to a team (two fewer to pay). Both codes are played internationally, although union is played by more countries.

**Rugby League:** Rugby is the main football game in New South Wales, Queensland and Canberra, where rugby league is the most popular code. Like Aussie rules, rugby league players are super fit, fast and tactically intelligent. The Winfield Cup is the world's premier rugby league competition and Australia is the world's leading rugby league nation, usually easily beating the main opposition in England, although it has few other international competitors. The national rugby league team is known as the Kangaroos.

There has been a battle for control of Australian rugby league in recent years between the National Rugby League (NRL) and the upstart Super League (established by Rupert Murdoch in 1995 to boost the audience for his Foxtel cable TV network), with a combined total of 14 teams. There has been a series of court battles over the reinstatement of teams such as the Sydney Souths, who were dropped from the league because of falling crowds and poor results. TV ratings have become of paramount importance and, if a team doesn't get the ratings, it's in danger of being dropped from the league. Matches are played on most Friday and Saturday evenings and Sunday afternoons between April and September.

Most rugby league teams are based in Sydney (12 of the top 14) with others in Melbourne, Canberra, and the Gold Coast of Queensland. Teams from New Zealand also compete in the Australian league. Sydney is the only major city in the world where rugby is more popular than soccer (it's estimated that some 80 per cent of the world's best league players live within 30km/18mi of downtown Sydney). League is popular among the masses, although attendances are much lower than for NFL (Aussie rules) games. Popularity has fallen sharply in recent years as a result of the controversy between the two leagues and continual scandals on and off the pitch. The State-of-Origin series between the Australian states in May/June is the premier interstate competition, although it's poorly supported by the public.

**Rugby Union:** Rugby union was once a strictly amateur code in Australia, but is now fully professional at the top level. The national team (called the Wallabies) were world champions in 1991, 1995 and 1999 and play around six internationals a year. Union is played at the highest level by (in addition to Australia), New Zealand (the All Blacks), South Africa (the Springboks), France, England, Ireland, Italy, Scotland and Wales (and at a lower standard by a number of other nations, including Argentina and Papua New Guinea). A few times a year, the ACT Brumbies, the NSW Waratahs and Queensland Reds state teams play each other in a 'state of the union' series.

# CRICKET

Cricket is a strange sport (baseball on Valium to outsiders) which usually takes uninitiated foreigners some time to understand (even many Australians don't understand the finer points). If you don't know the difference between a stump and a bail or an over and a wicket you may as well skip this bit, as any attempt to explain would take around 100 pages and almost certainly end in failure.

There are some 500,000 registered cricket players in Australia, where there are leagues at all levels from tots to oldies, for men and women, indoors and outdoors. Cricket, like footy, dominates its season (from October until March) and attracts big TV audiences. Half of all Australians watch cricket on TV and around 20 per cent go to matches, where tickets for top class games cost $30 for a one-day match and up to $120 for a five-day test match. State cricket is played to a high standard (higher than the English county game), although it isn't a fully professional sport. The main national competition is the interstate Sheffield Shield, in which matches are played over three or four days, and there's also high-quality district cricket. Cricket players aren't usually the fittest of sportsmen, which was highlighted in 1997 when concern was raised over the weight and fitness of some of Australia's elite cricketers (spin bowler Shane 'tubby' Warne walked out of a press conference when questions were asked about his paunch).

Cricket is also played at international level (called test matches) by a number of countries, including England, India, New Zealand, Pakistan, South Africa, Sri Lanka, the West Indies and Zimbabwe. Each year the Australian cricket team is usually engaged in one or two minor series of international matches (three tests) or a major series (five or six tests). If you thought four days (Sheffield Shield matches) were a long time for a single match to last, a test match lasts five days, usually with a rest day after two or three days' play. One-day internationals (usually day-night, played under floodlights with players wearing brightly-coloured 'pyjamas') are also played. Test matches in Australia are played in Adelaide (at the Adelaide Oval), Brisbane (the 'Gabba'), Melbourne (the Melbourne Cricket Ground/MCG), Perth (the Western Australian Cricket Association or 'WACA' cricket ground, pronounced 'whacker') and Sydney (the Sydney Cricket Ground). The Melbourne Cricket Club was established in 1838 and plays at the MCG (the world's largest cricket stadium).

The Australian cricket team also takes part in overseas tours during the Australian winter, when they play a series of test matches. The old enemy in cricketing terms is the Poms (English), with whom Australia competes every few years for the Ashes (not human, but from the stumps which were ritually incinerated when the Australian upstarts first beat England in 1882). A one-day, knockout World Cup competition also takes place every few years. Australian cricketing legends include Don Bradman (the greatest batsman ever), Ray Lindwall, Keith Miller, Richie Benaud, Dennis Lillee, Jeff Thompson, the Chappell brothers (Trevor, Greg and Ian), and Allan Border, as well as the present day crop of Shane Warne and the Waugh twins (Mark and Steve). Even today, people still talk about the bodyline series in 1932–33, in which the England bowlers broke the unwritten rules of cricket by bowling at the batsmen rather than at the wicket (a bit like the West Indies' fast bowlers in recent decades). It created a major diplomatic incident and almost caused Australia to cede from the British Empire (the Aussies were upset because they hadn't thought of it first!).

Thrashing the Poms and winning, or more likely keeping, the Ashes (which Australians think are the remains of the English game!) is sporting heaven to most Australians. However, some Australians have questioned whether it's worthwhile playing England in recent years, during which England have hardly been able to muster any sort of opposition. Even the apprentices in the Australian Cricket Academy can beat England these days and test matches are often no contests. Australian cricketers, like all Australian sporting heroes, have a ruthless streak, and have consistently hammered England since 1989. In the 1999 test series between the Aussies and Poms, the Aussies won 3-1 to retain the Ashes and in mid-2001 beat England in six consecutive one-day matches in the warm-up to the 2001 Ashes. The Aussies wanted to take the Ashes home with them (they're traditionally displayed at Lords Cricket Ground in London), although there's no way the Poms were going to let the Aussies have them (they may never have seen them again). Australia is the most successful country at international test cricket, although they haven't been so successful at limited-over, one-day matches in the World Cup. Australia is also a top nation in women's cricket and they won the women's World Cup in India in 1997 and were runners-up in 2000.

# SOCCER

Soccer is a minor sport in Australia, where's it's played mostly by immigrants (it's referred to insultingly as 'wogball' by footy fans) and is a poor cousin to the various rugby codes and Aussie rules. The professional National Soccer League (NSL) or A-League is played in the summer and attracts a relatively small following (most fans prefer overseas soccer), although it's gaining in popularity thanks to the success of the national team. Many top Australian players now play professional soccer overseas, notably in the English Premiership. The majority of clubs in the NSL are dominated by Italians, Greeks, Croatians, Slavs, Maltese, Dutch, Macedonians and assorted other 'foreigners' (who represent the ethnic origins of the local populace). The standard is on a par with top amateur teams in England and other European countries. Some Australian clubs have links with foreign clubs to develop young players (European professional clubs are looking to Australia to pick up cheap players, now that they've become so expensive in Europe).

The national team (called the 'Socceroos') has improved beyond all recognition in recent years and in 2001 won the Oceania Nations cup and qualified for the Confederations Cup. In mid-2001 the national team looked set to qualify for the 2002 World Cup in Korea and Japan. The 'Joeys' (under 17s) reached the final of the FIFA World Youth Cup in 2000. At home, the 2000 cup final set a record for attendance (some 1.2 million fans attended) and was won for the first time by the Wollongong Wolves. Australian soccer looks set for a bright future as major sponsorship has been found and some $21 million will be invested in the game over the next seven years. For true fans, all the latest information can be found on ▣ www. soccer australia.com.au.

# SKIING

Skiing in Australia dates back to the 1860s and is a popular sport, despite the fact that there's only one proper skiing area (the Australian Alps, straddling the New South Wales-Victoria border). A lot of money has been spent on improving the infrastructure in recent years, and the facilities and lifts at the larger resorts now compare favourably with the best that Europe and North America have to offer. Australia has an unreliable snow and in some years there's barely enough natural snow to cover even the highest slopes, and conditions can be hazardous for all but expert skiers. However, in the last decade snow cannons have been installed in most resorts, which can now guarantee at least some snow for part of the season (a lack of snow is no handicap to most Aussie skiers, as their main activity is getting drunk).

Many Australians ski in New Zealand which has a more reliable snow record and many more resorts (professional skiers and ski bums from the northern hemisphere also ski and train in New Zealand during the northern hemisphere's summer). There are artificial snow slopes at Corin Forest Alpine Recreation Area 30 minutes from Canberra, where wheeled bobsleds achieve speeds of up to 80kph (50mph) on a stainless steel slide. Australian resorts have a good safety record, although 18 people were killed in 1997 when a landslide swept away two ski lodges in Thredbo. Although most Aussies cannot ski for toffee, Zali Steggall won a bronze medal (in the slalom) at the 1998 winter Olympics in Nagano, Japan.

The ski season traditionally begins in early June (sometimes in May if there's good early snow) on the Queen's birthday weekend holiday and continues until around October. However, even in a good year there's usually adequate snow cover only in July, August and early September. Ski runs cater for all standards, from beginners to experts, although most long runs are relatively easy, while the more difficult runs are short. Snowboarding is increasingly popular in Australia (the major resorts have purpose-built runs and 'bowls') and equipment can be hired and lessons are available. The conditions are usually excellent for cross-country skiing (also called Nordic or 'langlauf' in Australia) and telemark skiing. The major resorts have ski schools and child-care centres. Ski lessons, including lift tickets cost around $65 per day (less for five or seven days) and the hire of boots and skis around $35 per day. (Costs are relatively high because of the short season). Major resorts have a reasonable choice of *après ski* entertainment and a selection of mountain restaurants, and there's a lot of partying among the lodges, although there's little night-life compared with most European and North American resorts.

It's possible to travel to the Snowy Mountains from Sydney or Melbourne for a day's skiing, although it's more practical to ski for at least a weekend or a few days. You can fly to Cooma from where it's just a short trip by road to most resorts. The NSW snowfields are around four hours by road from Canberra. Note that, if you drive, snow chains are compulsory (they can be hired) and there are heavy fines for motorists without them, even if there's no snow! Most resorts have a wide choice of accommodation, including hostel dormitories, luxury hotels and self-catering chalets and lodges, many of which are close to ski lifts and runs. The cheapest way to enjoy skiing is to rent a resort lodge or apartment with friends and bring most of your food and drink with you, as prices are high in resorts. Accommodation is cheaper in Cooma and Jindabyne, from where there's a bus service to the ski slopes. Accommodation at a lodge in Thredbo or Perisher costs from around $38 to $170 per person per day sharing a double room depending on the season.

**NSW:** Thredbo is Australia's leading ski resort (popular with overseas skiers) and has 65 marked runs (including the longest in the country of 5km/3mi) and a specially designed snowboarding park. A day ticket costs around $65 and a five-day pass around $275. Perisher Blue (1,680m/5,500ft) includes Perisher Valley, Smiggin Holes, Mount Blue Cow and Guthega, and has 30 lifts, some floodlit runs for night skiing and special snowboarding runs. Most accommodation is in nearby Jindabyne, which is cheaper as it's a 40-minute drive to the major resorts or a few minutes on the Skitube which links it to Perisher and Perisher Blue (previously named Blue Cow), the largest ski resort in the southern hemisphere with 506 acres of snow terrain. One of the advantages of staying in Jindabyne is that you can travel to whichever resort has the best snow conditions each day. Other resorts include Lake Crackenback and Charlotte Pass (1,780m/5,850ft), which is the highest and oldest ski resort in Australia and only reachable by snowcat from Perisher Valley (8km/5mi). Mount Selwyn (1,492m/4,900ft) is a day resort (no accommodation) with 12 lifts and is ideal for beginners. A one-day lift pass costs $38 and a five-day pass plus lessons $280.

**Victoria:** Victoria is home to the vast High Country and the southern end of the Great Dividing Range and the Victorian Alps, which have three major and six minor ski areas. The best resorts include Mount Buller, Mount Hotham, Falls Creek, Mount Buffalo, Mount Baw Baw and Lake Mountain. There's a resort entry fee of $17 per day in winter. Mount Buller is Australia's most popular resort with 80km/50mi of runs and an extensive lift system, within easy access of Melbourne's airport, rail and coach stations (from where buses take you directly to the resorts). Falls Creek has 30km/18mi of runs, 23 lifts and a vertical drop of 267m/875ft (you can also ski directly from the village to the lifts and back) and a recent merger with Mount Hotham has created a larger resort with improved facilities. There are also a number of cross-country ski centres in Victoria, e.g. Lake Mountain, which is the closest ski resort to Melbourne (just 100km/62mi away) with around 40km/25mi of trails. There's a $3 trail fee ($1 for children).

**Tasmania:** There are also some small snowfields in Tasmania, which has two minor resorts: Ben Lomond (60km/37mi from Launceston) and Mount Mawson (Mount Field National Park). These are less developed and even less challenging than the major resorts in NSW and Victoria. However, they're also much cheaper, e.g. a day pass at Mount Field and at Ben Lomond costs just $10.

A free monthly newspaper, *Alpine News*, is available from tourist offices in winter. Snow and road reports are available by telephone on ☎ 1900-912370 (recorded service) or 1900-934320 for Thredbo. Cross-country snow reports are available on ☎ 1900-926028.

# CYCLING

Most people in Australia buy bikes for getting around town rather than cycling purely for pleasure, exercise or sport (e.g. touring or racing). However, competitive cycling is also popular in Australia and includes road and track racing, cycle speedway, time-trial, cross-country racing, touring, bicycle moto-cross and even bicycle polo. Australia has had considerable success in international cycle racing in recent years, particularly track racing at the Olympics and world championships, and is fast becoming a major force in road racing (e.g. the Tour de France).

Apart from cycling to work or into town, cycling is an excellent way to explore the countryside at your leisure and get some fresh air and exercise at the same time. Note, however, that fresh air is in short supply in Australia's polluted cities, where you would be wise to wear a face mask to insulate yourself from traffic pollution (although, according to medical experts, they offer little or no protection against carbon monoxide). Cycling is an excellent way to get around most Australian cities (notwithstanding pollution), due to their relatively small size. Most Australian cities have an extensive network of cycle paths and tracks (Melbourne's cover 500km/310mi), with the exception of Sydney. Cyclists in cities such as Canberra and Perth can legally ride on footpaths and pedestrians can also use cycleways. There are children's off-road bike circuits in many cities and towns. In most cities, bikes can be transported on suburban trains free of charge or for a small fee during off-peak times; during peak periods (e.g. 6 to 9am and 3 to 6pm on weekdays) it may not be permitted or a special permit may be required. When transporting a bike on a plane or bus, you must usually dismantle and box it.

The climate and topography (in most regions) of Australia lends itself to cycling and is a good way to explore coastal areas. You can ride a long way in some regions without encountering any hills, although if you're actually looking for hills you're also well catered for. Long-distance bike riding or touring in Australia is a serious pursuit, although you must *never* go on a long trip in remote areas without being fully equipped and carrying sufficient water (always check local water sources when travelling in remote areas). When touring, you also need to be wary of poor roads, broken bridges, rabid dogs, crazy drivers and bad weather. You'll need a mountain bike if you want to get off the beaten track, where the terrain can be very demanding (on both riders and bikes). Note that cycling isn't permitted off sealed roads in national parks. A hat and a plentiful supply of sunscreen are necessary in hot weather. Many companies arrange organised tours throughout Australia inclusive of bikes (although you can use your own), a support vehicle, accommodation and meals.

A wide range of bikes is available to suit all pockets and needs, ranging from a basic 'town' bike costing a few hundred dollars to a professional racing cycle costing many $thousands. In between these extremes are shopping bikes, touring bikes, mountain bikes, BMX bikes, tricycles, tandems and bicycles with folding frames. Before buying a bike, carefully consider your needs, both current and future, obtain expert advice (e.g. from a specialist cycle store) and shop around for the best deal. Make sure you purchase a bike with the correct frame size. If you're a visitor and need a bike for touring, it's cheaper to buy a secondhand bike and sell it when you no longer need it (some cycle shops will buy back secondhand bikes at a guaranteed price).

A new fifteen-speed touring or mountain bike costs from around $300 (you can pay up to $10,000!), a good secondhand one from around $150 (try the weekly *Trading Post* in Sydney). Bicycle theft is common in Australia, so it's sensible to insure your bike if possible and buy a good lock. Most travel insurance companies offer policies for bikes.

Bikes can be rented in all cities and large towns, and may include tandems, tricycles and folding bikes. Ask at the local tourist office for information. Touring and mountain bikes can be rented from around $20 per day, $40 for a weekend and around $70 per week (add $10 to these rates in Sydney). They can sometimes also be rented by the hour from around $5 (there may be lower rates for children). Usually a deposit is required or you must leave your passport or a credit card as security. Many backpacker hostels provide free bikes for guests, although you should ensure that a rented or loan bicycle is insured against theft or damage and that you have a good lock.

It's important not to underestimate the dangers of cycling (particularly for children) in Australia, as many cyclists are killed or injured each year. Australian motorists don't respect cyclists as much as they do in some other countries, particularly in country areas (although many roads carry little traffic). Main roads can be particularly dangerous and many roads can deteriorate into gravel or rutted mud in country areas. Cycling in most cities is fairly safe, particularly where there are off-road cycle tracks and paths (Sydney is the main exception, where cyclists take their life in their hands). Cycling helmets are compulsory in all states and territories, and you can be fined on-the-spot (e.g. $25 to $50) for not wearing one. They can be uncomfortable in hot weather, but aren't as uncomfortable as brain surgery. Reflective clothing and bright (preferably flashing) lights at night may help to prevent an accident. If you have a child with a bicycle, it's important to impress upon him the need to take care and not take unnecessary risks, e.g. always observe traffic signals and signal clearly before making any manoeuvres. **Young children shouldn't be allowed to cycle on roads in towns and cities, as it's simply too dangerous.**

Many books are published for cyclists in Australia, including *Cycling Australia: Bicycle Touring Throughout the Sunny Continent* by Ian Duckworth (Van der Plas Publishing), *Cycling Around Sydney*, *Seeing Sydney by Bicycle*, *Discovering Melbourne's Bike Paths* and a series of *Cycling The Bush* (Hill of Content) books by Sven Klinge, which cover a number of states, plus *Cycling The Bush – The Best Rides in Australia*. Free brochures such as *Canberra Cycleways* are also available from tourist offices. Local cycling guides and maps are published by councils and conservation and cycling groups in many areas; many of these organisations also publish safety booklets and brochures for children. Cycling maps are available in the major cities from bookshops and local cycling clubs and organisations (the best are the government series of 1:250,000 scale).

If you're interested in joining a cycling club, your library should have information about local clubs, or you can contact the Australian Cycling Federation (☎ 02-9644 3002, 🖥 www.cycling.org.au). There are also bicycling organisations in all states such as the Bicycle Institute of New South Wales, GPO Box 272, Level 2, 209 Castlereagh Street, Sydney, NSW 2000 (☎ 02-9283 5200) and Bicycle Victoria, 19 O'Connell Street, North Melbourne, VIC 3051 (☎ 03-9328 3000).

## BUSHWALKING

Whether you call it walking, rambling, hiking, orienteering or bushwalking, getting from A to B for fun and pleasure (as opposed to not being able to afford a bus or train ticket) is popular in Australia and is the most common form of exercise – what's more it's free! Australians tend to call hiking 'bushwalking', even when it's done far away from the nearest bush. However, real bushwalking generally refers to long-distance, serious walking in the outback, from a day trip to a number of weeks. There are marked trails in most national parks and state forests, although some offer tough walking and only are for the seriously fit, and there's generally a lack of marked long-distance trails. If you're lucky, you may catch sight of some of Australia's rarer wildlife. You require a national park permit to enter certain parks and reserves; these cost around $10 per day for a vehicle or $50 to $60 per year. Day/night permits are also available in some areas for campers. Tracks are usually marked by coloured triangles on trees, posts, etc. Before setting out on a walk in a national park, you should sign on in the ranger's log book and sign off when you return, so that searches will be initiated if you get lost. When on a long walk, it's wise to let someone know your plans and when you expect to return. Some trails are closed in the summer because of fire risks.

It's important to be properly prepared and equipped when going on a long walk and staying out overnight. Self-sufficiency is important, as you cannot expect to find a hotel, restaurant or corner shop over every hill or around every bend. The outback doesn't suffer fools gladly and must be treated with respect, along with its flora and fauna. This means making adequate preparation (including fitness) and taking ample supplies of water, food, clothing, sun protection, maps and other essentials (such as an expert guide if you're inexperienced). Many shops sell or rent out bush clothing and equipment, and some youth hostels rent out equipment.

Australia has a wealth of beautiful, unspoiled hiking country in every state and territory. One of the major trails is the 5,000km/3,000mi National Trail from Cooktown (north of Cairns) to Melbourne, following the old stock routes, fire trails and bush tracks. Around Sydney, there's the Royal National Park, Ku-ring-gai Chase National Park, the Blue Mountains and Kosciusko National Park in the Snowy Mountains. A 250km/150mi walk links Sydney with the Hunter Valley, and in the west of the state the Hume and Hovell Track runs through high country between Albury and Yass. The Snowy Mountains (part of the celebrated Kosciusko National Park in NSW and Victoria) are a Mecca for bushwalkers, and Thredbo is a popular summer hiking resort with a chair-lift that takes you to the top of Mount Crackenback. One of NSW's most famous parks is the Warrumbungle National Park in the north of the state.

Victoria has some of the country's most spectacular and diverse walking country, including the Australian Alps Walking Track stretching for 655km/405mi from Walhalla (145km/90mi east of Melbourne near Mount Baw Baw) to the Brindabella

Ranges on the outskirts of Canberra. Other top walking areas in Victoria include the Little Desert National Park, Wilsons Promontory National Park, the Grampians National Park, Lederderg Gorge, the Great Dividing Range, Mount Bogong, the Coastal Walking Track and the Snowy River National Park (where the film *The Man From Snowy River* was shot). Tasmania has some of the best bushwalking in Australia, including the famous Overland Track from Cradle Mountain to Lake St. Clair (85km/53mi). A seventh of Tasmania is occupied by national parks, although they are under constant threat from mining and logging interests.

In South Australia, there's the Mount Lofty and Flinders Ranges, taking in the 1,500km/930mi Heysen Trail which crosses the state from Cape Jervis to Parachilna Gorge (in the Flinders Ranges). In Western Australia, there's the Stirling Range and Porongurup National Park (both north of Albany), and the Kalbarri, Karijini and Purnululu national parks. The 640km/400mi Bibbulman Track runs between Perth and Walpole on the south-eastern coast. There are also many excellent bushwalking possibilities in Queensland, including Lamington in the southern Border Ranges, Main Range in the Great Divide, Cooloola north of the Sunshine Coast and Bellenden Ker south of Cairns, plus coastal islands such as Fraser and Hinchinbrook. The Northern Territory provides a wealth of walking areas, including the Larapinta Trail in the Western MacDonnell Ranges (near Alice Springs), Trephina Gorge Nature Park in the Eastern MacDonnells, Gregory National Park, Kakadu National Park and Watarrka (Kings Canyon).

Orienteering is popular in Australia and is a combination of hiking and a treasure hunt, or competitive navigation on foot. It isn't necessary to be super fit and the only equipment that's required (in addition to suitable walking attire) is a good map and a compass. There are orienteering clubs in many areas and bushwalking clubs in most towns and areas. In many towns and country areas, guided walks are conducted throughout the year, ranging from sightseeing tours of towns to walks around local beauty spots, for which there may be a small fee. Walks are usually graded, e.g. easy, moderate or strenuous, and dogs can usually be taken unless otherwise stated. Many municipal councils public local walking guides and there are short guided walks in the major cities. Ask for information at tourist information centres or local libraries.

A wealth of bushwalking books is published in Australia, including *Bushwalking in Australia* by John Chapman (Lonely Planet), *Sydney and Beyond* by Andrew Mevissen, and a series of bushwalking books by Tyrone T. Thomas detailing walks in most states and popular walking areas, including the *20 Best Walks in Australia* (Hill of Content). Bushwalkers may also be interested in the Australian magazines, *Outdoor Australia* and *Wild*. There are bushwalking associations in all states and territories such as the NSW Confederation of Bushwalking, GPO Box 2090, Sydney 1043 (☎ 02-9294 6797, 🖳 www.bushwalking.org.au).

See also **Camping & Caravanning** on page 375 and **Parks, Gardens & Zoos** on page 376.

# MOUNTAINEERING, ROCK-CLIMBING & CAVING

Those who find walking a bit tame might like to try abseiling, rock-climbing, mountaineering, caving or pot-holing (subterranean mountaineering). If you're an inexperienced climber, you'd be well advised to join a climbing club before heading for the hills (an eight-hour beginner's course costs around $200). Contact the

Australian School of Mountaineering, 166b Katoomba Street, Katoomba, NSW 2780 (☎ 02-4782 2014, 🖳 www.ausmtn.com.au) for information. There are abseiling and climbing schools in all the major cities, many with indoor training apparatus (e.g. a climbing wall) for aspiring mountaineers. Ask about local clubs at climbing equipment stores.

Australia doesn't offer much in the way of mountaineering (Mount Kosciusko in the Snowy Mountains, NSW is the highest point at 2,228m/7,307ft), although it has some of the best and most varied rock climbing in the world. Caving is particularly popular in Tasmania, which has some of the most spectacular caves in Australia. Note, however, that some caves are open only to experienced cavers, including the Kubla Khan and Croesus caves and the Exit Cave (permits are necessary to enter most caves, many of which are kept locked). There are caving (speleological) clubs and societies in all major cities.

Note that a number of climbers, cavers and pot-holers are killed each year in Australia, many of whom are inexperienced and reckless. Many more owe their lives to rescuers who risk their own lives to rescue them. **It's extremely foolish, not to mention highly dangerous, to venture into the hills (or holes) without an experienced guide, proper preparation, excellent physical condition, sufficient training, and the appropriate equipment and supplies.**

# RACQUET SPORTS

There are excellent facilities in Australia for most racquet sports, including badminton, squash, racquetball and tennis. Some racquet clubs cater for both squash and tennis and possibly also badminton. Most private clubs have a resident or visiting coach, providing both individual and group lessons, and many sports clubs and resort hotels hold residential coaching courses and holidays throughout the year.

**Tennis:** Tennis is the most popular racquet sport and is played outdoors year round in most states. Public (council-owned) courts and those owned by local associations can be hired for around $10 to $15 an hour, although it can be difficult to book a court during popular times. Many hotels have tennis courts, and university courts can be hired during vacations for a token fee, e.g. from $2 an hour. Many companies and schools also have their own courts. There are also many private tennis clubs, although membership fees can be high and some have long waiting lists. Indoor courts are rare in Australia, where outdoor courts can be used year round in most regions. Most courts in Australia are hard courts and there are few grass courts left (the Australia Open used to be played on grass before moving to its current home).

Australia has a proud record in major competitions, particularly the Davis Cup (the world's premier team tennis competition), which Australia won 15 times between 1950 and 1969 and again in 1973, 1977, 1983 and 1986. Australians also won the Wimbledon men's singles title 15 times between 1952 and 1987 and the women's singles title five times between 1963 and 1980. Famous past players include Frank Sedgeman, Rod Laver, Lew Hoad, Ken Rosewall, John Newcombe, Tony Roache, Pat Cash, Margaret Court and Evonne Goolagong/Cawley. Although it's no longer the world-beater it once was, Australia remains a leading tennis nation. Today's top Australian male players include Pat Rafter, Mark Philippoussis, Todd Woodbridge, Jason Stoltenberg, Mark Woodforde, Sandon Stolle, Scott Draper and Lleyton Hewitt.

The Australian Open Tennis Championships are held in Melbourne at the National Tennis Centre at Flinders Park, where the main court is unique in that it has a roof which can be closed when it rains or during extreme heat (above 40°C/104°F). It's staged over two weeks in January and is the first of the world's four 'grand slam' tournaments (with Wimbledon and the US and French Opens), although it's ranked below the others in importance and many of the world's top players don't compete. Anyone can play at the National Tennis Centre (except when the Australian Open is being held) for around $25 per hour indoors and around $16 outdoors. Tours are also available, although in mid 2001 the National Tennis Centre was closed for refurbishment. Information is available from ▣ www.tennisaustralia.com.au.

**Squash & Racquetball:** Squash is also a popular racquet sport in Australia and there's an abundance of courts in the major cities and towns. The cost of hiring a court is around $15 per hour, and most clubs have club evenings when members can play for a few dollars. Racquets and balls can be hired. The club standard is among the highest in the world, and competitions are staged at all levels from club and state competitions to the Australian Open. Australia is one of the world's top squash nations. It has two men in the world's top 10 (Paul Price and David Palmer, 2001 British Open champion) and two of the world's top four women players (three-times world champion Sarah Fitz-Gerald and current world champion Carol Owens). Past champions include the legendary Geoff Hunt, the Martin siblings, Rod, Brett and Michelle, and Heather McKay, the last being unbeaten for an incredible 16 years. However, in the last five years squash has declined in popularity and the number of players has dropped by around 10 per cent. In some cities (e.g. Sydney), clubs have been closing in increasing numbers in recent years as the cost of maintaining or opening a club increases and property values rise (many former clubs have been redeveloped as office blocks, apartments and shops). For information contact Squash Australia, Sports House, Office 9, Level 1, Cnr Castlemaine & Caxton Sts, Milton QLD 4064 (☎ 07-3367 3200, ✉ squashoz@squash.org.au).

Racquetball (a variant of squash played with shorter racquets and a larger, bouncier ball) is played in Australia on a squash court and racquets and balls can be hired at some squash clubs.

**Badminton & Table Tennis:** Badminton is also a popular sport in Australia, particularly among migrants from countries such as China, Indonesia, Malaysia and Singapore, although it lags behind tennis and squash. Most badminton facilities are provided by public sports centres; private clubs are rare. Table tennis is also quite popular in Australia, where it's played both as a serious competitive sport and as a pastime in social and youth clubs. If you want to play seriously, there are clubs in most areas. Costs vary, although it's an inexpensive sport with little equipment necessary.

To find the racquet clubs in your local area look in the yellow pages, enquire at your local library or contact the appropriate national association.

# SWIMMING

There's a wealth of public heated indoor and outdoor swimming pools in all towns in Australia, where the entrance fee is usually around $5. There are also salt-water, tidal pools on many beaches and Olympic-size pools in all major cities. Many hotels, motels, apartment complexes and hostels also have their own swimming pools. In the major cities and resorts, there are swimming centres with a number of heated pools, diving area, solarium, sauna, spa and possibly a gymnasium. Outdoor pools may open only from around October until April in Melbourne and other southern cities.

Australia has over 7,000 beaches (long, white sandy beaches are common) and all Australian coastal cities have a number of beaches, all of which are open to the public. Sydney has miles of ocean beaches (48km/30mi in the Sydney metropolitan area alone) and also many along its harbour (e.g. Balmoral). Sydney's Bondi Beach is one of Australia's (and the world's) most famous beaches, particularly for surfing. Manly (11km/7mi from the city centre) is another famous Sydney beach resort and the TV programme 'Home and Away' is filmed at Sydney's Palm Beach. Topless bathing is common throughout Australia, although it isn't accepted on all beaches. South Australia was (surprisingly, considering they're supposed to be prudes) the first Australian state to have a legal nudist beach, and the law was recently changed in NSW to permit nude bathing on selected beaches. Local councils can, however, designate any beach a nudist beach. Nude sunbathing is illegal in WA. There are sunscreen patrols on many beaches in Australia to warn people of the need to protect their skin from the sun.

Beach culture is an important aspect of life in Australia, where kids usually learn to swim 'before they can walk'. Beach life led to the surf lifesaving movement (which is both a sport and a community service), the surf ski and the surfboat. Australian beaches are among the best guarded and patrolled in the world. All public beaches are patrolled by lifesavers, who may be volunteers (over 50,000) or paid by the local council. They work each day during the summer season and year round in some resorts. When swimming off a protected beach, it's important to stick to the 'flagged' areas patrolled by lifesavers. Protected beaches also have shark and jellyfish nets (Sydney has an 80km/50mi underwater shark net along its coast – in theory!), although they aren't failsafe. Note that there are dangerous rips (riptides), undertows and shallow sandbanks off some beaches, which claim a number of lives each year (particularly on beaches which aren't patrolled by lifesavers). If you get caught in a rip, you should swim with it rather than against it.

Efforts are made to keep surfers apart from swimmers on protected beaches. On surfing beaches, swimmers must stay within the swimming area defined by red and yellow flags, which may be hoisted from around 6am until 6 or 7pm in summer (year round on some beaches). They are placed to indicate the safest swimming area in the prevailing conditions and also indicate the area under closest scrutiny by lifesavers. **Because of the dangers, swimmers are urged by lifesaving associations never to swim outside patrolled areas (almost all beach drownings are on unpatrolled beaches).** If you get into trouble while swimming off a beach manned by lifesavers, you should raise one arm in the air to alert the lifesavers. Take care not to venture too far out, as it isn't uncommon for swimmers to be swept out to sea.

You should clear the water if a siren sounds, which may signal a shark sighting or a swarm of jellyfish. Shark attacks are rare (although widely reported) and on average only one Australian per year is killed by a shark. There's very little risk of being eaten alive by a shark, e.g. Sydney beaches have had only one fatal shark attack since 1937. The most common problem is jellyfish, particularly box jellyfish (known as sea wasps), whose sting can be fatal (another tiny jellyfish, irukandji, is found farther afield and is almost as deadly). During the jellyfish season, warning signs are posted along the Queensland coast from Mackay northwards and there's also a Poison Information Line (☎ local call rate 13-1126), which can provide information.

However, it's sensible to stay out of the sea during the wet season in the Northern Territory and northern Queensland (from October until May).

Saltwater crocodiles can be a danger near estuaries, and you should also keep a lookout for crocodiles if you're planning to swim in rivers in northern Queensland or the Northern Territory, or in swimming holes in the outback. You're apparently supposed to run away from a crocodile in a zig-zag pattern as they cannot run that way (unless the croc's had a few beers, in which case you could be in trouble!). Other dangers include poisonous coral, cone shells, stonefish, blue-ringed octopus, sea-snakes and catfish, all of which can kill you. In some places swimming is solely for sharks, crocodiles, jellyfish and idiots!

Note that the water off many Australian beaches is polluted, and many Australian rivers and lakes are also too polluted to swim in. Australians don't respect their beaches, and litter can be found everywhere (wilderness beaches are the cleanest). A recent survey by the Surfrider Foundation showed that around 20 per cent of Australian beaches are within 5km/3mi of a sewage outlet (three billion litres of raw sewage is pumped into the sea every day), a quarter have stormwater pipes draining onto beaches, almost three-quarters have developments within just 250 metres of the high-tide mark (25 per cent are also affected by further developments), and around 80 per cent are strewn with litter (including syringes left by drug addicts).

Many beaches have completely lost their sand dunes as a result of beachfront development, and environmental groups believe that urgent action is needed to save what's left of Australia's beaches. Some resorts have a hotline where a recorded message updates callers on pollution from stormwater or sewer outfalls (☎ freecall 1800-036677 in Sydney) and warns of other hazards such as stinging jellyfish and dangerous currents. Daily beachwatch reports are published in newspapers (e.g. the *Sydney Morning Herald*) giving the location of sewage and stormwater. Pollution warnings are posted on some beaches.

Children learn to swim at school in Australia and regularly swim in the school or local public pool (adult lessons are also given at most pools). Students are divided into classes according to age and swimming ability and are taught the finer points of swimming by qualified coaches. Students can obtain swimming certificates from junior through intermediate and senior up to lifesaver qualifications (to gold medal standard). Under a law that came into effect in 1997, all private pools in Australia must have fences higher than 1.5m and be inspected by local councils. Legislation is designed to reduce the incidence of drowning among children aged under five, which is the most common cause of death for children of this age (more than 300 people die from drowning annually).

Private swimming clubs abound in Australia and help produce tomorrow's Olympic team. Australians have an excellent record in the Olympics and World Swimming Championships and dominated the Sydney Olympics with several new world records. They also wipe the floor with other countries in the Commonwealth games held every two years. Australians also excel at water polo and diving.

# WATER SPORTS

All water sports, including sailing, windsurfing, water-skiing, rowing, power-boating, canoeing, surfing, parasailing and subaquatic sports, are popular in Australia, which is hardly surprising considering it has a coastline of 36,738km/22,826mi (some 80 per cent of Australians live within 30km/20mi of the coast) and numerous rivers and lakes. Boats and equipment can be rented from coastal resorts, lakes and rivers, and instruction is available for most water sports in holiday areas. Jet skis and surf skis can also be rented in an increasing number of resorts. Every beach resort worthy of the name stages a surf carnival in summer, in which individuals and teams compete for honours in swimming and surfboat races, board-paddling events, team lifesaving competitions and the highlight, iron-man/iron-woman competitions (a combination of swimming and surfski riding). There's even a professional iron-man circuit which tours Australia in the summer.

**Scuba Diving & Snorkeling:** Australia is a Mecca for scuba divers and snorkelers, particularly the Great Barrier Reef (2,000km/1,240mi in length), which offers some of the world's best diving and is one of the natural wonders of the world with some 400 different types of coral and around 1,500 species of fish. Experts enthuse about the diving on the outer reef wall and you can rent underwater photographic gear (some boats even have on-board film-processing equipment). You can also wreck dive on the Reef, which is the graveyard of over 500 ships. Many diving boats operate out of Cairns and other towns on the northern Queensland coast (boats are licensed to operate from around 20 sites). A day trip from Cairns costs around $80 for snorkelers and $110 for scuba divers, which includes two tank dives. Full snorkelling gear can be hired for around $15 a day, although some day trip organisers provide free snorkelling gear. Note, however, that during the wet season (January to March), floods can wash mud out into the ocean which can seriously reduce viability. There are rules regarding where you can dive on the reef and what you can do (e.g. spearfishing is generally prohibited). Diving shops abound in resort areas and the major cities.

Divers in Australia need a PADI (Professional Association of Diving Instructors) certificate. To obtain a certificate in Australia you usually require a doctor's certificate that you're fit to dive and you must usually show that you can tread water for ten minutes and swim 200m to be accepted on a course. Tuition in Australia is among the cheapest available in tropical waters and a PADI certificate course lasts five days for beginners and costs between $300 and $550. There are diving schools in many coastal towns in Queensland, among the most popular of which are Airlie Beach, Cairns and Townsville. Shop around and ask about courses and avoid cheap 'cowboy' operators, as beginners have occasionally died after receiving poor tuition from these. Always learn with a qualified and reputable outfit. Some diving clubs offer free introductory lessons in a local pool. Note that not all courses offer good value and with the cheaper courses you're likely to spend most of the time in a classroom or pool. A good mix is two days in the classroom and pool, a day trip to the reef, and perhaps two days on the reef spending the night on board. It isn't necessary to be a scuba diver or snorkeler to enjoy the Great Barrier Reef, which you can view from a glass-bottomed boat.

Although the Great Barrier Reef is the main destination for divers in Australia, there are interesting alternatives, including Fly Point at Port Stephens (north of Newcastle, NSW) and Ningaloo Marine Park (extending for 260km/160mi along the western side of the Northwest Cape in Western Australia), which is a smaller, more accessible version of the Great Barrier Reef (in places it's only a few hundred metres offshore). In some areas there are 18th century (e.g. off Rottnest Island near Perth, WA) and WWII wrecks, which make interesting dives.

**Surfing:** Surfing is a way of life rather than just a sport in Australia, where surfers (variously known as surfies, waxheads, seaweed munchers and shark-suckers) are mocked for their fanaticism. A number of international surfing competitions are staged in Australia, which has many top male and female professionals (Australian Mark Richards, who won the world title four times from 1979 to 1982, is considered the greatest competitive surfer of all time). There are surfing schools in all major (and many minor) surfing areas, which run beginners' courses usually lasting three to seven days. It's best to have a few lessons before buying your own board to see whether you take to it (surfboards can be hired for around $30 per hour and some resort hotels lend them to guests free of charge). A wetsuit is usually necessary in winter. Some schools operate surfing safari trips, where you camp in remote locations and learn how to surf, fish and look after yourself in the wild. Surfing variations include surf mats, surfoplanes and boogie boards (small boards that you lie on while learning to master a proper surfboard). **Note, however, that boogie boards can be dangerous and users comprise a large proportion of those rescued by lifesavers.** Surfers can be a hazard for swimmers and, if you impinge on the bathing areas of beaches, you'll be warned off by a lifesaver with a megaphone (if you fail to comply, your board may be confiscated).

The best surfing is usually in New South Wales and Western Australia. The best beaches in Sydney are on the south shore, including Bondi, Tamarama, Coogee, Maroubra and North Narrabeen. Cronulla, south of Botany Bay, is also popular, and there are many beaches between Manly and Palm Beach on the North Shore. Byron Bay in northern NSW is considered one of Australia's best surfing areas. If you live in Canberra, the nearest decent surfing is around 160km/100mi away at Batemans Bay. The best surf close to Melbourne is found at Mornington peninsula on the Great Ocean Road. Bells Beach, Jan Juc, Torquay, Anglesea and Lorne are also popular surfing venues in Victoria. In South Australia you need to travel to Pondalowie for the state's most reliable and strongest waves. Tasmania has some good surf beaches, the best of which is Marrawah on the west coast, although the sea is very cold. Surfing conditions are poor north of Brisbane, and Surfers' Paradise doesn't live up to its name. Cottesloe and Leighton are popular surfing venues in Perth, although the best surf is found at Yallingup further south.

Note that on some beaches the local surfies are protective of their patch and may discourage newcomers. In some areas, you can call a number (e.g. ☎ 1902-210990 in Sydney for $4 per minute!) to find out where the best waves are. Surf carnivals are held in popular surfing resorts during the season from December to April. Enthusiasts may wish to buy a copy of *Surfing Australia* by Mark Thornley (Periplus Publishing).

**Sailing:** Boats of all shapes and sizes (from Lasers and catamaran dinghies to motor cruisers and ocean-going yachts) can be rented from coastal locations throughout Australia. A luxury yacht with up to eight berths costs around $300 per day or around $50 per person per day (novices can charter a boat with a skipper). Some companies offer flotilla trips, where you travel in a group with an experienced skipper. Sailing schools abound in resort areas and offer introductory lessons and courses for beginners up to racing standard. Many Australians fulfil their dream of owning their own boat, and boat ownership is among the highest in the world. Airlie Beach and the Whitsunday Islands are the most popular sailing areas in Queensland, which is the centre of Australia's yacht charter business. In many resorts, it's possible to get a job or a free ride as a crew member on a yacht.

Yacht racing is popular in all areas, including 18-foot skiff (an Australian invention) races, which are staged in Sydney Harbour on most Saturdays during the summer. Australia has an excellent record in international sailing events (including the Olympics and world championships) and won the America's Cup in 1983 – the first nation to beat the Americans in over 100 years. One of Australia's major sporting events is the Sydney to Hobart yacht race (run annually since 1945), which starts on 26th December. It's a handicap race over 630 nautical miles and attracts entries from all over the world.

Note that vessels arriving in Australia must call at a 'proclaimed' port (all major ports), where customs, quarantine and immigration facilities can be completed (usually three hours' notice must be given via an OTC coastal radio station). Customs duty and sales tax is payable on any craft imported for private or commercial use and is payable on arrival, although those staying in Australia for less than 12 months can import a vessel duty and tax free (although a security bond may be required). A book entitled *Go Boating Safely* is published by the Australian Government Publishing Service.

**Miscellaneous:** Windsurfing is popular throughout Australia, and windsurfing schools abound in beach resorts and on inland lakes (you'll probably learn faster on an inland lake than on coastal waters). Tuition costs around $160 for two half-days with a wetsuit included; windsurfer hire costs around $60 per day. Water-skiing has a large following in Australia, where boats, skis and wetsuits can be hired in coastal resorts and on large inland lakes. Jet skis can be hired (around $50 for half an hour) in many beach resorts and on some inland lakes. However, unless you're an experienced rider, it's wise to steer well clear of jet skis, which can be deadly in the wrong hands (both to riders and anyone who comes into contact with them). There are restrictions on the use of jet skis in most resorts. Parasailing, where you're attached to a parachute pulled along by a motor boat and float off into the wide blue yonder, is possible in many beach resorts (it's less frightening than jumping out of a plane and you have a softer landing).

Rowing is a serious sport in Australia (Australia topped the Olympic medal table in Atlanta in 1996 and won five medals in the world rowing championships in 1997), and there are rowing clubs in all major cities and towns. Canoeing is popular on rivers and lakes, where there are numerous clubs offering courses, equipment hire and tours (the *Canoeing Guide to NSW* is published by the NSW Canoe Association (☎ 02-9552 4500, 🖳 www.canoe.org.au). White-water rafting is popular in Australia with its many excellent rapid rivers graded from 1 (easy) to 6 (heeelp!!!!!). Among Australia's wildest rivers are the Franklin and Gordon in Tasmania. The Caltex Avon Descent is Australia's greatest whitewater classic covering 133km/83mi on the Avon River in Western Australia from Northam to Perth. Australia has a number of world champion canoeists.

# AERIAL SPORTS

Most aerial sports have a wide following in Australia (which has an awful lot of airspace), particularly gliding, hang-gliding, paragliding, hot-air ballooning and microlighting. The main things most aerial sports enthusiasts have in common are madness and money, both of which are essential in liberal doses in order to fulfil man's ultimate ambition.

Hang-gliding has become increasingly popular in Australia in the last decade, and there are hang-gliding schools in many areas. Tuition costs round $70 for half an hour to fly in tandem with an instructor; a full course to obtain a pilot's licence (issued by the Hang Gliding Federation of Australia ☎ 02-6947 2888, 💻 www.hgfa.asn.au) costs around $1,500 and can be undertaken in a maximum of ten days. Paragliding or parascending is the cheapest and easiest way to fly and entails 'simply' jumping off a steep mountain slope with a parachute or being tow-launched by a vehicle or a boat. When you've gained enough height, you release the tow and float off on your own (or come crashing back to earth). Although generally safer than hang-gliding, paragliding is dangerous or even lethal in the wrong hands. Paragliders must complete an approved course of instruction, after which (if you survive) you receive a licence which allows you to purchase a paraglider and fly when supervised by an experienced pilot. Parasailing or paraflying is possible in many beach resorts and is like aerial water-skiing (a 10-minute 'flight' costs from $100).

Hot-air ballooning has a small but dedicated band of followers in Australia, although participation is generally limited to the wealthy on account of the high cost of balloons (lawyers and politicians usually get a reduction for supplying their own hot air). Alice Springs is the country's ballooning centre. A flight in a balloon costs from around $120 ($55 for children) and is an unforgettable experience and a spectacular way to see some of Australia's most stunning landscapes (e.g. Ayers Rock, where balloon operators offer 30 or 60-minute sunrise flights – including 'champagne' breakfast).

Aircraft and gliders (sailplanes) can be hired with an instructor or without (provided you have a pilot's licence) from many small airfields in Australia. There are many gliding clubs in Australia, and parachuting and free-fall parachuting (sky-diving) flights can be made from most private airfields. Schools offer tandem jumps for beginners (where you're strapped to an instructor), and a day's freefall course costs around $400. The latest craze to have taken off (literally) in Australia is the microlight (or ultralight), a low-flying go-cart with a hang glider on top and a motorised tricycle below. Microlights are designed to carry a maximum of two people and can be stored in a garage. It's one of the cheapest and most enjoyable ways of experiencing real flying without your own wings (you require a private pilot's licence). Flying lessons are cheaper in Australia than in most European countries and similar to North America. You can take a 'tourist' flight in a small plane from most airfields, and seaplane flights are also offered in some areas, e.g. Sydney harbour.

Note that most aerial sports or private aviation are specifically excluded from many insurance policies, including, for example, health insurance and mortgage life assurance policies. Before taking up any aerial sport, you should ensure that you have adequate health and accident insurance, sufficient life assurance and your affairs are in order. Why not take up fishing instead? A nice, sensible, *safe* sport – not that fish would agree!

# FISHING

Fishing (or angling) facilities in Australia are excellent and it's one of the biggest participant sports in the country. There's good fishing in Australian waters, both inland and offshore, the main attraction being big game fishing. There's good trout fishing on inland lakes and rivers in many states, particularly in Tasmania. However, you should be wary of eating fish caught in inland waters as many are polluted, despite $millions spent on cleaning them up (many rivers are used as waste disposal 'pipes' by industry). Over-fishing of certain species is also an increasing problem for

Australia's fishing industry. There are bag and size limits in most areas for certain species of fish, e.g. Victoria limits trout catches to ten a day, and a licence may be required when fishing in inland waters. In WA, fishing licences ($15 per week, $25 per month and $60 annually) are required only if you plan to catch marron and rock lobsters or will be using a net. Licences are available from the Fisheries Department. Some species such as turtles, clams, dugongs (sea cows) and triton shells are protected and may not be hunted in Australian waters.

The main Australian game fishing industry is based in Townsville, where game includes black marlin (the prize catch), sailfish, saltfish, wahoo, tuna and Spanish mackerel. The main season is from June to November. Australia's most prized game fish, black and blue marlin, are protected by law and *must* be returned to the sea whether dead or alive (often after being tagged) or you risk a fine of up to $12,500! The Coral Sea off Cairns is one of the few places in the world where large black marlin are found. Game fishing competitions are regularly staged – one of the major events is the Gove Game Classic (NT) which attracts fishermen from all over the world. A game fishing boat for eight can be rented for around $1,000 per day, although marlin fishing can cost $1,500 per day for four to six passengers. 'Bottom' fishing boats, carrying up to 30 passengers, are also available for hire. Reef fishing on the Great Barrier Reef is particularly popular, and fishing boats depart regularly from Cairns and Townsville for trips lasting eight to 15 hours.

Good game fishing is to be had in the waters off Broome (WA), where game includes mackerel, yellowfin tuna, wahoo, yellowtail, kingfish, hammerhead and bronze whale shark. There's also good game fishing off New South Wales (tailor fish, marlin, mulloway, black marlin), Victoria and Tasmania (mulloway, bluefin tuna and Australian salmon), South Australia (tuna), Perth (blue marlin) and Darwin (queenfish, Spanish mackerel, barramundi and barracuda). Other popular prey include brown trout, English redfin, perch, eel and native blackfish (off the west coast of Tasmania), Australian salmon, mulloway, shark, giant crab, trevally, whiting and crayfish (off South Australia) and salmon, herring, tailor, trevally, sea pike, samson fish, Spanish mackerel, bream, mulloway and crayfish (off the southern coast of Western Australia). Northern Australia is famed for its barramundi ('barra') fishing, found both offshore and inland. Fishing trips are organised from around $250 per day, usually between March and October, including accommodation, all meals, guides, boat rental, equipment, tackle and bait. Note that in the NT there are limits on catches of barramundi and mud crabs (contact the local fisheries management service for information).

Tasmania has Australia's best fresh-water fishing, including superb trout fishing (introduced in 1864 from England). A licence is required to fish in inland waters and there are bag, season and size limits for many species of fish. Licences cost $45 for the season, $35 for 14 days, $20 for three days and $12 for one day and are available from sports stores, post offices, and state travel and information centres. The fishing season in most inland waters is from the Saturday nearest to 1st August until the Sunday closest to 30th April. However, there's a shorter season in many areas and in some waters (a *Fishing Code* brochure is available detailing the seasons). Tasmania's coastal waters are also rich fishing grounds (fishing is permitted all year), where salmon, whiting and bream can all be caught from the shore.

# GOLF

Golf was introduced in Australia in the 1820s and today there are some 1,400 clubs and around a million golfers, making it the most popular participant sport in the country. Melbourne has more than 100 golf courses (it claims to have more than any other city in the world) and Sydney has almost 100. There are many beautiful and spectacularly sited courses throughout the country. Many are public courses, but the best courses are usually private. Most of these allow non-members to play, although you may need to be invited by a member. Many private golf clubs are part of a larger country club or hotel sports complex, where facilities may include a luxury hotel, restaurant, bar, tennis, squash, swimming pool and other facilities. Golf isn't an expensive sport in Australia, where a round usually costs $10 to $25. Golf clubs can be hired for around $20.

Many golf clubs have golf nets and covered driving ranges, and most also have professionals to help you reduce your number of lost balls (beware of courses with lots of water, which has a voracious appetite for golf balls). Driving ranges are also provided in most areas and have all-weather, floodlit bays, practice bunkers and putting greens. The big advantage of a driving range (apart from the reasonable cost of a few dollars for a basket of 50 balls) is that you don't need to go and find your balls in the undergrowth or buy new ones when they land in the water (there isn't any).

Australia has produced many top golfers, including Greg Norman, Peter Senior, David Graham, Craig Parry, Darren Cole, Peter O'Malley, Stuart Appleby, Robert Allenby, Brad King, Greg Chalmers and Robert Stephens. When not playing on the European or American circuits, Australia's top professionals play the ANZ PGA Tour of Australasia Order of Merit. The premier event is the Australian Open, staged in November at the Metropolitan Golf Club in Melbourne. Top Australian female golfers include Karrie Webb (who was world number one in 1997) and Karen Lunn. Crazy golf, miniature golf, pitch and putt, and putting greens (e.g. in public parks) are provided in most areas for those who set their sights a little lower than winning the Australian Open.

# GYMNASIUMS & HEALTH CLUBS

There are gymnasiums and health and fitness clubs (where sadists are employed and masochists go to torture themselves) in all cities and large towns in Australia, including multipurpose fitness centres with swimming pools, aerobics and fitness machines. Many private health and fitness clubs organise aerobics and keep-fit classes, and may have a sauna, solarium, Jacuzzi, steam bath and massage parlour. Many top class hotels also have health clubs and swimming pools, which are usually open to the general public, although access to facilities may be restricted to guests only at certain times.

All clubs and centres have tonnes of expensive, bone-jarring, muscle-wrenching apparatus, designed either to get you into shape or to kill you in the attempt. Middle-aged 'fatties' shouldn't attempt to get fit in 'five minutes' (after all it took years of dedicated sloth and over-eating to put on all that weight), as overexertion can result in serious injuries. A good gymnasium or health club will ensure that this doesn't happen and will carry out a physical assessment, including a blood pressure test, fat distribution measurements and heart rate checks. All clubs should provide a free trial and assessment and produce a personal training programme. In your rush to become one of the body beautiful, it pays to take the long route and give the intensive care unit (and mortuary) a wide berth.

Private health and fitness clubs have been popping up in all areas of Australia. The cost of membership varies considerably according to the city, area, the facilities provided and the local competition. Note, however, that there has also been a spate of closures in recent years, which have left annual members out of pocket. This has led to a new law prohibiting gyms from offering annual membership specials that are much cheaper than a monthly payment scheme. Beware of fly-by-night outfits and choose a reputable, long-established club. Membership fees and facilities vary considerably, so you should shop around. Many gymnasiums can be used by non-members on payment of an admission fee, where a day ticket usually costs around $25 (monthly membership is also usually available). Some gyms in major cities (e.g. Sydney) are open 24 hours a day from Mondays to Fridays. Some clubs offer reduced rates for couples and family membership.

## MISCELLANEOUS SPORTS

The following is a selection of other popular sports in Australia, most of which are practised throughout the country.

**Athletics:** Most towns have athletics clubs and organise competitions and sports days. Competitive running has a strong following in Australia, and jogging is popular in the main cities, where there are jogging tracks in many public parks and gardens. Races are organised throughout the year in all areas, from fun runs of a few miles up to half and full marathons. The ultimate 'jog' is the 1,060km/658mi ultrathon, the world's longest point-to-point race, run from Melbourne to Sydney in spring, taking over 50 days to complete. Australia isn't renowned for its prowess in athletics but has a number of world-class athletes, notably Cathy Freeman, who won the 400m at the 1997 world championships and the 2000 Olympics. However, athletics isn't a popular spectator sport in Australia (unless it's the Commonwealth, World or Olympic Games) and Australia has few world champions in track and field sports (compared with their huge success in other sports). Australia is one of only three countries (Britain and Greece are the others) to have competed at every modern Olympics and has hosted two Olympic Games (Melbourne 1956 and Sydney 2000).

**Baseball:** To the uninitiated, baseball is the only game that provides test cricket with any sort of challenge for the title of the most boring sport in the world (although it doesn't offer much competition, as games are far too short). Baseball is popular in Australia, particularly among insomniacs, who find that watching people run around in circles in pyjamas provides an instant cure. There's a national league and a national team, although it isn't a professional sport.

**Basketball:** A sport specially created for giants (and black American giants in particular), which is popular in Australia and one of the country's fastest-growing sports. There's a professional National Basketball League (NBL), and top matches are televised and attract crowds of over 15,000. The NBL has bolstered club standards, and the national team (the Australian Crocodiles) is now rated in the world's top ten. The import of foreign players is restricted in order to nurture home-grown talent.

**Bowls:** Once regarded mainly as a pastime for the elderly and retired, (lawn) bowls is increasingly popular with people of all ages, particularly the young (who are ruining the game's image). Top matches are well attended and televised. There are hundreds of bowling clubs throughout Australia (almost every city suburb has one), which is one of the world's top bowls nations and has produced many world champions.

**Boxing:** Boxing is popular throughout the country, particularly as a spectator 'sport' (many people enjoy watching a good fight, as long as they're out of arms' reach). Most towns have a boxing club, and gymnasiums for budding professionals are common in the main cities. Australia has produced a number of world champions over the years.

**Bungee Jumping:** This 'sport' was invented in New Zealand and is popular among macho Aussies. If your idea of fun is jumping 60m/200ft or more with an elastic rope attached to your body to prevent you from merging with the landscape, bungee jumping may be just what you're looking for. Jumps are usually made from specially constructed steel towers, but also from bridges, cranes, hot-air balloons, etc. It's a strictly regulated sport, which is actually very safe. You can also try rap-jumping in Australia which consists of rappelling (hence the name) or abseiling head first down a cliff at high speed (or you could go fishing).

**Darts:** Not actually a sport, but an excuse to get drunk (have you ever seen anyone playing darts in a milk bar?). A popular game in pubs, many of which have teams that compete in local leagues.

**Fencing:** A sport which has lost a lot of its popularity since the invention of the gun, although a hard core of enthusiastic 'swordsmen/women' are holding out in a small number of clubs.

**Frisbee:** Believe it or not, throwing plastic discs around has actually developed into a competitive 'sport' in Australia, with league and cup competitions.

**Gymnastics:** Another popular sport in Australia, and most schools and sports centres have 'gym' clubs.

**Hockey:** Hockey (grass) is a leading sport in Australia, and both the Australian men and women's hockey teams are among the best in the world (the sport is equally popular among both sexes). The national men's team is called the Kookaburras. (For the record, Australia won the men's underwater hockey world title in 1996 – a sport reserved for those who can hold their breath for a long, LONG time.)

**Horse & Greyhound Racing:** Horse racing is very popular in Australia, although not because Australians are a nation of equestrians or horse lovers, rather inveterate gamblers. Australia has a long tradition of horse racing and the Sydney Turf Club was established in 1825. Australia's premier horse race (and its greatest sporting event) is the Melbourne Cup run at the Flemington Racecourse in Melbourne on the first Tuesday in November. It's a blend of spectacle, carnival, fashion show, banquet and, yes, horse racing and brings the country to a total standstill. In addition to flat horse racing, trotting (pacers or harness racing) is popular in Australia (race meetings are always held at night). Greyhound racing is the poor relation of Australian racing and has a relatively small (but dedicated) following.

**Horse Riding:** Equestrianism (or horse riding to those who cannot spell the word) is popular in Australia, where there's an abundance of space to ride and it's relatively inexpensive to own and keep your own horse. On cattle and sheep ranches in the outback, horses remain the primary means of getting around. There are many riding schools in rural areas throughout the country, where horses can be hired. Trail rides abound in most areas, where most schools offer half and full-day trail rides; many also organise longer trips through the mountains, outback, rain forests and sand dunes. Australia has a proud tradition of horse breeding and horsemanship and is one of the world's leading equestrian nations. You can also try camel riding in many areas, particularly in the Northern Territory and around Alice Springs. Camel treks are organised for periods of up to 14-days (take plenty of salve for your bottom!).

**Martial Arts:** For those brought up on a diet of Bruce Lee, unarmed combat such as Aikido, Judo, Karate, Kung Fu, Kushido, Taekwon-Do and T'ai Chi Ch'uan, are taught and practised at clubs throughout Australia.

**Motor Sports:** Australians love all motor sports, including formula one, Indycar, touring car, rallying, motor cycling, speedway and moto-cross. The Australian grand prix (staged at Albert Park in Melbourne) is one of the best organised formula one races in the race calendar and has won the best race award on several ocassions. Australia has produced a number of formula one champions, including Jack Brabham and Alan Jones. An Indycar (USA) race is staged in Surfers' Paradise (QLD) in March and is the only Indycar race held outside North America. Touring car racing has a huge following in Australia and attracts heavy sponsorship and wide TV coverage. The highlight of the season is the Bathurst (150km/93mi west of Sydney) 1,000km (629mi) race held in October. The Australian Safari road rally is run over 6,000km (3,700mi) of rugged terrain in August, the route remaining secret until the night before each day's race. Australia has a peerless record in 500cc motorcycling in recent years and has produced many world champions, including one of the greatest motorcyclists of all time, Michael Doohan, who won the world 500cc motorcycle title for the fifth successive year in 1998 before retiring a year later.

**Netball:** The most popular women's team game in Australia. There are clubs in all towns, and competitions are staged at all levels, including a televised national competition. Australia won the netball world cup in both 1991 and 1995.

**Polo:** A minority sport for princes and Australian millionaires (e.g. Kerry Packer), where players attempt to hit a ball into a goal while riding a horse at speeds of up to 40mph/65kph without falling off.

**Roller-skating, Roller-blading, Skate-boarding and BMX:** Rinks and specially designed circuits are provided in many towns for skateboarding and BMX riding (acrobatics on a bicycle). Participants should be protected against falls by crash helmets and elbow and knee pads (although not mandatory). It's difficult to hire equipment, as it's too easily stolen, although BMX bikes can usually be hired. Roller-skating and roller-blading rinks are provided in major cities and towns, where skates can be hired and coaching is usually available. Many centres organise roller-discos for teenagers. The promenades of beach resorts are popular roller-skating/blading venues. Keen roller-skaters and roller-bladers also play roller hockey.

**Shooting & Hunting:** Shooting and hunting are extremely popular in Australia, which has a long tradition of firearms sports. However, shooters were dealt a blow in 1997 when many guns were outlawed after the Port Arthur massacre in Tasmania in 1996. Range shooting is popular in towns, and hunting has a large following in the outback, where locals will shoot anything that moves.

**Snooker & Billiards:** Many hotels, bars and sports clubs have billiard or snooker tables, and there are snooker and billiards clubs in the larger towns. American pool is also played in Australia.

**Softball:** Similar to baseball, softball is played with a larger, slightly softer ball, and teams have ten players instead of nine. It's a popular sport in Australia, where it's also played on the beach.

**Tenpin Bowling:** There are tenpin bowling centres in all the major cities in Australia, many with a restaurant and licensed bar. All centres stage competitions and there are tenpin bowling leagues and clubs in all areas (many companies have teams).

**Trampolining:** A popular sport among high fliers and gymnasts, with a large number of clubs (both junior and senior) around Australia, where courses are organised for all ages.

**Volleyball:** A fun game for all the family which is widely played both indoors and outdoors (particularly beach volleyball) in Australia.

**Wrestling:** When it comes to mass popularity, 'showbiz' wrestling (as seen on TV) is streets ahead of the real sport of wrestling (as practised in the Olympics).

**Other Sports:** Many foreign sports and pastimes have a group of expatriate fanatics in Australia, including American football, archery, boccia, croquet, Gaelic sports (hurling, Gaelic football), handball, lacrosse and pétanque (or boules). For information enquire at council offices, libraries, tourist offices, expatriate social clubs, embassies and consulates.

# 17.

# SHOPPING

Australia isn't one of the world's great shopping countries, either for variety or for bargains. Although the choice and quality of goods on offer has improved considerably in the last decade, it's still limited compared with Europe and North America, and many new products aren't available in Australia or cost a fortune. However, there's a wide choice of department, chain and international stores in the major cities, and exclusive boutiques and chic stores abound in arcades and shopping centres. In stark contrast to the cities, small country towns are only likely to have a general store and a few other shops. Prices are also necessarily higher in rural areas owing to freight costs, and most people who live in the country stock up on goods (and buy expensive items) when visiting a city or large town, or shop by mail-order.

There are many small, family-run stores in Australia, particularly in rural areas, small towns and the suburbs of major cities, although Australia's shopping scene has been transformed in the last few decades with the opening of numerous large shopping centres (malls) and vast supermarkets. Following the trend in most western countries, there has been a drift away from town centres by retailers to out-of-town shopping malls (introduced in the late '70s), which has left some town centres run down and deserted. The biggest drawback to shopping in cities is parking, which can be a nightmare. However, in some areas too many shopping malls were built for too few customers and many are now being redesigned, redeveloped, reinvented or even demolished. Towns are now turning to 'street-scaping', i.e. reviving streets by landscaping, installing traffic 'calmers' (speed bumps) or pedestrianising them, which many people prefer to bland malls. Australian cities invariably have excellent shopping centres, many housed in fine period buildings and pedestrianised streets.

Australia doesn't exactly have a free and open marketplace, and there are many protected industries, tariffs, monopolies and cartels, although competition reforms have been introduced in recent years. Consequently, consumers don't always get the best deal and often pay much higher prices than in other countries. In the case of expensive and luxury items, you may be better off buying them overseas by mail or via the Internet (see page 440). However, the price of many consumer goods such as TV and stereo systems, computers, cameras, electrical apparatus and household appliances has fallen dramatically in recent years. Furthermore, if your funds are in a currency that has increased in value against the Australian dollar in recent years (such as the £sterling or US$), you'll be pleasantly surprised how far your money will stretch.

There's generally no bargaining or bartering in Australia, although if you intend to spend a lot of money or buy something expensive, you should shop around and shouldn't be reticent about asking for a discount (except in department and chain stores and supermarkets, where prices are usually fixed). Many shops will also meet any genuine advertised price, although often reluctantly. Taxes are usually included in advertised prices, although for some items goods and services tax (GST – see page 346) may be added to the marked price. Always shop around before buying, but make sure that you're comparing similar goods or services, as it's easy to 'save' money by purchasing inferior products. In recent years, consumer confidence has been low and the retailing sector has been relatively flat since the recession in the early '90s. Australians have become a nation of bargain hunters and have deserted department stores for no-frills retailers and discount stores such as Harris Scarfe, Kmart and Big W.

To encourage Australians to buy Australian-made goods, the government introduced the Advantage Australia loyalty programme in 1997. Under this scheme, shoppers collect special stamps from companies selling Australian-made goods (including food) such as Ampol, Cadbury, Caltex, CSR and Edgell. When your stamp book is full, it can be used to redeem special offers, discounts and rewards, or you can donate it to a designated charity. There's also a schools programme, under which stamp books are donated to help pay for computers. Goods made in Australia often have a green and gold symbol to distinguish them from less expensive (and supposedly inferior) goods made in Asia. In general, Australian-made products are of high quality, although they're often more expensive than similar imported goods (top-branded, imported goods are much more expensive in Australia than in many other countries).

A wealth of quality arts and crafts are sold in Australia, including hand-woven and knitted woollen garments, leather goods, hides and skins (particularly sheep and lambskin products), rugs, jewellery (e.g. gold, opals, pearls and diamonds), handbags, embroidery, paintings, ceramics, glassware, woodwork and traditional Australian 'outback' clothing. Aboriginal art (of which there are many styles produced by different tribes) is popular and is best purchased directly from artists' co-operatives or Aborigine-owned stores, rather than from tourist shops. It's cheapest in Alice Springs, Darwin and outback towns, although genuine Aboriginal art can be expensive. Aboriginal Arts Australia (AAA) was established by the government to market Aboriginal and Torres Strait Islander arts and crafts, through its stores in Alice Springs, Darwin and Perth. Note that much 'Aboriginal' artwork is mass-produced junk, and cheap 'fake' Aboriginal souvenirs are also made in Asia, so before buying anything always check where it's made.

Most shops hold sales at various times of the year, the largest of which are held in December/January and July. The most popular sales are the post-Christmas (or end-of-year) sales, which traditionally start on 26th December, where savings of up to 60 per cent are possible. Some stores seem to have a permanent sale, although retailers aren't permitted to advertise goods as reduced when they've never been advertised or sold at a higher price.

Most shops accept major credit and debit (EFTPOS) cards, although you may be asked for proof of identification. Personal cheques aren't usually accepted, and some stores don't even accept cash in order to deter robbers. Note that, since the demise of one and two cent coins, prices have been rounded up or down to the nearest five cents (this sometimes also applies to electronic transactions, although there's no reason why it should). In major cities and tourist areas you *must* be wary of pickpockets and bag-snatchers, particularly in markets and other crowded places. Don't tempt fate with an exposed wallet or purse or by flashing your money around.

The quality of service and assistance in shops ranges from excellent to poor, depending on the type of store, although generally Australian storekeepers aren't renowned for their service. Many retail outlets require customers to allow staff to search their bags (excluding very small bags such as handbags) when paying or leaving a store. This is usually shown by a sign; by entering a store you consent to having your bags searched (no sign, no checks). If you have any questions about your rights as a consumer, contact your local consumer affairs office, fair trading bureau or citizens advice bureau. Most retailers, particularly department and chain stores, will exchange goods or give a refund without question, but smaller stores aren't so enthusiastic. See also **Consumer Rights** on page 442.

Shopping guides are available in many areas, including the essential *Bargain Shoppers* guides to Melbourne and Sydney (published by Universal Magazines, Unit

56-8, Byfield Street, North Ryde, NSW 2113) and *Shopping in Exciting Australia* by Ronald Krannich (Impact Publications). Many stores, particularly department and chain stores, provide free catalogues at Christmas and other times of the year. If you're looking for a particular item or anything unusual, you'll find that the yellow pages (see page 176) will save you a lot of time and trouble (and shoe leather). Shopping Tours have become popular in recent years whereby shoppers are guided round mainly discount and warehouse shopping in Sydney (e.g. Shopping Spree ☎ 02-9360 6220), Melbourne (e.g. Shopping Spree Tours ☎ 03-9596 6600) and Adelaide (e.g. Shopping Tours ☎ 08-8234 2400).

# SHOPPING HOURS

Shopping hours in Australia vary with the city or town, the state or territory and the day of the week, but generally are among the most liberal in the world. Shopping hours have been extended in recent years, and in some states (e.g. Victoria) stores can now open 24 hours a day, seven days a week, apart from a few public holidays (e.g. Good Friday, Christmas Day and before 1pm on ANZAC day). However, shops cannot be required to open on New Year's Day, Australia Day, Labour Day, Easter Monday, the Queen's Birthday or Melbourne Cup Day, and trading is optional on Sundays (in some states, e.g. Queensland, Sunday trading is a contentious issue).

In the major cities, many stores are open for up to 12 hours a day (some are even open 24 hours) and on Sundays, and many remain open all day Saturdays. Department stores may open on Sundays (e.g. from 10am to 4pm) and some open earlier on sales days, e.g. at 7.30 or 8am. City newsagents, chemists and delicatessens usually open on Sundays (e.g. from 8am until 8pm), and chemists may open up to 24 hours a day. There are 7-11 (modelled on the American 7-11 stores) and Food Plus stores in the major cities which, despite their name, open 24 hours a day and may have a petrol station 'attached'. Harbourside shopping centres in Sydney (such as Darling Harbour) are open from 10am to 9pm Mondays to Saturdays and from 10am to 6pm on Sundays. Many city bookshops are open during the evenings and throughout weekends. Even shops which aren't open all day and all night usually have late night shopping until 9 or 9.30pm one evening per week, usually Thursdays or Fridays.

In some areas, stores stay open an hour later in summer than in winter. Most shops in resorts such as the Gold and Sunshine Coasts are open at weekends and on public holidays as well as late at night. Normal shopping hours in country areas are usually from around 8.30 or 9am to between 5 and 6pm Mondays to Fridays, and from 9am until noon on Saturdays.

# MALLS & MARKETS

In the last few decades, numerous vast indoor shopping centres (called malls after their American counterparts) have sprung up in out-of-town areas throughout Australia. Malls usually contain a huge selection of shops, including a large department store and many of the most popular chain stores, and are open seven days a week. The main attractions are one-stop shopping and free parking, which usually means you can simply wheel your trolley full of purchases to your car. The largest malls incorporate a wide range of leisure attractions, including cinemas, games arcades, food halls, fun parks, children's play areas, and a variety of restaurants, cafés and pubs.

Most towns and cities also have covered shopping centres, although parking is often expensive and difficult in city and town centres, particularly on Saturdays, and parking areas may be located some distance from stores. Among the most famous city shopping centres are the vast Melbourne Central (home to 300 stores) and the Queen Victoria Building (200 stores), Strand Arcade, Centrepoint Shopping Complex and MLC Centre in Sydney. Many city malls are housed in restored period buildings (such as the converted GPO building in Sydney, now the New Mall), which are often connected by tunnels and walkways to other stores and centres.

**Markets:** Most small towns have markets on one or two days a week and in major cities and towns there may be a market (or a number) on most days of the week. Markets are cheap, colourful and interesting, and are often a good place for shrewd shoppers to pick up bargains, although you need to be careful what you buy (beware of fakes). Items commonly for sale in markets include fruit and vegetables, meat, fish and other food, clothes, arts and crafts, household goods, jewellery and books. Markets are the best place to buy fresh food, where the quality and variety rivals that of any country. Arts and craft markets are common in major cities and resort towns, where artisans can often be seen at work. Flea markets are popular in the major cities and sell secondhand goods, including clothes, books, records, antiques and miscellaneous bric-a-brac. Some towns have permanent covered or indoor market places where markets are held from Mondays to Saturdays, and in some cities there are also popular outdoor Sunday markets. Check with your local library, council or tourist office for information (guides are available to markets in some states, e.g. Victoria).

# FOOD & SUPERMARKETS

The quality and variety of food in Australia is superb and the equal of any country in the world. Food outlets include markets (where the freshest produce, meat and fish is usually available), delicatessens (delis), ethnic food shops, general and corner stores, and, of course, supermarkets. There's a wealth of gourmet food shops in the major cities offering everything from bread and cheese to fruit and vegetables, from cakes and pastries to coffee and tea. You can buy almost any ethnic food and ingredients somewhere in Australia, and in the major cities there are stores specialising in imported American and British foods, although prices can be high. Australia still maintains the quaint British tradition of delivering milk to homes in many towns and cities (home bread deliveries are also made), and many stores deliver groceries, either free or for a small fee.

Australians spend over $40 billion a year in supermarkets, which are (not surprisingly) among Australia's most profitable retailers. However, despite increasing pressure from the major supermarket chains, independent grocers are expected to survive by providing locally-oriented products and personal service. Supermarkets carry some 45,000 products in their major stores, although they've reduced the less popular brands in recent years. The biggest supermarket chains in Australia are Woolworths, Coles Myer and Franklins, which together account for more than three-quarters of the market, the remaining quarter being split between a few smaller players and independents. In mid-2001, Woolworths made a successful takeover bid for the 67 Franklins stores. Woolworths has 1,400 stores throughout Australia, including a chain of Metro supermarkets, and employs some 130,000 Australians (one in every 100 Australians of working age is employed by Woolworths!). Woolworths was the first Australian supermarket to introduce food shopping on the Internet, a service it calls 'Homeshop'. Minimum orders are $60 and deliveries are only available in metropolitan areas at present. Coles Myer also has Coles Express stores in city centres stocking around 13,000 products and offering up-market deli products, gourmet take-home meals, a home catering service and personalised cakes (e.g. for office celebrations).

Supermarkets aren't usually permitted to sell alcohol, which must be purchased from bottle shops (liquor stores/off-licences), grocers or hotels (pubs). However, in country areas, supermarkets and bottle shops may be combined. Supermarkets may have in-store bank kiosks and petrol stations, and they also have plans to introduce news agencies and pharmacies. Major supermarkets open seven days a week and in some cities remain open until midnight. They provide trolleys, which usually require a deposit of 20¢; some stores insist that customers use a trolley or basket even when they're buying only a few items. Many supermarkets provide free plastic carrier bags and boxes, and some provide staff to help you pack your purchases (although you may need to ask).

Australians have been eating more healthily in recent years, consuming less red meat (although they're still big meat eaters) and alcohol, and eating more fruit and vegetables. Meat is reasonable priced and of excellent quality, as generally is fresh fish and seafood (although it can be expensive). Most supermarkets have good fruit and vegetables, owing to the high turnover of stock (although you should avoid packaged produce, which may be stale or over-ripe as well as being more expensive). Many supermarkets bake their own bread on the premises and most have fresh fish, meat and cheese counters as well as their own delicatessens. Home cooking is one of the casualties of modern living and most Australians don't have enough time to shop and cook elaborate meals. Consequently, prepared, oven-ready meals, microwave food and take-away meals are increasingly popular, and all supermarkets cater for this lucrative growth market. Note, however, that some prepared and fast foods provide little or no nutritional value and in some cases you'd be better off eating the packaging!

Food prices vary with the city, the shop and the season. Adelaide and Melbourne are generally regarded as the cheapest cities for food, while Darwin is the most expensive, as most food must be transported from outside the territory. The current food prices in Australia's capital cities are listed in the monthly *Australian Outlook* newspaper (see **Appendix A**). Note that all foods are sold by the metric measure in Australia (see **Appendix C** for imperial comparisons).

**Labelling:** Many manufacturers make unsubstantiated and wild claims for their products, particularly 'health' foods and environmentally-friendly 'green' products, which are deliberately misleading and often illegal. You usually pay a premium for anything with a claim to be 'low fat', 'free-range' or 'low calorie', many of which are bogus, although stricter guidelines on food labelling have been introduced in recent years and claims such as 'low fat', 'high fibre', 'sugar-free', 'light' and 'low cholesterol' must meet specific standards.

There are also regulations concerning the vitamins and minerals that can be added to food and new rules about where food is produced. All highly perishable goods (e.g. fresh foods, dairy produce and prepared foods) must have a 'use by' date, after which their sale is illegal (perishable goods are usually discounted a day or two before the use by date). Note, however, that use by dates are widely ignored in country areas. Regulations regarding the handling and storage of food have also be tightened in recent years to curb outbreaks of food poisoning, which is estimated to make thousands of Australians sick each year.

**Scanning:** All supermarkets in Australia use computerised (electronic point-of-sale) pricing systems where a bar code is included on the labels of goods and is read by a laser reader at the checkout. Always check your receipt carefully, as customers are frequently overcharged, particularly on special offer items. Note, however, that unless you make a note of the price of everything you buy, any errors made when prices are entered into the computer may go unnoticed. In most supermarkets, if an item is scanned at a higher price than advertised (or displayed), you're usually entitled to it free under the voluntary code of practice of the Australian Supermarket Institute. Self-scanning, where customers scan their own goods, has been introduced in some supermarkets in recent years. Under this system, which reduces the time spent at checkouts, spot checks are made to deter cheats. In future, all supermarkets are expected to offer this option., although they won't do away with checkout staff (derogatorily called 'checkout chicks') and will still offer the regular checkout service for those who don't wish to do their own scanning (and those who like a modicum of personal service).

## ALCOHOL

The average Australian family spends around $25 per week on alcohol (liquor), which can be purchased from licensed bottle shops (also called grog shops), pubs and restaurants (it isn't usually sold in food shops or supermarkets). There are drive-in bottle shops (possibly with 'express' and 'browse' lanes) in major cities, where the biggest and cheapest chains include Liquorland and Liquor Mart. The largest single liquor store in Australia is Dan Murphy's Cellar in Melbourne with some 8 million bottles of wine (enough to throw a *really* good party!). Opening hours vary with the state or territory, e.g. from 8.30am until 8.30pm or 10am until 10pm, Mondays to Saturdays. There are reduced opening hours on Sundays. Wine can also be purchased in Australia by mail-order (e.g. from Cellarmaster Wines) and Australians buy some 15 per cent of all bottled wines by mail-order (compared with less than 2 per cent in most other countries). You must be aged over 18 to buy alcohol or consume it in a public place.

## Wine

Although part of the 'new world', Australia isn't exactly a newcomer when it comes to wine production; vines were imported in 1788 by the first fleet and commercial production started in the 1820s in NSW and Tasmania, which were followed by South Australia, Western Australia and Victoria in the 1840s. However, up to 1960, some 80 per cent of all Australian wine was fortified wine, for which the country is still noted. Today, over 90 per cent of Australian wine is table wine, the country has over 1,300 wineries and there are plans to double production by the year 2025. Only ten years ago, Australia imported more wine than it exported. Now wine is one of the country's fastest growing exports: it was worth some $1.5 billion in 2000, but the Australian wine industry has an ambitious long-term strategy known as Vision 2025, by which date Australian wine is expected to be worth $4.5 billion in annual sales and the industry to be the world's most profitable and influential. Exports (three-quarters from South Australia) are made to around 80 countries, the biggest markets being New Zealand (where Australian wine accounts for around a third of the wine market), Ireland (28 per cent) and Britain (17 per cent). However, while exports have soared, home sales have fallen in recent years, the average annual consumption per head being around 20 litres – Australians are increasingly choosing quality over quantity and drinking more premium wines, many of the best Australian wines rarely reaching foreign markets.

Australian wines have earned an increasing international reputation and respect in recent years, with their distinctive, deep fruity flavour, full-bodied character and consistency. Although many jokes have been cracked at the expense of Australian wine in the past, today's wines are certainly not just for sprinkling on your fish and chips. In fact, Australian wines have been astounding the judges and competitors at international wine exhibitions for over a century – one story tells of an Australian wine winning a competition in France in the 19th century and promptly losing it again when it was discovered where the wine was produced! Today, Australia is the most dynamic wine-producing country in the world (and easily the best of the new world producers) and the sophistication and quality of its wines have improved in leaps and bounds in the last few decades. Growers aren't afraid to experiment; indeed many go out of their way to introduce new grape varieties and create exciting new blends (they threw out the rule book decades ago). Australian winemakers have a pragmatic approach and are quick to introduce the latest technology; they're noted for their high yields and low production costs. The climate, soil, modern equipment and techniques, allied to the Australians' freedom from tradition and love of experimentation, combine to produce some of the best and most original wines in the world.

**Regions:** South Australia produces around 55 per cent of Australia's wine, New South Wales (including the ACT) 35 per cent, the remaining 10 per cent being shared between Tasmania, Western Australia and Victoria (there's also a small production in Queensland and in Alice Springs in the Northern Territory). The most famous wine regions are the Barossa Valley, Coonawarra and the Clare Valley in South Australia, the Hunter Valley in New South Wales (famous for its white wines, particularly chardonnay), Rutherglen/Milawa (port and muscat), the Yarra Valley where sparking wines are produced, the Geelong area and the Mornington Peninsula in Victoria, and the Margaret River and Swan River Valley in Western Australia. Although each region is noted for a particular style of wine and specific grape varieties, there's also a lot of experimentation and blending of grapes between regions. The main producers include Penfolds, Lindemans, Seppelt, Seaview, Orlando (producers of Jacob's Creek, Australia's best known international brand), Wyndham Estate, Hardys and Wolf Blass. There are also many small independent producers, often called boutique vineyards, making high-quality wines.

**Varieties & Grapes:** Australian wines are usually named after the grapes used rather than given fancy titles or called after the region in which they're grown. The best Australian wines are varietal (wines made from one grape variety), although they also produce many excellent wines made from a blend of grapes. Australia is best known for its superb cabernet sauvignon, pinot noir and shiraz (called syrah in other parts of the world). Blended wines are also common, including grenache/shiraz, grenache/cabernet sauvignon, merlot/cabernet sauvignon and cabernet sauvignon/malbec, some of which are unique to Australia. Australian wines are noted for their high alcohol content, which for reds can be up to 14.5 per cent. One of the most lauded and most expensive is Penfold's Grange Hermitage (recently declared a national icon!), which like some French wines is becoming too expensive to drink and is hoarded and traded like gold!

The most common white wine grapes are riesling, sauvignon blanc and chardonnay, although sémillon, gewürztraminer, muscadelle, colombard, chenin blanc, viognier, verdelho and marsanne are also grown. Blended white wines include sémillon/sauvignon, sémillon/chardonnay and Mitchelton's marsanne/viognier/roussanne (which must take first prize for originality and is also an excellent wine). Often grapes are blended from different regions, which is why Australia has no national wine appellation or quality control scheme. Buyers need to rely on the reputation of individual producers, which is generally an excellent guide, as there's little year-on-year variation in quality and reliability (you'll also rarely come across a bad, e.g. corked, bottle of Australian wine). Note that Australia has some 10,000 labels and interpreting them can be difficult for the uninitiated, although label information has improved considerably in recent years.

**Wineries:** Most producers welcome visitors and provide tastings, although you may need to make an appointment at the smaller wineries, which are often more attractive than the larger, more commercialised establishments. Some wineries charge a small fee of a few dollars (to deter freeloaders), which is refunded if you buy. Note, however, that wine at wineries isn't necessarily cheap and can be more expensive than at bottle shops. Some wineries have restaurants where you can sample local food and wines at the same time. Most regions have a visitors' centre, e.g. the Barossa Valley Visitors' Centre, which is open from 9am to 5pm Mondays to Fridays and from 10am to 4pm at weekends and on public holidays.

**Prices:** The price of Australian wine has been increasing steadily over the years and the best are now among the most expensive in the world. Even 'ordinary' wine is no longer the bargain it was some years ago and it's generally more expensive than in many European wine-producing countries owing to higher taxes. Prices have also increased in recent years owing to a shortage of quality grapes. A good 750ml bottle costs around $8 to $10, while $15 to $20 buys an excellent bottle. Imported wines are available in Australia, but are expensive compared with similar quality local wines.

Australia invented the wine box or cask ('chateau cardboard') in 1974; it consists of a plastic bag in a box with a built-in tap. Some two-thirds of all wine sold in Australia is sold in casks, over 60 per cent of which is dry or medium-dry white wine, 20 per cent dry red or sparkling wine, 10 per cent fortified and 10 per cent other types. Wine boxes are good value (but no longer the bargain they once were) and cost from $8 to $15 for three or four litres, up-market wines costing around $10 for a two-litre box. Most wine sold in boxes is every bit as good as the table wines sold in Europe and North America and some is outstanding. Boxes are particularly popular for parties and barbecues, and are also good for those who like the odd glass (the wine won't go off quickly as no air can get to it).

**Sparkling & Fortified Wines:** Australia also makes excellent sparkling wines (both red and white), which are produced by the *méthode champenoise* (fermented in the bottle), although they may no longer be called Champagne. An excellent bottle can be purchased for $12 to $16 (Yellowglen make some of the best). Australia is also noted for its fortified wines, although they aren't well known overseas. These include port (red and white), sherry, muscat, madeira, brandy and tokay (the last having little in common with the Hungarian wine after which it's named), the best of which are world-beaters. Port is a popular drink in Australia (it's made in Victoria), the best vintages selling for $80 to $100 per bottle (and a match for the best that Portugal has to offer), while a good non-vintage (such as Hardys Tall Ships Tawny Port) can be purchased for around $15.

**Information:** There are many books about Australian wine, including *Australian Wine - A Pictorial Guide*, *The Wines of Australia* by Oliver Mayo (Faber & Faber) and *The Penguin Good Australian Wine Guide* by Huon Hooke & Mark Shield (Penguin), which contains ratings for all of Australia's premium wines.

# Beer & Other Drinks

Before the second world war, Australia was largely a beer-drinking country, and Australians still consume far more beer than wine – over 100 litres per head annually. Bottled beer is sold in 375ml (stubbies) and 750ml bottles and in 375ml cans. The cost of a dozen 750ml bottles is around $30 to $40 or around $1.80 to $2.20 per bottle (a single 750ml bottle usually costs around $2.25). Most beer bottles have twist off caps, so no bottle-opener is required. Canned beer costs around $1.60 for single cans (375ml) reducing to around $1.20 per can when you buy a case of 24. Cheaper 'no name' beers cost around 20 per cent less than the market leaders and don't taste significantly different, although most people have their favourites. Aluminium cans are recycled, and there's a refund of a few cents per can to encourage the practice. For more information about Australian beer see **Bars & Pubs** on page 386.

Australians don't drink a lot of spirits such as whisky and gin (around a litre per head, per year). A bottle of Scotch whisky or London gin costs around $25 to $30 for the cheaper brands or around the same as in northern Europe. Australia's most famous spirit is rum, of which the Bundaberg ('Bundy') brand is the national spirit (there are also 'over-proof' varieties, which are lethal).

# DEPARTMENT & CHAIN STORES

Australia has a number of excellent department and chain stores. For the uninitiated, a department store is a large store, usually on several floors, which sells almost everything and may also include a food hall. Some stores have a department where shoe repairs, key cutting and engraving is done while you wait. Each floor is usually dedicated to a particular type of goods, such as ladies' or men's fashions or furniture and furnishings. Some stores are housed in beautiful art-deco or Victorian buildings and many are air-conditioned with a restaurant or cafeteria, telephones and toilets. Note that the floor at street level is designated the ground floor (not the first floor) in Australia, the floor above the ground floor is the first floor and the floor below the ground floor is usually called the basement.

The major department store chains in Australia include Grace Bros, Myer and David Jones. Sydney has David Jones (two stores, one with an excellent international food hall), Coles and Grace Bros, while Melbourne has Buckley & Nunn, Myer, Waltons, David Jones, George's (considered the 'Harrods' of Australia) and the Japanese store, Daimaru. Myer's store on Bourke Street Mall in Melbourne is the largest department store in the southern hemisphere and one of the ten largest in the world. Other department stores in Australia include David Jones, Myer and Fosseys in Canberra, Fitzgerald's and Myer in Hobart, Myer, David Jones and John Martin's (known locally as Johnny's) in Adelaide, Coles, David Jones and Myer in Brisbane, and Ahern's, Boans, Coles and Myer in Perth. Department stores have struggled in recent years, under pressure from no-frills retailers and discount stores, although some have been revitalised and are making a strong comeback.

A chain store is a store with a number of branches, usually in different towns, e.g. Woolworths, Target, Kmart and Harris Scarfe. There are dozens of chain stores in Australia, selling everything from electrical and household goods to books and clothes. Many department and chain stores provide customer accounts and allow the account balance to be repaid over a period of time, although this isn't usually wise as the interest rates are high. Many department and chain stores offer gift vouchers which can be redeemed at any branch. Department stores (and many smaller shops) provide a gift wrapping service, particularly at Christmas time, and will deliver goods locally or send them by post/courier, both within Australia and world wide.

# CLOTHES

Good clothes are relatively expensive in Australia, as there are high tariffs on imported clothing and footwear. The good news is that the mild climate most of the year means that most people don't need an extensive wardrobe.

It used to be said (with some justification) that fashions arrived in Australia a decade after they had swept Europe and North America, although this is certainly no longer the case. Today, Australian clothes stores offer a wide range of attire, from traditional made-to-measure clothing to the latest ready-to-wear fashions, with prices ranging from a few dollars to several thousand. Top quality and exclusive (i.e. expensive) international ladies' and men's fashion shops abound, and all the leading international labels are available in the major cities. In addition to department and chain stores, all towns and cities have a wealth of independent stores covering the whole fashion spectrum and all price brackets. Bush clothes (or 'bush chic') can be purchased at specialist shops, including R M Williams (whose clothing has achieved cult status) and the Thomas Cook Boot and Clothing Company in Sydney. Bush clothes include oilskin raincoats (e.g. Drizabone), riding boots, wide-brimmed Akubra hats, work shirts, moleskins (trousers made of closely woven cotton), sheepskin coats and leather belts.

In the early '70s, Australia had a thriving clothing manufacturing industry, but this has been decimated in the last 20 years. Australia also has a number of celebrated designers, some of whom have received international acclaim. Nowadays, most clothes are imported from Asia and many aren't up to the quality common in Europe and North America. However, although the quality of foreign-made clothes may occasionally be suspect, you usually get what you pay for. Most shops provide a tailoring or alteration service (for a small fee) and many stores also provide a made-to-measure service. Note that women's clothing manufacturers usually base their sizes on the average size 12, and many women find it difficult to find fashionable clothes that fit. Note also that the sizing of clothes in Australia follows the American rather than the UK system – i.e. 'medium' is usually on the large side (see **Appendix C** for a comparison of sizes).

Shopping malls and markets are the best place to shop for reasonably priced clothes, and mail order fashion offers (in newspapers and magazines) usually provide good value. Good clothes can also be purchased at huge savings from factory outlets, which also sell designer clothes (although you should try them for size and check for faults). If you're after designer clothes, the best time to buy is during the sales. There are vintage and secondhand clothing stores and markets in most Australian cities, plus clothes hire shops where you can hire anything from a ball gown to a wedding dress, a morning suit to evening dress (perfect for the office party).

**Shoes:** Many clothes stores sell shoes, and there's also a wide range of specialist shoe stores in Australia. Note, however, that Australia has few good shoemakers and quality imported shoes can be very expensive. Many people stock up on shoes before arriving in Australia and replenish their wardrobe on trips overseas. There are also sportswear shoe stores in most towns specialising in sports and leisure shoes (e.g. trainers). Shoe repair shops can be found in all towns and many department stores, and most high streets have a shop (or department) where repairs are carried out while you wait. Note, however, that the quality of repairs from a family cobbler may be superior to that of an 'instant' repair shop.

# NEWSPAPERS, MAGAZINES & BOOKS

Australians read more newspapers per head than most other nationalities, and some 600 are published, including national, state, city, regional and suburban newspapers. Most large regional cities have daily newspapers, and smaller towns publish weekly newspapers (there are also suburban weeklies in capital cities). There's an active foreign-language press in Australia catering to immigrants of many different nationalities and producing around 150 publications in 40 languages. In general, the Australian press is fairly parochial and provides scant coverage of foreign news (unless it's a major news item), and you shouldn't expect unbiased political reporting in Australian newspapers, which often reflect the political bias of their owners. The law regarding cross-media ownership is restrictive and has led to clashes between the government and media interests (foreign ownership is limited to 15 per cent).

Most major newspapers are owned by a few press barons, including Rupert Murdoch (whose News Corporation owns some 60 per cent of the Australian print media) and Kerry Packer (Publishing and Broadcasting). Daily and Sunday newspapers range from the broadsheet 'quality' newspapers (those that are difficult to read in confined spaces) for serious readers and the popular tabloids (for those who just like to look at pictures). There are just two national dailies, *The Australian* (including *The Weekend Australian* on Saturdays) and *The Australian Financial Review* (Mondays to Fridays only). *The Australian* is Australia's foremost newspaper and is printed simultaneously at six sites around the country from Mondays to Fridays. Other major papers are either published state-wide or limited to one city. Those with the largest circulation are *The Herald-Sun* (Melbourne), *The Daily Telegraph* (Sydney), *The Sydney Morning Herald* and *The West Australian* (Perth), *The Courier Mail* (Brisbane), *The Age* (Melbourne) and *The Advertiser* (Adelaide).

Most dailies publish larger Saturday editions, which usually sell around 50 per cent more copies than the weekly editions and may include weekend supplements, e.g. *The Weekend Australian* and the *The Sydney Morning Herald*. The major Sunday newspapers include *The Sunday Telegraph* (Sydney), *The Sunday Mail* (Brisbane), *The Sun-Herald* (Sydney), *The Sunday Herald-Sun* (Melbourne), *The Sunday Times* (Perth), *The Sunday Mail* (Adelaide) and *The Sunday Age* (Melbourne). Most Sunday newspapers are tabloids and aren't as good quality as some of the weekly newspapers. Most cities also have evening newspapers. The circulation figures of Australian newspapers are relatively small by international standards, ranging from around 130,000 for *The Australian* to 720,000 for *The Sunday Telegraph*.

Foreign newspapers are available from international news agencies in major cities and cost around $5, or $9 for the larger Sunday editions, although they're usually a few days old when they arrive in Australia. They are also available in some (e.g. state) libraries. Newspapers of particular interest to British expatriates include the *Guardian Weekly*, *Weekly Telegraph*, *International Express* and *UK Mail*, all of which are published weekly and contain a run-down of the week's most important news (they're also available on subscription).

**Magazines:** Australians are avid magazine readers, around 1,000 of which are published every month, plus a further 700 trade publications. Foreign magazines are also popular and widely available in the major cities (particularly British and American magazines). Popular Australian political and business magazines include the *Business Review Weekly*, The *Bulletin* (Australia's oldest magazine, but now effectively controlled by the American *Time* magazine), *Australian Business*, and an Australian edition of the American *Newsweek* magazine. Women's magazines abound and include *The Australian Women's Weekly* (which is actually published monthly and sells around 1 million copies), *Women's Day* (which is a weekly), *Family Circle*, *New Idea* and *Australian Good Housekeeping*. There are also Australian editions of many international women's magazines, including *Cosmopolitan*, *Marie Claire* and *Vogue*.

Newsagents in the ACT, New South Wales, Queensland and Victoria have a monopoly on newspaper distribution to homes, milk bars and convenience stores. Newsagents are open long hours in major cities and also on Sundays. Prices are generally higher in remote areas and states other than where a newspaper is published, owing to the high cost of distribution. Some cafés and tea rooms provide free newspapers for customers to read (not take home), and newspapers can also be read in public libraries and at newspaper offices. The good news for foreigners and computer users is that most Australian and foreign newspapers and magazines can be accessed via the Internet. You can also take out a subscription to your favourite foreign newspapers and magazines at a large saving over local newsagent prices (if you're willing to wait a few weeks or months for delivery).

**Books:** Australians are avid book readers, and all Australian cities have a wealth of bookshops (with luck all selling this book). Australia also has a flourishing publishing industry. Angus & Robertson's Bookworld and Dymocks are the largest chains of bookshops and are represented in most major cities (Dymocks in Sydney claims to be the largest bookshop in the southern hemisphere). Many department stores also have book departments. Melbourne is reckoned to be the best city for bookshops in Australia, with Sydney not far behind. Many bookshops are open during the evening (some until midnight) and at weekends in major cities. Several also offer Internet sales sites where you can purchase new and used books.

There are specialist bookshops in major cities covering topics such as travel, art, children's subjects, feminism, gay and lesbian interests, the new age, backpacking, 'Australiana' and antiquarianism. In many towns there are 'remainder' or cut-price bookshops, and in the major cities there are secondhand bookshops for collectors and bargain hunters. Many large bookshops in cities also have a selection of foreign-language books, and there are ethnic bookshops in some areas serving local ethnic communities. Government publications can be purchased at Commonwealth

Government Bookshops in the major cities or by mail from the Australian Government Publishing Service, GPO Box 84, Canberra, ACT 2601.

Note that books aren't sold at fixed prices in Australia, and locally published books are typically sold at a 10 per cent discount. However, imported books can be expensive and are usually marked up by 25 to 50 per cent. Book tokens are sold and accepted by most bookshops. Many organisations and clubs run their own libraries or book exchanges and public libraries usually have an excellent selection of books.

# FURNITURE

Furniture is usually good value in Australia, where there's a wide choice of modern and contemporary designs in every price range, although (as with most things) you generally get what you pay for. Exclusive imported furniture is available (with matching exclusive prices), although imports also include reasonably priced quality leather suites and a wide range of cane furniture from Asia. Among the largest furniture chain stores in Australia are Harvey Norman, Freedom Furniture and KC Country Furniture, plus the major department stores, all of which offer a wide range of top quality Australian-made and imported furniture. It costs around $10,000 to furnish an average three-bedroom home, although secondhand furniture is widely available. Furniture can also be rented for around $200 to $300 per month for an average home.

Note that, when ordering furniture, you may have to wait weeks or months for delivery. Try to find a store which has what you want in stock or which will give you a guaranteed delivery date (after which you can cancel and receive a full refund if you wish). A number of manufacturers sell direct to the public, although you shouldn't assume that this will result in huge savings and should compare prices and quality before buying. There are also stores specialising in beds, leather, reproduction and antique furniture, and a number of companies manufacture and install fitted bedrooms and kitchens. Note that fitted kitchens are an extremely competitive business in Australia and you should be wary of 'cowboy' companies who are specialists in shoddy workmanship.

If you want reasonably priced, quality, modern furniture, there are a number of companies (e.g. Ikea, which is hugely popular) selling furniture for home assembly (which helps keep down prices). Assembly instructions are generally easy to follow (although some people think Rubik's cube is easier) and some companies print instructions in a number of languages. Retailers will often assemble furniture for you, although this increases the price. All large furniture retailers publish catalogues, which are generally distributed free of charge. Some stores offer you $100 or $200 for your old suite when you buy a new one from them. However, this may not be much of a bargain, particularly if your suite is worth more than the amount offered, and you should always shop around for the best price and quality available.

Furniture and furnishings is a competitive business in Australia, and you can often reduce the price by some judicious haggling, particularly if you're spending a large amount of money. Some stores will match a competitor's price rather than lose a sale. Another way to save money is to wait for the sales. If you cannot wait and don't want to (or cannot afford to) pay cash, look for an interest-free credit deal. Check the advertisements in local newspapers and national home and design magazines such as *Australian Home Beautiful*, *Australian House & Garden* and *Better Homes and*

*Gardens*. See also *The Bargain Shoppers* guides to Melbourne and Sydney (see page 427).

# HOUSEHOLD APPLIANCES

Large household appliances such as cookers and refrigerators are usually provided in rented accommodation and may also be fitted in new homes. Many homeowners include fitted kitchen appliances such as a cooker, refrigerator, dishwasher and washing machine when selling their house or apartment, although you may need to pay for them separately. Dishwashers (the mechanical type, not the wife or husband) are still something of a luxury item in Australia and aren't usually found in rented accommodation. There's a wide range of household appliances in Australia, from both Australian and foreign manufacturers. Note that some appliances such as refrigerators cost twice as much to run as others (choose those with a high energy efficiency rating). Note that refrigerators/freezers in Australia are normally 'tropicised' or fan-assisted to cope with the high average temperatures.

If you wish to bring large appliances with you, such as a refrigerator, washing machine or dishwasher, note that the standard Australian unit width isn't the same as in other countries. Check the size and the latest Australian safety regulations before shipping these items to Australia, as they may need expensive modifications. On the other hand, if you already own small household appliances, it's worthwhile bringing them to Australia, as usually all that is required is a change of plug (but check first). If you're coming from a country with a 110/115V electricity supply (e.g. the USA), you'll need a lot of expensive transformers (see page 144). Don't bring a TV to Australia as it won't work (see page 182). A huge choice of home appliances is available in Australia, where smaller appliances such as vacuum cleaners, grills, toasters and electric irons aren't expensive and are usually of good quality. It pays to shop around, as quality, reliability and prices vary considerably (the more expensive imported brands are usually the most reliable).

Before buying household appliances, whether large or small, it may pay you to check the test reports in *Choice* magazine (see page 443) at your local library. The cost of major household items is listed in the free *Cost of Living and Housing Survey* published annually by the Commonwealth Bank of Australia.

If you need kitchen measuring equipment and cannot cope with decimal measures, you'll have to bring your own measuring scales, jugs, cups (American and Australian recipe cups aren't the same size) and thermometers (see also **Appendix C**). Note also that Australian pillows and duvets aren't the same size or shape as in many other countries.

# SECONDHAND BARGAINS

There's a lively secondhand market in Australia for almost everything, from antiques to motor cars, computers to photographic equipment. You name it and somebody will be selling it secondhand. With such a large secondhand market there are often bargains to be found, particularly if you're quick off the mark. Many towns have a local secondhand or junk store and charity shops (e.g. Salvation Army or Vincent de Paul), selling new and secondhand articles for charity, where most of your money goes to help those in need. There are a number of national and regional weekly newspapers devoted to bargain hunters such as the *Trading Post* in Sydney.

If you're looking for a particular item, such as a camera, boat or motorcycle, you may be better off browsing the small ads in specialist magazines than those in more general newspapers or magazines. Classified ads in local newspapers are also a good source of bargains, particularly for furniture and household appliances. Shopping centre (mall) and newsagent bulletin boards and company notice boards may also prove fruitful. Expatriate club newsletters are a good source of household items, which are often sold cheaply by those returning home. Another place to pick up a bargain is at an auction, although it helps to have specialist knowledge about what you're buying (you'll probably be competing with experts). Auctions are held in Australia throughout the year for everything from antiques and paintings to motorcars and property. Local auctions are widely advertised in newspapers and via leaflets.

There are antique shops and centres in most towns, and street markets and fairs are common in the major cities (where you can pick up interesting Australiana – but you must get there early to beat the dealers to the best buys). For information about markets, inquire at your local tourist office or library. Car boot (trunk) sales are gaining popularity in Australia, and yard sales, where people sell their surplus belongings at bargain prices, are also popular. Sales may be advertised in local newspapers and signposted on local roads (they're usually held at weekends).

# HOME SHOPPING

Home shopping by mail, phone, fax or computer (using on-line computer services or the Internet) has become increasingly popular in recent years. Direct marketing is worth some $5 billion a year in Australia, 75 per cent through direct mail and catalogues, with the remainder through tele-marketing. Mail-order catalogue shopping has long been popular in Australia, particularly among people living in remote areas. In addition to dedicated mail-order companies, most major department stores also provide mail-order catalogues. Direct retailing is fairly common in Australia, particularly for computers, office equipment and supplies, and financial and insurance services. TV shopping is also becoming increasingly popular and products sold through infomercials have already had a huge success. There are two, 24-hour pay TV shopping channels in Australia, the TV Shopping Network (TVSN) and The Value Channel (TVC). TVSN offers some 4,000 individual product lines, an unconditional money-back guarantee and delivery in five to ten working days (at a fixed rate anywhere in the world).

**Internet:** Shopping via the Internet is a fairly recent innovation but is growing at a huge pace (Australia is second only to the USA in the number of Internet users per head of population) and is expected to dominate retailing in the next century. Food retailers such as Woolworth and Coles Myer have introduced Internet food shopping, although deliveries are usually only to metropolitan areas. Under present rules, consumers are exempted from goods and services tax (GST) and customs duty when imported mail-order goods attract a total tax bill of less then $50. You can buy virtually anything over the Internet, and large savings can be made on goods that don't incur high postage or shipping costs. Australians are increasingly using the Internet to buy products such as CDs, books and sporting goods (e.g. fishing equipment) from the USA, on which savings can be substantial. Note that when buying expensive goods overseas, you should always insure them for their full value.

It's estimated that some $2 billion per year is lost in sales and taxes on overseas

Internet sales, which prompted the Australian government to launch an investigation. Australia is more concerned than many other nations, as overseas traders can easily undercut Australian prices and circumvent Australia's high import tariffs and taxes, which could become a real threat to Australia's economy. Note that Australian banks don't officially allow businesses to accept credit card orders over the Internet, although many businesses ignore this edict, as banks have no way of knowing whether an order was received over the Internet or by some other means.

Note that home shopping can be a minefield and, although you have the same rights as when shopping in-store, they're more difficult to enforce. However, new security standards have been introduced in recent years such as the Secure Electronic Transaction (SET) standard, which makes Internet shopping much safer. Nevertheless, before committing yourself to buying anything from home, always make sure you know your rights and don't send cash through the post or pay for goods in advance unless absolutely necessary (and you have a cast-iron, money-back guarantee). It's always sensible to investigate mail-order and Internet companies and to pay by credit card, as you may then have redress against the credit card company if goods don't materialise or aren't as advertised. If a local company is a specialist mail-order trading company, make sure they're a member of the Australian Direct Marketing Association (ADMA), which has a code of conduct and offers assistance to consumers (☎ 02-9368 0366, 💻 www.adma.com.au). The ADMA also offers extensive advice on e-commerce. You should be wary of doing business with companies in offshore locations, as there are a number of offshore scams (including fake credit cards, phoney lottery tickets, worthless phone cards, Internet gambling and pyramid schemes). **If anything sounds too good to be true, it almost certainly is!**

# DUTY-FREE ALLOWANCES

Visitors or migrants coming to Australia are permitted to import the following goods duty-free:

- 1,125ml (1.125 litres) of alcoholic drinks, including wine, beer or spirits, per person over 18 years of age;
- 250g of tobacco products (for customs purposes, 250 cigarettes are equal to 250g) per person over 18 years of age;
- all personal clothing and footwear (excluding furs);
- articles for personal hygiene/grooming such as toiletries, but excluding perfume concentrate;
- articles taken out of Australia on departure, but excluding articles purchased duty and/or sales tax free in Australia (any duty/tax free goods are counted against your duty-free allowance);
- any other articles (except alcohol and tobacco) obtained overseas or duty and sales tax free in Australia, up to a total purchase price of $400 per person aged 18 or over ($200 for under 18s) – this includes goods intended as gifts or received as gifts, whether personal or carried on behalf of others;

Members of the same family travelling together may combine their individual duty-free allowances. Duty and/or sales tax must be paid on any goods above the duty-free allowance, excess articles being valued for duty/tax on the price paid for them, converted to Australian dollars. However, duty and/or sales tax up to $50 is waived on goods in excess of duty-free concessions, provided that the goods are declared as excess to concessions and aren't for commercial purposes. If purchase receipts aren't available, alternative methods of valuation may be used. Some items (such as jewellery) are subject to high rates of duty and/or sales tax. Payment of duty and tax can be made in cash, by travellers' cheque (in A$) and by international credit card. Information can be obtained from state customs offices (see **Appendix A**) or the Australian Customs Service, GPO Box 148, Fyshwick, ACT 2609.

One unusual feature at Australian airports is in-bound, duty-free shops where you can buy alcohol and tobacco products and a limited range of perfumes and cosmetics before you reach immigration and customs. There are also city duty-free shops where you can buy duty-free goods (upon presentation of a valid international air ticket) before going to the airport to catch your plane. Check the prices here first as they're usually lower than at airports. Purchases must usually be taken from the shop in a sealed bag (marked 'Important – Duty-Free Goods in Possession') that you must keep intact until you've boarded your flight. Alcohol, cigarettes, perfume and jewellery must be purchased within ten days of your departure and kept sealed until you've left Australia. However, some goods such as cameras, film, watches and most electronic goods can be used as soon as they're purchased. The maximum permitted value of purchases is $400, which are listed on your ticket and must be shown to customs officers at airports, so you must take them with you as hand baggage when leaving the country (so don't buy a life-size toy kangaroo!).

**GST Tourist Refund:** A GST refund is available to tourists leaving Australia on goods to the value of over $300. In order to obtain the refund, the goods must be bought at a registered shop or business, where a tax invoice must be obtained, and must be exported within 30 days of purchase. When you leave Australia, you should present to a customs officer the tax invoice and you may also be required to present the purchased goods, your passport and your departure documents (e.g. airline ticket). If the amount refundable is less than $200, you'll probably receive it in cash. If the amount is larger, you must lodge a payment authorisation with instructions on how you wish the money to be repaid to you (by credit card, payment to an Australian bank account or by cheque). Note that GST refunds can be be reclaimed only at airports or seaports with a TRS verification facility. Note also that GST is not refundable on duty-free goods.

## CONSUMER RIGHTS

If you buy something which is faulty, damaged or doesn't work or measure up to the manufacturer's or vendor's claims, you can return it and obtain a replacement or your money back. Note that extended warranties or money-back guarantees don't affect your statutory rights as a purchaser, although the legal status of a warranty may be unclear. Some stores offer an unconditional refund or exchange of goods, which isn't required by law, although this guarantee is usually only for a short period and goods must be returned unused and as new.

You have the right to a refund or replacement goods if you buy a faulty product (with the exception of goods purchased at auction). Signs such as 'no refunds given', 'no responsibility for loss or damage', 'goods left for repair at your own risk' and 'all care but no responsibility taken' are meaningless and unlawful under state and federal laws. All goods must be of 'merchantable' (reasonable) quality and fit for the purpose for which they were sold, and it's illegal for sellers to include a clause in the conditions of sale that exempts them from liability for defects, product faults or lack of care. Most traders will back down once you show that you know the law and are determined to obtain your rights.

There are a number of consumers' organisations in Australia, including consumer affairs bureaux, fair trading bureaux, citizens' advice bureaux, ombudsmen and small claims tribunals (see also **Legal & General Advice** on page 458). A consumer affairs bureau will give general advice over the phone, but won't usually take any action on a complaint unless it's made in writing or in person. If you make a complaint, the bureau will give you advice, write to the trader concerned on your behalf, or may refer your complaint to another government or consumer body to investigate. Note, however, that callers are often given poor or incorrect advice. If you're unable to resolve a dispute with a trader or tradesman, you can take a dispute to a small claims or consumer claims court or tribunal for a small application fee. Note that claims are limited to $2,000 in Tasmania, $3,000 in New South Wales (up to $25,000 for building disputes) and $5,000 in all other states and territories. Traders who fall foul of the Trade Practices Act can be fined up to $20,000.

The consumers' champion in Australia is the Australian Consumers Association (57 Carrington Road, Marrickville, NSW 2204, ☎ 02-9577 3399, 🖳 www. choice. com.au), which publishes a number of magazines for consumers, including *Choice*, their general consumer magazine, *Health Reader*, *Money Choice*, *Computer Choice*, *Choice Travel* and *Consuming Interest* (a quarterly magazine about consumer issues). The ACA also publishes and distributes a wide range of consumer-oriented books. *Choice* contains independent tests of products and services and is essential reading when buying major household goods. Magazines are available only on subscription  and not from newsagents. The ACA also provides a Consumer Information Service (☎ 02-9577 3399).

# 18.

# ODDS & ENDS

This chapter contains miscellaneous information. Although all topics aren't of vital importance, most are of general interest to anyone planning to live or work in Australia, including everything you ever wanted to know (but were afraid to ask) about tipping and toilets.

# ABORIGINES

The ancestors of the Aborigines are thought to have travelled from south-east Asia and arrived in Australia at least 45,000 years ago, although some experts believe it could be nearer 60,000. When the first Europeans set up a colony in NSW in 1788, there were thought to be some 300,000 Aborigines living in Australia in tribes, either semi-nomadic or sedentary. Like most tribes, the Aborigines have always lived in harmony with their environment, which they've used to maximum advantage to live off the land, making the most of the adverse climatic and geographical conditions.

In spite of the Aborigine presence, the European settlers treated their new home as *terra nullius* (no man's land) and refused to recognise Aborigine land rights. Over the next two centuries Aborigines were driven from their land, systematically slaughtered or forced to do low-paid agricultural work, as well as suffering vast casualties from imported European diseases such as smallpox and influenza. In the early twentieth century, most Aborigines were confined to government reserves or in Christian missions. The Federation then introduced its now infamous 'assimilation policy', under which the federal government had complete jurisdiction over Aborigine lives including legal custody over Aborigine children, many of whom were taken away from their families and put into foster homes or training centres. This generation of Aborigines is now referred to as the 'stolen generation'.

It was not until 1976 that the first Aborigine Land Rights Act was passed in the Northern Territory, where about half of all land is now under Aborigine jurisdiction, including Uluru. In the rest of the country, very little land has been returned to the Aborigines. Aborigine welfare is a major problem facing Australia – Aborigines have a life expectancy of 20 years less than that of white Australians and an unemployment rate four times higher as well as numerous other problems such as alcohol and substance dependency. Amnesty International annually launches a scathing attack on Australia's treatment of Aborigines, and the biggest discrimination problem in Australia remains the 'Aboriginal question'. Australia's record in trying to improve the living standards of its indigenous peoples over the last 25 years is among the worst in the developed world, and many Aborigines live in squalor and serious disadvantage in a way that shames Australia to Australians and to the world. However, decent Australians are appalled by the plight of many Aborigines and most want them to get a better deal (provided it doesn't cost them any money or land). Although attitudes have improved, much is still left to be done in order to reconcile the two societies. The Labor Party has made an election pledge to formally apologise on behalf of the Australian people to the Aborigine people, and there is firm national support for official reconciliation.

# CITIZENSHIP

Immigrants are eligible for Australian citizenship after just two years residence in the previous five years, including the 12 months immediately prior to their application, which costs $120. Applicants must be permanent residents, be at least 18 years of age, have a basic knowledge of the English language, be capable of understanding the nature of their citizenship application and understand the responsibilities and privileges of Australian citizenship, be of good character, and be likely to live in Australia or maintain a close and continuing association with Australia. The ability to speak English doesn't apply to people over aged 50, and those over 60 aren't required to understand the responsibilities and privileges of Australian citizenship.

Exceptions to the above rules apply to armed forces personnel (who need only to have served for three months), former Australian citizens (who need only to have been resident for 12 months in the last two years), spouses, widows, widowers of Australian citizens (who normally need to have been resident only for the 12 months prior to their application), permanent residents not present in Australia but engaged in activities beneficial to Australia, and various others. In certain cases, such as that of spouses/widows/widowers of Australian citizens, applicants must show that they would suffer significant hardship or disadvantage if they weren't granted citizenship.

Most people born in Australia before 26th January 1949 automatically became Australian citizens on that day, and those born between 26th January 1949 and 20th August 1986 automatically became Australian citizens unless one of their parents was a foreign diplomatic or consular official. Since 20th August 1986, citizenship has been acquired if, at the time of a person's birth in Australia, at least one parent was either an Australian citizen or a permanent Australian resident. Those born overseas to an Australian citizen can apply for registration as an Australian citizen by descent if they meet certain criteria. A child who is a permanent resident and legally adopted in Australia (after 22nd November 1994) automatically acquires Australian citizenship if at least one parent is an Australian citizen at the time of the adoption.

New citizens must make a 'pledge of commitment': "From this time forward, under God, I pledge my loyalty to Australia and its people, whose democratic beliefs I share, whose rights and liberties I respect, and whose laws I will uphold and obey." (Note that the words 'under God' may be omitted). The benefits of citizenship include the right to run for public office and to enlist in the defence and police forces and undertake certain other public service jobs, the right to be protected under Australian diplomatic arrangements overseas, the right to claim full welfare benefits, the right to register children born overseas as Australian citizens and the right to vote (Australian citizens are not only obliged to enrol on the electoral register, but obliged to vote in general elections as well!). If you're granted Australian citizenship, you can retain your foreign passport (provided the country of issue permits dual nationality) and obtain an Australian passport. Once you're an Australian citizen, you must use your Australian passport to enter and leave Australia.

Around 16 million people have Australian citizenship and a further 970,000 are eligible for citizenship. Some 75,000 people are granted citizenship each year, although only around one in ten immigrants becomes an Australian citizen (despite the fact that some 80 per cent of immigrants interviewed within six months of their arrival claim they will take out citizenship). British immigrants are the least likely to become Australian citizens. In 2001 the government launched a citizenship 'drive' coinciding with the Federation Centenary Year to try to persuade permanent residents to become citizens. There's a comprehensive website available (⌨ www. citizenship.gov.au).

# CLIMATE

The biggest attraction of Australia for many immigrants, particularly those from the northern hemisphere, is its temperate climate and the lifestyle it affords. Australia is an 'upside down' country (weather-wise) with the warmest part (nearest the equator) at the top and the coldest at the bottom. It's less prone to climate extremes than other continents of comparable size, because it's surrounded by seas and has few high mountain masses. Australia's seasons are the opposite of the Northern Hemisphere, i.e. when it's summer in Europe it's winter in Australia and vice versa. The most pleasant seasons in most of Australia are spring and autumn, with the exception of Tasmania where summer is the most enjoyable season. Australia has climates to suit everyone (bar Eskimos), although it broadly has just two climatic zones. Some 40 per cent of Australia lies in the tropical zone, while the remaining regions (south of the Tropic of Capricorn) are in the temperate zone. The tropical zone has just two seasons: wet (November to April) and dry (May to October), while the temperate zones have four seasons: Spring (September to November), Summer (December to February), Autumn (March to May) and Winter (June to August).

The average hours of sunshine per day in Australia's capital cities ranges from five in Hobart to eight in Perth. January is the hottest month in most southern regions, while February is hottest in Tasmania and southern Victoria. Average summer temperatures in January range from around 17°C (63°F) in Hobart to 29°C (84°F) in Alice Springs and Darwin. Temperatures exceed 30°C (86°F) in most areas during summer, and temperatures occasionally soar to 45°C (113°F). The hottest place in Australia is Marble Bar (WA), where the temperature from October to March usually averages 40°C (104°F) or more. The highest recorded temperature in Australia is 53.1°C (127°F), measured at Cloncurry (QLD) in 1889. If you cannot stand extreme heat, choose Hobart, Adelaide, Melbourne or Sydney rather than Perth, Brisbane or Darwin.

Australia has the lowest rainfall of any continent after Antarctica, with average annual rainfall for the capital cities varying from 1,536mm (60.4in) in Darwin, which is in the monsoon region, to 530mm (21in) in Adelaide. During the wet season in the north (January to March), roads can quickly become impassable as tracks turn into raging rivers after a downpour. In contrast, large arid inland areas get less than 250mm (10in) of rain per year. In winter, temperatures can fall below 10°C (50°F) on winter nights in most regions, and sleet can fall on the urban areas of Hobart and even in Canberra and Adelaide. Snow is rare except in the Australian Alps, straddling the New South Wales/Victoria border, where it's possible to ski between June and October.

**NSW/Sydney:** New South Wales has a huge variety of weather, although it generally has an equable climate. Sydney has the highest rainfall of any Australian capital city at 1,140mm (45in), which is spread fairly evenly throughout the year, including summer. In Sydney it rains on some 150 days a year, the wettest months being April to June. It has mild winters, when daytime temperatures rarely fall below 10°C (50°F) and can reach 17°C (63°F). Summer temperatures average around 25°C (77°F), although they can be quite humid, particularly from January to March. Occasionally, the temperature in Sydney exceeds 40°C and can still be 30°C at midnight, although this is rare, as cool sea breezes help lower temperatures during heat waves. Sydney frequently has high pollution levels in summer.

**ACT/Canberra:** Canberra has four distinct seasons, with hot dry summers and cold winters. It's situated inland, so the climate isn't moderated by the ocean as in Australia's coastal cities. Canberra is the coldest capital city in winter, with temperatures plunging to around freezing at night, although it rarely snows. Winter mornings are frosty but most days are bright and sunny, temperatures averaging around 12°C (54°F). Annual rainfall is low at around 660mm (26in). The ACT has an average of seven hours sunshine per day, summer temperatures averaging around 27°C (81°F). Canberra is noted for its clean air and isn't prone to pollution in summer.

**Queensland/Brisbane:** Queensland has a sub-tropical climate in the south and is tropical in the north, with wet and dry seasons. Summer is the wet season, when rainfall averages around 1,000mm (40in), particularly in the north, where violent thunderstorms and floods are common. The state has the wettest town in Australia, Tully, with over 4,000mm (160in) of rain per year (four times that of Brisbane). Extremes of flood and drought are common in country areas. Brisbane is one of the sunniest cities in Australia, with an average of over 7.5 hours per day and mild sunny winters. Average temperatures are between 10°C (50°F) and 21°C (70°F) in winter and between 21°C (70°F) and 29°C (84°F) in summer. Summer temperatures can, however, exceed 38°C (100°F), and humidity can be very high, although it's usually tempered by cool sea breezes in coastal areas.

**Victoria/Melbourne:** The Victorian climate is somewhere between maritime and continental. The weather in Melbourne can be extremely changeable, and it's said that you can experience all four seasons in one day (rather like Britain). Victoria has a generally mild climate, although it can experience very hot and cold periods. Melbourne experiences cold, wet and windy weather in autumn and winter, although temperatures rarely fall below 5°C (41°F) with highs of around 14°C (57°F). Mountainous regions have snow in winter, when temperatures remain below freezing for long periods. It has low rainfall of around 660mm (26in), half that of Sydney and Brisbane, and this is fairly evenly spread throughout the year (June and July are the wettest months). Melbourne has mild autumns (the most pleasant season) and hot summers, when temperatures average 25°C (77°F) and occasionally soar to 40°C (104°F).

**South Australia/Adelaide:** South Australia has an almost Mediterranean climate, characterised by long, dry summers and short mild winters, and is said to have the best year-round climate in Australia. Adelaide is noted for its low rainfall (the lowest of any state capital) at just 530mm (21in), which falls mainly between April and October. South Australia is the driest state and its northern regions are mostly desert. It's sunny and not too cold in winter, when average temperatures are between 8°C (46°F) and 16°C (61°F). There's an average of four hours sunshine per day in winter and seven hours in summer. Summers are hot with maximum temperatures averaging over 27°C (80°F), although nights aren't usually too hot and there's low humidity. It's very hot in the northern desert regions, where summer temperatures are frequently over 40°C (104°F).

**Western Australia/Perth:** The southern areas of Western Australia enjoy a Mediterranean climate, while northern areas have a tropical climate with dry and wet seasons. Perth is the sunniest capital city in Australia with an average annual temperature of 18°C (64°F) and over eight hours sunshine per day. Spring and autumn are the most pleasant seasons. The average rainfall is low at 914mm (36in) per year (although it's over 1,500mm/60in on the south-west coast) and it falls mainly between April and October. The northern and eastern regions have very low rainfall and consist mostly of desert. Winters in Perth are mild and sunny but wet, with average temperatures of between 9°C (48°F) and 18°C (64°F), although frost is common away from the coastal areas. Summers are very hot, with daytime temperatures frequently between 30°C (86°F) and 40°C (104°F) and hot nights, although it's a dry rather than humid heat. The summer heat is mitigated by cool breezes that blow in off the sea from Fremantle west of Perth, called the Fremantle Doctor for its soothing effect (some enterprising locals bottle it and sell it to tourists!).

**Northern Territory/Darwin/Alice Springs:** The Northern Territory has a tropical climate with just two seasons: wet from November to April (also known as the 'green' season) and dry for the remainder of the year. Basically, the weather is as hot as hell all year round, with average daily temperatures in Darwin between 20 and 33°C (68 and 91°F) and reaching over 40°C (104°F) for weeks on end in the central desert regions (and Alice Springs). Rainfall is almost non-existent in Darwin from May to September, which is more than compensated for between December and March, when it's between 250 and 380mm (10 and 15in). The heat and humidity is often oppressive, with humidity as high as 95 per cent just before the start of the wet season. The Northern Territory is prone to cyclones and violent thunderstorms. Alice Springs has an average of 9.5 hours' sunshine a day, with warm winters and hot, dry summers. Summer evenings can be cool, while in winter the temperature often falls below freezing at night. Alice has low annual rainfall, with an average of around 40mm (1.5in) falling between December and February.

**Tasmania/Hobart:** Tasmania has a temperate climate, with four distinct seasons, but is without the extremes of the mainland cities. It's the coldest part of Australia and is occasionally hit by icy southerly winds from Antarctica, although it's still relatively mild by northern European standards. Nights can be cool throughout the year, although winters aren't as cold as in Canberra and Alice Springs. The average winter temperature in Hobart is between 5°C (41°F) and 12°C (54°F). It has around 620cm (25in) of rain per year (half that of Sydney and Brisbane), rain falling on around half the days of the year, mostly between July and October. In the west, rainfall is around four times that of Hobart. Hobart enjoys an average of around five hours of sunshine per day, maximum summer temperatures averaging around 21°C (70°F). Water temperatures are much lower than the rest of Australia, and it's generally too cold for sea bathing.

**Natural Disasters:** Australia is hit by frequent natural disasters, including droughts, floods, cyclones, bush fires, earthquakes and tropical storms. Periodic droughts are a way of life and a constant worry for farmers. In many rural areas, rivers are sucked almost dry by the demand for water for irrigation, causing many to slow to a trickle and the water to become polluted by toxic algae (rivers are also polluted by salt and are dying). There are frequent (sometimes permanent) water restrictions in most regions of Australia, even in the major cities. The Australian weather is periodically (e.g. in 1997) affected by *El Niño*, an ocean warming phenomenon where prevailing cold water currents along the west coast of South America become warmer, thus upsetting weather patterns and leading to floods in North and South America and droughts in Australia.

Bush fires are a constant threat in country areas (mainly in summer), which are often caused by lightning strikes (many are also deliberately lit). They often threaten country towns and occasionally major cities, and deaths among fire-fighters and homeowners are frequent (some people needlessly lose their lives because they refuse to abandon their homes). Lighting fires in a bush fire zone is strictly forbidden; even where it's permitted, you must ensure that every spark is extinguished before leaving and must *never* throw cigarette butts out of car windows. Earthquakes are rare in Australia, although in 1989 one struck Newcastle (NSW), killing 13 people, injuring 160 and causing damage costing $1.7 billion.

Cyclones (known as 'blows') are fairly common in the summer months (between November and April) in the northern regions of Australia (from Western Australia to Queensland). In 1974, cyclone Tracey flattened Darwin with gusts of up to 280kph (174mph). It killed 66 people and destroyed more than 5,000 homes leaving fewer than 500 intact in what was the worst natural disaster in Australia's modern history. The city has since been completely rebuilt to 'withstand' cyclones. More recently, Exmouth in Western Australia was devastated by Cyclone Vance in 1999. Violent tropical and electrical storms are common in the north of Australia, particularly northern Queensland. In January 1998, torrential rains in Townsville caused widespread flooding when 500mm (20in) of rain fell in just 12 hours.

Approximate average daily maximum/minimum temperatures for Australia's major cities are shown below in Centigrade and, in brackets, Fahrenheit. (A quick way to make a *rough* conversion from Centigrade to Fahrenheit is to multiply by two and add 30 – see also **Appendix C**.)

| City | Spring | Summer | Autumn | Winter |
|---|---|---|---|---|
| Adelaide | 22/11 (72/52) | 28/17 (82/63) | 22/12 (72/54) | 16/8 (61/46) |
| Alice Springs | 30/14 (86/57) | 35/21 (95/70) | 18/13 (82/55) | 20/7 (68/45) |
| Brisbane | 26/16 (79/61) | 29/21 (84/70) | 26/16 (79/61) | 21/10 (70/50) |
| Cairns | 29/21 (84/70) | 31/24 (88/75) | 29/22 (84/72) | 26/18 (79/64) |
| Canberra | 19/6 (66/43) | 27/12 (81/54) | 20/7 (68/45) | 12/1 (54/34) |
| Darwin | 33/24 (91/75) | 32/25 (90/77) | 32/23 (90/73) | 30/20 (86/68) |
| Hobart | 17/8 (63/46) | 21/12 (70/54) | 17/9 (63/48) | 12/5 (54/41) |
| Melbourne | 20/9 (68/48) | 25/14 (77/57) | 20/11 (68/52) | 14/7 (57/45) |
| Perth | 22/12 (72/54) | 29/17 (84/63) | 24/14 (75/57) | 18/9 (64/48) |
| Sydney | 22/13 (72/55) | 26/18 (79/64) | 22/14 (72/57) | 17/9 (63/48) |

The weather forecast is available via TV teletext services, in daily newspapers, and on TV and radio broadcasts. Warnings of dangerous weather conditions affecting motoring are broadcast regularly on ABC national and local radio stations. Many newspapers devote a full page (often in colour) to the weather, and news programmes on radio and TV are usually followed by detailed weather forecasts and analyses. Forecasts are usually extremely accurate, not least because of Australia's generally stable weather patterns.

# CRIME

Australia is a safe country by international standards, and you can walk almost anywhere at any time of the day or night in Australian cities without risking being mugged or murdered. However, it's important to take the usual safety precautions that you would in any country and to bear in mind that Australia has become a more violent society in the last decade. Crime rates vary from state to state: ACT and the

Northern Territory are the most dangerous places to live, while Victoria is the safest. House-breaking and burglary is rampant in Australian cities, particularly Sydney, and some 415,000 cases are reported a year. Car theft is also widespread in cities, although the incidence is decreasing. Beware of pickpockets and opportunist thieves such as bag snatchers in major cities and crowded places, and keep a close eye on your belongings when travelling on public transport and when staying in hotels or hostels. Ramraiding used to be widespread in Australian cities but has fallen off since retailers stopped displaying valuable goods in their windows.

Although basically honest, many Australians delight in 'beating the system', including cheating their employers (bludging), fiddling their income tax (e.g. by not declaring income) and not paying motoring fines – unpaid fines total $millions annually. Many people take their lead from politicians, officials and the police, among whom corruption is widespread. Organised crime is rife in Australia's major cities, where much crime is linked to Asian gangs, including Chinese, Thais and Vietnamese. It's estimated that crime costs Australia some $13 billion annually, including white-collar crime (e.g. fraud, forgery and false pretences) which is thought to cost over $3 billion per year alone and is the country's largest crime cost (it's also the biggest crime growth area and the hardest to prosecute). Around $8 billion per year is spent on public and private crime prevention.

Violent crime is still relatively rare in Australia, although it has increased considerably in the last decade or so (along with most other western countries). There has been a huge increase in armed robbery in the last decade, and rapes, murders and assaults have all increased dramatically, although muggings are still relatively rare. Violent crimes by the young have soared (many children and youths are totally out of control) and gun (see below) and knife culture is widespread. Armed robbery is becoming fairly common in Australia, where banks, retail outlets and petrol stations are the most common targets (particularly all-night stores and petrol supermarkets). As a result, some outlets have stopped accepting cash and many are considering closing at night. Women should avoid travelling alone at night, and hitchhiking can be dangerous for both sexes (there have been a number of murders of backpackers in recent years, many involving a serial killer, thankfully now behind bars).

**Drugs:** Illegal drug use and trafficking is a vast and growing problem in Australia, although the authorities in some states have taken a more enlightened view of the use of 'soft' drugs such as cannabis and marijuana in recent years, and there are nationwide moves to liberalise laws prohibiting their use.

Smoking pot (cannabis) is widespread in Australia, where around a third of the adult population uses or has used it and growing cannabis plants is a vast cottage industry (although the highest quality cannabis comes from Papua New Guinea). The law regarding its use varies considerably. It has been decriminalised in the ACT and South Australia, where there's a fine of $50 to $200 for its possession or production. However, its possession is still a criminal offence in New South Wales, Victoria, Queensland, Western Australia and Tasmania, where possession and/or production can result in a fine of $2,000 to $300,000 (Queensland) and/or up to 15 years in jail. Victoria has recently introduced a 'cannabis cautionary scheme' for first time offenders, who receive a formal caution and are then referred to a drug treatment centre. Police forces around the country are watching the scheme with interest and in some states are considering introducing a similar scheme for heroin offenders. Similarly, the law relating to marijuana use varies considerably: in some states it has been decriminalised and its use and possession is legal, while in others its use is punishable by huge fines and even imprisonment. Unlike hard drugs there's little crime associated with cannabis or marijuana use. In contrast, the use of hard drugs is responsible for a large proportion of crime in Australia, including over half of all thefts in the major cities (which are committed by drug addicts to finance their habit). It's also estimated that heroin trafficking is involved in some 40 per cent of serious crime. Despite the harsh penalties, Queensland is reckoned to be the worst state for drug use, particularly amphetamines such as ice, ecstasy and LSD. Some officials would like to decriminalise all drug use and treat users as victims rather than criminals, although this enlightened view cuts no ice with the USA, which has campaigned long and hard against any relaxation of international drug laws.

**Guns:** Like Americans, Australians have a fascination for guns and there are millions of legal and illegal guns in private hands. However, unlike America, the incidence of gun crime is remarkably low considering the number of weapons in circulation (only some 25 per cent of homicides involve the use of guns). Following the Port Arthur massacre in 1996 (when 35 people were shot dead when a gunman went on the rampage), the government instituted a buy-back of automatic and semi-automatic guns (including self-loading rifles and pump-action shotguns) financed by a Medicare levy. Owners were given 12 months to hand in guns but, when the amnesty ended in 1997, it was conservatively estimated that a million people still held illegal guns. There has been compulsory registration of firearms since 1st July 1997 and owners must be aged over 18, undergo a training and safety course and have a good reason to own a gun, such as belonging to a shooting club. New penalties for possessing illegal firearms include a $6,000 to $24,000 fine and up to four years imprisonment, depending on the type of firearm. However, Australia's gun laws are still among the most liberal in the world.

**Prisons:** Australia has a tough sentencing and prison regime (including controversial private prisons), and the prison population has doubled since 1990 (prison violence is widespread). The Northern Territory has the highest prison population. Tougher sentences have been introduced in recent years in many states, and sentence-reducing or remission have been abolished, although neither policy has had much effect on crime rates (the main reasons for crime are drug use, family breakdown, poverty and unemployment – particularly among youths). Many people are held on remand for up to 12 months in prison cells where conditions are often appalling, and around half of them are acquitted by the courts. A disproportionate number of Aboriginal and Torres Strait Islander people are convicted of crimes (mostly due to drunkenness and related crimes); these comprise just 2 per cent of the population but make up 15 per cent of prisoners in some states. Deaths in custody (including suicides) are high and include a disproportionately high number of Aborigines.

Although the foregoing catalogue of crime may paint a less than rosy picture of Australia, it's still a relatively safe place to live. In comparison with many other countries, Australia's crime rate isn't high and the incidence of violent crime is low. If you take care of your property and take precautions against crime, your chances of becoming a victim are small. Note that the rate of crime in Australia's cities varies considerably from suburb to suburb, and anyone coming to live in Australia would be well advised to avoid high crime areas.

**Further Information:** Police forces, central government, local authorities and security companies all publish information and provide advice on crime prevention.

Police forces have local crime prevention officers whose job is to provide free advice to individuals, homeowners and businesses. See also **Home Security** on page 142, **Car Theft** on page 268, **Legal & General Advice** on page 458 and **Police** on page 463.

# GEOGRAPHY

Australia is one of the world's oldest land masses (some of its rock was formed over 3 million years ago) and its largest island. Separated from other land masses, it evolved in partial isolation, resulting in its unique flora and fauna, and the development of the primeval Aboriginal race with a civilisation stretching back 40,000 years. The country extends 3,200km/1,988mi from north to south and 4,000km/2,485mi from east to west, covering an area of 7,682,300km≈ (2,966,144mi≈), including Tasmania, with a coastline of 36,738km (22,826mi). It's the world's sixth largest country (after Russia, Canada, China, the USA and Brazil) and is around the same size as the continental USA (minus Alaska), one and a half times the size of Europe (excluding Russia) and more than 30 times the size of Britain. Almost 40 per cent of the country lies north of the Tropic of Capricorn.

Australia lies in the southern hemisphere south-east of Asia between the Indian and Pacific oceans. Its nearest neighbour is Papua New Guinea (PNG), which is some 200km (125mi) north of Cape York in the north-west. Bali and other Indonesian islands lie off the north-west coast, and the French island of New Caledonia is situated to the north-east. New Zealand is around 1,700km (1,050mi) off the east coast, and to the south lies Antarctica. Australia is surrounded by four seas (Arafura, Coral, Tasman and Timor) and three oceans (Indian, South Pacific and Southern).

The Great Barrier Reef lies between 50 and 300km (31 to 186mi) off the north-east coast and stretches from the Torres Strait to Gladstone. It's the largest coral reef in the world, extending some 2,000km (1,260mi) and encompassing an area of around 200,000km≈ (77,226mi≈). The reef is the world's largest living entity and an important marine ecosystem containing many rare life forms (it has been declared a World Heritage site).

Australia is the world's flattest country, with an average elevation less than 500m/1,640ft (the world's average is 700m/2,296ft) and only around 5 per cent of it is more than 600m/1,968ft above sea level. The Great Western Plateau covers most of Western Australia, a large part of the Northern Territory and South Australia, and part of Queensland. East of the plateau are the Central Eastern Lowlands, extending from the Gulf of Carpentaria in the north to eastern South Australia and the western Victorian coast. The Great Dividing Range (or Eastern Highlands) follow the east coast southwards from northern Queensland to southern Tasmania, separating a narrow fertile strip of land on the coast from the arid inland areas. The vast, flat inland plain is broken only by a few low mountain ranges such as the Flinders and Macdonnell Ranges, the Olgas and Uluru (or Ayers Rock, the largest rock on earth, 9.4km/5.8mi in circumference – if you're tempted to climb it, bear in mind that it's Aboriginal sacred ground and many people have died of heart attacks in the attempt!). Other mountain ranges include the Hamersley Range, the Kimberleys and the Stirling Range in Western Australia, and the Snowy Mountains (Australian Alps) in Victoria, where Mount Kosciusko is the highest point (2,230m/7,316ft) in Australia.

Australia has the lowest rainfall of any continent after Antarctica and evaporation exceeds rainfall over 70 per cent of the country. Surface water is scarce and most lakes (with memorable names such as Lake Disappointment) and rivers are dry most of the year. Most of the centre and west of the country consists of desert (some 1.5 million km≈/579,195mi≈). A third is desert or arid lands, some 55 per cent semi-arid and shrub lands, and only around 6 per cent is cultivated for crops or used for grazing. Australia has three main deserts, the Great Sandy, the Gibson and the Great Victoria, and several smaller ones. Lush forests are found on the east coast, particularly in the far north. The country's longest rivers are the Murray, Darling, Ord and Swan. The main river is the River Murray, which with the River Darling has a catchment area covering Queensland, New South Wales and Victoria. Severe salting has occurred in recent years due to indiscriminate land clearing for agricultural use, which has reduced irrigation potential and lowered the quality of drinking water (if nothing is done, the Murray-Darling basin will be dead in 50 years time).

Australia is divided into six states (New South Wales, Queensland, South Australia, Tasmania, Victoria and Western Australia) and two territories (the Australian Capital Territory and the Northern Territory). The island of Tasmania (also called the Apple Isle) is larger than Denmark or the Netherlands and was founded by Dutchman Abel Tasman in 1642 and originally named Van Dieman's Land (changed to Tasmania in 1856). External territories include Norfolk Island (the territory of Ashmore and Cartier Islands), Christmas Island, the Cocos (Keeling) Islands and the Australian Antarctic Territory. Macquarie Island (around 1,600km/994mi south-east of Tasmania) is administered by Tasmania.

# GOVERNMENT

Australia has a three-tiered system of government: federal or Commonwealth, state and local.

**Commonwealth/Federal Government:** The Commonwealth of Australia was formed on 1st January 1901, when the states gained their independence from Britain, prior to which each state was an independent colony. Australia has a parliamentary system of government based on the British system, while the (written) constitution and federal structure is based on the US model. The powers of the Commonwealth parliament (the legislature) are laid down in the constitution, which can be amended only by a referendum carried by a majority of voters in a majority of the states, as well as an overall majority. The Australian constitution provides for a division of power between the Commonwealth and the states. The sovereign head of the Commonwealth of Australia is Britain's Queen Elizabeth II, who's represented in Australia by the Governor-General and state governors (see **Republic Debate** on page 457).

The Commonwealth government has constitutional power over Australian territories (ACT and NT) but not the states and can overturn laws made in the territories, e.g. the controversial euthanasia law enacted in the Northern Territory in 1995. It's responsible for income and sales tax, customs and excise, defence, foreign affairs, immigration, international trade and commerce, social services, postal services and communications, currency, banking and intellectual property (copyrights, patents and trademarks). The Commonwealth government raises around 80 per cent of total government spending.

Like Washington DC in the USA, Canberra is the purpose-built capital city and capital of the Australian Capital Territory (ACT). The ACT was created as a compromise when New South Wales and Victoria couldn't decide between them whether Sydney or Melbourne should be the capital of Australia. In 1911 the ACT, located roughly half way between Sydney and Melbourne, was acquired from the New South Wales government. The Northern Territory was transferred from the state of South Australia to Commonwealth administration in the same year. The Commonwealth government first convened in Canberra in 1927, prior to which Melbourne was the seat of federal government. A new Parliament House was inaugurated in 1988 on Capitol Hill. The Australian parliament is bicameral (consisting of two houses), the House of Representatives and the Senate (see below).

**House of Representatives:** The house of representatives (lower house) is elected every three years and is the premier house, whose members make up the government of the day and whose principal role is as legislator (the making of laws). It comprises 148 members (MHRs), each of whom represents a constituency with approximately the same population. The number of members allocated to each state and territory is proportionate to the number of residents, as follows: New South Wales (50), Victoria (37), Queensland (26), Western Australia (14), South Australia (12) Tasmania (5), the Australian Capital Territory (3) and the Northern Territory (1). The number of MHRs was to be increased in 2001 to 150, in line with recent population increase.

**Senate:** The senate (upper house) is composed of 12 senators from each state and two from each territory, making a total of 76. Senators are elected for a six-year term (except for Australian Capital Territory and Northern Territory senators, who serve for three years) by a system of proportional representation. In senate elections, the whole state constitutes the electorate. The senate represents state interests and reviews legislation passed by the lower house, which must pass both houses before becoming law.

**Political Parties:** Australia has six main political parties: the Australian Labor Party (ALP), the Liberal Party (LP), the Country Liberal Party (CLP), the National Party of Australia (NPA), the Independent Party (IND) and the Australian Democrats (AD). Some parties, such as the National Party of Australia (NPA), are regional parties and stand in only one or two states, and Australia essentially has a two-party system, comprising the Liberal and National Parties (conservative, right wing), who traditionally form a coalition, and the Australian Labor Party (socialist, left wing). The party with a majority of seats in the House of Representatives generally forms the government (although, if it has no overall majority and cannot find coalition partners, it could find itself in opposition). The leader of the largest party (or the largest party in a coalition) becomes the Prime Minister (currently John Howard), who presides over a cabinet of ministers.

The Labor Party, which held power from 1983 until 1996, is now a much more moderate party than it was in the '60s and '70s. The Liberal/National coalition triumphed in the 1996 and 1998 general elections, and the current state of the parties in the House of Representatives is Liberal Party 64, Labor Party 68 and National Party 16. In the Senate the Liberal Party has 31 seats, the Labor Party 29, Australian Democrats 9, National Party 3, and the Country Liberal, Greens, Independent and Pauline Hanson's One Nation Parties 1 each. Thus the Liberal/National coalition has a huge majority in the lower house, but needs support from the Australian Democrats to get legislation through the upper house. The next general election is due by January 2002, although the government may dissolve both houses in late 2001 and call a general election. It's generally thought by political analysts that the Liberal/National Coalition will have a hard task to win a third term. All Australian citizens must vote in Commonwealth elections or face a fine (although there's a move to change to voluntary voting). Only Australian citizens over 18 years of age and British subjects who were resident in Australia and on the electoral roll on 25th January 1984 may vote.

**State Parliaments:** Each state has its own parliament (with upper and lower houses, except for Queensland), a cabinet headed by a premier, a governor (who's the Queen's representative) and its own constitution. The head of the largest party in the NT and ACT is called the chief minister, and the Queen's representative is called the administrator. The lower house is called the Legislative Assembly or the House of Assembly and is usually elected for four years, while the upper house is usually called the Legislative Council and elected for twice the period of the lower house. Queensland, the Northern Territory (self-governing since 1978) and the Australian Capital Territory have a single house (the Legislative Assembly). State parliaments are generally elected under a preferential voting system for the lower house and by a variety of other systems for the upper house. Under the preferential voting system, each candidate is ranked in order of preference, which means that the person nominated as number one on most ballot forms isn't necessarily elected.

State government was long noted for its corruption and nepotism, although this is generally considered to be no longer the case. Many state politicians do hardly anything, and in some states (e.g. Victoria) the upper house rarely sits (upper houses are essentially just a 'rubber stamp' for the lower house). The states have control over education, health, housing, community services, infrastructure, justice, police, transport, roads, water, mineral resources, forestry, conservation, Aboriginal welfare and tourism. The states receive the bulk of their funding from the Commonwealth government, although they also levy stamp duty and charges on banking and other financial transactions, plus various other duties and taxes. They're continually in conflict with the Commonwealth government over funding for services such as health care and law enforcement.

**Local Government:** Local councils (including city, town, municipal and shire councils) provide services to their communities and control matters that cannot be handled by larger bodies (such as property zoning). There are some 900 local government authorities in Australia, whose powers and responsibilities vary from state to state, consisting largely of elected representatives who usually act in an honorary unpaid capacity. Although generally well run, some councils have run up huge debts, often through building and acquisition programmes. Councils are largely funded by property taxes (rates), business taxes and water rates, supplemented by state and federal funds. Local government is responsible for a number of services, including town planning, garbage collection, water and sewerage, the construction and maintenance of local roads and other infrastructure, public health, libraries, community services, weights and measures, parks and recreation grounds, swimming pools, and sports and community centres. Local government departments and officials are listed in telephone directories under 'Local Government'.

**Republic Debate:** There's an ongoing debate in Australia over whether the country should become a republic and replace the Queen by an elected president. The sovereign head of the Commonwealth of Australia is Queen Elizabeth II, the Queen of England, who's represented in Australia by the governor-general (G-G) and the state governors. The G-G is nominated by the Commonwealth government and appointed by the Queen and acts on the advice of ministers in virtually all matters. However, this system led to a major political crisis in 1975, when the G-G dismissed the elected Labor government of Gough Whitlam and called a general election after the government failed to pass the budget bill (this has in fact, occurred six times in Australia's parliamentary history). There's a huge gulf between republicans and monarchists, and a referendum was held in November 1999. In spite of previous indications that the republicans would win, 55 per cent of Australians voted against the republic. Only two states, ACT and Victoria voted clearly for a republic, while in the territories and other states (except Queensland and Western Australia) voting was very even. Therefore, for the time being, Queen Elizabeth remains as Australia's head of state.

# LEGAL & GENERAL ADVICE

Australian law is based on English common law, which it resembles closely. This is divided into statute law, enacted by legislature, and common law which is developed by the courts, both of which continually evolve as a consequence of precedents set by the courts. There's also a clear distinction between criminal law (acts harmful to the community) and civil law (disputes between individuals). If there's a dispute between federal and state law, federal law takes precedence. Less serious criminal cases are heard by magistrates or justices of the peace, while serious criminal and civil cases are held before a judge and jury (e.g. in a district or county court) consisting of 12 people in criminal cases (fewer in civil cases). There's no capital punishment in Australia, which has been abolished. Note that many minor offences incur fines, including topless and nude bathing (where prohibited), littering, smoking where it's prohibited, drinking under age and on trains outside the permitted hours, and taking alcohol on to Aboriginal lands (laws regarding these and other offences also differ from state to state).

Each state or territory has its own court system consisting of magistrates' courts, intermediate district or county courts and supreme courts. There are also state courts of petty sessions, children's courts, family courts (which handle divorce cases and the custody of children), small claims courts and industrial courts, which hear claims concerning industrial relations law. Some disputes such as family disputes and disputes between neighbours can be resolved by mediation. Most criminal cases in Australia are heard in state or territory courts. There are huge delays in hearing cases, and local courts are hugely over-burdened, some magistrates courts processing up to 60 cases per hour. In serious cases, the accused are held in prison on remand for up to a year before their cases are heard; when the accused is on bail, cases can take up to 18 months to come to court.

A federal system exists to deal with matters over which the Commonwealth government has jurisdiction. The highest court in the land is the High Court of Australia (created in 1976), which is the country's final court of appeal from the states' supreme courts. It's presided over by the chief justice and six other justices, all of whom are political appointees. In recent years, there has been an acrimonious relationship between the High Court and politicians (at stake is the balance of power between the judiciary and the government). Other federal courts include the Federal Court of Australia and the Family Court of Australia, both of which handle specialised cases involving federal law. In 1986, Australia changed the constitution to prevent

Britain making laws in Australia or having any government responsibility, thereby removing the ultimate legal appeal to the British Privy Council. At federal and state levels, the office of ombudsman deals with a variety of citizens' complaints against government administration. Administrative Appeals Tribunals hear appeals in cases involving freedom of information, immigration, pensions and tax.

If you're arrested, you aren't required to give your name or address and are permitted to contact a friend or lawyer (called solicitors in Australia) before answering any questions. The police will provide an interpreter if you're arrested and cannot speak English. It's best to say nothing until a lawyer is present and even then you have the right to remain silent (although this may change under a government review). In some states, interrogation is recorded on video. If you're charged with an offence, you may be released on a surety (bail) or remanded in custody (foreigners may have their passports confiscated to prevent them leaving the country). If necessary, the police will provide a duty solicitor. Your country's consulate or embassy in Australia can usually provide you with a list of local lawyers, if necessary speaking your native language.

Each state has a legal aid commission, and you may be able to obtain legal aid if you cannot afford a lawyer, although it's subject to a means test and is becoming increasingly difficult to obtain as a result of cuts; people are often refused help unless they're facing jail or a fine of over $1,000. Information about legal aid can be obtained from local courts. Free legal advice is also available in all states and territories (there's a nominal fee of $2 in Western Australia) from various organisations, including community legal or justice centres, legal aid commissions and citizens' advice bureaux.

As in most countries, civil liberties are constantly under threat, although Australia remains one of the most free and open countries in the world. For information regarding civil liberties in Australia, contact the Australian Civil Liberties Union (ACLU, PO Box 1137, Carlton, Melbourne, VIC 3053, ☎ 03-9347 8671, 🖳 www. go.to/aclu), which publishes an annual booklet, *Your Rights*, containing information about your legal rights in various situations. The booklet is available from ACLU and from newsagents for $6.50. See also **Consumer Rights** on page 442.

## MARRIAGE & DIVORCE

Like most western countries, Australia has a declining marriage rate and people are also marrying later – around 26 years of age for women and 28 for men. Many more people are choosing to remain single and there's an increasing number of single, childless women. In 1996, the lowest number of marriages per capita was recorded this century, although since then the number has risen slightly. An increasing number of marriages (around 45 per cent of the total) take place outside the traditional church. One of the reasons is that a traditional church wedding and reception costs upwards of $18,000, in contrast to a simple garden civil ceremony with a minister or a civil celebrant, which costs less than $200.

Some 70 per cent of Australian adults are married, around 15 per cent are lone parents and some 8 per cent (300,000 couples) live in *de facto* marriages (an unmarried couple living together as husband and wife). Although the law varies with the state, generally when a *de facto* marriage breaks up after two years, either party can apply for division of property, maintenance or custody of children as if they were formally married. Note, however, that *de facto* couples don't have the same inheritance rights as married couples and should therefore ensure that their wills reflect their wishes.

Anyone planning to marry must complete a *Notice of Intention to Marry* form and give it to the person (e.g. a minister or civil marriage celebrant) who will be conducting the marriage. Notice must be given between one and three months before the planned date of the marriage. Both parties must provide their birth certificates and a divorce decree or death certificate if they've been divorced or widowed. A man must usually be 18 to marry and a woman 16, although anyone aged under 18 must have their parents' consent to marry and permission from a judge or magistrate. A marriage must be witnessed by two people aged over 18. A legal marriage that takes place overseas is almost always recognised in Australia. A woman usually takes her husband's surname when she marries, although it isn't obligatory and she can retain her maiden name.

**Divorce:** Australia has the third highest divorce rate in the world, marriages lasting an average of less than eight years (there's around one divorce for every two marriages). 1999 saw the highest number of divorces (around 52,000) for 23 years. Under the Family Law Act, the only grounds for divorce in Australia are the irretrievable breakdown of a marriage; fault (e.g. adultery, cruelty or desertion) no longer constitutes grounds for divorce. Under the law, a marriage has irretrievably broken down if a couple has lived apart for one year and there's no reasonable likelihood of a reconciliation. It's also possible for these conditions to be met when a couple live separately and apart in the matrimonial home, although it's difficult to prove. If a couple have been married for less than two years, they must usually have considered reconciliation with the assistance of a marriage guidance counsellor before a court will hear divorce proceedings.

The average cost of a divorce in court fees alone (excluding your solicitor's fees) is around $1,700, with a fee of $460 payable simply to file an application. Extra fees apply to obtaining court orders on access to and custody of children and property orders. Parents seeking ancillary relief in the Family Court (which normally entails child custody or access) must pay $150, and a parent defending such an action must also pay the fee. A one-off hearing, which can be imposed by the court if parents disagree on access, costs each parent $300. If parents go to court to decide alimony, proceedings can cost up to $10,000 per day and some divorced people have little left after paying legal costs.

One of the court's main duties is to protect and promote the welfare and rights of dependent children. Both parents have joint custody of a child under Australian law, although one parent can ask for and be granted sole custody, in which case the wishes of the child are taken into consideration. Before maintenance is granted, the age, health, financial resources and obligations of each party are taken into consideration (the same applies to the division of matrimonial property). Matters concerning the division of property, maintenance and custody of children must be decided before a divorce can be granted. After one month, a decree becomes absolute and parties are free to re-marry.

# MILITARY SERVICE

There's no conscription (draft) in Australia, where all members of the armed forces are volunteers. The Australian Defence Force (ADF) comprises three services: the

Australian Army, the Royal Australian Air Force and the Royal Australian Navy. The combined strength of the ADF (including reservists and civilians) is around 94,000 (51,000 permanent service personnel, 26,700 reservists and the remainder civilians). Some 10 per cent (13 per cent of regular service personnel) are women, who are eligible for 99 per cent of navy and air force positions and around two-thirds of army positions (women are banned from carrying combat arms). In recent years, there has been an exodus from the services, the army having a 14 per cent attrition rate (the rates for the air force and navy are slightly lower). Many young people have different career expectations, and the armed forces are finding it difficult to recruit.

All soldiers initially enlist for a minimum of four years under the Open Ended Enlistment Scheme and after four years can apply for discharge by giving six months' notice. Applicants for the ADF must be Australian citizens or be eligible for grant of citizenship or must undertake to apply for citizenship when they become eligible. They must be aged at least 17 and under 35 (42 if they have a particular skill) and must be at least 152cm (5ft) tall. Reservists serve a minimum of 26 days a year (14 full-time). In recent years, a new form of reserve service has been introduced. Under the Ready Reserve programme, members serve full-time for 12 months and then train for 50 days per year for four years. Soldiers may also transfer from the regular army or army reserve to the Ready Reserve, in which case they're committed to five years' part-time training.

Australia is a member of a number of defence treaties, including the Five Power Defence Arrangement (FPDA) with Malaysia, Singapore, New Zealand and Britain, and the ANZUS alliance with the USA and New Zealand. The country also has a close military relationship with Indonesia, with whom it conducts combined exercises. Australian troops were deployed in East Timor during 1999 and 2000 and were responsible for most of the evacuation of UN personnel and the restoration of calm. Australia spends some $12 billion per year on defence (1.8 per cent of its GDP) and there are plans to modernise the defence forces over the next ten years at a cost of $5 billion.

# PETS

Pets can be imported into Australia from most countries, although there are rigorous controls and it's very expensive. All imports are subject to quarantine, and an import permit must be obtained prior to shipment. Applications should be made at least two months prior to the intended date of importation to the Australian Quarantine Inspection Service (AQIS) in the state where you'll be living. The application fee is $60 and the import permit takes up to four weeks to be issued and is valid for two months. Dogs and cats must have been continuously resident for six months (or since their birth if less than six months old) in the country of origin immediately prior to shipment to Australia and must not have been in quarantine or under quarantine restrictions during the 30 days prior to export. Both dogs and cats must be aged at least 12 weeks at the time of export. Certain breeds of dogs that are considered dangerous aren't eligible for importation, including the pitbull terrier or American pitbull, dogo Argentino, fila Brazileiro and Japanese tosa. The importation of birds and small mammals such as hamsters is also prohibited.

Imported dogs and cats must be identified by a microchip, for which there's a one-time fee of around $35 ($15 for pensioners). Microchipping of imported animals is voluntary in most states, although there are plans to make it compulsory (as it is for Australian born pets) in more states, e.g. NSW. All dogs aged over three months must be registered annually with your local council. If your dog has been microchipped and 'desexed', the charge is $35; if it still has its reproductive organs intact, you'll have to pay $100!

All imported cats and dogs must have current vaccinations. Dogs must have vaccinations for distemper, hepatitis, parvovirus and para-influenza, and must also test negative for canine brucellosis, leptospirosis and canine tropical pancytopenia within 30 days of export. Cats must have vaccinations for feline enteritis, rhinotracheitis and calicivirus. Vaccinations must have been given at least 14 days prior to shipment and not more than 12 months previously. All dogs and cats must be treated for internal parasites within 14 days of shipment and for external parasites within 96 hours of export, and must pass a clinical examination within 48 hours of shipment. Note that, if dogs and cats exported to Australia don't meet all the pre-export and post-arrival testing, vaccination, health and certification requirements, they may need to be re-exported, treated or destroyed or remain in quarantine until any disease concerns have been resolved.

**Quarantine:** Dogs and cats from New Zealand, Norfolk Island and the Cocos (Keeling) Islands aren't required to undergo quarantine. Dogs and cats from approved rabies-free countries and territories, including Cyprus, Hawaii, Ireland, Japan, Malta, Norway, Singapore, Sweden, Taiwan and the UK are quarantined for 30 days. Dogs and cats from countries and territories where rabies is considered to be well controlled (including Austria, Belgium, Canada, Denmark, Finland, France, Germany, Greece, Hong Kong, Israel, Italy, Luxembourg, Malaysia, the Netherlands, Portugal, Spain, Switzerland and the USA) are quarantined for a minimum of 30 days and a maximum of 120. Pets from certain other approved rabies-free countries (mostly Pacific islands) must spend 60 days in quarantine. The import of dogs and cats from countries and territories where dog-mediated rabies is endemic is permitted only indirectly via an approved country, where the animal must be resident for at least six months prior to export to Australia. Many pet owners decide that the cost and strain of quarantine on their pets (and themselves) is too much to bear and find their pets new homes.

Pets must be shipped by air to Australia in an International Air Transport Association (IATA) approved container available from pet shipping agents such as Par Air Services (UK ☎ 01206-330332, 🖳 www.parair.co.uk) and Airpets Oceanic (UK ☎ 01753-685571, 🖳 www.airpets.com) in the United Kingdom. Animals are inspected at airports by a veterinary surgeon prior to shipment. Animals can only arrive at the following airports in Australia: Kingsford Smith Airport (Sydney), Tullamarine Airport (Melbourne) and Perth Airport. Other entry points require AQIS consent. On arrival in Australia, dogs and cats are quarantined in an approved animal quarantine station at Spotswood (Victoria), Eastern Creek (NSW) or Byford (Western Australia). Quarantine costs are around $12 per day for a cat and $16 for a dog. Weekly visits are permitted during the quarantine period. Other charges include $68 for the examination of the animal, $30 for document clearing and $95 for transport. These charges are higher if the animal arrives in Australia outside business hours (8am to 4pm). For further information contact the Australian Quarantine Inspection Service (AQIS), GPO Box 858, Canberra, ACT 2601 (☎ freecall 1800-020504 or 02-6272 3933, 🖳 www.aquis.gov.au). AQIS publish a leaflet *The Importation of Dogs and Cats into Australia* (AQIS information sheet 2) as well as comprehensive information and forms online.

# POLICE

Each state and the Northern Territory has its own independent police force, and there's also an Australian Federal Police (AFP) force, which is the federal government's primary law enforcement agency. The AFP are responsible for protecting federal property and enforcing federal laws such as those concerning drug trafficking, organised crime, terrorism, fraud, counterfeiting, money laundering and illegal immigration. The AFP also provides community police services in the Australian Capital Territory and in Australia's external territories. The National Crime Authority (which deals with organised crime) also has a policing role. Most police forces have special squads to handle VIP protection and specific crimes such as homicide, armed robbery, illegal drug trafficking and use, and fraud. There are also water police in cities and coastal areas.

There have been numerous police corruption scandals in recent years in Australia, which, if the allegations are true, has one of the most corrupt police forces in the western world. After investigations in NSW, some 200 police officers were found to have criminal records. Corruption varies from minor infringements such as accepting free food and drinks and tipping off window and other repair companies in return for a commission, to selling inside information to criminals, taking bribes, extortion, fabrication of evidence, stealing goods and money, assaults and sexual harassment, selling confiscated drugs and involvement in organised crime. Freebies and kickbacks are considered to be a legitimate perk of the job by many officers.

An almost impenetrable police culture protects crooked officers, and the authorities find it virtually impossible to obtain convictions (and, in any case, don't like to wash their dirty linen in public). Whistle-blowers who shop their colleagues or don't 'play the game' are likely to be hounded out of the force or transferred to the 'back of Bourke'. The anti-corruption record of the Police Integrity Commission (PIC) has been described by some politicians as a joke. Sexism and racism are widespread in Australia's police forces and female officers generally have poor promotion prospects compared with male officers. There are an increasing number of complaints by the public against the police in some states (23,000 in NSW alone in 1996–97). Not surprisingly, the police have a poor public image and are often seen as a law unto themselves.

All police in Australia are armed and in addition to guns carry other 'weapons' to pacify 'dangerous criminals', such as extendable batons and capsicum (pepper) sprays (used by NSW officers to disable armed attackers). Police officers in NSW have been issued with new semi-automatic pistols (15-shot .40 calibre) in order to confront armed gangs. General police policy if threatened is to shoot first and ask questions afterwards, although this is changing after a number of 'accidental' deaths in recent years. There have been frequent incidents where police have shot dead unarmed assailants or even innocent bystanders (the Australian police shoot more innocent people than crooks). Since 1990, some 75 people have been shot dead by the police and around 90 others have died from their injuries. Most people believe that the police ought to be able to deal with a man armed with a knife without shooting him dead, e.g. by using nets, poles, sprays and batons. The number of deaths in custody has also risen alarmingly in recent years, including many Aboriginals (blacks are around 20 times more likely to die in custody than whites).

Police in some states (e.g. Victoria) have stopped attending routine calls (such as security alarms, the vast majority of which are false) in an effort to redirect sources to fighting crime. In some areas the police have drastically reduced the number of incidents they visit in order to cut their workload and allow more police to patrol the streets. Instead of sending a car, they may ask callers to report minor incidents by phone or go to a police station.

Details of your rights regarding arrest, questioning, statements or detention by the police are explained in the ACLU publication *Your Rights* (see page 442). The police emergency number varies with the state – if in doubt call the operator on 1234 or the national emergency line on 000. See also **Car Theft** on page 268, **Crime** on page 451, **Home Security** on page 142 and **Legal & General Advice** on page 458.

# POPULATION

The population of Australia in 1999 was just under 19 million and has increased by over four million in the last 20 years. However, population growth slowed in the '90s because of lower net immigration and low birth rates, and the growth rate in 1999 was 1.3 per cent, although this is still higher than many other industrialised nations. Australia has an ageing population and a declining birth rate, as more women are choosing to marry later and have fewer children. At the present birth-rate of 1.76 births per woman (half the birth rate in 1961) and current rates of immigration, the population is expected to grow relatively slowly in the 21st century. It's expected to be 21 million by 2010, 22 million by 2020 and between 24 and 28 million by 2050 (although other projections have come up with a much lower figure of 20 million by 2050 if current population trends continue). In the last 20 years, there has been a huge rise in the number of people aged over 65 (who accounted for 12 per cent of the population in 1999) and in particular those aged over 85. By 2020 the over 65s are expected to comprise around 16 per cent of the population. The average age in 1999 was around 36 years.

The indigenous Aboriginal and Torres Strait Islander population of Australia is around 300,000, over half of whom live in New South Wales and Queensland. The Aboriginal population was estimated at between 200,000 and 750,000 when Australia was colonised by the English in 1788, although it was reduced dramatically in the 19th and early 20th centuries, since when it has recovered. Until 1961, population estimates in Australia excluded full-blooded Aboriginal people.

Australia is a highly urbanised society. Only some 15 per cent of Australians live in rural areas, while around 85 per cent live in urban areas (up from just over 60 per cent in 1921). Over 70 per cent of the population live in the major cities, which are situated on or near the coast. Some 80 per cent of Australians live within 30km (20mi) of the coast, over 40 per cent in Sydney and Melbourne alone, and 35 per cent in New South Wales. Over 60 per cent of New South Wales' population lives in Sydney and its suburbs. Almost two-thirds of the nation's population growth is in the eight capital cities, of which Brisbane, Darwin and Perth are Australia's fastest-growing cities.

In recent years, Australians have been moving to the north and west of the country, fleeing the arid interior and clinging to the coast with more enthusiasm than ever. Rapid population growth in some areas of Queensland has placed a huge burden on the infrastructure such as roads, hospitals and schools, and is also having important environmental and ecological consequences in some areas. Some environmentalists believe that Australia already has more people than its natural resources can sustain, despite the huge size of the country and the low population density, while others argue that the country can sustain a much larger population. In recent years, the post-war slogan of 'populate or perish' has been changed to 'populate *and* perish' by those who would like to see immigration drastically reduced.

The long-term population shift away from the south-east to the west and the tropics has continued unabated in the '90s. Victoria has lost thousands of people to other states in the last decade or so, although by 1997 the exodus had slowed to a trickle (most people move from Victoria to Queensland). South Australia and Tasmania have been losing the most people in recent years (Tasmania recorded a net loss in 1999) and the ACT is also losing residents at a high rate. The flood of migrants (particularly retirees) to Queensland has slowed in recent years but showed a 30 per cent increase in the last decade. Queensland is the fastest-growing state (most new arrivals are interstate migrants, many moving there on their retirement) and it's expected to replace Victoria as the second most populous state by around 2025.

The average population density in Australia, where vast areas are vitually uninhabited, is just two people per km≈ (compared with 85 people per km≈ in Asia). The capital, Canberra, has a density of just 20 people per km≈ or around a tenth of the population density of most European cities. Victoria is the most densely populated state. The population of states and territories and their capital cities in 1999 was as follows:

| State | Population | |
|-------|-----------|--|
|       | **State** | **Capital** |
| ACT   | 310,000   | Canberra (308,000) |
| NSW   | 6.4 million | Sydney (4 million) |
| NT    | 193,000   | Darwin (86,500) |
| QLD   | 3.5 million | Brisbane (1.6 million) |
| SA    | 1.5 million | Adelaide (1.1 million) |
| TAS   | 470,000   | Hobart (128,500) |
| VIC   | 4.7 million | Melbourne (3.3 million) |
| WA    | 1.9 million | Perth (1.1 million) |

Since the war, there has been an influx of migrants from continental Europe, including large numbers of Greeks and Italians, plus Lebanese, Turks, Yugoslavs and various others. All major cities contain suburbs with predominantly 'foreign' communities and atmospheres, including Chinese, Greek, Italian, Lebanese and Yugoslav. Sydney is home to more New Zealanders than most cities in New Zealand, and Melbourne's Greek population is the third largest in the world (after Athens and Thessalonica). Since the end of the official 'white Australia' policy in 1975, Australia has also admitted large numbers of Asian immigrants, including many refugees from Indochina. There are also significant numbers of immigrants from the Pacific, Middle East, Central and South America, and South Africa. Around 75 per cent of the population is Australian born. In 1997, over 90 per cent of the population was of European descent, 5 per cent Asian and 1.5 per cent Aboriginal. Within the next 50 years, around 25 per cent of Australia's population is likely to be of Asian origin.

# RELIGION

Australia has a tradition of religious tolerance, and every resident has total freedom of religion without hindrance by the state or community. Australia is a secular society and has no official state religion (25 per cent of Australians claim to have no religion), although around 70 per cent of the population are Christians. Churches, particularly the Catholic Church, play a large role in education, and many schools are partly church funded. Church attendance is low in Australia. In general, Australians are fairly laid-back about religion and there are few religious zealots and bible-thumpers, as are common in the USA and some other countries.

Roman Catholic (4.8 million) and Anglican (3.9 million) are the two main religions followed by the Uniting Church (1.3 million), Presbyterian (675,000), Orthodox (500,000), Baptist (295,000), Lutheran (250,000) and Pentecostal (174,000) churches. Most Protestant churches have merged to become the Uniting Church, although the Church of England has remained independent. Unlike most Christian religions, the Orthodox Church thrives in Australia, particularly in Melbourne and Sydney. There are also sizeable Buddhist, Muslim and Jewish communities in the major cities. There has been a wider tolerance of smaller religious groups in the last decade, during which mainstream Christianity (apart from Catholicism) has declined while 'nature-based' religions such as witchcraft, druidism and paganism have proliferated. Eastern and minority religions have also gained in popularity, including Taoism, Japanese Mahikari and Shinto. There's no recognised Aboriginal religion, although the Aboriginal people have many sacred sites throughout the country.

Every town and city has an Anglican and a Catholic church, and Uniting churches are also common. Religious centres for all the world's major religions are found in the major cities and details of church and religious services are published in local newspapers throughout the country.

# SOCIAL CUSTOMS

All countries have particular social customs and Australia is no exception. Australians are generally very informal in their relationships and won't be too put out if you break the rules, provided your behaviour isn't outrageous. On the other hand, in some circles, eccentricity is much prized and you may be invited to some social functions *only* if you act disgracefully (but make sure you don't confuse the Vicar's tea party with the local wife-swapping club). However, bear in mind that Australia is a multicultural society, and many people retain the same customs as their forefathers in their 'home' country, even when their family has been in Australia for generations. As a foreigner you may be forgiven if you accidentally insult your host, but you may not be invited again. The following are a few Australian social customs:

● When introduced to someone, you generally follow the cue of the person performing the introduction, e.g. if someone is introduced as Bruce you can safely call him Bruce; however, if someone is introduced as the Reverend Piddleton, it might not be wise to address him as 'Piddles' (unless he asks you to). After you've been introduced to someone, you usually say something like 'Pleased to meet you', 'hello' or even 'g'day mate' and shake hands. Among friends, it's common for men to kiss ladies on the cheek (or once on either cheek). Men don't usually kiss or embrace each other in Australia (although it depends on their nationality and sexual orientation). Australians are informal, and even total strangers are called mate (even women), particularly in working class circles (so don't be surprised if your plumber calls you mate). Note that 'mateship' (which roughly equates to the American term 'buddy') is a different thing altogether. It applies only to men and to be someone's life-long mate is considered an honour and a big compliment.

• Australians are a lot more casual than their British or European cousins and more direct in asking questions and voicing their opinions (like Americans). Don't be surprised if an Aussie gives you the 'third degree' when you meet for the first time. It's nothing personal – they're just being curious and are genuinely interested in strangers. Australians are usually friendly and hospitable to strangers and will often go out of their way to help you. If you're travelling around Australia, don't hesitate to use your contacts to obtain a free bed (Australians you meet may offer to put you up or volunteer their friends and family). It's considered quite normal to take people up on these offers, even if they're total strangers.

• It's common for neighbours to invite newcomers around for a cup of tea (or something stronger), although in cities (where people often live next to each other and remain strangers) you may have to go out of your way to meet your neighbours. A good way to meet the locals is to hold a barbie (although difficult in an apartment) and invite all your neighbours. If you're invited to a barbie, it's common to take a bottle of wine or some beer and you may be asked to bring your own meat (or whatever else you wish to eat). Some invitations ask guests to bring along a 'plate', e.g. a buffet dish from which everyone can help themselves. Men and women tend to congregate separately at social occasions such as parties or barbies. You are, however, permitted to fraternise with members of the opposite sex.

• Australians tend to dress casually, e.g. to wear shorts to the office in summer, and it isn't usual to wear a suit or tie unless you're a high-powered manager or executive or a salesperson. Smart casual dress is adequate for most informal occasions, e.g. when visiting restaurants and night clubs. When going anywhere that may be formal (or particularly informal), it may be wise to ask in advance what you're expected to wear. On the rare occasions when dress is formal, such as evening dress or dinner jacket, it will be stated in the invitation and you'll be unlikely to be admitted if you turn up in the wrong attire. If you're invited to a wedding, always enquire about the dress, unless you want to stick out like a sore thumb. In Australia, black or dark dress is usually worn at funerals.

• Guests are normally expected to be punctual with the exception of certain society parties, when late arrival is *de rigueur* (unless you arrive after the celebrity guest), and at weddings, when the bride is always late. Anyone who arrives late for dinner or, horror of horrors, doesn't turn up at all, should expect to be excluded from future guest lists (unless he has a *very* good reason).

# TIME DIFFERENCE

There are three different time zones in Australia, which is one of the few countries in the world to use a half-hour split time zone (CST):

| Zone | GMT + | States |
|------|-------|--------|
| Eastern Standard Time (EST) | 10 hours | ACT, NSW, TAS, QLD, VIC |
| Central Standard Time (CST) | 9.5 hours | NT, SA |
| Western Standard Time (WST) | 8 hours | WA |

All states and territories except WA, QLD and the NT operate 'daylight saving' from October to March, when clocks are advanced one hour. To add further confusion, states don't always change their clocks at the same time. In Tasmania, daylight saving starts a month earlier and ends up to a month later than in other states (it lasts for six months). In NSW, the ACT, Victoria and South Australia, the changeovers take place on the last Sunday in October and the last Sunday in March. Clocks move forward (or back) at 2am. This leads to as many as five different time zones between October and March, e.g. when it's 9am in Western Australia it's 10.30am in the Northern Territory, 11am in Queensland, 11.30am in South Australia and noon in NSW, Victoria and Tasmania. Attempts are being made to rationalise summer time zones. Time changes are announced in local newspapers and on radio and TV.

Australia hasn't converted to the 24-hour clock, and times in many timetables are given using the 12-hour clock (i.e. am and pm), with before noon times printed in light type and afternoon times printed in **bold** type. Note that, because of the huge time difference between Australia and many other continents (e.g. there are 10 or 11 hours' difference between Europe and EST), you should always check the local time when making international calls (one sure way to upset most people is to wake them at 3am). The time difference between Australia and most countries is listed at the back of the white pages under 'Telstra 0011 International and Telstra Faxstream 0015 International'. You can also obtain world time information and a time converter for over 220 countries via the Internet (🖳 www.telstra.com.au). The time difference between Sydney (at noon in January) and some major international cities is shown below:

| SYDNEY | LONDON | CAPE TOWN | TOKYO | LOS ANGELES | NEW YORK |
|--------|--------|-----------|-------|-------------|----------|
| NOON | 1AM | 3AM | 10AM | 5PM | 8PM |
| | | | | (both previous day) | |

# TIPPING

Tipping isn't a general practice in Australia (Americans please note!), although you may wish to leave a tip when you've had exceptional service or have received good value. People almost never tip taxi drivers in Australia, unlike in the vast majority of other western countries. However, it's common practice to round up taxi fares to the nearest dollar, although a cab driver may round the fare down rather than give you change. Porters (who usually have set charges), hairdressers, hotel staff, cloakroom attendants and garage staff (who clean your car's windscreen or check its oil or tyre pressures) also don't expect to be tipped (but won't complain if they are). Tipping in hotels depends where you're staying – it's unnecessary in tourist or medium class hotels, although staff in grand establishments are used to receiving tips from their wealthy clients. Note, however, that tips are regarded by some Australians as patronising or even insulting.

One of the few exceptions to the 'no tipping' rule is top class restaurants, where it's customary to tip waiters up to 10 per cent of the bill for good service. Restaurant tips can be included in cheque or credit card payments or given as cash. The total on credit card counterfoils may be left blank to encourage you to leave a tip, so don't forget to fill in the total before signing it, or the waiter may enter his own 'tip'. Note that service charges aren't usually added to bills by hotels and restaurants. It isn't customary to tip a barman in a bar or pub, although many people leave their small change.

# TOILETS

Public toilets in Australia are usually free, generally clean and are commonly found in parks, council and tourist offices, shopping centres, department stores, and bus and train stations. The most sanitary (even luxurious) toilets are found in hotels, restaurants and department stores, and are usually only for customers. Clean toilets are also found in public and private offices, museums and galleries, airports, car parks, petrol stations and near beaches. Pub toilets vary from 'no-go areas' to spotless.

Australians don't use the terms powder room, washroom or bathroom when referring to a toilet, but use a variety of (often colourful) names, including lavatory (lav), loo, toot, dunny (an outside toilet in country areas, often consisting of a wooden hut with an earth floor), bog, thunder box, public convenience, ladies' or gents' (room), WC (water closet), crapper (after Thomas Crapper who invented the WC), privy and ablutions (many of these are of British origin, but are in general use in Australia). Some toilets have nappy (diaper) changing facilities and facilities for nursing mothers, and there are also special toilets for the disabled at airports, bus and rail stations and in shopping centres in major cities. Roadhouses in country areas have toilets and showers. When using a public toilet, make sure you use the correct one, as it's sometimes difficult to tell the difference between the stylish male and female signs.

# 19.

# THE AUSTRALIANS

**W**ho are the Australians? What are they like? Let us take a candid and totally prejudiced look at the Australian people, tongue firmly in cheek, and hope they forgive my flippancy or that they don't read this bit (which is why it's hidden away at the back of the book). The typical Aussie is sophisticated, bronzed, classless, unpretentious, garrulous, friendly, generous, materialistic, matey, casual, down to earth, sincere, a compulsive gambler, tough, naive, crude, delinquent, jingoistic, arrogant, an ocker, irreverent, parochial, tardy, xenophobic, macho, brave, a republican, fiercely competitive, a carnivore, unreliable, eccentric, a philistine, hospitable, handsome, frank (to the point of bluntness), open, homophobic, a cricket and footy fan, laid back, insular, inebriated, a surfie, unambitious, proud, honest, sociable, an inveterate traveller, relaxed, informal, hedonistic, idealistic, boorish, cosmopolitan, loud, amusing, outspoken, optimistic, an anarchist, egoistical, chauvinistic, a beach bum and a foreigner.

You may have noticed that the above list contains 'a few' contradictions (as does life in Australia), which is hardly surprising as there's no such thing as a typical Australian and few people conform to the popular stereotype (whatever that is). Australia is one of the most cosmopolitan and multicultural countries in the world and a nation of 'foreigners' (except for a few hundred thousand native Aborigines), who have as much in common with each other as Icelanders with Africans or Tibetans with South Americans. However, despite its diverse racial mix, Australia isn't a universal melting pot, but a potpourri of ethnic splinter groups living separate lives with their own customs, neighbourhoods, shops, clubs, restaurants, newspapers, sports, and even TV and radio stations.

Australians pride themselves on their lack of class-consciousness and don't have the same prejudices and pretensions common in the old world, although Australia has never been an egalitarian society. However, Australia is far from being a classless society, and status is as important here as it is anywhere else, although it's usually based on money and character rather than birthright. Australia generally has no 'old school tie' barriers to success and almost anyone, however humble his origins, can fight his way to the top of the heap (although colour barriers aren't so easy to overcome). Despite the fact that the vast majority of Australians are misplaced Britons and assorted Europeans on the wrong side of the world, modern Australia has more in common with America in its lifestyle, attitudes and ambitions than with Britain or Europe.

Australians are noted for their insularity (which is hardly surprising when your nearest neighbours are thousands of miles away) and xenophobia – no doubt due to being inundated by foreigners, many of whom cannot (or won't) speak English. Nobody knows better than the Aussies that foreigners were created solely to be loathed and detested (Australians have a wealth of derogatory terms for immigrants) and transmit exotic diseases – which is why their planes are fumigated before they're allowed to set foot on Australian soil. Many Australians are prejudiced against all foreigners, who only come to Australia to steal their jobs and 'bludge' (scrounge) off the state, and don't care much for anyone who isn't a dinky die Aussie (newcomers are derisively called 'new Australians'). The culture gap is widest between Australians and Asians (the White Australia policy was officially abandoned in 1973 – but not in the nation's psyche), who are better educated, more hard-working *and* often more intelligent – enough to incense anyone. However, for better or worse, the country has belatedly (and reluctantly) concluded that its future lies in trading with its Asian neighbours rather than maintaining its traditional ties with Britain.

The natives have a particular abhorrence for the ubiquitous British (Poms) and New Zealanders (Kiwis), both of whom are the prime culprits in stealing Aussie jobs (when not dole bludging on Australian beaches). Kiwis have free access to Australia and wash up on Australian shores in vast numbers (Bondi Beach is 'home of the NZ government in exile'); not surprisingly, they're the butt of many Australian jokes (e.g. Q. 'What do you call a New Zealand sheep farmer?' A. 'A pimp.') However, Aussies reserve a special place in their hearts for those from the mother country, endearingly referred to as whinging Poms or Pommy bastards, to whom they're inexorably drawn by mutual antipathy. Making fun of the Poms is a popular pastime and has given rise to a surfeit of Pommy jokes (e.g. Q. 'What's the difference between a 747 and a Pom?' A. 'When you switch off the engines, the 747 stops whining.'). The Aussies cannot bear to be constantly reminded of their convict ancestry, while the Poms are mortified that they gave the Aussies free passage (admittedly brig class) to their land of sunshine and plenty, while they froze at home in the cold and rain. Aussies are an ungrateful shower and don't appreciate what the Poms have done for them, such as teaching them how to play cricket and rugby, introducing them to British culinary delights, and generally educating them on how to behave in polite society (admittedly this hasn't been an unqualified success – but what can you expect from 'Neanderthals' who live at the end of the earth, thousands of miles from the nearest civilisation?).

Australia is a hotbed of ethnic friction, although, apart from a small minority, most Australians *aren't* racist or even xenophobic. If it's any consolation to foreigners, Aussies don't exactly get on with their fellow countrymen and delight in abusing their neighbours at every opportunity. All Australians look down on those from other states and love to make fun of them. The inhabitants of Australia's two major cities have a shared loathing for the 'other lot' and the only thing that's (sometimes) worse than a whinging Pom to a Sydneysider is a Melbournite (and vice versa). Interstate rivalries, particularly between Victoria and New South Wales, have been a brake on economic progress for decades. To outsiders, Sydney is full of homosexuals (it's the gay capital of the world), crooks, posers and yuppies; it's always raining in Melbourne (bleak city) where the locals are staid and snobbish and consist mostly of Greeks and Italians (called Mexicans by those from NSW, as they're 'south of the border'); Queenslanders (banana benders) are red-necked fascists (somewhere to the right of Attila the Hun) and uncivilised ockers; Canberra has been described as 'the ruination of a perfectly good sheep station' and is a deadly-boring place (it's often likened to a cemetery) inhabited by civil servants and politicians (enough said) – if you develop a yearning to live in Canberra, seek immediate psychiatric help; Adelaide is conservative and dull and inhabited by prudes and killjoys (wowsers) – South Australians are disparagingly termed crow-eaters after the eating habits of the early settlers; Western Australians (sandgropers) are aliens, backward and country bumpkins who inhabit a different planet (Perth is the most remote city in the world); Northern Territorians (topenders) are primitives, drunks and Crocodile Dundee types, who are either paid to stay or cannot afford to leave; and Tasmanians (taswegians) are puritans, radical conservationists and dimwits (all that in-breeding), descended from convicts and still living in the 19th century.

Being (relatively) intelligent people, Australians have a *laissez-faire* attitude to business and work, which lag well behind having a good time. They down tools at the drop of a spanner (Australia has some of the most militant trade unions in the world) and think nothing of having a day off work (sickie) when they've something better to do, which is most of the time. If Australians worked as hard as they played (particularly at sport), they'd put even the Japanese to shame. Contrary to the widely held misconception that 'hard work never did anyone any harm', Aussies know only too well that hard 'yakka' is bad for your health and can prove fatal. They prefer to make (or more often lose) their fortune at gambling, the only acceptable way to get rich, and will bet on almost anything, including lotteries, football pools, horse and greyhound racing, bingo, casinos, poker machines (pokies), two-up, general elections, toad, cockroach and lizard races, which politician will get caught next with his hand in the till, or even (in desperation) two flies climbing a wall. Gambling on sporting events is a national obsession.

Australians are passionate about sport ('life be in it'), which is an integral part of Australian culture. The country is highly successful in international competitions, particularly swimming, which isn't surprising as training includes trying to out-swim a great white shark! Australians can be found in their natural state on a beach or anywhere where there's water (when not in a pub). However, with the exception of those who spend their time wrestling crocodiles, boxing kangaroos or out-running water buffalo, the nearest most Australians get to working up a sweat is their TV. Despite the popular image of Australians as bronzed, muscular lifesavers and bathing beauties, the majority are overweight and unfit – a popular 'sport' in the outback is 'whammying', where fatties attempt to knock each other over with their beer bellies! Nevertheless, when achievements are measured against population, Australia is the foremost sporting nation in the world (but don't tell the Aussies – they're conceited enough as it is). Australia has fierce sporting rivalry with its neighbour New Zealand (particularly in rugby), although the most popular sport is Pommy bashing, which reaches its peak in the annual humiliation of the Poms at cricket. However, although they're sports fanatics, Australians believe in fair play and love to root for the underdog – unless it's the English, in which case they yearn to see them ground into the dust.

It's a common misconception among foreigners that Australians speak English – amazingly some people even go to Australia to *learn* English! However, don't expect Australians to speak British English or even American English (the Mad Max movies had to be dubbed for American audiences!). The only people who speak proper English in Australia are the foreigners, apart, that is, from the million or so migrants who hardly speak a word of it. Australians converse in a secret language (slanguage) called 'strine', full of strange words, ungrammatical phonetic spelling, rhyming slang, blasphemy, profanity and fun (Aussies have some of the most colourful abuse in the world). Aussies routinely abbreviate everything, as it's usually too hot to say the whole word (and opening your mouth lets the flies in); most syllables are omitted to save energy – besides which, enunciating clearly is difficult when you're pissed.

Which brings us to the Aussies' favourite pastime – boozing. The Aussies' natural habitat is a pub (preferably close to a beach), where they spend their waking hours between visits to the dole office and the meat pie van. Their favourite tipple is ice-cold beer, otherwise know as amber nectar, neck oil, a cold one, etc., or a glass of Chateau Chumbawumba for the wimps. Aussies are passionate about their local beers and aren't particularly complimentary about brands brewed in other states (outside Queensland, XXXX stands for CRAP). In truth, Aussies don't really care much for beer, which is just an excuse for a good vomit (chunder, technicolor yawn, kark, laugh at the ground, shout for Ruth, big spit, etc.). However, despite their awesome reputation as a nation of drunks, Aussies aren't generally great drinkers and they consume less alcohol per head than the inhabitants of most European countries (which is best not mentioned in your local pub in Oz). Recent figures published by World Drink Trends showed Australia languishing in an ignominious 20th place.

Australia has long been famous for its 'cultural cringe' and is still occasionally typecast as a land of mutton-eating philistines, although it's no longer the cultural desert some would have you believe. It may come as a surprise that not all Aussies are beer-swilling, loud-mouthed, uncultured yobbos and some have even been known to visit theatres and listen to classical music (Australia even has an opera house!). Nowadays Australians export their culture in the guise of films, TV programmes, art and music, which are disseminated around the globe. It's even possible to take a degree in Australian studies, which lasts for *a whole week* and includes an in-depth study of Fosters, barbies, surfing, Neighbours, cricket, Germaine Greer, Skippy, Mad Max, Olivia Newton John, Crocodile Dundee, footy, Rolf Harris, Kylie, the bush, Clive James, the Sydney Opera House, Dame Edna Everage and the Bee Gees. Note, however, that although they have a sharp (crude) sense of humour, the Aussies are somewhat lacking in mirth when it comes to attacks on their culture, and newcomers should tread warily.

Aussies are infamous for their macho, ocker image and a peculiar Aussie male bonding called mateship (similar to American buddyship). Australian men are men's men, and mainstream males (i.e. the heterosexual half of the nation) have no time for limp-wristed gays. However, rumour has it that Australian men are becoming more sensitive (heaven forbid!), that ockerism is dead and Aussie men are now sensitive new age guys – although anyone who believes that is a few snags short of a barbie (a sensitive Aussie is an oxymoron). The lifestyle magazine Ralph (Responsible And Lovable Piss-Head) is much nearer the mark and is targeted at the ubiquitous incorrect bloke interested mainly in sport, beer, sex, humour, motors, boys' toys and trivia (not necessarily in that order – some Aussies actually prefer sex to beer, but most have a bigger capacity for booze).

Aussie males are rampant chauvinists (not surprisingly, women's lib passed Australia by), and some of their more flattering terms for women include bush pigs, swamp hogs and maggots – a good looking Sheila is a 'glamour maggot' or 'glam mag'. Paradoxically, Australia was the one of the first countries in the world to give women the vote, although they were still banned from the pub (not that most women would have been seen dead in one). When attending social functions, men traditionally congregate at one end of the room (or garden), usually where the booze is, and the Sheilas at the other (attending to the food). Despite their ocker image, many Australians are apparently (according to a recent 'survey') considerate lovers when sober, although they're also among the world's fastest performers (they don't want to waste valuable drinking time). To the average Aussie male, foreplay is 'hey Sheila, you wanna ****?' and sex drive is doing it in the back of a panel van. (While on the subject of sex, readers may wish to know that if they go to their corner shop and ask for some Durex, they're likely to end up with a roll of sticky tape.)

Australian politicians (pollies) are world leaders in mismanagement and some of the most hilarious and entertaining in the world (you have to laugh, otherwise you'd cry). In a less liberal country they'd all be locked up, although this would deprive Aussies (not to mention a legion of journalist, cartoonists, broadcasters, etc.) of their best source of jokes. Whatever momentous events are happening elsewhere in the world, you can always rely on Aussie politics for some amusing diversions such as party infighting, defections, sackings, lurks and perks, rorts (scams) and scandals, although strangely there are very few sex scandals – could they all be gay? When not junketing around the world (or abusing their official credit cards, etc.), pollies spend their spare time (well at least a few days a year) hurling personal abuse at each other in parliament (not surprisingly, there are relatively few women politicians in Australia). Aussies have a healthy disrespect (contempt) for their politicians and need to be forced to vote under the threat of fines. The seat of government (Canberra) is appropriately located in the wilds of New South Wales – well away from civilisation and normal people.

Immigration has undeniably made Australia a culturally richer, more diverse and infinitely more interesting country. However, today's Australia is closed to many of the immigrants who have made Australia one of the best countries in the world. (First you were transported for free, then you had to pay £10 and now they won't even let you visit without a visa – if you want to stay, you need to be under 30, speak fluent English, and have a couple of university degrees and ten years' work experience.) However, if you're rejected, try to look on the bright side. The Australian Dream isn't always what it's cracked up to be, and a 1997 survey found that almost half of recently arrived migrants believed they were better off at home (admittedly most were unemployed without access to social security).

Australia's other problems include high suicide and crime rates, high unemployment (plus job insecurity), homelessness, a spiralling drug problem, child poverty, pollution, welfare dependency, a high divorce rate, and a shameful record on preserving its environment, animal life and indigenous peoples (see **Aborigines** on page 446). Many Australians have little optimism, particularly the young, many of whom are in a desperate plight and have been largely abandoned by politicians and business. In the last decade or so, the country has been ravaged by high unemployment, which together with the burgeoning number of single-parent families and low pay, is increasingly creating two Australias: the haves and the have-nots. Pressure on poor families is blamed for causing family breakdowns, domestic violence and lawlessness. Many Australians work too hard, travel too far, arrive home too late, and have kids who go to schools too far away. These problems are by no means unique to Australia in today's ever-competitive world and are shared by most western countries. However, how Australia faces up to them and the challenges of the new millennium will shape its future for generations to come.

Australians were profoundly shocked by the recession in the early '90s, which destroyed the myth of economic security and eternal prosperity. In the '90s, Australians were under siege from all sides, with many of their traditional beliefs and values swept away by events largely beyond their control (such as Asia's economic meltdown). In recent years, Australia has appeared to be retreating from the rest of the world (the great leap backwards), introverted and inward-looking, unable to come to terms with its past, frightened by the future, and with political 'leaders' who lack strategy or direction. Many people consider that the current Liberal-National coalition government represents the old (widely discredited) conservative approach, and not the brave new world and opportunities that Australia needs to grasp in order to establish itself as a dynamic force in the modern world.

**And now for the good news!** Australia is one of the most open, liberal, stable and tolerant societies in the world. It has a strong economy, with political stability, abundant natural resources, a skilled workforce, steady population growth, and substantial domestic and foreign capital investment. It's renowned for its wonderful climate, rugged beauty, outdoor lifestyle, superb beaches, unique wildlife, excellent restaurants (and barbecues), friendly people, creativity, open spaces, excellent sports facilities, cultural diversity, freedom, good transportation and health care, excellent local government and things that work.

Australia is rated as one of the top countries in the world for its quality of life, and Sydney was ranked first and Melbourne fifth in a 1997 survey of the 'best' cities in the world by the American *Travel and Leisure* magazine. Some say that Sydney is like America before the innocence faded, a truly cosmopolitan, international city. Australians rank among the world's most contented people and are generally happy with life, although paradoxically many people reckon that life is getting worse. However, most Australians are eternal optimists, although newcomers should be aware that 'she'll be right' is code for 'everything that can go wrong will' and 'no worries' means 'it has screwed up again'. Aussies are informal, casual (relaxed to the point of sleep) and straight talkers ('tell it as it is'), and will expect you to be open and friendly also. One of the things that endears Aussies to foreigners is their outrageous sense of humour and ability to poke fun at themselves and everyone else. Australians generally take people as they find them and, if you're friendly and make an effort to adapt to their way of life, they may even take to you.

Australia is nothing if not a land of contradictions and, despite the gloomy predictions from some quarters, most Australians have remarkable faith in themselves and optimism for the future. Although immigrants may criticise some aspects of Australian life, relatively few seriously consider leaving and most are proud to call themselves Aussies. In fact, immigrants from a vast range of backgrounds firmly believe that Australia is the best country in the world. Few other nations offer such an irrepressible and exciting lifestyle. For sheer vitality and *joie de vivre*, Australia has few equals and, for the fortunate few who are lucky enough to secure a residence visa, it's a land where you can turn your dreams into reality. Australia remains a country of great opportunity, although perhaps no longer the Lucky Country (if it ever was – you make you're own luck in Oz through hard yakka). Provided you maintain a sense of humour about everything, you too may find that 'she will indeed be all right'!

**A few final words of caution – whatever you do don't whinge!** Newcomers should never compare Australia unfavourably with their home country (the worst sin is to say repeatedly, 'we do it like this/better at home'). However, if you really want to rile the Aussies, you could complain about their boring blue skies; tell them their beer's too cold and their wine's too warm, the sun's too hot (and gives you cancer), there are too many flies and bugs, their birds squawk instead of singing, much of the wildlife is out to eat or kill you, and everywhere you turn there are smiling, friendly Aussies.

One last tip, don't believe everything you read; for example, despite what it says above, the Poms adore the Aussies – but we do occasionally like to get our own back for all those humiliating cricket defeats!

**Long Live Australia! God Save the Queen! Up the Republic!**

# 20.

# MOVING HOUSE OR LEAVING AUSTRALIA

W hen moving house or leaving Australia, there are many things to be considered and a 'million' people to be informed. The checklists contained in this chapter are designed to make the task easier and with luck help prevent an ulcer or a nervous breakdown, provided of course you don't leave everything to the last minute (only divorce and bereavement cause more stress than moving house). See also **Moving House** on page 140 and **Relocation Consultants** on page 121.

## MOVING HOUSE

When moving house within Australia, the following items should be considered:

- If you live in rented accommodation, you must give your landlord notice (the period will depend on your contract). You may need to remain until a minimum period has elapsed and, if you don't give your landlord sufficient notice, you'll be required to pay the rent until the end of your contract or for the full notice period. This will also apply if you have a separate contract for a garage or other rented property, e.g. a holiday home.

- Inform the following:

  - Your employer.

  - If you're a homeowner and are moving to a new council area, you should inform your present council when you move and re-register in your new council area after arrival. When moving to a new area or state, you may be entitled to a refund of a portion of your property taxes (rates).

  - Your electricity, gas and water companies.

  - Your telephone company (or companies).

  - Your insurance companies (for example health, car and home), banks, building societies, credit union, post office, stockbroker and other financial institutions, credit and charge card companies, hire purchase companies, solicitor and accountant, and local businesses where you have accounts.

  - Your family doctor, dentist and other health practitioners. Health records should be transferred to your new doctor and dentist, if applicable.

  - Your children's schools. If applicable, arrange for schooling in your new area. Try to give a term's notice and obtain a copy of any relevant school reports or records from your children's current schools.

  - All regular correspondents, social and sports clubs, professional and trade journals, and friends and relatives. Give or send them your new address and telephone number. Arrange to have your mail redirected by Australia Post (see **Change of Address** on page 160).

  - If you have an Australian driving licence or an Australian registered car, give your local state traffic authority (see **Appendix A**) your new address as soon as possible after moving.

  - Your local consulate or embassy, if you're registered with them (see page 115).

- Return any library books or anything borrowed.

- Arrange removal of your furniture and belongings by booking a removal company (see page 121) well in advance. If you have only a few items of furniture to move, you may prefer to do your own move, in which case you may need to hire a van.

- Arrange for a cleaning company and/or decorating company for rented accommodation, if required.

- If you're renting, make sure that you get your bond returned.

- Cancel milk and newspaper deliveries.

- **Ask yourself (again): 'Is it really worth all this trouble?'**

## LEAVING AUSTRALIA

Before leaving Australia permanently or for an indefinite period, the following items should be considered *in addition* to those listed above under **Moving House**:

- Give notice to your employer, if applicable.

- Check that your family's passports aren't out of date.

- Check whether any special requirements (e.g. visas, permits, inoculations) are necessary for entry into your country of destination by contacting your local embassy or consulate in Australia. An exit permit or visa isn't required to leave Australia.

- Book a removal company (see page 121) well in advance. International shipping companies usually provide a wealth of information and may also be able to advise you on various matters concerning your relocation. Find out the exact procedure for shipping your belongings to your country of destination from the relevant embassy in Australia (don't rely entirely on your shipping company). Special forms may need to be completed before arrival. If you've been living in Australia for less than a year, you're required to export all personal effects, including furniture and vehicles that were imported tax and duty free.

- Arrange to sell anything that you won't be taking with you, e.g. house, car and furniture.

- You may qualify for a rebate on your tax payments (see page 354). If you're leaving Australia permanently and have been a member of a superannuation scheme, your super benefits won't be paid until you reach the 'preservation' age, i.e. 55 for those born before 1st July 1960 and 60 for those born after 30th June 1964. Contact your employer's personnel office or your superannuation company for information.

- If you have an Australian-registered car which you're permanently exporting, you should ask your local state traffic authority to de-register the vehicle, and register it in your new country of residence on arrival (as necessary).

- Depending on your destination, your pets may require special inoculations or may need to go into quarantine for a period (see page 461).

- Contact your telephone and other utility companies well in advance, particularly if you need to get deposits repaid.

- Arrange health, travel and other insurance as necessary (see **Chapter 13**).

- Depending on your destination, arrange health and dental check-ups for your family before leaving Australia. Obtain a copy of all your health and dental records and a statement from your health insurance company noting your present level of cover.

- Terminate any outstanding loan, lease or hire purchase contracts and pay all outstanding bills (allow plenty of time, as some companies may be slow to respond).

- Check whether you're entitled to a rebate on your car and other insurance. Obtain a letter from your Australian motor insurance company stating your number of years without claim.

- Sell your house, apartment or other property, or arrange to let it through a friend or a letting agency (see **Chapter 5**). If you sell a second home in Australia, you may need to pay capital gains tax on any profit made on the sale (see page 359).

- Check whether you need an international driving permit or a translation of your Australian or foreign driving licence for your country of destination.

- Give friends and business associates in Australia a temporary address and telephone number where you can be contacted overseas.

- If you're travelling by air, allow plenty of time to get to the airport, register your luggage and clear security and immigration.

- Buy a copy of *Living and Working in* ******** before leaving Australia. If we haven't written it yet, drop us a line and we'll get started on it right away!

**Have a safe journey!**

# APPENDICES

## APPENDIX A: USEFUL ADDRESSES

# Embassies and Consulates (Canberra)

A full list of embassies and consulates in Australia is contained in two booklets (*Diplomatic List* and *Consular List*) published by the Department of Foreign Affairs and Trade and available from the Australian Government Publishing Service. Note that business hours vary considerably and all embassies close on their national holidays as well as on Australian public holidays. Always telephone to check opening hours before visiting. A selection of embassies in Canberra is listed below:

**Austria:** 12 Talbot Street, Forrest, ACT 2603 (☎ 02-6295 1533/1376, 🖥 www. austriaemb.org.au).

**Belgium:** 19 Arkana Street, Yarralumla, ACT 2600 (☎ 02-6273 2501).

**Canada:** Commonwealth Avenue, Yarralumla, ACT 2600 (☎ 02-6270 4000).

**China:** 15 Coronation Drive, Yarralumla, ACT 2600 (☎ 02-6273 4780).

**Denmark:** 15 Hunter Street, Yarralumla, ACT 2600 (☎ 02-6273 2195).

**Finland:** 10 Darwin Avenue, Yarralumla, ACT 2600 (☎ 02-6273 3800, 🖥 www. finland.org.au).

**France:** 6 Perth Avenue, Yarralumla, ACT 2600 (☎ 02-6216 0100, 🖥 www.france. net.au/official).

**Germany:** 119 Empire Circuit, Empire Cct Yarralumla, ACT 2600 (☎ 02-6270 1911, 🖥 www.germanembassy.org.au).

**Greece:** Cnr Turrana Street, Yarralumla, ACT 2600 (☎ 02-6273 3011).

**Indonesia:** 8 Darwin Avenue, Yarralumla, ACT 2600 (☎ 02-6250 8600).

**Ireland:** 20 Arkana Street, Yarralumla, ACT 2600 (☎ 02-6273 3022).

**Israel:** 6 Turrana Street, Yarralumla, ACT 2600 (☎ 02-6273 1309).

**Italy:** 12 Grey Street, Deakin, ACT 2600 (☎ 02-6273 3333, 🖥 www.ambitalia. org.au).

**Japan:** 112 Empire Circuit, Yarralumla, ACT 2600 (☎ 02-6273 3244, 🖥 www. japan.org.au).

**Korea:** 113 Empire Circuit, Yarralumla, ACT 2600 (☎ 02-6273 3044).

**Malaysia:** 7 Perth Avenue, Yarralumla, ACT 2600 (☎ 02-6273 1543).

**Netherlands:** 120 Empire Circuit, Yarralumla, ACT 2600 (☎ 02-6273 3206).

**New Zealand:** Commonwealth Avenue, Canberra, ACT 2600 (☎ 02-6270 4211).

**Norway:** 18 Mugga Way, Red Hill, ACT 2603 (☎ 02-6295 1048).

**Papua New Guinea:** 39-41 Forster Crescent, Yarralumla, ACT 2600 (☎ 02-6273 3322).

**Philippines:** 1 Moonah Place, Yarralumla, ACT 2600 (☎ 02-6273 2535, 🖥 www. philembassy.au.com).

**Portugal:** 23 Culgoa Circuit, O'Malley, ACT 2606 (☎ 02-6290 1733).

**Russia:** 76 Canberra Avenue, Griffith, ACT 2603 (☎ 02-6295 9033).

**Singapore:** 17 Forster Crescent, Yarralumla, ACT 2600 (☎ 02-6273 3944).

**South Africa:** Corner State Circle and Rhodes Place, Yarralumla, ACT 2600 (☎ 02-6273 2424, 🖳 www.rsa.emb.gov.au).

**Spain:** 15 Arkana Street, Yarralumla, ACT 2600 (☎ 02-6273 3555).

**Sweden:** Turrana Street, Yarralumla, ACT 2600 (☎ 02-6273 3033).

**Switzerland:** 7 Melbourne Avenue, Forrest, ACT 2603 (☎ 02-6273 3977).

**Thailand:**111 Empire Circuit, Yarralumla, ACT 2600 (☎ 02-6270 2700).

**United Kingdom:** Commonwealth Avenue, Canberra, ACT 2600 (☎ 02-6270 6666, 🖳 www.uk.emb.gov.au).

**USA:** 21 Moonah Place, Yarralumla, ACT 2600 (☎ 02-6214 5600).

# Australian Customs Service

**Australian Capital Territory:** Australian Customs Service, 5 Constitution Avenue, Canberra, ACT 2601 (☎ 02-6275 6666).

**New South Wales:** Regional Director of Customs, Sydney Central Building, 477 Pitt Street, Sydney, NSW 2000 (☎ 02-9213 2000).

**Northern Territory:** Regional Director of Customs, 21 Lindsay Street, Darwin, NT 0800 (☎ 08-8946 9999).

**Queensland:** Regional Director of Customs, Terrica Place, 140 Creek Street, Brisbane, QLD 4000 (☎ 07-3835 3444).

**South Australia:** Regional Director of Customs, 220 Commercial Road, Port Adelaide, SA 5015 (☎ 08-8847 9211).

**Tasmania:** Regional Director of Customs, Imports/Exports, Level 1, 25 Argyle Street, Hobart, TAS 7000 (☎ 03-6230 1201).

**Victoria:** Regional Director of Customs, Lexington Building, 414 Latrobe Street, Melbourne, VIC 3001 (☎ 03-9244 8000).

**Western Australia:** Regional Director of Customs, 2 Henry Street, Fremantle, WA 6160 (☎ 08-9430 1444).

# Motor Vehicle Registration Authorities

**Australian Capital Territory:** Transport Regulation, GPO Box 582, Dickson, ACT 2602 (☎ 02-6207 7000).

**New South Wales:** Registrar of Motor Vehicles, Roads and Traffic Authority, GPO Box K198, Haymarket, NSW 2000 (☎ freecall 1800-624384 or 02-9218 6888).

**Northern Territory:** Motor Vehicle Registry, GPO Box 530, Darwin, NT 0801 (☎ 08-8999 3150).

**Queensland:** Queensland Transport, Registration Division, GPO Box 2451, Brisbane, QLD 4700 (☎ 07-3253 4700).

**South Australia:** Technical Department, State Wide Compliance Management Group, Katena Street, Regency Park SA 5010 (☎ 08-8348 9599).

**Tasmania:** Registrar of Motor Vehicles, GPO Box 1002K, Hobart, TAS 7000 (☎ 03-6233 5201).

**Victoria:** Vic Roads, 60 Denmark Street, Kew, VIC 3101 (☎ 13-1171 or 1800-814762).

**Western Australia:** Department of Transport, Licensing Division, 21 Murry Road South, Welshpool, WA 6101 (☎ 08-9351 1680).

# Miscellaneous

**Australian American Association**, Level 1, 2 Eden Street, Sydney, NSW 2000, Australia (☎ 02-8920 0641, 💻 www.aaafed.asn.au).

**Australian-Britain Society**, National Office, PO Box 9088, Deakin, ACT 2600, Australia (☎ 02-6273 5818, 💻 www.aust-britsociety.org.au).

**Australian-British Chamber of Commerce**, 393 Strand, London WC2R 0LT, UK (☎ 020-7379 0720, 💻 www.britishchamber.com).

**Australian Embassy**, 1601 Massachusetts Ave., NW, Washington, DC 20036, USA (☎ 202-797-3000, 💻 www.austemb.org).

**Australian High Commission**, Australia House, Strand, London WC2B 4LA, UK (☎ 020-7379 4334, 💻 www.australia.org.uk).

**Australian Taxation Office**, 2 Constitution Avenue, Canberra, ACT 2601, Australia (Excise Inquiry Line ☎1300-657 162, 💻 www.ato.gov.au).

**Australian Tourist Commission**, 1st Floor, Gemini House, 10-18 Putney Hill, London SW15 6AA, UK (☎ 020-8780 2227, 💻 www.australia.com).

**BDS Challenge International**, 80 Tribune Street, Brisbane, QLD 4101, Australia (☎ 07-3844 8093, 💻 www.bdstech.com.au). International employment agency.

**Department of Industrial Relations, Employment, Training & Further Education**, 1 Oxford Street, Darlinghurst, NSW 2010, Australia (☎ 02-9243 8888, 💻 www.dir.nsw.gov.au).

**Financial and Migrant Information Service**, Commonwealth Bank of Australia, Senator House, 85 Queen Victoria Street, London EC4V 4HA, UK (☎ 020-7710 3990, 💻 www.firb.gov.au). Publishes a free annual booklet for prospective migrants.

**Foreign Investment Review Board**, Department of the Treasury, Parkes Place, Parkes, ACT 2600, Australia (☎ 02-6263 3795). Provide information about buying property in Australia for non-residents and retirees.

**United Kingdom Settlers' Association (UKSA)**, PO Box 707, South Yarra, Victoria 3141, Australia (☎ 03-9787 3112, ✉ endeavour@start.com.au).

# APPENDIX B: FURTHER READING

There are many useful reference books for those seeking general information about Australia, including the *Year Book Australia* published annually by the Australian Bureau of Statistics. The Australia Government Publishing Service (AGPS, GPO Box 84, Canberra, ACT 2601) publishes and distributes a wealth of useful publications for prospective migrants, businessmen and visitors, and professional publications can be obtained from Australian Professional Publications, 220 Pacific Highway, Crows Nest, NSW 2065. A selection of books about Australia is listed below (the publication title is followed by the name of the author and the publisher's name in brackets). Books prefixed with an asterisk (*) are recommended by the author. Some of the books listed are out of print, but you may still be able to find a copy in a bookshop or library.

## Living & Working

**The Australian Immigration Book** (Made-To-Measure)

***The Cost of Living and Housing Survey Book** (Commonwealth Bank of Australia)

***Getting a Job in Australia**, Nick Vandome (How To Books)

**Live and Work in Australia and New Zealand**, Fiona McGregor, Charlotte Denny (Vacation Work)

**Live, Work & Play in Australia**, Sharyn McCullum (Kangaroo Press)

**Living & Working in Australia**, Laura Veltman (How To Books)

## Tourist Guides

***Australia** (Lonely Planet)

***Australia: Insight Guide** (Insight Guides)

***Australia: The Rough Guide**, Margo Daly et al (The Rough Guides)

***Australia & New Zealand Travel Planner** (TNT Magazine - See **Magazines & Newspapers**)

**Australia & New Zealand, Travellers Survival Kit**, Susan Griffith & Simon Calder (Vacation Work)

**Berlitz Pocket Guide to Australia** (Berlitz)

***Discover Australia**, Ken Bernstein (Berlitz)

**Essential Australia** (Automobile Association)

**Explore Australia: 2002** (Viking Australia)

***Frommers Australia from $50 a Day** (Macmillan Travel)

***Insider's Australia Guide**, Harry Blutstein (MPC)

**Let's Go 2001: Australia** (Pan)

***Maverick Guide to Australia**, Robert W. Bone (Pelican)

***Sydney Time Out Guide** (Penguin)

Note also that Lonely Planet and The Rough Guide publish numerous state, city and activity guides to Australia.

# Travel Literature

**Australia: True Stories of Life Down Under** (Traveler's Tales)
**Daisy Bates in the Desert**, Julia Blackburn (Minerva)
**\*Down Under**, Bill Bryson (Doubleday)
**\*In The Land Of Oz**, Howard Jacobson (Penguin)
**Outdoor Traveller's Australia** (Stewart, Tabori, Chang)
**A Ride in the Neon Sun**, Josie Dew (Little, Brown & Company)
**\*The Ribbon and the Ragged Square**, Linda Christmas (Penguin)
**\*Sean and David's Long Drive**, Sean Condon (Lonely Planet)
**\*Sydney**, Jan Morris (Penguin)
**Tracks**, Robyn Davidson (Vintage)

# The Great Outdoors

**Australian Bushcraft**, Richard Graves (Taylor-Type)
**Bicycle Touring in Australia**, Leigh Hemmings (Mountaineer Books)
**\*Bushwalking in Australia**, John Chapman (Lonely Planet)
**Bush Tucker: Australia's Wild Food**, Tim Low (Angus & Robertson)
**Cycling Australia**, Nicola Wells (Lonely Planet)
**Discover Australia by 4WD** (Hema Maps Pty Ltd)
**How to Survive Australia**, Robert Treborlang (Major Mitchell Press)
**\*Outback Australia** (Lonely Planet)
**Outback Australia? No Worries!**, Peter Wearing Smith (Omni Travel)
**\*Safe Outback Travel**, Jack Absalom (Five Mile Press)
**\*Stay Alive, A Handbook on Survival**, Maurice Dunlevy (AGPS)

# Australians

**12 Edmondstone Street**, David Malouf (Penguin)
**The Australians, In Search of an Identity**, Ross Terrill (Bantam)
**\*The Australian People**, Craig McGregor (Hodder & Stoughton)
**Christina Stead**, Hazel Rowley (William Heinemann)
**Contemporary Australians**: (DW Thorpe)
**Culture Shock! Australia**, Ilsa Sharp (Kuperard)
**\*A Fortunate Life**, Albert Facey (Viking)

*From Strength to Strength, Sara Henderson
*More Please, Barry Humphries (Penguin)
*Patrick White: A Life, David Marr (Vintage)
*Robert J Hawke, Blanche D'Alpuget (Penguin)
*Unreliable Memoirs, Clive James (Picador)
Wild Card, Dorothy Hewett (Virago)

# History/Culture

Australia's Immigrants 1788-1978, Geoffrey Sherington (Allen & Unwin)
*The Fatal Shore, Robert Hughes (Pan)
*The Lucky Country: Australia in the Sixties, Donald Horne (Angus & Robertson)
*The Penguin History of Australia, John Malony (Penguin)
*The Road to Botany Bay, Paul Carter (Faber & Faber)
*A Secret Country, John Pilger (Vintage)
A Short History of Australia, Manning Clarke (Penguin)

# Aboriginal Australia

Aboriginal Art, Wally Caruana (Thames & Hudson)
Aboriginal Australians, K. Suter, K. Stearman (Minority Rights Group)
Charles Perkins, Peter Read (Viking)
Mutant Message Down Under, Mario Morgan (Thorsons)
*The Other Side of the Frontier, Henry Reynolds
*My People, Kath Walker (Jacaranga Wiley)
*My Place, Sally Morgan (Virago)
Seeing the First Australians, Ian & Tamsin Donaldson (Allen & Unwin)
*The Songlines, Bruce Chatwin (Picador)
*Triumph of the Nomads, Geoffrey Blainey (Macmillan)
*Wandering Girl, Glenys Ward (Virago)

# Miscellaneous

The 100 Things Everyone Needs to Know About Australia, David Dale (Pan McMillan)
Australia (Commonwealth of Australia)
*Australia & New Zealand by Rail, Colin Taylor (Bradt)
*The Book of Australia (Watermark Press)
*The Great Barrier Reef (Readers Digest)

**How to Be Normal in Australia**, Robert Treborlang (Major Mitchell Press)

**The Little Aussie Fact Book**, Margaret Nicholson (Penguin)

***The Penguin Australian Encyclopaedia**, Sarah Dawson (Penguin)

***The Sydney Morning Herald Good Food Guide**, Terry Durak & Jill Dupleix

**Traditional Australian Cooking**, Shirley Constantine (McPhee Gribble/Penguin)

***The Wines of Australia**, Oliver Mayo (Faber & Faber)

# Magazines & Newspapers

**Australia News**, Outbound Newspapers, 1 Commercial Road, Eastbourne, East Sussex BN21 3XQ, UK (☎ 01323-726040, 🖥 www.outbound-newspapers.com).

**Australian Outlook**, Consyl Publishing, 3 Buckhurst Road, Bexhill-on-Sea, East Sussex TN40 1QF, UK (☎ 01424-223111, 🖥 www.consylpublishing.co.uk).

**Southern Cross**. Free weekly newspaper for homesick Aussies (published by TNT – see below).

**TNT Magazine**, 14-15 Child's Place, Earls Court, London SW5 9RX, UK (☎ 020-7373 3377, 🖥 www.tnt-live.com). Free weekly magazine for expatriate Australians.

# APPENDIX C: WEIGHTS & MEASURES

Australia uses the metric system of measurement (although some goods are still sold in imperial sizes and weights). Nationals of a few countries (including the Americans and British) who are more familiar with the imperial system of measurement will find the tables on the following pages useful. Some comparisons shown are only approximate, but are close enough for most everyday uses. In addition to the variety of measurement systems used, clothes sizes often vary considerably with the manufacturer (as we all know only too well). Try all clothes on before buying and don't be afraid to return something if, when you try it on at home, you decide it doesn't fit (most shops will exchange goods or give a refund).

## Women's Clothes

| Continental | 34 | 36 | 38 | 40 | 42 | 44 | 46 | 48 | 50 | 52 |
|---|---|---|---|---|---|---|---|---|---|---|
| UK | 8 | 10 | 12 | 14 | 16 | 18 | 20 | 22 | 24 | 26 |
| USA | 6 | 8 | 10 | 12 | 14 | 16 | 18 | 20 | 22 | 24 |

## Pullovers

| | Women's | | | | | | Men's | | | | |
|---|---|---|---|---|---|---|---|---|---|---|---|
| Continental | 40 | 42 | 44 | 46 | 48 | 50 | 44 | 46 | 48 | 50 | 52 | 54 |
| UK | 34 | 36 | 38 | 40 | 42 | 44 | 34 | 36 | 38 | 40 | 42 | 44 |
| USA | 34 | 36 | 38 | 40 | 42 | 44 | sm | medium | large | | | xl |

**Note: sm = small, xl = extra large**

## Men's Shirts

| Continental | 36 | 37 | 38 | 39 | 40 | 41 | 42 | 43 | 44 | 46 |
|---|---|---|---|---|---|---|---|---|---|---|
| UK/USA | 14 | 14 | 15 | 15 | 16 | 16 | 17 | 17 | 18 | - |

## Men's Underwear

| Continental | 5 | 6 | 7 | 8 | 9 | 10 |
|---|---|---|---|---|---|---|
| UK | 34 | 36 | 38 | 40 | 42 | 44 |
| USA | small | medium | large | extra large | | |

## Children's Clothes

| Continental | 92 | 104 | 116 | 128 | 140 | 152 |
|---|---|---|---|---|---|---|
| UK | 16/18 | 20/22 | 24/26 | 28/30 | 32/34 | 36/38 |
| USA | 2 | 4 | 6 | 8 | 10 | 12 |

## Children's Shoes

| Continental | 18 | 19 | 20 | 21 | 22 | 23 | 24 | 25 | 26 | 27 | 28 | 29 | 30 | 31 | 32 |
|---|---|---|---|---|---|---|---|---|---|---|---|---|---|---|---|
| UK/USA | 2 | 3 | 4 | 4 | 5 | 6 | 7 | 7 | 8 | 9 | 10 | 11 | 11 | 12 | 13 |

| Continental | 33 | 34 | 35 | 36 | 37 | 38 |
|---|---|---|---|---|---|---|
| UK/USA | 1 | 2 | 2 | 3 | 4 | 5 |

## Shoes (Women's and Men's)

| Continental | 35 | 35 | 36 | 37 | 37 | 38 | 39 | 39 | 40 | 40 | 41 | 42 | 42 | 43 | 44 | 44 |
|---|---|---|---|---|---|---|---|---|---|---|---|---|---|---|---|---|
| UK | 2 | 3 | 3 | 4 | 4 | 5 | 5 | 6 | 6 | 7 | 7 | 8 | 8 | 9 | 9 | 10 |
| USA | 4 | 4 | 5 | 5 | 6 | 6 | 7 | 7 | 8 | 8 | 9 | 9 | 10 | 10 | 11 | 11 |

## Weight

| Avoirdupois | Metric | Metric | Avoirdupois |
|---|---|---|---|
| 1 oz | 28.35 g | 1 g | 0.035 oz |
| 1 pound* | 454 g | 100 g | 3.5 oz |
| 1 cwt | 50.8 kg | 250 g | 9 oz |
| 1 ton | 1,016 kg | 500g | 18 oz |
| 1 tonne | 2,205 pounds | 1 kg | 2.2 pounds |

**\* A metric 'pound' is 500g, g = gramme, kg = kilogramme**

## Length

| British/US | Metric | Metric | British/US |
|---|---|---|---|
| 1 inch | 2.54 cm | 1 cm | 0.39 inch |
| 1 foot | 30.48 cm | 1 m | 3 feet 3.25 inches |
| 1 yard | 91.44 cm | 1 km | 0.62 mile |
| 1 mile | 1.6 km | 8 km | 5 miles |

**Note: cm = centimetre, m = metre, km = kilometre**

## Capacity

| Imperial | Metric | Metric | Imperial |
|---|---|---|---|
| 1 pint (USA) | 0.47 litre | 1 litre | 1.76 UK pints |
| 1 pint (UK) | 0.57 litre | 1 litre | 0.26 US gallons |
| 1 gallon (USA) | 3.78 litre | 1 litre | 0.22 UK gallon |
| 1 gallon (UK) | 4.54 litre | 1 litre | 35.21 fluid oz |

## Square Measure

| British/US | Metric | Metric | British/US |
|---|---|---|---|
| 1 square inch | 0.45 sq. cm | 1 sq. cm | 0.15 sq. inches |
| 1 square foot | 0.09 sq.m | 1 sq. m | 10.76 sq. feet |
| 1 square yard | 0.84 sq. m | 1 sq. m | 1. 2 sq. yards |
| 1 acre | 0.4 hectares | 1 hectare | 2.47 acres |
| 1 square mile | 259 hectares | 1 sq. km | 0.39 sq. mile |

## Temperature

| ° Celsius | ° Fahrenheit | |
|---|---|---|
| 0 | 32 | freezing point of water |
| 5 | 41 | |
| 10 | 50 | |
| 15 | 59 | |
| 20 | 68 | |
| 25 | 77 | |
| 30 | 86 | |
| 35 | 95 | |
| 40 | 104 | |

**Note: The boiling point of water is 100°C / 212°F.**

## Oven Temperature

| Gas | Electric | |
|---|---|---|
| | °F | °C |
| - | 225–250 | 110–120 |
| 1 | 275 | 140 |
| 2 | 300 | 150 |
| 3 | 325 | 160 |
| 4 | 350 | 180 |
| 5 | 375 | 190 |
| 6 | 400 | 200 |
| 7 | 425 | 220 |
| 8 | 450 | 230 |
| 9 | 475 | 240 |

For a quick conversion, the Celsius temperature is approximately half the Fahrenheit temperature.

## Temperature Conversion

Celsius to Fahrenheit: multiply by 9, divide by 5 and add 32.
Fahrenheit to Celsius: subtract 32, multiply by 5 and divide by 9.

## Body Temperature

Normal body temperature (if you're alive and well) is 98.4° Fahrenheit, which equals 37° Celsius.

# APPENDIX D: MAP OF AUSTRALIA

The map of Australia opposite shows the states of Australia, which are listed below along with their capital cities.

| State/Territory | Capital |
| --- | --- |
| Australian Capital Territory (ACT) | Canberra |
| New South Wales (NSW) | Sydney |
| Northern Territory (NT) | Darwin |
| Queensland (QLD) | Brisbane |
| South Australia (SA) | Adelaide |
| Tasmania (TAS) | Hobart |
| Victoria (VIC) | Melbourne |
| Western Australia (WA) | Perth |

# INDEX

# F

# J

# L

# M

# T

# U

# V

# W

# Y

# Z

# LIVING AND WORKING SERIES

*Living and Working* books are essential reading for anyone planning to spend time abroad, including holiday-home owners, retirees, visitors, business people, migrants, students and even extra-terrestrials! They're packed with important and useful information designed to help you **avoid costly mistakes and save both time and money.** Topics covered include how to:

- Find a job with a good salary & conditions
- Obtain a residence permit
- Avoid and overcome problems
- Find your dream home
- Get the best education for your family
- Make the best use of public transport
- Endure local motoring habits
- Obtain the best health treatment
- Stretch your money further
- Make the most of your leisure time
- Enjoy the local sporting life
- Find the best shopping bargains
- Insure yourself against most eventualities
- Use post office and telephone services
- Do numerous other things not listed above

*Living and Working* books are the most comprehensive and up-to-date source of practical information available about everyday life abroad. They aren't, however, boring text books, but interesting and entertaining guides written in a highly readable style.

**Discover what it's *really* like to live and work abroad!**

Order your copies today by phone, fax, mail or e-mail from: Survival Books, PO Box 146, Wetherby, West Yorks. LS23 6XZ, United Kingdom (☎/🖨 +44 (0)1937-843523, ✉ orders@ survivalbooks.net, 💻 www.survivalbooks.net).

# ORDER FORM

## ALIEN'S GUIDES / BEST PLACES / BUYING A HOME / DISASTERS / WINES

| Qty. | Title | Price (incl. p&p)* | | | Total |
|---|---|---|---|---|---|
| | | UK | Europe | World | |
| | The Alien's Guide to Britain | £5.95 | £6.95 | £8.45 | |
| | The Alien's Guide to France | £5.95 | £6.95 | £8.45 | |
| | The Best Places to Buy a Home in France | £13.95 | £15.95 | £19.45 | |
| | The Best Places to Buy a Home in Spain | £13.45 | £14.95 | £16.95 | |
| | Buying a Home Abroad | £13.45 | £14.95 | £16.95 | |
| | Buying a Home in Britain | £11.45 | £12.95 | £14.95 | |
| | Buying a Home in Florida | £13.45 | £14.95 | £16.95 | |
| | Buying a Home in France | £13.45 | £14.95 | £16.95 | |
| | Buying a Home in Greece & Cyprus | £13.45 | £14.95 | £16.95 | |
| | Buying a Home in Ireland | £11.45 | £12.95 | £14.95 | |
| | Buying a Home in Italy | £13.45 | £14.95 | £16.95 | |
| | Buying a Home in Portugal | £13.45 | £14.95 | £16.95 | |
| | Buying a Home in Spain | £13.45 | £14.95 | £16.95 | |
| | How to Avoid Holiday & Travel Disasters | £13.45 | £14.95 | £16.95 | |
| | Renovating & Maintaining Your French Home | Autumn 2003 | | | |
| | Rioja and its Wines | £11.45 | £12.95 | £14.95 | |
| | The Wines of Spain | £15.95 | £18.45 | £21.95 | |
| | | | | **Total** | |

Order your copies today by phone, fax, mail or e-mail from: Survival Books, PO Box 146, Wetherby, West Yorks. LS23 6XZ, UK (☎/▤ +44 (0)1937-843523, ✉ orders@survivalbooks.net, 🖥 www.survivalbooks.net). If you aren't entirely satisfied, simply return them to us within 14 days for a full and unconditional refund.

Cheque enclosed/please charge my Amex/Delta/MasterCard/Switch/Visa* card

Card No. _ _ _ _    _ _ _ _    _ _ _ _    _ _ _ _

Expiry date _____    Issue number (Switch only) _____

Signature _____    Tel. No. _____

NAME _____

ADDRESS _____

_____

_____

\* Delete as applicable (price includes postage – airmail for Europe/world).

# BUYING A HOME SERIES

*Buying a Home* books are essential reading for anyone planning to purchase property abroad and are designed to guide you through the jungle and make it a pleasant and enjoyable experience. Most importantly, they're packed with vital information to help you **avoid the sort of disasters that can turn your dream home into a nightmare!** Topics covered include:

- Avoiding problems
- Choosing the region
- Finding the right home and location
- Estate agents
- Finance, mortgages and taxes
- Home security
- Utilities, heating and air-conditioning
- Moving house and settling in
- Renting and letting
- Permits and visas
- Travelling and communications
- Health and insurance
- Renting a car and driving
- Retirement and starting a business
- And much, much more!

*Buying a Home* books are the most comprehensive and up-to-date source of information available about buying property abroad. Whether you want a detached house, townhouse or apartment, a holiday or a permanent home, these books will help make your dreams come true.

**Save yourself time, trouble and money!**

Order your copies today by phone, fax, mail or e-mail from: Survival Books, PO Box 146, Wetherby, West Yorks. LS23 6XZ, United Kingdom (☎/▤ +44 (0)1937-843523, ✉ orders@ survivalbooks.net, ▣ www.survivalbooks.net).

# ORDER FORM

## LIVING & WORKING SERIES / RETIRING ABROAD

| Qty. | Title | Price (incl. p&p)* | | | Total |
|---|---|---|---|---|---|
| | | UK | Europe | World | |
| | Living & Working Abroad | £16.95 | £18.95 | £22.45 | |
| | Living & Working in America | £14.95 | £16.95 | £20.45 | |
| | Living & Working in Australia | £14.95 | £16.95 | £20.45 | |
| | Living & Working in Britain | £14.95 | £16.95 | £20.45 | |
| | Living & Working in Canada | £16.95 | £18.95 | £22.45 | |
| | Living & Working in the Far East | Winter 2003 | | | |
| | Living & Working in France | £14.95 | £16.95 | £20.45 | |
| | Living & Working in Germany | £16.95 | £18.95 | £22.45 | |
| | Living & Working in the Gulf States & Saudi Arabia | £16.95 | £18.95 | £22.45 | |
| | Living & Working in Holland, Belgium & Luxembourg | £14.95 | £16.95 | £20.45 | |
| | Living & Working in Ireland | £14.95 | £16.95 | £20.45 | |
| | Living & Working in Italy | £16.95 | £18.95 | £22.45 | |
| | Living & Working in London | £11.45 | £12.95 | £14.95 | |
| | Living & Working in New Zealand | £14.95 | £16.95 | £20.45 | |
| | Living & Working in Spain | £14.95 | £16.95 | £20.45 | |
| | Living & Working in Switzerland | £14.95 | £16.95 | £20.45 | |
| | Retiring Abroad | £14.95 | £16.95 | £20.45 | |
| | | | | **Total** | |

Order your copies today by phone, fax, mail or e-mail from: Survival Books, PO Box 146, Wetherby, West Yorks. LS23 6XZ, UK (☎/▤ +44 (0)1937-843523, ✉ orders@ survivalbooks.net, 💻 www.survivalbooks.net). If you aren't entirely satisfied, simply return them to us within 14 days for a full and unconditional refund.

Cheque enclosed/please charge my Amex/Delta/MasterCard/Switch/Visa* card

Card No.  __ __ __ __   __ __ __ __   __ __ __ __   __ __ __ __

Expiry date _____   Issue number (Switch only) _____

Signature _____   Tel. No. _____

NAME _____

ADDRESS _____

_____

_____

* Delete as applicable (price includes postage – airmail for Europe/world).